CAMBRIDGE GREEK AND LATIN CLASSICS

D0322142

PLINY THE YOUNGER
EPISTLES
BOOK II

EDITED BY
CHRISTOPHER WHITTON
*Lecturer, Faculty of Classics, University of Cambridge
and Fellow of Emmanuel College*

CAMBRIDGE
UNIVERSITY PRESS

CAMBRIDGE
UNIVERSITY PRESS

University Printing House, Cambridge CB2 8BS, United Kingdom

Published in the United States of America by Cambridge University Press, New York

Cambridge University Press is part of the University of Cambridge.

It furthers the University's mission by disseminating knowledge in the pursuit of
education, learning and research at the highest international levels of excellence.

www.cambridge.org
Information on this title: www.cambridge.org/9780521187275

© Christopher Whitton 2013

First published 2013

A catalogue record for this publication is available from the British Library

Library of Congress Cataloguing in Publication data
Pliny, the Younger
Pliny, the younger : Epistles book II / edited by Christopher Whitton, Lecturer, Faculty of
Classics, University of Cambridge and Fellow of Emmanuel College.
pages   cm
Includes bibliographical references and indexes.
ISBN 978-1-107-00689-8 (hardback)
1. Pliny, the Younger – Correspondence.   I. Whitton, Christopher, editor
of compilation.   II. Title.
PA6638.A32W45   2013
876'.01 – dc23   2013006881

ISBN 978-1-107-00689-8 Hardback
ISBN 978-0-521-18727-5 Paperback

CONTENTS

PREFACE

This commentary aims to provoke and assist readers to engage with a book of Pliny's *Epistles* in Latin. It was written in the conviction that so rich a work can only be appreciated in its original language, that slow reading is essential to an understanding of Pliny's art, and that approaching the *Epistles* through anthologies is to miss fundamental levels of meaning. Pliny's stock is on the rise: a series of articles and monographs in the last two decades has affirmed the value of engaging with his prose not just as document but (also) as literature. Yet literary readers are scarcely served by modern commentaries in any language, and *Epistles* 2 has so far escaped sustained attention in any form – two reasons to hope that the volume in your hands is timely. It has the aspiration to help readers construe Pliny's Latin, to situate his work in a historical (and scholarly) context and to offer a literary interpretation which opens rather than closes discussion. *Atque haec ego sic accipi uolo, non tamquam assecutum esse me credam . . .* (2.5.9).

I have been spoiled over three years with excellent libraries and good company in Cambridge, Munich and Berlin, and with generous help from many people. Anna Anguissola, David Butterfield, Emily Gowers, Harry Hine, Richard Hunter, Myles Lavan, Lucia Prauscello and David Sedley gave advice, and Amanda Claridge, James Diggle, Catharine Edwards, Peter Garnsey and Ingo Gildenhard commented on parts of the book in draft. Neil Hopkinson, Michael Reeve and Tony Woodman offered valuable criticisms of the whole, as did series editors Philip Hardie and Stephen Oakley, generous in their encouragement, and John Henderson, supervisor and mentor of unstinting kindness over many years. With Roy Gibson, exemplary reader, correspondent and host, I have enjoyed *uices pulchrae iucundae*: it is a pleasure to advertise here his forthcoming commentary on *Epistles* 6 in this series. Moreed Arbabzadah and James McNamara cheerfully undertook long hours of reference-checking, and it was a great luxury to have Andrew Dyck as copy-editor. To all these my sincere thanks.

Thanks most of all, though, to my parents David and Hilary, to my sister Dominique, and to Michael Squire, ten extraordinary and very happy years on.

July 2012   CLW

ABBREVIATIONS

GENERAL

AE	*L'Année épigraphique*, Paris 1888–
ANRW	*Aufstieg und Niedergang der römischen Welt*, Berlin 1972–
BNP	Cancik, H. and H. Schneider, eds. *Brill's new Pauly. Encyclopedia of the ancient world*, Leiden 2002–10
CIL	*Corpus inscriptionum Latinarum*, Berlin 1863–
G–L	Gildersleeve, B. L. and G. Lodge. *Gildersleeve's Latin grammar*, 3rd edn, London 1958
G–M	Gibson, R. K. and R. Morello. *Reading the letters of Pliny the Younger: an introduction*, Cambridge 2012
H–S	Hofmann, J. B. and A. Szantyr. *Lateinische Syntax und Stilistik*, Munich 1965
IG	*Inscriptiones Graecae*, Berlin 1873–
ILS	Dessau, H., ed. *Inscriptiones Latinae selectae*, Berlin 1892–1916
K–H	Kühner, R. and F. Holzweissig. *Ausführliche Grammatik der lateinischen Sprache. Erster Teil: Elementar-, Formen- und Wortlehre*, 2nd edn, Hannover 1912
K–S	Kühner, R. and C. Stegmann. *Ausführliche Grammatik der lateinischen Sprache. Zweiter Teil: Satzlehre*, 2nd edn, 2 vols, Hannover 1912
Lausberg	Lausberg, H. *Handbook of literary rhetoric* (tr./ed. M. T. Bliss et al.), Leiden 1998
Leumann	Leumann, M. *Lateinische Laut- und Formenlehre*, new edn, Munich 1977
LSJ	Liddell, H. G., R. Scott, H. S. Jones. *Greek-English lexicon*, 9th edn (with revised supplement), Oxford 1996
LTUR	*Lexicon topographicum urbis Romae*, Rome 1993–2000
MGH	*Monumenta Germaniae historica*, Berlin 1826–
NLS	Woodcock, E. C. *A new Latin syntax*, London 1959
N–W	Neue, F. and C. Wagener. *Formenlehre der lateinischen Sprache*, 3rd edn, 4 vols, Leipzig 1892–1905
OCD	Hornblower, S., A. Spawforth, E. Eidinow, eds. *Oxford classical dictionary*, 4th edn, Oxford 2012
OLD	Glare, P. G. W., ed. *Oxford Latin dictionary*, 2nd edn, Oxford 2012
PIR	*Prosopographia imperii Romani saec. I, II, III*, Berlin 1847–98 (*PIR²* = 2nd ed., 1933–)
RE	*Pauly-Wissowa Realenzyklopädie der klassischen Altertumswissenschaft*, Stuttgart 1893–1980

TLL   *Thesaurus linguae Latinae*, Munich 1900–

vdH²   van den Hout, M. P. J. *M. Cornelii Frontonis Epistulae . . . iterum edidit*, Leipzig 1988

EDITIONS, COMMENTARIES AND TRANSLATIONS
(*EPISTLES* 1–9)

Only works to which reference is made are listed; fuller catalogues of editions are given by Gierig I xxxiv–xxxvi and Aubrion 1989: 368–72 (inaccurate). Commentaries on other texts are included in the general bibliography.

Aldus	Aldus Manutius, 1508 (2nd edn, 1518, correcting misprints only), Venice
Boyle	Boyle, J. (Earl of Orrery). 1751. *The letters of Pliny the Younger, etc.*, 2 vols, London
Cataneus	Cataneus, 1519 (2nd edn), Venice
Cortius	Cortius and Longolius, 1734, Amsterdam
Cowan	Cowan, J. 1889. *Pliny's letters books I and II*, London
Döring	Döring, M. 1843. *C. Plinii Caecilii Secundi Epistolae*, 2 vols, Freiberg
Duff	Duff, J. D. 1906. *C. Plini Caecili Secundi Epistularum liber sextus*, Cambridge
Förtsch	Förtsch, R. 1993. *Archäologischer Kommentar zu den Villenbriefen des jüngeren Plinius*, Mainz
Gierig	Gierig, G. E. 1800–2. *C. Plinii Caecilii Secundi Epistolarum libri decem*, 2 vols, Leipzig
Guillemin	Guillemin, A.-M. 1927–8 (2nd edn, 1959–62). *Pline le Jeune. Lettres I–IX*, 3 vols, Paris
Keil	Keil, H. 1870. *C. Plini Caecili Secundi Epistularum libri novem, etc.*, Leipzig
Kukula	Kukula, R. C. 1912. *C. Plini Caecili Secundi Epistularum libri novem, etc.*, 2nd edn, Leipzig
Lehmann-Hartleben	Lehmann-Hartleben, K. 2007. *Plinio il giovane / Lettere scelte. Con commento archeologico di K. Lehmann-Hartleben* [orig. 1936], *introduzione di Paul Zanker, aggiornamento bibliografico a cura di Anna Anguissola*, Pisa
Mayor	Mayor, J. E. B. 1880. *Pliny's letters book III*, London
Merrill	Merrill, E. T. 1919. *Selected letters of the younger Pliny*, 2nd edn, London [incl. 2.1, 2.6, 2.11–14, 2.17, 2.20]
Merrill 1922	Merrill, E. T. 1922. *C. Plini Caecili Secundi Epistularum libri decem*, Leipzig
Mynors	Mynors, R. A. B. 1963. *C. Plini Caecili Secundi Epistularum libri decem*, Oxford (corrected reprint 1968)

Pflips Pflips, H. 1973. 'Ciceronachahmung und Ciceroferne des jüngeren Plinius: Ein Kommentar zu den Briefen des Plinius über Repetundenprozesse (epist. 2,11; 2,12; 3,9; 4,9; 5,20; 6,13; 7,6)', diss. Bamberg

Philips Philips, H. [= H. Pflips]. 1986. *C. Plini Caecili Secundi Epistulae (in Auswahl)*, Paderborn [incl. 2.6, 2.11, 2.14]

Radice Radice, B. 1963. *The letters of the Younger Pliny*, London/ Radice, B. 1969. *Pliny. Letters and Panegyricus*, 2 vols, Cambridge, MA (the same translation)

Scarcia Scarcia, R. 1967. *Plinio il Giovane. Lettere scelte*, Rome [incl. 2.3, 2.5, 2.14, 2.18]

Schuster Schuster, M. (rev. R. Hanslik). 1958 (3rd edn). *C. Plini Caecili Secundi Epistularum libri novem, Epistularum ad Traianum liber, Panegyricus*, Leipzig

S-W Sherwin-White, A. N. 1966. *The letters of Pliny. A historical and social commentary*, Oxford (corrected reprint 1985)

S-W 1967 Sherwin-White, A. N. 1967. *Fifty letters of Pliny*, Oxford [incl. 2.1, 2.6, 2.11, 2.20]

Trisoglio Trisoglio, F. 1973. *Opere di Plinio Cecilio Secondo*, 2 vols, Turin

Walsh Walsh, P. G. 2006. *Pliny the Younger. Complete letters*, Oxford

Westcott Westcott, J. H. 1965. *Selected letters of Pliny*, Norman, OK

Zehnacker Zehnacker, H. 2009–12. *Pline le Jeune. Lettres I–IX*, 3 vols (French translation by N. Méthy from vol. 2), Paris

IMAGINARY PLAN OF THE
LAURENTINE VILLA

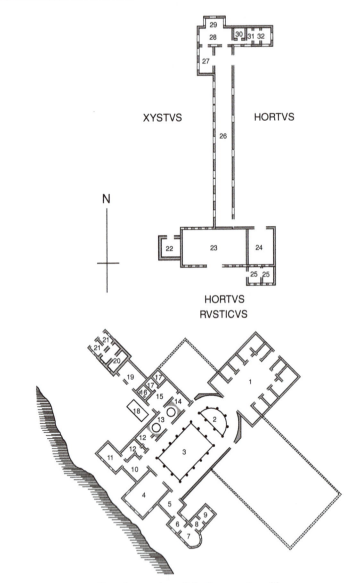

Imaginary plan of the Laurentine villa
(as reconstructed by Winnefeld 1891: see p. 222)

Key

INTRODUCTION

1 EPISTLES IN BRIEF

The early second century AD saw publication of the *Epistles*, a nine-book collection of 247 letters. Together with the *Panegyricus* (an address to Trajan) and 124 letters to and from Trajan known as *Epistles* 10,[1] this collection comprises the surviving literary legacy of Pliny the Younger.

The second book is a typical medley of twenty pieces addressed to a range of elite personal acquaintances. Their status as letters is self-evident from the formulaic trappings of heading (e.g. C. PLINIVS ROMANO SVO S.) and sign-off (VALE) and from the invocation of epistolary topoi – brevity, intimacy, humility – marking them as specific, personal and occasional.[2] Yet these conventions are not uniformly invoked: nothing about 2.7, for instance, beyond heading and sign-off marks it as a letter, while explicit signs of epistolarity are confined to the opening and close of the long, elaborate 2.11 (Priscus) and 2.17 (villa). Editing is obvious: details, dates and names have been smoothed away, the particular is turned to the general, and the sheer complexity of structure and literary texture strains against ephemerality. As a scripted collection (this commentary will argue), *Epistles* 1–9 constitutes an open, public and monumental work of very grand design.

Not all readers have seen it that way. In recent generations Pliny has served primarily as historical source-book and as fodder for beginner Latinists. Sherwin-White did great service to both industries with his landmark *Historical and Social Commentary* of 1966 and the little *Fifty Letters of Pliny* (1967) that followed. The latter typifies the anthologising urge that persisted through the twentieth century, sorting and selecting letters for palatable consumption, showing students the Pliny they might be assumed to like, and eradicating in the process such meaning as may reside in sequence and interplay within and between books. The former, for all its many virtues, is unwelcoming to the novice, parsimonious – as the title warns – on linguistic and literary comment, and scarcely available outside libraries. That leaves a significant hole given the lack of alternative: no other English commentary has been addressed to even a single complete book of the *Epistles* in over a century.[3] Little wonder that most students (and many scholars)

---

[1] *Epistles* 10 has letters conventionally numbered 1–121 but including 3B, 17B and 86B. Probably published posthumously and added to *Epp.* 1–9 in late antiquity (see however Stadter 2006, Woolf 2006, Noreña 2007), it might best be called a semi-detached adjunct to *Epistles* 1–9; together with *Pan.*, it plays a subordinate role in this volume.

[2] For these and other topoi see Trapp 2003, especially 1–46. Other helpful introductions to ancient epistolography are Rosenmeyer 2001: 1–12, Edwards 2005, Gibson–Morrison 2007, Ebbeler 2010.

[3] Mayor (1880) on book 3 is the only substantial commentary on a book; there are student editions of books 1–2 by Cowan (1889, the last on book 2 in any language) and

experience Pliny through the distorting lens of a translation, and very few engage with complete books, let alone the collection. More recently, however, the *Epistles* has undergone its literary turn: a series of books and articles have begun to demonstrate the rewards that follow from approaching it as a crafted literary work and one in which the books, and the whole, make meaningful units.[4] Not that selective reading is 'wrong' as such: as in many poetic books, the fragments offer themselves as easy prey to excerptors, while ancient indexes facilitated browsing (§8); above all it is the tension between the autonomy of the letter and its subordination to larger structures that is fundamental. A commentary seems a useful format with which to give voice to this equivocation, open as it is to selective reading while gesturing towards interpretation of the whole. For – Pliny's mastery of prose apart (§§4–6) – it is in the interstice between ephemerality and eternity, between the fragment and the masterpiece, that the *Epistles* finds its essence.

* * *

A collection of purportedly private letters from a consular orator directs the reader first and foremost to Cicero, the salient peak in the Roman epistolary landscape: we have over 900 letters, and Pliny may have known twice as many.[5] Prized for their historical and literary interest, they offer apparently unmediated access to the inner life of one of Rome's great icons. Pliny's *Epistles* names Cicero ten times, makes several prominent allusions to his letters, and integrates abundant smaller motifs and phrases.[6] Emulation goes far beyond the literary: as a provincial 'new man' and beacon of oratorical, political and cultural prestige, Cicero provides Pliny with a model for life as well as letters – or at least for life within letters.[7] For all that – indeed, not least because he serves as far more than a model letter-writer – it is clear that Pliny's *Epistles* is a very different creature from the letters of Cicero. Cicero's correspondence is collected in books, of varying length, according to addressee (*Ad Atticum*, *Ad Quintum fratrem*, etc.), and includes around a hundred letters written by others;[8] Pliny's books are remarkably consistent in length, give no voice to others, and show no obvious organisation by

---

book 6 by Duff (1906). History repeats itself: 'Pliny's Letters have hitherto been known to schoolboys chiefly by selections . . . ' (Cowan v).

[4] See Ludolph 1997 and Hoffer 1999 (book 1), Henderson 2002a (book 3); also G–M 36–73 (book 6), Bernstein 2008 and Whitton 2010 (book 8), Gibson forthcoming (book 9); and Beard 2002 (Cicero), Cancik 1967 and Richardson-Hay 2006 (Seneca), Gibson 2013c (Sidonius). For readings of *Epp.* 1–9 (or 1–10) as a whole, see Marchesi 2008 and G–M.

[5] White 2010: 171–5, in an essential study of Cicero's letters; see also Hutchinson 1998, Beard 2002, Hall 2009.

[6] See pp. 32 and 41 and index s.v. Likewise, *Pan.* looks often (but not only) to Cicero's foundational panegyric, *Pro Marcello* (Durry 1938: 28–33).

[7] Weische 1989, Riggsby 1995, Lefèvre 1996 (= id. 2009: 111–22), Marchesi 2008: 207–40, Gibson–Steel 2010, G–M 74–103.

[8] Beard 2002, White 2010: 31–61. The sixteen books of what we call *Ad familiares* were probably known singly to Pliny as *Ad Lentulum*, *Ad Tironem*, etc. (Peter 1901: 54–7, Beard 2002: 117–18, White 2010: 171).

correspondent. Cicero's vary in their headings and sign-offs, routinely address multiple topics, and include abundant unexplained names, obscure references and in-jokes – all the paraphernalia whose absence makes Pliny's letters so accessible to a remote readership. Most importantly, Cicero's letters were edited and published posthumously: whatever plans he may have had for wider circulation, his extant epistles were intended for single or select readers; those of Pliny (at least books 1–9, our concern here) are self-published.[9] To a later reader (such as Pliny) Cicero's letters offer incidental fragments of a biography. Pliny's *Epistles*, by contrast, comprises the planned fragments of an autobiography (§2).

'It is a great jump from the letters of Cicero to those of Pliny. The gap is not bridged by the metrical Epistles of Horace or by the letters in prose of Seneca to Lucilius' (S-W 2). We might be less dogmatic (and add Ovid). In prose, Seneca's *Epistulae morales* offer the primary and radical alternative to Cicero. One hundred and twenty-four letters in twenty books,[10] all addressed to his friend Lucilius, add up to a correspondence course in Stoic self-scrutiny. Since Sherwin-White wrote, the epistolarity of what used to be called essays in disguise has been explored and emphasised,[11] and it is no surprise to find Seneca as a second significant influence on Pliny's *Epistles*. He is named only once (5.3.5) but is a recurrent if often hazy intertextual presence,[12] offering in particular a primary paradigm for the epistolary villa-portrait (2.17.intro.).[13] There, as elsewhere, resemblances also point contrasts: unlike the severe sexagenarian who confides in Lucilius alone, forty-something Pliny is in the prime of life, scripting buoyant epistolary interactions with a hundred-odd addressees,[14] and too jovial to don the iron mantle of asceticism. Seneca does not bridge a gap from Cicero to Pliny: he provides a different, and very pertinent, model for epistolary self-exposure.

Yet prose is only part of the story. Horace's two books of hexameter *Epistles* and Ovid's *Tristia* and *Epistulae ex Ponto* (elegiac letters of lament from exile) harnessed epistolarity for ethical self-representation and crafted letters into poetic books.[15] Their intertextual presence in Pliny seems slight, but the precedent in

---

[9] On *Epp.* 10 see n.1 above. The details regarding Cicero are much debated: White 2010: 31–61.

[10] Pliny knew more: Gell. *NA* 12.2 quotes from 'book 22', and there may have been losses within our 124 letters too (Inwood 2007a: xiii).

[11] Signal contributions are Wilson 2001, Henderson 2004a, Inwood 2007b. The 'real' vs 'literary' debate that formerly dominated had been as unproductive for Seneca as it is for Pliny (below).

[12] E.g. 2.5.13n. *ne*, 2.6.5n. *si gulae*, 2.8.2n. *numquamne*, 2.10.3n. *claustra*, 2.10.4n. *a*, 2.15.1n. *nihil*. On Seneca and Pliny see Lausberg 1991: 91–100, Cova 1997, Griffin 2007 and indexes to Henderson 2002a, Marchesi 2008, G–M s.v.

[13] As well as for the format (2.1n. C. PLINIVS, 2.1.12n. VALE) and for highly clausulated letters (n.172). For a possible allusion to Sen. *Ep.* 1.1 see 2.1.1n. *post*.

[14] The precise number is elusive, given doubts over identification (Birley 2000a: 17–21).

[15] On Horatian epistolarity see de Pretis 2002; for Ovid see Williams–Walker 1997, Gaertner 2005: 6–9 and his index s.v. 'epistolography'; also Kennedy 2002 on *Heroides*. Single verse epistles are found already in Catullus (e.g. 65, 68A).

structure and composition significant.[16] Certainly they exemplify the epistolary conceit central to Pliny's (and Seneca's) letters, that we readers are eavesdropping on private conversations.[17] So too the equivocation – also familiar from Catullus, or Horace's *Odes* – between the ephemeral (a poem for a specific reader and occasion) and the eternal (poetry for all readers and all time). That same equivocation was shared by two recent poetic collections: Martial's *Epigrams* (AD 80s–100s) and Statius' *Siluae* (AD 90s). Both have been proposed as models for Pliny, Martial for his lively miniatures of Roman society and epigrammatic wit, Statius for his 'occasional' poetry and sustained ecphrastic description.[18] Pliny no doubt knew both; he makes Martial's death a significant point of closure in his *Epistles* (3.21) and may hint at Martialesque closure in *Epistles* 2;[19] certainly Statius' verbalised villa (*Siluae* 2.2) is in view as we tour that of Pliny (2.17.intro.). None of these poets is so pervasive a point of reference as Cicero, but together they serve as a reminder that Pliny's generic frame of reference extends more widely than prose, and more widely too than self-proclaimed letters.

Scholarly debate over these different antecedents has been heavily coloured by the question of 'authenticity': those committed to finding 'real' letters in Pliny's collection are likely to emphasise Cicero, dismissing Seneca and poets, while at another extreme Martial and Statius have bolstered the arguments of the minority who see the *Epistles* as a wholly 'literary' work, each letter invented for publication.[20] The argument has been persistent, and sterile. Several letters deal with demonstrably historical persons and events (though it is rash to put faith in reality markers such as 'yesterday');[21] we have no reason to doubt that Pliny wrote off a debt for Calvina (2.4) or canvassed for Clarus (2.9), or for that matter that he reported the Priscus trial to Arrianus (2.11–12) or told Gallus why he was so fond of his Laurentine villa (2.17): letters played a large part in elite life, and he might have written several thousand each year.[22] Yet the simple fact of publication opens an interpretative chasm no different – if we set aside prejudices about an assumed prose/verse divide – from that faced by the reader of a Horatian ode

---

[16] Possible hints of Hor. *Epp.* at 2.17.29n. *maxima*, 2.18.5n. *tam* (see also 2.2.1n. *quod*, 2.2.2n. *nascitur*, 2.10.4n. *monimento*). On structure (and Ov. *Ex P.*) see below, §3.

[17] Spectacularly pricked by Hor. *Ep.* 1.20, addressing the book itself. Ov. *Ex P.* 3.9.51–2 offers a disingenuous closing denial: *nec liber ut fieret . . . propositum curaque nostra fuit.*

[18] Guillemin 1929: 147 (Martial), Peter 1901: 114–18 (Statius); also Syme 1991: 646. Both collections include prefatory prose epistles (Pagán 2010).

[19] 2.20.intro. See also 2.6.2n. *nam sibi*, 2.10.3n. *ut*, 2.20.8n. *Regulo*. On 3.21 see Henderson 2001a, id. 2002a: 44–58.

[20] The extreme poles are occupied by Lilja 1969 (also Bell 1989) and Guillemin I xxix–xxx respectively. For a review of the debate see Gamberini 1983: 122–36. The historian Sherwin-White, while granting editing its place, staunchly defended the letters' 'historicity' (S-W 11–20).

[21] 2.7.1n. *here*; also 2.14.6 *here*.

[22] Cf. Hall 2009: 16 on Cicero.

or an Ovidian epistle: who could say whether Gallus received two lines or two hundred, or any at all, in some earlier version? The archaeological search for a substratum of putative 'originals' has limited rewards, and this commentary joins other recent studies in preferring to read and respond to these pieces in the edited collection in which they are presented to us: not so much 'Pliny's letters' (plural) as 'Pliny's *Epistles*' (singular).[23]

Not that epistolarity is unimportant: on the contrary, the very intransigence of the 'authenticity' debate is telling. Poised on the boundaries of real and literary, of private and public, of occasional and eternal, the *Epistles* is defined by indeterminacy. Its range of addressees situates Pliny in a (Ciceronian) milieu of senators and equestrians, with a heavy bias towards his native Transpadana (Italy north of the Po), and this milieu forms part of his identity.[24] But what we see is an idealised version of that society, just as each letter is an idealised transcript of any original communication. Indeed, we learn remarkably little about his addressees, who thus serve above all as mirrors reflecting Pliny's own image. The ambitions and self-awareness of the *Epistles* suggest that he is not writing first and foremost for his 'primary' reader, nor even for the 'secondary' readership of intimate *litterati* – a subset of the address-book on display – who share and savour each other's elegant epistolary efforts,[25] but for an external, one might say 'tertiary', readership of eavesdroppers such as us.[26] That Pliny never, after the prefatory 1.1, refers to the circulation of letters beyond his private circle and says nothing of the hours he spent writing them (up)[27] is part and parcel of the epistolary conceit, flattering us with fantasy membership of that inner sanctum and superiority even to the readers of his speeches.[28] The repeated intimations of immortality through literature (as in 2.10), quickening in the final book, dwell on poetry, history, oratory – anything but letters. Yet it is the *Epistles* – along with *Panegyricus* – that has lived on, proving itself, for all its

---

[23] Or, if you prefer, *Letters* (sg.). On the origins of the shifting but deep-rooted dichotomy 'epistle' (distant, literary, canonical) vs 'letter' (approachable, 'real', casual) see Rosenmeyer 2001: 5–12.

[24] Transpadanes comprise around a quarter of Pliny's addressees and receive towards a third of his letters (Syme 1968, Birley 2000a: 17–21, Bradley 2010: 415); as for social editing, meanwhile, 'no letter to a doctor, a philosopher, a free[d]man' (Syme 1985a: 343). On Cicero's social mix see White 2010: 59.

[25] 2.2.intro., 2.13.7n. *epistulas*. The constructedness of Pliny's literary community is well analysed by Johnson 2010: 32–73. Gurd 2012: 105–26 (developing a slightly different argument) distinguishes this 'genetic' public from Pliny's 'general' public.

[26] Particular signs of consideration towards such readers are noted in 2.11.10n. *erat*, 2.20.7n. *quia*.

[27] In 9.19.1 Ruso has read a letter to Albinus (6.10), proof only of personal circulation (Murgia 1985: 200–1; cf. Cic. *Att.* 4.6.4). Some see signs of publication in 9.11.1 *libris* and 9.23.2–3 *studiis*, but neither clearly concerns letters. Hours of writing: G–M 118.

[28] 2.5.4n. *ad*, 2.19.9n. *eruditissimum*. The *Epistles*' equivocal status is subtly explored by Fitzgerald 2007a (especially 193).

professedly humble, ephemeral and peripheral status, to be a very serious bet on posterity.

2 PLINY'S WORLD

The man we call Pliny the Younger was born C. or L. (Gaius or Lucius) Caecilius Secundus in AD 61 or 62. The name is deduced from epigraphical evidence, the date from the *Epistles* – two attempts at self-immortalisation which have succeeded in leaving us an unusually full biography.[29] His father, L. Caecilius Secundus, was an equestrian of Comum (modern Como, near Milan); his mother Plinia was sister of the prominent equestrian C. Plinius Secundus (Pliny the Elder), now best known for his *Natural History*. When the father died, the boy became the ward of a senior senator, Verginius Rufus (2.1.8n. *tutor*); in 79 he was adopted by the elder Pliny in his will (5.8.5) and accordingly became C. Plinius (Caecilius) Secundus.[30] Within a year or two he was practising as an advocate in Rome and, as *decemuir stlitibus iudicandis* in *c.* 80/81, presiding over the centumviral court, the primary civil tribunal (2.14.1n. *centumuiralibus*); soon afterwards he served as military tribune in Syria, and by the late 80s he had entered the senate as *quaestor Caesaris* (one of the emperor's personal officials: 2.9.1n. *quam*). He pursued a swift *cursus*: tribune of the plebs, praetor, prefect of the military treasury and prefect of the treasury of Saturn (2.8.2n. *angor*). Pliny was suffect consul for September and October 100, an augur from 103 or 104 (2.1.8n. *illo*) and curator of the Tiber *c.* 104–6; around this time he also served in the *consilium principis*, the emperor's informal cabinet. In *c.* 110 he was posted as governor to Bithynia-Pontus, where he stayed for somewhat less than two years (Williams 1990: 13). He is widely assumed, *ex silentio*, to have died in that office at the age of around fifty.

Rightly or not, we tend to define imperial history almost wholly by reigning *principes*. In those terms, Pliny was born under Nero (ruled 54–68) and adopted by a man somewhat intimate with Vespasian (69–79) and his son Titus (79–81);[31] he owed his senatorial status and career thereafter to Titus' brother Domitian (81–96). That debt became awkward when Domitian was assassinated in September 96 and condemned as a vicious and bloodthirsty tyrant, but the embarrassment was not unique to Pliny, whose career shows no sign of retardation during the sixteen-month principate of the elderly Nerva (96–8) or under his adopted successor Trajan (98–117).[32] Five to ten years Pliny's senior, Trajan too had fared

---

[29] The following account skims over controversies: for detail see Birley 2000a: 1–17, superseding S-W 69–82; also Syme 1991: 551–67, G–M 108–10, 265–73.

[30] See Salway 1994: 132 for the name, Champlin 1991: 144–6 on testamentary adoption. Pliny seems not to have used 'Caecilius', distinguishing him from his uncle, except in the most formal contexts (Birley 2000a: 1), how early it featured in the title of his *Epistles* (cf. Stout 1954: 16) is unclear.

[31] Working intimacy with Vespasian is advertised in 3.5.9, with Titus in the preface to his *Natural History*.

[32] For the historical context see e.g. Griffin 2000, Bennett 2001, Grainger 2003.

well enough under Domitian, as had one and all of the men promoted in the years following his accession: this was less a revolution than a coup within the governing class. Nevertheless, 96 is enshrined in historians' minds as a watershed, thanks not least to the rhetoric of Pliny and Tacitus.[33] The *Panegyricus* tirelessly works a dichotomy between *pessimus* Domitian and *optimus* Trajan; *Epistles* 1–9 features the same dichotomy, but more discreetly.[34] Pliny is rarely seen intersecting directly with emperors, and the *Epistles* has its centre of gravity away from the Palatine. Nevertheless, in its understated way, it is emphatic in distancing its author from Domitian and in associating him with Nerva and Trajan.

Like Tacitus (*Agricola* 1–3, *Histories* 1.1–3) but less explicitly, Pliny makes Domitian's death the enabling force for an entire (literary) career. It features early (1.5.1 *post Domitiani mortem*) and plays a central role in the suicide of old Corellius Rufus (1.12.8), while upbeat signs of revived intellectual life conjure up a restoration mood for book 1 as a whole.[35] Those two letters typify Pliny's epistolary construction and negotiation of the watershed: contrasts are strong, but the focus is less on emperors than on subjects. In 1.5 Pliny introduces Regulus as a Domitianic creature and polar opposite of himself, while 1.12 presents Corellius, family friend and mentor, as Domitian's bitter enemy; both letters thus – with typical obliquity – set Pliny on the (new) side of right.[36] In book 2 this pair is reversed and varied: 2.1 commemorates the death of another 'good' elder statesman, Verginius Rufus, who is tied to both Nerva and Pliny, while 2.20 returns to the 'bad' senator Regulus. Meanwhile the short 2.18 incidentally parades intimacy with Junius Mauricus and Arulenus Rusticus, so contributing to a running project of associating Pliny with senatorial victims of Domitian.[37] His own Domitianic past, though not erased (2.9.1n. *quam*), receives scant mention.[38]

No emperor is named in book 2: a *princeps* or *Caesar* is sighted now and then, largely in passing, but Pliny never specifies which (2.1.3n. *reliquit*). Trajan's adoption (Oct. 97), accession (Jan. 98) and entry to Rome (late 99, glimpsed in 3.7.6–7), all of which (could) fall within the time-frame of the book,[39] pass unnoticed. The result, besides keeping modern historians exercised, is a flawless transition from Nerva (book 1) to Trajan (book 3), constructing a single reign, as it were, of Nerva–Trajan and so underlining the gulf between this new regime

---

[33] On this violent rhetoric of periodisation see first Ramage 1989. How far it reflects changed reality is debatable (Waters 1969, Coleman 2000, Saller 2000b, Wilson 2003).

[34] Hoffer 1999, especially 61–6, Beutel 2000: 129–270; also Hoffer 2006 on 10.2. Reference to Domitian in the Bithynia correspondence, by contrast, is businesslike (10.58, 10.60, 10.65.3, 10.66.2, 10.72).

[35] Notably 1.10, 1.13: Hoffer 1999 *passim*, G–M 24–5.

[36] So too 1.18.3 (Pliny recalls former fears of opposing *Caesaris amicos* in court).

[37] 2.18.intro. The theme perhaps makes 2.18–20 a triptych (2.19n. CERIALI).

[38] For speculation on it see Giovannini 1987, Soverini 1989, Strobel 2003.

[39] Namely 97–100 (below, §3), though Oct. 97 precedes its earliest datable event (Verginius' funeral in Nov./Dec. 97).

and that of Domitian.[40] The lack of triumphal apparatus also quietly emphasises the *ciuilitas* of Trajan, who benignly presides over the central parade of senatorial (and Plinian) vigour, the Priscus trial, and to whom one may credit – though Pliny does not do so directly – the *otium* on display in 2.17 and elsewhere (pp. 10–11). Contrast with the cowed senate of Domitianic days, laboured in *Pan.* 76.1–4 (describing the same occasion), is delicately drawn (2.11.10n. *erat*): after *Epistles* 1, and the reminder at the start of this book (2.1.3n. *Caesares quibus*, 4n. *in*), it can be taken as read that the happy present is played out in implicit comparison with a gloomy past.[41] Like the *Panegyricus*, the Priscus letter binds Pliny to Trajan, but here in miniature and with Pliny, not Trajan, centre-stage (2.11.intro.):[42] imperial politics are refracted rather than projected in these professedly private letters.

This (quiet) celebration of Nervan/Trajanic present over Domitianic past is complicated, however, by a contrasting strain of nostalgia and dissatisfaction with modernity. Perverse hospitality (2.6), debased oratorical practice in the courts (2.14) and 'legacy hunting' (2.20) all prompt satirical attacks on contemporary society; generals are not what they used to be (2.7.1) and even the senate cannot be trusted to vote wisely (2.12).[43] Pliny's response ranges from constructive (2.6, 2.7) to resigned, with especially gloomy prognosis ending 2.14 and 2.20. Is the Trajanic future not so bright after all? The narrative of decline was a constant in Roman literature: *hoc maiores nostri questi sunt, hoc nos querimur, hoc posteri nostri querentur* (Sen. *Ben.* 1.10.1).[44] Things were always better in a hazy, distant past, when men were real men and virtue was real virtue. But such pessimism over the *longue durée* should not be mistaken for criticism of a ruling emperor: Seneca, for instance, could refer to a Rome *in qua ciuitate numquam deest patronus peioribus* in one of his most panegyrical works (*De clementia* 1.15.2). Indeed, the weaknesses of society and the senate can be marshalled as justification precisely for a *princeps*, a man (or more) to save Rome from itself.[45] All the same, a striking negativity imbues the close of book 2. Especially given Regulus' association with Domitian, this gives the impression that all is not (yet) well with the world: Rome wasn't rebuilt in a day.[46]

---

[40] Hoffer 1999: 142–3, G–M 24. Later books tell a different story of Nerva (G–M 27–35; already 4.22.4–6 reveals him dining with *delatores*), as does *Pan.*, where his weakness is a source of Trajan's legitimacy (Kienast 1968, Méthy 2006).

[41] Pliny returns to attack Domitian explicitly in 4.11 and 8.14; see also 3.9.31 and 33, 4.9.2, 4.22, 7.27.12–14, 9.13.

[42] Not that readers of *Pan.* should miss Pliny's self-projection there (Henderson 2002a: 151, id. 2011).

[43] See intro. to each letter and 2.18.2n. *sperare*, 2.20.12 *in*; see also Lefèvre 2009, Strunk 2012.

[44] E.g. Cat. 64.397–408, Sall. *Jug.* 3–4, Hor. *C.* 3.6.46–8, Livy *praef.* 9, Vell. 2.92.5, Tac. *H.* 1.18.3.

[45] 3.20.12 and 4.25.5, each with heavenly allusion (2.4.3n. *decurrit*); Trajan comes to the senate's rescue again in 5.13.7–8.

[46] On this 'narrative of decline', and its modification by later books, see pp. 16–17, 19–20.

The failings of modernity serve not least, however, to sharpen the contrast with the exemplary individuals in Pliny's circle. In contrast to the usual Roman search for exemplars in the distant past, the *Epistles* is notable for its celebration of contemporary *exempla*,[47] first among them four 'elders and betters' (G–M 104–35): Verginius Rufus (2.1), Vestricius Spurinna (2.7, 3.1), Corellius Rufus (1.12) and the elder Pliny (3.5). Not that Pliny elevates modernity over antiquity: what makes these men great is their comparability with men of an earlier age.[48] Celebrating them has a pay-off for Pliny, who basks in reflected glory whenever he praises the good (1.17.4 *scias ipsum plurimis uirtutibus abundare qui alienas sic amat*; cf. 4.27.6, Krasser 1993a), and, in the case of these father-figures, in quasi-inherited glory too (2.1.8n. *tutor*). Others earn admiration as well: the rhetor Isaeus (2.3), though he represents an entirely different walk of life, and younger men like Erucius Clarus (2.9), Voconius Romanus (2.13) and the dead Cottius (2.7); fellow senators also merit passing compliments in 2.11, above all Tacitus (cf. also 2.1.6n. *laudator*, pp. 33–4 below). Conversely, counter-exemplary figures demonstrate how not to behave: the inhospitable host of 2.6, the corrupt senators Priscus and Firminus (2.11–12) and above all Pliny's *bête noire* Regulus (2.11.22, 2.20).

Celebrating the *exempla* of others, however, is only part of the story: Pliny also provides one himself. The bad host of 2.6 makes a counter-example for Avitus, but the letter is centred on Pliny's contrasting model etiquette (2.6.3–5). 2.14 dissociates him from the common crowd of advocates, 2.12 even from the senate herd (and by 9.13 he will be in a virtuous minority of one: 2.11.intro.). From *protégé* of Verginius Rufus (2.1) Pliny rapidly becomes a father-figure (2.4, 2.18) and patron (2.5.3, 2.9, 2.13), in a miniaturised version of his development through the *Epistles*.[49] He is thus revealed, within his epistolary society, as a crucial link in the chain of exemplarity, passing on to the next generation what he learnt from the last;[50] but he also serves, of course, as teacher and exemplar for his wider readership. Not only does Pliny provide us with a repository of model letters[51] – how to handle a tricky will (2.4, 2.16), recommend a friend (2.9, 2.13), tease but persuade (2.10), help with a favour (2.18) – he presents at every turn a model life in the fragmentary self-portrait that is the *Epistles*.[52] This may be

[47] See Gazich 2003, and for the few past *exempla*, Méthy 2003 (cf. Gowing 2005: 123–30 and Henderson 2011 on *Pan.*). More broadly on exemplarity see e.g. Mayer 1991, Chaplin 2000, Morgan 2007: 122–59.

[48] See 2.1.7n. *exemplar aeui prioris*, 2.7.1n. *assequebantur*, 2.9.4n. *antiquus*, 6.21.1; Döpp 1989.

[49] G–M 62–3, 131–5; 2.6n. Avito, 2.18.intro.

[50] And restoring a virtuous cycle almost lost in Domitian's principate (8.14.2–10 with Gazich 2003: 127–31).

[51] A real 'etiquette book' of model letters survives from antiquity (2.4.intro.).

[52] The staging of the self in *Epistles* has been a major theme of recent study: see especially Ludolph 1997 and Henderson 2002a and 2003; also Radicke 1997, Hoffer 1999, Gibson–Morello 2003 and G–M *passim*. Syme 1958: 98 already saw the *Epistles* for 'the closest that was decent or permissible to the autobiography of an orator and a statesman' (also

no Senecan course in Stoicism; but as an exemplary guide to ethics, a practical demonstration of life lived, these letters too could aspire to the title *Epistulae morales*.[53] Whether it is an example we could ever hope to follow – where, that is, to draw the line between didaxis and egotistical display – is another question.[54]

Pliny's life, as distilled in the *Epistles*, is marked by social success, happy relations, jovial generosity, buoyant optimism, a strong sense of duty to society and state, but also space for *otium* and so devotion to literature. Faced with such a picture of perfection, *quis credet? nemo, hercule, nemo . . .*[55] Certainly it does not win universal admiration from modern readers, whether (in part) because we derive our entertainment from human weakness, or because of a profound expectation that life under autocracy should not be cheerful.[56] Pliny's unfashionable aura of self-satisfaction does little to help: few are fooled by his false modesty (2.4.intro.) or willing to play along with the conceit that we are accidental, not intended, readers. At the same time, the rare intimacy (purportedly) on offer in this behind-the-scenes *exposé*, as with Cicero's letters, has perhaps inevitably damning effect: *maior e longinquo reuerentia* (Tac. *An.* 1.47.2). Worse still, he has seemed to some an intellectual lightweight.[57] Such value-judgments belong best with the individual reader, but it is worth underlining that Pliny's portrait is perfect not least in its imperfection. Through the stage-curtain he invites us to glimpse not just triumphs but also foibles: here is a man who is not ashamed to enjoy a little laziness (2.2.2n. *desidia*) and who yearns for respite from his duties (2.8.2n. *angor*, 2.14.14n. *ratio*). The humanising *captatio beneuolentiae*, cajoling the reader and sugaring the didactic pill (or smoothing the egotism) with confessed weakness – staking a paradoxical claim to exemplarity in and through being normal – at least aims to take the edge off Pliny's self-advertisement. It also directs us to the spiritual core of the *Epistles*, the world of *otium*.

For all the celebration of statesmanship and social grace, the private, leisured sphere has a special place in this portrait of Pliny's 'private' self. *Otium* is the prerequisite not just for relaxation but for the *studia* (literary activities) that are the life-blood of the *Epistles* and the route to eternity: 3.7.14 [*uitam*] *si non datur factis, certe studîs proferamus* 'if we may not extend our life with deeds, let us at least do so with our efforts on the page'.[58] Late in book 2 we reach the sanctum that is the Laurentine villa, site of and metonym for literary devotion (2.17.intro.); late

---

p. 664 and id. 1985a: 350). Another branch of scholarship has preferred to take Pliny at his word: Bütler 1970, Trisoglio 1972, Méthy 2007, Lefèvre 2009.

53 On Pliny's pragmatic philosophy see André 1975, Griffin 2007.

54 One tied up with the question of readership – senators? provincial elite? posterity? (I privilege the last: pp. 1–6 above).

55 Fielding *Tom Jones* viii 1 (after Persius).

56 Two reasons for Tacitus' generally greater appeal. Hoffer 1999 is the signal attempt at locating 'anxieties' in the cracks of Pliny's smooth façade.

57 An epitome of mediocrity for Norden 1898: 318; Pausch 2004: 51–3 collects more recent gems. Prose artistry, for this reader, is Pliny's highest claim on posterity.

58 2.2.2nn. *partim, studîs, otio*, Bütler 1970: 28–40, Méthy 2007: 378–413.

in that letter we reach the inner sanctum of the villa itself, Pliny's private suite for undisturbed meditation and composition. Both as concept and as consummation of textual art, the villa carries immense weight in the economy of the *Epistles*, as its final letter confirms: the last thing we see, as his epistolary life-blood fades away, is Pliny in his Laurentine study, dictating and reworking into oblivion (9.40.2 *illa quae dictaui identidem retractantur*).[59] Here at the heart of his Laurentine retreat, that most intimate spot, we find perhaps the ultimate intrication of life, letters and literature in Pliny's epistolary monument: *ipse posui* (2.17.20).

3 A BOOK OF LETTERS

For most readers of Pliny in the last century or more, the book has been a unit of limited interest. Modern editions either give *Epistles* 1–9 complete (usually together with book 10, sometimes also the *Panegyricus*) or present excerpts from across the collection, regardless of book-divisions. For Pliny and his contemporary readers, however, *Epistles* 1–9 took the form of nine separate book-rolls, and entered a culture in which the book (or books) of miniatures was a prized and highly determined literary form.[60] That at least is the standard modern view of Augustan poetic books, such as Virgil's *Eclogues* or Propertius' elegies, and of their Hellenistic forebears; the trenchant assumption that prose is essentially different from verse has until recently left Pliny and other prose-artists largely out of the picture.[61] Yet the form of the *Epistles* has a good deal in common with that of poetic collections: book 2, for instance, comprises – like Horace's *Epistles* 1 or *Odes* 2 – twenty self-contained miniatures, each as a rule distinct from its neighbours in addressee, topic, style and length, yet coherent in all these respects as a group. Individual letters are strongly demarcated, not just by the adamant VALE and the obvious rounding-off devices of ring-composition, a *sententia* or an advertisement of epistolarity,[62] but also – again like poems in a collection – by the closural effect intrinsic to their internal structure.[63] But, for all this autonomy, each letter is also part of multiple larger units: the linear sequence, the cycle (e.g. by theme or addressee), the book, the series of books, the collection.[64] It is becoming cliché

[59] Whitton 2013. These Laurentine dictations, we can (by then) infer, are court-speeches (G–M 219–20), but the lingering final scene of literary composition must (also) import epistolary self-referentiality (cf. 2.17.24n. *studis*).

[60] On the book-roll see e.g. Van Sickle 1980, Johnson 2004. On the (over)determination of the poetic book, see Barchiesi 2005 and, among a vast bibliography, e.g. Rudd 1976, Santirocco 1986 and n.64 below.

[61] For correctives see Marchesi 2008: 12–52 (poetic approaches to the *Epistles*), G–M 36–73, especially 36–45 (book 6), and above n.4.

[62] Ring-composition: 2.1.6n. *huius*; *sententia*: pp. 26–7; epistolarity: e.g. 2.1.12, 2.5.13, 2.11.25; see also Winniczuk 1975.

[63] From the smallest scale (2.15) to the largest (2.11, 2.17): see intro. to each letter. On the closural force of structure see Herrnstein Smith 1968, especially 38–150.

[64] Epigram collections offer a parallel: e.g. Gutzwiller 1998, ead. 2005b, Krevans 2007 (Hellenistic); Fowler 1995, Scherf 1998 (Martial).

to speak of Pliny's epistolary 'mosaic', a work of art in which each 'tile' is both autonomous and part of a larger whole, or now also a 'kaleidoscope' whose pieces fall out differently at every shaking.[65] While the *Epistles* invites reading for the letter, then, it also calls attention to the larger canvas: the book, and the set, is a fragmented totality in which each member is a *pars... perfecta* 'perfect part' (2.5.12), both self-standing and subordinate to the whole.

These assertions are harder to substantiate than to make, given the inherent evasiveness of the *Epistles*. The first letter, doubling as editorial preface, promises a selection of 'somewhat carefully' (*paulo curatius*) written letters, organised at random: *collegi non seruato temporis ordine (neque enim historiam componebam), sed ut quaeque in manus uenerat* 'I have collected them without keeping chronological order (for I was not writing a history), but as each one came into my hands' (1.1.1). Prefaces are a notorious site of disingenuity, and even a cursory reader of Pliny's manicured prose can see the urbane understatement in *paulo curatius*, to be taken no more literally than Statius' advertisement of careless haste in the prefaces to his *Siluae*.[66] The same 'air of agreeable carelessness' (Merrill xxxviii) infuses the claim to accidental ordering: not to mention chronology (yet), the randomness is too studied to be accidental, and Pliny is explicit elsewhere about his commitment to variety (2.5.7n. *uarietas*). Disingenuity is doubled, however, if his proemial phrase alludes to Ovid *Epistulae ex Ponto* 3.9.53 *postmodo collectas utcumque sine ordine iunxi* 'afterwards I collected [my letters] and put them together somehow or other, not in any order',[67] since that claim ends a very elaborately structured collection of poetic epistles.[68] Reference to Ovid in so prominent a place constitutes a pressing invitation to set aside prejudice about prose, and to approach Pliny's *Epistles* with an eye to the frames, sequences, juxtapositions, symmetries – and wit – that lie amid and between its 247 constituent parts.

Like a book of Virgil's *Georgics* or (again) Horace's *Odes*, Pliny's books lead on their *doctus lector* with evasive structural games, hinting now at one principle, now at another, in an 'endless tease of disguised patterning and forsworn composition' (Henderson 2002a: xi): this languid elegance will not be caught being too systematic. Tracing such patterns is necessarily fraught and, like explaining a joke, misses the point of the tease, the *delectatio* of discovery (and of foiled expectations).[69] As with intertextuality (§6), this is an area more for suggestive exploration than for prescriptive analysis. But setting Pliny's letters (back) into

[65] 'Mosaic': Altman 1982: 167–84 (on the epistolary novel); 'kaleidoscope': Henderson 2002a: xi with n.5; id. 2003: 125.

[66] For Pliny's genteel turn of phrase see 2.1.4n. *durior*, 2.5.2n. *absolutiora*, 2.17.2 *paulo grauius*.

[67] Syme 1985b: 176, Marchesi 2008: 20–2 (Froesch 1968: 51 already saw the resemblance).

[68] Gaertner 2005: 2–5 (*Ex P.* 4 came later).

[69] Cf. Merwald 1964: 154–8, especially 157 'the result of this game, in which the balls are thrown this way and that between reader and author, is extreme aesthetic *delectatio*' (my translation).

their books and into the collection is not only to pay due respect to the integrity of an aesthetically arranged work of art, it is essential to an appreciation of it.

* * *

Epistles 2 contains twenty letters, the fewest of any book.[70] Addressed to eighteen men and one woman, they range from 48 to 1,083 words (the equivalent, roughly, of 8 to 180 Virgilian hexameters).[71] The book presents itself, characteristically, as an unsorted medley, jumbling letters long and short, serious and light, more and less overt in their epistolarity,[72] to senators and equestrians at Rome and afar, showing Pliny at work and at leisure, in Rome and out of it, content and discontented. So far so various, but variety (a governing principle for Sherwin-White and for many) seems not to be the sole arbiter of arrangement. The book finds cohesion first in its framing letters: similar in length, each addressed to a provincial equestrian and favoured correspondent, one gravely celebrates Verginius Rufus, exemplary consular and true friend to Pliny, the other satirically attacks Aquillius Regulus, counter-exemplary senator and false friend to the dying. Epistle 2.1 moves from the public stage (Verginius' funeral) to the private (intimacy with Pliny), 2.20, conversely, from the *cubicula* of Regulus' victims to a climax of oratorical indignation: these book-ends offer contrast and chiastic ring-composition, with perhaps a dash of intratextuality (2.1.12n. *et*, 2.20.14n. *et*), on the grand scale. A second large-scale contrast concerns 2.11 and 2.17, by far the two longest letters of the book. One crowns Pliny's success in the Priscus trial, the other ushers us into his Laurentine retreat. As instantiations of urban *negotium* and suburban *otium*, of public (as it were) and private, these two letters stage a defining Plinian dichotomy, and in a remarkable way. Uniquely in a collection which – unlike Cicero's or Seneca's – eschews arrangement by addressee, 2.11 is extended into a diptych by 2.12, a second letter to the same person, Maturus Arrianus, on the same topic. Taken together, this diptych runs to 1,082 words, a near-exact match for the 1,083 words of 2.17: these 'twin peaks', towering over book 2, play out quite precisely Pliny's work/life balance.[73] The precision is in part illusory, given the scope for quibbles (*quo modo* or *quomodo*?),[74] and given that ancient prose seems to have been measured not in words but in *uersus* 'lines', where a 'line' was a fixed number of syllables.[75] Still, on this scale it does not

---

[70] At around 6,200 words, however, it is a fraction above average (*c.* 6,100 words) in length.

[71] Namely 2.15 and 2.17 (see 2.15.intro.). Pliny's shortest letter is 9.32 (36 words), his longest 5.6 (1,520 words).

[72] Contrast e.g. 2.7, featuring no engagement with the addressee, with 2.6.6–7 before and 2.8.1 after.

[73] Whitton 2010: 120 n.13, G–M 218–19 (with slightly different figures). Word-counts here exclude letter-heading and VALE.

[74] A further problem is textual corruption: the present count excludes 2.17.14 *et* and 2.17.15 *gestationi* (both excised) but includes 2.17.16 *singulae sed alternis pauciores*, which, while corrupt, seems not to be wholly extraneous.

[75] See 4.11.16 (below, p. 22), Lang 1999.

especially matter what units you count: both aurally and visually, 2.11–12 and
2.17 are a finely balanced pair of highlights for the book.

Do these balances go further? Perhaps so: 2.1–3 and 2.18–20, the first and
last three letters of the book, add up to 843 and 842 words respectively, while
2.4–8 (at 1,083 words) make a match for 2.17. That leaves 2.9–11 (1,298 words)
against 2.12–16 (1,088 words), just failing to balance either side of the book's
middle, which (in terms of word-count, and so physical position on the scroll)
falls a little before the end of 2.11.[76] Could it be that Pliny has measured out his
book so carefully? We are not used to such grand designs in Roman prose, and
circumspection is in order: pattern-hunting, after all, is self-fulfilling for those
who look hard enough.[77] The balance of 2.11–12 and 2.17, however, is sufficiently
obtrusive to prompt at least an open mind.[78]

The behaviour of 2.11 shows characteristic structural fluidity. On the one
hand, together with 2.12 it presents (as we have seen) an exceptional diptych,
straddling the physical centre of the scroll. Yet 2.10–11, numerically central among
the 20 letters, also makes a fitting double-spread, pairing the urgent topic of
literary immortality (albeit jovially treated) with Pliny's great performance in
the Priscus trial (2.10.intro.). There again, 2.11 stands independently of both
neighbours, to judge from the arrangement of the three longest letters of the
book, 2.11~2.14~2.17, and again in the symmetrical framing of 2.11 by 2.9 and
2.13 (a complementary pair of recommendation letters, each to a consul of 97).[79]
These shapes challenge, or rather complement, a reading in terms of word-counts
and of diptychs.

Epistles 2.1–9, by contrast, suggest more thoroughgoing symmetries. Here
four odd-numbered letters hold up individuals, first old, then young, for praise:
2.1 (Verginius), 2.3 (Isaeus), 2.7 (Spurinna and Cottius) and 2.9 (Clarus). The
even-numbered letters, which tend to be shorter, present a pattern too: 2.2 and

---

[76] On 'centre' so defined, see Whitton forthcoming. It reveals that several other major
letters traditionally considered off-centre actually stand at the middle of their books: 3.9
(Classicus trial), 5.8 (writing history), 8.14 (slaves and slavishness). Centres signify within
letters too: e.g. 2.4.2n. *famam*, 2.11.14n. *dixi*, 2.17.15n. *hortum*.

[77] The excesses of Virgilian numerology offer a warning (e.g. Duckworth 1962 and its
reviews).

[78] Cf. G–M 39–43 on the (thematic) 'symmetry' of 6.1–3 and 6.32–4, and n.76 above
for some smaller-scale comparanda.

[79] 2.13.intro. Pliny specifies the consulate of neither: if the date is not coincidence, it
evidences patterning at vanishing-point. Given that no individual (Arrianus apart) receives
more than one letter in book 2, further arrangement by addressee – a principle familiar
from Hor. *Epp.* 1 and Ov. *Ex P.* 1–3 – is buried at best: the identification of five is uncertain
(2.2, 2.3, 2.7, 2.14, 2.19) and four others are scarcely known (2.4, 2.5, 2.10, 2.17). Measuring
by rank, one might observe that 2.1, 2.11–12 and 2.20 are addressed to equestrians, 2.2,
2.3 and 2.18 (probably) to senators: if Cerialis (2.19) was also a senator, that makes a
symmetrical scheme across 2.1–3, 2.11–12 and 2.18–20. Again, 2.7–9, 2.11–12 and 2.14 are
all addressed to fellow Transpadanes (men from Pliny's native region), as could be 2.10 and
2.13, to make a run of eight. If age is a factor, Pliny does not supply enough details to show
it; and if any of this is patterning, it is forsworn indeed.

2.8 are a pair of *otium*-miniatures (Pliny is at leisure in 2.2, longs for it in 2.8), while 2.4 and 2.6 each feature his *frugalitas*. This scheme was discerned by Merwald, the keenest student of Pliny's structures, who identified a series of concentric frames, 1~9, 2~8, 3~7, 4~6, with 2.5 at the centre.[80] It looks neat – too neat – and is certainly liable to objections: 2.1, for instance, pairs better with 2.7 (obituary letters) than with 2.9, and Plinian *frugalitas* is a secondary theme at most in 2.6. Yet what is especially interesting – albeit unnoticed – about Merwald's scheme is the letter at its heart. For 2.5 features the clearest meta-epistolarity (self-reflexive literary comment) of the book in its manifesto for a fragmentary aesthetic (2.5.intro.), signposted with an exceptional instance of gluing between letters: the two analogies in 2.5.8–11 (dinner and statue) return as topics of 2.6 (dinner) and 2.7 (statue). Such a pronounced invitation to read for sequence is rare (underlining the special status of 2.5), but another case appears in 2.15, where Pliny cuts himself short with a warning against endless complaints – a witty perversity in this, the briefest letter of the book, but well justified as comment on the preceding 2.14, the most sustained expression of discontent in book 2.[81] Meta-epistolary self-consciousness also threatens to tweak the reality effect at the start and end of the book, with delicate hints back to book 1 and forward to book 3 (2.1.1n. *post*, 2.20.9n. *sufficiunt*). These evanescent gestures of self-awareness, like the evasive structural patterns surveyed, slyly undercut the impression of real correspondence thrown together, or even a simple principle of variety: the *Epistles* will allow the reader to overlook such hints, but has more to offer for those who accept the invitation to dance.

* * *

What, though, of sequential reading? Narrative progression is one of the most obvious artistic structural devices and a given in such modern epistolary novels as Richardson's *Clarissa*, Goethe's *Die Leiden des jungen Werthers* or Laclos' *Les Liaisons dangereuses*. In Roman poetry the position is more complicated: Catullus' poems, for instance, notoriously jumble his relationship with Lesbia. Readers familiar with the letters of Cicero and Seneca, however, would have every reason to expect at least loose chronological progression, and they would not be disappointed on unrolling Pliny's collection. Although his letters are never dated and never – with the signal exception of 6.16.4 (the eruption of Vesuvius) – specify dates within them, and despite the disclaimer in 1.1.1 *non seruato temporis ordine*, ordering by time is routine in serial letters addressing the same topic and/or person (as e.g. 2.12, reporting a debate of February 100, follows 2.11, on January events). Other letters – still a minority – can be dated relatively or absolutely through information about Pliny's and others' movements and careers (much

---

[80] Merwald 1964: 49–59, adding some small (too small?) verbal connections: 2.2.2 *occupatior* ~ 2.8.3 *occupationum*, 2.4.3 *ne sit mihi onerosa* ~ 2.6.5 *non est onerosum*. He sees *Epistles* 2 (ibid. 39–60) as two panels 2.1–9 and 2.11–20, with 2.10 as the 'hinge'; his analysis of 2.11–20 (and of *Epistles* 1–9) suffers from tendentious rigidity, but includes shrewd comment.

[81] See 2.9.1n. *anxium* for mood similarly trickling between adjacent letters.

of it laboriously reconstructed from the *Epistles* itself). Sherwin-White, author of the most detailed and authoritative analysis,[82] demonstrated that the books proceed in overlapping sequence: *Epistles* 1 has a time-frame or 'book-date' of AD 96/7–98/9,[83] book 2 runs 97–100, book 3 covers 99–103, and so on to book 9, dated to 106–108/9.[84] Within books, by contrast, he argued that (serial letters such as 2.11–12 apart) the items were ordered at will – an important reminder that the *apparent* date of the letter (the 'dramatic date', as it were) is not necessarily identical with the date of editing (or even, we might add, of composition). Can this be shown for our book?

In *Epistles* 2 the following can be assigned some sort of dramatic date: 2.1 (Nov. or Dec. 97), 2.7 (before 28 Jan. 98), 2.8 (Jan. 98 to Aug. 100), 2.9 (late 99 or late 100), 2.11 (Jan. 100), 2.12 (Feb. 100), 2.13 (probably 100), 2.14 (before Jan. 98 or after Oct. 100), 2.16 (perhaps after Aug. 100), 2.19 (after Jan. 100);[85] in 2.5 Pliny is revising a speech given before Jan. 98 or after Oct. 100.[86] Several of these dates derive from Pliny's time as prefect of the treasury of Saturn (Jan. 98 to Aug. 100), during which he claims not to have practised as a civil advocate (10.3A.1), and his consulate (Sept.–Oct. 100), a topic reserved for *Epistles* 3 (below, p. 18). If we assume that no letters later than October 100 are included and that Pliny would only revise speeches in their immediate aftermath, 2.14 and 2.19 alone would demonstrably defy chronological sequence; remove those assumptions and (for what it is worth) no letter, in this book at least, would break ranks.[87]

It may be more pertinent, however, to ask how far the letters *intend* to be datable: these dramatic dates depend on often complex reconstructions, and even relative dating is restricted to 2.12.1 *proxime*, binding the exceptional diptych 2.11–12. Unless Pliny's sole intended audience was his immediate circle, he can fairly be said to have made the task extraordinarily difficult. Whether the letters of book 2 are in chronological sequence, then, is a less relevant consideration for the reader (if not for the historian) than the *impression* of sequence, the narrative, which they present. One reading might run as follows: Pliny mourns the death of his old *tutor* and patron (and so spreads his wings) in 2.1, presides as *pater*/patron to Calvina (2.4), Comum (2.5) and Avitus (2.6), triumphs in the Priscus trial (2.11) but adds a gloomy postscript (2.12), is depressed by the civil courts (2.14)

---

[82] S-W, especially 20–65, building (especially) on Mommsen 1869.

[83] 96/7–98 in S-W 27, 41, 103 (though p. 122 implies 97–8), 96–9 in S-W 1967: 73.

[84] 106–8 for S-W, extended to 109 by Syme 1985b. Book 10, though mostly dwelling *c.* 110–12, begins afresh in 98.

[85] See 2.1.6n. *laudatus*, 2.7.1n. *principe*, 2.8.2n. *angor*, 2.9.2n. *a Caesare*, 2.11.10n. *in*, 2.11.24n. *referri*, 2.13.2n. *longum*, 2.14.intro., 2.16.4n. *si*, 2.19.8n. *nobis*.

[86] 2.5.1n. *actionem*.

[87] S-W need not be wrong on other books, but further weak links include 1.18 (S-W 28: Pliny mentions a dream from before Jan. 98 – but also long before the time of writing) and 3.2, which S-W set in late 103 (thus much later than 3.4, in 99) through a false assumption about its addressee (S-W 58–9, 210: see Birley 2000a: 100).

and has bad news from Comum (2.15), lingers at Laurentum (2.17) and finally bursts with impotent ire at Regulus' unchecked success (2.20). Seen through this prism, *Epistles* 2 presents itself as an arc with the Priscus trial at the summit but a narrative of decline and withdrawal thereafter. Of course other letters show Pliny patronising and indulging in literary pursuits as usual (2.9, 2.10, 2.13, 2.16, 2.18, 2.19), but it is striking that 2.11, 2.14 and 2.20 each end with shadows: 2.11 in the glimpse of Regulus stalking backstage (2.11.22) and its 'appendix' 2.12, 2.14 with unusual resignation at its close and its own tail-letter 2.15 (above, p. 15), 2.20 with the Domitianic creature Regulus triumphant. The beginnings of a pattern? Only the *Laurentinum* needs to be added to make a sequence 2.11~2.14~2.17~2.20, a sequence which easily extends back to 2.8, the prime note of frustration in the book's first half. From this vantage-point, Pliny's villa letter, for all its sunny radiance, could (also) appear as a signal of retreat from Rome to the suburban periphery.

In the world of the *Epistles*, such a narrative is fragmentary, a suggestive gesture at best; Pliny assured us that he was not writing a history (1.1.1 *neque enim historiam componebam*).[88] Yet readers are prone to seek out (or impose) a narrative, however jumbled the fragments may look, and the impression sketched out here suggests that Pliny's book, in its own oblique way, exploits and caters to that urge. At all events, it is striking that the second half of book 2 is freighted with discontent: the reader leaves the book with a less cheery impression of Pliny than is usually ascribed to him, foreshadowing perhaps the darkness that sets on at the end of *Epistles* 1–9.[89] But that prompts another question, how to read book 2 itself in the broader sweep of the collection.

* * *

Epistles 1–9 presents itself as an organic artistic unity, above all through the ring-composition that binds the first and last books: scholars have noted the reversal of 1.1.1 *frequenter hortatus es* ~ 9.1.1 *saepe te monui*, the pairs of letters to Tacitus (1.6~9.10 and 1.6~9.14), on political 'revenge' (1.5~9.13) and on oratory (1.20~9.26), the chiastic closing reprise of the great villa letters (2.17 and 5.6) in 9.36 and 9.40, and a framing pun between the addressees of 1.1 (Clarus, 'Mr Bright' or 'Mr VIP') and 9.40 (Fuscus, 'Mr Shady').[90] There are hints too of an inner ring spanning the second and eighth books: Priscus (2.11–12) finds a match in the central 8.14, the villa a partner in 8.20 (to the same Gallus), and 2.20 a reply in the foiled *captatio* of 8.18.[91] And at the mid-point of the central book we find *suades ut historiam scribam* (5.8.1), in striking reprise of *neque enim historiam componebam*

---

[88] With manifest irony: Ash 2003.

[89] On which see Gibson forthcoming. The gloom of 2.20 was once taken to show a Domitianic date (e.g. Merrill xl, 263–4).

[90] See Murgia 1985: 198–9 and Whitton 2012 and 2013 (with further references). On Clarus/Fuscus see Barchiesi 2005: 331–2, Marchesi 2008: 249–50, Gibson 2011b.

[91] 2.12.intro., 2.17n. GALLO, 2.20.1n. *fabulas*. In other ways book 8 looks back to book 1 (Whitton 2013 at n.41).

(1.1.1)[92] – another adumbration of grand designs. Yet what Pliny promised was an open-ended, unplanned series of books (1.1.2 *ita enim fiet ut eas quae adhuc neglectae iacent requiram et si quas addidero non supprimam*). Once again the *Epistles* is marked by indeterminacy, presenting itself both as unified whole and as an accretive scripting of 'real-life' epistolarity in process.[93]

As we have seen, Sherwin-White's generally accepted book-dates show a progression through the nine books from AD 96/7 to 108/9; but these dramatic dates prove nothing about the editorial process. Most scholars have assumed serial publication, whether in single books (Mommsen), triads (Peter),[94] or irregular groupings such as 1–3, 4–5, 6–7 and 8–9 (Syme), or 1, 2 (or 1–2), 3, 4–6 and 7–9 (Sherwin-White);[95] Murgia added the important suggestion that the whole set might have been revised and re-released in *c.* 109 to form *Epistles* 1–9 as we have it.[96] Adjudication between these positions is difficult. On one side, small signs of linguistic change over the collection (2.4.3n. *nec*, 2.6.7n. *igitur*) may imply serial composition (without excluding a final stage of editing); likewise, to mention just one detail, the presence of Vibius Maximus (addressee of 3.2), who suffered *damnatio memoriae* in 107.[97] On the other, there are indications at least of forward planning from one book to the next, as when 3.20 expresses foreboding which finds fulfilment in 4.25, or even (at an extreme) in 1.5, whose open-ended threats of reprisals against Regulus only come good, obliquely, in the attack on Publicius Certus described in 9.13 (Whitton 2013); like other responsions between books 1 and 9, however, this could have been engineered in retrospect. Absences are equally suggestive: *Epistles* 1–2 suppresses mention of the Classicus trial and Pliny's forthcoming consulate, reserving them (along with his adoptive father Pliny the Elder) for book 3,[98] and says nothing of his new wife Calpurnia (2.17.20n. *amores*) or of the great Etruscan villa (2.17.intro.). Yet our ability to mine the creative process (was book 3 a possibility, a sketch, a draft when book 2 was composed?) is limited, as the disagreements between Syme, Sherwin-White and others make clear. Greater rewards may lie in considering how the collection behaves, as a series of books each (like the letters within it) marked off as units but also part of a growing whole.

Certainly *Epistles* 2 invites a reading not just as a single book but also as the second half of a diptych: at least when viewed from book 3, *Epistles* 1–2 makes a tightly knit pair of 'preconsular' books. Although they differ (as do all consecutive pairs) in the number of letters (24 in book 1, 20 in book 2), the sense of

---

[92] 'Mid-point' in terms of the scroll (above, n.76).

[93] Cf. MacArthur 1990: 128 (of a real-life letter collection): 'textual construction "en devenir"'.

[94] Mommsen 1869: 36–53, Peter 1901: 105–9 (and others).

[95] Syme 1958: 662–4, S-W 30 (and 45).

[96] Murgia 1985: 191–202; see also Hoffer 1999: 9–10. Bodel (n.d.) proposes multiple stages of extension and revision.

[97] On his identity see S-W 210, Syme 1968: 143.

[98] 2.12.intro., 2.11.19n. *Cornutus*, 2.1.8n. *tutor*.

a diptych is encouraged by an unusual degree of similarity in content,[99] by the Nerva–Trajan overlap (above, pp. 7–8), and by the pairing of letters to an extent unmatched in subsequent books: 1.3~2.8 (to Caninius on *otium*), 1.4~2.4 (female addressees), 1.5~2.20 (Regulus), 1.7~2.10 (to poet Octavius), 1.8~2.19 (hesitation over publishing/reciting a speech), 1.10~2.3 ('Greek intellectuals'), 1.11~2.2 (brief demand for news), 1.12~2.1 (death of an elder statesman and personal patron), 1.14~2.18 (to/about Acilianus), 1.15~2.6 (dinner), 1.17~2.7 (statue).[100] Even the longest letters (1.20, on length, and 2.17, the villa), for all their differences, find analogous positions in their books. Any patterning to this arrangement shimmers typically almost out of view (1.10–11–12 ~ 2.3–2–1 catches the eye), with only the two notes to women (1.4~2.4) sharing the same position, and the picture is complicated by double pairings: 1.5, for instance, also resonates (through addressee Romanus) with 2.1 and (through mention of Mauricus) with 2.18, while 2.4 (munificence to Calvina) finds a match not just in 1.4 (to a woman) but also in 1.19 (munificence to Firmus). Nor need we insist on the identification of any particular 'pair' to see how closely (yet subtly) these two first books cohere.

Accordingly 2.20 may be read as the close not just of its book but of *Epistles* 1–2 together, reprising as it does the subject and manner of 1.5 (the first substantial letter of book 1) to reveal Regulus' *flagitia* . . . *tectiora* (1.5.1) in ring-composition (2.20.1n. *nec*). Yet this letter is also the site of closure unravelled: the next book begins with another letter to the same Calvisius (3.1), palliating the bitter aftertaste of 2.20 with the savoury example of Vestricius Spurinna, while book 3 as a whole, with Regulus forgotten and Pliny now consul, reframes book 2 and its narrative of retreat as the fall before a rise.[101] Across *Epistles* 2–3 paired letters are less frequent but still present, whether numerical, as 2.1~3.1 (portrait of an elder statesman) and 2.13~3.13 (about/to Voconius), or thematic, as 2.11~3.9 (central senatorial trial), 2.19~3.18 (reciting speeches). Some of the pairs of books 1–2 extend into trios, as 1.11~2.2~3.17 ('no letters'), 1.15~2.6~3.12 (dinner), 1.17~2.7~3.6 (statue), while 1.10~2.3 (Greek portraits) finds partial continuation in 3.11 (Artemidorus). *Epistles* 3 will end on a heavily closural note, with Martial's death, Pliny as a new Cicero and the motif of literary eternity (3.21), so end-stopping a triad *Epistles* 1–3 (see 2.10.intro.) – but that closure is already (retrospectively) challenged by the preceding 3.20, a set-up for 4.25 (above). And so on.

As the collection proceeds, reframing continues: the large Laurentine villa, for instance, will be revealed by book 5 as mere prelude to the still greater Etruscan estate (2.17.intro., 29n. *uillulae*). But the most telling instance concerns Regulus, subject of vicious attack in 1.5 and 2.20 and a passing shot in 2.11.22. The arrival

---

[99] In Sherwin-White's terms, a similar distribution of 'letter-types' (S-W 42–7).
[100] This list varies and extends S-W 54.
[101] 2.20.intro.; for the effect cf. Cic. *Att.* 3.27 *nos funditus perisse uideo* (a gloomy end to his exile book) ~ *Att.* 4.1.1 *cum primum Romam ueni* . . . with Beard 2002: 126–7. For 'retreat' see above, pp. 16–17.

of book 3, as we have noted, sets the gloom of 2.20 in a new light, but revision of that letter continues in book 4, with wicked emplotment. In 2.20.5–6 we see Regulus commit perjury on his son's life; when his next appearance begins with the words *Regulus filium amisit* (4.2.1), the poetic justice is too good to miss.[102] He is also, more obliquely but (as Gibson and Morello have demonstrated) quite clearly, connected to another instance of pessimism overturned, this time in 2.14, Pliny's excoriation of his fellow civil advocates (G–M 68–73, 2.14.intro.). Although Regulus is not mentioned in that letter, in books 4–6 his waning influence and death are accompanied by a rise in Pliny's centumviral glory and a concomitant resurrection of the court itself, a hint perhaps that the discontent of 2.14 is to be associated with his continued influence back then. Taken together, these adjustments to our experience of *Epistles* 2, unpicking its completeness (and revising much of its gloom), suggest that the single book, like the single letter, has its internal cohesion but also finds new meaning from its context in the collection. Which is the 'right' meaning is a different, perhaps the wrong, question: the *Epistles* is no jigsaw puzzle to solve, but neither are its shifting sands wholly indeterminate. Patterns, frames, sequence and narrative within and between its individual books fade in and out of view, teasing the reader with evanescent glimpses of meta-epistolarity: such is Pliny's evasive epistolary game in these nine suites of semi-autonomous 'perfect parts'.

4 PROSE D'ART

The primary colours of Pliny's Latin are brevity, clarity and rhetoricity. From this palette he creates a subtly varying style which is both distinctive and flexible, embracing a wide range of manners – grand, chatty, frank, delicate, satirical, kindly, businesslike, coquettish – all within the miniature confines of the *pressus sermo purusque* 'succinct and simple language' that is the professed norm of epistles (7.9.8). Elements gesture towards the axiomatic conversationality of letters (2.5.13n. *tecum*), but this prose is nothing if not intensely worked in its artful semblance of spontaneity.[103]

Rhetoric was heavily theorised in antiquity, as Pliny, practising orator and pupil of Quintilian (2.14.9n. *Quintiliano*), well knew.[104] The following discussion introduces technical terms used in the commentary and offers an overview of Pliny's manner. This might first be characterised in opposition to the so-called

---

[102] 2.20.6n. *in*, Syme 1958: 663, Murgia 1985: 193, giving good reason to suppose that Pliny published only after Regulus' death (6.2). S-W 55, 203 (concerned with dates of publication) resolutely misses it.

[103] Pliny's language is discussed by Niemirska-Pliszczyńska 1955, Aubrion 1975: 113–30, Gamberini 1983. Grammar and syntax, (drily) covered in Kraut 1872 and Lagergren 1872, are largely left for the commentary.

[104] Ancient discussions and examples are collected in Lausberg, to which I routinely refer.

periodic style. Often considered a defining feature of the 'classical' Latin prose of Caesar and Cicero, **periodic sentences** build tension through participles and subordinate clauses before the main verb releases it at the end.[105] Such periods are rare in the *Epistles*, which tends rather to be 'additive', presenting information in smaller units that often lead sequentially one to the next: explanations more commonly follow than precede, and information is frequently tacked on after the main clause (2.1.1 *perinde felicis*) or Pliny modifies a statement as if thinking aloud (2.4.4 *tamen... sed... uero*). **Participles** are used relatively lightly, and **parataxis** (lack of subordination) is common (2.5.2n. *rogo*). **Hyperbaton** (the 'artificial' separation of words which belong together) is used, sparingly, for rhetorical or stylistic effect.[106] As in Cicero's letters and dialogues,[107] **verbs** are prone to fall early (e.g. 2.14.1 *uerum opinaris: distringor... sunt enim... raro incidit...*), though this is no absolute rule: they may be final, juxtaposed mid-sentence (2.4.1 *debuisset, fuisset*), framing a clause (2.6.3 *animaduertit... interrogauit*) or a combination of these (2.1.2n. *triginta*).

A defining feature of Pliny's prose, as of much early imperial Latin, is **antithesis**, the setting of two or more ideas in opposition. These may be single words (2.17.4 *frugi nec tamen sordidum*, 2.17.23 *aut effundit aut retinet*) or groups of words, known for these purposes as 'members' or cola (sg. **colon**):[108] 2.3.1 *dicit semper ex tempore,* | *sed tamquam diu scripserit*, 2.13.6 *aut fidelius amico* | *aut sodale iucundius.* The ideas being paired can be opposites or complementary. The cola may be coordinated by conjunctions, sometimes flagged by a concessive particle (*fortasse, licet, quidem*), or by **polysyndeton** (multiple conjunctions, e.g. *et... et*); also by subordination (2.12.5 *cum sit impar prudentia, par omnium ius est*), or – very commonly – in **asyndeton**, lack of connection.

Asyndetic antithesis is superabundant in Pliny, often underlined with **rhyme** (2.20.11 *putabat... instabat*)[109] or **anaphora** (opening repetition: 2.13.5 *ille meus in urbe,* | *ille in secessu contubernalis*), when possible with **polyptoton** (multiple inflections: 2.17.3 *multi greges ouium,* | *multa ibi equorum boum armenta*),[110] more affective and affirmatory than, say, *multi greges et armenta*. Word-order is commonly inverted across the cola in **chiasmus** (AB~BA: 2.4.3 *quod cessat ex reditu* | *frugalitate*

---

[105] Periods are notoriously difficult to define, and the term 'periodic' much abused: see Adams–Lapidge–Reinhardt 2005: 7–14, problematising the notion of a golden periodic ideal; also Mayer 2005: 208.

[106] Rhetorical: e.g. 2.1.1n. *insigne*, 2.4.2n. *magnum*, 2.11.3n. *uir*. Stylistic: 2.1.1n. *in*, 2.9.1n. *anxium*, 2.11.5n. *censuit*.

[107] For Cicero's epistolary style see Hutchinson 1998, von Albrecht 2003: 52–72, Hallaaho 2011. On the position of verbs see Linde 1923 (pp. 155 and 166 for Pliny).

[108] On the vagaries of this term see Lausberg §§928–34, Habinek 1985: 1–17. The sign | indicates a break between cola.

[109] E.g. 2.12.3n. *non*, 2.14.10n. *immodicum*, 12n. *quae*, all examples of homoeoteleuton (end-rhyme); other types at e.g. 2.5.7n. *sicut*, 2.6.5n. *quibus*, 2.12.5n. *numerantur*, 2.15.2n. *materna*, 2.17.29n. *maxima*.

[110] Anaphora: e.g. 2.1.2n. *legit*, 6n. *magnum*, 7n. *plenus*, 12n. *Verginium*, 2.3.2n. *multa*. With polyptoton: e.g. 2.3.3n. *crebra*, 2.18.4n. *hanc*.

suppletur);[111] more often, and arguably more artificially,[112] it is matched in **parallelism** (AB~AB: 2.3.9 *legendi semper occasio est,* | *audiendi non semper,* 2.20.11 *obseruauit scribentem,* | *inspexit an scripsisset*).[113] In either case, concinnity (exact harmony) is often moderated by intervening words (e.g. *occasio est* in 2.3.9) or by formal or syntactical variation (*ex reditu* against *frugalitate* in 2.4.3, participle *scribentem* against indirect question *an scripsisset* in 2.20.11). When there are three (or more) elements, total symmetry (2.11.13n. *ut,* ABC~CBA) and total parallelism (2.19.2n. *omnibusque,* ABC~ABC) are rare:[114] Pliny prefers a mixture of chiasmus and parallelism, e.g. 2.17.2 *iunctis paulo grauius et longius,* | *equo breue et molle* (ABC~ACB), 2.7.5n. *acuent* (ABCD~ACBD), 2.11.8n. *ex* (ABCDDC~ADBC).[115]

Such **bicola** (pairs of cola) take three shapes. The frequent **rising bicolon** (2.11.13 *quem… tuebatur,* 11~21 syllables) conforms to an observed tendency in rhetoric ('the law of rising members'),[116] a tendency which makes a **falling bicolon**, with its unexpectedly short second member, the more striking (2.6.7 *cum sint turpissima discreta ac separata,* | *turpius iunguntur,* 13~6 syllables).[117] Especially common in Pliny, however, is the pairing of equal members in **isocolon**: 2.3.6 *quid in senectute felicius* | *quam quod dulcissimum est in iuuenta?* (10~10).[118]

Counting **syllables** may seem eccentric to the modern mind, but it is clearly how Quintilian and others weighed their cola;[119] when Pliny jokes that he will count (in our terms) 'every word' of a reply, what he says is *ego non paginas tantum sed uersus etiam syllabasque numerabo* 'I will count not just the pages but even the lines and the syllables' (4.11.16). Balance is relative, however, and the number of syllables need not match precisely,[120] so that 2.6.2 *nam sibi et paucis opima quaedam,* | *ceteris uilia et minuta ponebat* (10~12) can reasonably be called isocolon;[121] in any case, uncertainties over how to treat **elision** make syllable-counts more indicative than determinative.[122] This antithetical balancing extends to larger structures

---

[111] E.g. 2.1.3n. *Caesares… euasit,* 2.2.1n. *non,* 2.7.6n. *amaui,* 2.11.21n. *in,* 2.15.2n. *materna.*

[112] Chiasmus may be the more 'natural' word-order (Leeman 1963: 22), but its rhetorical use was also routine (H–S 696–8). See also Steele 1902.

[113] E.g. 2.2.2n. *haec,* 2.5.3n. *in,* 2.6.2n. *non,* 2.10.2n. *tibi,* 2.20.11n. *Aurelia;* cf. 2.11.4n. *magna* (parallel alliteration) and larger-scale parallel antithesis at e.g. 2.11.8n. *ex,* 2.17.13n. *turbati,* 14n. *gestatio.*

[114] There is an unusual bunching in 2.11 (2.11.3n. *omniaque,* 6n. *quae,* 6n. *acres,* 7n. *quod*).

[115] And e.g. 2.5.7n. *ut,* 2.12.5n. *nam,* 2.17.3n. *multi,* 6n. *altera,* 17n. *quantumque,* 24n. *nec,* 26n. *suggerunt,* 2.18.3n. *cum,* 2.19.9n. *a te.*

[116] 2.1.1n. *insigne* and e.g. 2.1.8n. *primum,* 2.6.5n. *illa,* 2.7.5n. *et,* 2.11.6n. *acres,* 2.18.1n. *sedeo.*

[117] E.g. 2.1.12n. *ciues,* 2.6.4n. *liberti,* 2.12.5n. *numerantur,* 5n. *nam,* 2.15.2n. *habent.*

[118] Quint. 9.3.80, Lausberg §§711–32, Calboli 1969: 336–8. E.g. 2.5.7n. *ut,* 2.6.1n. *ut,* 2.7.7n. *non,* 2.11.22n. *ut,* 2.14.7n. *plerique,* 2.18.1n. *quid.*

[119] E.g. Quint. 9.3.79–80, 'Demetrius' *On style* 25. Lausberg §721 is strangely insistent that ancients counted words, not syllables; many other modern scholars assume the same.

[120] *Rhet. Her.* 4.27–8.

[121] So e.g. 2.3.2n. *multa* (8~7), 2.9.5n. *omnes* (14~16), 2.11.4n. *magna* (6~7), 2.11.7n. *quod* (12~14), 2.14.5n. *uocantur* (14~15).

[122] Elision is assumed here to occur within but not between cola. See Riggsby 1991, and n.162 below. There is scope for doubt too with e.g. *nihil/nil, prehendere/prendere,* and forms in *-(i)i-* (2.1.5n. *male,* 2.2.2n. *studis,* 2.11.2n. *petit,* 23n. *Mari*).

too: the two *cum*-clauses in 2.4.2 are balanced at 48~50 syllables, while the short letter 2.15, clearly divided into two segments (*quomodo te ... | me ...*), not only has matching truisms ending each half (17~16), but makes an isocolon in itself (50~53). Scaling up (and switching to word-counts for the sake of practicality), the close balance between 2.11–12 and 2.17 (above, pp. 13–14) captures an antithesis of *negotium* and *otium* in an isocolon (as it were) of extraordinary proportions.

Besides the bicolon, the **tricolon** is popular with Pliny as with all rhetoricians. Polysyndeton is quite rare (2.3.5 *aut ... aut ... aut*),[123] partial connection ('X Y *et* Z') commoner,[124] asyndeton very frequent. **Rising tricolon** famously makes for high rhetoric in Cicero; for Pliny it is one option among several.[125] He also likes what might be termed **extended tricolon**, in which the third colon alone is markedly longer (2.1.12 *Verginium cogito, Verginium uideo, Verginium ... teneo*, 7~7~26);[126] equal or near-equal members are also common (2.2.1 *iniquus interdum, impotens saepe*, μικραίτιος *semper*, 6~5~6).[127] Longer accumulations in **tetracolon** and **pentacolon** are generally restricted to single words or very short units, listing qualities (2.9.4 *sanctus antiquus disertus atque in agendis causis exercitatus*, 2.9.3n. *probissimum*, 2.13.7n. *excelsum*) and actions (2.20.3 *componit uultum, intendit oculos, mouet labra, agitat digitos, computat*, 2.3.3n. *prohoemiatur ... excelse*); often a longer or shorter final member marks the end (2.9.4 *atque ... exercitatus* and 2.20.3 *computat* in the phrases just quoted). Here too variety reigns: instead of AB~AB~AB,[128] Pliny routinely mixes parallelism and chiasmus to give AB~AB~BA (2.17.1 *gratiam uillae, opportunitatem loci, litoris spatium*),[129] AB~BA~AB (2.1.8n. *eadem*, 2.13.4n. *pater ... clarus*) or AB~BA~BA (2.8.1n. *lacus*);[130] the same goes for longer sequences (2.17.22n. *non*).[131]

Whatever their length, cola frequently rise in intensity (**gradation**): e.g. 2.1.8 *regio ~ municipia ~ agri* (homing in geographically), 2.11.8 *fustibus caesus ~ damnatus in metallum ~ strangulatus in carcere* (progressively more outrageous).[132] The last member of a graded sequence is often marked with *atque etiam* or with *denique* or *etiam* (second word).[133] Common too is the **asyndetic tricolon of**

---

[123] Also e.g. 2.3.6, 2.7.1, 2.10.7 (X *et* Y *et* Z); 2.10.1 (X *uel potius* Y *ac paene* Z).

[124] 2.1.2n. *triginta*. X Y *que* Z *que* is also possible, but rarer (2.11.3n. *deprecatusque*).

[125] See 2.1.8n. *eadem* (6~9~13) and e.g. 2.8.1n. *lacus* (4~11~17), 2.11.1n. *solet* (22~33~40), 10n. *princeps* (12~31~49), 2.19.2n. *iudicum* (16~23~35).

[126] Noted by Ax 1930: 747. E.g. 2.4.3n. *modicae* (7~7~23), 2.7.1n. *numquam* (8~7~20), 2.17.5n. *a tergo* (3~2~9). More rarely the second and third members are both much longer than the first, e.g. 2.1.8n. *sic* (12~33~36), 2.14.4n. *conuenitur* (6~21~17).

[127] E.g. 2.9.1n. *meus* (4~7~5), 2.10.5n. *tam* (4~5~6), 2.11.1n. *personae claritate famosum* (10~10~9). Others dip in the middle: 2.1.6n. *magnum* (8~5~8), 2.15.1n. *quomodo ... ?* (11~7~11).

[128] Found occasionally, e.g. 2.2.1n. *iniquus*, 2.11.18n. *senatum*.

[129] And e.g. 2.9.4n. *summa*, 2.11.2n. *fidei*, 2.17.12n. *latissimum*.

[130] E.g. 2.8.2n. *omnia*, 2.11.8n. *fustibus*, 2.19.2n. *iudicum*; also 2.4.3n. *modicae* (AB~BA~BAA).

[131] In all this Pliny keeps company with Livy, Seneca and others (Steele 1902, Kraus 1994: 22–3).

[132] See Lausberg §§403, 406, Lagergren 1872: 48, Niemirska-Pliszczyńska 1955: 111–12 and e.g. 2.3.3n. *apte*, 4n. *nihil*, 2.7.1n. *numquam*, 2.11.4n. *magna*, 2.14.6n. *hoc*.

[133] 2.1.6n. *etiam*, 2.3.8n. *denique*.

single words, found over a hundred times in the *Epistles* (2.8.2 *uinum balinea fontes*, 2.9.6 *diligeris coleris frequentaris*), besides more than twenty tetracola or longer sequences (2.11.17 *subtilis dispositus acer disertus*);[134] here too the last member may be capped with *etiam* or *denique* and/or extended (2.13.10 *studia mores omnem denique uitam*). Often this entails **redundance**, the use of two (or more) synonymous or near-synonymous words where one would do. This manner of emphasis, for which Cicero is notorious, is much affected by Pliny especially in **doublets** (usually with a conjunction), whether in grandeur (2.1.1n. *insigne*) or in limpid description (2.17.9 *digerit et ministrat*, 2.17.25 *obuius et paratus*).[135]

In all its varieties, then, antithesis is at the core of Pliny's prose style. Like other imperial prose authors, he has been faulted for it by generations of scholars raised to admire periodic Latin as the golden ideal; but within the tight parameters of the antithetical manner his capacity for variation is all the more impressive. The variety is subtle – demure by comparison with Tacitus' celebrated war against concinnity[136] – and the scale small (as fits his epistolary stage); but the product is anything but bland.

* * *

Letters purport to be conversation (2.5.13n. *tecum*), and rhetorical formalism is combined with (refined) casual touches, reminiscent of but different from Cicero's epistles: **parenthesis** is very frequent (2.3.2n. *sed*); **Greek** implies epistolary intimacy (2.2.1n. μικραίτιος) but self-consciously so (often with bilingual word-play);[137] **direct speech**, for all its apparent conversationality, is highly stylised: a pregnant epigram from Verginius (2.1.9), a string of crafted bicola in 2.6.3–4, clausulated wheedling from Regulus in 2.20.4.[138] There is little place for the chatty particles that spice up Seneca's letters (Summers 1910: xlix–l), and even informal phrases are integrated into the most honed of structures, as in 2.20.2 *Verania Pisonis grauiter iacebat, huius dico Pisonis quem Galba adoptauit*, where the casual *huius dico* articulates precise isocolon (13~13). The combination typifies the balancing act of these published 'private' letters and their display of lazy learning (2.2.intro.).

This blend of casual and formal is evident not least in Pliny's abundant **brevity**. Terse expression was a rhetorical desiderandum of the age, and the

---

[134] See Kraut 1872: 44–5, 2.3.1n. *facultas*, 2n. *surgit*; also e.g. 2.1.12n. *cogito*, 2.17.29n. *incolere*. Asyndetic tricola are widespread in Latin (H–S 830); Oakley 2009: 197 n.13 collects Tacitean examples.

[135] See e.g. 2.1.4n. *durior*, 7n. *quaerendus*, 2.7.4n. *uita*, 2.14.12n. *funditus*.

[136] Norden 1898: 332–4, Sörbom 1935 and e.g. indexes to Damon 2003 and Ash 2007 s.v. *uariatio*.

[137] E.g. 2.3.8n. ἀφιλόκαλον, 2.11.23n. *superest*, 2.14.5n. Σοφοκλεῖς. At 2.3.10 λαμπροφωνότατος and 2.11.17 σεμνῶς the Greek is choice and grand; 2.20.12 ἀλλὰ τί διατείνομαι is an allusion. The villa letter is studded with transliterated Greek (2.7.8n. *cubiculum*).

[138] On the clausulae see below, p. 30. Direct speech also at 2.3.10, 2.14.11, 2.20.8, 10; P. puts words into his correspondent's mouth in 2.2.2, 2.3.9, 2.10.5.

Panegyricus shows how even a very long work can strain for concision in single phrases (Durry 1938: 48). But brevity is scripted into the *Epistles* at every level, highly self-conscious as these letters are of their generically determined status as miniatures. **Asyndeton**, a marker of plain style (Marouzeau 1962: 228–33), is ubiquitous: it makes for efficient lists (2.1.2n. *triginta*), swift sketches (2.3.1–4) and narratives (parts of 2.11 and 2.20), casual camaraderie (2.15) and plain talk (*passim*): in short, a wide range of uses, often interspersed – in typical variety – with connected sentences.[139] **Verbal ellipse** is very common, with *esse* of course (including in subordinate clauses),[140] but also with other verbs, making for swift narrative or argument (2.6.6 *quorsus haec?*, 2.14.11 *iterum clamor*, 2.20.3 *nihil*) or epigrammatic kick (2.20.8n. *Regulo*), and gesturing towards the (much more) elliptical style of many Ciceronian letters. **Pronouns** are easily omitted from indirect statement (2.11.9n. *fore*) and *is qui* is routinely shortened to *qui* (2.1.10n. *qua*), while other words are used compendiously, e.g. 2.1.5 *consulatu* 'inauguration as consul'. Pliny also likes the **substantival participle**, making a single word work hard (2.3.9n. *dicentis*), and the efficient free use of the **future participle** (2.1.5n. *acturus*).

Brevity is often served by the construction **apo koinou** (ἀπὸ κοινοῦ 'in common'),[141] where a word or phrase is stated once but understood twice (2.13.5 *cum hoc seria* [*sc. miscui*], *cum hoc iocos miscui*). A common feature of spoken language, it becomes more mannered when shared words are distributed across two or more cola in what may be called **double apo koinou** (2.3.2 *multa lectio in subitis*, *multa scriptio elucet*, i.e. prosaically *multa lectio et scriptio in subitis elucet*).[142] A construction well established in prose as in verse (e.g. Caes. *BG* 1.1 *qui ipsorum linguā Celtae*, *nostrā Galli appellantur*, Hor. *Ep.* 1.1.1 *prima dicte mihi*, *summa dicende Camena*), it is much affected by Pliny, often as here in 2.3.2 with anaphora further stylising the form (and creating tension between brevity and expansiveness).[143] More pregnant still is **syllepsis**, in which the reader must not only reuse but also adapt the shared word. The adaptation may be **syntactic**, as in 2.1.2 *legit scripta de se carmina*, *legit historias* [*sc. de se scriptas*], or **semantic**, where the common word has two different senses, or works more naturally in one colon than another, e.g. 2.17.10 *plurimo sole*, *plurimo mari lucet* 'is bright with abundant sun and abundant sea'.[144]

This last example captures Pliny's intense working of **lexis**. Villa-jargon aside, his vocabulary can seem deceptively simple, and **neologism** (coining new

---

[139] Asyndeton is notably spare in the reasoning of 2.5 and 2.19.
[140] 2.2.1n. *quod*.
[141] Lausberg §§692–708, Mayer 1994: 25–8 (a helpful discussion of Horace). Various terms have been used in antiquity and modernity (e.g. H–S 824–5, 834–6, Panhuis 1980).
[142] 2.1.6n. *ornamentum*.
[143] 2.9.2n. *ego*, 2.11.15n. *tantum*, 2.13.5n. *ille*, 5n. *cum*, 6n. *mira*.
[144] The latter is now often called zeugma. See 2.1.2n. *legit* (syntactic), 2.1.4.n. *pari* (semantic) and index s.v.

words) plays a relatively small role (2.3.3n. *prohoemiatur*); **metaphor** is fairly frequent (index s.v.), with a curious tendency to switch referents mid-way (2.4.4n. *ita*). **Alliteration** is routine, as in so much Latin, often expressive (2.1.5n. *per*, 2.6.1n. *ut*, 2.11.3n. *uela*), balancing a bicolon (2.11.4n. *magna*, 2.17.15n. *hac*) or pointing wordplay and paradox (2.1.2n. *gloriae*, 2.5.1n. *perpolitur*, 2.11.23n. *superest*). Most important, though, is the careful selection and use of ordinary words: much of Pliny's language could fairly be called plain (precisely what it strives to be), and what marks the more mannered moments, above all in the villa letter, is the audacity that subtends the smooth diction. Take an upstairs room with a view: *latissimum mare, longissimum litus, uillas amoenissimas possidet* (2.17.12). The unremarkable verb *possidet* acquires a novel meaning ('commands a view of') while creating the piquant expression 'owns [other people's] villas'. Then comes a room *in quo sol nascitur conditurque* 'in which the sun is born and laid to rest' (2.17.13): no rare words here, but the combination is poetic and the image paradoxical. In these and numerous examples, Pliny follows Horace's advice (*Ars poetica* 47–8), to make a familiar word new through a clever combination. It is a minute artistry, impossible to appreciate in translation, and characteristically belied by the plain surface of the text: *ars adeo latet arte sua* (2.2.intro.).

A helpful term for this manner of composition is **point** (sharpness), the ingenious concision that attracts attention through surprise. It was a prized commodity in early imperial rhetoric: Ovid, Seneca and Tacitus, to name three, are famous (or infamous) for it.[145] Common techniques include **paronomasia** (wordplay: 2.15.2 *habent hunc finem assiduae querellae, quod queri pudet*), especially with polyptoton (2.3.11 *ut audias Isaeum uel ideo tantum ut audieris*), rhyme (2.6.5 *tua continentia... aliena contumelia*) and **oxymoron**, the paradoxical combination of apparently contradictory ideas (2.17.21 *et distinguit et miscet*). Any phrase can be 'pointed', like the examples from the villa letter above, but a particular instantiation of this mode is the *sententia*, a clever one-liner used especially to round off an argument or (in modern terms) paragraph. This term is much contested in its definition (giving fresh meaning to the adage *quot homines, tot sententiae*) and requires a brief discussion.

*   *   *

A **sententia** is a formulation that captures a truth or the attention, preferably both. Modern scholars often distinguish between the *gnōmē* (γνώμη 'maxim, aphorism'), a telling encapsulation of some universal human truth (*omnia uincit amor*),[146] and the 'epigram', a witty comment often marked by point (*capax imperi, nisi imperasset*).[147] Both were known in Pliny's time as *sententiae*, as Quintilian's

---

[145] Summers 1910: xv–xli is an engaging but moralising account of 'the pointed style'; see more sympathetically Voss 1963.

[146] V. *Ecl.* 10.69.

[147] Tac. *H.* 1.49.4 on Galba ('capable of rule, if he had not ruled'). For the spelling *imperi* (yielding 5-syllable isocolon) see 2.11.23n. *Mari*.

discussion (*Inst.* 8.5, AD 90s) makes clear: his survey ranges from *sententiae* 'properly called' (the *gnōmē*) through to 'newer types' (the epigram), and demonstrates with more than thirty examples a wide variety of formulations, which he corporately terms oratorical *lumina* 'highlights' (*Inst.* 8.5.2, 29).[148] They have three related functions: persuasive, decorative and structural. A *sententia* persuades by giving the speaker an aura of wisdom and authority or by charming the audience with epigrammatic gratification (the pleasure of recognising and decoding paradox); it decorates with its brilliance; and it contributes to structure through its frequent use to round off an argument or section.

Plinian *sententiae* are sometimes gnomic, sometimes epigrammatic, often both. Take for instance *habent hunc finem assiduae querellae, quod queri pudet* (2.15.2) and *nam cum sit impar prudentia, par omnium ius est* (2.12.5). The first, offering a universal truth about complaint, is gnomic, the second, commenting on a specific situation (voting rights in the senate), epigrammatic. Each features antithesis in falling bicolon with chiasmus, wordplay and incongruity; each implicitly claims authority for itself while capturing the reader's attention. Accordingly *sententia* and 'sententious' are used in this commentary not only to mean 'aphoristic' but also as a synonym for 'epigrammatic'; often it covers both, or hovers between the two, as in 'power corrupts; absolute power corrupts absolutely'.[149] The *sententia* was a vehicle for wit as well as wisdom (1.9.8 *satius est enim, ut Atilius noster eruditissime simul et facetissime dixit, otiosum esse quam nihil agere*).[150] Yet artificiality does not (for Pliny) preclude sincerity. In 4.11.2 he quotes a *sententia* by the exiled senator-turned-rhetor Licinianus, who addressed Fortune with the words *'facis enim ex senatoribus professores, ex professoribus senatores'*. Pliny continues, *cui sententiae tantum bilis, tantum amaritudinis inest ut mihi uideatur ideo professus ut hoc diceret* 'there is such bile, such bitterness in this *sententia* that I think he became a rhetor just to deliver it'.[151] Licinianus' gnomic epigram draws attention through its rhetorical construction[152] and the witty appropriation of the commonplace that Fortune is fickle,[153] but Pliny focuses on its emotive power. His sententious riposte seems intended to have similarly authoritative effect.[154]

If to modern taste the frequency of *sententiae* and their air of omniscience can make them pall, they were evidently felt by Pliny (and contemporaries) as not just witty but powerful. Accordingly they find a particular place as

---

[148] On this and other ancient accounts of *sententiae* see Lausberg §872–9, Sinclair 1995: 152–63, Kirchner 2000: 20–41.

[149] After Acton. Gallent-Kočevar 1933 and Vielberg 2003, by contrast, concern themselves only with gnomic statements, brief or not. Tacitean studies (e.g. Kirchner 2000) similarly tend to exclude epigram; see however Oakley 2009: 202–3.

[150] Cf. 2.14.2 *expresse* (of the same Atilius).

[151] Pliny uses *sententia* with this meaning only here and at 1.16.2.

[152] Namely *commutatio* (2.6.4n. *liberti*).

[153] An 'applied' or 'personalised' *gnōmē* (Quint. 8.5.6–7).

[154] For this type of point (self-collapsing hyperbole) see 2.3.11n. *uel.*

punctuation at the ends of letters,[155] whether proffering a truth (e.g. 2.6.7, 2.7.7) or alluding to an axiom (2.9.6, 2.17.29, 2.18.5), whether with paradox (2.4.4) or wordplay (2.13.11, 2.15.2); especially with falling bicolon (2.1.12, 2.4.4, 2.15.2) they carry a memorable 'sting' in the tail.[156] They find a place within letters too (e.g. 2.1.3, 2.11.7, 2.12.5, 2.14.8) and often gravitate to the centre (2.10.4, 2.15.1, 2.16.2); runs of two or more in quick succession are relatively infrequent (2.11.7, 2.12.5, 2.14.6 and 8).[157] Together these *lumina* strive to articulate, to entertain and to persuade.

Antithesis, casual formality, brevity and point – together with rhythm, discussed separately below – are the core constituents of Pliny's language, subtly blended and shaded in homogeneous variety. Often understated, always highly worked, his Latinity lays claim to a place among the great achievements of Roman prose.

5 RHYTHM

The *Epistles* demands to be read as much by ear as by eye.[158] Prose rhythm is 'a vast and varied jungle', more flexible than verse and inadequately theorised in antiquity and modernity alike,[159] but one area in which we are relatively well informed is the use of certain rhythmic combinations ('clausulae') to end cola and sentences in a form of aural punctuation.[160] Imported from Greek by Cicero and others, the principles of such punctuation were by Pliny's time widely applied in oratory and literary prose. The study of clausulae helps editors determine orthography and choose between textual variants,[161] assists readers in dividing up cola and so construing the Latin, and reveals a vital and omnipresent aspect of Pliny's prose artistry.

---

[155] Cf. Herrnstein Smith 1968: 151–86 on closural markers in poetry, including epigram, 'unqualified assertion' (cf. *gnōmē*) and above all 'the sense of truth'.

[156] For the image of the sting see 2.19.4n. *aculeis*. A biting *sententia* ends many paragraphs in Tacitus' earlier works (Damon 2003: 15–16, 302–4, Ash 2007: 21–4).

[157] The absence of *sententiae* from the villa letter, for all its point, is striking.

[158] Mynors xxii: 'auribus enim, non oculis modo uerum etiam auribus legendus est noster'.

[159] Wilkinson 1963: 139–40 professes only to have 'hovered over the jungle in a helicopter', but his survey of the terrain (pp. 135–64 and 237–42) is judicious and accessible; cf. (briefly) *OCD* 'prose rhythm, Latin' and, on internal cola, Nisbet 1990. Pliny's clausulae have a dedicated study in Hofacker 1903; see also Bornecque 1907: 326–40 (using a different method), Pflips 392–405, Durry 1938: 50–2 (on *Pan.*).

[160] Discussion here is restricted to endings; for some unusual opening rhythms see 2.9.1n. *anxium*, 2.10.1n. *hominem*, 2.17.1n. *miraris*. It also ignores stress-accent and word-division, which clearly play a part (e.g. type 4 below routinely ends with a word shaped ◡◡◡ or ◡◡–, e.g. *cécidit/métuunt*). See Spatzek 1912 (claiming that the clausulae of *Pan.* are based solely on stress), Müller 1954: 755–82 (a helpful study of Curtius Rufus).

[161] E.g. 2.1.5n. *male*, 2.2.2n. *studís*, 2.11.23n. *Mari* (not that rhythm is a panacea: 2.11.2n. *petít*, 2.14.5n. *uocantur*, 2.17.16n. *singulae*).

Syllables are counted heavy or light as in verse, and the same norms of elision apply;[162] the final syllable is indifferent, counted heavy either way.[163] It takes more confidence with quantities to scan prose than poetry, but Pliny's frequent use of a small number of endings makes the task both approachable and useful. Most of his clausulae are constructed from a few standard building-blocks: the cretic (– ◡ –), spondee (– –) and trochee (– ◡); from these the dispondee (– – – –) and ditrochee (– ◡ – ◡); also the molossus (– – –) and hypodochmiac or cretic–iamb (– ◡ – ◡ –).[164] A heavy syllable can be 'resolved' into two light syllables, to make, e.g., a 'resolved cretic' (– ◡ ◡ ◡ – or ◡ ◡ ◡ –). Pliny's favourite combinations in *Epistles* 1–9 are as follows:

1	– ◡ – – ×	cretic–spondee[165]	(ends 29% of sentences)
2	– ◡ – ×	ditrochee[166]	(17%)
3	– ◡ – – ◡ ×	double cretic	(15%)
4	– ◡ – ◡ ◡ ×	cretic + resolved spondee	(10%)
5	– – – ×	dispondee	(6%)

These percentages are derived from Hofacker 1903; they are indicative at best, but allow some observations to be made.[167] Five patterns account for three-quarters of all sentence-ends. In prose written without attention to rhythm, cretic–spondees might be expected to end about 7% of sentences,[168] but they end 29% of Pliny's; conversely, the dispondee, which might 'naturally' end 24% of sentences, is reduced to 6%.[169] It is clear that Pliny (however consciously) strongly favoured the former and avoided the latter.[170] Comparison with statistics for the *Panegyricus*

[162] Elision seems to be the rule within cola, even if some instances give pause for thought (e.g. 2.13.10 *in primis ama hominem*). In verse of course hiatus, though avoided, is not forbidden.

[163] For these essentials see e.g. Raven 1965: 22–30. The final syllable is either heavy by quantity or *breuis in longo* ('light in place of heavy'), though some distinction was felt (Cic. *Or.* 194, despite ibid. 217; Quint. 9.4.93–4); the *anceps* symbol ('×') is adopted here for convenience.

[164] Quint. 9.4.107–8 advises against this last, but it had been Cicero's sixth-favourite (e.g. Dyck 2008: 245–6); Hofacker 1903: 18 ranks it eleventh in Pliny. Common word-divisions are 2.3.3 (*de*)*lectat afficit* and 2.3.8 *audias ueni*.

[165] Some scholars prefer 'cretic–trochee', which amounts to much the same thing (above, n.163).

[166] Often preceded by a cretic or molossus.

[167] I have rounded percentages to whole numbers. Even this degree of accuracy is specious: for critique of such analysis see Orlandi 2005, id. 2008: 405–532.

[168] De Groot 1921: 106 (the methodology was crude).

[169] For some notably spondaic endings, and their effect, see 2.11.20n. *Pompeium*, 2.16.1n. *non*, 2.20.6n. *pueri*; but see also 2.5.10n. *et*.

[170] Stylisation is also clear in the avoidance of final monosyllables (except prodelided *es*(*t*), e.g. 2.3.7 *ferreusque es*) and the restricted number of 'heroic' clausulae (2.3.3n. *narrat*). *Epistles* 10 has proved harder to judge: Hofacker 1903: 37 finds Pliny's practice unchanged; Bornecque 1907: 337–40 sees many more 'faults' (in his terms) on Pliny's part, and total indifference on Trajan's. Unsystematic observation suggests something between the two; that the letters of book 10 are stylistically less mannered is clear (Gamberini 1983: 332–76; Coleman 2012).

(type 1 = 28%, 2 = 20%, 3 = 15%, 4 = 7%, 5 = 6%) shows scant variation between these 'private' *Epistles* and that public oratory:[171] here Pliny differs from Cicero, whose letters are far more varied in their degree of clausulation than his other works.[172] He differs too in his preferences: while the first three clausulae are among Cicero's favourites,[173] type 4 is not: it ends only around 2% of his sentences,[174] and never a speech. Pliny, by contrast, has it often, and it ends four of the twenty letters in book 2 (2.3, 2.9, 2.10, 2.19). This is no quirk of his: the resolution became fashionable early in the first century AD, and is routine in (for instance) both Senecas, Pliny the Elder and Quintilian.[175] To call Pliny's rhythms Ciceronian (Hofacker 1903: 49–52) is thus misleading: his preference here, as in many aspects of his style, is representative of his own age.[176]

Clausulae routinely end not just sentences but also internal cola, in letters both grand and intimate. Even 'realistic' fragments of conversation are as mannered in their rhythm as in their rhetorical structures: e.g. 2.6.3 *'quam consuetudinem sequeris?'* [type 4] *'eadem omnibus pono:* [1] ... *' 'etiamne libertos?'* [1] *'... non libertos puto'* [molossus–cretic], or Regulus at 2.20.4 *'quod ut tibi magis liqueat,* [4][177] *haruspicem consulam* [3] *quem sum frequenter expertus'* [1]. Some clausulae perhaps lend themselves better to moments of grandeur – the three paragraphs of 2.1 (as edited here) end with the impressive *eloquentissimus* [3], *haberem, tibi mandarem* [cretic–molossus] and *gloria neminem* [3] – but such evaluations are subjective and fragile: the faux-petulant 2.2 that follows also ends with a double cretic. In characteristic fashion, Pliny's practice combines strong preference for a small number of patterns with flexibility in their application: the clausulae in an antithesis, for instance, may match (2.3.1n. *dicit*), vary (2.6.2n. *non*) or do both (2.11.1n. *personae claritate famosum*).

For example, 2.2 may be clausulated as follows.

$$- \;\; \cup \;\; - \;\; - \;\; \cup\!\times \;| \qquad\qquad\qquad \textit{double cretic}$$
$$- \qquad \cup \;\; - - \;\; \times \;| \qquad\qquad \textit{cretic–spondee}$$

irascor, nec liquet mih(i) an debeam, sed irascor.

$$\textit{3} \times \textit{cretic–spondee}$$
$$- \;\; \cup \;\; - \;\; - \;\; \times \;| \; - \;\; \cup \;\; - - \;\; \times \;| \; - \;\; \cup\!- \;\; - \;\; \times$$

scis quam sit amor iniquus interdum, impotens saepe, μικραίτιος semper;

---

[171] Indeed, Bornecque 1907: 332 finds *Epp.* slightly more 'polished' than *Pan.*

[172] Hutchinson 1998: 9–12. Cicero's practice varied over time, complicating the picture. Seneca's letters are as rhythmic as Pliny's (with slightly different preferences: Bornecque 1907: 109, Bourgery 1910: 167).

[173] Statistics for Cicero (speeches) after Zieliński 1904 (fold-out chart): type 1 (23%), type 2 (29%), type 3 (11%), type 4 (2%), type 5 (6%).

[174] 1.6% for Zieliński 1904, 2.8% for De Groot 1921: 107.

[175] All of whom much prefer it to the *esse uideatur* ($- \cup \cup \cup - -$) and $\cup \cup \cup - - -$ resolutions favoured by Cicero. The statistics of De Groot 1921: 108–9 set them all in a similar range to Pliny (whom he unfortunately excludes).

[176] See 2.11.2n. *petit* for the possibility that Pliny moderates his clausulae for the Ciceronian 2.11. Historical prose is a different creature (Aili 1979), with which Pliny shows little affinity.

[177] For *tibī* see 2.6.4n. *magno*.

– ◡ – × | – ◡ – – × | *ditrochee* | *cretic–spondee*
haec tamen causa magna (e)st, nesci(o) an iusta;

– ◡ – – ◡× | *double cretic*
sed ego, tamquam non minus iusta quam magna sit,

       resolved cretic–spondee | *cretic–spondee*
◡ ◡◡ – – × | – ◡ – – × |
grauiter irascor quod a te tam diu litterae nullae.

– ◡◡ – – ◡ × | *resolved molossus* + *cretic*
exorare me potes uno modo,

– ◡ – – ◡× | *double cretic*
si nunc saltem plurimas et longissimas miseris.

–◡– – × | – ◡ – – × | 2 × *cretic–spondee*
haec mihi sola excusatio uera, ceterae falsae uidebuntur.

       cretic–spondee | *cretic* + *resolved cretic*
– ◡ – – × | – ◡ – ◡◡ ◡ × |
non sum auditurus 'non eram Romae' uel 'occupatior eram';

◡ ◡ – – – ◡ – | *resolved molossus* + *cretic*
– ◡ – – ◡× | *double cretic*
illud enim nec di sinant, ut 'infirmior'.

       molossus–cretic | *dactyl* + *cretic*
– – – – ◡ × | –◡◡– ◡× |
ipse ad uillam partim studîs,[178] partim desidia fruor,

– ◡– – ◡× | *double cretic*
quorum utrumque ex otio nascitur. VALE.

All twenty-one cola (including two that overlap)[179] end with an identifiable clausula. Unresolved cretic–spondee (type 1) and double cretic (type 3) account for more than half of them, including all six sentence-ends, with the cretic–spondee especially frequent (nine in total). This short letter happens not to exemplify two of Pliny's 'top five' (types 4 and 5 above), but its blend of favourite rhythms with a few less common variants is characteristic. Greek is integrated

---

[178] For the spelling see 2.2.2n. *studîs*.
[179] For the notion of overlapping clausulae (open to theoretical objections), see Hutchinson 1995: 494–6.

into the rhythm as usual; the final VALE (also as usual) is not. There is mannered patterning in antithesis (three matching clausulae for the tricolon *iniquus . . . semper*, a pair for the bicolon *haec . . . uidebuntur*), tempered with variety in the three imagined excuses (*'non eram Romae'*, etc.) and the two (slightly) different clausulae of *ipse . . . fruor* near the end. In rhythm, as in all aspects of his prose, Pliny's extreme stylisation is clear; to ignore it is to overlook an essential aspect of his art.

6 INTERTEXTUALITY

One last strand of Pliny's epistolary texture calls for a few words, given its importance and topicality. The interrelationship of texts has long been a central theme of scholarship on Latin poetry, and more recently prose. Whereas nineteenth-century scholars stripped texts back to their 'sources', many modern critics prefer to empower the later text, which is said to recall and rework earlier texts in allusion; the reader who recognises such allusion gains access to further levels of meaning. For others, 'allusion' is too fraught with hazards of intentionality (the presumption that we can reconstruct the author's line of thought), and it is safer to speak of 'intertextuality', whereby (in its strongest sense) resonances between texts are determined only at the point of reception.[180] This commentary occupies a middle ground: sometimes I assert allusion in the strong sense; elsewhere the catch-all 'cf.', while offering parallels, leaves open the possibility of directed recall without insisting on it.[181] The nature of allusion, infinitely more evasive than the modern footnote, demands such openness, all the more so in the *Epistles*, a work which – quotations apart[182] – generally looks to earlier literature with characteristic obliquity. Cicero's letters are very often in the air, a sort of 'background music' (Marchesi 2008: 214) whose volume varies letter by letter,[183] while his oratory and treatises feature especially in 2.10–12, as well as in 2.1.10–12 and 2.20.12. Evocations of Cicero thus end the first and last letters of the book as well as dominating its central panel – and is it a coincidence that the *Verrines*, a recurrent point of reference for 2.11, make a fleeting allusive target at the end of the book?[184] Certainly Ciceronian echoes play an ongoing but discreet part in constructing Pliny as orator and statesman, as does (briefly) the allusion to

---

[180] The essential point of departure is Hinds 1998 (on verse). A. J. Woodman has been a pioneer in prose allusion (e.g. Woodman 1998 and 2012). On Plinian allusion see especially Schenk 1999 and Marchesi 2008.

[181] The openness of this signpost can thus be potent as well as frustrating (cf. e.g. Gibson 2002).

[182] Above all of Homer (Deane 1918: 50–1) and Virgil (Krasser 1993b).

[183] See index. Marchesi 2008: 252–7 gives a catalogue of 'potential links' in other books.

[184] 2.20.12n. *nequitia et.*

Demosthenes in 2.20.12. Horace, Ovid, Seneca, Martial and Statius were mentioned above (pp. 3–4);[185] to his uncle Pliny seems to owe words and phrases (though certainly not his style) without making pointed allusion;[186] conversely, his teacher Quintilian is an unsurprising but underestimated presence, not least in one of the most telling allusions of the book (2.5.intro.).[187]

Tacitus, Pliny's near-contemporary, fellow provincial *nouus homo* and favourite correspondent (with eleven letters in total), is a special case.[188] Subtle allusion to *Agricola* (AD 98) seems likely in 2.1 (2.1.10n. *si*), but similarities to *Dialogus* and *Histories* are caught up in a complex web of mutually dependent dating.[189] *Epistles* 6 contains a clear allusion to *Dialogus* (6.21.1 ~ *D.* 15.1, following a long letter to Tacitus),[190] and the direction of travel may be the same in book 2. In 2.5.9 ~ *D.* 10.3 similarity of phrasing may reflect only linguistic usage of the day, while in 2.3.8 ~ *D.* 7.4 and 8.1 the topic is related but the language not close; at 2.10.7 ~ *D.* 6.4, however, both language and content may suggest that Pliny is evoking and inverting Aper's argument.[191] Certainly it is striking that each of these three concerns the same speech of Aper (*D.* 5–10), also the object of allusion in 9.10.2 (and, some believe, 1.6.2).[192] With the *Histories* things are little clearer. In 2.6.6 *ne tibi . . . luxuria specie frugalitatis imponat* ~ *H.* 1.30.1 '*falluntur quibus luxuria specie liberalitatis imponit*' the lexical similarities look too close for accident, but we are hard pressed to say which came first.[193] Another instance may incline to making Tacitus the alluder (2.1.2n. *cum*), as perhaps does an intertext between *Epistles*

---

[185] Epic and tragedy play a lesser part. The two most 'poetic' letters evoke Catullus (2.2) and Ennius (2.10.2), perhaps along with Virgil and Ovid; for Virgil see also 2.5.11n. *auulsum*, 2.17.1n. *miraris*, 1n. *delectet*, 2n. *saluo*, 5n. *longinquo*, 15n. *hortus*, 24n. *personat* (some of these with Homer too).

[186] 2.1.10n. *quibus*, 2.6.7n. *cum*, 2.12.2n. *cum*, 2.13.2n. *nec*, 4n. *citerioris*, 11n. *rogat*, 2.17.3n. *uilla*, 9n. *dormitorium*, 9n. *suspensus*, 13n. *turbati*, 16n. *cum*, 17n. *teporem*, 22n. *media*. On the elder Pliny's notoriously terse and difficult Latin see Pinkster 2005.

[187] See also e.g. 2.3.4n. *studio*, 6n. *res*, 2.9.2n. *uereor*, 3n. *ut*, 2.14.12n. *pudet*, 2.18.5n. *in*.

[188] On this famous relationship see Griffin 1999, Whitton 2012.

[189] For the date of *Dialogus* see Syme 1958: 670–3 (AD 102 or *c.* 106), Murgia 1980 and 1985 (before *Epp.* 1 and before mid-97), Brink 1994 (99–103), Woodman 2009a (after *Epp.* 1); much of the debate centres on alleged intertexts with the *Epistles*. The *Histories* is first known (intertextuality aside) from Pliny *Ep.* 6.16 (with a dramatic date of *c.* 106), which supplies material about AD 79; assuming Tacitus wrote sequentially, he was beyond our extant text (*H.* 5, on AD 70) by then. The final version of *Pan.* (a speech delivered on 1 Sept. 100) has been dated as early as autumn 100 (Seelentag 2004: 218), as late as 107 (Woytek 2006); a date in between seems likely. For the *Epistles*, see above, p. 18; dating any given phrase earlier than a possible final revision in *c.* 109 is difficult. On *Germania* (AD 98) see 2.7.2n. *Bructerum*, 2n. *quod*.

[190] As Roy Gibson observed *per epistulas*. Cf. also 7.9.8 *pressus sermo purusque* ~ *D.* 2.2 *Secundo purus et pressus . . . sermo non defuit* (noted by Tony Woodman).

[191] See respectively 2.5.9n. *haec* (also 2.7.4n. *uita*, 2.9.1n. *anxium*); 2.3.8n. *Gaditanum*, 8n. *ab*; 2.10.7n. *imaginor*.

[192] Cf. *D.* 9.6 (reprised at *D.* 12.1) with (e.g.) Murgia 1985: 173–81, Marchesi 2008: 118–35, Woodman 2009a: 32–3. But see also 2.9.1n. *anxium*, 2.11.1n. *personae*.

[193] See also 2.17.16 *serenus dies et immotus* ~ Tac. *H.* 1.86.1 *sereno et immoto die*.

4 and *Histories* 1,[194] but certainty in such matters is rarely possible,[195] not least given the likelihood that 'publication' was preceded by more intimate sharing and circulation.[196] At all events, the prejudice which inclines many readers to assume that Pliny might have 'imitated' Tacitus (cf. 7.20.4 *maxime imitabilis, maxime imitandus*), but not vice versa,[197] is not borne out by the hints of Pliny in the *Annals*, all but certainly composed after his death.[198]

7 AFTERLIFE

posteris an aliqua cura nostri, nescio . . . (9.14). In antiquity Pliny's hopes for immortality were best realised through the *Panegyricus*, which became a model of its genre; but the letters also played their part. So far as we can tell, Pliny (like Tacitus and others) meets with studied silence from several generations; the *Panegyricus* first stirs in the AD 280s, *Epistles* 1–9 in the late fourth century.[199] So the *communis opinio*; but three reasons suggest that Juvenal should be added as an early reader.[200] Syme suggested that Marius Priscus' double appearance in the *Satires* was prompted not by his trial but by the (later) publication of Pliny's letter on it (2.11.intro.). More pressingly, several of the aristocrats who people Juvenal's poems have names familiar from Pliny's circle; none makes a conclusive link, but neither is there reason to deny connection each time.[201] Third, there are signs of allusion to 2.6 (*Satires* 1 and 5), 4.11 (*Satires* 7) and 8.18 (*Satires* 10).[202] Few would date any of these poems earlier than *Epistles* 1–9, making Juvenal, along

---

[194] 4.11.8 *ad supplicium nescio an innocens, certe tamquam innocens ducta est* ∼ *H.* 1.6.1 *tamquam innocentes perierant*, both working the same point (executions, justified or not, unjustly performed): Tacitus is sharper and so perhaps later – but such arguments are fragile. Conversely, in 8.14 Pliny seems to allude to *H.* 1 (Whitton 2010: 126–8).

[195] *Pace* Woytek 2006, intervening in an old and still unsettled debate about *H.* ∼ *Pan.*

[196] Advertised in 7.20 and 8.7 (probably books of *H.*, S-W 427, rather than *D.*, Syme 1958: 113, 673). See Durry 1938: 60–6 and bibliography in 2.10.6n. *recita.*

[197] An assumption based on the loftier stature widely attributed to Tacitus (influentially by Syme 1958: 112–20 and *passim*) and from taking epistolary humility literally (correctives in Marchesi 2008: 97–206 and above, n.188).

[198] Bruère 1954: 174–6, Woodman 2009a: 34–5, Whitton 2012: 349; also perhaps 4.11.7 *nunc ad Vestam, nunc ad ceteros deos manus tendens* ∼ *An.* 12.65.3 *modo ad deos, modo ad ipsum tendere manus* (cf. n.194 on the same letter), *Pan.* 46.4 *scaenici imperatoris* ∼ *An.* 15.59.2 *ille scaenicus*, and the speculation in Whitton 2010: 135.

[199] 10.96–7 (the 'Christians' letters), however, were known to Tertullian in 197. On the early reception of *Epp.* see Cameron 1965 (with id. 1967), largely followed by von Albrecht 1997: 1154–5, Wolff 2003: 95–8; on *Pan.* see Rees 2011.

[200] As perhaps of *Pan.* (Hardie 1997–8, especially 118).

[201] 2.4n. CALVINAE, 2.20.10n. *Aurelia.* See also 2.3.1n. *Isaeum.*

[202] See respectively 2.6.intro., Courtney on Juv. 7.197–8 (adding that Juvenal, like Licinianus, crafts a *commutatio*), Syme 1979b: 253–4; also 2.17.6n. *altera.* Each letter has a satirical streak which 'stands in sharp contrast to [Pliny's] normal bland benevolence' (Syme ibid., on 8.18); two of them may also have caught Tacitus' eye (above).

with Tacitus, Pliny's first attested reader.[203] As for his younger friend Suetonius, extant works show little sign of intertextuality with the *Epistles*.[204]

Thereafter the silence is striking, not least from Fronto: another provincial *nouus homo*, epistolographer and panegyrist, he has not a word for Pliny.[205] Nor have Apuleius or Aulus Gellius: in the 'archaising turn' of the mid-second century earlier imperial authors were out of fashion.[206] In the late fourth century Pliny's epistolary stock rises: he is alluded to or quoted by Ausonius in the *Cento nuptialis* (*c.* 374),[207] in the anonymous *Epitome de Caesaribus* (*c.* 400?),[208] by a commentator on Juvenal,[209] and several times by Jerome (380s onwards);[210] whether Ammianus Marcellinus (380s/390s) had read him is uncertain (2.6.5n. *quibus*).[211] The ten-book letter collections of Ambrose (before 395) and Symmachus (probably after 402) are widely thought to show Plinian influence;[212] certainly the flourishing late-antique genre of self-consciously learned letters found a primary generic forebear in his collection.[213]

By far the most engaged ancient reader of *Epistles* 1–9, however, was Sidonius Apollinaris, Gallic bishop, politician and man of letters. His own nine-book collection of epistles, published around 480, explicitly invites comparison with that of Pliny (Sid. *Ep.* 1.1.1, 9.1.1)[214] and shows substantial textual and

---

[203] And not a sympathetic one, if the names are indeed connected (the allusions, on the other hand, show no antipathy). Freudenburg 2001: 215–42 sees Juv. 1–5 satirising if not Pliny, then the cultural discourse he represents. Juvenal's dates still give food for debate, but most follow Syme 1979b and assume publication beginning in the 110s (e.g. Braund 1996a: 16).

[204] Suetonius is addressee of 1.18, 3.8, 5.10 and 9.34, and subject of 1.24, 10.94–5. On their relationship see Power 2010, who sees allusion to him in 5.10. In book 2 similarities of language, as often between Pliny and the declamations attributed to Quintilian, suggest common contemporary coin rather than intertextuality (e.g. 2.5.11n. *congruentiam*, 2.19.8n. *leges*, though see 2.1.7n. *illis*).

[205] Rees 2011: 175–7. Who published Fronto's letters, and when, is not agreed.

[206] See e.g. Cameron 2010: 399–405.

[207] *Cento* epilogue (~ 4.14.4 and 9). See Green 1991: 518 for the date. Allusion is certain (ibid. 524–5, adding *quippe eruditi* ~ 4.14.4 *erit eruditionis tuae*); Cameron 2010: 416 (correcting id. 1965: 294–5).

[208] *Epit.* 12.5 makes substantial use of 4.22 (McDermott 1970: 147). If Barnes 1976: 260–1 were right in making Marius Maturus (early 3c.) an intermediary, it would be a unique sign of life for *Epp.* between the early 2c. and late 4c.

[209] 2.3.1n. *magna*. For the date, see Cameron 1965: 292.

[210] 2.3.8n. *numquamne*, 10n. τί δέ (see Cain 2008 for dates and bibliography; also Adkin 2011). Like many since, Jerome confused the elder and younger Plinys (Cameron 1965: 289–91).

[211] On Macrobius *Saturnalia* 5.17 (*c.* 430), which concerns *Pan.* but may hint at letters too, see Cameron 1965: 295 n.4, Kelly 2013.

[212] A key factor is the (supposed) arrangement of each as 9+1 books (Gibson 2012: 59–60), but there is scope for doubt: e.g. Cameron 2010: 415, Salzman–Roberts 2012: lxii–lxiii and Kelly 2013 (Symmachus), Savon 1995 with the reply of Zelzer–Zelzer 2002 (Ambrose). A possible Symmachean intertext at 2.12.3n. *in* (and, doubtfully, 2.5.13n. *ne*).

[213] Gibson 2012 offers a survey of the landscape.

[214] Also in *Epp.* 2.10.5, 4.3.1, 4.22.2 and 8.10.3.

architectural engagement.[215] Although his rich prose style is quite unlike Pliny's pared-down lucidity, he frequently reworks turns of phrase, some of them straight-forward (2.1.6n. *hic*, 2.3.11n. *quae*, 2.7.3n. *rarum*, 2.9.6n. *diligeris*); more often he notices point and replies in kind (2.3.1n. *magna*, 2.13.11n. *rogat*, 2.17.10n. *plurimo*) or (re)appropriates a rare word (2.14.6n. *mesochorus*, 2.20.3n. *climactericum*), not without fun at Pliny's and his own expense (2.17.11n. *baptisteria*, 12n. *calidissimo*, 16n. *cryptoporticus*, 22n. *andron*). These allusions are particularly dense in his *Epistles* 2.2, a villa letter which unites – among other intertextual targets – the Lauren-tine and Etruscan villas of Pliny (2.17 and 5.6):[216] like his predecessor, Sidonius makes the villa a rich expression of textually negotiated cultural identity.[217] As for architecture, Roy Gibson has observed (*inter alia*) the significant total of 147 let-ters (against Pliny's 247), that his first two books are pre-episcopal as Pliny's are pre-consular, and that his 2.11–12 responds to the unique pairing of addressees in Pliny's 2.11–12.[218] More systematic patterning in Sidonius' second book (with its fourteen letters against Pliny's twenty) is harder to identify, but this combination of artistry, wit and evasiveness shows him to be an exceptionally perceptive and sympathetic reader of Pliny's letters.

After Sidonius, *Epistles* 1–9 show sporadic signs of life including a possible echo in a sixth-century Greek epigram (2.20.2n. *Verania*) and a certain borrowing in a ninth-century letter (2.1.10n. *tanti*);[219] but the flame is carried most visibly by the manuscript tradition, surveyed below. The letters reached Italy, the hotbed of humanism, in stages in the fifteenth and early sixteenth centuries; *Epistles* 1–7 and most of book 9 were first printed in 1471, *Epistles* 1–9 in 1490, *Epistles* 1–10 (so fixing the collection as it is known today) by Aldus in 1508.[220] Pliny's humanist reception seems to set the tone for the next five hundred years, as that of a prized if not quite top-rank canonical author,[221] though he exerted wide influence on elegant *lettres d'art* and (with Seneca) on the essay form.[222] For much of the twentieth century he was valued as a historical source but widely patronised as a writer and

[215] On allusivity see Geisler 1887: 356–8 (full but undiscriminating); on architecture (and Sidonian wit), Gibson 2011b, 2013a and 2013c. Sidonius never mentions or alludes to *Epp.* 10, suggesting that his copy contained only books 1–9.

[216] See 2.17.intro.; also Pavlovskis 1973: 48–50 (unsympathetic); for 5.6 see e.g. Sid. *Ep.* 2.2.3 (~ 5.6.3) and 2.2.20 (~ 5.6.41–4), and Gibson 2013a on the addressees; 4.30 is also in mind (2.17.10n. *plurimo*). See also 2.17.12n. *erigitur* and 23n. *quem* on Sid. *Carm.* 22.

[217] Mratschek 2008: 373–4.

[218] Gibson 2013a, 2013c, 2.12.intro.

[219] Also e.g. a tenth-century citation of 1.5.15 in Rather of Verona, *Phrenesis* 22 (= Migne, *Patrologia Latina* 136: 391–2).

[220] Editions are listed in Aubrion 1989: 369–72.

[221] On humanism see Schmidt 1983, Gamberini 1984, Kemper 2000 (Römer 1989 for *Pan.*), 2.3.8n. *numquamne* (Petrarch). Thereafter there is no systematic study, but see Allain 1901–4: III 229–378 (a promenade through the ages, tenuously relevant to Pliny), Wolff 2003: 97–8 (select second-hand anecdotes), Lefèvre 1988 ≈ id. 2009: 252–72 ('nature' letters), du Prey 1994 (villas).

[222] Sallmann 2010, Redford 2012.

thinker; more recently, fresh recognition of the *Epistles*' intense artistry suggests that we may at last be catching up with Sidonius, and with Pliny.

8 TRANSMISSION, TEXT, INDEXES

The *Epistles*, especially its first books, has reached modernity relatively intact.[223] Editors have classified the hundred or so extant MSS into three families, designated by their reconstructed archetypes (common ancestors) as α ('nine-book'), β ('ten-book') and γ ('eight-book'). Two of these (αγ) are closely related, forming a line of descent separate from β,[224] but all stem ultimately from a single source, the hypothetical archetype of books 1–9 (to whose text β, uniquely, added book 10). By tracing the text back along these branches, editors hope to recover Pliny's original words.[225] For the most part they are believed to have succeeded, and textual problems are discussed rarely in the commentary (differences from other modern editions are listed below, p. 42). Nevertheless, an understanding of the landscape is essential background to such difficulties as arise, and is central to the story of Pliny's epistolary afterlife.[226]

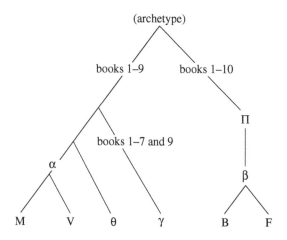

The ten-book family β was perhaps the most influential in securing Pliny's survival. Its most important representatives are the ninth-century *Beluacensis* (**B**) and the widely copied eleventh-century *Florentinus* (**F**), both containing most of

---

[223] The tale is best told by Mynors v–xxii (in Latin) and Reynolds 1983; Stout 1954 is the fullest discussion. On the independent transmission of *Pan.* see Mynors 1964: v–xi. Present text and discussion derive from published work only.

[224] Argued by Stout 1924 and 1954, accepted by Mynors and Reynolds 1983, doubted by Schuster xi–xii, ignored by Zehnacker.

[225] For a brief introduction to textual criticism see Reynolds–Wilson 1991: 207–41.

[226] Stemma after Mynors 3.

1.1–5.6.[227] They share an archetype β descended from Π, a fifth- or early sixth-century MS which survives as a tiny fragment (2.20.13–3.5.4) but once contained all or most of *Epistles* 1–10; this appears to be the *Parisinus*, a ten-book MS discovered, used and lost again in the years around 1500.[228] The nine-book family α is represented primarily by two ninth-century MSS, *Mediceus* (**M**) and *Vaticanus* (**V**). V contains only books 1–4 but M has most of 1.1–9.26.9, which may have been the extent of α.[229] That in turn shared an archetype with the head of the eight-book family, γ (*Veronensis deperditus*), a perhaps ancient MS rediscovered at Verona in 1419, copied and used to 'correct' F texts (αB were unknown), and subsequently lost. Containing *Epistles* 1–7 and 9 (up to 9.40), with some letters missing and others out of order, it had a wide progeny but is the most difficult text to reconstruct, especially in the early books, where it was widely 'contaminated' with (combined with readings from) F. Two of the best sources are *Dresdensis* Dc 166 (**D**) and *Holkhamicus* 396 (**H**), an anthology of 167 letters.[230]

Epistles 2 is well represented among the three families: MVFD have the whole book, B a little over half (with a lacuna from 2.4.2 *solus* to 2.12.3 *praebere*), H letters 1–10, 13, 16 and 18 (not in that order), Π a few words (2.20.13–14). In the search for Pliny's original text, critics first reconstruct where possible the readings of α, β and γ. When these differ, as they often do, we can adjudicate according to several (sometimes conflicting) principles including Latinity, Plinian usage, rhythm and the likelihood of specific copying errors or interpolation. No single family is routinely reliable or unreliable. Given that αγ share an archetype, their agreement against β is not proof of a better reading, though β (especially the influential F) is more prone to interpolation.[231] When α and γ differ, either can be right but β often settles it, since agreement of αβ or βγ should show a reading common to both branches αγ and β and thus to the archetype. Yet minor slips might be made independently by two different copyists, as e.g. 2.11.10 *ad hoc* (*adhuc* Fγ), 2.14.9 *me memini* (*memini* αβ), and 2.17.22 *sonum* (*somnum* Bγ);[232] alternatively, these and more substantial similarities may reflect contamination between families.[233] When αβγ all agree, the archetype is not in doubt, but this need not be a faithful reproduction of Pliny's text. We have no

---

[227]   For the shelf-marks of the αβ MSS mentioned here see Mynors 3.

[228]   Mynors xix, generally accepted (*contra* Schuster v–vi). Yet Π had an index for book 3 (see below) and presumably every book; Aldus, who used *Parisinus* for his 1508 edition (if perhaps hastily: Stout 1954: 68–80), makes no mention or use of any such. Π is reproduced, transcribed and discussed in Lowe–Rand 1922.

[229]   M ends mid-page with an *explicit*. It can be viewed at teca.bmlonline.it.

[230]   On these and **m** (below, n.240) see Stout 1954: 16–24 (who calls γ 'δ' and H 'l'); H is described in Reynolds forthcoming. Traces of another lost nine-book MS, θ, become visible only in later books (Stout 1954: 33–44, Mynors xiv–xvi, Reynolds 1983: 321).

[231]   α interpolates too, e.g. 2.6.3 [*respondi*] *eadem*. F alone preserves the tricky 2.11.23 λιτούργιον and 2.17.4 *in D litterae*.

[232]   See also 2.1.12n. *uolui*, 2.7.1n. *here*.

[233]   E.g. 5.6.15 *prominulam* M, *pro modo longam* βγ. The latter (printed by Mynors) is preferable in rhythmic and stemmatic terms, but is a pat substitute for *prominulam*, which is

evidence that β parted company from αγ before the fourth or fifth century, leaving perhaps three hundred years and any number of copyings for corruption or interpolation to creep in.[234] Conjectural emendation should not be undertaken lightly,[235] but excision seems required in 2.14.5n. *uocantur* and in a difficult passage of the villa letter (2.17.14n. *aperto*, 2.17.15n. *adiacet*) which has also suffered corruption in the archetype (2.17.16n. *singulae*).[236]

A peculiarity of Pliny's MSS concerns the tables of contents (usually called 'indexes') and letter-headings. In modern editions, which do not print (and barely discuss) the indexes, the headings have a uniform appearance (2.1n. C. PLINIVS), except that each addressee is identified by a single name in *Epistles* 2 and 6–9 but by a double name in books 3–5 and in most of book 1. This variation is doubtless an accident of transmission, apparently along the following lines. Someone in antiquity, perhaps Pliny himself, supplied a table of contents for each book, listing addressees with double names and the opening few words of each letter.[237] These survive in Π (book 3) and B (books 1–5, with deficiencies in 1–2).[238] The index to book 3 in B, for instance, begins as follows:[239]

Ad Caluisium Rufum ·	nescio an ullum
Ad Vibium Maximum ·	quod ipse amicis tuis ·
Ad Caerelliae Hispullae · [*sic*]	cum patrem tuum ·

In F these indexes have been dropped, but double names are sporadically interpolated into the text (as in book 1 of B), so beginning the trend that continues in printed editions today. There is no sign of indexes in α and only one (independently constituted) in γ;[240] if they did indeed feature in the archetype, they

scarcely explicable as a corruption (Goold 1964: 324). The recurrent difficulty of isolating γ readings in the first place obscures the picture.

[234] Deufert 2008: 68–71. Relevant factors are (*i*) the estimated age of Π, (*ii*) the possibility that Symmachus and Ambrose knew a ten-book, Sidonius a nine-book version (above, nn.212, 215), and (*iii*) the suggestion that *Epp.* 1–10 were first combined when the codex came into fashion (Reynolds 1983: 317), though *Epp.* 1–9 might have gone their own way in β before book 10 was added. The thesis of Barwick 1936: 439–45, that αγ and β represent two editions both produced by Pliny, has persuaded few.

[235] It is rejected at 2.10.3n. *quidam*, 2.17.15n. *uinea* and 2.18.4n. *nisi*, accepted at 2.4.4n. *facile* and 2.19.5n. *quae* (in neither of which do αβγ all agree). Liberman 2009a exemplifies the dangers of excess, as did Guillemin's *Budé* (1927–8), littered with Postgate's emendations (see Zehnacker 2009, with the reply of Liberman 2009b).

[236] Corruption too, perhaps, at 2.3.2 *subitis*, where γ has *subditis*, as apparently did β (visibly corrected to *subitis* in BF, according to Zehnacker). If so, α corrected tacitly. See also 2.19.9n. *omnesque*, 2.20.7n. *quia*.

[237] See Barwick 1936: 423–39 (largely followed here); also Robbins 1910, Gibson 2011b.

[238] B stops at 5.6.32, but its index includes all of book 5. The index in Π is transcribed in Lowe–Rand 1922: 24–5 (with photographs in plates II–III), the B indexes in Robbins 1910: 476–8. On book 1 see Barwick 1936: 426–7 (*contra* Robbins 1910: 481).

[239] As transcribed in Robbins 1910: 476–7 (capitalisation and word-division normalised).

[240] **m** (Venice, Marc. Lat. XI.37, foll. 95–102) has a text of book 1, with single-name indexes of addressees for books 1 and 2 (Merrill 1917: 259). The omission of certain letters

were lost from αγ at an early stage. The general consistency with which MSS name any given person by *gentilicium* or *cognomen* and the routine agreement between αβγ suggest that the letter-headings contained only single names; this in turn implies that Pliny provided two-name indexes alongside them, since it is unlikely that a later scribe or scholar could have provided second names so consistently.[241]

The surviving index to book 2, however, has lost all double names and acquired several errors.[242]

Ad Romanum post aliquos annos in-	Ad Paulinu irascor nec liquet michi
Ad Nepotem · magnis aeuum fama ·	Ad Galuinam si pluribus pater tuus
Ad Lupercum actionem · aet a te frequent ·	Ad Auitum · longum est altius repet
Ad Magnum · nere a senatu Vestricio ·	Ad Caninium studes an piscoris an
Ad Apollinare · anxium me et inquet ·	Ad Octauium · hominem te patient
Ad Arrianum · ΔIHOYPΓION illud quod	Ad Priscu et tu occasiones oblig–
Ad Maximum · uerum opinaris ·	Ad Valerium quomodo te ueteres
Ad Annium · tu quidem pro cetera ·	Ad Gallum miraris cur me Laurent
Ad Marcium · quid at te mihi	Iucundius
Ad Cerialem · hortaris ut orationem ·	Ad Caluisium · assem para et accipe

It seems that the list was lost early on, recompiled from the single-name headings,[243] then copied at least once without reference to the text: this best explains the omission of the long 2.11 (whose entry, like that of 2.12, began *Ad Arrianum*) and the difference between the opening words of 2.18 in the index (*mihi iucundius*, the text of αγ) and in the text of this same MS (*iucundius mihi*).[244] The preservation of a double-name index would have spared much confusion, given that several addressees share a *cognomen*;[245] still, even this depleted version adds a witness to Pliny's text.[246] The existence of ancient indexes also has interesting implications for reading strategies, allowing readers to track correspondents across the collection (if not within this book, where no two letters except 2.11– 12 share an addressee) or to browse by letter-openings; in addition, they may

from both text and indexes shows that the latter were compiled or copied from its exemplar, not imported from β (Barwick 1936: 437). That exemplar may have been γ itself.

[241] Barwick 1936: 428–35; for possible indications to the contrary see 2.8n. CANINIO, 2.16n. ANNIANO.

[242] Again from Robbins (as n.239), with abbreviations expanded.

[243] Barwick 1936: 435–6.

[244] Robbins 1910: 479. The division of 2.18 (*Ad Marcium . . . Iucundius*) across both columns looks like a scribe trying to make the table up, after the loss of 2.11, to a round twenty items.

[245] See e.g. 2.3n. NEPOTI, 2.13n. PRISCO, 2.14n. MAXIMO.

[246] 2.7.1n. *here*, 2.11.23n. *superest*, 2.16n. ANNIANO.

have served as yet another prompt to situate Pliny's work against its Ciceronian forebears.[247]

9 *AD LECTOREM*

The aim of this commentary, as of the series, is 'to provide the guidance that the reader needs for the interpretation and understanding of the book as a work of literature'. Longer notes are graded, with linguistic help coming first. Glosses attempt to produce a semblance of English rather than translationese; syntactical and rhetorical analysis regularly follows. Greek is translated. I frequently refer to the *OLD* (less because meanings can be tidily fixed than to save citing parallels given there), sparingly to the *TLL*. The degree to which Pliny's language conforms to the 'classical' usage of the first century BC is emphasised less than it used to be: the currency of a word or construction can be seen by glancing at an *OLD* paragraph cited, and comparison with contemporary authors often proves more illuminating.

All references within the *Epistles* include the book-number (e.g. 2.6.3). The frequent cross-references within the commentary, intended to help the reader while retaining brevity, take the form '2.12.1n. *proxime*', or simply '2.12.1n.' when the lemma begins with the word already under discussion; 'intro.' means the introduction to the commentary on that letter, 'Intro.' the general Introduction. For other authors and works I adopt *OLD* style or obvious abbreviations (e.g. Cic. *De or.*, Pl. *NH*, Tac. *H.*; Seneca's dialogues are given by name). Pliny's works other than *Epistles* 2 are quoted from the Oxford texts of Mynors (*Epistulae* 1963, *Panegyrici Latini* 1964), other authors from current Oxford or Teubner texts, with some changes to spelling and punctuation. Statements about frequency of words are based on searches of the Packard Humanities Institute and Brepolis databases. The symbol | marks line-breaks in verse, colon-breaks in prose; the sign ~ invites comparison between cola or texts.

Debts to, differences from and coincidences with former commentators (pp. x–xi, among whom I have learned most from Gierig and Merrill, alongside S-W) are signalled sparingly, since they can easily be traced; in citing other bibliography I have tried to err on the side of generosity. For prosopography Birley 2000a is useful but relatively hard to obtain; I also therefore refer to *PIR* and elsewhere. G–M contains, besides a wealth of stimulating readings, catalogues of contents and persons, a structured bibliography and a map of 'Pliny's Italy'.

---

[247] 'Yet another': see pp. 2, 32. The earliest and best MS of Cic. *Fam.* has tables of contents for most books (Shackleton Bailey 1977: 1 19), e.g. *Fam.* 2.1 *M. Cicero salutem dicit Curioni* | *quamquam me nomine*; their origin is conceivably – especially in the light of Pliny – ancient. Analogous lists of incipits were also compiled for epigram books (Krevans 2007: 133); and Pl. *NH* includes a (rather different) table of contents and sources. The import of Pliny's indexes has been barely discussed, but see now Bodel n.d., G–M 45–7 and Gibson 2013b (to whom, as ever, I am indebted).

No new collation of MSS has been undertaken for this volume, and there is no *apparatus criticus*. Differences from Mynors and/or Schuster are listed below and discussed in the commentary; orthography has also been adapted tacitly in several places where rhythm is unaffected (e.g. 2.6.2 *paruulis* not *paruolis*, 2.8.1 *affatim* not *adfatim*, 2.14.8 *quomodo* not *quo modo*), and a few oddities in section numbering have been corrected (2.14.5n. *et*, 7n. *nam*, 2.17.4–15n., 18n. *haec*). Paragraphing often agrees with that of Schuster. Punctuation is largely aligned with modern English usage: explanations (*nam, enim*, asyndetic) are usually preceded by a colon; asyndeton is punctuated except in a series all or mostly of single words (e.g. 2.13.10 *studia mores omnem denique uitam*). I have been relatively sparing with commas, both Germanic (e.g. before *ut*) and rhythmic (cf. Mynors xxii), so offering fewer hurdles to fluent readers, if also fewer staging-posts for beginners: help in the notes, I hope, will compensate.

VALE.

	Mynors	Schuster	Whitton
2.1.5	coiit	coit	coît
2.1.7	abit	abit	abît
2.1.12	uolo	uolui	uolui
2.2.2	studiis	studiis	studîs
2.11.2	petiit	petit	petît
2.11.6	sola frequens.	sola frequens.	sola. frequens
2.11.23	unguentarii	unguentari	unguentari
2.14.1	negotii	negotii	negoti
2.14.5	ἀπὸ... καλεῖσθαι	[ἀπὸ... καλεῖσθαι]	[ἀπὸ... καλεῖσθαι]
2.14.10	audit, repetit	audit, repetit	audît, repetît
2.14.11	quaesiit, perît	quaesiit, perit	quaesît, perît
2.16.1	sint	sunt	sint
2.17.7	triclinii	triclinii	triclini
2.17.8	bibliothecae	bybliothecae	bybliothecae
2.17.14	et quamquam	et quamquam	[et] quamquam
2.17.15	gestationi	gestationi	[gestationi]
2.17.16	singulae et alternis pauciores	singulae et alternis pauciores	†singulae sed alternis pauciores†
2.17.24	studiis	studiis	studîs
2.18.1	studiis	studiis	studîs
2.19.2	recitantur	recitantur	recitentur
2.20.3	audiit	audiit	audît
2.20.5	filii	filii	fili

C. PLINI CAECILI SECVNDI
EPISTVLARVM LIBER SECVNDVS

C. PLINI CAECILI SECVNDI
EPISTVLARVM LIBER SECVNDVS

I

C. PLINIVS ROMANO SVO S.

Post aliquot annos insigne atque etiam memorabile populi Romani oculis **1**
spectaculum exhibuit publicum funus Vergini Rufi, maximi et clarissimi
ciuis, perinde felicis. triginta annis gloriae suae superuixit, legit scripta de **2**
se carmina, legit historias, et posteritati suae interfuit. perfunctus est tertio
consulatu, ut summum fastigium priuati hominis impleret, cum principis
noluisset. Caesares quibus suspectus atque etiam inuisus uirtutibus fuerat **3**
euasit, reliquit incolumem optimum atque amicissimum, tamquam ad
hunc ipsum honorem publici funeris reseruatus. annum tertium et octo- **4**
gensimum excessit in altissima tranquillitate, pari ueneratione. usus est
firma ualetudine, nisi quod solebant ei manus tremere, citra dolorem
tamen. aditus tantum mortis durior longiorque, sed hic ipse laudabilis.
nam cum uocem praepararet acturus in consulatu principi gratias, liber **5**
quem forte acceperat grandiorem et seni et stanti ipso pondere elapsus est.
hunc dum sequitur colligitque per leue et lubricum pauimentum fallente
uestigio cecidit coxamque fregit, quae parum apte collocata reluctante
aetate male coît. huius uiri exsequiae magnum ornamentum principi, **6**
magnum saeculo, magnum etiam foro et rostris attulerunt: laudatus est
a consule, Cornelio Tacito: nam hic supremus felicitati eius cumulus
accessit, laudator eloquentissimus.

Et ille quidem plenus annis abît, plenus honoribus, illis etiam quos **7**
recusauit; nobis tamen quaerendus ac desiderandus est ut exemplar
aeui prioris, mihi uero praecipue, qui illum non solum publice quantum admirabar tantum diligebam: primum quod utrique eadem regio, **8**
municipia finitima, agri etiam possessionesque coniunctae; praeterea
quod ille mihi tutor relictus affectum parentis exhibuit: sic candidatum me
suffragio ornauit, sic ad omnes honores meos ex secessibus accucurrit,
cum iam pridem eius modi officiis renuntiasset, sic illo die quo sacerdotes solent nominare quos dignissimos sacerdotio iudicant me semper
nominabat. quin etiam in hac nouissima ualetudine, ueritus ne forte inter **9**
quinqueuiros crearetur qui minuendis publicis sumptibus iudicio senatus
constituebantur, cum illi tot amici senes consularesque superessent, me
huius aetatis per quem excusaretur elegit, his quidem uerbis: 'etiam si
filium haberem, tibi mandarem.'

10 Quibus ex causis necesse est tamquam immaturam mortem eius in sinu tuo defleam, si tamen fas est aut flere aut omnino mortem uocare,
11 qua tanti uiri mortalitas magis finita quam uita est. uiuit enim uiuetque semper, atque etiam latius in memoria hominum et sermone uersabitur
12 postquam ab oculis recessit. uolui tibi multa alia scribere, sed totus animus in hac una contemplatione defixus est. Verginium cogito, Verginium uideo, Verginium iam uanis imaginibus, recentibus tamen, audio alloquor teneo; cui fortasse ciues aliquos uirtutibus pares et habemus et habebimus, gloria neminem.

VALE.

2

C. PLINIVS PAVLINO SVO S.

1 Irascor, nec liquet mihi an debeam, sed irascor. scis quam sit amor iniquus interdum, impotens saepe, μικραίτιος semper; haec tamen causa magna est, nescio an iusta; sed ego, tamquam non minus iusta quam magna
2 sit, grauiter irascor quod a te tam diu litterae nullae. exorare me potes uno modo, si nunc saltem plurimas et longissimas miseris. haec mihi sola excusatio uera, ceterae falsae uidebuntur. non sum auditurus 'non eram Romae' uel 'occupatior eram'; illud enim nec di sinant, ut 'infirmior'. ipse ad uillam partim studîs, partim desidia fruor, quorum utrumque ex otio nascitur.

VALE.

3

C. PLINIVS NEPOTI SVO S.

1 Magna Isaeum fama praecesserat, maior inuentus est. summa est facultas copia ubertas; dicit semper ex tempore, sed tamquam diu scripserit. sermo Graecus, immo Atticus; praefationes tersae graciles dulces, graues
2 interdum et erectae. poscit controuersias plures; electionem auditoribus permittit, saepe etiam partes; surgit amicitur incipit; statim omnia ac paene pariter ad manum, sensus reconditi occursant, uerba (sed qualia!) quaesita et exculta: multa lectio in subitis, multa scriptio elucet.
3 prohoemiatur apte, narrat aperte, pugnat acriter, colligit fortiter, ornat excelse. postremo docet delectat afficit; quid maxime, dubites. crebra ἐνθυμήματα, crebri syllogismi, circumscripti et effecti, quod stilo quoque assequi magnum est. incredibilis memoria: repetit altius quae dixit ex

tempore, ne uerbo quidem labitur. ad tantam ἕξιν studio et exercita- **4**
tione peruenit: nam diebus et noctibus nihil aliud agit, nihil audit, nihil
loquitur. annum sexagensimum excessit et adhuc scholasticus tantum **5**
est, quo genere hominum nihil aut sincerius aut simplicius aut melius.
nos enim qui in foro uerisque litibus terimur multum malitiae quamuis
nolimus addiscimus; schola et auditorium et ficta causa res inermis **6**
innoxia est nec minus felix, senibus praesertim: nam quid in senectute
felicius quam quod dulcissimum est in iuuenta? quare ego Isaeum non **7**
disertissimum tantum uerum etiam beatissimum iudico; quem tu nisi
cognoscere concupiscis, saxeus ferreusque es.

Proinde si non ob alia nosque ipsos, at certe ut hunc audias ueni. **8**
numquamne legisti Gaditanum quendam Titi Liui nomine gloriaque
commotum ad uisendum eum ab ultimo terrarum orbe uenisse, statimque ut uiderat abisse? ἀφιλόκαλον illitteratum iners ac paene etiam
turpe est non putare tanti cognitionem qua nulla est iucundior, nulla
pulchrior, nulla denique humanior. dices: 'habeo hic quos legam non **9**
minus disertos.' etiam, sed legendi semper occasio est, audiendi non semper. praeterea multo magis, ut uulgo dicitur, uiua uox afficit. nam licet
acriora sint quae legas, altius tamen in animo sedent quae pronuntiatio
uultus habitus gestus etiam dicentis affigit – nisi uero falsum putamus **10**
illud Aeschinis, qui cum legisset Rhodiis orationem Demosthenis admirantibus cunctis, adiecisse fertur 'τί δέ, εἰ αὐτοῦ τοῦ θηρίου ἠκούσατε;' et
erat Aeschines, si Demostheni credimus, λαμπροφωνότατος, fatebatur
tamen longe melius eadem illa pronuntiasse ipsum qui pepererat. quae **11**
omnia huc tendunt, ut audias Isaeum uel ideo tantum ut audieris.

VALE.

4

C. PLINIVS CALVINAE SVAE S.

Si pluribus pater tuus uel uni cuilibet alii quam mihi debuisset, fuisset fort- **1**
asse dubitandum an adires hereditatem etiam uiro grauem. cum uero ego **2**
ductus affinitatis officio, dimissis omnibus qui non dico molestiores sed
diligentiores erant, creditor solus exstiterim, cumque uiuente eo nubenti
tibi in dotem centum milia contulerim praeter eam summam quam pater
tuus quasi de meo dixit (erat enim soluenda de meo), magnum habes
facilitatis meae pignus, cuius fiducia debes famam defuncti pudoremque
suscipere.

Ad quod te ne uerbis magis quam rebus horter, quidquid mihi pater
tuus debuit, acceptum tibi fieri iubebo. nec est quod uerearis ne sit mihi **3**

onerosa ista donatio: sunt quidem omnino nobis modicae facultates, dignitas sumptuosa, reditus propter condicionem agellorum nescio minor an incertior; sed quod cessat ex reditu frugalitate suppletur, ex qua uelut

4 fonte liberalitas nostra decurrit. quae tamen ita temperanda est, ne nimia profusione inarescat – sed temperanda in aliis; in te uero facile ei ratio constabit etiam si modum excesserit.

VALE.

5

C. PLINIVS LVPERCO SVO S.

1 Actionem et a te frequenter efflagitatam et a me saepe promissam exhibui
2 tibi, nondum tamen totam: adhuc enim pars eius perpolitur. interim quae absolutiora mihi uidebantur non fuit alienum iudicio tuo tradi. his tu rogo intentionem scribentis accommodes: nihil enim adhuc inter manus habui
3 cui maiorem sollicitudinem praestare deberem. nam in ceteris actionibus existimationi hominum diligentia tantum et fides nostra, in hac etiam pietas subicietur. inde et liber creuit, dum ornare patriam et amplificare
4 gaudemus pariterque et defensioni eius seruimus et gloriae. tu tamen haec ipsa quantum ratio exegerit reseca: quotiens enim ad fastidium legentium deliciasque respicio, intellego nobis commendationem et ex
5 ipsa mediocritate libri petendam. idem tamen qui a te hanc austeritatem exigo, cogor id quod diuersum est postulare, ut in plerisque frontem remittas. sunt enim quaedam adulescentium auribus danda, praesertim si materia non refragetur: nam descriptiones locorum, quae in hoc libro frequentiores erunt, non historice tantum sed prope poetice prosequi
6 fas est. quod tamen si quis exstiterit qui putet nos laetius fecisse quam orationis seueritas exigat, huius (ut ita dixerim) tristitiam reliquae partes
7 actionis exorare debebunt. annisi certe sumus ut quamlibet diuersa genera lectorum per plures dicendi species teneremus, ac sicut ueremur ne quibusdam pars aliqua secundum suam cuiusque naturam non probetur, ita uidemur posse confidere ut uniuersitatem omnibus uarietas
8 ipsa commendet. nam et in ratione conuiuiorum, quamuis a plerisque cibis singuli temperemus, totam tamen cenam laudare omnes solemus, nec ea quae stomachus noster recusat adimunt gratiam illis quibus capitur.
9 Atque haec ego sic accipi uolo, non tamquam assecutum esse me credam, sed tamquam assequi laborauerim, fortasse non frustra, si modo
10 tu curam tuam admoueris interim istis, mox iis quae sequuntur. dices te

non posse satis diligenter id facere, nisi prius totam actionem cognoueris. fateor; in praesentia tamen et ista tibi familiariora fient, et quaedam ex his talia erunt ut per partes emendari possint. etenim, si auulsum statuae **11** caput aut membrum aliquod inspiceres, non tu quidem ex illo posses congruentiam aequalitatemque deprendere, posses tamen iudicare an id ipsum satis elegans esset; nec alia ex causa principiorum libri circumfer- **12** untur quam quia existimatur pars aliqua etiam sine ceteris esse perfecta.

Longius me prouexit dulcedo quaedam tecum loquendi; sed iam finem **13** faciam ne modum quem etiam orationi adhibendum puto in epistula excedam.

VALE.

6

C. PLINIVS AVITO SVO S.

Longum est altius repetere, nec refert, quemadmodum acciderit ut homo **1** minime familiaris cenarem apud quendam, ut sibi uidebatur, lautum et diligentem, ut mihi, sordidum simul et sumptuosum: nam sibi et paucis **2** opima quaedam, ceteris uilia et minuta ponebat; uinum etiam par- uulis lagunculis in tria genera discripserat, non ut potestas eligendi sed ne ius esset recusandi, aliud sibi et nobis, aliud minoribus amicis (nam gradatim amicos habet), aliud suis nostrisque libertis. animaduertit qui **3** mihi proximus recumbebat et an probarem interrogauit. negaui. 'tu ergo' inquit 'quam consuetudinem sequeris?' 'eadem omnibus pono: ad cenam enim, non ad notam inuito, cunctisque rebus exaequo quos mensa et toro aequaui.' 'etiamne libertos?' 'etiam: conuictores enim tunc, non libertos **4** puto.' et ille: 'magno tibi constat.' 'minime.' 'qui fieri potest?' 'quia scilicet liberti mei non idem quod ego bibunt, sed idem ego quod liberti.' et her- **5** cule si gulae temperes, non est onerosum quo utaris ipse communicare cum pluribus. illa ergo reprimenda, illa quasi in ordinem redigenda est si sumptibus parcas, quibus aliquanto rectius tua continentia quam aliena contumelia consulas.

Quorsus haec? ne tibi, optimae indolis iuueni, quorundam in mensa **6** luxuria specie frugalitatis imponat. conuenit autem amori in te meo, quo- tiens tale aliquid inciderit, sub exemplo praemonere quid debeas fugere. igitur memento nihil magis esse uitandum quam istam luxuriae et sor- **7** dium nouam societatem, quae cum sint turpissima discreta ac separata, turpius iunguntur.

VALE.

7

C. PLINIVS MACRINO SVO S.

1 Here a senatu Vestricio Spurinnae principe auctore triumphalis statua decreta est, non ita ut multis, qui numquam in acie steterunt, numquam castra uiderunt, numquam denique tubarum sonum nisi in spectaculis audierunt, uerum ut illis qui decus istud sudore et sanguine et factis 2 assequebantur. nam Spurinna Bructerum regem ui et armis induxit in regnum, ostentatoque bello ferocissimam gentem, quod est pul- 3 cherrimum uictoriae genus, terrore perdomuit. et hoc quidem uirtutis praemium, illud solacium doloris accepit, quod filio eius Cottio, quem amisit absens, habitus est honor statuae. rarum id in iuuene, sed pater hoc quoque merebatur, cuius grauissimo uulneri magno aliquo fomento 4 medendum fuit; praeterea Cottius ipse tam clarum specimen indolis dederat ut uita eius breuis et angusta debuerit hac uelut immortalitate proferri. nam tanta ei sanctitas grauitas auctoritas etiam, ut posset senes 5 illos prouocare uirtute quibus nunc honore adaequatus est. quo quidem honore, quantum ego interpretor, non modo defuncti memoriae, dolori patris uerum etiam exemplo prospectum est: acuent ad bonas artes iuuentutem adulescentibus quoque, digni sint modo, tanta praemia constituta, acuent principes uiros ad liberos suscipiendos et gaudia ex superstitibus et ex amissis tam gloriosa solacia.

6 His ex causis statua Cotti publice laetor, nec priuatim minus: amaui consummatissimum iuuenem tam ardenter quam nunc impatienter requiro. erit ergo pergratum mihi hanc effigiem eius subinde intueri, 7 subinde respicere, sub hac consistere, praeter hanc commeare. etenim, si defunctorum imagines domi positae dolorem nostrum leuant, quanto magis hae quibus in celeberrimo loco non modo species et uultus illorum sed honor etiam et gloria refertur!

VALE.

8

C. PLINIVS CANINIO SVO S.

1 Studes an piscaris an uenaris an simul omnia? possunt enim omnia simul fieri ad Larium nostrum: nam lacus piscem, feras siluae quibus lacus 2 cingitur, studia altissimus iste secessus affatim suggerunt. sed siue omnia simul siue aliquid facis, non possum dicere 'inuideo'; angor tamen non et mihi licere, qui sic concupisco ut aegri uinum balinea fontes. numquamne

hos artissimos laqueos, si soluere negatur, abrumpam? numquam, puto. nam ueteribus negotiis noua accrescunt, nec tamen priora peragun- 3 tur: tot nexibus, tot quasi catenis maius in dies occupationum agmen extenditur.

VALE.

9

C. PLINIVS APOLLINARI SVO S.

Anxium me et inquietum habet petitio Sexti Eruci mei. afficior cura 1 et quam pro me sollicitudinem non adii quasi pro me altero patior; et alioqui meus pudor, mea existimatio, mea dignitas in discrimen adducitur. ego Sexto latum clauum a Caesare nostro, ego quaesturam impetraui, 2 meo suffragio peruenit ad ius tribunatus petendi, quem nisi obtinet in senatu, uereor ne decepisse Caesarem uidear. proinde annitendum est 3 mihi ut talem eum iudicent omnes qualem esse princeps mihi credidit. quae causa si studium meum non incitaret, adiutum tamen cuperem iuuenem probissimum grauissimum eruditissimum omni denique laude dignissimum, et quidem cum tota domo. nam pater ei Erucius Clarus, uir 4 sanctus antiquus disertus atque in agendis causis exercitatus, quas summa fide, pari constantia nec uerecundia minore defendit; habet auunculum C. Septicium, quo nihil uerius, nihil simplicius, nihil candidius, nihil fidelius noui. omnes me certatim et tamen aequaliter amant, omnibus 5 nunc ego in uno referre gratiam possum. itaque prenso amicos, supplico ambio, domos stationesque circumeo, quantumque uel auctoritate uel gratia ualeam precibus experior; teque obsecro ut aliquam oneris mei partem suscipere tanti putes. reddam uicem si reposces, reddam et si non 6 reposces. diligeris coleris frequentaris: ostende modo uelle te, nec deerunt qui quod tu uelis cupiant.

VALE.

10

C. PLINIVS OCTAVIO SVO S.

Hominem te patientem uel potius durum ac paene crudelem, qui tam 1 insignes libros tam diu teneas! quousque et tibi et nobis inuidebis, 2 tibi maxima laude, nobis uoluptate? sine per ora hominum ferantur isdemque quibus lingua Romana spatiis peruagentur! magna et iam longa exspectatio est, quam frustrari adhuc et differre non debes. enotuerunt 3

quidam tui uersus, et inuito te claustra sua refregerunt; hos nisi retrahis
4 in corpus, quandoque ut errones aliquem cuius dicantur inuenient. habe
ante oculos mortalitatem, a qua asserere te hoc uno monimento potes:
nam cetera fragilia et caduca non minus quam ipsi homines occidunt
5 desinuntque. dices, ut soles: 'amici mei uiderint.' opto equidem amicos
tibi tam fideles, tam eruditos, tam laboriosos ut tantum curae intentionisque suscipere et possint et uelint; sed dispice ne sit parum prouidum
6 sperare ex aliis quod tibi ipse non praestes. et de editione quidem interim
ut uoles; recita saltem quo magis libeat emittere, utque tandem percipias
7 gaudium quod ego olim pro te non temere praesumo. imaginor enim qui
concursus, quae admiratio te, qui clamor, quod etiam silentium maneat;
quo ego, cum dico uel recito, non minus quam clamore delector, sit modo
8 silentium acre et intentum et cupidum ulteriora audiendi. hoc fructu tanto
tam parato desine studia tua infinita ista cunctatione fraudare; quae cum
modum excedit, uerendum est ne inertiae et desidiae uel etiam timiditatis
nomen accipiat.

VALE.

II

C. PLINIVS ARRIANO SVO S.

1 Solet esse gaudio tibi si quid acti est in senatu dignum ordine illo:
quamuis enim quietis amore secesseris, insidet tamen animo tuo maiestatis publicae cura. accipe ergo quod per hos dies actum est, personae
claritate famosum, seueritate exempli salubre, rei magnitudine aeternum.
2 Marius Priscus accusantibus Afris, quibus pro consule praefuit, omissa
defensione iudices petît. ego et Cornelius Tacitus, adesse prouincial-
ibus iussi, existimauimus fidei nostrae conuenire notum senatui facere
excessisse Priscum immanitate et saeuitia crimina quibus dari iudices
possent, cum ob innocentes condemnandos interficiendos etiam pecu-
3 nias accepisset. respondit Fronto Catius deprecatusque est ne quid
ultra repetundarum legem quaereretur, omniaque actionis suae uela uir
mouendarum lacrimarum peritissimus quodam uelut uento miserationis
4 impleuit. magna contentio, magni utrimque clamores, aliis cognitionem
senatus lege conclusam, aliis liberam solutamque dicentibus quantumque
5 admisisset reus tantum uindicandum. nouissime consul designatus Iulius
Ferox, uir rectus et sanctus, Mario quidem iudices interim censuit dandos,
6 euocandos autem quibus diceretur innocentium poenas uendidisse. quae
sententia non praeualuit modo sed omnino post tantas dissensiones fuit

sola. frequens annotatumque experimentis quod fauor et misericordia acres et uehementes primos impetus habent, paulatim consilio et ratione quasi restincta considunt; unde euenit ut quod multi clamore permixto 7 tuentur nemo tacentibus ceteris dicere uelit: patescit enim, cum separaris a turba, contemplatio rerum quae turba teguntur.

Venerunt qui adesse erant iussi, Vitellius Honoratus et Flauius Mar- 8 cianus; ex quibus Honoratus trecentis milibus exsilium equitis Romani septemque amicorum eius ultimam poenam, Marcianus unius equitis Romani septingentis milibus plura supplicia arguebatur emisse: erat enim fustibus caesus, damnatus in metallum, strangulatus in carcere. sed Hon- 9 oratum cognitioni senatus mors opportuna subtraxit, Marcianus inductus est absente Prisco. itaque Tuccius Cerialis consularis iure senatorio postulauit ut Priscus certior fieret, siue quia miserabiliorem siue quia inuidiosiorem fore arbitrabatur si praesens fuisset, siue (quod maxime credo) quia aequissimum erat commune crimen ab utroque defendi et, si dilui non potuisset, in utroque puniri.

Dilata res est in proximum senatum, cuius ipse conspectus augustis- 10 simus fuit: princeps praesidebat (erat enim consul); ad hoc Ianuarius mensis, cum cetera tum praecipue senatorum frequentia celeberrimus; praeterea causae amplitudo auctaque dilatione exspectatio et fama insitumque mortalibus studium magna et inusitata noscendi omnes undique exciuerat. imaginare quae sollicitudo nobis, qui metus, quibus 11 super tanta re in illo coetu praesente Caesare dicendum erat. equidem in senatu non semel egi, quin immo nusquam audiri benignius soleo; tunc me tamen ut noua omnia nouo metu permouebant. obuersabatur 12 praeter illa quae supra dixi causae difficultas: stabat modo consularis, modo septemuir epulonum, iam neutrum; erat ergo perquam onero- 13 sum accusare damnatum quem ut premebat atrocitas criminis, ita quasi peractae damnationis miseratio tuebatur. utcumque tamen animum cog- 14 itationemque collegi, coepi dicere non minore audientium assensu quam sollicitudine mea. dixi horis paene quinque: nam duodecim clepsydris quas spatiosissimas acceperam sunt additae quattuor. adeo illa ipsa quae dura et aduersa dicturo uidebantur secunda dicenti fuerunt; Caesar qui- 15 dem tantum mihi studium, tantam etiam curam (nimium est enim dicere sollicitudinem) praestitit ut libertum meum post me stantem saepius admoneret uoci laterique consulerem, cum me uehementius putaret intendi quam gracilitas mea perpeti posset. respondit mihi pro Marciano Claudius Marcellinus; missus deinde senatus et reuocatus in posterum: 16 neque enim iam incohari poterat actio nisi ut noctis interuentu scinderetur.

17 Postero die dixit pro Mario Saluius Liberalis, uir subtilis dispositus acer disertus; in illa uero causa omnes artes suas protulit. respondit Cornelius **18** Tacitus eloquentissime et, quod eximium orationi eius inest, σεμνῶς. dixit pro Mario rursus Fronto Catius insigniter, utque iam locus ille poscebat, plus in precibus temporis quam in defensione consumpsit. huius actionem uespera inclusit, non tamen sic ut abrumperet; itaque in tertium diem probationes exierunt. iam hoc ipsum pulchrum et antiquum, senatum **19** nocte dirimi, triduo uocari, triduo contineri! Cornutus Tertullus consul designatus, uir egregius et pro ueritate firmissimus, censuit septingenta milia quae acceperat Marius aerario inferenda, Mario urbe Italiaque interdicendum, Marciano hoc amplius Africa. in fine sententiae adiecit, quod ego et Tacitus iniuncta aduocatione diligenter et fortiter functi essemus, arbitrari senatum ita nos fecisse ut dignum mandatis partibus **20** fuerit. assenserunt consules designati, omnes etiam consulares usque ad Pompeium Collegam: ille et septingenta milia aerario inferenda et Marcianum in quinquennium relegandum, Marium repetundarum poenae **21** quam iam passus esset censuit relinquendum. erant in utraque sententia multi, fortasse etiam plures in hac uel solutiore uel molliore: nam quidam ex illis quoque qui Cornuto uidebantur assensi hunc qui post ipsos cen- **22** suerat sequebantur. sed cum fieret discessio, qui sellis consulum astiterant in Cornuti sententiam ire coeperunt. tum illi qui se Collegae annumerari patiebantur in diuersum transierunt, Collega cum paucis relictus. mul- tum postea de impulsoribus suis, praecipue de Regulo, questus est, qui se in sententia quam ipse dictauerat deseruisset. est alioqui Regulo tam mobile ingenium ut plurimum audeat, plurimum timeat.

23 Hic finis cognitionis amplissimae; superest tamen λιτούργιον non leue, Hostilius Firminus legatus Mari Prisci, qui permixtus causae grauiter uehementerque uexatus est. nam et rationibus Marciani et sermone quem ille habuerat in ordine Lepcitanorum operam suam Prisco ad turpissimum ministerium commodasse stipulatusque de Marciano quin- quaginta milia denariorum probabatur, ipse praeterea accepisse sestertia decem milia foedissimo quidem titulo, nomine unguentari, qui titulus a **24** uita hominis compti semper et pumicati non abhorrebat. placuit censente Cornuto referri de eo proximo senatu: tunc enim, casu an conscientia, afuerat.

25 Habes res urbanas; inuicem rusticas scribe. quid arbusculae tuae, quid uineae, quid segetes agunt, quid oues delicatissimae? in summa, nisi aeque longam epistulam reddis, non est quod postea nisi breuissimam exspectes.

VALE.

12

C. PLINIVS ARRIANO SVO S.

Λιτούργιον illud quod superesse Mari Prisci causae proxime scripseram, 1
nescio an satis, circumcisum tamen et arrasum est. Firminus induc- 2
tus in senatum respondit crimini noto. secutae sunt diuersae sententiae
consulum designatorum: Cornutus Tertullus censuit ordine mouendum,
Acutius Nerua in sortitione prouinciae rationem eius non habendam.
quae sententia tamquam mitior uicit, cum sit alioqui durior tristiorque.
quid enim miserius quam exsectum et exemptum honoribus senatoriis 3
labore et molestia non carere? quid grauius quam tanta ignominia affectum non in solitudine latere sed in hac altissima specula conspiciendum
se monstrandumque praebere? praeterea quid publice minus aut con- 4
gruens aut decorum, notatum a senatu in senatu sedere ipsisque illis a
quibus sit notatus aequari, summotum a proconsulatu quia se in legatione
turpiter gesserat de proconsulibus iudicare, damnatumque sordium uel
damnare alios uel absoluere? sed hoc pluribus uisum est. numerantur 5
enim sententiae, non ponderantur, nec aliud in publico consilio potest
fieri. in quo nihil est tam inaequale quam aequalitas ipsa: nam cum sit
impar prudentia, par omnium ius est.

Impleui promissum priorisque epistulae fidem exsolui, quam ex spatio 6
temporis iam recepisse te colligo: nam et festinanti et diligenti tabellario
dedi – nisi quid impedimenti in uia passus est. tuae nunc partes, ut primum 7
illam, deinde hanc remunereris litteris quales istinc redire uberrimae
possunt.

VALE.

13

C. PLINIVS PRISCO SVO S.

Et tu occasiones obligandi me auidissime amplecteris, et ego nemini 1
libentius debeo: duabus ergo de causis a te potissimum petere constitui 2
quod impetratum maxime cupio. regis exercitum amplissimum: hinc tibi
beneficiorum larga materia; longum praeterea tempus quo amicos tuos
exornare potuisti: conuertere ad nostros, nec hos multos – malles tu 3
quidem multos, sed meae uerecundiae sufficit unus aut alter, ac potius
unus.

Is erit Voconius Romanus. pater ei in equestri gradu clarus, clarior 4
uitricus, immo pater alius (nam huic quoque nomini pietate successit),

mater e primis. ipse citerioris Hispaniae (scis quod iudicium prouinciae
5 illius, quanta sit grauitas) flamen proxime fuit. hunc ego, cum simul
studeremus, arte familiariterque dilexi: ille meus in urbe, ille in secessu
contubernalis; cum hoc seria, cum hoc iocos miscui. quid enim illo aut
6 fidelius amico aut sodale iucundius? mira in sermone, mira etiam in ore
7 ipso uultuque suauitas. ad hoc ingenium excelsum subtile dulce facile eruditum in causis agendis; epistulas quidem scribit, ut Musas ipsas Latine
8 loqui credas. amatur a me plurimum nec tamen uincitur. equidem iuuenis
statim iuueni quantum potui per aetatem auidissime contuli, et nuper ab
optimo principe trium liberorum ius impetraui; quod quamquam parce
9 et cum delectu daret, mihi tamen tamquam eligeret indulsit. haec beneficia mea tueri nullo modo melius quam ut augeam possum, praesertim
cum ipse illa tam grate interpretetur ut dum priora accipit posteriora
mereatur.
10   Habes qualis quam probatus carusque sit nobis, quem rogo pro ingenio, pro fortuna tua exornes. in primis ama hominem: nam licet tribuas
ei quantum amplissimum potes, nihil tamen amplius potes amicitia tua;
cuius esse eum usque ad intimam familiaritatem capacem quo magis
scires, breuiter tibi studia mores omnem denique uitam eius expressi.
11 extenderem preces nisi et tu rogari diu nolles et ego tota hoc epistula fecissem: rogat enim, et quidem efficacissime, qui reddit causas
rogandi.

VALE.

14

C. PLINIVS MAXIMO SVO S.

1 Verum opinaris: distringor centumuiralibus causis, quae me exercent
magis quam delectant. sunt enim pleraeque paruae et exiles; raro incidit
2 uel personarum claritate uel negoti magnitudine insignis. ad hoc pauci
cum quibus iuuet dicere; ceteri audaces atque etiam magna ex parte
adulescentuli obscuri ad declamandum huc transierunt, tam irreuerenter et temere ut mihi Atilius noster expresse dixisse uideatur, sic in foro
pueros a centumuiralibus causis auspicari ut ab Homero in scholis. nam
3 hic quoque ut illic primum coepit esse quod maximum est. at hercule ante
memoriam meam (ita maiores natu solent dicere) ne nobilissimis quidem
adulescentibus locus erat nisi aliquo consulari producente: tanta uener-
4 atione pulcherrimum opus colebatur. nunc, refractis pudoris et reuer-
entiae claustris, omnia patent omnibus, nec inducuntur sed irrumpunt.

sequuntur auditores actoribus similes, conducti et redempti. manceps conuenitur; in media basilica tam palam sportulae quam in triclinio dantur; ex iudicio in iudicium pari mercede transitur. inde iam non inurbane 5 Σοφοκλεῖς uocantur; isdem Latinum nomen impositum est Laudiceni; et tamen crescit in dies foeditas utraque lingua notata. here duo nomencla- 6 tores mei (habent sane aetatem eorum qui nuper togas sumpserint) ternis denariis ad laudandum trahebantur: tanti constat ut sis disertissimus. hoc pretio quamlibet numerosa subsellia implentur, hoc ingens corona colligitur, hoc infiniti clamores commouentur cum mesochorus dedit signum. opus est enim signo apud non intellegentes, ne audientes quidem: nam 7 plerique non audiunt, nec ulli magis laudant. si quando transibis per 8 basilicam et uoles scire quomodo quisque dicat, nihil est quod tribunal ascendas, nihil quod praebeas aurem; facilis diuinatio: scito eum pessime dicere qui laudabitur maxime.

Primus hunc audiendi morem induxit Larcius Licinus, hactenus tamen 9 ut auditores corrogaret. ita certe ex Quintiliano praeceptore meo audisse me memini. narrat ille: 'assectabar Domitium Afrum. cum apud cen- 10 tumuiros diceret grauiter et lente (hoc enim illi actionis genus erat), audît ex proximo immodicum insolitumque clamorem. admiratus reticuit; ubi silentium factum est, repetît quod abruperat. iterum clamor, iterum 11 reticuit, et post silentium coepit. idem tertio. nouissime quis diceret quaesît. responsum est: "Licinus." tum intermissa causa "centumuiri" inquit "hoc artificium perît."' quod alioqui perire incipiebat cum perisse 12 Afro uideretur; nunc uero prope funditus exstinctum et euersum est. pudet referre quae quam fracta pronuntiatione dicantur, quibus quam teneris clamoribus excipiantur. plausus tantum ac potius sola cymbala et 13 tympana illis canticis desunt: ululatus quidem (neque enim alio uocabulo potest exprimi theatris quoque indecora laudatio) large supersunt.

Nos tamen adhuc et utilitas amicorum et ratio aetatis moratur ac 14 retinet: ueremur enim ne forte non has indignitates reliquisse sed laborem fugisse uideamur. sumus tamen solito rariores, quod initium est gradatim desinendi.

VALE.

15

C. PLINIVS VALERIANO SVO S.

Quomodo te ueteres Marsi tui? quomodo emptio noua? placent agri, 1 postquam tui facti sunt? rarum id quidem: nihil enim aeque gratum est

2 adeptis quam concupiscentibus. me praedia materna parum commode
tractant, delectant tamen ut materna, et alioqui longa patientia occallui:
habent hunc finem assiduae querellae, quod queri pudet.

VALE.

16

C. PLINIVS ANNIANO SVO S.

1 Tu quidem pro cetera tua diligentia admones me codicillos Aciliani, qui
me ex parte instituit heredem, pro non scriptis habendos, quia non sunt
2 confirmati testamento; quod ius ne mihi quidem ignotum est, cum sit iis
etiam notum qui nihil aliud sciunt. sed ego propriam quandam legem
mihi dixi, ut defunctorum uoluntates, etiam si iure deficerentur, quasi per-
3 fectas tuerer. constat autem codicillos istos Aciliani manu scriptos. licet
ergo non sint confirmati testamento, a me tamen ut confirmati obseru-
4 abuntur, praesertim cum delatori locus non sit. nam si uerendum esset
ne quod ego dedissem populus eriperet, cunctantior fortasse et cautior
esse deberem; cum uero liceat heredi donare quod in hereditate subsedit,
nihil est quod obstet illi meae legi, cui publicae leges non repugnant.

VALE.

17

C. PLINIVS GALLO SVO S.

1 Miraris cur me Laurentinum uel, si ita mauis, Laurens meum tanto opere
delectet; desines mirari cum cognoueris gratiam uillae, opportunitatem
loci, litoris spatium.
2   Decem septem milibus passuum ab urbe secessit, ut peractis quae
agenda fuerint saluo iam et composito die possis ibi manere. aditur non
una uia: nam et Laurentina et Ostiensis eodem ferunt, sed Laurentina a
quarto decimo lapide, Ostiensis ab undecimo relinquenda est. utrimque
excipit iter aliqua ex parte harenosum, iunctis paulo grauius et longius,
3 equo breue et molle. uaria hinc atque inde facies: nam modo occurren-
tibus siluis uia coartatur, modo latissimis pratis diffunditur et patescit.
multi greges ouium, multa ibi equorum boum armenta, quae montibus
hieme depulsa herbis et tepore uerno nitescunt.
4   Villa usibus capax, non sumptuosa tutela. cuius in prima parte atrium
frugi nec tamen sordidum; deinde porticus in D litterae similitudinem

circumactae, quibus paruula sed festiua area includitur. egregium hae
aduersus tempestates receptaculum: nam specularibus ac multo magis
imminentibus tectis muniuntur. est contra medias cauaedium hilare, mox 5
triclinium satis pulchrum quod in litus excurrit ac, si quando Africo mare
impulsum est, fractis iam et nouissimis fluctibus leuiter alluitur. undique
ualuas aut fenestras non minores ualuis habet atque ita a lateribus, a
fronte quasi tria maria prospectat, a tergo cauaedium porticum aream
porticum rursus, mox atrium siluas et longinquos respicit montes.

Huius a laeua retractius paulo cubiculum est amplum, deinde aliud 6
minus quod altera fenestra admittit orientem, occidentem altera retinet;
hac et subiacens mare longius quidem sed securius intuetur. huius cubiculi 7
et triclini illius obiectu includitur angulus qui purissimum solem continet
et accendit. hoc hibernaculum, hoc etiam gymnasium meorum est; ibi
omnes silent uenti, exceptis qui nubilum inducunt et serenum ante quam
usum loci eripiunt. annectitur angulo cubiculum in hapsida curuatum 8
quod ambitum solis fenestris omnibus sequitur. parieti eius in bybliothecae speciem armarium insertum est, quod non legendos libros sed
lectitandos capit. adhaeret dormitorium membrum transitu interiacente, 9
qui suspensus et tubulatus conceptum uaporem salubri temperamento
huc illuc digerit et ministrat. reliqua pars lateris huius seruorum libertorumque usibus detinetur, plerisque tam mundis ut accipere hospites
possint.

Ex alio latere cubiculum est politissimum, deinde uel cubiculum 10
grande uel modica cenatio quae plurimo sole, plurimo mari lucet; post
hanc cubiculum cum procoetone, altitudine aestiuum, munimentis hibernum: est enim subductum omnibus uentis. huic cubiculo aliud et procoeton communi pariete iunguntur. inde balinei cella frigidaria spatiosa 11
et effusa, cuius in contrariis parietibus duo baptisteria uelut eiecta sinuantur, abunde capacia si mare in proximo cogites. adiacet unctorium
hypocauston, adiacet propnigeon balinei, mox duae cellae magis elegantes quam sumptuosae; cohaeret calida piscina mirifica ex qua natantes
mare aspiciunt, nec procul sphaeristerium quod calidissimo soli inclinato 12
iam die occurrit. hic turris erigitur sub qua diaetae duae, totidem in
ipsa, praeterea cenatio quae latissimum mare, longissimum litus, uillas
amoenissimas possidet.

Est et alia turris. in hac cubiculum in quo sol nascitur conditurque; 13
lata post apotheca et horreum. sub hoc triclinium quod turbati maris non
nisi fragorem et sonum patitur eumque iam languidum ac desinentem,
hortum et gestationem uidet qua hortus includitur. gestatio buxo aut rore 14

marino, ubi deficit buxus, ambitur (nam buxus, qua parte defenditur tectis, abunde uiret; aperto caelo apertoque uento quamquam longinqua
15 aspergine maris inarescit); adiacet interiore circumitu uinea tenera et umbrosa nudisque etiam pedibus mollis et cedens. hortum morus et ficus frequens uestit, quarum arborum illa uel maxime ferax terra est, malignior ceteris. hac non deteriore quam maris facie cenatio remota a mari fruitur; cingitur diaetis duabus a tergo, quarum fenestris subiacet uestibulum uillae et hortus alius pinguis et rusticus.

16 Hinc cryptoporticus prope publici operis extenditur. utrimque fenestrae, a mari plures, ab horto †singulae sed alternis pauciores†. hae, cum serenus dies et immotus, omnes, cum hinc uel inde uentis inquietus,
17 qua uenti quiescunt sine iniuria patent. ante cryptoporticum xystus uiolis odoratus: teporem solis infusi repercussu cryptoporticus auget, quae ut tenet solem sic Aquilonem inhibet summouetque, quantumque caloris ante tantum retro frigoris; similiter Africum sistit, atque ita diuersissimos
18 uentos alium alio latere frangit et finit. haec iucunditas eius hieme, maior aestate. nam ante meridiem xystum, post meridiem gestationis hortique proximam partem umbra sua temperat, quae ut dies creuit decreuitue
19 modo breuior, modo longior hac uel illa cadit. ipsa uero cryptoporticus tum maxime caret sole cum ardentissimus culmini eius insistit. ad hoc patentibus fenestris Fauonios accipit transmittitque, nec umquam aere pigro et manente ingrauescit.

20 In capite xysti, deinceps cryptoporticus horti, diaeta est, amores mei, re uera amores: ipse posui. in hac heliocaminus quidem alia xystum, alia mare, utraque solem, cubiculum autem ualuis cryptoporticum, fenestra
21 prospicit mare. contra parietem medium zotheca perquam eleganter recedit, quae specularibus et uelis obductis reductisue modo adicitur cubiculo, modo aufertur. lectum et duas cathedras capit; a pedibus mare, a tergo uillae, a capite siluae: tot facies locorum totidem fenestris et
22 distinguit et miscet. iunctum est cubiculum noctis et somni. non illud uoces seruulorum, non maris murmur, non tempestatum motus, non fulgurum lumen, ac ne diem quidem sentit nisi fenestris apertis. tam alti abditique secreti illa ratio, quod interiacens andron parietem cubiculi hortique distinguit, atque ita omnem sonum media inanitate consumit.
23 applicitum est cubiculo hypocauston perexiguum quod angusta fenestra suppositum calorem, ut ratio exigit, aut effundit aut retinet. procoeton inde et cubiculum porrigitur in solem, quem orientem statim exceptum
24 ultra meridiem obliquum quidem sed tamen seruat. in hanc ego diaetam cum me recepi abesse mihi etiam a uilla mea uideor, magnamque eius uoluptatem praecipue Saturnalibus capio, cum reliqua pars tecti licentia

dierum festisque clamoribus personat: nam nec ipse meorum lusibus nec illi studîs meis obstrepunt.

Haec utilitas, haec amoenitas deficitur aqua salienti, sed puteos ac 25 potius fontes habet: sunt enim in summo. et omnino litoris illius mira natura: quocumque loco moueris humum, obuius et paratus umor occurrit, isque sincerus ac ne leuiter quidem tanta maris uicinitate corruptus. suggerunt affatim ligna proximae siluae, ceteras copias Ostiensis colonia 26 ministrat; frugi quidem homini sufficit etiam uicus quem una uilla discernit. in hoc balinea meritoria tria, magna commoditas si forte balineum domi uel subitus aduentus uel breuior mora calfacere dissuadeat. litus 27 ornant uarietate gratissima nunc continua, nunc intermissa tecta uillarum, quae praestant multarum urbium faciem, siue mari siue ipso litore utare, quod non numquam longa tranquillitas mollit, saepius frequens et contrarius fluctus indurat. mare non sane pretiosis piscibus 28 abundat, soleas tamen et squillas optimas egerit; uilla uero nostra etiam mediterraneas copias praestat, lac in primis: nam illuc e pascuis pecora conueniunt, si quando aquam umbramue sectantur.

Iustisne de causis iam tibi uideor incolere inhabitare diligere secessum? 29 quem tu nimis urbanus es nisi concupiscis. atque utinam concupiscas, ut tot tantisque dotibus uillulae nostrae maxima commendatio ex tuo contubernio accedat!

VALE.

18

C. PLINIVS MAVRICO SVO S.

Quid a te mihi iucundius potuit iniungi quam ut praeceptorem fratris tui 1 liberis quaererem? nam beneficio tuo in scholam redeo et illam dulcissimam aetatem quasi resumo, sedeo inter iuuenes ut solebam atque etiam experior quantum apud illos auctoritatis ex studîs habeam. nam proxime 2 frequenti auditorio inter se coram multis ordinis nostri clare iocabantur; intraui, conticuerunt. quod non referrem, nisi ad illorum magis laudem quam ad meam pertineret, ac nisi sperare te uellem posse fratris tui filios probe discere. quod superest, cum omnes qui profitentur audiero, quid de 3 quoque sentiam scribam, efficiamque, quantum tamen epistula consequi potero, ut ipse omnes audisse uidearis. debeo enim tibi, debeo memo- 4 riae fratris tui hanc fidem, hoc studium, praesertim super tanta re: nam quid magis interest uestra quam ut liberi – dicerem tui, nisi nunc illos magis amares – digni illo patre, te patruo reperiantur? quam curam mihi

5 etiam si non mandasses uindicassem. nec ignoro suscipiendas offensas in
   eligendo praeceptore, sed oportet me non modo offensas uerum etiam
   simultates pro fratris tui filiis tam aequo animo subire quam parentes pro
   suis.

VALE.

19

C. PLINIVS CERIALI SVO S.

1 Hortaris ut orationem amicis pluribus recitem: faciam quia hortaris,
2 quamuis uehementer addubitem. neque enim me praeterit actiones quae
   recitentur impetum omnem caloremque ac prope nomen suum perdere,
   ut quas soleant commendare simul et accendere iudicum consessus,
   celebritas aduocatorum, exspectatio euentus, fama non unius actoris
   diductumque in partes audientium studium, ad hoc dicentis gestus incessus discursus etiam, omnibusque motibus animi consentaneus uigor cor-
3 poris. unde accidit ut ii qui sedentes agunt, quamuis illis maxima ex
   parte supersint eadem illa quae stantibus, tamen hoc quod sedent quasi
4 debilitentur et deprimantur; recitantium uero praecipua pronuntiationis
   adiumenta, oculi manus, praepediuntur: quo minus mirum est si auditorum intentio relanguescit, nullis extrinsecus aut blandimentis capta aut
   aculeis excitata.
5   Accedit his quod oratio de qua loquor pugnax et quasi contentiosa est;
   porro ita natura comparatum est ut ea quae scripsimus cum labore cum
6 labore etiam audiri putemus. et sane quotus quisque tam rectus auditor
   quem non potius dulcia haec et sonantia quam austera et pressa delectent?
   est quidem omnino turpis ista discordia, est tamen, quia plerumque euenit
   ut aliud auditores, aliud iudices exigant, cum alioqui iis praecipue auditor
   affici debeat quibus idem, si foret iudex, maxime permoueretur.
7   Potest tamen fieri ut quamquam in his difficultatibus libro isti nouitas
   lenocinetur – nouitas apud nostros: apud Graecos enim est quiddam
8 quamuis ex diuerso, non tamen omnino dissimile. nam ut illis erat moris
   leges quas ut contrarias prioribus legibus arguebant aliarum collatione
   conuincere, ita nobis inesse repetundarum legi quod postularemus cum
   hac ipsa lege tum aliis colligendum fuit. quod nequaquam blandum
   auribus imperitorum tanto maiorem apud doctos habere gratiam debet
9 quanto minorem apud indoctos habet; nos autem, si placuerit recitare,
   adhibituri sumus eruditissimum quemque.

Sed plane adhuc an sit recitandum examina tecum, omnesque quos
ego moui in utraque parte calculos pone, idque elige in quo uicerit ratio:
a te enim ratio exigetur, nos excusabit obsequium.

VALE.

20

C. PLINIVS CALVISIO SVO S.

Assem para et accipe auream fabulam, fabulas immo: nam me priorum 1
noua admonuit, nec refert a qua potissimum incipiam.

Verania Pisonis grauiter iacebat, huius dico Pisonis quem Galba adop- 2
tauit. ad hanc Regulus uenit. primum impudentiam hominis qui uenerit
ad aegram, cuius marito inimicissimus, ipsi inuisissimus fuerat! esto, si 3
uenit tantum; at ille etiam proximus toro sedit, quo die, qua hora nata
esset interrogauit. ubi audît, componit uultum, intendit oculos, mouet
labra, agitat digitos, computat. nihil. ut diu miseram exspectatione sus-
pendit, 'habes' inquit 'climactericum tempus, sed euades. quod ut tibi 4
magis liqueat, haruspicem consulam quem sum frequenter expertus.'
nec mora, sacrificium facit, affirmat exta cum siderum significatione 5
congruere. illa ut in periculo credula poscit codicillos, legatum Regulo
scribit. mox ingrauescit, clamat moriens hominem nequam perfidum ac
plus etiam quam periurum, qui sibi per salutem fili peierasset. facit hoc 6
Regulus non minus scelerate quam frequenter, quod iram deorum, quos
ipse cotidie fallit, in caput infelicis pueri detestatur.

Velleius Blaesus ille locuples consularis nouissima ualetudine con- 7
flictabatur, cupiebat mutare testamentum. Regulus, qui speraret aliquid
ex nouis tabulis, quia nuper captare eum coeperat, medicos hortari rogare, quoquo modo spiritum homini prorogarent. postquam signatum est 8
testamentum, mutat personam, uertit allocutionem, isdemque medicis:
'quousque miserum cruciatis? quid inuidetis bona morte, cui dare uitam
non potestis?' moritur Blaesus et, tamquam omnia audisset, Regulo ne
tantulum quidem.

Sufficiunt duae fabulae, an scholastica lege tertiam poscis? est unde fiat. 9
Aurelia ornata femina signatura testamentum sumpserat pulcherrimas 10
tunicas. Regulus cum uenisset ad signandum, 'rogo' inquit 'has mihi
leges.' Aurelia ludere hominem putabat, ille serio instabat; ne multa, 11
coegit mulierem aperire tabulas ac sibi tunicas quas erat induta legare;
obseruauit scribentem, inspexit an scripsisset. et Aurelia quidem uiuit,

ille tamen istud tamquam morituram coegit. et hic hereditates, hic legata quasi mereatur accipit.

12 Ἀλλὰ τί διατείνομαι in ea ciuitate in qua iam pridem non minora praemia, immo maiora nequitia et improbitas quam pudor et uirtus

13 habent? aspice Regulum, qui ex paupere et tenui ad tantas opes per flagitia processit ut ipse mihi dixerit, cum consuleret quam cito sestertium sescentiens impleturus esset, inuenisse se exta duplicia, quibus portendi

14 miliens et ducentiens habiturum. et habebit, si modo, ut coepit, aliena testamenta, quod est improbissimum genus falsi, ipsis quorum sunt illa dictauerit.

VALE.

COMMENTARY

I

Verginius Rufus has received a state funeral. He was not only great but fortunate, living thirty years beyond his moment of glory, dying under a good emperor, and receiving a funeral oration from Tacitus. He had a good life, but we shall miss him, I myself especially: as my guardian he showed me the love of a parent and more. Hence my grief – but I am consoled by his undying glory.

Book 2 opens in grand style and with a grand subject. As governor of Germania Superior in AD 68, Verginius Rufus had crushed Julius Vindex's revolt against Nero, then pledged loyalty to Galba rather than pursue the throne himself; he returned to prominence as an octogenarian consul in Nerva's new principate (Jan. 97). His death and funeral, and the dramatic date of this letter, can be fixed to the last two months of that year (§6n. *laudatus*). P. revisits his great deeds in 6.10 and 9.19, quoting Verginius' self-composed epitaph (*hic situs est Rufus, pulso qui Vindice quondam | imperium asseruit non sibi sed patriae*); he begins here with his death.

The letter begins with news of the funeral (§§1–6), which embraces a miniature account of Verginius' later years and death, alluding briefly (but pregnantly) to his 'refusal' of the principate (§2n. *cum*, §7n. *illis*). This is framed as a story of *felicitas*; even his unglamorous broken hip was sustained in the most senatorial of ways, as Verginius prepared for the speech of thanks he would deliver to Nerva upon assuming the consulate. The literary celebration of deaths ('*exitus* literature') was in vogue, both in poetry (Titinius Capito in 1.17.3) and prose (C. Fannius in 5.5; Titinius Capito (again) in 8.12.4; 6.16, the *exitus* of Uncle Pliny; and the death scenes of Tac. *Ag.*, *H.* and esp. *An.*). Where other writers heroised victims of earlier principates, P. presents a noble death in the service of the new regime (Pausch 2004: 88–113).

Yet this public stage occupies less than half the letter. From Tacitus' funeral oration (§6) P. moves to the private sphere, where he remains for most of §§7–12, staking his personal claim to sorrow: Verginius was the exemplary compatriot, guardian and mentor for whom P. was the best son he never had (§§8–9). With this rhetoric of surrogate paternity P. presents himself as virtual successor to a man known to us – thanks to these letters – as a key figure of the Nervan 'gerontocracy'. At the same time, this personal (and so suitably epistolary) tribute complements, or competes with, Tacitus' public oration. P. typically says nothing of his words, but seems to engage allusively with his *Agricola* (§10n. *si*) as well as with Cicero's *Laelius* (*De amicitia*), an apt model for this exemplary friendship across generations (§11n. *uiuit*). Like those works, this letter ends in an intimate *consolatio*, so completing its transformation into a virtual funeral speech of its own, albeit within the putative intimacy of epistolarity.

The death of a senior consular and professed intimate recalls 1.12, on the suicide of Corellius Rufus (Hoffer 1999: 141–59), a central letter in its book with the death of Domitian at its middle (1.12.8). P. characteristically varies the pattern here (Intro. 18–19), setting Verginius first in the book and referring more obliquely (though still clearly) to Domitian (§3n. *Caesares quibus*). There is some paradox in making death, a conventional closural motif, a beginning (as does Cicero in the *Brutus*; cf. also Tac. *H.* 1.4.2 and *An.* 1.6.1 with Woodman 1995: 259), but where Cicero and Tacitus generate gloom, the death of Verginius, inaugural figure *par excellence*, betokens new life for Rome, for P., and for a second book of *Epistles*.

As a book-opening, the weighty 2.1 contrasts strongly with the slight 1.1 (as, conversely, the long 2.11 contrasts with the miniature 1.11), while finding a match in 3.1, a letter of almost identical length (396~410 words) which celebrates a living elder statesman, Vestricius Spurinna (2.7.intro.). A different set of contrasts builds the frame of book 2, with 2.20 (again comparable, at 366 words) dwelling on the counter-exemplary life of Regulus (2.20.intro.); whereas 2.1 moves from high political to personal, 2.20 moves chiastically from the private realm to the state at large (2.20.12n. *in*, Intro. 13). Within the nine-book collection, 8.23, a eulogy for young Junius Avitus and the penultimate letter of book 8, just fails, in a characteristic structural tease, to provide symmetrical balance (Whitton 2013 at n.45).

On P. and Verginius see Pausch 2004: 99–113, Marchesi 2008: 158–60 and 189–99, Lefèvre 2009: 23–36, G–M 126–35. On Plinian consolation see Gnilka 1973.

C. PLINIVS ROMANO SVO S. (= s<*alutem dicit*>) 'Gaius Pliny sends greeting to his friend Romanus', the definitive marker of epistolarity (Augustine *Retract.* 2.20 *epistula est: habet quippe in capite quis ad quem scribat*; Cugusi 1989: 384–6). Every letter in books 1–9 is headed by such a formulaic *inscriptio*, varying only in the addition of *prosocero* and *socrui* to his grandfather-in-law and mother-in-law; book 10 is similarly routine (*C. Plinius Traiano imperatori* – no *suo* here – and *Traianus Plinio*). In book 2 and (it seems) originally throughout, the addressee is abbreviated to a single name, usually as here a *cognomen*, more rarely a *gentilicium* (family name) to avoid ambiguity (2.8n. CANINIO; see also 2.16n. ANNIANO); it seems that an index originally supplied both (Intro. 39–41). The style resembles contemporary letters from Vindolanda (in Bowman–Thomas 1983 and 1994, with comment at 1983: 49–50; also Birley 2000a: 32–3) and the prefatory letters of Statius and Martial, though P.'s use of his *praenomen* (C.) is a rarity (shared with Quintilian's prefatory epistle). The stark routine (like Seneca's unchanging *Seneca Lucilio suo salutem*) strikes a contrast with the variety of Cicero's headings (cf. Cugusi 1983; Corbinelli 2008: 176–82) and with the correspondence of Fronto later in the second century (Birley 2000a: 33–4).

The addressee is C. Licinius Marinus Voconius Romanus (*PIR*[2] L 210), the equestrian friend and coeval from Saguntum (Sagunto) in Hispania Citerior whose career P. advances in 2.13 and whose promotion to senatorial status he requests of Trajan in 10.4 (apparently unsuccessfully: 2.13.intro.). With eight letters he is P.'s third-favourite correspondent (after Tacitus and grandfather-in-law Calpurnius Fabatus), but content too marks him as a key figure: besides 6.15 (Javolenus), 8.8 (*fons Clitumnus*) and 9.7 (Como villas), his letters include 1.5 on Regulus, 3.13 on *Pan.*, 6.33 on Viriola (P.'s greatest centumviral triumph) and finally 9.28, in which his letters are characterised as mirrors of P.'s own (2.13.7n. *epistulas*): see G–M 149–54. Through him 2.1 is bound to 1.5, the other most explicitly political letter of book 1 (see intro. on 1.12), on the death of Domitian and concomitant role-reversal of the 'good' Pliny and 'bad' Regulus (2.20.intro.). His name is resonant for this epistolary inauguration on the public stage (cf. §1n. *populi*). For hints of Plinian name-play see §6n. *laudator*, 2.2n. PAVLINO, 2.11.14n. *secunda*, 2.11.23n. *superest*, 2.14.8n. *eum*, 2.15n. VALERIANO, Gibson 2011b: 659 n.23, G–M 42 n.15 (and cf. Woodman 1998: 219–22 on Tacitus). There are plenty of opportunities that P. does not take: no eighth letter for Octavius (2.10, 1.7), for instance, nor obvious play on Priscus (2.11.2n. *Marius*) or 'kinglet' Regulus (2.20).

1 A grand sentence (in the small-scale terms of the *Epistles*) builds to a series of climaxes: the delayed grammatical subject (*publicum funus*), the topic of the letter (*Vergini Rufi*) and lastly the theme-word for §§1–6 (*felicis*). The high style and absence of epistolary niceties (Romanus first appears in §10 *in sinu tuo*) sets a public stage, at least for the opening of this quasi-funeral oration. Few letters begin without a second-person reference (2.3, 2.6; also 2.7, close to this letter in theme and manner). **Post aliquot annos** 'after several years' *sc.* without such splendid events, aggrandising (albeit with epistolary mildness: not *multos annos*) and setting a restoration mood through oblique reference to Domitian. The words also invite meta-epistolary reading – how many years have passed since book 1? (not many: Intro. 16) – but do so delicately: contrast Martial's explicit comment on the progress of his books (e.g. *Epig.* 2.93, 3.1), and that of P.'s epigone Sidonius (G–M 45). Time is thematised in 1.1.1 *non seruato temporis ordine* (alluding to another time-focused opening, Sen. *Ep.* 1.1: Whitton 2010: 130 n.74) and 3.1.1 *nescio an ullum iucundius tempus exegerim*; cf. also 4.1.1 *cupis post longum tempus.* **insigne atque etiam memorabile ... spectaculum** 'a splendid and indeed memorable spectacle'. Hyperbaton (the separation of adjectives and noun by *populi Romani oculis*) throws weight onto *spectaculum* through delay, as does the redundance of *insigne ... memorabile*. The adjectives are a rising pair (3~5 syllables), reflecting (as usual) Behagel's 'law of rising members' ('Gesetz der wachsenden Glieder': West 2007: 117–19). *atque etiam*, which routinely accompanies gradation (Intro. 23), implies that *memorabile* surpasses *insigne* in meaning too. **populi Romani:** a cliché of public discourse, rare in the *Epistles* (1.17.4; 8.6.7, quoting a decree). **oculis** 'to the view' (*OLD* 3a), indirect object of *exhibuit*, intensifying the visuality of *spectaculum*. **spectaculum exhibuit** 'presented a spectacle', a standard use of *exhibeo* (*OLD* 3, *TLL* v.2 1430.4–46) but unusually with *publicum funus*, not a person, as subject (cf. Mart. *Spect.* 24(21).2 *exhibuit ... harena*).

The predominance of perfect tenses in §§1–6 (*superuixit, legit,* etc.) gives an aura of detached report (Rosén 1980: 29–31), with which the personal tone and mixed tenses of §§7–12 will contrast. **publicum funus** 'state funeral', paid for at public expense and presided over by magistrates (S-W, Vollmer 1893, Toynbee 1971: 55–6). Very few are attested for non-members of the imperial family; Licinius Sura, another triple consular, received one in 110 (Dio 68.15.3²). Deaths populate the *Epistles* (2.7, 2.20, 1.5.1, 1.12, 3.7, 3.10, 3.14, 3.21 etc.) but funerals are rare: one in passing at 3.16.4, a funereal *spectaculum* (ending a book) at 6.34.2. **Vergini Rufi:** L. Verginius Rufus (*PIR* V 284), born AD 13/14 (§4n. *annum*), consul in 63 (*ord.*), 69 (*suff.*) and 97 (*ord.*, with Nerva), a rare tally (§2n. *perfunctus*). To be 'ordinary' consul, opening and so naming the calendar year, was more prestigious than to be one of the 'suffect' consuls, who might now number ten each year. On his role in 68, when he refused to challenge Galba, but only after possibly suspect hesitation, see Tac. *H.* 1.8, 1.52; Levick 1985; Syme 1991: 512–20, 641–5 (sceptical about his power), *BNP* 'Verginius II.1' (Eck), §2n. *cum.* For P.'s naming practice see Vidman 1981, Jones 1991, Birley 2000a: 21–34. The manner here (*gentilicium* and *cognomen* at first mention, then a single name later, in §12) is most common, e.g. 2.7.1–2, 2.9.1–2, 2.11.2–5, 2.14.10–12, 2.20.7–8, though not uniform. The spelling *Vergini* (some MSS have -*ii*) is guaranteed by rhythm (a cretic–spondee) and P.'s normal usage (2.11.23n. *Mari*). **maximi et clarissimi** 'most important and distinguished' (*OLD clarus* 6), a common pair (e.g. Cic. *Fam.* 11.14.3, Livy 28.12.13, Sen. *Polyb.* 11.12.3); *clarissimus* was by now a *uox propria* for senators, as e.g. 3.8.1 (*OLD* 7, *TLL* III 1275.8–42). The phrase is varied and the name inverted at the head of the next Verginius letter: 6.10.1 *Rufi Vergini . . . optimi illius et maximi uiri.* **perinde felicis** '(and) no less fortunate', i.e. *felicissimi etiam* (*perinde* + positive after a superlative, unique to P., is also at 1.8.12 *utilissimum munus, sed non perinde populare*). The short, asyndetic tail (cf. Sall. *H.* 2.77 *Mithridates corpore ingenti, perinde armatus,* Flor. 1.37 *atrox caelum, perinde ingenia,* but without their syllepsis) sets the theme §§2–6 (cf. §6 *felicitati*). For the consolatory motif cf. Cic. *Brut.* 4–5 *felicitate . . . felicitatem,* 329 *fortunatus illius exitus,* Tac. *Ag.* 45.3 *tu uero felix*; but Hortensius and Agricola were fortunate in dying before rather than enduring terrible times, Verginius is *felix* in living so long and into the happy present. P. often uses *felix* as 'lucky' (Zieske 1972: 307–10), but there is a hint of divine favour here (§3n. *tamquam*).

2 triginta annis gloriae suae superuixit, | legit scripta de se carmina, legit historias, | et posteritati suae interfuit: tricolon (13~15~11 syllables), arranged ABA (A = clause-final verb + dat., B = clause-initial verbs + acc.); for the connections 'X Y *et* Z' / 'X Y Z*que*' (and sim.), rarer in 'classical' Latin (Caesar, Cicero), see e.g. 2.9.4n. *summa,* 2.17.5n. *et* (Kraut 1872: 45, K–S II 32, *OLD* -*que* 2b). Asyndeton predominates in §§2–4 (a list of reasons for calling Verginius *felix*) and widely in the *Epistles* (Intro. 21). The variation in verb-placement continues below: *perfunctus est* (initial) . . . *euasit, reliquit* (juxtaposed in mid-sentence, a favourite arrangement of P.), *excessit* (middle), *usus est* (initial) . . . *elapsus est* (final) . . . *fregit* (final) . . . *coît* (final). *triginta annis* is 'for thirty years' (abl. of duration, common since Livy: *NLS* §54.i) or 'by thirty years' (abl. of degree of difference: *NLS* §82.ii), AD 68–97 by the usual inclusive reckoning. **gloriae suae superuixit** 'he outlived his glory', flirting with paradox until the reader (re)construes *gloria* as 'glorious action' (*OLD* 3); *superuiuere* (+ dat.) is first attested here (cf. Apul. *Met.* 1.14 *ipse mihi superuiuens*). Allusion, perhaps, to Livy 2.7.8 *superstitem gloriae suae*, describing Valerius Publicola, *cos.* 509 BC and thus an apt inaugural model for this figurehead of the Nervan revival. In Publicola's case survival was problematic, as for Pompey in Lucan 8.28–9 *uita superstes | imperio*: better to die at the apex of one's fame (a topos: Cic. *Lael.* 11 with Powell, *Tusc.* 1.85–6, Juv. 10.278–82). P. advocates the reverse (as does Cicero in *Pro Marcello*), that long enjoyment of glory is the true desiderandum. Light alliteration and assonance (*su- su-*) points the paradox; cf. Tac. *Ag.* 3.2 *nostri superstites sumus* and the similarly sibilant 9.13.7 *'salui simus qui supersimus'*. **legit scripta de se carmina, legit historias** 'he read poems and histories written about himself', with *legit* in affective anaphora; *scripta de se* is sylleptic (understand *scriptas de se* in the second colon: on syllepsis see Intro. 25). **carmina:** unknown; possibilities include epigram, occasional poetry like Statius' *Siluae*, panegyric (cf. *Laus Pisonis*, the only extant encomium of a *priuatus* from the 1C. AD) or historical epic; Verginius need not have been the sole subject (next n.). **historias** *sc. de se scriptas*, an exaggeration for 'histories in which he featured', such as those of Cluvius Rufus (9.19.5) and Tacitus (*H.*); also presumably the elder Pliny's history *a fine Aufidi Bassi* (3.5.6). P. neglects to mention that these were not all laudatory: contrast 9.19.5 (Cluvius speaking to Verginius) *'si quid in historiis meis legis aliter ac uelis'* (Gibson forthcoming); for Tacitus see below on *cum*. **et posteritati suae interfuit** 'and was part of his own posterity', sententious paradox (on 'sententious', i.e. gnomic/surprising/witty, see Intro. 26–8). *posteritas*, posthumous reputation (*OLD* 3), is a prime concern of P., esp. 9.3.1 *ego beatissimum existimo qui bonae mansuraeque famae praesumptione perfruitur, certusque posteritatis cum futura gloria uiuit* (cf. Quint. 12.11.7). For the paradox, cf. Mart. 7.47.10 *frueris posteritate tua*. **perfunctus est tertio consulatu:** a third consulate was a rare honour: only emperors held more. Verginius was Nerva's sole triple consular; only three *priuati* are recorded under the Flavians (Mucianus, Vibius Crispus, Fabricius Veiento) and three under Trajan: Frontinus, *ord.* 100 (2.11.22n.), L. Julius Ursus, *suff.* 100 (Syme 1985b: 276, *BNP* 'Iulius II 140' (Eck), *pace* S-W and others, who gave his post to Vestricius Spurinna), L. Licinius Sura, *ord.* 107. Verginius completed his third term (*perfunctus*) – in absence? – and died later in the year (§4n. *durior*). **ut summum fastigium priuati hominis impleret** 'so that he fulfilled the highest rank [*OLD fastigium* 7] of a subject'. For *implere*, cf. Tac. *An.* 4.38.1 *locum principem impleam*, *An.* 11.16.3 *principem locum impleat* (*TLL* VII.1 636.26–31, *contra OLD* 8b). This gloss on *perfunctus est tertio consulatu* might be taken as a result clause, or as a pseudo-final clause ascribing purpose to destiny ('so as to fulfil': *OLD ut* 28f,

Nisbet 1923, Heubner on Tac. *H.* 1.48.1, Oakley on Livy 7.1.7, Watt 1990: 87 on *Pan.* 50.5). *summum fastigium priuati hominis* looks like oxymoron, since *summum fastigium* refers naturally to the principate itself: *Pan.* 52.2, Sen. *Marc.* 4.4, Tac. *An.* 3.56.2, 13.17.3, 15.65 (the context of Lucian *Macrobii* 7 εἰς τὴν τελεωτάτην... τάξιν 'to the highest rank' is uncertain: imperial adoption?). *priuatus* 'not holding office' describes a non-magistrate in the Republic, a non-emperor in the principate (*OLD priuatus*² 1). Its adjectival use (*OLD priuatus*¹ 2b) with *homo* is quite rare: Sen. *Clem.* 1.8.6 (opposed to *regibus*), Tac. *Ag.* 39.3 *priuati hominis nomen supra principem attolli*, *An.* 15.61. P. works the alliterative antithesis *priuatus/princeps* hard in *Pan.* (e.g. 7.2 *sub bono principe priuatus esse desisti*; cf. Tac. *Ag.* 39.3, just quoted). **cum principis noluisset** *sc. fastigium*, 'when/although he had refused that of emperor', in AD 68 (intro.), completing a characteristic *sententia*. Verginius' 'great deed' (6.10.4 *diuinum illud et immortale factum*) is briefly stated (this is no history: cf. 1.1.1), but worked into pointed antithesis; P. makes capital out of it again in §7 *illis etiam quos recusauit*. Cf. Tac. *H.* 1.8.2 (on Verginius) *an imperare noluisset dubium; delatum ei a milite imperium conueniebat* 'it was uncertain whether he had refused rule; what *was* agreed was that rule had been conferred on him by the soldiery'. Tacitus' *noluisset* (nowhere else in P. or Tac.) may imply a correction of P.'s version (Damon ad loc.), though the relative chronology of *H.* 1 and *Epp.* 2 is unclear (Intro. 33–4); if so, he exercises precisely the independence Verginius wanted (9.19.5, Whitton 2012: 351–2). See also §6n. *laudator*.

3 Caesares ... euasit, reliquit ... amicissimum: chiastic. For both antithesis and diction cf. *Pan.* 95.4 *in tantum diligo optimum principem | in quantum inuisus pessimo fui*, setting P. himself in the role played by Verginius here. **Caesares quibus suspectus atque etiam inuisus uirtutibus fuerat** 'the emperors who had suspected and even hated him for his excellence' (*uirtutibus* abl. of cause: *NLS* §45), alluding primarily but obliquely to Domitian (never named in *Epistles* 2): cf. 8.14.7 *cum suspecta uirtus*, *Pan.* 14.5 *alienisque uirtutibus... inuidus imperator*, 95.4 (previous n.), and see Kraus–Woodman on Tac. *Ag.* 41.1 *infensus uirtutibus princeps* (again Domitian) for the commonplace that tyrants hate merit. *Caesar* (*OLD* 3) is a routine synonym for *princeps*; the plural anonymises and aggrandises ('more hysterically than historically', Merrill), and emphasises the longevity of a man whose life spanned twelve emperors. For *atque etiam* see §1n. *insigne.* **euasit** 'escaped' (*OLD* 5b); cf. Tac. *An.* 16.8.3 *Neronem... euasere*, *Ag.* 44.5 *euasisse postremum illud tempus* (Domitian's last years). **reliquit incolumem optimum atque amicissimum** *sc. Caesarem*, 'he left secure an excellent and most devoted one' (*OLD relinquo* 8a, 9b). *incolumis* suggests both living (*OLD* 1c) and reigning (*OLD* 2a), notionally coterminous in the case of an emperor; cf. 10.35.1 *pro incolumitate tua*, 10.100 *florentem et incolumem* (cf. *Pan.* 55.1), *Pan.* 53.6 *incolumem imperatorem* (effectively 'the present emperor'). Almost certainly Nerva, a better fit than Trajan for *amicissimus* given his age, fixing the death (and Tacitus' consulate: §6n. *laudatus*) to 97. For the pair *optimum atque amicissimum* cf. 3.4.3, 4.19.1 and e.g. Cic. *Red. sen.* 12, *Att.* 1.8.1; it balances and varies *suspectus atque etiam inuisus* (8~9 syllables, nom. ~ acc.). *optimus* was a common imperial honorific (Frei-Stolba 1969: 21–8, Woodman on Vell. 2.126.5); P. apparently reserves for Trajan the moniker '(the) *princeps optimus*' (2.13.8n.), but Nerva is '(an) *optimus princeps*' again at 9.13.23 and *Pan.* 88.5, and *optimus* at *Pan.* 7.4 and 89.1; cf. Frontin. *Aq.* 64.1 *optimi diligentissimique Neruae principis* (suspected by Rodgers ad loc.). P. nowhere names Nerva or Trajan in book 2 (and never uses *Traianus* in the private letters): the unspecific *princeps* (2.7.1, 2.11.10) and *Caesar* (2.9.2, 2.11.11, 15) tend to obscure any boundary within the new regime (Intro. 7–8). On his terms and names for emperors see also S-W 125, Birley 2000a: 28–9. **tamquam … reseruatus** 'as if kept for', hinting at divine providence. *tamquam* holds out the possibility without confirmation or denial (*pace OLD* 5b: G–L §602 n.3, K–S 1 790–1). **publici funeris:** gen. of definition with *honorem* (*NLS* §72.5, *OLD honor* 2a; cf. 2.7.3 *honor statuae*).

4 annum tertium et octogensimum excessit 'he lived beyond his eighty-third year' (*OLD excedo* 7b), i.e. died aged 83. That was in late 97 (§4n. *durior*), giving him a birth-year of late AD 13 or early 14. **in altissima tranquillitate** 'in the most profound peace' (*OLD altus* 10b), referring to an easy old age (cf. 3.7.9 on Silius Italicus, another name tied to AD 68 (3.7.10–11), 4.23.4, 2.8.1n. *altissimus*) and evoking the consolatory topos of a peaceful death (Pausch 2004: 108 n.314); coming after §3, it also has a political edge: for 'deep peace' as the inverse of tyranny, see Sen. *Clem.* 1.1.8 *securitas alta*, *Thy.* 576 *alta pax*, Lucan 1.249 *pax alta* with Roche, and Corellius' death *florente re publica* (1.12.11). Whether Nerva's principate really was tranquil is a different matter (9.13 with G–M 23–7). **pari uenera-tione** '(and) equal reverence' (*OLD par* 10a), abl. of attendant circumstances (*NLS* §47; cf. 2.11.14 *dicere … audientium assensu*, Lavency 2002: 246–7). For the use of *par* (cf. §1 *perinde felicis*), cf. 1.10.7 *sanctitas summa, comitas par* (likewise asyndetic) and *TLL* x.1 267.69–80; here it may be sylleptic (semantically strained: Intro. 25), since *ueneratio* is nowhere else called *alta*. Verginius was thus *in otio cum dignitate* (Cic. *De or.* 1.1, Gierig); for reverence in retirement cf. Quint. 12.11.7 *sentiet uiuus eam quae post fata praestari magis solet uenerationem*; but see §2n. *historias*. **usus est firma ualetudine** 'he enjoyed good health' (*OLD utor* 11, *firmus* 2b); *firmus* is common for 'healthy' (cf. 1.12.12 *firmissimi*) in Cicero, first of *ualetudo* in Sen. *Ep.* 28.6 (*TLL* VI.1 814.59–69, 2.2.2n. *infirmior*). **nisi quod** 'but for the fact that', *OLD nisi* 8. **ei** 'his', a so-called 'sympathetic dative' (*NLS* §63) or 'dative of personal interest' (G–L §350). **tremere:** as commonly in old age. **citra dolorem tamen** 'but without pain' (*OLD citra²* 5, post-Augustan). **aditus … mortis** 'the approach to death', a choice variant on *uia mortis*: cf. Quint. 8.5.5 (quoting a tragedy) *aditus ad mortem* and the poets' *ianua leti* (Lucr. 1.1112, etc.). **tantum** 'only', adv. (*OLD* 8a). **durior longiorque** 'rather hard and long' (*OLD durus* 8a), nearly a year (§5n. *cum*, §6n. *laudatus*). *durior* perhaps has a poetic ring (Hor. *Sat.* 2.2.88 *dura ualetudo*, V. *Georg.* 3.68 *durae … mortis*, *Aen.* 10.791, Lucr. 3.460 *durumque dolorem*;

though cf. Cic. *Fin.* 1.43 *durissimis animi doloribus*, Sen. *Marc.* 1.8). Comparatives are
common in P. as a genteel substitute for the positive, as 2.2.2 *occupatior... infirmior*,
2.5.2 *absolutiora* (Quint. 9.3.19, G–L §297.2, K–S II 475–6). A clause-final word-
pair with *-que* is a recurrent mannerism, often with a degree of redundance
and rhythmically convenient: §5 *sequitur colligitque*, 2.10.4 *occidunt desinuntque*, 2.12.2
durior tristiorque, 2.17.13 *nascitur conditurque*, 17 *inhibet summouetque*, 19 *accipit transmit-*
titque and e.g. 1.1.1 *colligerem publicaremque*, 1.5.2, 17, 1.14.1, 1.20.4, 1.22.8, 1.23.3.
Kraus 1992: 323, restricting herself to 'sentence-end' (any punctuation stronger
than a comma), counts 39 such, far more than Cicero (6×) and surpassed only by
Livy (266×), the elder Pliny (205×) and Tacitus (102×) among authors surveyed.
For its use with comparatives, as here, cf. 2.12.2 (above), 5.6.33 *opacior nigriorque*,
6.16.17 *nigrior densiorque*, 7.27.2 *grandior pulchriorque*, 8.4.8 *tardius cautiusque*, 9.13.6
cunctantior cautiorque, 9.26.12 *custoditius pressiusque*. **hic ipse** = *aditus mortis*, now
specifically its beginning. Supply *erat*, or take as an appositional addition (*TLL*
VI.3 2725.40: see 2.13.2n. *nec*). **laudabilis:** a stock *desiderandum* (Edwards 2007
passim). By collapsing Verginius' fall and long subsequent illness (*longior*) into a
single event, P. constructs from the mundanity of a broken hip a pseudo-heroic
death in the service of oratory and the state (§5 *acturus in consulatu principi gratias*):
Pausch 2004: 110 and 112 (*contra* Ludolph 1997: 80, who thinks P. diminishes
Verginius).

5 cum uocem praepararet 'when he was warming up his voice'. In Quintilian (10.7.2, 11.3.22) the phrase refers to warm-up exercises, not general rehearsal.
Since Verginius was presumably out of practice, P. probably refers to prepara-
tions on the day of his speech, 1 January, a fitting date for a first letter. His death
by *studia* (2.2.2n.), like that of Uncle Pliny (6.16), generates nobility from accident; it has distinguished (and more dramatic) precedent in L. Licinius Crassus,
hero of Cicero's *De oratore*, who contracted pleurisy after a vigorous senatorial
performance and died a week later (*De or.* 3.6). **acturus ... principi gratias**
'to deliver his speech of thanks to the emperor'. P. is free with the future participle, which affords brevity (Gamberini 1983: 462); its use to express purpose
(also 2.20.10 *signatura*) is routine in prose from Livy on (*NLS* §92d, Oakley on
Livy 6.22.9). On the *gratiarum actio*, a speech of thanks by a consul entering office,
see *Pan.* (the only extant published example) with Durry 1938: 3–5, Fedeli 1989:
400–4, Seelentag 2004: 217–24, id. 2011: 81–7. **in consulatu:** brachylogy for
'on his inauguration as consul'. **liber quem forte acceperat grandiorem**
'a rather large scroll he had happened to take' *sc.* from a slave. *grandiorem* is
predicative in the relative clause (lit. 'and which was rather large / too large [for
him]'); the adjective is a colloquial and/or dignified alternative to *magnus* (Brink
on Hor. *Ep.* 2.2.178–9, Adams 2005: 86; both are apt here). *liber* 'scroll' was the
ancient equivalent to a book. P. commonly uses it for a speech, revised and written up after the event (2.5.3, 2.19.7, 1.2.1, 1.20.4 etc.), but not always (e.g. 2.17.8);
this one is not Verginius' *gratiarum actio* (cf. *forte*). Scrolls were not particularly
heavy (Casanova 1998: 121 guesses 300–500 grams here) but could be unwieldy,

certainly for an octogenarian with tremor. On the (varying) shapes and sizes of book-rolls see Kenney 1982: 24–5, Johnson 2010: 17–22 and, most fully, Johnson 2004 (noting this passage on p. 151 n. 72). **et seni et stanti ipso pondere elapsus est** '(he was old and standing up) slipped from his hands [*OLD elabor* 1a] by its sheer weight'. *seni* and *stanti* (dat. of disadvantage) could be taken as nouns or adjectives; either way, they supply further reasons, besides *ipso pondere* (causal abl.), for his dropping the scroll. **hunc dum sequitur colligitque** 'as he reached after it and gathered it up': Verginius 'chases' (*OLD sequor* 2a–b) and gathers together (*OLD colligo* 1a) the unrolling scroll. For the verb-pair with *-que* see §4n. *durior.* **per leue et lubricum pauimentum fallente uestigio** 'losing his step on the smooth and slippery floor' (marble or mosaic), lit. 'his footing failing him . . . ' (*OLD fallo* 3b, *uestigium* 2a), with *fallente* continuing the alliteration of *leue et lubricum.* The preposition *per*, which has caused commentators trouble, means lit. 'across' (motion is implied in *fallente* and stated in *sequitur*). **cecidit coxamque fregit** 'he fell and broke his hip' (strictly the top of the femur). After *hunc . . . uestigio* has built tension (helped by the redundant pairs *sequitur colligitque* and *leue et lubricum*), the sharp and alliterative *cecidit coxamque* captures his sudden fall. **parum apte collocata** 'not very well set'. *parum* (*OLD* 3b) is a soft negative common in P. (e.g. 2.10.5 *parum prouidum*, 2.15.2 *parum commode*, 1.8.6 *parum aequis*, 10.94.2 *parum felix* [i.e. infertile] *matrimonium*). *collocare* is only here of setting fractures: P. is perhaps avoiding technical language. The procedure was established (cf. the Hippocratic *On fractures, c.* 400 BC). **reluctante aetate** 'his (old) age refusing to cooperate' (with the treatment), abl. abs., personifying *aetas* (cf. Sen. *Tranq.* 9.7.2 *reluctante natura*) and inverting the commoner use of (*re*)*luctor* 'struggle (to stay alive)' (V. *Aen.* 4.695 *luctantem animam*, Sen. *Oed.* 344, Sil. 6.126, *TLL* VII.2 1731.78–1732.8). P.'s use of the ablative absolute is studied by Steele 1904. **male coît** 'healed badly' (*OLD coeo* 5), compressed and euphemistic coverage of a long illness and death. The MSS are divided between *coit* (αγ) and *coüt* (β), as often in perfects of 3rd/4th conjugation verbs and compounds of *ire.* Recovering orthography is hazardous, since scribes often but inconsistently normalised spellings (in §7, e.g., α has *abiit*, βγ *abit*), but given that they were more likely to 'correct' *-it* to the more familiar *-iit* (the circumflex adopted here is a modern convenience, not found in MSS), *coit* looks the better text (Stout 1954: 140; cf. Goold 1964: 326). The MSS agree on *-it* at e.g. 2.14.10 *audit*, 2.14.11 *perit*, 1.5.11 *petit*, 5.20.2 *petit* (all pf.) and rhythm supports short forms when the MSS are divided at e.g. §7 *plenus annis abit* and 5.4.1 *a senatu petit*, Quint. 7.1.61 *aduocatus petit* (all double cretic). Sen. *Ep.* 56.9 *excisa desit* (ditrochee). The longer form finds some (not unequivocal) rhythmic support at 2.11.2 and 8.23.5 (see 2.11.2n. *petît*); here it yields a slightly commoner resolution (resolved cretic + resolved spondee), but both possibilities are rare. Assuming P. did not write *-iit* while sometimes or always hearing *-it*, he either varied his spelling (quite possible: 2.2.2n. *studîs*) or wrote *-it* throughout, a form whose currency is well attested (G–L §131.2, K–H 784, N–W III 446–8, Winterbottom on [Quint.] *Decl. min.* 270.16) and which is adopted here. See also 2.14.11n. *quaesît*, 2.20.3n. *ubi.*

6 huius uiri exsequiae 'this is the man whose funeral rites', summing up §§2–5 (for this use of *hic*, often at letter-end, cf. 7.31.7 *hunc hominem*, 2.7.6 *his ex causis*, 2.10.8 *hoc fructu*; also 2.6.6 *quorsus haec?*), and chiastically reprising with variation *funus... Rufi*. Ring-composition is frequent in P., sometimes explicit (e.g. 1.23.5 *iterum dicam*, 3.16.13 *quod initio dixi*), more often by repetition and variation. See index s.v. and Winniczuk 1975; it frequently binds a complete letter (§12n.), often a part as here (e.g. 2.3.7n. *Isaeum*, 2.3.11n. *quae*), sometimes a sentence (2.2.1n. *irascor*); also the book (2.20.14n. *et*), and *Epistles* 1–9 (Intro. 17). **magnum ornamentum principi, magnum saeculo, magnum etiam foro et rostris:** graded tricolon (8~5~8 syllables) with anaphora. The form A+B+{C+D}, popular with Cicero, recurs in §8. **ornamentum... attulerunt** 'conferred... distinction' (*OLD ornamentum* 6, *affero* 4b; cf. Sil. 16.254 *amplius attulerint decoris*, Tac. *An.* 15.43.5 *decorem... attulere*). The words, both *apo koinou* (construed 'in common': Intro. 25) with all three members of the tricolon, are characteristically distributed, with the verb at the end and the non-verbal *ornamentum* in the first member: e.g. 2.2.2 *mihi... uidebuntur*, 2.5.3 *existimationi... subicietur*, 2.11.4 *cognitionem... dicentibus*, 2.11.15 *mihi... praestitit*. **principi:** it does Nerva credit to have honoured a great man (strictly, to have overseen the honour done by the senate): cf. 1.17.4 *scias ipsum plurimis uirtutibus abundare qui alienas sic amat* and 2.7.1 *principe auctore*. **saeculo** 'the age', common in P., 'used with a certain self-conscious rectitude for the [*sc.* Nervan–]Trajanic period to mark the beginning of an era of "good" emperors' (S-W). So too Tac. *Ag.* is framed with *beatissimum saeculum* (3.1 and 44.5); the singular reinvents and demythologises the 'Golden Age(s)' (*aurea saecula*) of Virgil (*Aen.* 6.792–3, after *Ecl.* 4) and Seneca (*Apoc.* 4.1, *Clem.* 2.1.3); see also Roche 2006. **etiam:** frequently added by P. as second word to the last item in a list, whether bicolon (2.6.2, 2.11.2, 15, 20, 2.13.6, 2.17.7), tricolon (§8, 2.7.4, 2.10.8, 2.19.2) or longer (2.3.8, 9, 2.10.7). Like *atque etiam* (§1n. *insigne*), it routinely accompanies gradation (*pace* Kraut 1872: 28, Cowan on 1.22.7). Here it underlines *forum et rostra* as the most important item, inviting the justification that follows. **foro et rostris:** a surprisingly rare pair, symbolic for Lucan (4.799, 7.65) of peaceful constitutionality (also in Sen. *Ben.* 6.32.1, Pl. *NH* 10.121, Sil. 7.543). The *rostra* (speaker's platform in the forum: *BNP* 'rostrum') was evidently still a site for public oratory. **laudatus est a consule, Cornelio Tacito** 'he received a eulogy from the consul, Cornelius Tacitus', asyndetically explaining *etiam foro et rostris*. On funeral orations see Kierdorf 1980, Flower 1996: 128–58; for a consul as encomiast cf. Quint. 3.7.2 *funebres laudationes... ex senatus consulto magistratibus saepe mandantur*. Only one other *priuatus* is known to have received such a speech *pro rostris*, M. Vinicius in AD 46 (Dio 60.27.4). P. characteristically gives no report of the content (2.11.14n. *dixi*), predictable and replaced by his letter. This is the sole positive evidence for the year of Tacitus' consulate, universally accepted as 97 (§3n. *optimum*). His tenure is excluded by the *Fasti Ostienses* from the first eight months of the year; a military diploma published in 1984, if it has been correctly dated, further rules out

Sept.–Oct., so fixing his consulate and this funeral in Nov.–Dec. (Roxan 1994: 255–6, confirming the hunch of Vidman 1982: 91–2, Syme 1991: 518). On Tacitus' career generally see Alföldy 1995, Birley 2000b. The word order (*consul* then name in apposition, *TLL* IV 564.31–50) is much rarer than the converse; it first presents the explanation of *magnum ornamentum . . . foro et rostris attulerunt* (Verginius was praised by a consul), then reveals who that consul was. **nam** explains the addition of *Cornelio Tacito* (*OLD* 2c).   **hic supremus felicitati eius cumulus accessit** 'this came as the crowning glory of his *felicitas*' (*OLD cumulus* 4a, *accedo* 15a), referring forward to *laudator eloquentissimus* in apposition (cf. Sid. *Ep.* 1.7.1 *namque hic quoque cumulus accedit laudibus imperatoris, quod . . .*, 3.5.1; on Sidonius see Intro. 35 7). *cumulus accedit* is a favourite with Cicero, who construes it with *ad*; P.'s dative is contemporary: [Quint.] *Decl. mai.* 6.1 (*dolori*), Suet. *Tib.* 17.1 (*gloriae*). The hyperbaton (*supremus . . . cumulus*) is stylised: Cic. *Att.* 4.19.2 *magnus . . . cumulus*, *Marc.* 34 *maximus hoc tuo facto* [abl.] *cumulus accesserit*, Val. Max. 6.8.7 *perfectissimum . . . cumulum*; it also matches §1 *insigne . . . oculis spectaculum exhibuit* in syntactic ring-composition.   **felicitati:** cf. §1 *felicis*, the third and strongest reprise of §1 (cf. *huius uiri exsequiae* and previous n.), tightly binding §§1–6.   **laudator eloquentissimus:** strong praise; cf. 2.11.17 *respondit Cornelius Tacitus eloquentissime*, two of P.'s four uses of this superlative (2.3.7n. *disertissimum*). Here it is emphasised by its final position, outside the ring-frame *laudatus . . . laudator*, and making an impressive single-word clausula (popular with Cicero, if not with Quint. 9.4.63–6); any pun on *tacitus* is muffled. Tacitus' historical presentation of Verginius (*H.* 1.8.2, 1.52.3–4, 2.51, 2.68.4) is ambivalent (critical for e.g. Shotter 1967: 379–80, Syme 1991: 517; favourable for Townend 1961: 337, Hainsworth 1964, Cole 1992: 236–7; see §2n. *cum*). That hardly makes it surprising that he could have delivered a glowing funeral eulogy, never a time for balanced assessment (cf. Cic. *Brut.* 62 *multa enim scripta sunt in eis* [= *mortuorum laudationibus*] *quae facta non sunt, etc.*).

7 Et ille quidem . . . abît 'and so he died' (*OLD abeo* 5). Three overlapping uses of *quidem* may be identified here: (*i*) contrasting, preparing an antithesis with *tamen*, like μέν . . . δέ (*OLD* 3a, Solodow 1978: 30–66, esp. 31); (*ii*) concessive ('it is true that . . . ': *OLD* 4, Solodow 1978: 44–6); (*iii*) *et . . . quidem*, like (καὶ) μέν, concludes one topic (Verginius' *felix mors*) in preparation for a new one (P.'s grief), as 2.7.3 *et hoc quidem*; also Sen. *Apoc.* 4.2 and Apul. *Met.* 4.12 (ending death scenes): Solodow 1978: 46–7.   **plenus annis abît, plenus honoribus** 'he died having had his fill of years, his fill of honours' (*OLD plenus* 8a, with the contemporary abl.: Quint. 9.3.1), anaphora with *abît* taken apo koinou (§2n. *legit*). *plenus annis* picks up a consolatory motif: Lucr. 3.938 *plenus uitae*, Sen. *Ep.* 98.15, Stat. *Silu.* 2.2.128–9 *abire paratum | ac plenum uita* (*TLL* X.1 2412.47–52), Cic. *Marc.* 25 'satis diu . . . uixi', Sen. *Ep.* 61.4; P. elaborates it first with *plenus honoribus* (magistracies, priesthoods etc.: *OLD honor* 5a; cf. *Pan.* 57.1 *honoribus . . . expletus*) and then further, into paradox (next n.). For *abît* see §5n. *male*.   **illis etiam quos recusauit** 'even of those that he refused', turning the glory of refusing the principate to paradox (cf. Suet.

Iul. 79.1 *gloriam recusandi*). *illis* perhaps has a shade of 'those famous ones' (*OLD* 4b), but P. often reflects the contemporary weakening of *ille* in oblique cases into a near-equivalent of *is* (e.g. *illum* below, §8 *illo die quo*; see 2.18.1n. *illos*), making any distinction between this phrase and e.g. 2.16.2 *iis etiam . . . qui* subtle (cf. also *Pan.* 25.3 *illi etiam quibus*, 78.2 *illorum etiam qui*). Yet the six statements of *ille* in §§7–9, four of them referring to Verginius, seem cumulatively emphatic. **nobis tamen** contrasts with *ille quidem*; the (true) plural *nobis* also contrasts with the following *mihi uero.* **quaerendus ac desiderandus est** '[we] must miss him and long for him' (*OLD* quaero 2a, desidero 1a, gerundives of obligation), redundant doublet, as Livy 24.45.10 *desiderari quaerique.* P.'s pair is typically graded (*desiderare* is stronger than *quaerere*): cf. 6.2.1 *soleo . . . quaerere M. Regulum (nolo enim dicere desiderare).* P. feels that loss in 6.10.1–2, visiting Verginius' old house (*desiderium . . . requirebant*). **ut** 'as' (*OLD* 10). **exemplar aeui prioris** 'a model of a former age'; cf. 5.14.3 *ad exemplar antiquitatis* (Cornutus Tertullus), 7.33.9 *exemplum . . . simile antiquis* (provided by P.). The crucial phrase, and the last words before the personal turn (*mihi uero praecipue*), stand at the centre of the letter (197 words precede, 196 follow). *aeui prioris* doubles as 'previous generation' and, with grander gesture, 'former age', the great Romans (*antiqui*: cf. 2.9.4n. *antiquus*) of unspecified times gone by (*contra* Lefèvre 2009: 28, who sees Verginius as specifically 'republican'). See Woodman on Vell. 2.92.5 and Intro. 9–10; the transfer of exemplary role from Verginius to P. is neatly caught in the pair 6.10–11 (6.10 on Verginius; 6.11 on P. as model for two young orators: G–M 62–3). **mihi uero praecipue:** the pivot of the letter: *uero* is emphatically adversative (*OLD* 7b, K–S ii 80–1; cf. Kroon 1995: 281–332, esp. 328), distinguishing P. from everyone else (including Tacitus); for the motif cf. Ov. *Am.* 2.6.11–12 *omnes . . . tu tamen ante alios* with McKeown. P. reasserts his intimacy with Verginius in 9.19.5 *ipse sum testis, familiariter ab eo dilectus probatusque* (with Bernstein 2008: 205), and indirectly in 6.10.1 (a stay at Verginius' old villa at Alsium, now the possession of P.'s mother-in-law Pompeia Celerina – sign of a family connection?). **qui illum . . . quantum admirabar tantum diligebam** 'who loved him no less than I admired him', one up on Cic. *Leg.* 2.4 *eorum quos diligimus aut admiramur.* P. routinely has the indicative in explanatory relative clauses, e.g. 1.23.2 *errauerim fortasse qui . . . putaui, Pan.* 58.4 *miseros ambitionis, qui . . . erant!*, only occasionally the 'classical' subjunctive (2.10.1n. *qui*). Cicero has indicative sometimes (e.g. *Att.* 3.18.2 *homo mirus, qui me tam ualde amat*), Seneca regularly (Summers 1910: lxii; see K–S ii 292–3. Any distinction between indicative 'fact' and subjunctive 'ground' (G–L §626, *NLS* §159) seems more pertinent to high 'classical' prose. Love and affection are widely shared in the *Epistles* (2.2.1n. *amor*, 2.13.5n. *dilexi*) but combine with admiration only in the case of selected senior senators: Corellius Rufus (3.3.1 *suspexerim magis an amauerim dubitem* (see 2.4.3n. *nescio* for the syntax), 4.17.4 *ex admiratione diligere coepissem*); the 'Stoics' Musonius (3.11.5 *cum admiratione dilexi*) and Arulenus Rusticus (1.14.1 *scis . . . quanto opere . . . suspexerim dilexerimque*; see 2.18.intro.); Verginius again, now with Frontinus, at 9.19.2 *utrumque dilexi, miratus sum.* **non solum publice** 'not only in my capacity as a citizen' *sc.* but also personally (*publice* lit. 'in terms of the state (*res publica*)', *OLD* 1, 3). For the opposition, here with the second part unstated, cf. 2.7.6 *publice laetor, nec priuatim minus*, 5.14.6, 10.1.2, *Pan.* 90.1; also 6.11.3 *aut publice . . . aut mihi.*

8 primum quod . . . praeterea quod: two reasons for *non solum publice*, in a rising pair (*praeterea quod . . .* extends to the end of §9). **utrique** *sc. erant*, possessive dat. **eadem regio, municipia finitima, agri etiam possessionesque coniunctae:** rising AB~BA~AB tricolon (6~9~13 syllables); the gradation (homing in through region ~ town ~ estates; cf. 7.23.1 *et domi et intra domum atque etiam intra cubiculi limen*) is pointed by *etiam* (§6n.). Rising tricolon reflects high rhetoric in Cicero (Lindholm 1931: 165–7); it becomes commoner in the principate (ibid. 200–16) and is one variant among several for P., perhaps with a feeling of oratorical grandeur (e.g. §9, 2.10.7, 2.11.1, 8, 11, 18; see also §1n. *insigne* on rising pairs); for the form A+B+{C+D}, see §6n. *magnum.* **regio** 'district', in Transpadana (4.6.1), northern Italy (formerly Cisalpine Gaul). It was a large area but P. uses the word affectively, not legally: Syme 1968: 135–7 identifies 'Pliny country' as the eastern part of *Regio* XI (Transpadana), extending slightly into *Regio* X (Venetia). **municipia:** P. was a native of Comum (Como), Verginius of Mediolanum (Milan), *c.* 40km (a day's journey: 6.8.2 with S-W) south. **agri . . . possessionesque** 'lands and holdings' (*OLD possessio* 3), legally slightly different (Florent. *Dig.* 50.16.211, Fest. 233) but used here as redundant synonyms, as Cic. *Off.* 1.151 *se . . . in agros possessionesque contulit.* **coniunctae** modifies both nouns, agreeing with the nearer (G–L §286). **praeterea quod** 'secondly because' (above on *primum*). **ille mihi tutor relictus affectum parentis exhibuit** 'having been left as a guardian to me, he showed me the love of a parent', *OLD relinquo* 6b, *affectus* 7a. *ille* props up *mihi* (*apo koinou* with *relictus* and *exhibuit*) and asserts the bond through the proximity of pronouns. **tutor:** a boy who lost his father was assigned a *tutor* until the age of 14 (Buckland 1963: 142–65, Crook 1967a: 113–18, Saller 1994: 181–203); given high death-rates, such tutelage was very common. P.'s father, absent from the *Epistles* except by implication here and 7.11.5 *praediis . . . paternis*, therefore died before *c.* 76 (his mother lived until at least 79: 2.15.2n. *praedia*). Guardianship differed from adoption, which conferred property and title; P. acquired his name in 79 from his maternal uncle, Pliny the Elder, by testamentary adoption (Intro. 6). There is no sign of a paternal uncle, a favourite candidate for *tutor* (Saller 1994: 196–7, e.g. Mauricus in 2.18), and the elder Pliny was probably away from Italy during the early 70s (Syme 1991: 508; ibid. 510–11 speculates that Verginius was a relative through the elder Pliny's wife; for another possible family connection see §7n. *mihi* on his villa). Uncle Pliny was mentioned in passing in 1.19.1 *auunculo meo*, but full introduction is reserved for 3.5 (then 5.8.5 and 6.16; see also Gibson 2011a on 5.6), leaving books 1–2 dominated by P.'s 'virtual' fathers, the senators Corellius Rufus (1.12) and Verginius: see Cova 2001: 65 (Verginius as P.'s 'true model') and Bernstein

2008, id. 2009 on P.'s 'fictive paternity'. **affectum parentis:** demonstrated
in what follows. Cf. Cic. *Brut.* 1 *in parentis eum* [= Hortensius] *loco colere debebam*
(the other side of the coin), Tac. *An.* 4.8.4 *quamquam esset illi propria suboles, ne secus*
quam suum sanguinem foueret. **sic . . . sic . . . sic** = *affectu parentis.* Rising tricolon
(12~33~36 syllables), with main verbs at end ~ middle ~ end. **candidatum**
me suffragio ornauit 'he honoured me with his support when I was standing
for office' (*OLD suffragium* 5, *orno* 6), as Corellius did (4.17.6 *ille meus in petendis hon-*
oribus suffragator et testis). *suffragium* was the exercise of influence with the emperor
(2.9.2) or other important individuals such as fellow senators (3.20.5, 4.15.13)
to secure someone's election or appointment (Pavis d'Escurac 1992: 56–7). **ad**
omnes honores meos ex secessibus accucurrit 'he hurried to all my magistracies from his place of retreat' (*OLD honor* 5a); P. usually has *secessus* (2.8.1n.
altissimus) sg., but pl. also at 4.23.4 and (in slightly different sense) *Pan.* 49.1, 83.1.
A hyperbolical way of saying that Verginius attended P.'s inaugurations (*honores*
is brachylogical) despite living in retirement at his Alsium villa (§7n. *mihi*), 35km
up the coast. The construction of *accucurrit* (lit. 'ran (to help)'), usually with *ad +*
place/person, is rare (cf. Tac. *An.* 2.31.2 *ad gemitum*). With this good office compare again Corellius at 4.17.6 *ille in incohandis* [*honoribus*] *deductor et comes*, 1.5.11 *in*
praetoris officio with Merrill, 9.37 (P. apologises for being unable to attend Paulinus'
installation as consul). **cum iam pridem eius modi officiis renuntiasset**
'although he had long since renounced obligations of that kind', *OLD pridem* 3,
modus 12c, *officium* 2a, 3a, *renuntio* 8 (+ dat.). We know nothing else of Verginius'
career between 70 and 97; this passage implies that he was 'retired' at least during
P.'s adulthood, rhetorically advantageous both in distancing him from Domitian
and in emphasising his devotion to P. But *eius modi officiis* is vague, and does not
preclude continued involvement in senatorial life. **renuntiasset:** P. strongly
prefers syncopation in *-a(ui)sse-* forms (*c.* 25:1; Cicero has *c.* 4:1); the opposite
obtains for pf. and fut. pf., with e.g. 3.20.1 *excitarit, Pan.* 53.2 *amarit* in the minority,
c. 1:8 (at 1.20.25 *erraro* (Mynors) is a less likely reading than *errare*: Goold 1964:
324). **illo die quo sacerdotes solent nominare quos dignissimos sac-**
erdotio iudicant 'on the day when priests by custom nominate those whom
they judge most worthy of a priesthood', wordy and apparently formulaic, though
this 'day of nomination' (cf. 4.8.3, below) is otherwise unknown. Priests seem to
have been elected by the senate, following and perhaps rubber-stamping *commen-*
datio by the emperor; how the *nominatio* fitted in is uncertain (S-W 273, Talbert
1984: 345–6). P. got his augurate in 103/4 (S-W 79–80, Birley 2000a: 16; he puns
on it in 7.33.1), for which he credits Trajan's *iudicium* (4.8.1, cf. 10.13.1), but he also
mentions that Frontinus (§2n. *perfunctus*) had nominated him repeatedly (4.8.3 *me*
nominationis die per hos continuos annos inter sacerdotes nominabat). A priesthood was a
desirable office for a senator, especially one in the four major colleges (*pontifex,*
augur, quindecimuir sacris faciundis, septemuir epulonum). These had a total membership
of 60 and office was for life, making it no prerogative even for consulars, who
might number 150–200 at any one time (S-W 272). See Beard–North–Price 1998:

1 98–108, 134–7, Scheid 1978, Várhelyi 2010. **semper nominabat** 'he used always to nominate me' (*OLD semper* 2, with a 'usitative-distributive' imperfect for clarity after *illo die*, Rosén 1980: 30); cf. Cic. *Brut.* 1 (also mentioned above on *affectum*) *cooptatum me ab eo* [Hortensius] *in collegium* [of augurs] *recordabar*. P. is not afraid to let us see that Verginius' requests were unsuccessful. Even as a *nouus homo* he might have hoped for a high priesthood before the consulate (Tacitus was *quindecimuir* in 88), but competition was stiff, and the point here is the esteem Verginius demonstrates for P.: cf. 4.8.3 (previous n.), with a possible epigraphic parallel in *CIL* vi 41075.9, as supplemented by Gordon 1952: 254–6 (though not by *CIL* or *AE* 1954.4). That P. later became an augur need not mean that Verginius was too.

9 quin etiam 'what is more' (*OLD quin* A 2–3), for the ultimate proof of *affectus parentis*. An unusually 'periodic' sentence, with a chain of subordinate clauses building to the main clause (*me . . . elegit*), capped in turn with the brief, telling words of Verginius himself. **nouissima ualetudine** 'final illness' (*OLD nouissimus* 2a, 3a, *ualetudo* 3), as 2.20.7, 5.16.3, 7.24.1. **ueritus:** if the broken-hipped Verginius really was a potential appointee, physical disability must have been a greater feature of public life than the silence of our sources suggests (Garland 2010). **quinqueuiros . . . qui minuendis publicis sumptibus iudicio senatus constituebantur** 'the board of five that was being established by the verdict of the senate for reducing the public expenses': wordy officialese, generating the long ascent to a punch-line. *iudicium* [*OLD* 6–7] *senatus* is tantamount to 'senatorial decree': cf. 4.15.5 *iudicia principis* (i.e. edicts) and e.g. Cic. *Agr.* 2.57 *iudicio senatus*, Tac. *An.* 3.32.1 *iudicioque patrum*. P. is equally insistent on the senate's part in appointing this commission at *Pan.* 62.2. It was charged with cutting expenditure from the *aerarium Saturni* (2.8.2n. *angor*, 2.16.3n. *delatori*; on Nerva's finances see Grainger 2003: 52–65). **minuendis:** dative gerundive of purpose governed by *constituebantur*, a routine construction with names of offices (K–S I 748, §133d). On the dative gerund(ive) in general, see ibid. 746–9, *NLS* §207.4c. Unlike Tacitus, P. is sparing and conservative with it: cf. only 7.31.4 *emendis diuidendisque agris adiutor assumptus* (again an official title and with a verb) and 1.8.7 *agendae rei necessaria* (governed by an adj., as normal in prose from Livy: K–S I 746–7, §133a). Platner 1888 catalogues P.'s gerund(ive)s, excluding the gerundive of obligation. **crearetur** 'be appointed' (*OLD* 5a). **cum** 'although'. **illi . . . superessent** 'he still had' (*OLD supersum* 7). **senes consularesque** '[who were] older men and consulars'. To be *consularis* (former consul) was a status for life. P., in his thirties, was a more junior *praetorius* (former praetor). **huius aetatis** 'at my age', i.e. 'despite my youth', gen. of description (*NLS* §85.1.b); the concessive force is implicit in the antithesis with *senes*. For this 'ploy of legitimizing precociousness' (Henderson 2002b: 218 n.9), presenting P. as mature before his time, cf. 2.13.8 *per aetatem*, 1.19.1, 3.11.5. **per quem excusaretur** 'to present his excuses' (lit. 'through whom he might be excused', *OLD excuso* 3), relative purpose clause. **his**

quidem uerbis 'with these very words' (*quidem* 'these and no other': *OLD* 1c, 5a, Solodow 1978: 103), as at 3.9.13, 8.6.10 (also in Nepos and Quint.).   **'etiam si filium haberem, tibi mandarem'** 'even if I had a son, I would be asking you' (lit. 'I would be entrusting [this] to you', *OLD mando* 5a). The brief direct speech encapsulates and exceeds §8 *affectum parentis*, sententiously capping the paragraph: P. was better even than a son to Verginius (for the pointed close cf. §12 *gloria neminem*, Intro. 24, 27–8). The rare absolute use of *mandare* (cf. Pl. *NH* pr.20 *heredi mandare*) and the heavy clausula (cretic–molossus: for the quantity of *tibī* see 2.6.4n. *magno*) give pregnant brevity to the two-word close. For the conceit of surpassing a parental relationship, see 2.18.4n. *nisi*, 8.11.1 *etiam materna indulgentia molliorem* (Calpurnia's aunt), and the prayer at *Pan.* 94.5 that Jupiter grant Trajan a (natural) heir 'whom he has . . . made to resemble an adoptive son' (*similemque fecerit adoptato*). A climactic single line of direct speech is used again at 3.9.25, 6.16.11, 9.13.23, and on a smaller scale 2.14.11, 7.6.12; cf. also 2.6.4. These words were not Verginius' last, but within P.'s text they acquire the force of an *ultima uox*; cf. 6.16.11, a sole, heroising quotation of the elder Pliny.

10 Quibus ex causis: a summing-up formula 7× in P. (first in Pl. *NH*), drawing together §§7–9.   **tamquam immaturam mortem eius . . . defleam** 'lament his death as premature', with lugubrious alliteration in *tamquam . . . mortem* (seven heavy syllables). *immatura mors* is common, *mortem deflere* moderately so (e.g. Cic. *De or.* 3.9 [*mors Crassi*] *defleta*). Verginius' death was anything but premature (§7 *ille quidem plenus annis abît*), hence *tamquam* 'as (if)' (§3n.), knowingly irrational; cf. also 5.5.4 *mihi uero semper acerba et immatura mors eorum qui immortale aliquid parant*, relativising (for a different reason) 'premature'.   **in sinu tuo** 'in your bosom'; cf. 8.16.5 *si in amici sinu defleas* (ending a letter on deaths), Sen. *Contr.* 7.6.16 *quantum in sinu filiae fleuit!* The first sign of epistolarity is an extravagant version of the conceit that a letter substitutes for face-to-face conversation (2.5.13n. *tecum*).   **si tamen fas est aut flere:** for *si tamen* 'if, that is' ('limiting' *tamen*) see *OLD si* 8b, *tamen* 5b, K–S II 429 §12b. Here it implies 'but it is not', correcting the previous statement in *reprehensio* (Sandys on Cic. *Or.* 135, Lausberg §§784–6): cf. *Pan.* 20.4 *quam dissimilis . . . transitus! si tamen transitus ille, non populatio fuit*; other *reprehensio* at e.g. 2.4.4, 2.19.7, 1.12.1, 3.9.28. *si fas est* is common (*TLL* VI 288.52–63, 292.38–58) but P.'s alliteration evokes Naevius' supposed self-epitaph *immortales mortales si foret fas flere*, | *flerent diuae Camenae Naeuium poetam . . .* (Gell. *NA* 1.24, Courtney 1993: 47–50); for the injunction cf. also Tac. *Ag.* 46.1 [*uirtutes*] *quas neque lugeri neque plangi fas est*. Here the letter turns to *consolatio*, a stock closing element of the funeral speech, so completing its transformation into a virtual *laudatio funebris* of its own. Synthesis of letter with its subject is a recurrent technique: e.g. 2.11, 2.12, 3.9, 8.14, 9.13. In this case, however, P. is reperforming not his own speech but that of Tacitus, whose *Agricola* seems to be in mind (Syme 1958: 121, Marchesi 2008: 189–99). The engagement is subtle (multiple points of similarity, all handled differently, and combined with extensive allusion to Cicero: §11n. *uiuit*) but seems the more likely given the coincidence of topic (consolatory celebration of a father-figure), Tacitus' role in the funeral (§6) and the Agricolan tones of the third Verginius letter (9.19.3 ~ *Ag.* 1, esp. *magnum aliquid memorandumque fecerunt* ~ *magna aliqua et nobilis uirtus*; 9.19.4 *in praedicando uerecundia . . . gloria* ~ *Ag.* 8.3 *uerecundia in praedicando . . . gloriam*). That letter may also respond to Tac. *H.* (Whitton 2012: 351–2); the other Verginius letter, 6.10, follows 6.9 to Tacitus. P. engages extensively with *Ag.* in 8.14 (Whitton 2010; see ibid. 123 nn.29–30 on 6.16.1 and *Pan.*). **omnino** 'at all' (*OLD* 3b). **qua** '(that) by which', attracted to the gender of *mortem*. Its antecedent is an implied *id*, object of *uocare* (such antecedents are routinely suppressed, e.g. 2.4.4 [*id*] *quod*, 2.5.2 [*ea*] *quae*, 2.11.8 [*ei*] *qui*, 2.20.8 [*ei*] *cui*; Kraut 1872: 11–12, K–S II 281–2; also 2.7.2n. *quod* and Shackleton Bailey 1965–70: VII 66 s.v. 'ellipse' for instances in Cic. *Att.*). **tanti uiri mortalitas magis finita quam uita est** 'the mortality rather than the life of so great a man has been brought to an end', setting up a mild paradox which the following sentence will resolve: *uita* here means 'life' as fame (*OLD* 6a): cf. Cic. *Phil.* 9.10 *uita enim mortuorum in memoria est posita uiuorum*; Sen. *Ep.* 93.5 *quid quaeris quamdiu uixerit? uiuit: ad posteros usque transiliut et se in memoriam dedit.* P.'s words receive a rare Carolingian reworking in a letter by Einhard (AD 836) on his wife's death, *cuius mortalitatem magis quam uitam finitam esse uidebam* (*MGH Epist.* VI 10.6–7).

11 uiuit enim uiuetque semper: *uiuit* picks up *uitam* in 'noun–verb modification': cf. 7.19.3–4 *dolore . . . doleo enim*, Wills 1996: 327–8. The verbal polyptoton of pres. + fut. is common (Wills 1996: 302; Martin–Woodman on Tac. *An.* 3.12.5), but P. seems to recall Cic. *Lael.* 102 *mihi quidem Scipio, quamquam est subito ereptus, uiuit tamen semperque uiuet: uirtutem enim amaui illius uiri, quae exstincta non est* etc. Laelius' self-consolation at the loss of a dear friend, concluding a dialogue on friendship and following comments on *amicitia* across generations (*Lael.* 101–2), sets apt precedent for P.'s mini-tract on his intimacy with old Verginius. Cicero's phrase had been reworked before: Vell. 2.66.5 (of Cicero) *uiuit uiuetque per omnem saeculorum memoriam*, Sen. *Marc.* 6.1.3 *cuius uiget uigebitque memoria*, Tac. *Ag.* 46.4 *quidquid ex Agricola amauimus . . . manet mansurumque est in animis hominum*, though this last looks also, or rather, to Cic. *Leg.* 1.1 *manet uero, Attice noster, et semper manebit* on the eternal power of literature (with *agricolae* a few words later). P.'s formulation is closer to Cicero than to Tacitus, though that could itself be taken as an indirect response to the strong Ciceronianism of *Ag.* 46 (Marchesi 2008: 192 nn.82–3). Cf. also Cic. *Lael.* 23 *uerum enim amicum qui intuetur tamquam exemplar aliquod intuetur sui; quocirca et absentes adsunt et . . . mortui uiuunt.* **atque etiam:** §1n. *insigne*; here *etiam* is felt closely with *latius* (*OLD etiam* 4b). **in memoria hominum et sermone:** cf. Cic. *Rab. Post.* 2 *sermone hominum ac memoria patrum uirtutes celebrantur*, with the same *coniunctio* (the placing of *hominum* between the ablatives, a form of hyperbaton: cf. *Rhet. Her.* 4.38 with Calboli, H–S 693). Again P.'s Ciceronianism matches that of Tac. *Ag.* 46.4 (*in animis hominum*, 8× in Cicero). **uersabitur** 'will dwell' (lit. 'will be constantly'), *OLD* 11b (*in animo, ante oculos*, etc.) and 11c (*in ore*, etc.).

The diction is Ciceronian: cf. (again) Cic. *Lael.* 103 *nec mihi soli uersatur ante oculos* [cf. Pliny's *ab oculis*] . . . *sed etiam posteris erit clara et insignis*; the combination *sermone uersari* is exclusive to Cicero (*De or.* 1.12, *Phil.* 2.57), as is *memoria uersari*, if read at *Leg.* 1.4. Elsewhere P. prefers *obuersari oculis* (4.17.4, 8.23.6, in similar contexts). Like the close of *Ag.* (46.4 *superstes erit*), but less obtrusively, the future tense is performative: P.'s letter itself is part of the process of memorialising Verginius (§12n. *gloria*).   **postquam ab oculis recessit** 'now that he has withdrawn from sight' (*OLD oculus* 4, *recedo* 1c); for *postquam* 'now that' (*OLD postquam* 3, G–L §564) cf. 2.15.1, *Pan.* 13.5, 32.1.

12 uolui tibi multa alia scribere, sed totus animus . . . defixus est: cf. 8.23.8, ending laments for Junius Avitus, *in tantis tormentis eram cum scriberem haec <ut haec> scriberem sola: neque enim nunc aliud aut cogitare aut loqui possum*. The MSS are divided between *uolui* (α) and *uolo* (βγ), making *uolo* (adopted by Mynors) theoretically more likely (Intro. 38), but *uolui* is also at 3.18.11, 8.16.5 and 8.23.8, all easily taken as 'I intended [when I started writing]' (not the 'epistolary' perfect: 2.5.1n. *exhibui*). *uolo* finds defence in Fronto *M. Caes.* 2.11.2 (p. 31.1 vdH²) *uolo ad te plura scribere, sed nihil suppetit*, but cf. Fronto *Ant. Pium* 4.2 (p. 164.16 vdH²) *te . . . scire uolui.*   **multa alia:** brevity and incompleteness are epistolary stock-in-trade (though P.'s letters are usually highly complete in themselves), and in ignoring *multa alia* P. abides by his usual one-letter-one-theme rule (S–W 43–4, Lefèvre 2009: 24–5), but the point here is the overwhelming focus on Verginius. Marchesi 2008: 194 moots allusion to V. *Georg.* 4.501–2 and *Aen.* 2.790–1 *multa uolentem | dicere*, dismissed by Bradley 2010: 418–19.   **in hac una contemplatione** 'in sole contemplation of this' (as e.g. *hic metus* 'fear of this'): the activity is mental (cf. *totus animus*; *OLD contemplatio* 2), but the noun's primary meaning ('viewing') generates, together with the following *uideo* and §11 *ab oculis*, ring-composition with §1 *oculis spectaculum*. The noun (first in Cicero) also features in Tac. *Ag.* 46.1 *ad contemplationem uirtutum tuarum.*   **defixus est** 'remains fixed', *OLD* 3a + *in* + abl. (first in Ov. *Her.* 21.113: *TLL* v.1 341.6–20). The tense is normal ('has become and still is fixed').   **Verginium . . . Verginium . . . Verginium:** the name, not voiced since §1, returns for emotive anaphora in an extended tricolon (7~7~26 syllables; see Intro. 23). The single name at second mention follows P.'s rule (§1n. *Vergini*), and is suitably intimate. Like V. *Georg.* 4.525–7 (*Eurydicen* ×3) and Stat. *Theb.* 12.805–7 (*Arcada* ×3), the effect, despite the case, is of invocation. Threefold repetition of the deceased's name was ritual (Hom. *Od.* 9.65, Aristophanes *Frogs* 184, 1175–6, Theocritus 23.44, V. *Aen.* 6.506 *manes ter uoce uocaui* with Austin; Weinreich 1928: 201); cf. also the funeral pronouncement *uale uale uale* (Servius on V. *Aen.* 1.219), which Verginius' *u* alliteration (anticipated in *uiuit . . . uiuet . . . uersabitur . . . uolui*) conveniently shadows.   **cogito . . . uideo . . . audio alloquor teneo:** *OLD cogito* 8a 'call to mind, think about' + acc. (esp. Cic. *Scaur.* 49 *te . . . uideo, . . . non cogito solum*), *teneo* 2b 'embrace'. Graded tricolon of trisyllabic verbs, the third member (*audio alloquor teneo*) itself a graded tricolon, as the sensations and actions intensify; for the emotive trio cf. 2.17.29 *incolere inhabitare diligere*, though P. has such asyndeton frequently (Intro. 23–4). A characteristically minute development of a cliché (e.g. Petr. 42.4 *uideor mihi cum illo loqui*), inverting 1.16.9 *uidere alloqui audire complecti... contingit* (living people). With *teneo* cf. Tac. *Ag.* 46.3 *formamque ac figuram animi... complectantur.* **iam uanis imaginibus** 'likenesses now empty', both insubstantial (*OLD uanus* 1b; cf. Hor. *C.* 1.24.15 *uanae... imagini* (Quintilius' ghost) with Nisbet–Hubbard) and futile (*OLD uanus* 2a; cf. Stat. *Silu.* 2.7.128 *solacia uana*, the bust of Lucan over his widow's bed, with Newlands). More empty *imagines* at Tac. *Ag.* 46.3 and *Pan.* 55.10–11 (reworking *Ag.*: Bruère 1954: 163–4), but those are statues, these fantasies. **recentibus tamen** 'yet fresh': for *recens* 'fresh in the mind', i.e. 'vivid, clearly conceived', see *OLD* 5 (Quint. 10.7.14 *recentes rerum imagines* seems to mean both 'new' and 'vivid'). 'Recent' would be otiose (Gierig). For freshness after death cf. Hor. *C.* 3.30.6–8 *non omnis moriar... crescam laude recens* with Nisbet–Rudd. **fortasse** 'it may be that'. **ciues aliquos... pares...,** **gloria neminem:** the steeply falling bicolon (20~6 syllables), its pregnant ending similar to §1 *perinde felicis*, §9 *tibi mandarem*, offers a memorable parting *sententia* (Intro. 26–8): others may reach *summum fastigium priuati hominis* (§2), but none with the added *gloria* of refusing the principate. **uirtutibus** 'in excellence' (§3n. *Caesares quibus*), abl. of respect (*NLS* §55). **pares:** cf. Hor. *C.* 1.24.6–8 *cui Pudor... quando ullum inueniet parem?* **et habemus et habebimus:** the polyptoton recalls §11 *uiuit enim uiuetque*, ring-composing the *consolatio* and throwing weight onto *gloria neminem*, standing outside the frame thus established. Verbal polyptoton (§11n. *uiuit*) is common in P. (e.g. 2.11.14n. *dicturo*, 2.13.11n. *rogat*; Niemirska-Pliszczyńska 1955: 107–11; cf. Summers 1910: lxxxvi on Seneca), yet it is striking that another pair with *habere* ends the book at 2.20.13–14 *habiturum. et habebit.* **gloriā neminem** sc. *parem aut habemus aut habebimus*, a pithy close (above on *ciues*). The final judgment puts full weight on the importance of renown (cf. Cic. *Planc.* 60 *etenim honorum gradus summis hominibus et infimis sunt pares, gloriae dispares*) – such as this letter can supply (so too 6.10.6 concludes with Verginius' *claritas*, 9.19.8 with his path to *gloria*): cf. Tac. *Ag.* 46.4 (also in antithesis) *multos... obliuio obruit, Agricola... superstes erit.*

VALE: this detached adjunct, never integrated into syntax or rhythm, ends every letter in *Epistles* 1–9 (but none in book 10), as it does those of Seneca; the stylised routine contributes to the 'literary' feel of the collection. Real *subscriptiones* (sign-offs, often handwritten) were usually variants on the theme *cura ut ualeas, uale mi carissime*, etc., as evidenced by Cicero's letters and the Vindolanda tablets (Bowman–Thomas 1983, id. 1994); cf. Cugusi 1983: 28–9 and 56–64.

2

I am angry – perhaps unjustly, but love is not just – because you have not written. Only long and numerous letters will assuage me. I am at my villa, mixing writing and idleness.

An 'epistolary visiting card' distinguished by 'vacuity' and 'the light bantering tone of *iocatio*, hardly rising to the level of wit' (S-W 111, 43) – or a microcosm of P.'s epistolary art? The cliché lament at 'no news', the humour and several turns of phrase contribute to the feel of this 'exquisitely Ciceronian' note (Cugusi 1983: 224), but the crafting goes beyond even Cicero's epistolary elegance. Allusions also evoke a poetic world, matched by P.'s affected, elegiac petulance (Marchesi 2008: 88–96), and phrasing and structure are characteristically manicured.

P.'s sole 'news' is confined to a parting comment (ironically brief, given his demand for abundant long letters from Paulinus) that he is enjoying a mixture of *studia* (literary work) and *desidia* (laziness), 'both of which are born of *otium* [leisure]'. This fleeting glimpse of villa life is notable not just for the self-ironising validation of idleness, but also as a gloss on this letter itself, with its paradoxical combination of languor and intense art. That paradox is staked out clearly in 7.13, to Ferox: *eadem epistula et non studere te et studere significat. aenigmata loquor? ita plane, donec distinctius quod sentio enuntiem. negat enim te studere, sed est tam polita quam nisi a studente non potest scribi; aut es tu super omnes beatus, si talia per desidiam et otium perficis.* 'The same letter shows that you are not working and that you are working. Am I speaking in riddles? Evidently so, until I explain more clearly what I mean. It says that you are not working, but it is as polished a letter as can only be written by someone working; otherwise you are luckiest of all, if you can produce material like that in idle leisure.' Ferox, it should be clear, is a mirror for P., his letter a mirror for P.'s letters. Epistle 2.2, short (because P. is idle) but exquisite (because P. is a man of *studia*), encapsulates and exhibits a fundamental aesthetic of the *Epistles* as a whole, a version of the rhetorical *desiderandum* that art conceal its own art (cf. Quint. 4.2.127 *desinat ars esse si apparet*, Ov. *Met.* 10.252 *ars adeo latet arte sua*, Merwald 1964: 155–6, Calboli on *Rhet. Her.* 4.10).

This short and jocular piece makes an obvious contrast with the gravity and high emotion of 2.1, and shines an early ray of leisured light into a book where *negotium* will weigh heavily (G–M 218). The brevity and 'no news' theme match (and are restricted to) 1.11 and 3.17, in a typical distribution across books 1–3 (Intro. 18–19), while, at greater remove, intratextuality (§2n. *plurimas*) and addressee (below) open a dialogue with 9.2–3. The (lack of) balance between this and 2.17 is also reversed in book 5 (§2n. *partim*). The shortest letters of book 2 are distributed 2.2 ~ 2.8 ~ 2.15; compare (and contrast) the previous book, 1.1 ~ 1.11 ~ 1.21.

PAVLINO: probably C. Valerius Paulinus (*PIR* V 107, Syme 1953: 158, S-W 146) from Gallia Narbonensis, *cos. suff.* 107, who receives 4.16 (celebration of forensic *studia*), 5.19 (P. sends his reader to Paulinus' villa at Forum Iulii), 9.3 (a call to eternity to a fellow man of letters) and 9.37 (P. cannot attend his installation as consul). 9.3 may allude to Seneca *De breuitate uitae*, also addressed to a Paulinus (Marchesi 2008: 233–6); the apt name (*breu-* ~ *Paul-*) perhaps earns him this brief note too. In 4.9.20–1 he demonstrates *iustitia* and *constantia* in the Bassus trial; in 10.104–5 he is dead, having made P. an heir.

1 Irascor . . . irascor: P. frequently opens with a main verb, more often second-person (2.8.1 *studes*, 2.11.1 *solet*, 2.14.1 *uerum opinaris*, etc.; Niemirska-Pliszczyńska 1955: 77–8), and/or with some varied repetition (2.3.1 *magna . . . maior*, 2.17.1 *Laurentinum . . . Laurens*, 2.20.1 *fabulam, fabulas immo*, 1.6.1 *ridebis . . . rideas* etc.); here *irascor* rings the sentence precisely in the figure called κύκλος or *redditio* (Lausberg §625), e.g. Cic. *Pis.* 2 *Piso est a populo Romano factus, non iste Piso*, V. *Aen.* 3.435 *unum illud tibi, nate dea, proque omnibus unum*. The petulant opening, underlined by the unusual rhythm (four heavy syllables to open: 2.17.1n. *miraris*), shares something with Sen. *Ep.* 60.1 *queror litigo irascor*, but P.'s 'neoteric irony' (Castagna 2003: 158) is closer in tone to Catullus 38.6 *irascor tibi: sic meos amores?* (Marchesi 2008: 91–2) and Stat. *Silu.* 4.9.53 *irascor tibi, Grype* (ending a Catullan 'letter' on poetic exchange). The play-anger contrasts with other brief notes, 1.11 and (more strongly) 3.17, where anxiety rules. Like all epistolary humour, it serves to construct intimacy (cf. 1.6 with G–M 162), reproducing 'conversation' on the page (2.15.13n. *tecum*). **nec liquet mihi an debeam** 'and I am not sure whether I should (be)', *OLD liqueo* 3b, *an* 6a (now a common alternative to *num*: K–S II 523–4). The first of a string of equivocations: cf. 1.15.3 *dure fecisti: inuidisti, nescio an tibi, certe mihi, sed tamen et tibi*. **scis quam sit amor . . . :** cf. Cic. *Att.* 2.24.1 *non ignoro quam sit amor omnis sollicitus atque anxius, Fam.* 7.15.1 *'quam sint morosi qui amant'* (quoting a poet). P. characteristically takes a commonplace (*scis . . .*) but subjects it to (mannered) variation (Gallent-Kočevar 1933: 58–61). **iniquus interdum, impotens saepe, μικραίτιος semper** 'sometimes cruel, often headstrong, always petulant', AB~AB~AB tricolon (6~5~6 syllables, each with cretic–spondee), with graded adverbs. For *iniquus* see *OLD* 4a ('of actions, laws, etc.') but also 5a ('of persons'), flirting with personification of *Amor*: cf. Prop. 1.19.22 *iniquus Amor*, Serv. *ad Aen.* 4.520 *Cupidini . . . cui curae est iniquus amor*. Although P. more often uses *amor* of non-sexual love between friends (*OLD* 3a), e.g. 2.6.6 *amori in te meo*, than of sexual love (e.g. 6.31.4, 7.5.1) – to use a crude dichotomy (Gunderson 1997: 225–6) – the erotic overtone here is clear, as he writes with the petulance of a jilted lover (cf. Cat. 50 with Gunderson 1997). On *amicitia*, a *fil rouge* of the *Epistles*, see Castagna 2003. **impotens:** *OLD* 3a; with *amor* at Cat. 35.12 *illum deperit impotente amore*. **μικραίτιος:** from μικρ- 'small, slight' + αἰτία 'reason', hence 'touchy, irascible' (Lucian *Fugitiui* 19 pairs it with ὀξύχολος 'short-tempered'), a rare synonym for φιλαίτιος (used by Cic. in *Att.* 13.20.2, *Fam.* 3.7.6). The Greek compound is a surprise, trumping an expected tricolon in *in-*. Like Cicero (in his epistles), P. both quotes Greek and includes occasional words, often as here contemporary (not classical Attic) forms. Single words in book 2 at 2.3.3, 4, 8, 2.11.17, 23, 2.12.1, 2.14.5; quotations at 2.3.10, 2.20.12; numerous transliterated Grecisms ornament the villa letter (2.17.8n. *cubiculum*). The frequency is comparable with Cicero *Ad familiares* (the letters to Atticus have Greek around six times more often: Hutchinson 1998: 14). There is no call to doubt P.'s fluency in Greek (*pace* Weische 1989: 377; Guillemin 1929: 77–8 is unduly cautious): quite apart from the cultural norm of code-switching (Adams 2003a), see next n., 2.3 (Isaeus), 6.6.3 (studies with Nicetes Sacerdos), 7.4.2 (wrote Greek tragedies

aged 14), 7.9.2 (the value of Greek/Latin translation). On Greek in the *Epistles* see
p. 24, Deane 1918, Venini 1952, Niemirska-Pliszczyńska 1955: 48–58; for Cicero
see Baldwin 1992, Dankel 2000, Swain 2002, Adams 2003a: 308–47; for Seneca,
Bowersock 2003. In *Pan.* (like Cicero in speeches), P. avoids it. **haec tamen
causa magna est** 'but *this* reason is a large one', inverting μικραίτιος (*causa* =
αἰτία, *magn-* ≠ μικρ-). Other bilingual wordplay at 2.3.8n. ἀφιλόκαλον, 2.11.23n.
superest and 1.5.15 δυσκαθαίρετον ~ 1.6.1 *cepi* (Whitton 2012: 357). **nescio an**
'perhaps not' (*OLD nescio* 4b; K–S II 522 n.4), as always in P., except *Pan.* 45.4
'perhaps' (*OLD nescio* 4a). The latter is the earlier and Ciceronian use; by P.'s time
both were available. **iusta** 'fair' (*OLD* 5b), inverting *iniquus*. For the combination with *magna causa*, cf. Cic. *Fam.* 13.29.2 *magna iustaque causa*, *Phil.* 5.40, Ov. *Her.*
17.156; Sen. *Ira* 2.10.2 *maior est excusatio et iustior*. **tamquam** 'as if' + subj.: *OLD*
4a, 5a; G–L §602 (= *tamquam si*). **non minus iusta quam magna:** chiastic
with *magna...iusta*. **grauiter irascor** 'I am deeply angry' (*OLD grauiter* 10)
returns us, after all the vacillations, to the opening, making a trio of *irascor*, now
expanded with the mock-ponderous adverb. *grauiter irasci* is just what good friends
do not do (Cic. *Off.* 1.88). **quod a te tam diu litterae nullae** sc. e.g. *sunt/sint
redditae* 'that in all this time no letters [have come] from you'; for *irasci quod* (+
indic. or subj.) cf. 3.9.29 *iratus quod euocatus esset inuitus* and e.g. Cic. *Fam.* 7.13.1
(next n.), Sen. *Contr.* 9.3.11 *irascitur mihi quod [duos] educaui*. Word-order and ellipsis
point the pique, leading P. at last to the cause of his 'anger'. The complaint is
an epistolary topos (Cugusi 1983: 76, id. 1989: 408 n.117): cf. 1.11.1 *olim mihi nullas
epistulas mittis*, Cic. *Att.* 1.15.2 *nullae mihi abs te sunt redditae litterae*, 12.38.1 *non dubito
quin occupatissimus fueris qui ad me nihil litterarum*, *Q. fr.* 2.3.7 (and often). Hor. *Ep.*
2.2.22 *ad te quod epistula nulla rediret* is a numerologically neat comparandum here in
2.2 (Marchesi 2008: 89); for the diction cf. also Cic. *Fam.* 7.13.1 *ut tibi irascerer quod
parum mihi constans... uiderere ob eamque causam me arbitrare litteras ad te iam diu non
misisse*. P. routinely omits *esse* and other verbs (Lagergren 1872: 42–4, Merrill 461,
Gamberini 1983: 467–70), including in subordinate clauses (a rarer trait: Leo 1878
I 187; H–S 419–23, esp. §223b; but see e.g. Charney 1943 on Seneca); cf. 2.17.16n.
cum. **litterae:** the plural can mean either 'letter' (e.g. 1.8.1) or 'letters' (1.10.9);
cf. *OLD* 7a, *TLL* VII.2 1522.17–68 and 1525.84–1526.8. The latter is suggested by
§2 *plurimas* and 1.11.1 *nullas epistulas* (previous n.). *epistula* was now the usual word
(*c.* 100× in P.), with *litterae* virtually obsolete except in historians (Adams 1972a:
357, id. 2003c: 570). P. has it about 20×, lightly recalling Cicero, in whose letters
litterae outnumbers *epistula* by around 3:1. Any difference in nuance between them
(Gavoille 2000, on Cicero) seems to have been lost.

2 exorare me potes uno modo, si... miseris: cf. Cic. *Att.* 12.6.2 *quomodo
hoc ergo lues? uno scilicet, si mihi librum miseris* (Guillemin 1929: 115); for *exorare* of
assuaging anger, cf. 9.21.3 *irasci...exoratus*. A logical 'mixed' conditional, with
pres. apodosis (*potes*, easily understood as embracing the future too; cf. *NLS*
§194a) and fut. protasis (*miseris* is the usual fut. pf.; for future *nunc* see *OLD*

5a). **plurimas et longissimas** *sc. litteras*, an ironically unreasonable demand given the brevity of this short and so far sole epistle to Paulinus (cf. 9.32 *fit ut scribere longiores epistulas nolim, uelim legere*, in the last such 'courtesy note'). The same superlatives return, with reversal of roles, in 9.2.1 *non solum plurimas epistulas meas uerum etiam longissimas flagitas* (Marchesi 2008: 230–3), so spanning an arch 2.2~9.2; the conclusion of that letter (9.2.5 *est enim summi amoris negare ueniam breuibus epistulis amicorum*) makes a good gloss on this one. As a reader P. enjoys length in letters (9.20.1) as in oratory (1.20.4); his own longer ones often end with jocular requests for reciprocity (2.11.25n. *aeque longam*) and/or mock-apologetic reference to the 'rule' that letters should be brief (2.5.13n. *orationi*; 'Demetrius' *On style* 228; Trapp 2003, index s.v. 'brevity') e.g. 3.9.27 *dices '. . . quid enim mihi cum tam longa epistula?'* and 5.6.41–4 (arguing, at the end of his longest letter, that length is relative). **haec mihi sola excusatio uera, ceterae falsae uidebuntur** 'this excuse alone will seem true to me, others false': parallel antithesis with *mihi* and *uidebuntur* distributed in double *apo koinou*, and with syllepsis (*sc. uidebitur* in the first colon: 2.1.2n. *legit*); for the position of *mihi* see 2.17.24n. *in.* P.'s last letter to Paulinus (9.37) is one long excuse for his absence from Rome. **excusatio uera:** cretic–spondee; unlike in *ratio* (2.4.4n.) and despite e.g. Juv. 1.79 *indignatio* (where metre dictates a short *o*), the final *o* seems to be felt long, and so scanned heavy, in nouns ending −‿−, e.g. 2.10.7 *admiratio te* (ditrochee), 2.19.4 *intentio relanguescit* (cretic–spondee), 9.14.1 *silentio protulit* (double cretic). For the term 'cretic-*spondee*', despite *ueră*, see Intro. p. 29 n.163. **non sum auditurus** 'I am not prepared to hear': the periphrastic future has a nuance of intent (Palmer 1956: 326–7; Kooreman 1996). **occupatior** 'too busy' or 'rather busy' (2.1.4n. *durior*). A reason for short, infrequent or non-existent letters in 3.17.1 *occupatus*, Cic. *Att.* 10.6.1 *occupatior*, 12.38.1 (in §1n. *quod*), *Fam.* 8.4.3 (Caelius) *occupatiorem*; Sen. *Ep.* 106.1 calls it a poor one. P. does not let business stop *him* writing (e.g. 2.8). **illud enim nec di sinant, ut 'infirmior'** *sc.* e.g. *audiam, dixeris*, 'because as for "under the weather", the gods forbid!', completing a tricolon; *illud enim* implies 'I shan't even mention the old line . . . ' (cf. *OLD ille* 14a), branding this last excuse as especially feeble. **nec di sinant:** lit. 'let the gods not allow'; cf. Curt. 10.6.20 *'nec di sierint'*, Petr. 103.1 *nec istud dii hominesque patiantur*, 112.7 *'nec istud'* inquit *'dii sinant, ut . . . '*, Tac. *An.* 1.43.2 *'neque enim di sinant ut . . . sit'*, a fossilised use of archaic *nec* 'not' (*OLD neque* 1, Löfstedt 1956: 1 338–40). The gods' role in P.'s world is largely formulaic (Bütler 1970: 10–15, Liebeschuetz 1979: 182–92, Ameling 2010: 272–80, Méthy 2010). **ut** expands *illud* (*OLD ut* 39a), as Sen. *Contr.* 1.1.17 *ne* [*nec* Löfstedt] *di istud nefas patiantur, ut diu rogauerit*, Petr. 112.7 (previous n.). The construction with *sinere*, usually rare (Briscoe on Livy 34.24.1), is routine with this phrase. **'infirmior'** 'too unwell' or 'rather unwell' (as *occupatior*). *infirmus* (*OLD* 2b) is P.'s standard term for 'ill' (cf. 2.1.4n. *usus*); it makes another poor excuse at 9.12.33 *fuit . . . , ut excusabatur, infirmus*. For *occupatior . . . infirmior* as reasons not to write letters, cf. Suet. *Life of Horace* (*De poet.* 24.19–22 Rostagni) (a letter from Augustus to Maecenas) *ante ipse sufficiebam scribendis epistolis amicorum, nunc* *occupatissimus et infirmus Horatium nostrum a te cupio abducere.* **ipse** abruptly turns to P., for the briefest of news (neither *plurimum* nor *longissimum*). **ad uillam** 'on my estate' (*OLD ad* 13a), a variant for *in uilla* since Cic. *Rosc. Am.* 44, only here in P. (*TLL* I 522.14–20; K–S I 520, Kraut 1872: 19). As usual for his class, P. had multiple country estates (S-W on 5.6.45): the *Laurentinum* 'Laurentine' and *Tusci* 'Etruscan' villas described in 2.17 and 5.6, and *plures* around his native Comum (9.7.2). The dominance in book 2 of the Laurentine villa, and the absence of the Etruscan, invites a view of him here, as in 1.9 and 1.22.11, at Laurentum (S-W reaches the same view, for biographical reasons). This is his last snatch of villa life before 2.17; at 2.8 he will be pining for it. **partim studîs, partim desidia fruor** 'I am enjoying a mixture of literature and laziness' (*OLD partim* 1b, *fruor* 2a + abl.): cf. 5.18.2 *ego in Tuscis et uenor et studeo*, a short letter near the end of the book dominated by the *Tusci* villa (thus loosely mirroring the place of 2.2 in book 2). The combination recalls Hor. *Sat.* 2.6.61 (dreaming of *otium*) *nunc ueterum libris, nunc somno et inertibus horis*; cf. also perhaps Stat. *Silu.* 2.pr.19–21 *Vrsum ... sine iactura desidiae doctissimum* (generally taken as 'not wasting his *otium*', but more pointed as 'without impinging on his *desidia*', i.e. has time for both idleness and learning). **studîs:** *OLD* 7a 'intellectual activity, esp. of a literary kind', abl. with *fruor*. For P. *studia* embrace education (3.3.3), philosophical study (5.16.8 *altioribus studiis*) and all the 'literary arts', *viz.* rhetoric (6.6.3) and oratory (1.2.6 and *passim*), but also the whole gamut of composition: cf. 3.5.5 *omne studiorum genus*, 9.29.1 *uariis ... studiorum generibus*; 8.12.1 *colit studia* (Capito, who writes *exitus* and urged history on P. in 5.8). Of course that includes not least, in these *Epistles*, epistolary writing: cf. 7.13 (cited in intro.), Intro. 10–11. The form *studîs* (= *studiis*) is strongly suggested by clausulae here, 2.18.1 *ex studîs habeam*, 1.3.3 *secessu studîs asseris*, 3.2.3 *in studîs utor* and often (as e.g. Sen. *NQ* 4a.pr.14 *me studîs tradidi*, Quint. 10.3.31 *in studîs paruum (e)st*, Tac. *D.* 10.4 *artium studîs credo*); similarly with other nouns in *-ium / -ius* at e.g. 4.17.6 *officîs nostris*, Pan. 17.1 *extorto socîs auro*, Sen. *Ep.* 91.21 *supplicîs taedio*, Tac. *D.* 35.2 *ingenîs afferant*; it is guaranteed by metre at e.g. Sen. *Phoen.* 625 *exilîs*, Mart. 1.117.17 *denarîs* and is common epigraphically (N–W I 189–90, K–H 464–5). Unless P. could write *-iis* but hear *-is* (cf. 2.1.5n. *male*), editors have little reason, then, to follow the uniform *-iis* of MSS, which may merely reflect (admittedly thorough) 'correction' in a later, less rhythmically sensitive age. Conversely, *studiis* finds support at 3.18.5 *habitum putem an stud(i)is* and 9.23.2 *et quidem ex stud(i)is* (the two times P. has it last rather than penultimate in a clausula), where it makes a familiar cretic + resolved spondee (even if a cretic–iamb with *studîs* would be unexceptional: 2.11.2n. *petit*). Perhaps, given his apparent preference for *-it* and *-i* over *-iit* and *-ii* (2.1.5n. *male*, 2.11.23n. *Mari*), P. used *-is* throughout; but he may have varied his forms to suit the rhythm, as one did with e.g. verbs in *-a(ui)sse* (Quint. 9.4.59; 2.1.8n. *renuntiasset*). In this edition the short form is adopted here and in 2.18.1, where rhythm demands it (as by some editors of Seneca: Reynolds 1965: I xvi, Hine 1981: 357–8; Winterbottom 1970: 69 resists the temptation), and, given the balance of probabilities, in 2.17.24. **desidia** 'laziness', thematised by

P., exceptionally, as a personal trait: 1.2.3 *me longae desidiae indormientem*, 1.2.6 *audis desidiae uotum*, 1.6.1 *inertia mea*, 1.8.2 *ab homine desidioso*, 9.38.2 *delicatus* and esp. 3.5.19 (comparing himself with his workaholic uncle Pliny the Elder) *sum desidiosissimus*. For other authors the word is routinely pejorative, marking the 'wrong' sort of leisure (e.g. Cic. *Brut.* 8 *non inertiae... sed oti, Fam.* 15.4.16 *oti ac desidiae* (i.e. *oti desidiosi*), Sen. *Ep.* 68.3, Tac. *D.* 4.1; Statius, however, validates it as *otium* at *Silu.* 2.*pr.*19–21 (above), 4.4.38, 4.6.31). For P. too it is negative: 4.16.3 (to Paulinus) *studeamus* vs *desidiae*, 4.23.4 *quando secessus mei non desidiae nomen sed tranquillitatis accipient?*; branding philistines at 1.13.5 *auditorum uel desidia uel superbia*, 1.20.23 and 6.2.5. Given the demonstration throughout the *Epistles* of P.'s vigour in both *negotium* and *studia*, the self-disparagement here is evidently ironic, humanising through 'gentle humour' (von Albrecht 1989: 162, on 1.6): no stern Seneca here (*pace* Lefèvre 2009: 126, 299–300, who diagnoses 'intellectual paralysis' in this 'aesthete'). The goal is clear in 7.13 (intro.): effort should conceal effort, as art conceals art. **quorum utrumque** 'both of which', a Horatian claim (above on *partim*). **otio:** *OLD* 2a 'freedom from business or work..., esp. as devoted to cultural pursuits'. It is a leitmotif of P.'s epistolary life, routinely, however, in productive tension with its opposite, *negotium* (advocacy, public office, personal duties): see Bütler 1970: 41–57, Ussani 1981, Pani 1995, Hoffer 1999: 111–18, Leach 2003, G–M 169–97, and for the broader picture André 1966, Toner 1995, Fagan 2006. Marchesi 2008: 92–6 reads this letter against *Cat.* 51.13–16 (*otium, Catulle, tibi molestumst...*) as a politicised endorsement of imperial *otium*; with or without Catullus, P.'s leisured contentment here and (at length) in 2.17 is open to a reading as indirect Trajanic encomium (for *otium* as panegyric see e.g. Hor. *C.* 4.15.17–20; V. *Georg.* 4.564 *studiis florentem ignobilis oti*). **nascitur** 'are born of' (*OLD* 10). *ex otio nascitur* may invert an Ovidian cadence: *Am.* 1.9.41 *ipse ego segnis eram discinctaque in otia natus*, *Tr.* 3.2.9 *securaque in otia natus*, also *Met.* 15.711 *in otia natam* (Naples), an aptly elegiac and self-depreciatory echo for this languorous close.

3

Isaeus has proved a superlative declaimer in all respects. What a wonderful life, far from the unsavoury realities of court practice! You must come to hear him: reading can never match delivery in person.

P. sings the praises of Isaeus, a Syrian sophist (declaimer) recently arrived in Rome. The letter is a rare Roman appreciation of the Greek rhetor's art, and of course a crafted style-piece in itself.

As a 'portrait', 2.3 answers 1.10, on the Syrian sophist-philosopher Euphrates. There too is a celebration of Rome's flourishing *liberalia studia* (1.10.1), there too an open-armed response to the Greek arts – a far cry from Crassus' rejection of rhetors in Cic. *De or.* 2.75 *nec mihi opus est Graeco aliquo doctore, qui mihi peruulgata praecepta decantet, cum ipse numquam forum, numquam ullum iudicium aspexerit* (cf. 2.14.2n. *audaces*). In part this reflects changing realities: P.'s generation witnessed the first real influx of eastern senators (Levick 1967: 103–20, Halfmann 1979: 71–3), and the second-century integration of sophists into the Roman elite was perhaps under way (Bowersock 1969, Bowie 1982). Yet P. is no philhellenist *tout court*: like Cicero, he can vary his tone to suit the occasion, as when he dismantles an opposing speaker in 5.20.4: *est plerisque Graecorum ut illi pro copia uolubilitas* (Swain 2004: 7–10). Nevertheless, his admiration for Isaeus' declamations is exceptional both as a Roman celebration of Greek rhetoric, and as a celebration of show declamation in either language. In the bigger picture, Isaeus and his like come second to practical men of Rome, like Titius Aristo, who spends his days in the real work of advocacy instead of amusing himself with long disputations (1.22.6), and – of course – like P. himself. The line between rhetor and senator is still clear (4.11.1–2, 2.5.intro.), and P. is recommending that Nepos come to hear Isaeus, not imitate him (§11n. *quae*). But as one tile in the mosaic of P.'s life, a touch of 'escapism' (Hömke 2002: 80), Isaeus has his place as proper refreshment from the *malitia* of the courts (§5), an urban complement to the rustic *desidia* of 2.2.

The letter is in two unequal parts, beginning with an encomiastic sketch of Isaeus (§§1–7). The style suits the man, with an unusual density of mannered figures as well as rhetorical terms, some Greek but most Latin, as befits this semi-detached cultural appropriation. §7 bridges into the second, protreptic section (§§8–11), urging Nepos to come and hear Isaeus. Here the language is more relaxed, matching the more conversational content, with its anecdotes of Livy and Aeschines, one Roman and one Greek, the second aptly set (by one reckoning) at the dawn of the 'Second Sophistic'.

On declamation at Rome see e.g. Bonner 1949, Kennedy 1972: 312–37, Hömke 2002: 45–82 (79–80 on 2.3); on the 'Second Sophistic', e.g. Kennedy 1972: 553–613, Whitmarsh 2005. P.'s response to Greek culture is considered by Galimberti Biffino 2007; on 'portrait' letters see Leach 1990, Krasser 1993a, Hoffer 1999: 119–40, Henderson 2002a: 7–10 (on 1.10) and esp. Pausch 2004: 51–146 (129–33 on 2.3). See also Cova 1966: 14–15, Picone 1978: 37–40, 86–8, Gamberini 1983: 49–55.

NEPOTI: not a rare name (Mynors, index s.v.), but similarities of content encourage identification with the Nepos who receives 3.16 (a quasi-portrait of Arria) and 4.26 on the editing of speeches (also identifying him as governor of a major province). The index for book 4 gives 'Maecilius', a rare *gentilicium* easily emended, as by most since Mommsen, to Metilius, giving a probable but not certain fit in P. Metilius Sabinus Nepos, *cos. suff.* 103, *cos.* II 128 (*PIR*[2] M 545), who may also receive 6.19. He is probably not the Sabinus of 6.18, 9.2, 9.18, both for historical reasons (Birley 2000a: 64, 71–2, 90) and given the MSS' usual consistency in single names (2.1n. C. PLINIVS). On this prosopographical knot see Jones 1968: 124–5, Syme 1985a: 331 and 344 (self-contradictory), Birley 2000a: 71–2; *contra* S-W.

1 Magna Isaeum fama praecesserat, maior inuentus est: bicolon antithesis with a crispness of which Isaeus might have approved (Phil. *VS* 514), leaving no room for any nod to addressee or letter form. For the idea (reality exceeds expectation) cf. Livy 28.35.5–6 (Scipio)... *maior praesentis ueneratio cepit*, and for its converse *B.Alex.* 48.1 *periculo magno, tum etiam maiore periculi fama*, Tac. *Ag.* 25.3 *magno paratu, maiore fama*. 'Amplifying antithesis' (a positive adjective trumped by its comparative) is very widespread (Oakley on Livy 6.11.1 and e.g. Cic. *Quinct.* 98, Sall. *Jug.* 92.1, Sen. *Tro.* 912–13, Mart. 8.56.1, Tac. *An.* 1.17.1) and not rare in P., e.g. 4.16.3, 10.41.2, *Pan.* 27.1 (all *magnus*... *maior*), 1.5.15 *multi*... *plures*, 2.13.5 *clarus, clarior*, 6.2.4 *bene*... *melius*. Here the parallelism is complicated by an unannounced change of subject between the cola. Quoted by a fourth-century scholiast (*Schol. vet.* ad Juv. 3.73, himself allegedly quoting Suetonius: Cameron 1965: 292–3, id. 1967: 421–2), it also caught Sidonius' eye: Sid. *Ep.* 3.7.2 *persona siquidem est, ut perhibent* [NB], *magna exspectatione, maior aduentu, relatu sublimis, inspectione sublimior*.   **Isaeum:** a sophist from Syria, where P. had served as military tribune (1.10.2 with S-W), though he seems to have met him only in Rome. See Grimal 1955: 381–3, Smith 1997; Phil. *VS* 512–14 gives a potted biography and account of his style, which was 'neither exuberant nor meagre, but simple and natural and suited to the subject matter' (tr. Wright) – a 'moderate' style like that favoured by Quintilian and P. (S-W 86–90; below on *Atticus*). Like them, he deplored 'sing-song' delivery (*VS* 513; 2.14.13n. *canticis*). Juvenal makes Isaeus a byword for Greek volubility (3.73–4 *sermo*... *Isaeo torrentior*). He is otherwise known from two verse inscriptions, *IG* II/III² 3632 and 3709 (with Oliver 1949: 248–52), the first of which reports that he taught Hadrian, perhaps around this time (Hadrian, born AD 76, would be in his early twenties). P. typically uses the single *nomen* for Greeks and other non-citizens (Jones 1991: 158; Vidman 1981: 589 makes him a citizen); this one is shared with one of the ten canonical Greek orators (*OCD* 'Isaeus 1'). **inuentus** 'found [to be]', *OLD* 5d.   **facultas copia ubertas** 'facility, resources, fertility', three synonyms for the trained orator's arsenal. For *facultas*, see Lausberg §1151, *TLL* VI.1 152.3–153.76; for *copia OLD* 1c, 6 and Lausberg §51; for *ubertas OLD* 3a. On asyndetic trios of single words, see Intro. 23–4; they may or may not be synonymous (§2n. *surgit*). Three more come within a few lines in this highly worked passage: *tersae graciles dulces* (extended to a tetracolon), *surgit amicitur incipit, docet delectat afficit*.   **dicit semper ex tempore, sed tamquam diu scripserit** 'he always speaks off the cuff [*OLD tempus* 10b], but as if he has spent a long time writing [it]', chiastic isocolon (8~8 syllables) with paired clausulae. Contrast Phil. *VS* 514 'his declamations were not actually off the cuff [αὐτοσχεδίους], but he meditated from dawn to midday' (though planning and improvising are not mutually exclusive).   **sermo Graecus** *sc. est*, with taut asyndeton.   **immo Atticus** 'or, rather, Attic', *OLD immo* (e). The dialect of classical Athens was widely held to be the purest form of the language. Greek writers of the period, the so-called Second Sophistic, were much preoccupied with recovering and imitating it (Kennedy 1972:

553–65, Anderson 1993: 86–100, Whitmarsh 2005: 41–56), as were P. and friends
(4.3.5). P. never uses *Atticus* as 'Atticist', nor does he ever use *Asianus* 'Asianist'
(for the ancient 'quarrel' between elaborate and pared-down styles see *OCD*
'Asianism and Atticism', Quint. 12.10.16–26 with Austin, Leeman 1963: 91–111,
136–67). **praefationes:** the declamation was preceded by a preamble called
(προ)λαλία or διάλεξις (Russell 1983: 77–9, Anderson 1993: 53–5): cf. 4.11.2. For
analogous prefaces to Latin recitations, see 1.13.2, 8.21.3. In 4.5.3 and 4.14.8
P. figures his own letter as *praefatio* to an enclosed speech. **tersae graciles
dulces, graues interdum et erectae** 'polished, simple, charming; occasionally weighty and noble'. The adjectives progress through the three *genera dicendi*
('plain', 'middle' and 'grand' styles) well established in rhetorical theory (Quint.
12.10.58–62 with Austin, Lausberg §§1078–82). Quintilian brings *tersus* (*OLD* 3)
into literary criticism for clarity and elegance (10.1.93 *tersus atque elegans*, 10.1.94
tersior et purus, 12.10.50 *tersum ac limatum*); for *gracilis* see Quint. 12.10.66 [*genus*]
gracile (= the 'plain' style) and *OLD* 4b. The middle style is evoked by *dulcis* (e.g.
Quint. 12.10.64), the grand by *graues . . . et erectae*, with appropriate extra weight.
Isaeus is tastefully sparing with this last (*interdum*). Mixing styles was axiomatic:
cf. Cic. *De or.* 3.177, Quint. 12.10.69 *utetur . . . omnibus* [*generibus dicendi*]; progression
up the scale was canonical within a speech as a whole (§3 notes).

2 poscit controuersias plures 'he invites several themes': for *controuersia*
'theme' (ὑπόθεσις) see *TLL* IV 782.82–783.81. After the general comment on
praefationes, historic present (G–L §229) slips us into a miniature narrative of the
performance proper (μελέτη), in which the sophist argues a hypothetical legal
case. Isaeus perhaps lets the audience choose between suggestions, as at Lucian
Rhet. praec. 18, Phil. *VS* 529 with Russell 1983: 79, Korenjak 2000: 116–20. Speakers in Cicero's dialogues despise such *impudentia*, which originated with Gorgias
(*De or.* 1.102–3, *Fin.* 2.1–2, *Lael.* 17). Quintilian is also scornful: some even allow
their opening word to be specified (Quint. 10.7.21 *peruersa ambitio . . . friuolum ac
scaenicum*). **partes:** which side of the case he should argue (*OLD* 15). **surgit
amicitur incipit:** asyndetic tricolon. In §1 it piled up synonyms (for verbs, see
e.g. Cic. *Pis.* 1 *decepit fefellit induxit*; a bicolon at 2.20.7 *hortari rogare*), here it covers
three actions in swift succession (e.g. 2.1.12 *audio alloquor teneo*, Tac. *Ag.* 37.2 *sequi
uulnerare capere*). The preamble was usually delivered seated (Russell 1983: 77, and
for Roman examples Sen. *Contr.* 1.*pr.*21, 3.*pr.*11). **amicitur** 'wraps his cloak
around him' (Radice), uniquely of arranging clothing already worn. This is the
Greek *pallium* (as at 4.11.3), which like the toga was large and difficult to control.
Quint. 11.3.137–47 gives elaborate rubrics for state of dress at different points in
the speech. **statim . . . exculta:** 12~8~12 syllables. **statim . . . ac paene
pariter** 'at once . . . and almost at the same time', hyperbole for 'at once . . . in
quick succession'; this temporal use, *OLD pariter* 4, is common in P., e.g. *Pan.*
8.6 *omnia pariter et statim factus es*. The adverbs frame *omnia* in *coniunctio* (2.1.11n.
in). **omnia . . . ad manum** *sc. ei sunt* 'he has everything at his fingertips' (lit.

'to hand', *OLD manus* 4, *TLL* VIII 362.62–82). **sensus reconditi occursant** 'recondite conceits come flying' (lit. 'keep coming into his mind', *OLD occurso* 3b). For *sensus* (the clever thought that underlies a *sententia*), see *OLD* 9c, Quint. 8.5.2, Tac. *D.* 20.4 with Gudeman. Isaeus' epigrams would be an obvious attraction to P. **uerba** *sc. occursant*. (**sed qualia!**) '– and *what* words! –': P. interrupts himself (*OLD sed* 1) with an admiring exclamation, a device at home in low and high styles: Mart. 10.10.6 *sed quanto blandius!*, Sil. 14.505 *pro qualis!* Parenthesis is very common in P. (2.4.2n. *erat* and index, Niemirska-Pliszczyńska 1955: 122–5, Melzani 1992: 231–4, Häusler 2000). Its routine designation as colloquial (as by the three scholars just cited) is problematic, given its frequency in (e.g.) Quintilian and Tacitus, its theorisation in ancient rhetoric (e.g. von Albrecht 1964: 15, 21–3), and the range from very short interjections to grander 'floor-holding' types (2.7.2n. *quod*); see Halla-aho 2011: 431–2. On parenthesis (*interiectio*) in general see Lausberg §860, H–S 472–3, 728–9, von Albrecht 1964, Bolkestein 1998. On P.'s penchant for admiring exclamations (1.16.5, 3.1.6, 7.25.1) see Niemirska-Pliszczyńska 1955: 119–22; cf. Cic. *Leg.* 3.20 *(quos et quantos uiros!)* with Dyck. **quaesita et exculta** 'recherché and polished' (*OLD quaesitus* 2; for *excolere* 'polish' see Quint. 2.6.2, *TLL* V.2 1278.42–52). **multa lectio in subitis, multa scriptio elucet:** anaphoric isocolon (8~7 syllables) with *in subitis . . . elucet* distributed in *apo koinou* (2.1.6n. *magnum*). Isaeus' improvisations (*OLD subitus* 5b) display the extensive reading and writing on which they are built. Such training was essential for any orator: see §4 notes, and Cic. *Brut.* 92 *nulla . . . res tantum ad dicendum proficit quantum scriptio* with Douglas. For the anaphora and diction, cf. 5.21.5 *quantum legit, quantum etiam scripsit!* Lucian takes a typically sardonic view of a rhetor: *Pseudologistes* 6 'he was completely unconvincing in delivery, stringing together what he had probably studied and practised for a long time'.

3 prohoemiatur . . . excelse: five parallel two-word cola swiftly track the four canonic divisions of a speech and (fifthly) its *ornatus*. On the four divisions, which together comprise *inuentio*, see Quint. 4–6, Lausberg §§260–442, de Brauw 2007.   **prohoemiatur** 'he proemises', a neologism (or at least first preserved here) by analogy with προοιμιάζεται (Consoli 1900: 62), followed by Sid. *Ep.* 4.3.2 among others; other apparent coinages (two of them Greek) at 2.7.6n. *erit*, 2.11.23n. *superest*, 2.17.16n. *cryptoporticus*; see also 2.17.5n. *cauaedium*, 13n. *gestationem*. We begin with the introductory προοίμιον or *exordium*.   **apte** = πρεπόντως, 'fittingly'. For the importance of *aptum* or *decorum* (τὸ πρέπον) see Cic. *Or.* 70–4, Quint. 11.1, Lausberg §1244 'aptus', *TLL* II 333.40–52, 335.20–1. It is often associated with relative simplicity (Plato *Statesman* 284e τὸ μέτριον καὶ τὸ πρέπον 'what is moderate and fitting', Cic. *De or.* 2.56 *aptus et pressus*), and is recommended for proems (Quint. 4.1.52–71, Seguerianus 19, 237, 240 Dilts–Kennedy). The gradation of adverbs from *apte* to *excelse* both in meaning and in weight (climaxing in *excelse*, – – –) mimics the stylistic crescendo of a speech.   **narrat aperte** 'narrates lucidly': the διήγησις or *narratio*, a persuasive exposition of the events, proposal or dispute in question (Quint. 4.2.31). *narratio aperta* is a stock desiderandum (Lausberg §315, *De or.* 2.80 with Leeman–Pinkster–Nelson, 2.329). The words make a heroic clausula (–⏑⏑––), avoided by many prose writers for its similarity with a hexameter ending (other things being equal, it might be expected to end around 8% of sentences: De Groot 1921: 106, albeit a rough and ready statistic). Like Cicero and others, P. allows it especially when the last word comprises 4 or 5 syllables and so makes an unlikely verse-ending (H–S 714–15, Laurand 1911: 86, Woodman on Vell. 2.95.2), as e.g. 2.11.22 *deseruisset*, 2.14.12 *excipiantur*, 2.17.25 *(a)qua salienti*, 2.18.2 *conticuerunt*, 2.19.4 *praepediuntur*, 2.20.14 *-ens habiturum* (all strong breaks; similar heroics end 1.10 and 7.29), and, ending internal cola, 2.6.5 *est onerosum* and *-nem redigenda est*, 2.7.5 *suscipiendos*, 2.16.2 *deficerentur*. But, again like Cicero (e.g. *Phil.* 11.33 *summaque uirtus*), P. sometimes neglects that 'rule', as here, 2.11.2 *-antibus Afris*, and (at strong breaks) 1.19.4 *milia nummum*, 3.9.26 *ad breue tempus*, 4.3.1 *dicere nemo*, 5.5.6 *et fuit idem*, 8.2.2 *non satis aequum* (1.7.4 is a verse quotation). Brakman 1925: 93–4 inaccurately lists twenty sentence-final heroics in the *Epistles*; around fifty in *Epistles* and *Pan.* are catalogued (in different terms) by Bornecque 1907: 326, 238–9, 422–3.   **pugnat acriter** 'fights vigorously, keenly': the *narratio* is followed by the 'proofs' (πίστεις, *probatio* or *confirmatio*), where fierce argument (*OLD acriter* 4) is required, especially in contesting the claims of one's opponent (ἐλέγχων ἀπαίτησις or *refutatio*: Quint. 5.13). The metaphor of *pugna forensis* (Quint. 5.12.17) is common (*OLD pugno* 4b).   **colligit fortiter** 'sums up powerfully' (*OLD colligo* 10, *fortiter* 2): the ἐπίλογος or *peroratio*, where high emotions have their special place (Quint. 6.1; Seguerianus 238 Dilts–Kennedy prescribes a 'bold . . . and daring' style).   **ornat:** ornament or 'finish' (κατασκευή, *ornatus*) covers word-choice and figures of speech (Quint. 8.3), or taken more broadly the whole gamut of lexis, tropes, rhythm and sentence construction (Lausberg §§538–1054).   **excelse** 'sublimely', a defining marker for P. of great oratory in the grand style (e.g. 2.13.7, 1.20.19) but not in the philosophical sense of 'Longinus' (Armisen-Marchetti 1990).   **postremo** 'in a word' (*OLD* 4).   **docet delectat afficit:** the famous tripartite definition of the orator's art, deriving from Aristotle (Hendrickson 1905: 260): Cic. *De or.* 2.115 ('to prove that what we are defending is true [=*docere*], to win over our listeners [=*delectare*], to draw them to whatever emotion the case requires [=*afficere*]', Quint. 8.*pr.*7 *docendi mouendi delectandi*. The three functions were associated with the plain, middle and grand styles respectively (Cic. *Or.* 69, Quint. 12.10.59).   **quid maxime:** *sc. efficiat* or similar (indirect question).   **dubites** 'you would find it hard to say', potential generalising subjunctive (*NLS* §119).   **crebra ἐνθυμήματα, crebri syllogismi:** isocolon (6~6 syllables) with anaphora and polyptoton. **ἐνθυμήματα** 'enthymemes'. An *enthymema* is an elliptical syllogism (next n.): Cic. *Top.* 55 gives the example *hoc metuere, alterum in metu non ponere!* 'to fear this, to have no fear for that!' (*sc.* 'is inconsistent'). See Burnyeat 1994; also Cic. *Top.* 53–7 with Reinhardt, Lausberg §371, Anderson 2000: 44–8 and, for the background, Arist. *Rhet.* 1.2 = 1356a35–1358a35. Quintilian and others latinise the word (as P. does *syllogismi*); for the Greek form cf. Cic. *Att.* 1.14.4, a letter (also) in mind at 1.2.4 *Marci nostri* ληκύθους. On P.'s use of Greek, see 2.2.1n. μικραίτιος; the bunching in this letter (§4, §8, §12) fits the subject. **syllogismi** 'syllogisms'. A syllogism is a deduction in which a conclusion is derived from two or more premises: e.g. in Aristotelian logic 'A belongs to all B, B belongs to all C; therefore A belongs to all C', or in Stoic logic 'If the first, the second; but the first; therefore the second'. Unlike in an enthymeme, the deduction is spelled out explicitly (Lausberg §371). The word first appears in Latin in the younger Seneca. **circumscripti et effecti** 'concise and (yet) complete' (*OLD et* 14a, *efficio* 9b), probably describing both ἐνθυμήματα and *syllogismi* (for the agreement, see 2.1.8n. *coniunctae*). Epigrammatic concision was a particular forte of Isaeus (Phil. *VS* 514). **quod stilo quoque assequi magnum est** 'which it is no small feat to achieve even in writing'. For *stilo assequi* cf. 4.3.3; also 1.8.8 (*prosequi*). The antecedent of *quod* is '[producing] concise and yet complete enthymemes and syllogisms'. **incredibilis memoria:** a crucial skill, and gift, in an orator (Calboli on *Rhet. Her.* 3.28–9, Lausberg §§1083–90, Yates 1966). A poor memory is one of Regulus' many defects (6.2.2). **repetit... labitur:** asyndeton, with framing verbs. **repetit altius** 'he recalls at length' (*OLD altus* 8a 'remote in time'). *alte/-ius repetere* (*TLL* I 1786.16–39) is common for 'begin far/further back' in a narrative (2.6.1n. *longum*), but P. refers here to recapitulation (*OLD* 6c 'recall'; *memoria* preceded, and *quae dixit* follows). Perhaps he means ring-composition, perhaps repetition necessitated by late arrivals in the audience (Quint. 11.2.39): as a rule, sophists prided themselves on not reusing material. **labitur** 'goes wrong' (*OLD labor*[1] 9c–10). Cf. Cic. *Brut.* 301, expressing awe at Hortensius' delivering an entire speech word-perfect from memory. Such claims imply equal powers of memory in the reporter.

4 ἕξιν 'habileté' (Walsh), 'skill', defined by Quint. 10.1.1 as *firma quaedam facilitas* built on long and diligent study, the *habitus* of Cic. *Inv.* 1.36 (Lausberg §7, Cousin 1979: 3, 292); ἕξις first appears in Latin at Sen. *Contr.* 7.pr.2, another (less laudatory) portrait of a rhetor. There is no short cut to facility: 3.13.3 *disponere apte, figurare uarie nisi eruditis negatum est*, 7.9.6. The polemic (against 'naturalists' who relied on talent alone) was live: see Quint. 2.11–12 with Reinhardt–Winterbottom. **studio et exercitatione:** cf. Quint. 12.9.20 *disciplina et studium et exercitatio dederit uires etiam facilitatis.* **peruēnit:** perfect. **diebus et noctibus** 'night and day', i.e. 'continuously' (*OLD dies* 1a). For the abl. (post-Augustan) cf. 5.8.3, *Pan.* 67.8. **nihil... loquitur:** anaphoric tricolon, with gradation in the verbs (moving from study to practice).

5 annum sexagensimum excessit: he is (at least) sixty (2.1.4n. *annum*). **et** 'and (yet)' (§3n. *circumscripti*). **scholasticus tantum** 'only a man of the schools', detached from the practical oratory of the forum (cf. Quint. 12.11.16 *in foro nos experiri potuimus dum scholastici sumus* with Austin). The word is commonly used with disdain: Kennedy 1999: 174–5 on Petronius' *scholastici*, Suet. *Gramm.* 30.2 *usquequaque scholasticus* (with Kaster) and other instances in *OLD scholasticus* 2a. P., who would never call himself a *scholasticus* (9.2.3) except in jest (2.20.9 *scholastica lege*), is unusual in using it kindly – from the patronising position of a securely established 'real' advocate – here and at 1.24.4 (Suetonius). The (naturalised) Greek term is precisely apt for a rhetor. **aut sincerius aut simplicius aut melius:** slightly falling tricolon (5~5~4 syllables), climaxing in the simplest, all-embracing term. A striking counter-claim to the usual allegations of bombast and pretension (e.g. Petr. 1–2, Tac. *D.* 35.5 *ingentibus uerbis*), and to Quint.'s view that declamation, though a vital pedagogical tool, is emphatically not an end in itself (Quint. 2.10 with Reinhardt–Winterbottom, Bonner 1949: 80–2, Hömke 2002: 52–9). What P.'s Isaeus offers, however, is not a threat to proper forensic practice, but a complement. For *simplex + sincerum*, see Cic. *Off.* 1.13 (later Gell. *NA* 13.27.3); cf. 2.9.4 *uerius . . . simplicius . . . candidius.* '*simplicitas* is a canonical virtue among the "sincere" circle of P. and friends' (Guillemin 1929: 52 (translated); Hoffer 1999: 162 n.4). **nos enim qui** 'for we who' (if Nepos is an advocate: cf. 4.26.2 *disertissimus*), or 'for those of us who' if not; authorial plural (§8n. *nos*) seems less likely, given what follows. It establishes the crucial dichotomy between Isaeus' harmless pursuit and the reality of a senatorial orator's duties. **in foro uerisque litibus** 'in the real battles of the courts' (*OLD forum* 5): hendiadys, cf. 7.9.13 *in foro causisque*, 1.22.6 *in toga negotiisque.* The courts of the forum are the home of real-life rhetoric: Cic. *Brut.* 283 *foro, cui nata eloquentia est*, Sen. *Contr.* 9.*pr.*5; Brink 1989: 476 n.24, 488 n.60. **terimur** 'wear ourselves out' (*OLD* 7), a colourful substitute for *uersari.* **malitiae** 'malice', partitive genitive. Despite the best efforts of some readers (Cowan 'used here in its better sense', Leeman 1963: 496 'finesse'), the meaning is clear; on *malitia* of lawyerly tricks see Fantham 2008, esp. 327–8. Elsewhere P. distances himself from imperfect and immoral trends in advocacy, which can be tidily pinned on 'delators' such as Regulus (2.14, 2.20.intro., 1.5.11–12; cf. Winterbottom 1964 on Quint.). Here he shows vice rubbing off even on the good men like him (cf. 8.14.2–10 with Whitton 2010: 126), as suits his emphasis on the contrasting 'innocence' of Isaeus and his sort. **quamuis:** with subjunctive, as often at this period (*OLD* 4b). **addiscimus:** the prefix adds little (*OLD addisco* 1b), but makes a double cretic.

6 schola et auditorium et ficta causa | res inermis innoxia est nec minus felix: tricolon subject, then a complement (*res*) with a divided tricolon of adjectives; chiasmus sets *causa ~ res* together mid-way. The triple subject is in antithesis to §5 *foro uerisque litibus.* For the *uerum/fictum* dichotomy, cf. Quint. 10.2.12, Tac. *D.* 31.1 (Messalla, less favourably) *fictis nec ullo modo ad ueritatem accedentibus controuersiis.* **res inermis innoxia:** a uniquely idealistic take on declamation, both in boyhood (*quod dulcissimum est in iuuenta*) and in adult life (*quid in senectute felicius?*). For Quintilian it is the most useful school exercise but often badly taught and studied (2.10); in Tac. *D.* 35 Messalla is roundly damning. See Bonner 1949: 71–83, Hömke 2002: 45–82. In adulthood, private amateur declamation was widely valued as cathartic recreation for an advocate from the hurly-burly of the forum: e.g. Cic. *De or.* 1.149, *Att.* 9.4.3, Sen. *Contr.* 4.*pr.*6, Quint. 10.5.14 *alitur enim atque enitescit uelut pabulo laetiore facundia et assidua contentionum asperitate fatigata renouatur* (Kennedy 1972: 335–7, Hömke 2002: 23–4); it is taken for granted at Tac. *D.* 14.3. Yet P. extends this commendation to public show-declamations by professional rhetors, a genre implicitly condemned by Quint. 2.10.6 (on school declamation: *nam si foro non praeparat, aut scaenicae ostentationi aut furiosae uociferationi simillimum est*) and all but ignored in Tac. *D.* (Hömke 2002: 60–73, 81; hints in *D.* 31.1 and *D.* 39.1 *auditoria* with Gudeman). **nec minus felix:** as in 2.1.2 *perinde felicis,* the 'tail' adds the most important term. **senibus praesertim:** a second tail, leading into the *nam*-clause, like 3.1.2 *senum praesertim: nam*; cf. 2.5.5, 2.16.3, 2.18.4 (all *praesertim... nam*), 2.17.28 *lac in primis: nam.* **quid in senectute felicius | quam quod dulcissimum est in iuuenta?** chiastic isocolon (10~10 syllables); *senectute felicius* is also chiastic with *felix senibus.* The *sententia per interrogationem* (a rhetorical question adding up to a gnomic statement: Quint. 8.5.5–6) rests on the dubious premises that old men share the taste of the young and that declamation is the best thing about adolescence. Language and theme recur at 2.18.1 *illam dulcissimam aetatem quasi resumo.* Petrone 2003: 20–2 alleges allusion to Petronius.

7 quare ego... quem tu sums up the encomium (for this use of *quare* cf. 3.8.4, 4.17.11, 5.20.8, all letter-ends) and bridges to the protreptic second part, in which Nepos (*tu*) replaces Isaeus as focal point. *ego* makes an antithesis with *tu* and 'focuses' (emphasises) *quare* (Adams 1994b: 141–51). *quare ego* is favoured by P. (3.8.4, 4.17.11, *Pan.* 5.7, none with following *tu uel sim.*); it otherwise begins a statement only at Sall. *Cat.* 52.36 *quare ego ita censeo.* **Isaeum:** repetition seals a ring with §1. **disertissimum:** high praise, applied perhaps to the same Nepos in 4.26.2 (also 2.14.6n. *tanti*), but a step down from *eloquentissimum,* reserved for a senator's eloquence at 2.1.7 and 2.11.17 (Tacitus) and 4.11.1, which draws clearly the distinction between advocate and sophist: *hic modo inter eloquentissimos causarum actores habebatur; nunc eo decidit ut... rhetor de oratore fieret* (also, coquettishly, for the poetry of Vergilius Romanus in 6.21.4). By contrast, Cic. *De or.* 1.94–5 and Quint. 8.*pr.*13 reserve *eloquens* for the orator most skilled in *ornatus.* **uerum etiam:** P. prefers this to *sed etiam* by an exceptional degree (43:1). Others favour the latter (Cic. 287:920, Pl. *NH* 11:18, Quint. 22:129, Apul. 6:44); Seneca (0:51) rejects *uerum etiam* altogether, while Tacitus (0:10) confines even *sed etiam* to his early works (*Ag., G., D.*). **beatissimum:** picking up *felix,* a virtual synonym (1.3.2 *felix beatusque,* 3.7.2 *beatus et felix*). **iudico** marks P.'s role as competent judge and mediator of fame. **concupiscis** 'you long for' (2.8.2, 2.17.29), a strong verb, first in Cicero and common in his letters. **saxeus ferreusque es:** a concise blend of two proverbial expressions mostly found in poetry: Otto 1890: 134, 310; Nisbet–Hubbard on Hor. *C.* 1.3.9. For the combination, cf. Eur. *Med.* 1279 ὡς ἄρ' ἦσθα πέτρος ἢ σίδαρος 'rock or iron you are, then', Tib. 1.1.63–4 *ferro... silex.* This metaphorical use of *saxeus* is rare (*OLD* 5 gives Vitr. 8.3.22, citing an epigram).

8 si non . . . at certe 'if not . . . then at least': cf. *Pan.* 32.2 *si non . . . at, OLD at*
13b; 3.7.14 *si non . . . certe.* **nosque ipsos** 'or me myself' (*OLD -que* 7), authorial
plural. P. uses it freely (index s.v.), often in close proximity to a singular (2.4.3n.
nobis); nuances are hard to pin down (K–S 1 87–8, H–S 19–20, Marouzeau 1962:
224–6, S-W on 1.8.4, Lilja 1971), but see 2.4.3n. *sunt*, 2.5.3n. *nostra.* **uĕni:** Nepos
is away from Rome but not (as in 4.26) on service. **numquamne legisti:** *legisti,*
not *audisti,* perhaps because the story precedes living memory; perhaps a joke
about Nepos' preference for books (§9; at 3.16.2 *tibi . . . legenti* he again depends
on P. as conduit); perhaps a self-conscious reference to the power of the written
word. Indeed, the tale owes its survival to this letter; Jerome demonstrated his
own reading in a close reworking, *Ep.* 53.1 *ad Titum Liuium lacteo eloquentiae fonte
manantem uisendum de ultimo terrarum orbe uenisse Gaditanum quendam legimus;* see also
§10n. *qui,* §10n. τί and, on the same letter, 2.5.13n. *ne* (see Intro. 35 n.210). Cf.
Petrarch *Res memorandae* 2.19 *Titum Livium . . . cuius eloquentie fama de ultimis mundi
regionibus admirantes claros uiros Romam usque perduxit. Quod et Plinius scribit et post illum
Ieronimus . . . testatus est; Ep. fam.* 24.8 'if you [Livy] had been alive' *ego . . . visitatorum
unus ex numero tuorum [fierem], profecto non Romam modo te videndi gratia, sed Indiam ex
Gallis aut Hispania petiturus).* Petrarch, who clearly had a different text of Jerome
Ep. 53.1 (*Gaditanum,* if right, is corrupt in the MSS, and other versions read *de
ultimis Hispaniae Galliarumque finibus quosdam uenisse nobiles legimus:* Wright 1997:
69–71), somehow knew Jerome's source; if he found it himself (Kemper 2000:
15–19), this is rare evidence that he knew the *Epistles.* Ogilvie 1965: 4 wonders
if Livy had told the story himself (cf. Tacitus' brag in 9.23.2–3). **Gaditanum
quendam:** a man from Gades (Cadiz) in Baetica. P. routinely omits names,
here because it is irrelevant (Jones 1991: 168–9; 2.6.1n. *quendam*). In Tac. *D.* 7.4
Aper talks up the eagerness of provincials arriving at Rome to see celebrity
orators in the flesh. **Titi Liui:** the historian Livy, famous in his lifetime and
standard reading in the 1c. AD. Quintilian (2.5.19, 10.1.101–2) makes him (almost)
Sallust's equal and mentions him often; teenager P. notoriously finds him more
interesting than an erupting volcano (6.20.5). P. tends to refer to historians by
two names (e.g. Cornelius Nepos at 5.3.6); poets by contrast are usually mentioned with just one; orators vary (Jones 1991: 159–61). **nomine gloriaque:**
the same doublet ('name and fame') or hendiadys ('glorious name') at Cic. *Diu.*
1.31, Sall. *Jug.* 18.12, Tac. *H.* 2.37.1; cf. Tac. *G.* 13.3 *id nomen, ea gloria.* It varies the
commoner *nominis gloria.* **commotum** 'stirred' (*OLD* 8–10). **ad uisendum
eum:** gerund(ive) of purpose. There is some slippage in P.'s argument: coming
to *see* a celebrity is a different sort of *cognitio* (§8) from *hearing* a performer (was
Livy giving recitals?). **ab ultimo terrarum orbe** 'from the farthest end of
the earth' (*OLD orbis* 12). Cadiz defined the western extremity of the inhabited
world: Mayor on Juv. 10.1, Nisbet–Hubbard on Hor. *C.* 2.6.1. The language
exoticises (cf. Hor. *Epod.* 1.13 *Occidentis usque ad ultimum sinum* with Mankin, Lucan
4.1 *procul extremis terrarum . . . in oris,* Sil. 7.108–9), amplifying the pilgrimage. At
Tac. *D.* 8.1 Aper bets that the advocates Eprius and Vibius are as famous *in*

extremis partibus terrarum as in their home towns. **statimque ut** 'as soon as', Ciceronian. **uiderat** varies *uisendum*. By classical 'rules', subordinate verbs in indirect statement are subjunctive unless the author wants to emphasise their factual veracity, but P. is flexible in his choice of moods (e.g. 2.11.19 *acceperat*, 22n. *qui*; Kraut 1872: 38–9, Philips 83–4), not unusually for his time (*NLS* §286, K–S II 544–5). **ἀφιλόκαλον** 'boorish' (Radice), lit. 'without love for beauty/virtue'. The positive φιλόκαλος ranges from the philosophical (Plato *Phaedrus* 248d, Cic. *Fam.* 15.19.3) to the aesthetic ('connoisseur', of Silius Italicus in 3.7.7), frequently implying 'cultured' (often in Plutarch and Lucian). The antonym (first here and in Plut. *Quaest. conu.* 672c) makes a bilingual tricolon with *illitteratum* and *iners* through the cognate prefixes *in-/ἀ-* (cf. 1.20.15 *omnia... omnia...* πάντα), extended to a tetracolon by *ac paene etiam turpe*. All describe the following infinitival phrase *non... putare*. **illitteratum** 'uncultured', a pentasyllabic synonym for ἀφιλόκαλον. **ac paene etiam:** a rare variant on *atque etiam* (2.1.1n. *insigne*), similarly marking gradation but highlighting the final *turpe* (2.6.7n.) as especially bold, indeed over-bold (*paene*). Also at 9.7.4, Pl. *NH* 34.1, Gell. *NA* 18.13.5. **putare tanti** 'think it worthwhile', *OLD puto* 4b + gen. of value. **cognitionem** 'making (his) acquaintance' (*OLD cognitio* 4), picking up §7 *cognoscere*. **qua:** abl. of comparison. **nulla... nulla... nulla:** another tricolon of praise (cf. §5 *nihil aut sincerius...*), slightly rising (6~5~8 syllables), this time with anaphora. **iucundior... pulchrior... humanior:** the first two are paired again at 7.20.2 *o iucundas, o pulchras uices!* (also in Cic., Sen., Tac.), the latter two at 8.21.1 *pulcherrimum et humanissimum*. The adjectives look graded, climaxing with *humanior* (but cf. 8.24.9 *humanior melior peritior*, Pan. 59.3 *iustissimus humanissimus patientissimus*). **denique**, like *etiam* (2.1.6n.), commonly bolsters the last member in a list (tricolons again at 2.7.1, 2.13.10; tetracolon at 2.9.3). **humanior** 'more humane' (*OLD* 6). Like *iucundior* and *pulchrior* it modifies *cognitio*, but resonates with the man himself and the learning he imparts: cf. 1.10.2 (Euphrates) *plenusque humanitate quam praecipit*. The quality, which might be summarised as an enlightened empathy for fellow (and lesser) men, is liberally spread across the *Epistles*; it is often associated, as here, with literary study (e.g. 4.3.4) and with Greece, its cradle (8.24.2). See Braund 1997 and (on P.) Zucker 1928, Rieks 1967: 225–53, Bütler 1970: 107–18, Cova 1978: 107–13, Méthy 2007: 25–58.

9 dices: a standard rhetorical technique of forestalling an objection (*occupatio*: Cic. *De or.* 3.205, *Or.* 138, Quint. 4.1.49, Seyffert 1855: 128–35). P. has it often, e.g. 2.5.10, 2.10.5. **quos legam** 'people to read' (as we talk of 'reading Pliny'), relative purpose clause. **etiam, sed** 'yes, but...' (*OLD etiam* 5b), a usage peculiar to P. (5.3.7, 6.2.8, 6.28.3; K–S II 52); similarly 1.20.23 *est, sed*, 5.8.7 *utinam! sed*, 8.14.8 *sed*, all quashing an objection (cf. Oakley on Livy 9.4.11–15). **legendi semper... audiendi non semper:** parallel antithesis, with *occasio est* taken *apo koinou*. **multo:** abl. of degree of comparison (*NLS* §82). **uiua uox:** the power of the 'living voice' was proverbial (*ut uulgo dicitur*): Cic. *Att.* 2.12.2 *ubi sunt* *qui aiunt* ζώσης φωνῆς? (i.e. 'that old line about *uiua uox* is quite wrong'), Sen. *Contr.* 1.*pr.*11 *quod uulgo aliquando dici solet*, Quint. 2.2.8 *uiua illa, ut dicitur, uox*, etc.: Otto 1890: 378. **nam...affigit** 'for even if what you read is more powerful, nevertheless words make a deeper impression when enhanced by the voice, the expression, the comportment and the gesture of a speaker' (lit. '...nevertheless those things [*sc. ea*] sit more deeply which the voice...of a speaker has embellished'). Nepos may have better orators (the classics) to read at home, but Isaeus' performance will make him more memorable. **licet...sint:** concessive (*OLD licet* 4a, *NLS* §248), as e.g. 2.13.10, 2.16.3. **acriora:** in oratory *acer* describes a vigorous style that makes a sharp impact, e.g. 1.2.4 *acres enim non tristes esse uolebamus*, 6.33.9 *acribus...et erectis*, *TLL* I 362: 45–72. **legas:** generic subjunctive (*NLS* §155), probably in the generalising second person (making a universal statement, rather than commenting on Nepos' library). **altius...sedent:** *OLD altus* 15a, *sedeo* 10b. **pronuntiatio uultus habitus gestus etiam:** *etiam* caps the list (2.1.6n.). These four essential elements of *actio* (performance) are treated in *Rhet. Her.* 3.19–28, Cic. *De or.* 3.213–27 and most extensively Quint. 11.3; see e.g. Gunderson 2000, Corbeill 2004, Hall 2007. P. asserts their value again, now in advocacy, at 2.19.2. *pronuntiatio* is usually used of 'delivery', encompassing both voice and gesture (Quint. 11.3.1, *OLD* 4b), as in 2.14.12, 2.19.4, *Pan.* 67.1. Here alone in P. it seems restricted to voice, as at Val. Max. 8.10 (*TLL* x.2 1918.27–31), avoiding repetition of *uox*. **dicentis** 'of [someone] speaking'. This substantival use of the participle is common in P., especially but not only in the present tense, e.g. 2.4.2 *defuncti*, 2.5.2 *scribentis*, 2.11.14 *audientium* and index s.v. (Kraut 1872: 5–6; more generally, Adams 1973a).

10 nisi uero 'unless, that is', ironic (as usually): Ciceronian, otherwise only in Quint. 6.2.30 and P. (7.17.2, *Pan.* 25.2). **putamus:** associative plural, binding speaker and addressee and thus urging assent (Marouzeau 1962: 223–4, Sinclair 1995: 53–6). **illud Aeschinis** 'that remark of Aeschines' (*OLD ille* 14b). The anecdote (revisited in 4.5) is familiar from Cic. *De or.* 3.213 *illud ab Aeschine dictum...*, Val. Max. 8.10.*ext.*, Quint. 11.3.7, all on the importance of delivery; it is also in Pl. *NH* 7.110, [Plut.] *Orat. Vit.* 840d–e, Phil. *VS* 510, Jer. *Ep.* 53.2 (below) and a life of Aeschines (*Vita Aesch.* 3.4 Dilts, 1C. AD or later): Kunst 1917. The poet Julius Montanus produced a comparable apophthegm on Virgil: *eosdem...uersus ipso pronuntiante bene sonare, sine illo inanes esse mutosque* (Donatus *Life of Virgil* 29). Aeschines and Demosthenes are the only Greek orators quoted by P. (Aeschines again at 9.26.10–13); Lysias (1.20.4) and Isocrates (6.29.6) get brief mention. **qui cum legisset...admirantibus cunctis:** cf. Cic. *De or.* 3.213 *quam* [*orationem*] *cum...legisset admirantibus omnibus*, Jerome *Ep.* 53.2 *mirantibus cunctis atque laudantibus*. P. uses *cuncti* sparingly (again in this book at 2.6.3) and with a touch of grandeur; on this official and/or highbrow alternative to *omnes* (common esp. in such abl. abs.) see Adams 1973b: 129–31. **Rhodiis:** dative. Aeschines retired to Rhodes and established a rhetorical school there after his defeat by Demosthenes in the Ctesiphon case of 330 BC (on the trial see Yunis 2001: 7–12, MacDowell 2009: 382–6). According to Philostratus, this was the foundation of the Second Sophistic (*VS* 481; Kindstrand 1982: 90–5). Whether that idea was already current at P.'s time is not clear (cf. Sen. *Contr.* 1.8.16 with Fairweather 1981: 115, Quint. 2.4.41–2 with Reinhardt–Winterbottom); if it was, the anecdote is well chosen for this 'sophist' letter.   **orationem Demosthenis:** *oratio* is P.'s default word for speech, whether delivered or written/recited (both, e.g., at 6.33.7). According to Cicero (above), Aeschines recited first his own speech *Against Ctesiphon* (*Ctes.*), then, on the following day, Demosthenes' reply *On the crown* (*Cor.* = *De corona*). Like Quintilian (above), P. keeps the narrative crisp by omitting the first speech and leaving the moral of the story, spelled out by Cicero, implicit. Demosthenes is the pinnacle of Greek oratory for P. as for others (9.26.8 *ille norma oratoris et regula*, Quint. 10.1.76 *paene lex orandi*, 10.2.24 *perfectissimus Graecorum*, Tac. *D.* 25.3; cf. Drerup 1923, Pernot 2006) and the model for his own sometimes exuberant rhetorical style (9.26.8–9). He is the first and last author named in the *Epistles* (1.2.2, 9.26.11), an orator P. can only dream of imitating (1.2.2, 7.30.5), though he is happy to invite the comparison, as at 6.33.11 *ut inter meas* ὑπὲρ Κτησιφῶντος ('an *On the crown*, so far as any of my speeches could be') and in 4.5 and 9.23.4–5; see also 2.17.22n. *ac.*   **'τί δέ, εἰ αὐτοῦ τοῦ θηρίου ἠκούσατε;'** 'what if you had heard the beast himself?' For the lively, elliptical τί δέ, εἰ = *quid si* (*OLD quis*[1] 13a) see LSJ τίς B.I.8f, Stevens 1976: 30–1 (Attic verse examples), and e.g. [Plato] *Theages* 125c7. Other versions are tamer (e.g. Cic. *De or.* 3.213 *quanto... magis miraremini, si audissetis ipsum!*); P. is the first Roman author to give it in Greek (as fits his subject) and to include the 'beast'. Though the word is a common term of abuse in Demosthenes and Aeschines, particular inspiration may lie in Aesch. *Ctes.* 182, attacking Demosthenes as τοῦ θηρίου τούτου 'this beast'; cf. also Cic. *Or.* 26 *beluam* (translating Aesch. *Ctes.* 167 κίναδος 'beast'). But the motif may have been in wider circulation: it also appears in *Vita Aesch.* 3.4 Dilts (above on *illud*): 'you wonder how I lost, because you did not hear that beast for yourselves [οὐκ ἠκούσατε ὑμεῖς τοῦ θηρίου ἐκείνου]'. Jerome *Ep.* 53.2 translates and again (above on *qui* and §8n. *numquamne*) expands: *quid si ipsam audissetis bestiam sua uerba resonantem?* Perpillou 1995 would have θηρίον mean 'worm' or 'cancer', evidently not a view shared by P., Jerome et al.   **et** 'and what is more' (*OLD* 2a), not, with most translators, 'and yet'. The sentence from here to *pepererat* is affirmative: loosely, 'and Aeschines was no mean speaker himself – yet all the same he professed Demosthenes superior'. The same two-stage affirmation (*et erat... tamen*) at *Pan.* 41.3 *et erant principes ipsi sua sponte auidi...; plura tamen semper a nobis... didicerunt* ('and it is not as if emperors were not already miserly... yet they still learnt more meanness from us'). The full stop usually printed after λαμπροφωνότατος obscures the structure; a comma instead of a semi-colon is adopted here to avoid confusion with a Greek question mark.   **si... credimus** flags up the quotation.   **λαμπροφωνότατος** 'very clear-voiced', quoting Dem. *Cor.* 313. Demosthenes' compliment is double-edged (in paraphrase, 'Aeschines, you only display your oratorical skills when attacking a fellow-countryman'), as P. surely knew (in 4.7.6 he mocks Regulus with similarly ironical praise from *Cor.* 291): he is either sanitising (Schenk 1999: 121) or reflecting a broader tradition of taking the praise straight (Aeschines is λαμπρόφωνος in [Plut.] *Vit. orat.* 840a, *Vita Aesch.* 1.3 Dilts; Kindstrand 1982: 17–18). P. quotes six speeches of Demosthenes, none more often than *On the crown* (again at 2.20.12n. ἀλλά, 4.7.6–7, 9.26.8–9), which he also names at 6.33.11 (above on *orationem*): cf. Aelius Aristides *Orations* 28.75 'if you know no other Demosthenes, you will at least know *On the crown*...'; Pernot 2006: 177–8. On P.'s Greek quotations, also embracing Homer, Hesiod, Thucydides, Euripides, Aristophanes and Eupolis, see Deane 1918: 50–4, adding Plato (4.25.5). **fatebatur** 'he confessed'; for the imperfect, cf. 2.14.10 *narrabat*, 1.16.6 *dicebat*, 4.22.1 *negabatur* (all introducing indirect speech: Rosén 1980: 36–8). **longe melius:** a post-Augustan alternative to *multo melius*. **ipsum** *sc. eum*, subject of the acc.+inf. after *fatebatur*. **pepererat:** for *parere* 'give birth' of artistic composition see *OLD* 4; for the indicative, §8n. *uiderat*.

11 quae omnia huc tendunt, ut audias Isaeum 'all of which is driving to this conclusion: you must hear Isaeus' (*OLD huc* 2c, *tendo* 10). Ring-composition (§8 *ut hunc audias*) and the summing-up draw together the second, protreptic part of the letter. For the formula cf. 7.20.7 *quae omnia huc spectant, ut* and Sid. *Ep.* 4.8.4 *quae cuncta praemissa... huc tendunt, ut* (with Amherdt); for *huc... ut* see also *TLL* VI.3 3070.65–81 (esp. Sen. *Ep.* 20.8 *huc... cogitationes tendant, ut*); 2.6.6 *quorsus haec?* has the same function. Unlike Euphrates (cf. 1.10.11 *audiendo discendoque* and *illi te expoliendum limandumque permittas*), Isaeus is to be heard as entertainment, not as a teacher. **Isaeum** completes a ring with §1 *Isaeum* (so superseding the ring §1 ~ §7 *Isaeum*). He has been named three times, all acc., at beginning, middle and end. In 1.10 Euphrates' name occurs three times, in different cases, and less precisely distributed. **uel ideo tantum ut audieris** 'if for no other reason than to have heard him', a *sententia* amounting to 'just for the sake of it': cf. *Pan.* 59.2 *nec ideo tantum uelle consules fieri ut fuerint*, also with verbal polyptoton; the pf. subj. marks completion (G–L §512 n.1). *ideo tantum ut* is a contemporary phrase (Mart., [Quint.], Tac.), also used for point at Mart. 1.*pr*.21 *an ideo tantum ueneras, ut exires?*, [Quint.] *Decl. mai.* 7.2 *ideo tantum occisus est, ut uiderem*. Also contemporary is *uel ideo ut/ne* (first in Quint. 4.1.33), used with circular polyptoton also at Tac. *D.* 39.1 *paruum et ridiculum fortasse uidebitur quod dicturus sum, dicam tamen, uel ideo ut rideatur*.

4

You should accept your father's inheritance, indebted though it is. I shall provide for you, whether I can afford it or not.

The first of several letters showing P.'s equitable dealings in matters of inheritance (2.16, 4.10, 5.1, 5.7, 7.11, 7.14), and his munificence.

Calvina's father has died in debt. P. urges her to accept his estate rather than allow dishonour to her father, promising to write off the debt as a gift. She need not be concerned: he can afford it – or, even if he cannot, he will make an exception for her. The indelicacy and immodesty on display make this letter a test case of the complicity which the *Epistles* demands of its reader, our willingness to collude in the pretence that we are eavesdropping on a private correspondence. At the same time, it stands proud as a practical (public) demonstration of *liberalitas*, accompanied by a good dose of self-praise.

Praise of the self was problematic in antiquity as today (if not straightforwardly transcultural), as notoriously in the case of Cicero (Sen. *Breu.* 5.2 *non sine causa sed sine fine*, Quint. 11.1.16–28, Plutarch *Comparison of Demosthenes and Cicero* 2, Allen 1954; also Plutarch *On praising oneself inoffensively*, Rutherford 1995, Spatharas 2011); on P. see Rudd 1992, Eck 2001, Gibson 2003a, Gauly 2008. Often P. achieves it indirectly through citing *iudicium aliorum* (2.11.14n. *non*), but he also embraces direct self-promotion, at least in the letters. He tackles the subject head on in 1.8, justifying (and performing to his epistolary audience) the advertisement of his public munificence at Comum (Leach 1990: 28–31, Griffin 2003a: 104 and 2007: 470–2). The very act of writing forces deeper contemplation of his generosity (1.8.9 *multum ac diu pensitatus amor liberalitatis*), so making it more exceptional and praiseworthy, the product not of impulse but of careful thought (*non impetu quodam, sed consilio*). A similar claim justifies extensive praise in *Pan.* 38–41 of Trajan for relaxing the inheritance tax: *augeo, patres conscripti, principis munus, cum ostendo liberalitati eius inesse rationem: ambitio enim et iactantia et effusio et quiduis potius quam liberalitas existimanda est cui ratio non constat (Pan.* 38.4; see §4n. *facile*). Whereas Cicero condemned *liberalitas* undertaken for the sake of glory as *ostentatio* and *uanitas (Off.* 1.44), P. focuses on the other side of the coin, the glory that accrues from well-directed munificence.

The grinding calculations and equivocations (§§3–4: can he afford it or not?) thus stake P.'s claim to being truly *liberalis*, performing out loud the thought-process behind this exemplary kindness: cf. Cic. *Off.* 1.49 (the best *beneficia* are those *quae iudicio considerate constanterque delata sunt*) and Sen. *Ben.* 4.10.2 *non est autem beneficium nisi quod ratione datur*; see also Aristotle *NE* 4.1 = 1119b22–1122a17. Yet he will have his cake and eat it: the letter ends by undercutting precisely that insistence on *ratio*, in a gesture of human(e) sentimentality (§4n. *etiam*): for Calvina he will spend even beyond his means. P.'s claims to munificence are borne out by the historical record: Duncan-Jones 1982: 27–32 finds his charity unmatched by any other *priuatus* of the time; at all events P.'s success in memorialising it was unique.

Despite the conventional sentence numbering, the letter falls into two almost equal halves (§2n. *famam*), setting out three benefactions in extended tricolon (§2n. *cum*). The first half, up to §2 *suscipere*, (*i*) tells Calvina that P. has paid off her father's other creditors since his death (§2n. *uiuente*), and (*ii*) recalls his help with her dowry; in the second half, from §2 *ad quod*, he (*iii*) undertakes to write off the whole debt, assuring her that he can (almost) afford it. Within books 1–2, the letter complements 1.19, gifting 300,000 sesterces to Romatius Firmus (with Henderson 2002b), as well as 1.4 (below, CALVINAE).

On wills and heredity, a preoccupation of the Roman elite and P.'s primary sphere of expertise in court (2.14.intro.), cf. 2.14, 2.16, 2.20, and *OCD* 'inheritance, Roman', *BNP* 'inheritance law', 'wills and testaments IV', Crook 1967a: 118–32, Champlin 1989, id. 1991. Receipt of an inheritance or legacy (or failure to receive one) was a stock epistolary theme, to judge from the model letters in *Papyri Bononienses* 5 (Montevecchi 1953: 18–28). On inheritance and the *Epistles* see Pavis d'Escurac 1978, Tellegen 1982 (esp. 18–29 on 2.4) with Mayer-Maly 1984, Corbier 1985, Ducos 1998, Carlon 2009: 109–16 ('women and legacies'). The theme also occupies a substantial portion of *Pan.* (2.16.3n. *delatori*).

CALVINAE: mentioned only here; a relative of P. by marriage (§2n. *ductus*) who was, or had been, married herself (§2 *dotem*). The cognomen is associated with Domitii and Junii (Raepsaet-Charlier 1987 §§321, 431, 470); Syme 1985a: 351 n.155 produces a possible father in L. Junius Calvinus, an official in Cyrene in 72. Juv. 3.133–4 has a Calvina selling favours to legacy hunters, one of his 'possible digs at Pliny's friends' (Highet 1961: 292–4; others include 2.20.10n. *Aurelia* and Hispulla, name of several of P.'s relatives by marriage: see Intro. 34–5).

Nine of the 247 letters in *Epistles* 1–9 are addressed to women: P.'s second (or third) wife Calpurnia (6.4, 6.7, 7.5) and her aunt Hispulla (4.19, 8.11); his first mother-in-law Pompeia Celerina (1.4); Corellia Hispulla (3.3) and Corellia (7.14), daughter and sister of respected mentor Corellius Rufus. 3.10 is addressed to Vestricius Spurinna (2.7.1n.) jointly with his wife Cottia. All but Cottia seem to be related to P. (Syme 1985a: 351, id. 1991: 510, 542, Carlon 2009: 76, G–M 106); Syme and G–M add Cottia for good measure, perhaps justly, though as a co-addressee she is a slightly different case. Cicero's correspondents included, besides his wife and daughter (*Fam.* 14), at least one unrelated woman, Caerellia (*Frag. ep.* XII Watt). Most of these letters (not e.g. 1.4) show P. defending the weaker sex as virtual *paterfamilias* of his extended family, as here he displaces Calvina's debt-ridden father as prudent and kindly provider (Carlon 2009: 100–3, 123–5). Letters to women tend to be short, and in books 1–4 are distributed one per book; the placing of 1.4, 2.4 and 6.4 also looks like the beginning of a pattern (matching Ov. *Ex P.* 1.4: Bodel n.d.). On women in P. see Shelton 1987 and 1990, Vidén 1993: 91–107, Posadas 2008, Carlon 2009. The Vindolanda Tablets include several letters to and from women, e.g. Bowman–Thomas 1994 §§257, 291–4.

1 Si: this is the only letter to begin with a counterfactual (*si* also opens 1.10, 4.15, 6.6, 9.8, 10.24, 10.73). The extensive subordination in §§1–2 is unusual, advertising careful thought already taken and marking perhaps a delicate subject (as e.g. 8.10–11 on Calpurnia's miscarriage): Gamberini 1983: 477; Halla-aho 2011: 436. **pluribus . . . uel uni cuilibet alii quam mihi** 'to more than one person . . . or to any single person other than me', dat. with *debuisset*. **pater**

tuus: words repeated twice in §2. In 2.18 *frater tuus* (×4) masks a famous name; here we can surmise only a 'Calvinus'. Calvina is defined from the outset in terms of her father: cf. 3.3.1 (to Hispulla) *cum patrem tuum . . .* (other women stand on their own feet, e.g. 1.4, 7.14). A stream of first- and second-person pronouns and adjectives parades the intimacy of this transaction: §1 *tuus, mihi*, §2 *ego, tibi, tuus, meo, meo, meae, te, tuus, tibi*, §3 *mihi, nobis, nostra*, §4 *te.* **debuisset** 'had been in debt' (*OLD* 1a). **fuisset fortasse dubitandum** 'it would perhaps have been a matter for doubt', impersonal gerundive of obligation. The juxtaposition *debuisset, fuisset* (2.1.2n. *triginta*) intensifies the *sse* alliteration and assonance, besides making chiasmus of word-length and alliteration in *deb- f- f- dub-*. Cicero also liked the first effect: *Fam.* 7.3.2 *fore, et fuisset fortasse*; *Flacc.* 82 *fortasse fecisset.* **an adires hereditatem** 'whether you should accept an inheritance' (*OLD adeo*[1] 10c), indirect question (2.2.1n. *an*); *adires* is deliberative (for direct *adeam?* 'am I to accept?'). Technical language: an *extraneus heres* 'independent heir' had the choice whether to accept an inheritance (Gaius *Institutiones* (*c.* AD 160) 2.162–73), which s/he did with the formula *eam hereditatem adeo cernoque* (Gai. *Inst.* 2.166); cf. 10.75.2 *rogauit enim testamento ut hereditatem suam adirem cerneremque.* Reasons for hesitation were the concomitant executive duties (disbursing legacies, paying the 5% inheritance tax), the costly upkeep of *sacra familiae* (cf. 6.10.5 *heredum officia*; Smith 1890: 998 '*sacra priuata*', *BNP* 'sacra') and sometimes, as here, debts – a so-called *damnosa hereditas* (Gai. *Inst.* 2.163, Crook 1967a: 124). By most accounts Calvina would not have had this option unless she had been released from *patria potestas* (*OLD extraneus* 1c; Gai. *Inst.* 2.156), whether through marriage *cum manu* (rare) or emancipation (*OCD* '*patria potestas*'). Alternatively, P. uses *adire* loosely (Tellegen 1982: 21–9). Calvinus could have spared her the dilemma by bequeathing his debts to a slave as *heres necessarius* (*OLD heres* 1b), a standard procedure; his failure to do so may imply that he died intestate (Tellegen 1982: 19–20), or that he had failed to update his will (instances of the latter at 5.5.2 and 8.18.5). **etiam uiro grauem** '(which would be) burdensome even for a man', *sc.* 'still more for a woman'. For *grauis* (*OLD* 10a, c), cf. *Pan.* 37.1 (on inheritance tax) *tributum . . . heredibus . . . graue*, Scaev. *Dig.* 26.7.59 *cum hereditas patris aere alieno grauaretur* (describing how a woman was saved from inheriting her father's debt). P. operates with the customary pre-modern gender opposition. Why it should be harder for a woman is unclear, perhaps because (it is assumed) women had less legal experience (Centlivres Challet 2008: 312). Around a fifth of known litigants were female, by one count (Bablitz 2007: 72–3). On women's legal rights and status (often hard to unravel) see S-W 204, 347, Champlin 1991: 46–9, Dixon 2001: 73–88 (also Thomas 1992, Gardner 1986, Centlivres Challet 2008).

2 cum . . . exstiterim, | cumque . . . contulerimpraeter . . . (. . . meo): two long explanatory clauses (*cum* + pf. subj.), finely balanced (48~50 syllables) but varied (the first has the long abl. abs. *dimissis . . . erant* sandwiched within it, the second carries a *praeter* phrase as an appendix), set out P.'s recent and earlier generosity. These two acts will be capped by the third, *iubebo*, whose working out will occupy the rest of the letter, making an extended tricolon. *cum uero ego* (cf. 2.1.7n. *mihi*) flags his saving intervention. **ductus affinitatis officio** 'induced by the obligation of a family connection' (*OLD duco* 16c, *officium* 3a). On *officium*, a staple of *amicitia*, see Hellegouarc'h 1972: 152–63. For *ductus* cf. Quint. 12.11.6 *humanitatis . . . communi ductus officio* (also Sen. *Ira* 1.12.5); for *affinitatis officio* 'the obligation of [i.e. which comes with] a family connection', cf. 8.9.2 *amicitiae officium* (*TLL* IX.2 519.26–7, 41–55); also 3.9.31 (*inquisitionis*), 3.18.1 (*consulatus*). *affinitas* (*OLD* 1a) is usually connection through marriage, perhaps here through one of P.'s wives. It is this connection that justifies, even compels, the kindness; P. mentions no quality of Calvina's (contrast Firmus in 1.19) beyond an unspecified special claim to his generosity (§4 *in te uero . . .*). **dimissis omnibus qui** 'having paid off all those who' (abl. abs.), *OLD dimitto* 3b. **non dico molestiores sed diligentiores** 'on the scrupulous side, let me say, rather than troublesome' (see 2.1.4n. *durior* for the genteel comparatives). For *diligens* 'careful (with money)' (*OLD* 3), cf. 2.6.1 *diligentem* (≠ *sumptuosum*), 4.13.8 *de suo diligentes*, 6.8.5 *sui diligens*; see 2.16.1n. *pro.* For *molestus* (*OLD* 1a), cf. Sen. *Ep.* 21.11 *non . . . molestus creditor: paruo dimittitur.* Extra-syntactic *non dico* rejects the first word as too strong: cf. 9.14.1 *non dico ingenio (id enim superbum) sed studio et labore . . .*, 7.9.9, 7.17.9, 8.6.2; similarly 8.12.3 *ne dicam.* At *Pan.* 22.1 it rejects a term as too weak: *non dico quadriiugo curru . . . sed umeris hominum, quod arrogantius erat.* Both are types of the figure *praesumptio* (Quint. 9.2.18, K–S I 824–5, Lausberg §785). P. displays his own *diligentia* in 6.8, pursuing inherited debt with interest on a friend's behalf. **creditor solus exstiterim** 'I have come to be the sole creditor', *OLD exsisto* 2a. **uiuente eo nubenti tibi** 'while he was alive . . . (on) you at the time of your marriage', a parallel pair of abl. abs. and dat. (indirect object of *contulerim*). **in dotem centum milia** [*sc. nummum*] **contulerim** 'I bestowed a hundred thousand [sesterces] for a dowry' (*OLD in* 22a, *mille* 5c, *confero* 5a); for language and gift (textbook liberality: Cic. *Off.* 2.55), cf. 6.32.2 *puellae nostrae confero quinquaginta milia nummum* (50,000). *dotem conferre* sounds formal: cf. Lex Cincia *frag. Vat.* 304 (quoted as *Leg. publ.* 5 in *OLD confero* 5a) and jurists in *TLL* IV 176.57, 181.73–4, 184.78–80. P.'s gift, the only sum named in the letter, is substantial but not exceptional: besides 6.32 above, cf. 1.19 (300,000); 7.14 (P. sells land for 200,000 under its value). 'Pliny spares Calvina no detail' (S-W), but it is hard to judge whether contemporaries would have found such candid maths distasteful. At 3.19.8 P. is equally open about his own financial limitations (on a higher scale, of course). On dowries see *OCD* 'marriage law, Roman', Buckland 1963: 107–12, Treggiari 1991: 323–64. **praeter** 'over and above' (*OLD* 4a). **eam summam:** the size of her father's contribution (greater or smaller than P.'s?) is unspecified. **quasi de meo** 'effectively at my expense' (*OLD quasi* 8, *de* 7a). **dixit** 'set down' (*OLD* 11). P. evokes but avoids the common phrase *dotem dicere* (*TLL* V.1 978.32–7), so leaving it unclear whether he or the father had been legally responsible for the dowry (*contra* Tellegen 1982: 20), part of his self-promotion as virtual *pater* (above on CALVINAE). **(erat enim**

soluenda de meo) '(for it had to be paid at my expense)' (*OLD soluo* 19b; supply *ea summa* as subject), justifying *quasi de meo*. On parenthesis see 2.3.2n. *sed*; explanations with *enim* or *nam* are especially frequent: 2.6.2, 2.11.10, 2.13.4, 2.14.10, 13, 2.17.14 (so e.g. Tac. *H.* 2.18.1 with Ash; for *enim*, see *TLL* v.2 578.50–70, 582.80–583.33). Repetition in the parenthesis of a term outside it (*de meo*) is common (Oakley on Livy 8.7.2). Even the part of the dowry paid by her father was a loan from P., or (tendentiously) money that could otherwise have been used to repay him.   **magnum . . . pignus** 'substantial proof' (*OLD pignus* 3a), embracing the brief main clause (reached at last) in hyperbaton.   **facilitatis** 'readiness' (*OLD* 4, 6), a euphemism for generosity (cf. 8.2.8 *magno mihi seu ratio haec seu facilitas stetit, Pan.* 51.5 *congiari facilitas*).   **cuius fiduciā** 'trusting in which' (*OLD fiducia* 2b).   **debes** 'you must' (*OLD* 6a), a piquant choice of word in this debt-ridden letter (§1 *debuisset*; *debuit* below), especially given the *f* and *d* alliteration in *fiducia debes famam defuncti* (§1n. *fuisset*).   **famam defuncti pudoremque suscipere** 'take up the reputation and honour of the deceased', chiastically and sententiously reprising §1 *adires hereditatem* at the half-way point (75 words out of 157; 179 syllables out of 368); *defuncti* is substantival (2.3.9n. *dicentis*). *suscipere* (lit. 'catch') embraces 'make one's concern' (*OLD* 7a, 1.19.1 *suscipere augere dignitatem*), 'defend' (*OLD* 5a, 5.1.6 *defunctae pudorem tueretur*) and 'take up (a burden)' (2.9.5n. *suscipere*); her father's reputation is indeed a burden, not least thanks to this letter. The pairing of *pudor* 'self-respect' (*OLD* 3) with *fama* is common (e.g. Cic. *Fam.* 7.3.1, Sall. *Cat.* 16.2, V. *Aen.* 4.322–3); P. also matches it with *existimatio* + *dignitas* (2.9.1), *reuerentia* (2.14.4), *uirtus* (2.20.12), *maiestas* (3.20.4). On Roman ideas of 'honour' see first Lendon 1997: 30–106. If Calvina refused the inheritance, her father would suffer the *ignominia quae accidit ex uenditione bonorum* (Gai. *Inst.* 2.154) or from defaulting in death: she is obliged, then, not only by P.'s generosity, but also ethically. On the word-order (*coniunctio*) see 2.1.11n. *in.*

Ad quod te ne . . . horter 'so as not to urge this upon you . . . ' (lit. 'urge you to this'; *quod* = *famam . . . suscipere*). The second half of the letter (previous n.) will hold up for inspection P.'s third and principal benefaction.   **uerbis magis quam rebus horter:** cf. Livy 21.42.1 *rebus prius quam uerbis adhortandos*, Sall. *H.* fr. inc. 9 M. *ut res magis quam uerba agerentur*. The antithesis goes back to Thucydides' λόγῳ . . . ἔργῳ 'in word . . . in deed'.   **quidquid . . . debuit** 'all your father's debts to me' (*OLD quisquis* 2), object of *iubebo*.   **acceptum tibi fieri iubebo** 'I shall have . . . credited to you', i.e. I shall instruct my bankers to record the debts as paid. *acceptum* is a participle agreeing with *quidquid . . . debuit*; the phrase *acceptum facere/fieri* + dat. is an accounting term (*OLD acceptus* 2b, *TLL* 1 314.49–63): cf. 6.34.3 (metaphorical) *meruisti ut acceptum tibi fieret* 'you deserved to take the credit for it'; also 2.11.23 *accepisse* (with n.), 3.19.8 *accipiam* (borrowing), 7.14.1 *ut accipi iubeam a te* (receipt of a payment). P.'s bankers would be private staff rather than public *argentarii* (Andreau 1999, *BNP* 'argentarius [2]'). After the intricacies that preceded, this sentence proceeds in efficient tricolon (purpose, relative, main clauses, 13~11~11 syllables) to the commanding simplicity of *iubebo*, P.'s third, final and immediate demonstration of generosity.

3 nec est quod uerearis 'you have no reason to fear', anticipating Calvina's protests. For the prohibition *non est quod* + subjunctive, preferred by P. to *noli(te)* + infin. and to *ne* + pf. subj., see K–S II 278–9. He shifts during the *Epistles* from *non/nec est quod* (2.11.25, 1.2.5, 1.6.2, 3.14.5), the form preferred by Seneca (Hine 2005: 225 with n.47), to the *nihil est quod* used by Cicero (2.14.8, 4.29.1, 7.16.4).   **ne sit mihi onerosa ista donatio** 'that this gift will be a burden on me'; *onerosa* varies §1 *grauem*. On the legalities of gifts see S-W on 5.1.2.   **sunt quidem omnino nobis** 'I have, it is quite true, . . . '; *quidem* is concessive (2.1.7n.). *omnino* could be too (5.9.7, 6.15.3, *OLD* 6), but that would make unusual tautology; it seems rather to underline the whole assertion, as e.g. 1.17.3 and 3.11.1 *est omnino* + dat. (here *quidem* has displaced it from *sunt*); cf. 2.19.6 *est quidem omnino turpis ista discordia*. The first of a series of oscillations, as P. denies and yet implies that his generosity is excessive (*sed . . . §4 tamen . . . sed . . . uero*). He slips into an authorial plural (2.3.8n. *nosque*) for this discussion of his wealth, 'loftily modest' perhaps (Hoffer 1999: 104 on 1.8.6). For the free alternation of sg. and pl., cf. e.g. 1.8.4–5 *cunctationem nostram . . . cunctationis meae*, 2.13.10, 2.19.9 and (probably) 2.11.11; it is not special to P. (K–S I 88).   **modicae facultates** '(only) moderate means' (*OLD* 5 *facultates* 5b, the discreet term for wealth), opening an extended tricolon (7~7~23 syllables), AB~BA~BAA, each with different clausula. P.'s wealth, mostly in land (3.19.8), has been estimated at 12–15 million (S-W 149), 17 million (Duncan-Jones 1982: 20) or 20 million (Saller 2000a: 823) sesterces. Whatever the objective value of such calculations (De Neeve 1990: 370–1, id. 1992: 337), they indicate *modicae facultates* by comparison with super-rich Seneca and Narcissus, at 300 and 400 million respectively (see the 'rich list' in Duncan-Jones 1982: 343–4; also 2.20.13n. *sestertium*). Nevertheless, P. was perhaps somewhat above the senatorial average (Talbert 1984: 53 n.59). To modern taste his modesty verges on *illa iactatione* ['boasting'] *peruersa, si abundans opibus pauperem se . . . uocet* (Quint. 11.1.21).   **dignitas sumptuosa** 'expensive status' (*OLD dignitas* 3a), alluding politely to P.'s senatorial career (cf. 1.14.5), a costly business even in the principate: 6.32.1 *ratio ciuilium officiorum necessitatem quandam nitoris imponit*, 7.11.4 *ludis meis*, Talbert 1984: 54–66.   **reditus** 'revenue' (*OLD* 3), comprising rent from tenant-farmers (S-W 254–5), income from produce and occasional property sales. P. took 400,000 in a year from his Etruscan estates alone (10.8.5); S-W estimates an annual total towards one million.   **agellorum:** this faux-modest and perhaps affective diminutive, common in Martial (and well established before him: Hanssen 1953: 126–7), refers to P.'s and others' estates at 1.24.1, 5.14.8, 6.3.1, 8.15.2. On P's diminutives, a suitably informal element of his epistolary style (as of Cicero's), see D'Agostino 1931, Niemirska-Pliszczyńska 1955: 9–18, Guerrini 1997; also, generally, Hanssen 1953 (163–226 on Cicero).   **nescio minor an incertior** 'as slight as it is uncertain' (lit. 'I know not whether [to say] slighter or more uncertain'). For the pose of uncertainty (*dubitatio*), tantamount to strong assertion, cf. 3.3.1 *patrem tuum . . . suspexerim magis an amauerim dubitem* (my admiration and love were both immeasurable), 5.18.2, 8.12.1, Whitton 2011a. P. comments on his poor returns again at 2.15.2; see also 3.19.7 with S-W, 9.20.2, 9.37.2 with S-W; he takes voluntary losses in 7.14 and 8.2. On the hazards of agrarian investment see e.g. Purcell 1985; on P. as landowner see De Neeve 1990, id. 1992, Lo Cascio 2003 (with ample bibliography, p.282 n.6). **quod cessat ex reditu | frugalitate suppletur** 'the shortfall in revenue is made up by modest living', chiastic. A paradoxical way of saying that P.'s outgoings are still lower than his income: cf. 6.8.5 (thrifty Atilius Crescens) *nullus illi nisi ex frugalitate reditus, Pan.* 41.1 *an tantas uires habet frugalitas principis ut tot impendiis . . . sola sufficiat?*, Cic. *Par.* 49–51 *non intellegunt homines quam magnum uectigal sit parsimonia . . . non esse cupidum pecunia est* etc.; Sen. *Tranq.* 9.1 *cum . . . possit ipsa paupertas in diuitias se, aduocata frugalitate, conuertere.* Such *frugalitas* features recurrently in P.'s lexicon of praise (1.22.4, 4.19.2, 5.19.9, *Pan.* 3.4, etc.) and is prominent in 2.6.4–5. His generosity seems regularly to come from spare annual income (S-W 150). **cessat** 'is lacking' (*OLD* 7b, *TLL* III 961.54–67): cf. 6.34.3 *Africanae* ['wild beasts'] *. . . cessauerint,* Mart. 9.98.2 *prouentus cessauerit,* [Quint.] *Decl. mai.* 12.4 *fructus cessauit.* **ex qua uelut fonte:** *fons* 'source, origin' is a common metaphor (*OLD* 4), but P. flags it with an apologetic *uelut* ('as it were', *OLD* 4) and spins it out (*decurrit, profusione inarescat*), still working the paradox of *frugalitas* as an active source of money. The image opens discussions of *liberalitas* at Cic. *Off.* 2.52 *largitio . . . fontem ipsum benignitatis exhaurit* and Val. Max. 4.8.1 (below on *ei*). Cicero (*Off.* 1.42–9, 2.52–5) warns against excess, but endorses considered assistance with *inter alia* dowries and debt. **liberalitas:** the key term. Whatever Cicero's ideals (*Off.* 2.52–3), *liberalitas* is always, for P. at least, a matter of cash (e.g. 5.7.4, 6.34.2). When practised properly (9.30) it is a virtue, not least of emperors (*Pan. passim,* Noreña 2001: 160–4). P.'s own *amor liberalitatis* (1.8.9) was well proved already in book 1: cf. 1.8 with Hoffer 1999: 93–110, 1.19 with Henderson 2002b; Manning 1985: 74–5, Griffin 2003a: 103–6, Griffin 2007, and intro. **decurrit** 'flows down' (*OLD* 2a). Verb and metaphor recur at 3.20.12 *uelut riui ex illo benignissimo fonte decurrunt,* where Trajan is the *fons* (touched with divinity by allusion to Sen. *Ben.* 4.4.3, as he is in the paired 4.25.5 by quotation of Plato) and senatorial participation in governance is the flowing largesse. This correspondence between P.'s noble generosity and Trajan's may be coincidence, as P. mirrors on a smaller scale the virtues of his *princeps* (2.6.3n. *cunctisque*; cf. 6.31.14 and 6.32, modest Trajanic and Plinian munificence juxtaposed; on imperial *liberalitas* see Kloft 1970, Manning 1985), the flipside of the 'leader as example' topos (Woodman on Vell. 2.126.5, Edwards 1993: 28).

4 quae = *liberalitas.* **tamen . . . sed . . . uero:** §3n. **sunt. temperanda est** 'must be moderated' (*OLD* 4a). **ita . . . ne nimia profusione inarescat** 'in such a way that it does not dry up from too abundant a flow' (after Radice). The metaphor continues with *inarescat* (cf. Pl. *NH* 31.51 *inarescunt fontes*) and etymological play on *profusio,* a noun commonly used of spending (*OLD* 3 'extravagance') but watery in derivation (*OLD* 1–2a). The referent has switched from *frugalitas* to *liberalitas* (for comparable shifts in metaphor see 2.8.3n. *tot*, 2.10.4n. *a qua*, 2.12.3n. *exsectum*). The last hurdle to P.'s munificence, which he surmounts but leaves clearly visible, is the risk that it is extravagant. **sed temperanda in aliis; in te uero . . . constabit:** self-correction (2.1.10n. *si*) through repetition of *temperanda* (*sc. est*). The chiastically opposed *in aliis* | *in te* (*OLD in* 42 'in the case of'), together with *uero*, adversative and climactic (1.7n. *mihi*), drives home the message that Calvina is receiving exceptional treatment. **facile ei ratio constabit** 'its books will easily balance', 'it will be easily accounted for'. *ei* (= *liberalitati*) is Keil's correction of *et* (Fγ, omitted in α), supported by *Pan.* 38.4 *cui ratio non constat*. The book-keeping metaphor *ratio constat* (*OLD consto* 10b, *TLL* IV 533.44–61), hitherto quite rare, is popular with P. (1.5.16, 1.9.1 etc.). Here he blends the metaphorical use with the literal, since accounting is precisely the point (Sen. *Ben.* 4.10.2 *non est autem beneficium nisi quod ratione datur*): cf. Val. Max. 4.8.1 *liberalitatis . . . duo sunt maxime probabiles fontes, uerum iudicium et honesta beneuolentia: nam cum ab his orietur, tunc demum ei ratio constat.* As in 1.8 and *Pan.* 38.4 (intro.), P. insists that generosity is truly generous only when it is calculated. **ratio:** probably *ratiŏ*. Correption (shortening of the final vowel) in *-io* nouns was by now widespread; although dactylic verse retains (as it must) *ratiō* (Sil. *Pun.* 8.330, Juv. 7.1), the rhythms of P., as of Seneca and Quintilian, strongly suggest *ratiŏ* (contrast 2.2.2n. *excusatio*). It makes a common clausula (resolved cretic + spondee) here and at 1.5.16 *ratio constabit*, 1.8.4 *deducet*, 5.8.14 *nascatur*, 9.1.4 *praecīdit*, *Pan.* 25.2 *seruata est*, 38.5 *non constat*, and others at 3.6.6 *permiserit*, 4.15.13 *contulerit*, 5.12.1 *recitandi* and 6.16.16 *rationem*. **etiam si modum excesserit** 'even if it exceeds the (proper) limit' (fut. pf.), a final paradoxical twist: the books will balance despite P.'s spending beyond the limit that his *modicae facultates* should allow. He thus undercuts one last time the claim that he *can* afford his kindness, and cheerfully ignores Cic. *Off.* 1.42–4 *ne maior benignitas sit quam facultates*, 2.55 *modus adhibeatur isque referatur ad facultates*, showing that for all his carefully worked *ratio* a human, sentimental generosity wins out. Of course *optimus . . . modus est: quis negat?* (1.20.20), but P. similarly fails to observe due limits in praise of friends (7.28.1) and in his love for them (8.24.10; Caninius returns the favour in 6.21.6). *modum excedere* gravitates strikingly to the ends of letters (2.5.13, 2.10.8, 3.11.8, 8.6.17) and books (7.33.10, 8.24.10; 10.116–17 just fails to follow the trend, so glancingly evoking the epistolary concern for brevity (2.2.2n. *plurimas*).

5

Here is part of the speech you have been asking for. Be severe, but indulgent too. As in a dinner, not everything may please everyone, but variety should give universal appeal. I know it is hard to judge out of context, but like the limb of a statue it can be assessed on its own merits. I have gone on too long: my letter, like the speech, should be moderate.

An important and programmatic letter, placed a quarter of the way through the book. The revision and publication of speeches is a key theme, established in 1.2 and kept running throughout the *Epistles* (2.19.1n. *recitem*), and this speech incidentally reveals P. patronising his home town Comum, making a patronal trio with needy Calvina (2.4) and young Avitus (2.6), and pointing the difference between the abstract delights of Isaeus (2.3.intro.) and the real-world import of P.'s own rhetorical pursuits. Yet epistolarity is equally if not more in sight, as P. stakes a double claim for variety (§7, at the centre) and the fragment (§§10–12), two core features of his epistolary aesthetics. The letter is framed with allusions to the opening and close of book 1 of the *Institutio oratoria*, the great tract on oratorical training published recently (AD 90s) by P.'s former mentor Quintilian (§1n. *efflagitatam*, §13n. *longius*; 2.14.9n. *Quintiliano*). P. thus advertises proemial status (through the choice of Quintilian's first book) and pointedly shrinks over 17,000 words of oratorical tract to a 371-word miniature, playing out his epistolary programme for the small scale and flagging up this manifesto for the paradoxical 'perfect part' (§12 *pars... perfecta*). Meta-epistolary intent is subtly underlined by the pair of analogies, dinner and statue, which – surely not by accident – provide the subjects of the following letters, 2.6 (dinner) and 2.7 (statue). The fifth position also seems significant, aligning it with the important 1.5 (Regulus, and P.'s oratory) and 3.5 (Pliny the Elder), while the addressee pairs it with 9.26, P.'s great, late defence of the grand style and the last long letter of the collection. Epistle 9.26 in turn responds clearly to 1.20, the longest letter of book 1 (advocating length in oratory), which introduces the topic of variety (1.20.12–13) developed here. A letter which at first sight typifies P.'s epistolary slightness thus turns out also to be an important programmatic piece which could well be called a 'second proem' (Whitton forthcoming).

LVPERCO also receives 9.26 (above, §5n. *idem*); he is otherwise unknown, unlikely to be the Lupercus(es) mocked in Mart. 1.117, 3.75, 4.28, etc. S-W 150 finds a possible match in Gallia Narbonensis.

1 Actionem... exhibui tibi 'here is the speech... for you to look at'. P. restricts *actio* (*OLD* 5) to forensic speeches (2.11.16, 2.19.2, 1.18.1, etc.), usually emphasising speech as (original) performance: cf. 1.20.9 *aliud est actio* ['speech'] *bona, aliud oratio* ['script'] and the antitheses in 4.21.3 *actione mea librisque*, 5.20.3 *actionibus... liber*; Quint. 12.10.49–51. Here, however, as at 5.20.8, it describes the written-up version. P. does not specify the occasion (typical of his 'evasive display', Morello 2003: 196–202), but it was evidently on behalf of his *patria* Comum (§§3, 5), perhaps in a case concerning municipal property, like that in 6.18; it presumably preceded Jan. 98, when P. dropped all advocacy for three years (Intro. 16). This cannot be the civic (non-forensic) speech of 1.8, nor the complete speech of 1.2 (*pace* S-W). **et a te frequenter efflagitatam et a me saepe promissam:** the bicolon (11~8 syllables) puts more weight on Lupercus' demands than P.'s promises. For the synonymous adverbs cf. [Quint.] *Decl. min.* 362.1 *saepe... frequenter* and the responsion of 1.1.1 *frequenter hortatus es* ~ 9.1.1 *saepe te monui*. **efflagitatam:** the verb recurs at 5.10.1 *efflagitantur*, of

Suetonius' poetry (see Power 2010: 152–3). The simplex *flagitare* is commoner (1.8.1, 4.14.1, 9.2.1, 9.25.1), but the compound has apt epistolary precedent in Cic. *Q. fr.* 2.10(9).1 *epistulam hanc conuicio efflagitarunt codicilli tui*, 3.1.11 *orationes efflagitatas... exsolui*, and also Quint. *pr.*1–3 (his prefatory letter) *efflagitasti cotidiano conuicio ut libros... emittere inciperem... efflagitantur*; this last will emerge as a primary target (§13n. *longius*). From beginning to end of the collection P. justifies his letters with others' demands: 1.1.1 *frequenter hortatus es ut epistulas... publicarem*; 9.40.1 *scribis pergratas tibi fuisse litteras meas* (cf. 2.19.1 *hortaris*, about a recital). Such openings may be 'formulaic' (S-W 6–7), but *frequenter* is only here and 1.1.1: a hint at the programmatic importance of this letter? **exhibui tibi** 'I offer for your inspection, I show you', *OLD exhibeo* 1a, as 1.2.1, 3.10.4, 4.27.5, 7.2.2 (at 5.10.1 it is different, a legal joke: *OLD* 1b). The perfect is 'epistolary', adopting the reader's point of view. It is common in Cicero, especially with verbs of writing and sending at the opening or close of a letter, e.g. *Att.* 1.19.10 *commentarium... misi ad te* (K–S 1 156–9, Mellet 1988: 189–206, Rauzy 2002). P. uses such tenses far less (3.13.1 and 7.12.1 *misi*, 7.19.11 and 8.23.8 *scriberem*, 8.15.1 *oneraui te*; also 6.4.2 *cupiebam*); contrast 1.2.1 *librum... exhibeo*, and see 2.1.12n. *uolui*, 2.14.1n. *miraris*. As in Cicero, the tense switches freely to present (§2 *rogo*) and indeed future (§13 *faciam*). On P.'s epistolary tenses see Kraut 1872: 38; Stout 1949 denies their existence. **nondum tamen totam** sets the theme, the fragment. **perpolitur** 'is receiving the final [*per-*] polish'. *polire* is a standard term in literary criticism; *perpolire* is first attested in *Rhet. Her.* 4.18, defining oratorical *compositio*, and is common in Cicero. The metaphor was more live in a world of papyrus rolls, whose ends were smoothed off (*expoliri*) with pumice (cf. Cat. 1.2 with Quinn). The alliterative paradox in *pars... per-*, incompletion and completion, is reprised in §12 *pars... perfecta*.

2 quae...uidebantur 'the parts that seemed' (*sc. ea*: 2.1.10n. *qua*), subject of the infinitive *tradi* after *non fuit alienum*. **absolutiora:** less assertive than *absoluta*, whether the comparative is true ('more finished' *sc.* than the rest) or genteel (2.1.4n. *durior*; cf. 1.1.1 *paulo curatius*). **uidebantur...fuit:** epistolary tenses (§1n. *exhibui*). **non...alienum** 'not inappropriate' (*OLD* 9), faux-diffident litotes. **iudicio:** terms for critical judgment (*OLD* 11a–b) and taste, scrupulously varied, abound in this tract on variety: §3 *existimationi*, §4 *fastidium... deliciasque, commendationem*, §5 *auribus*, §7 *genera lectorum, naturam, commendet*, §8 *laudare, stomachus*, §11 *iudicare*, §12 *existimatur*. **tradi** 'to be entrusted' (*OLD* 6), with *iudicio tuo* instead of *tibi* as indirect object (e.g. Sall. *Cat.* 35.6 *tuaeque fidei trado*). **rogo...accommodes** 'please... give', *OLD accommodo* 4b (only here in P.). Paratactic indirect command (jussive subjunctive, instead of an *ut*-clause) is very frequent in P.'s letters (Lagergren 1872: 161–2, Schuster 1926: 54–5), as in Cicero's. The effect seems colloquial (though that is a slippery term: Chahoud 2010 and e.g. 2.3.2n. *sed*). **intentionem** 'attention, devotion', common in P. (Cowan and Merrill on 1.3.2). Literally 'tension' (*OLD* 1), it often implies (determined) application (e.g. 1.3.2 *intentione rei familiaris*, 3.5.17 of workaholic Pliny the

Elder). **scribentis** 'of a writer' (substantival: 2.3.9n. *dicentis*), *sc.* not merely of a reader. Cf. Quint. 10.1.20 on the need to study the best authors *diligenter ac prope ad scribendi sollicitudinem* (Gierig); also *Ep.* 7.9.2 *quae legentem fefellissent transferentem* ['someone translating'] *fugere non possunt.* **nihil...deberem:** an assertion which makes P.'s failure to identify it the more remarkable, but which also eases the slippage between speech and letter in what follows (intro.). **inter manus habui** 'I have had in hand', as 5.5.7 (*OLD manus* 13a). *inter manus* (*TLL* VIII 364.39–53) is rarer than *in manibus*, which P. normally favours (4.13.1 etc.). Tac. *D.* 3.1 and *An.* 3.16.1 has scrolls being held *inter manus*, a subsidiary sense here. **sollicitudinem praestare** 'accord... care', *OLD sollicitudo* 3 (esp. Quint. 10.1.20, quoted above), *praesto* 9, doubly varying *intentionem... accommodes.* **deberem:** generic subj. For the imperfect subjunctive after a main verb translated as 'present perfect' (as *habui* must be), violating the so-called 'sequence of tenses', cf. e.g. §7 *teneremus*, 2.16.2 *tuerer*, 1.1.1 *frequenter hortatus es ut epistulas... colligerem publicaremque.* It is not special to P.: e.g. Cic. *Pis.* frag. 1, Sen. *Clem.* 1.1.1, Juv. 7.3–5 with Kenney 1962: 21 n.4; K–S II 179.

3 in ceteris... in hac: parallel antithesis, with *existimationi hominum* and *subicietur* in double *apo koinou*; supply *subiciuntur* in the first colon by syllepsis (2.1.2n. *legit*). **existimationi** 'judgment' (*OLD* 2a), varying §2 *iudicium.* **diligentia... fides... pietas:** graded tricolon. *diligentia* is P.'s routine care, not least in court (1.20.11); *fides* 'honour, integrity' is *inter alia* a canonical lawyerly virtue (2.9.4, 2.11.2, 3.4.4, etc.); Plinian *fides* is discussed by Barbuti 1994. The two are paired again in 8.6.10 (a senatorial decree). The emotionally resonant *pietas*, loving duty to family or homeland, caps them both (cf. *etiam*). **nostra:** authorial plurals cluster in §3 and §§6–7, tending to attach themselves to P. the orator and (public) writer, while P. the correspondent tends to be sg. (Marouzeau 1962: 225, S–W 511; cf. 2.3.8n. *nosque*). **etiam** 'in addition' (*OLD* 3a). **inde:** from the fact that *pietas* is also at stake. **et:** along with P.'s *sollicitudo.* **liber** 'scroll', i.e. 'book', commonly of a written-up speech (2.1.5n.), as here. **creuit:** the seed of a horticultural metaphor which sprouts in §4 *reseca.* **dum** 'as', *OLD* 4a. It opens a bicolon (14~17 syllables) with verbs framing their object in the first colon (*ornare patriam et amplificare*), objects framing the verb in the second (*defensioni... seruimus et gloriae*), in varied *coniunctio* (2.1.11n. *in*). **ornare patriam et amplificare** 'honour and extol my native land' (*OLD orno* 6, *amplifico* 3), i.e. enlarge its reputation through oratory (not with cash, *pace* S–W): cf. Cic. *De or.* 1.221 *orator... dicendo amplificat atque ornat*, Quint. 3.7.6 *proprium laudis est amplificare et ornare*, Cic. *Leg.* 1.5 *patriae... quae... sit ornata* (by a work of history); for such encomia of places see Quint. 3.7.26–7. The passage from *De legibus* takes *patria* as *res publica*, as does Val. Max. 3.2.6 *pro amplificanda et tuenda patria*; for P. here, as usual, it means his home town, Comum. P. amply stages his love for it in letters (even if he spends far more time in Etruria: Champlin 2001), and proved it in life with benefactions; the latter were immortalised on stone (*CIL* v 5262 = *ILS* 2927: Eck 2001, G–M

270–3). **gaudemus** 'take/took delight in' + infin. (quite rare): *OLD* 1e, esp. Quint. 1.2.30 (the orator's *animus*) *aliquid magnum agere gaudet*. The English tense depends whether one takes *creuit* as 'grew' or 'has grown' (probably the latter: §5n. *erunt*); *dum* takes present tense either way. **pariterque et:** *-que* links back, *et* ('both') looks forward, with *pariter* embracing *defensioni* and *gloriae* (as always with *pariterque et... et*: 1.8.1, Livy 31.35.6, Ov. *Met.* 11.556 etc.). **defensioni:** evidently Comum was the defendant (*possessor*) in the case. Others conjure up unlikely new meanings. **seruimus** 'put myself at the service of', a standard metaphor from slavery (*OLD* 3a). For *gloriae seruire* (common in Cicero, e.g. *Cat.* 1.23 *seruire meae laudi et gloriae*) cf. 1.8.13 *propriae laudi seruisse*; with *defensioni* the compound *deseruire* might otherwise be expected (cf. 7.7.2 *deseruire studiis*, 7.15.1 *amicis deseruio*), aural considerations apart (*de- de-*). **gloriae:** the acme is saved for last.

4 haec ipsa: the passages in praise of Comum. **quantum ratio exegerit** 'as much as necessary' (lit. 'as much as reason demands', fut. pf., *OLD ratio* 5a, *exigo* 9): cf. (only) 2.17.23 *ut ratio exigit*, Sen. *Ep.* 14.2 *cum exiget ratio*, Quint. 4.1.24 *id exiget ratio*. Commoner are *ratio/res poscit/postulat* (e.g. 7.12.1). **reseca** 'prune'. As well as Hor. *C.* 1.11.7 *spem longam reseces*, the metaphor is several times in Cicero (*OLD* 1b). **ad fastidium legentium deliciasque respicio** 'I consider the fastidiousness and caprices of readers' (*OLD fastidium* 5, *delicia* 5c, *respicio* 6b), the third *coniunctio* within a few lines (§3n. *dum*). *fastidium* is pejorative of (hyper)critical attitudes: Kaster 2001, esp. 167–8 on 6.17.5; cf. 7.12.3 (playfully) *beneficio fastidi tui*. P. often uses *deliciae* affectively (e.g. 1.3.1 *Comum, tuae meaeque deliciae*); he applies it to literary taste only here and, damningly, 1.20.23 *inertibus quorum delicias desidiamque quasi iudicium respicere ridiculum est*. Here he is less adamant, criticising bad taste but accepting (in some measure) its demands. P.'s disdain (a *fastidium* of its own: cf. Kaster 2001: 188) matches Sen. *Contr.* 3.*pr*.14–15 *utrum ergo putas hoc dicentium uitium esse an audientium? non illi peius dicunt, sed hi corruptius iudicant*, Quint. 10.1.43 *recens haec lasciuia deliciaeque et omnia ad uoluptatem multitudinis imperitae composita*. But where Seneca and Quintilian criticise oratorical audiences, P. is criticising readers of the published speech, a much smaller group. He does the same in 1.8.17, implicitly calling that readership a *uulgus*; the effect is to situate readers of the *Epistles* as confidants, members of a fantasy inner circle who can share P.'s disdain for the 'common' reader. Cf. 2.19.9n. *eruditissimum*, Intro. 5. **respicio, intellego:** standard juxtaposition at clause-break. **commendationem** 'approval' (*OLD* 4). **et** 'also'. **mediocritate:** moderation in length, not P.'s usual preference for speeches (1.20, 9.4, Gamberini 1983: 32–7) but an epistolary leitmotif (§13n. *longius*). **petendam** sc. *esse*, gerundive of obligation, an obligation P. accepts only with reluctance.

5 idem tamen qui a te hanc austeritatem exigo 'yet at the same time as demanding this severity from you' (lit. 'yet I the same man who...', *OLD idem* 10b). For *austeritas* 'severity' cf. Sen. *Polyb.* 8.4, also of composition and likewise contrasted with *remissa frons* (*TLL* II 1557.26–34); also Hor. *AP* 342 *austera poemata* (unappealing to the young: cf. *adulescentium* below). It would seem to come naturally to Lupercus as a critic (9.26.5, 13). **cogor:** more obligation (cf. §4 *exegerit, petendam*, §5 *exigo*), now the other way, in staged vacillation (cf. §4 *tamen* . . . §5 *tamen*). **in plerisque** 'in many places'. **frontem remittas** 'put severity aside', 'be indulgent' (lit. 'relax your brow'). *frons* (*OLD* 2) often expresses censorial severity; Seneca first has it with *remittere* (*Polyb.* 8.4, as above). Cf. 9.17.2 *uis tu remittere aliquid ex rugis?* 'will you stop frowning a bit?' **sunt enim quaedam . . . danda** 'for admittedly some concessions must be made' (*OLD do*[1] 16a). The position of *sunt* implies the concession ('admittedly'), countered in §6 *tamen*. **adulescentium auribus** 'to the taste of the young', a common use of *aures* (*OLD* 4). Such indulgence is advocated by Cic. *De or.* 2.88, *Brut.* 326, Quint. 2.4.3–14, 11.1.31–2. The phrase *auribus danda* is matched only by Quint. 12.10.45 *ne illis quidem nimium repugno qui dandum putant nonnihil esse temporibus atque auribus nitidius aliquid atque affectius postulantibus*, a comparable concession (see Quint. 12.10.45–8 and 2.10.10 *paulum aliquid inclinare ad uoluptatem audientium debemus*), though P. goes a little further (below). **materiā** 'topic, material' (*OLD* 7a). **non refragetur** (< *refragari*) 'does not militate against'. The subjunctive generalises ('universal present', G–L §595 R.3). **descriptiones locorum . . . non historice tantum sed prope poetice:** history was *proxima poetis et quodam modo carmen solutum* (Quint. 10.1.31) but P. ventures a half-step (*prope*) further. The adverb *historice* is attested only here before the 4c. AD. Topographical descriptions were a convention in historiography (Martin–Woodman on Tac. *An.* 4.33.3 *situs gentium*; Lucian *De hist. conscr.* 57 warns against overenthusiasm), and Quintilian mentions *descriptio regionum* (4.3.12) as suitable for a digression, where a little *historico . . . nitore* (10.1.33) is permissible. So far P. is in line with that, but in flirting with poetry (*prope poetice*) he accommodates modern taste (Tac. *D.* 20.5 (Aper) *exigitur enim iam ab oratore etiam poeticus decor* with Gudeman) at the risk of violating his teacher's precepts: cf. Quint. 2.4.3 *descriptionibus, in quas plerique imitatione poeticae licentiae ducuntur*, 10.2.21 *id quoque uitandum, in quo magna pars errat, ne in oratione poetas nobis et historicos . . . imitandos putemus*. Yet in declamations Quintilian makes some allowances: 10.5.15 *historiae nonnumquam ubertas in aliqua exercendi stili parte ponenda . . . ne carmine quidem ludere contrarium fuerit*. That last passage is clearly in mind at *Ep.* 7.9.8–9 *nam saepe in oratione quoque non historica modo sed prope poetica descriptionum necessitas incidit . . . fas est et carmine remitti . . . lusus uocantur* [cf. Quintilian's *ludere*], *sed . . .*, where P. reprises both *non historice tantum sed prope poetice* and *fas est* from the present passage. What was for Quintilian the stuff of exercises (*exercendi stili*) becomes in P. the acceptable manner for published speeches: a turn away from the master's attempt to restrict oratory to a forensic ideal detached from poetry, that *genus ostentationi comparatum* (Quint. 10.1.28–9), towards a view of the published oration as an epideictic genre in itself. Cf. 2.3, 2.10.7n. *qui*, 2.19.intro. **frequentiores** 'rather frequent' (2.1.4n. *durior*). **erunt:** the growth of the book (§3 *creuit*) is not yet complete, even as P. requests pruning. **prosequi** 'give treatment to' (*OLD* 8b). **fas** 'not forbidden', certainly in 7.9.9 (above), and so probably here too, with Quint. 10.5.15 as his authority (cf. Veyne 1967: 726–7).

6 quod: acc. object of *fecisse*, referring to *descriptiones...prosequi*. **exstiterit** 'is found, comes along' (*OLD exsto* 3a, Cic. *Cael.* 33), fut. pf. **putet:** generic subjunctive. **laetius fecisse** 'done so more richly'. For the use of *facere* to reprise an earlier verbal idea (here *prosequi*), see *OLD* 26a, not necessarily absolute (*quod...fecisse* here, and e.g. §10 *id facere*, 2.20.6 *facit hoc*). In *laetus* P. marries the plant metaphor of §3 *creuit* and §4 *reseca* (*OLD laetus* 1a) with critical terminology (*OLD* 2; Reinhardt–Winterbottom on Quint. 2.4.4). It connotes poetical licence in lexis and metaphor (e.g. Quint. 11.1.34, commenting on Cic. *Arch.* 19 *saxa atque solitudines uoci respondent*): cf. 9.33.1 *laetissimo...planeque poetico ingenio*; also 3.18.10 *laetioris stili*, describing *Pan.*, with Picone 1978: 82. **orationis** 'oratory', as a genre: cf. 5.8.9, *TLL* IX.2 880.58–881.10. **ut ita dixerim:** a variant on the common *ut ita dicam*, first in Quintilian (3×) and only here in P. (he has *ut ita dicam* 3×, and *ut sic dixerim*, also first in Quintilian, at *Pan.* 42.3). **tristitiam** 'austerity' (*OLD* 3), implying excessive *seueritas* (cf. 1.10.7), hence the tempering *ut ita dixerim*: cf. Cic. *Or.* 53 *et seueritatem quandam...et...quasi maestitiam*. **actionis:** §1n. **exorare** 'mollify', apt here as (possibly) a rhetorical term (Quint. 11.1.52, *TLL* V.2 1587.22–8); the construction with abstract subject and especially object (*tristitiam*) looks poetic (*OLD exoro* 1a, end of entry; Sil. *Pun.* 11.549), a nice irony if so. **debebunt** 'ought to'.

7 annisi...sumus 'I have done my best' (*OLD* 2a). This crucial sentence sits at the mid-point: *annisi...teneremus* is preceded by 178 words, followed by 180. **certe** 'at any rate' (*OLD* 2a). **ut quamlibet diuersa genera lectorum | per plures dicendi species teneremus** 'to hold the attention of every different sort [lit. 'sorts however diverse'] of reader by using more than one type of oratory', *OLD teneo* 22a, *species* 10a; ABC~ACB isocolon (13~13 syllables). P. echoes the manifesto of Quint. 12.10.69–72 (esp. 12.10.69 *plures igitur etiam eloquentiae facies...utetur enim* [*orator*], *ut res exiget, omnibus*), but where Quintilian talks of varying style as the moment demands, P.'s concern is with the differing tastes of his audience: so too 1.20.12–13 *aliud alios mouet...uaria sunt hominum iudicia...omnibus ergo dandum est aliquid quod teneant*; 4.14.3 *ipsa uarietate temptamus efficere ut alia aliis, quaedam fortasse omnibus placeant*. For the tense of *teneremus* see §2n. *deberem*. **sicut...ita** 'although...nevertheless' (*OLD sicut* 1c), a large-scale bicolon (28~28 syllables) with rhyming initial main verbs and paired subordinate clauses (*ueremur ne* ~ *uidemur posse confidere ut*), arranged ABCD~BACD (*quibusdam pars* [variety] *probetur* ~ *uniuersitatem omnibus* [variety] *commendet*), with further variety in their verbs (passive/active) and so cases (nom. *pars* ~ acc. *uniuersitatem*). **ne quibusdam...non probetur:** 'that some may not approve of' (lit. 'that...may not meet with the approval of some'); *quibusdam* is dat. with *probari* (*OLD* 2b, passive). **secundum suam cuiusque naturam** 'each according to his temperament' (*OLD natura* 11), i.e. 'taste' (Cowan). *suam* refers to the logical subject (*quibusdam*), not the grammatical one (G–L §309.2). **uidemur posse confidere:** confidence is carefully hedged around. **ut . . . commendet:** a unique purpose clause after *confidere*, by analogy with other verbs of expectation (K–S II 225, reading '2.5.7' for '9.26.13'), and generating the parallel *ueremur ne ~ uidemur . . . ut.* **uniuersitatem** 'the entirety' of the speech; cf. 3.15.5 *de uniuersitate . . . de partibus*, 9.4.2. **uarietas ipsa commendet:** *OLD commendo* 6a 'make attractive'. The delights of variety were proverbial (μεταβολὴ πάντων γλυκύ 'change is pleasant in all things', Otto 1890: 361, Tosi 1991: 361), and *uarietas* is famously a hallmark of P.'s letters: these words accordingly demand to be read as comment not just on his speeches but also on the *Epistles* themselves (Peter 1901: 110, Goetzl 1952, Cova 1966: 37–8, Picone 1978: 65–6, Pausch 2004: 67–8).

8 et 'likewise' (*OLD* 5a), introducing an implicit analogy. **in ratione conuiuiorum** = *in conuiuiis*, a Ciceronian periphrasis in which *ratio* has lost almost all meaning: e.g. Cic. *Brut.* 120 *in ratione dicendi* 'in (the business of) speaking', *Att.* 1.2.1 *in ratione petitionis* 'in the campaign' (Shackleton Bailey); so too Quint. 2.5.9 *in ratione eloquendi*, *Ep.* 1.8.13 *in ratione edendi* (*OLD ratio* 13d 'procedure' is unhelpful). The comparison of writer to host, reader to diner is widespread, not least in Quintilian (e.g. 10.1.19): Bramble 1974: 45–59, Gowers 1993: 41–2, 220–79, esp. 267–79 on 1.15 as epistolary *hors d'oeuvre*; cf. 7.3.5 *ut enim si cenam tibi facerem, dulcibus acres acutosque miscere*. See especially Hor. *Ep.* 2.2.61–4 (trying to please readers who demand *uario multum diuersa palato*), Mart. 10.59.3–4, Quint. 1.12.5 *. . . sicut in cibis, quorum diuersitate reficitur stomachus et pluribus minore fastidio alitur*, 10.1.58 (on *uarietas*). Coincidence of topic with the following 2.6 underlines the meta-epistolary intent (intro.). **quamuis a plerisque cibis singuli temperemus** 'although each of us may hold back from many of the dishes', *OLD plerusque* 4 (or 3 'most'), *tempero* 3a. A diner might sample only some of the dishes offered (cf. Ov. *Ars* 1.577–8 *et quemcumque cibum digitis libauerit illa,* | *tu pete*); they came in succession, like the sections of the speech, rather than all at once. Similarly 9.4.2 advises dipping in and out of a speech (a strategy easily transferred to a letter-collection: §4n. *mediocritate*). With *temperemus* P. has moved from 'all-accommodating host' to 'suave guest' (Gowers 1993: 268), styling himself one of the reading community. **nec ea quae stomachus noster recusat adimunt gratiam illis quibus capitur** 'and the things that our palate rejects do not diminish the attractions of those that please it' (lit. ' . . . do not remove the attraction from those things by which it is pleased'; *illis* is dative of disadvantage), *OLD gratia* 6a, *capio* 17, with typical verbal juxtaposition (*recusat adimunt*). For *stomachus* 'palate' (*OLD* 3a), cf. 7.3.5 *stomachus . . . excitaretur*, Quint. 1.12.5 (above).

9 haec ego sic accipi uolo, non tamquam . . . sed tamquam 'I want this to be taken as implying not that . . . but rather that' (*OLD accipio* 21a, *tamquam* 7a; K–S II 456 §8b); *haec* (neut. pl.) refers to what precedes (primarily *uidemur posse confidere*), while *sic* looks forward to *tamquam*. The language looks contemporary: Quint. 2.3.10 *quod . . . sic accipi potest tamquam*, Tac. *D.* 10.3 *neque hunc meum sermonem*

sic accipi uolo tamquam. **assecutum** 'achieved' (*OLD* 3). **laborauerim:** P.
prefers non-syncopated to syncopated perfect forms of *-are* verbs by about 4:1 (for
pluperfects see 2.1.8n. *renuntiasset*); rhythm is often a factor, though often (as here)
either form makes a common clausula: variety seems to play a part. **si modo
tu curam tuam admoueris** 'if you will only give your attention' (*OLD si* 8a,
admoueo 7c, fut. pf.), emphatically reintroducing Lupercus (*tu . . . tuam*) and varying
the request of §2 *his tu rogo intentionem . . . accommodes.* **interim istis, mox iis
quae sequuntur** 'for now to what you have here, in due course to what follows',
OLD iste 5b; for *mox* 'in due course, presently' (not 'soon') see Rose 1927. The
present tense is logical and perhaps casual (e.g. Cic. *Diu.* 1.126 *cur . . . ea . . . quae
sequuntur futura sint, Fam.* 2.10.4, 2.15.1); the variant *sequentur* (F) looks like a scribal
'correction' (Intro. 38).

10 dices: *occupatio* (2.3.9n.). For a similarly forestalled objection to reading unfin-
ished works, see 8.4.6–7 (P. offering to read fragments) *spectabuntur ut membra* (cf.
membrum below, §11). **cognoueris:** pf. subj., representing fut. pf. in direct speech
(*NLS* §280; the forms in this case are identical). **fateor** accepts the objection
before persisting (*tamen*): cf. 1.12.11–12 *scio* (×3) *. . . ego tamen* and 2.3.9n. *etiam.* P.
makes a similar move, on the same topic, in 8.4.7 (*scio. itaque . . .*). **in praesentia** 'for now', listed in *OLD praesens* 16b, but probably abl. fem. sg. of *praesentia*
(*TLL* x.2 857.49–52; cf. ἐν τῷ παρόντι). **et ista tibi familiariora fient, |
et quaedam ex his talia erunt ut per partes emendari possint** 'you
will become more familiar with this part, and some of the rest will (also) be
suitable for emendation in sections'. The (slightly strained) antithesis *ista . . . his*
reprises and extends §9 *istis . . . iis quae sequuntur* in parallel, referring again first to
the present enclosure (*ista*), then to future instalments (*his*, the parts still with P.).
Other translators, despite this parallelism and *erunt* (not *sunt*), make *quaedam ex his*
a subset of *ista.* The variation (*iis ~ his*) is not quite certain (the words are easily
confused in MSS, and αβγ all differ here), but is logical (*iis* introduces a relative
clause, *his* does not). The weighty ending (eleven heavy syllables) does not seem
pointed.

11 etenim: introduces the final truism, in the form of a second implicit analogy.
For *etenim* flagging an assertion (around half of Pliny's uses of it), cf. 1.8.6, 3.9.10,
5.17.3, 7.31.4, 9.3.2 and (at letter-end) 2.7.7, 4.12.7. **auulsum statuae caput
aut membrum aliquod:** *statuae* is dat. of disadvantage. Comparison of oratory
to statuary was common (Calboli on *Rhet. Her.* 4.9), not least in Cicero (Mankin on
De or. 3.26) and in Quintilian (12.10.1–9 with Austin, and smaller-scale analogies
at e.g. 2.1.12, 7.*pr.*2, 11.3.51; Aßfahl 1932: 54–6); cf. Isocrates 9.73–5, 15.7 (also Pind.
Nem. 5.1 'I am not a statue-maker . . . '), and the idea of speech as body in Plato
Phaedrus 264c (similarly Arist. *Poet.* 23.1 = 1459a20–1 (poetry), Polybius 1.3.4 with
Walbank (history)); see also Varro *LL* 9.78–9 (on noun-endings) *ut signa quae non
habent caput aut aliquam aliam partem . . .* (Scarcia). P.'s violent image of decapitation
evokes in lexis and rhythm V. *Aen.* 2.558 (Priam) *auulsumque umeris caput* before
returning to the prosaic (*aut membrum aliquod*). The choice of body-part is natural

(heads were the most frequently detached and exchanged parts of statues: Stewart 2003: 49–59), but also perhaps implies that Lupercus is receiving the proem (cf. Lucian *How to write history* 23 for proems as 'heads'; also §12n. *principiorum*). Similar imagery in 8.4.7 *spectabuntur ut membra* (sections of a work in progress), 7.9.6 *noua uelut membra peracto corpori intexere*, 3.10.6 (writer as sculptor). If the dining analogy of §8 prefigures 2.6, this one looks to the following 2.7: a strong meta-epistolary hint for this defence of the fragment (intro.). **inspiceres . . . posses** 'were examining . . . could', present counterfactual. **non tu quidem . . . posses** 'it is true that you could not . . .'. *tu* is pleonastic, providing a prop for *quidem* (concessive: 2.1.7n.) although it is not the term of contrast: cf. *Pan.* 6.3 *olim tu quidem adoptari merebare . . .* (where *olim* is the term of contrast). For this use of a pronoun, commonest with *ille* and esp. popular with Cicero, see K–S I 623–4, Samuelsson 1908: 50–66, Solodow 1978: 37–42. *non tu quidem* is also Ciceronian (Cic. *Mur.* 64, *Phil.* 2.23, and six more). P. has it only here; elsewhere he allows (un-Ciceronian) *non quidem* (1.22.6, 5.3.6, 6.32.1, *Pan.* 32.4), for which see Oakley on Livy 9.19.14. **congruentiam aequalitatemque** 'symmetry and proportion', two abstracts in practically unique uses (*OLD congruentia* 3b, *aequalitas* 6, adding Sen. *NQ* 4b.11.3, of a round ball), evoking the canonical artistic ideal of συμμετρία 'symmetry' (*TLL* IV 301.83), on which see Pollitt 1974: 256–8. For *congruens* of bodies, cf. Sen. *Ep.* 92.9 *male congruentibus membris*, Apul. *Met.* 2.2 *cetera corporis . . . adamussim congruentia*, and for the word-pair, Suet. *Tib.* 68.1 *ceteris quoque membris . . . aequalis et congruens.* **deprendere** 'grasp', i.e. 'recognise' (*TLL* v.1 609.31–2). **satis elegans** 'tolerably elegant'. *elegans* 'elegant, polished' is common in rhetorical criticism (*OLD* 4a). *satis* adds a casual air: it is not *total* perfection that P. desires (yet: *perfecta* follows soon).

12 principiorum libri 'books of prefaces' (*OLD principium* 5b), presumably compilations. Demosthenes and Cicero collected prefaces for personal use (Janson 1964: 16–17, MacDowell 2009: 6–7; Cic. *Att.* 16.16.4), but P. refers to published work; one might perhaps compare the *prolaliae* 'preambles' of Lucian and others (2.3.1n. *praefationes*, Nesselrath 1990), literary works in their own right. P.'s analogy perhaps implies that he is sending the opening of his speech (cf. also §11 *caput*), and may offer another hint of programmatic status (§1n. *efflagitatam*). **circumferuntur** 'are in circulation' (*OLD* 4c), as *Pan.* 50.5, Quint. 2.13.15, 2.15.4. **pars . . . perfecta:** the alliteration recalls §1 *pars . . . perpolitur*, completing a ring before the coda (§13), and with a bolder claim (*perfecta* supersedes §2 *absolutiora*). A common term both in art criticism (= τέλειος: cf. Pollitt 1974: 416–22) and in rhetoric (*TLL* X.1 1374.4–47), *perfecta* neatly ties up the statue/speech analogy, as well as making a suitably paradoxical end before the coda: P.'s letters themselves are nothing if not perfect fragments.

13 Longius me prouexit dulcedo: *longius . . . prouexit* 'has carried me too far' (*OLD longe* 1c, *proueho* 3) works a stock nautical metaphor, e.g. Cic. *Q Rosc.* 31, *Fin.* 3.74, Quint. 4.*pr.*4, 12.*pr.*2. The abstract subject *dulcedo*, however, is rarer: Sen. *Suas.* 1.8 *longius me fabellarum dulcedo produxit*, Quint. 1.12.19 *sed nos haec ipsa* *dulcedo longius duxit.* The latter, ending a book, makes a pointed precursor to P.'s version: his letter would then close with allusion to the last sentence of *Institutio* 1, as it began with what now seems a very likely evocation of the preface (§1n. *efflagitatam*). This letter has *not* been remarkably long (at 371 words, it is a little more than average within the roughly 6,200-word book), and so scarcely needs apology (contrast 2.11.25n. *aeque*, and cf. 2.17.29n. *iustisne*): P. has pointedly miniaturised Quintilian's massive precepts in this manifesto for the miniature. On the axiomatic brevity of letters see 2.2.2n. *plurimas.* **dulcedo quaedam** 'what I might call the pleasure' (lit. 'sweetness'). *quaedam* softens the metaphor (*OLD quidam*[1] 3b), and draws attention to the allusion. **tecum loquendi:** the letter is famously defined by 'Demetrius' as half of a dialogue (εἶναι γὰρ τὴν ἐπιστολὴν οἷον τὸ ἕτερον μέρος τοῦ διαλόγου, *On style* 223), and this idea of conversation on the page is widespread, e.g. Cic. *Att.* 12.39.2 *loquor tecum absens, Fam.* 9.21.1, Sen. *Ep.* 75.1; Thraede 1970 *passim*, Trapp 2003: 39–40 with n.164. The metaphor is similarly live at 5.6.3 *et tibi auditu et mihi relatu iucunda erunt*; elsewhere P. is happy just talking to his books (1.9.5 *mecum tantum et cum libellis loquor*). **finem faciam:** a sign-off otherwise restricted to 5.21.6 *finem epistulae faciam* (ending a book) and 6.16.21 *finem ergo faciam* (ending a long letter): another striking feature in this letter of only moderate length. **ne modum . . . excedam:** cf. Sen. *Ep.* 45.13 (also at letter-end) *sed ne epistulae modum excedam . . .* , but also 2.4.4 *etiamsi modum excesserit*, perhaps binding 2.5 to 2.4, as it is certainly bound to 2.6 and 2.7 (intro.). Symmachus *Ep.* 3.69.1 *multiplex iniuria modum epistulae familiaris excedit* is scant proof of allusion to Pliny (so rightly Kelly 2013; see Intro. 35), Jerome *Ep.* 53.9 *cernis me scripturarum amore raptum excessisse modum epistulae . . .* more persuasive, given his use of P. earlier in the same letter: cf. 2.3.8n. *numquam* and *Ep.* 53.6 *neque enim epistularis angustia euagari longius patiebatur* ~ 4.17.11 *latius . . . quam epistularum angustiae sinunt* (Trisoglio 1973: 366). **orationi . . . epistula:** *orationi* 'the speech' reprises with variation §1 *actionem*. P. simultaneously distinguishes letter from speech and blurs the boundary, applying to his letter the *modus* that, he has told us, must be applied to the speech: cf. (also at letter-end) 4.9.23 *habebis hanc interim epistulam ut* πρόδρομον ['advance messenger'], *exspectabis orationem plenam onustamque*, 9.13.26 *habes epistulam, si modum epistulae cogites, libris quos legisti non minorem*; comparable play at 4.5.3–4, 6.33.7. **adhibendum** *sc. esse.*

6

I recently dined with a man who serves different fare to his guests according their 'rank'. As I told my neighbour at table, my own practice is quite different. Restraint, not meanness, is the proper form of moderation. I wanted to tell you this so you could learn what to avoid yourself.

P. describes a counter-exemplary dinner at which the host served different grades of food to different guests: an occasion that should be defined by communality became the site of offensive hierarchy. Dining was a favourite moralising theme (Purcell 2005, Stein-Hölkeskamp 2005) and food a core satirical

motif (Gowers 1993); notable literary failures in conviviality are the dinners of
Nasidienus (Hor. *Sat.* 2.8), Trimalchio (Petr. 28–78) and Virro (Juv. 5). Like Juvenal
(who may draw on P. here: §3n. *ad*, §5n. *si*, §5n. *quibus*, §7n. *istam*), and like Martial
in several epigrams (§2n. *nam sibi*), P. condemns the host's behaviour in a letter
which is negative from start to finish. Yet unlike the satirists, P. observes from a
privileged position, and as a regular host himself; amid the castigation is a central
panel (§§3–5) in which he presents his own positive example for Avitus' edification.
The motif of (self-proclaimed) frugal guest and luxurious host is familiar from
Seneca *De tranquillitate animi* 1.4–9, though P.'s host goes a step further in being
extravagant and mean at once. Seneca also provides a model both for egalitarian
self-denial (§5n. *si*) and for the epistolary light touch: quick-fire dialogue (§3n.
animaduertit) waters down acerbity (and self-satisfaction) with lively variety. This
variety, and the subject, see P. duly following the meta-epistolary recipe set out
in the dining analogy of 2.5.7–8 (2.5.8n. *in*).

This letter about division is constructed from a succession of bicola, whether
isocolon (e.g. §1n. *ut*) or pointedly unbalanced (§4n. *liberti*, §7n. *cum*), and a stream
of *sententiae* from P., both *qua* narrator and in the staged dialogue (§§3–4). Near
the mid-point come the key words *exaequo . . . aequaui*, pronouncing the corrective
to this boorish host's behaviour. The ideal of simple conviviality has already been
set out in 1.15, to which this letter makes a pendant, as it does to the suavely
moderate dinner of 3.12 and the antique table manners of Vestricius Spurinna in
3.1.9 (§1n. *ut*). At the same time the closing focus on *frugalitas* perhaps pairs this
letter, across the cardinal 2.5, with 2.4 (§5n. *non est*, Intro. 14–15).

2.6 is included in most anthologies of P., and receives rhetorical analysis in
Philips 1976. Stein-Hölkeskamp 2002 is a cultural study of the contemporary *cena*.

Avito: probably the Junius Avitus whose early death is lamented in 8.23, rather
than the Julius Avitus, another *optimae indolis iuuenis* (§6n.), who has died young in
5.21.3–6. Junius' defining quality was his willingness to learn (8.23.2–5), especially
from P., his *formator morum* (8.23.2); his name ('Ancestral') also suits the old-
fashioned moderation being advocated here. He died an aedile-elect (thus in his
late twenties) in 108 or later (S-W 475), making him around twenty in book 2: just
as P. has learned from exemplary older senators like Verginius Rufus (2.1), so he
plays his part in educating the young. For P. as moral guide see 6.11, 6.29, 8.13,
9.13, Bütler 1970: 89–93, Gazich 2003 (see also van der Blom 2010: 311–15 on
Cicero); for P. as pseudo-father see 2.18.intro. To modern taste, he is perhaps not
as successful as Spurinna in avoiding the impression of preaching (3.1.6 *quamuis
ille hoc temperamentum modestiae suae indixerit, ne praecipere uideatur*).

1 Longum est altius repetere 'it would take too long to give the whole
story'. For modal *est* 'would be' see K–S I 171. *altius repetere* (*OLD altus* 8a, *repeto*
7a) means 'begin from further back' (4.13.10 *altius et quasi a fonte repetenda*, 4.11.15,
7.4.2; 2.3.3n. *repetit*) and thus 'go (more) deeply into' (e.g. Sen. *Contr.* 2.5.14). The
resemblance of *longum . . . repetere* ~ 2.5.13 *longius . . . prouexit* delicately strengthens

the meta-epistolary bond (2.5.8n. *in*). **nec rēfert** 'and it is not important'
(*OLD rēfert* 1a). **quemadmodum acciderit ut** 'how it came about that' (*OLD
accido* 7a), indirect question after *repetere* (rare, but cf. Cic. *Off.* 1.50 *quae natura
principia sint... repetendum uidetur altius*). **homo minime familiaris** 'though
I was by no means on close terms [with him]', lit. '[being] a man not at all
intimate', in apposition to the unstated subject (*ego*), as 3.5.7 [*sc. ille*] *homo occupatus*,
4.9.6 *homo simplex et incautus*. Less formal and assertive than *uir*, *homo* ranges
from pejorative to neutral, usually in P. the latter (Santoro-L'Hoir 1992: 146–62
concentrates on the former); see on 2.10.1, 2.11.23, 2.13.10, 2.20.2, 7, 11. Here
it provides a prop for *familiaris* (*OLD homo* 4a) and compensates for the lack
of a participle 'being'. For its use in self-reference, cf. 1.8.2 *ab homine desidioso*
and e.g. Cic. *Diu. Caec.* 32. *familiaris* qualifies more intimate friendship (cf. 4.17.2
[*sc. amicitia*] *non plane familiaris sed tamen amicitia*); elsewhere P. speaks of *familiares
amici* (7.17.11, 9.34.1, 9.37.1). **apud quendam:** the boor remains anonymous:
like wise Euphrates (1.10.7), P. *insectatur* ['harries'] *uitia, non homines* (cf. Mart.
10.33.10 *parcere personis, dicere de uitiis*). For the discreet *quidam* see §6 *quorundam*,
3.11.2, 6.8.3, 6.17.1, 8.22.4, 9.12.1, 9.26.1, 9.27.2; the anonymity is not reserved
for objects of criticism: e.g. 2.3.8 *Gaditanum quendam*, 9.27.1. **ut sibi uidebatur,
lautum et diligentem, | ut mihi, sordidum simul et sumptuosum**
'at once elegant and sensible in his view, mean and extravagant in mine' (*OLD
lautus* 2, *sordidus* 8, *sumptuosus* 2; for *diligens* 'sensible (with money)' see 2.4.2n.);
uidebatur and *simul* are distributed in double *apo koinou*. Isocolon (13~13 syllables)
with matching ditrochaic clausulae. *sordidum... sumptuosum* chiastically 'corrects'
lautum... diligentem, substituting different ways of seeing the same thing (the figure
distinctio: Quint 9.3.65, Lausberg §805); the chiasmus is combined with parallel
antithesis of opposites (*lautum* ~ *sordidum* lit. 'clean' ~ 'dirty', *diligentem* ~ *sumptuosum*
'careful' ~ 'wasteful'). P.'s critical view, with its hissing alliteration, takes winning
second place and invites curiosity with its oxymoron (cf. 4.2.5 (Regulus) *in summa
auaritia sumptuosus*). With the (desirable) pair *lautum et diligentem*, cf. 3.1.9 (Vestricius
Spurinna's *cena*) *non minus nitida quam frugi*; another model opposite in 3.12.1
[*cena*] *sit parca, Socraticis tantum sermonibus abundet*. *lautus* (*OLD* 3) is common in the
context of dining (frequent, with irony, in Petronius' *cena Trimalchionis*: Sullivan
1968: 148–9); within *Epistles* 1–2 it points to 1.15.2 *lauta*, describing (in moralising
jest) the simple, honest dinner on offer chez P. The conviviality and cheer of that
letter make a clear contrast with this castigation of perverted hospitality. Another
lautissimam cenam at 9.17.1, where (unlike here) P. urges 'live and let live' (*uis tu
remittere aliquid ex rugis?*, etc.).

2 nam sibi et paucis opima quaedam, ceteris uilia et minuta ponebat
'for he was serving choice delicacies to himself and a few, cheap and meagre
stuff to the rest' (*OLD opimus* 4, *uilis* 1, *minutus* 1b, *pono* 5: the servants, as in
English idiom, go unnoticed), explaining the paradox *sordidum simul et sumptuosum*
(hence *nam*) and setting the scene (hence the imperfect; similarly the pluperfect
discripserat below). Isocolon antithesis (10~12 syllables) combining parallelism

(dat. acc. ~ dat. acc.) with chiasmus (word-pairs frame the single words *opima* and *ceteris*) pointing the perversity. Such culinary stratification is a routine complaint in Martial (3.60.2 *cur mihi non eadem quae tibi cena datur?*, 1.20, 1.43, 2.43, 3.82, 6.11) and is central to Juv. 5, a client's-eye-view fantasy of tasteless Virro's banquet; cf. also Lucian *Saturnalia* 22 (graded food and wine), *On salaried posts* 26 (one deprived guest). Julius Caesar punished his baker for serving two different breads (Suet. *Iul.* 48); Pl. *NH* 14.91 hankers after the elder Cato's day, when such behaviour was unknown (*pace* S-W). **etiam:** the wine arrangements are a step worse: for the gradation and word-order see 2.1.6n. **paruulis lagunculis:** a scornful pair of diminutives (*laguncula* < *lagona* 'wine-flask'); contrast the homely *lagunculam* of 1.6.3 (and see 2.4.3n. *agellorum*). P. rarely uses diminutives pejoratively (2.14.2 *adulescentuli*, 3.9.13 *amicula*), as befits his usual benevolence. For *paruulus* + diminutive see e.g. Cic. *Tusc.* 3.2, Val. Max. 8.8.*ext.*1 (D'Agostino 1931: 119, Hanssen 1953: 125–6). **in tria genera:** still worse than the hosts who serve two different wines in Mart. 4.85 and 10.49 (surpassed differently by Virro, who even has two grades of water: Juv. 5.24–52). Pl. *NH* 14.97 says Julius Caesar once served four different wines at one feast, apparently offering a choice. **non ut potestas eligendi | sed ne ius esset recusandi:** take *esset* twice. Isocolon (9~9 syllables), varied clausulae, parallel synonyms *potestas* (*OLD* 5a) ~ *ius* (*OLD* 11) and antonyms (the gerunds *eligendi* ~ *recusandi*). **aliud sibi et nobis, aliud minoribus amicis . . . , aliud suis nostrisque libertis:** rising tricolon (7~10~11 syllables) with anaphora for the *tria genera*, interrupted by a key detail in parenthesis. *sibi et nobis* = *sibi et paucis* (above), revealing that P. (of course) was one of the favoured few: unlike the satirists (above on *sibi*), he surveys the scene from the comfort of top table. The inclusion of freedmen, even by a bad host, is taken for granted; comparative evidence is slim, but Suet. *Aug.* 74 counts it noteworthy that Augustus excluded them. On freedmen see Mouritsen 2011. **nam gradatim amicos habet** 'for he classifies his friends' (*OLD gradatim* 2b, as 8.2.8 *distincte gradatimque*); the parenthesis explains *minoribus amicis* (2.4.2n. *erat*). On P.'s liking for adverbs in -*im* see Niemirska-Pliszczyńska 1955: 45–6, and cf. Kenney on Apul. *Met.* 6.1.5, Kraus on Livy 6.36.12. Similar moralising at *Pan.* 47.5 *contumeliarum gradus* (under Domitian), Sen. *Ben.* 6.33.4 *non sunt isti amici . . . qui in primas et secundas admissiones digeruntur*, *Ep.* 47.8 *conuiuarum censura*, Suet. *Tib.* 46 (three *classes* of retinue); Sen. *Ben.* 6.34.2 traces the custom back to Gaius Gracchus. P. never admits to doing the same (*pace* S-W): 7.3.2 *amicitiae tam superiores quam minores* surely means 'relations with one's social superiors and inferiors' (cf. Sen. *Ep.* 94.14); 9.30.1 advocates generosity to *amicis . . . pauperibus* (≠ *minoribus*). For him, *amicitia* must always look level, though he has no desire for equality in society at large (2.12.5n. *nihil*): a typical Roman balancing act, not least at the dinner table (cf. D'Arms 1990, Gowers 1993: 212).

3 animaduertit . . . interrogauit: framing main verbs; pf. tense opens the 'action', a brief dialogue first reported, then in direct speech. The value of *sermocinatio* to enliven a narrative was well known to ancient orators (Quint.

9.2.29–30, Lausberg §820–5). Seneca similarly leavens his preaching (e.g. *Ep.* 12.2–3); on Cicero's artful epistolary use of dialogue see Hutchinson 1998: 113– 38. **mihi proximus recumbebat** 'was reclining next to me' (*OLD recumbo* 3a); cf. 4.22.4 *Veiento proximus* [*sc. Neruae*] *recumbebat*, 9.23.4. A *triclinium* tradition- ally comprised three couches, each for three people, arranged as three sides of a square. This could be multiplied for larger parties; hence *animaduertit* (*sc.* 'at another "table"', S-W). **an probarem:** indirect question (2.1.2n.). **negaui:** characteristic narrative brevity, e.g. 2.14.11 *clamor*, 2.20.3 *nihil*, 10.56.4 *negauit* (con- jectured). **'tu ergo . . . quam consuetudinem sequĕris?'** 'so what custom do *you* keep?' (*OLD ergo* 3a, *sequor* 10a), slipping into conversational direct speech; cf. Cic. *Att.* 4.18.2 *dices 'tu ergo haec quomodo fers?'* **eadem omnibus pono:** inverting §2 *sibi . . . ponebat*. P.'s practice responds in parallel to the host's, §3 food (apparently), §4 wine. **'ad cenam . . . non ad notam inuito'** 'I invite (peo- ple) to dinner, not to a humiliation', syllepsis (2.1.4n. *pari*) for a perverse practice. *nota* (*OLD* 4c) is a metaphor from the *nota censoria*, a public mark of censure (*BNP* s.v.), with perhaps a whiff of *nota* 'quality (of wine)' (*OLD* 5a). Juv. 5.9 *ini- uria cenae* decocts the pair into oxymoron; on specific intertextuality between 2.6 and Juv. 5 (ignored by Adamietz 1972: 85–96 and Juvenal's commentators), see Cova 1972: 22–4 (and briefly Scivoletto 1957: 143–4), though it seems unlikely that P. is alluding to Juvenal (*pace* Cova), given that most date Juv. 5 to the AD 110s (Intro. 35). *cenam* is choice, if P. felt an etymological link with *communis* (§4n. *conuictores*). **'cunctisque rebus exaequo quos mensa et toro aequaui'** 'I level out in all respects those whom I have levelled with table and couch' (i.e. with a dinner invitation), the first of two embedded *sententiae*. Isocolon (8~7 syllables); *exaequo* and *aequaui* are varied in tense and as simple~compound (on the latter, widespread phenomenon see Kenney on Lucr. 3.261, Oakley on Livy 10.24.14) yet matched in rhythm, ‒‒‒ (cf. *Pan.* 94.2 *audisti . . . exaudi*); the key-word *aequaui* is near the centre of dialogue and letter. *cunctis* (instead of *omnibus*) perhaps adds grandeur (2.3.10n. *qui*); for the cliché *mensa + torus* see e.g. Tibullus 2.5.100, Lucan 4.245, Stat. *Silu.* 5.1.125. §§4–5 show that this levelling includes P. himself; he thus follows Cic. *Lael.* 71 *qui sunt in amicitiae . . . necessitudine superiores, exaequare se cum inferioribus debent* and the perfect patron of *Laus Pisonis* 109–32 (especially 117 *unus amicitiae summos tenor ambit et imos*), and matches Trajan's idealised *mensa communis* (*Pan.* 49.4; for the mirroring of subject and prince see 2.4.3n. *decurrit*).

4 'etiamne libertos?' 'etiam' 'Even freedmen? – Yes, even them': the answer repeats the question (*TLL* v.2 931.40–7). Inviting freedmen is not in doubt (§2n. *sibi*), but treating them equally is presented as rare. S-W suggests that dinner has here replaced the *sportula* (2.14.4n.), as if clients were always freedmen. P. regularly advertises his *humanitas* towards slaves (1.4.4, 5.19, 8.1) and freedmen (4.10, 7.11, 7.14); on this well-worn topic see e.g. Yuge 1986, Gonzalès 2003, Lefèvre 2009: 181–94. He cashed it out in death, bequeathing *c.* 1.7 million sesterces to a hundred freedmen probably created by testamentary manumission (*CIL* v 5262:

see 2.5.3n. *ornare*). For comparable ethics see Cic. *Fam.* 16 (to and from Tiro), Sen. *Ep.* 47 (esp. §2 *rideo istos qui turpe existimant cum seruo suo cenare*). **'conuictores enim tunc, non libertos puto'** (*OLD puto* 5a 'think of . . . as') repeats in form and content §3 *ad cenam enim, non ad notam inuito*. A *conuictor* is a close friend, as Horace to Maecenas (Hor. *Sat.* 1.6.47), but the etymology *conuictor < conuiuere > conuiuium* is doubtless live (Cic. *Fam.* 9.24.3 *nos 'conuiuia'* [*sc. uocamus*] *quod tum maxime simul uiuitur*, Cato 45; Braund 1996b: 37–9). **'magno tibi constat'** 'that must cost [lit. 'costs'] you a lot' (*OLD consto* 11a with abl. of price). The clausula is probably cretic–spondee: if P. took the variable second syllable of *mihi, tibi*, etc. (*TLL* v.2 255.30–256.39) as short, it would make a disproportionate number of 'heroic' clausulae (2.3.3n. *narrat*): 2.16.2 *legem mihi dixi*, 2.20.10 *has mihi leges*, 1.5.17 *haec tibi scripsi*, 3.1.12 *eundem mihi cursum*, etc. (so too Hofacker 1903: 41–2). **'minime'** 'not at all', *OLD* 2b. **'qui fieri potest?'** 'how can that be?', *OLD qui²*. **'quia scilicet'** 'because, of course' (*OLD scilicet* 5a), as if he could imagine no alternative. The phrase is at home in dialogue (4.9.17, Hor. *Sat.* 2.2.36, Petr. 50.4) but is not confined to it (6.29.5, Sen. *NQ* 2.5.1 etc.). **'liberti mei non idem quod ego bibunt, sed idem ego quod liberti'** *sc. bibo*: rather than upgrading their wine, he downgrades his own. A second *sententia*, formed from apparent paradox, chiasmus and a figure of inversion called *commutatio* (Lausberg §800–3): cf. 6.29.5 *commode agendo factum est ut saepe agerem, saepe agendo ut minus commode*, 8.8.4, 9.6.3, 9.36.2, and (non-chiastic) 1.8.15 *non ideo praedicare quia fecerint, sed ut praedicarent fecisse creduntur*, 3.12.3. The falling bicolon (13~8 syllables) gives a kick to the punchline, and the clausula (‒ ‒ ‒ ‒) adds weight. For the sententious end to a tableau, see 2.1.9n. *etiam*. According to §5 P. is not condescending, but demonstrating laudable temperance (presumably he found other occasions to drink his best wines). The need for moderation at table will ring the next *cena* letter: 3.12.1 *teneat modum . . .* 3.12.4 *modus constet*.

5 et hercule 'and indeed', unpacking the *sententia* with a general truth (cf. 1.20.4, *Pan.* 45.3; Sen. *NQ* 1.16.4 and Pl. *NH* 7.5 *at hercule*) and effecting a seamless exit from mini-narrative into precepts. *hercule* is common in P.; originally 'by Hercules' (*OLD hercle*), it was now an asseverative particle like *certe*, 'direct, personal and rhetorical' (Syme 1958: 708, on *at hercule*) – not colloquial (*pace multorum*: it is frequent in Cic., Quint., [Quint.], Tac. *D.*, rare in Petronius, largely restricted to speeches in historiography, though cf. Tac. *An.* 1.3.5 with Goodyear). **si gulae temperes** 'if you moderate your greed' (*OLD gula* 2a, *tempero* 2a), subjunctive for generalising second person ('you/one': *NLS* §195). Lit. 'throat', *gula* is a vivid and moralising metaphor (e.g. Hor. *Sat.* 2.2.40; often in Seneca, Martial, Juvenal), only here in P. He advertised his own restraint in 2.4 (next n.) and now advocates Senecan asceticism: cf. Sen. *Ep.* 47.8 *intemperantia . . . gulae*, 108.14 *circumscribere gulam, Tranq.* 9.2 *discamus . . . continentiam augere, luxuriam coercere, gloriam temperare . . . frugalitatem colere* (where *gloriam* has been suspected as a corruption of *gulam*); cf. also Tac. *H.* 2.62.1 *si luxuriae temperaret*. On Seneca and P. see Intro. 3, index. **non est onerosum:** cf. 2.4.3 *ne sit mihi onerosa*, similarly showing how *frugalitas* makes generosity easy (Merwald 1964: 58–9). **quo utaris ipse** 'what you yourself eat and drink' (*OLD utor* 2a), object of *communicare* (*id* is omitted as usual before the relative: 2.1.10n. *qua*). Subjunctive as *temperes* above. **communicare** 'to share' (*OLD* 1), alluding perhaps to the ideal of *mensa communis* (*Pan.* 49.4; [Quint.] *Decl. min.* 301.11); cf. Juv. 8.177–8 *communia pocula . . . nec mensa remotior ulli*; §3n. *ad.* **illa ergo reprimenda, illa quasi in ordinem redigenda est** 'so that is what must be restrained [*OLD reprimo* 5a], that is what must be as it were cut down to size', rising bicolon (7~11 syllables). *illa* (= *gula*), in asseverative anaphora, is personified by the metaphor *in ordinem redigere* (lit. 'reduce to the ranks', of a soldier or magistrate: *OLD ordo* 6, Cowan on 1.23.1 *in ordinem cogi*): cf. Sen. *Clem.* 1.26.4 *crudelitatem suam in ordinem coactam*. The figurative language is softened, and flagged up, by *quasi* (*OLD* 9a). For the heroic clausula see 2.3.3n. *narrat.* **si sumptibus parcas** 'if you are cutting down your expenses' (*OLD sumptus* 1a, *parco* 1); subjunctive as *temperes* above. Cf. Juv. 5.156–8 *forsitan impensae Virronem parcere credas. | hoc agit, ut doleas: nam quae comoedia, mimus | quis melior plorante gula?*, a further twist (Virro is mean not for economy but for fun), perhaps following P.: *gula* occurs only twice in Juv. 5 and is here personified (cf. previous n.); *impensae parcere* is unparalleled and *sumptibus parcere* rare. **quibus aliquanto rectius tuã continentiã quam alienã contumeliã consulas** 'which [= expenses] it is considerably better to watch through personal self-control than through insults to others' (*OLD aliquanto* a, *recte* 6, *continentia* 2, *alienus* 1c, *consulo* 6b); *quibus* (antecedent *sumptibus*) is dat. with *consulo*. The *sententia* is crafted with parallelism (*tua continentia* ~ *aliena contumelia*), rhyming isorhythmic nouns (‒◡‒◡‒) and further rhyme in *aliquanto* ~ *aliena*, *aliena contumelia* and *contumeliã consulãs*. For *rectius . . . consulas*, cf. Amm. 16.12.8 *utilitati securitatique recte consulens*, one of several minor similarities, none of which settles the question whether or not Ammianus had read P.: 2.8.1n. *affatim*, 2.16.4n. *cunctatior*. With the climactic *contumelia* cf. Juv. 5.9 *iniuria cenae*, introducing Virro's feast (§3n. *ad*); for the Senecan tone see above on *si gulae*.

6 Quorsus haec? ne tibi . . . imponat 'Why all this? So that . . . will not deceive you', *OLD impono* 16. The ellipse of a verb of saying or leading is common with *quorsus*; with a purpose clause also at 6.8.3 *quorsus haec? ut scias* and e.g. Cic. *Off.* 3.67 *quorsus haec? ut illud intellegas*, Cato 42, Sen. *Ep.* 66.27, *NQ* 2.26.6; *OLD quorsum* 2b. For the concluding exhortation, cf. 2.3.11 *quae omnia huc tendunt.* **optimae indolis iuueni** 'a young man of excellent character' (*OLD indoles* 1a, gen. of characteristic), a cliché: 5.21.4 (Julius Avitus) *tantae indolis iuuenis*, 6.11.1 *summae indolis iuuenes*, 6.23.4 (the *iuuenis* Ruso) *indolis optimae*, and e.g. Vell. 2.61.2, Val. Max. 1.6.11, Sen. *Ep.* 98.9. **quorundam in mensã luxuriã specie frugalitatis** 'the extravagance of some people's dinners . . . through a false impression [*OLD species* 7c] of frugality', with symmetrical cases (ABCBA). The genteel anonymity continues (§1n. *quendam*), now with the philosophical topos of vice masquerading as virtue: Ov. *Rem.* 323–4 *mala sunt uicina bonis*..., Sen. *Clem.* 2.4.4 <*per speciem enim seueritatis in crudelitatem incidimus*>, *per speciem clementiae in misericordiam*, Juv. 14.109 *fallit enim uitium specie uirtutis* with Mayor. Such moralising on *luxuria* is rare in P. (Leach 2003: 149–52). Tacitus gives a similar line, with the same rare use of *imponere*, to emperor *manqué* Piso in *H.* 1.30.1 '*falluntur quibus luxuria specie liberalitatis imponit*'. Where Tacitus sets an adjacent virtue and vice together (in *distinctio*, §1n. *ut*), P. has more paradoxical opposites; still, if one inspired the other, it is hard to determine which came first (2.1.2n. *cum*, Intro. 33–4). **conuenit** 'befits', *OLD* 6b. **autem** 'also': the first reason was Avitus' excellence, the second P.'s affection. **amori in te meo:** cf. 8.24.1 *amor in te meus cogit*... *ut*... *moneam*, 9.12.2 *haec tibi admonitus*... *exemplo pro amore mutuo scripsi*, and 2.2.1n. *amor*. **inciderit:** probably fut. pf. (*NLS* §217.6), or perhaps generalising pf. subj. (*NLS* §217c.ii; for *quotiens* + subj. cf. 1.12.7, 3.16.4, *Pan.* 13.1, all historic). **sub exemplo praemonere** (*OLD sub* 11b, *praemoneo* 2): cf. 3.18.2 *ut futuri principes*... *sub exemplo praemonerentur*, *Pan.* 53.5 *futuros* [*sc. principes*] *sub exemplo praemonere*, 4.24.7, 6.22.7, 7.1.7, 9.12.2. Exemplarity is a leitmotif of the *Epistles* (Intro. 9–10, 2.1.7n. *exemplar*), advising others a mainstay of true friendship (Cic. *Lael.* 91 *monere et moneri proprium est uerae amicitiae* – though P. is more prone to *monere* than *moneri*). **quid debeas fugere** 'what you must avoid' (*OLD fugio* 11a), indirect question: a staple of moral philosophy (e.g. Cic. *Fin.* 4.46 *quid fugere debeant*, Sen. *Ep.* 71.2 *quid fugiendum sit*); with P.'s paternal guidance, cf. Hor. *Sat.* 1.4.105–6 *insueuit pater optimus hoc me,* | *ut fugerem exemplis uitiorum quaeque notando* with Gowers.

7 igitur: scarce in *Epp.* 1–6 (once per book on average), more frequent in *Epp.* 7–9 (11×); in the longer *Epp.* 10 (3×) and still longer *Pan.* (7×) it is fairly rare (*itaque*, by contrast, generally occurs 3 or 4 times per book, with equivalent frequency in book 10 and *Pan.*). Until book 7 it is always clause-first (as usually in Sallust and Tacitus); in books 8–10 and *Pan.* it alternates between that and clause-second (the preference of Cicero). On authors' different tastes see Quint. 1.5.39 and the statistics in *TLL* v.2 760–1. **memento:** the didaxis turns direct. **esse uitandum** varies *debeas fugere.* **istam luxuriae et sordium nouam societatem** 'that new partnership [*OLD societas* 3] of extravagance and meanness', varying §1 *sordidum simul et sumptuosum* in chiastic ring-composition. *nouam* claims topicality as if Martial had never written (§2n. *nam sibi*). *societatem* adds alliteration and paradoxical bite: *societas* 'fellowship' (*OLD* 4a) is far from this host's table(s). Juv. 1.139–40 *sed quis ferat istas* | *luxuriae sordes?* recasts the paradox as oxymoron (cf. §3n. *ad*); cf. Juv. 5.113 *diues tibi, pauper amicis.* **quae** = *luxuriae* and *sordes*, combined as neut. pl. (G–L §286.3). **cum sint turpissima discreta ac separata, turpius iunguntur** 'are utterly disgraceful separate and apart, but more disgraceful (still) in combination' (lit. '... are joined more disgracefully'). The closing *sententia* combines chiasmus (*sint turpissima* ~ *turpius iunguntur*) with parallelism (*turpissima discreta ac separata* ~ *turpius iunguntur*) and variety (adjective ~ adverb), in a falling bicolon (13~6 syllables) with short but heavy punchline, as §4n. *liberti*.

For the redundant pair *discreta ac separata*, cf. Pl. *NH* 19.55 *aquae quoque separantur et ipsa naturae elementa ui pecuniae discreta sunt* (moralising on gastronomic segregation), Tac. *H.* 5.5.2 *separati epulis, discreti cubilibus*. **turpissima . . . turpius:** a favourite moralising adjective; the superlative also at e.g. 2.11.23 *turpissimum*, 5.9.6, 8.18.3. For the sententious capping of superlative with comparative, cf. *Pan.* 85.8 *ardentissime diligas . . . ardentius diligaris*, 89.1 *optimus . . . meliorem*, 92.4 and e.g. Cic. *Marc.* 33 *maximas . . . maiores*, Livy 4.13.1 *pessimo . . . peiore*, Sen. *Ira* 3.17.4 *dissimillimus . . . dissimilior*, Quint. 2.19.3 *optimā melior*.   **iunguntur:** a pointed word, like *societatem* and following hard on *discreta ac separata*, to end this tale of segregation. The grave closing molossus (– – –) is matched in books 1–3 only by 3.21.6 *tamquam essent futura* (sealing Martial's epistolary tomb, and book 3).

7

Yesterday the senate awarded a triumphal statue to Vestricius Spurinna, richly deserved. His son Cottius was awarded a posthumous statue, a rare honour given his age, a fine incitement to virtue and parenthood and a great consolation to me, who loved him so dearly.

A letter of moderate length but high style which matches and varies 2.1. Again P. moves from celebrating the public honour done to a grandee of the new regime (§1n. *Vestricio*) to (self-)consolation for a death; this time, however, exemplary *senex* Spurinna lives on while an exemplary *iuuenis* is mourned. What begins as celebration of Spurinna ends up as a miniature funeral oration for Cottius, a rare shift, though a single theme could be identified as *statua triumphalis*. The explicit treatment of exemplarity in §5, and the focus on an upstanding *iuuenis*, also attach 2.7 to 2.6, with its exemplary instruction of young Avitus (§5n. *exemplo*). The styles contrast strongly, 2.6 mixing table-talk with Senecan moralising, 2.7 rising to oratorical grandeur: P. thus cashes out the meta-epistolary promise of 2.5 with these complementary yet varied fragments (see 2.5.intro. on the sequence 2.5–6–7).

As often, the letter finds a partner in book 1: the awarding of public statues recalls and varies 1.17, on Capito's private dedication of a statue in the forum. There P. is explicit about the kudos which attaches to honouring the dead: 1.17.4 *scias ipsum plurimis uirtutibus abundare qui alienas sic amat*, a cue for how to read 2.7, and the *Epistles* (Krasser 1993a; Pausch 2004: 94). But 2.7 is most strikingly bound into book 3. First, 3.1 takes up Spurinna, sketching a full portrait to which §§1–3 thus becomes a precursor (Pausch 2004: 117–18). Second, 3.6 replaces Cottius with the statue and 'supplementary *alter ego*' (Henderson 2002a: 161) that P. plans to erect in Comum, so completing a graded tricolon of epistolary sculpture across three books: 1.17 (private) ~ 2.7 (public) ~ 3.6 (*Pliny's Statue*); in book 4 Regulus (of course: 2.11.22n.) will provide a twin appendix on the *wrong* use of statues (mourning his son), 4.2.5 and 4.7.1 (Henderson 2002a: 30–2). Third, 3.10 to Spurinna and his wife announces P.'s composition of two books on the life of Cottius, 'revealing' 2.7 as a sketch for that Life, and trumping this statue (and that of 3.6?) with a literary *monumentum* better than any physical one (§4n. *hac*). Finally, *Epistles* 3 will feature (in 3.13 and 3.18) P.'s 'most monumental portrait' (Leach 1990: 36): the *Panegyricus*. Trajan gets a literal statue from P. in 10.8.4–9.1. On Spurinna see §1n. *Vestricio*; on the *Epistles* as (self-)portraiture, see bibliography in 2.3.intro., esp. Henderson 2002a, who erects the statue of 3.6 as governing metaphor for the *Epistles*. Strube 1964 is a rhetorical analysis of 2.7.

MACRINO: six letters are addressed to 'Macrinus': 2.7, 3.4 (the Classicus trial), 7.6 and 10 (the Varenus trial), 8.17 (the Tiber flood), 9.4 (a short, intensely metaepistolary note: G–M 240). The index for book 3 specifies Caecilius Macrinus, who is a likely candidate for the similar 7.6 and 10 (cf. 2.12.intro.) and probably, like all recipients of senatorial trial letters (S-W 274), equestrian: perhaps T. Caecilius Macrinus of Milan (Syme 1968: 146). It is economical, if speculative, to give him the rest too (S-W 153, Birley 2000a: 43), though Minicius Macrinus, the Transpadane equestrian (1.14.4–5) for whose son P. makes a match in 1.14 (2.18.intro.), cannot be ruled out. A Macrinus has lost his wife in 8.5.1.

1 An unusually grand sentence evocative of an oration. The main verb still comes relatively early (*decreta est*), but there are gestures at periodic style, with all verbs at clause-end and a long tail establishing tension (*non ita . . .*) resolved only by the final word, *assequebantur*. Cf. 2.1.1n. **Here:** the contemporary spelling of *heri* (Quint. 1.4.8, 1.7.22), to which it has been corrupted in Fγ (*here* is preserved in α and corrupted to *nere* in B's index: Intro. 40). 'The closest indication of time in the Letters, and a sure sign that this letter originated as a genuine epistle' (S-W 154): the first assertion overlooks 2.14.6 *here* and 3.16.2 *hesterno*, the second is empty. For the topicality, cf. 2.11.1 *per hos dies*; only the similar 2.1 also begins with a time expression (*post aliquot annos*). **a senatu Vestricio Spurinnae principe auctore:** a triad centred and weighted around Vestricius (4~7~5 syllables) and with the senate leading, in the (miniaturised) fulsome propriety of officialese (e.g. *CIL* III 2830 *huic* [*senatus a*]*uctore* [*imp*(*eratore*) *Tra*]*iano Hadriano* [*Au*]*g*[*usto*] *ornamenta triu*[*mp*]*halia decreuit*); contrast the cynical Tac. *Ag.* 40.1 *triumphalia ornamenta . . . decerni* in *senatu iubet* [*sc.* Domitianus], *An.* 3.37.1 *auctore principe ac decreto senatus* (with Woodman–Martin). **Vestricio Spurinnae:** T. Vestricius Spurinna, *cos.* II *suff.* 98 (*PIR* V 308, *RE* II/16 1791–8, Syme 1958: 634–5, id. 1991: 541–50; now known not to be *cos.* III 100, as previously thought: 2.1.2n. *perfunctus*). He stars in 3.1, aged 77 (3.1.10), as the model of a retired statesman (Henderson 2002a: 58–66; Pausch 2004: 114–29); and receives 3.10 (intro.), and 5.17, on poetry and an exemplary *iuuenis* (cf. esp. 5.17.6 on *imagines* as incitement to virtue). Their paraded intimacy binds P. to another *senex* of the new regime (see 2.1.intro.). Elsewhere he names him just *Spurinna* (1.5.8–9, 3.1.1, 4.27.5); the double name here fits the solemn context (Jones 1991: 156) and grand manner: cf. 2.1.1 *Vergini Rufi*. **principe auctore** 'on the emperor's instigation' (*OLD auctor* 12c). The unusual word-order (*auctore* usually leads, e.g. Suet. *Tib.* 47.1, Tac.

An. 15.22.1, inscriptions *passim*: *TLL* II 1198.27–37) brings together *senatu Vestricio Spurinnae principe*, a harmonious trio (4.12.3 *Caesare auctore* may also be stylistically determined). The *princeps* is generally taken to be Nerva (S-W 153–4, Syme 1958: 660, Birley 2000a: 74–5; on P.'s vagueness see 2.1.3n. *reliquit*) on the fairly firm basis that Cassius Dio (68.15.3², 68.16.2) does not include Spurinna among four consulars granted statues by Trajan (see also 2.9.2n. *Caesarem*), so giving a likely year of 97 (when he was also designated a consul for 98), or at least before Nerva's death on 28 Jan. 98. Triumphal statues were always proposed by the emperor (Alföldy 2001: 25 n.84; above on *a senatu*) in a *relatio*, a proposal made in person or in writing (Talbert 1984: 165–7, 234–6). For the implied compliment see 2.1.6n. *principi*. **triumphalis statua:** a statue in triumphal garb, probably in the Forum Augustum or Forum Romanum (Maxfield 1981: 105–9; see Alföldy 2001: 18–23 for locations). It routinely accompanied the award of *ornamenta triumphalia* (the closest to a triumph that a *priuatus* could obtain: Eck 1984: 142–3), as e.g. Tac. *Ag.* 40.1, *CIL* VI 1386 and 1444 (both Trajanic), but seems also to have been granted independently, as here and perhaps Tac. *H.* 1.79.5. Loyalty to the regime was doubtless at least as significant as military achievement (Alföldy 2001). Such statues were objects of reverence, used for the swearing of oaths (Juv. 8.142–4; *TPSulp.* 13, 14, 27 in Camodeca 1999). **non ita ut multis** 'not as [*sc.* was decreed] to many'; *multis* could be tendentious, but non-military awards of *statuae triumphales* may have been common, such perhaps as those disdained by Juv. 1.129–31. Spurinna's own award may have been connected with political services rendered to Nerva (S-W 153–4, previous n.). Epistle 8.6 damns the honours given Pallas under Claudius (8.6.6 *prolatos imperi fines... credas*; cf. 8.6.2). **numquam ... numquam ... numquam ... audierunt:** extended tricolon (8~7~20 syllables) with homoeoteleuton (-*erunt*) and indignant gradation (fight in a battle ~ serve in the army ~ go to the theatre). **in acie steterunt:** *OLD sto* 2a. **castra uiderunt:** *OLD uideo* 12 'have experience of'; cf. Licinius Crassus fr. 45 M. (= Cic. *De or.* 2.226) *an rei militari* [*sc. studes*], *qui numquam castra uideris?*, Cic. *Balb.* 9, *De or.* 2.76; also *Pan.* 15.2 *prospexisse castra* (= *breuis militia*). **denique** caps the tricolon (2.3.8n.). **nisi in spectaculis:** a sneer. Like Seneca (Lausberg 1991: 97–9), P. is generally hostile to mass entertainment (4.22, 9.6), but he can be flexible when occasion suits (6.34 with G–M 41, *Pan.* 33.1; see similarly Nisbet on Cic. *Pis.* 65), and again like Seneca (e.g. *Ep.* 7.3) he allows us to see him attending them (7.24.6). Trumpets regularly featured in public shows (*OLD tuba* 1b, V. *Aen.* 5.113, Juv. 6.250 with Courtney) as well as in battle (*OLD tuba* 1a, *bellicus* 3). **uerum ut illis:** rhyming the antithesis with *ita ut multis*. A mere 22 syllables of valour will outweigh the preceding 41 syllables of cowardice (*non ... audierunt*). **assequebantur** 'used to achieve' (*OLD* 3), a final verb and one-word clausula (2.1.6n. *laudator*) to round off the grand sentence. The tense adds a past/present dichotomy to what started as a contrast between deserved and undeserved honours. Nostalgia for the great men of a hazy past, ubiquitous in Roman literature, provides the terms of reference for celebrating modern heroes like Spurinna (e.g. 3.1.6, cited below; 2.9.4n. *antiquus*, Intro. 8–9). **decus** 'distinction' (*OLD* 2b, *Pan.* 13.5). **sudore et sanguine et factis** 'sweat and blood and deeds': a laconic trio for these men of action, in sharp riposte to the long *numquam* tricolon. 'Blood and sweat' was proverbial (Otto 1890: 334); P. modifies it with the terse but telling *factis* (for such modification see 2.2.1n. *scis*). Such are the tales he hears chez Spurinna in 3.1.6 *quantum ibi antiquitatis! quae facta, quos uiros audias!* A different view in 3.7.14 (we cannot become famous *factis: nam horum materia in aliena manu*).

2 Bructerum regem ui et armis induxit in regnum 'installed the king of the Bructeri in his kingdom by force of arms', *OLD induco* 8a (first here in prose). *Bructerum* shows the old gen. pl. ending (contrast *Bructerorum* at Tac. *H.* 5.18.1, *An.* 1.60.3) used often in poetry, sometimes in prose (only here in P.), for names of peoples: e.g. Caes. *BG* 7.77.12 *Teutonum*, Livy 24.49.7 *Celtiberum* (N–W 1 181–4); cf. perhaps *CIL* v.2 8768 B<small>RVCHERVM</small> (*TLL* 11 2206.43–4). The resulting jingle *Bruc̲terum reg̲em . . . induxit in reg̲num*, each a cretic-spondee (the quantity in *Bructĕrum* is shown by e.g. Strabo 7.1.3 Βροῦκτεροι, Claudian *IV cons. Hon.* 45), marks Spurinna's intervention as self-evidently right. The Bructeri lived on the Rhine (Rives 1999: 255–6); Spurinna presumably installed this king (*OCD* 'client kings') when governor of neighbouring Germania Inferior (a post inferred only from this passage; cf. 3.1.12 *prouincias rexit*, probably an aggrandising plural). Tac. *G.* 33.1 reports the massacre of 60,000 Bructeri by neighbouring tribes that left them *penitus excisis* 'wholly annihilated'; the relative chronology with the event mentioned here, despite modern historians' desire to make them coincide, is uncertain (Rives 1999: 257–8), not least given the likelihood that P. and/or Tacitus is being tendentious. The date of Spurinna's governorship is uncertain, but a short tenure around 97 seems most likely (Syme 1985c: 275–7, id. 1991: 543–5, *BNP* 'Vestricius' (Eck)): the widely favoured alternative, *c.* 83 (or even earlier, S-W 155), is hard to square with Cottius' death, which is topical here and in 3.10, and which must coincide with Vestricius' command (§3 *absens amisit* can hardly refer to a separate trip, *pace* Dessau *PIR²* V 308, S-W 155–6). Active military service as a septuagenarian sounds arduous, but there are parallels (S-W on 3.1.10), and the travel may have been the worst of it (below). **ui et armis:** a common hendiadys, esp. in Cicero and Livy. **ostentatoque bello** 'and with [only] the threat of war', *OLD ostento* 7; cf. Tac. *H.* 3.78.2 *ostentare potius urbi bellum quam inferre*. Epexegetic *-que* (*OLD* 6) introduces a second description of the same event. S-W 155 calls it a 'campaign', but P. may be talking up pacific diplomacy (below on *terrore*). **ferocissimam gentem . . . perdomuit:** a cliché, perhaps an official one: e.g. Livy 43.4.5 and Pl. *NH* 5.127 (*domare*), Sen. *Polyb.* 15.5 (*subicere imperio*), and esp. Tac. *An.* 3.47.4 (loosely quoting Tiberius) *ferocissimas gentis perdomitas* (with Woodman–Martin for the animal-taming metaphor). P. turns it to point with *terrore* (below). The Bructeri had amply proved their *ferocia* (the quintessential barbarian quality: Woodman–Martin on Tac. *An.* 3.40.2) in the 1c. AD (Rives 1999: 256), before their 'extermination' (above). **ferocissimam ... pulcherrimum:** two resonant superlatives, befitting the high style (§3 *grauissimo*, §6 *consummatissimo*, §7 *celeber-rimo*). **quod est pulcherrimum uictoriae genus** '– the most glorious [*OLD pulcher* 2b] sort of victory –' (lit. '[that] which is . . . '): *quod* (= *id quod*, 2.1.10n. *qua*) refers to the sentence it interrupts, *ferocissimam gentem terrore perdomuit* (Kraut 1872: 9, H–S 571 §308g.α). The parenthesis enhances that claim, emphasising through delay *terrore perdomuit*; cf. 2.11.17 *quod eximium eius orationi inest* and esp. 2.20.14 *quod est improbissimum genus falsi.* This parenthetical use of *quod*, commenting on the surrounding sentence and/or the following word or phrase, is common in P. (e.g. 2.11.9 *quod maxime credo*, 3.6.6 *quod mauis*, 6.22.7 *quod abominor*). Certainly in its longer forms it is not so much colloquial (despite many scholars: 2.3.2n. *sed*) as a rhetorical 'floor-holding' device (a term of Bolkestein 1998): e.g. Cic. *Quinct.* 83, Livy 6.24.9 with Kraus, Quint. 1.3.14, Tac. *Ag.* 9.4, *H.* 1.8.2 (most of these also with superlatives). The tendentious claim that bloodless victory is the most glorious recurs in *Pan.* 16.4 and 56.7–8; cf. Tac. *G.* 33.1 *non armis telisque Romanis sed, quod magnificentius est* [NB], *oblectationi oculisque ceciderunt.* **terrore perdomuit:** the jingle marks point: utter conquest (*OLD perdomo* 2) through fear (alone). Cf. *Pan.* 14.1 *ferociam superbiamque Parthorum ex proximo auditus magno terrore cohiberes* (Trajan's early service in Syria) and contrast Sen. *NQ* 3.*pr.*10 *et, qua maior nulla uictoria est, uitia domuisse.* If P. means diplomacy, this is a triumph of rhetorical hyperbole (cf. *sudore et sanguine et factis . . . ui et armis . . . terrore*). *terror* is the sentiment desirable in potentially unruly provincials: cf. *Pan.* 12.1 *nunc redit omnibus* [*sc.* 'provincials'] *terror et metus* (thanks to Trajan).

3 et hoc quidem uirtutis praemium, illud solacium doloris accepit 'and that is what he received as reward for his valour; but he also received this [= the following] as solace for his grief', with homoeoteleutic chiasmus *uirtutis praemium ~ solacium doloris*. The *praemium/solacium* pair, perhaps standard (e.g. [Quint.] *Decl. min.* 324.4 *ita illic praemium est, hic solacium*) returns in §5. For *et . . . quidem*, see 2.1.7n. *et*, with Solodow 1978: 67–9 on the lack of *sed/tamen*; together with *hoc . . . illud* it articulates the turn from the first topic, Spurinna's statue, to the second, that of Cottius. **quod** '(the fact) that', *OLD* 2a. **Cottio:** son of Vestricius and his wife Cottia (3.10), known only from these letters. If Cottia were a relative of P., as Syme guessed (2.4n. CALVINAE), Cottius would be too. Among his names (evidently) were Vestricius Cottius, combining paternal and maternal *gentilicia* in a form of elite polyonymy by now common; cf. C. *Bruttius* Praesens L. *Fulvius* Rusticus (addressee of 7.3), son of Bruttius and Fulvia (Salway 1994: 131–3). **quem amisit** 'whom he lost', standard euphemism (*OLD amitto* 9b). **absens** glances at a stock topos of lament, not to have been at the side of a dying relative: 8.23.8 (Avitus: §6n. *priuatim*), Tac. *Ag.* 45.4 with Ogilvie–Richmond. **habitus est honor statuae** '[Cottius] was honoured with a statue' (lit. 'the honour of a statue was done [to Cottius]'), *OLD honor* 3a, *TLL* VI.3 2443.11–14; *statuae* is gen. of definition (2.1.3n. *publici*). Presumably not a triumphal statue like his father's, given that P. does not say so. The consular Licinius Sura also received a posthumous statue, in 110 (Dio 68.15.3²), of which type it is unclear. **rarum id in iuuene** *sc. est.* At §5 Cottius is (by implication) *adulescens.* Such terms are affective and flexible, and Cottius (whose father was in his mid- to late seventies, §1n. *Vestricio*) might well have been in his thirties or more: S–W 155 has him already an ex-praetor, like the *iuuenis* and *adulescens* Minicius of 1.14.3, 10. Perhaps echoed in Sid. *Ep.* 7.2.5 *quod tam laudandum in iuuentute quam rarum* (with van Waarden). **pater hoc quoque merebatur** 'his father deserved this as well', *sc.* as his own statue. **cuius grauissimo uulneri magno aliquo fomento medendum fuit** 'whose wound so deep needed healing with some great remedy', working out the common medical metaphor of grief as 'wound' (*OLD grauis* 14b, *uulnus* 3, *fomentum* 1b 'dressing', *medeor* 2a), a consolatory commonplace (5.16.11, Tac. *Ag.* 45.5; Morford 1973: 29–31): cf. 4.21.4 *magno tamen fomento dolor meus acquiescet*, 5.16.11, 6.7.2. *medendum fuit* is impersonal passive, governing dat. *uulneri*, and with *fomento* abl. of means. Medical imagery is frequent in P., in analogies (1.8.12, 8.24.5), similes (2.8.2n. *ut aegri*, 4.22.7) and metaphors (2.11.6n. *acres*, 3.20.7–8, 6.16.13, *Pan.* 6.1, 30.5, 45.4).

4 praeterea continues the sentence beginning §3 *sed.* **tam clarum specimen indolis dederat** 'had furnished such clear/splendid proof of excellent character' (*OLD clarus* 4 'distinct', 8 'splendid', *specimen* 1a, *do* 14; for *indolis* see 2.6.6n. *optimae*). For the motif, cf. 5.21.4 (young Julius Avitus) *in flore primo tantae indolis iuuenis exstinctus*, Livy 35.15.3, grief for a prince who had shown such promise (*id enim iam specimen sui dederat*) of kingly character (*magni iustique regis . . . indolem*). P. apparently gave some such proof himself (3.11.5 *non nullius indolis dedi specimen*). **uita eius breuis et angusta . . . hac uelut immortalitate:** equal and opposite noun-phrases (9~9 syllables). The redundant pair *breuis et angusta* also at e.g. Cic. *ND* 2.20, Tac. *G.* 6.1, *D.* 30.5 (Murgia 1985: 188; the 'other resemblances to the *Germania*' which he attributes to 2.7 are very slight, but see §2n. *quod*). **debuerit:** pf. subj. 'to imply final result' (G–L §513). **hac uelut immortalitate proferri:** *OLD uelut* 4 'as it were', *profero* 10b 'extend, prolong' (cf. 3.7.14 [*uitam*] *studîs proferamus*). A key image near the centre of the letter. For the 'immortality' bestowed by a public statue, see 1.17.4, Cic. *Phil.* 9.10, Phaedrus 2.9.2 *aeterna in basi*. But physical monuments were evidently impermanent (*Pan.* 52.3–5, Cic. *Phil.* 9.14; Fejfer 2008: 63–5, 390–3; cf. Verginius' uncompleted tomb in 6.10), and this one will be trumped by P.'s literary portrait, his Life of Cottius (3.10.6 *non fragilem et caducam sed immortalem . . . effigiem*; cf. 2.10.4). As with statues (intro.), Regulus will provide the counter-example, with an absurd Life of his dead son (4.7). **ei:** possessive dat. (*sc. erat*). **sanctitas grauitas auctoritas etiam** 'probity [*OLD* 3], gravity, authority indeed': asyndetic tricolon with homoeoteleuton (-*itas*). Three qualities associated particularly with older men (e.g. 4.3.1 *sanctitate . . . auctoritate aetate quoque*), especially *auctoritas* (the *apex senectutis* in Cic. *Cato* 60), which therefore comes third, with a 'capping' *etiam* (2.1.6n.). On

Plinian *sanctitas*, see Méthy 2007: 121–8. **ut posset senes illos prouocare uirtute quibus nunc honore adaequatus est** 'that he could rival in valour those older men to whom he has now been made equal in honour' (*OLD prouoco* 5b, *Pan.* 51.3), with chiasmus in *posset . . . prouocare uirtute ~ honore adaequatus est.* The noun *honor* glides between English 'honour' (*OLD* 1) here and §7, and '(an) honour' (*OLD* 2) in §§3, 5. **senes illos:** *illos* gestures to all those statues one sees (§7n. *in*), but also perhaps to those great men of former times (§1n. *illis*). One could be called *senex* from mid-forties (hence 'older' in previous n.), though usage generally implies something older (Powell 1988: 2 n.8); P.'s polarity of *iuuenis* Cottius vs *senes* maximises a potentially slight difference.

5 quo quidem honore: *quidem* marks a new turn in the argument (Solodow 1978: 115–16), to exemplarity. The common alliteration with *quo* is bolstered by the surrounding words: *adaequatus . . . quo quidem . . . quantum.* **quantum ego interpretor** 'as I at least understand it' (*OLD interpretor* 4, with *quantum* internal acc.: *NLS* §13.iii), varying the Ciceronian *ut ego interpretor* and grander than *ut puto.* **non modo . . . uerum etiam:** abundant in Cicero (> 150×), then scarce except in P. (2.18.5, 5.13.1, 8, 9.19.3) and Apuleius (21×); see also 2.3.7n. *uerum.* **defuncti memoriae, dolori patris:** chiasmus, reprising (also chiastically) §4 *Cottius ipse . . .* and §3 *pater hoc.* The last mention of Spurinna, reduced to the supporting role of grieving parent, as Cottius (soon joined by P.: §6n. *priuatim*) fills the stage. **exemplo:** exemplarity trumps *memoria* and *dolor*, as P. emphasises the didactic value of the statue (Leach 1990: 21). See intro., 2.1.7n. *exemplar.* In the preceding letter P. was the *exemplum* for Avitus (2.6n. AVITO); now it is a young man's turn to instruct. **prospectum est** 'thought has been taken for' (*OLD prospicio* 6, impersonal passive) + dat. (*memoriae, dolori, exemplo*); the closing rhythm (six heavy syllables) underlines the gravity. **acuent . . . praemia constituta, acuent . . . gloriosa solacia:** *OLD acuo* 3 'incite'; cf. *Pan.* 44.7 *acuuntur isto integritatis . . . pretio similes.* Two balanced clauses (33~40 syllables) with homoeoteleuton (*praemia constituta ~ gloriosa solacia*), arranged ABCD~ACBD (A = *acuent*, B = *ad . . .*, C = object, D = subject phrase); there is further variety in *ad bonas artes* (noun) ~ *ad liberos suscipiendos* (gerundive) and in the subject phrases, one bulked out with *digni sint modo*, the second doubled (*et . . . et*). **bonas artes** 'noble behaviour' (*OLD ars* 4a). *bonae artes* can mean the liberal arts (1.22.1, *OLD ars* 6a), but here has the moralising sense (as in 5.17.1, to Spurinna) especially popular with Sallust (incl. *Jug.* 4.7: cf. below on *tanta*), Seneca and Tacitus. **iuuentutem adulescentibus:** juxtaposed synonyms, the first direct object of *acuent*, the second indirect object of *constituta.* **quoque:** as well as for older men. **digni sint modo** 'if only they prove worthy' (*OLD modo* 4; *sint* is jussive, 'let them only . . . '). **tanta praemia constituta** 'the granting of such high rewards' (Radice), *OLD consisto* 8. On this common construction (noun + participle for English abstract noun + gen.), see *NLS* §95. Sall. *Jug.* 4.5–6 reflects on the exhortatory effect of statues; Polyb. 6.53–4 describes young men inspired by *imagines* at a Roman funeral. **principes uiros** 'leading men', i.e. the elite: cf. 4.8.3 (*uir*), 7.6.1 (*uiri*), 7.24.4 (*femina*). Quite common, it perhaps has a whiff of officialese (e.g. Aug. *RG* 12, Vell. 2.89.4) suited to the grand tone; Suetonius uses it regularly, Tacitus rarely. **ad liberos suscipiendos** 'to father children' (cf. *OLD suscipio* 4a–b). The need to encourage elite child-raising is evident from the Augustan marriage laws, *ingentia praemia et pares poenae* (*Pan.* 26.5). The expense of education and the *cursus honorum* deterred, as did the potential rewards of childlessness through *captatio* (2.20.intro.): Hopkins 1983: 120–200. There were similar difficulties with the *plebs* (1.8.11, *Pan.* 26–7). Desire to raise children is also a reflection of a good emperor (10.2.2, *Pan.* 22.3, 26.5, 27.1; Woodman on Vell. 2.103.5; Sen. *Contr.* 2.5.2). **suscipiendos:** heroic clausula (2.3.3n. *narrat*). **et gaudia ex superstitibus et ex amissis tam gloriosa solacia** 'the joy they will have from them if they survive, the solace so glorious [*OLD gloriosus* 2] if they are lost' (*OLD ex* 18). Chiastic rising bicolon (9~14 syllables) puts weight on the patriotic paradox that the prospect of dead children will be an equal incentive to parenthood; *gloriosa solacia*, paired only here, makes point. An opposite oxymoron attends Regulus as he erects statues to his dead son, 4.2.5 *in summa infamia gloriosus* ('self-important [*OLD gloriosus* 1] in all his disrepute').

6 His ex causis: summing up the reasons for P.'s 'public' grief (2.1.6n. *huius*). The formula is unique to him (5×); cf. 2.1.10n. *quibus ex causis*. **statuā:** abl. of cause (*OLD laetor* 1b), completing rings with §3 *honor statuae* and §1 *triumphalis statua*. The theme-word has now been stated three times, each time in a different case: cf. 1.10 (in 2.3.11n. *Isaeum*), and contrast the ring-composition of 1.17.1 *statuam... in foro ponere* ~ 1.17.4 *statuam in foro... ponere*, and of 3.6.1 *signum* ~ 3.6.6 *signum*. *Cotti* reminds us that Spurinna's statue is forgotten. **publice laetor, nec priuatim minus** 'I am delighted as a citizen; and I am no less delighted on a personal level': the 'personal' reasons follow, in chiastic antithesis to *his ex causis*. For the opposition, see 2.1.7n. *non*, marking a similar move from public to private and asserting P.'s special claim to grief; here that claim continues in *mihi* and even §7 *nostrum*. With no child of his own (2.18.intro.), he 'good as borrows a son' (Henderson 2002a: 32–3) – a dead one now, after Avitus in the last letter (2.6n. Avɪᴛᴏ) – and appropriates Spurinna's grief for himself (cf. Stat. *Silu.* 5.5). Fuller lament, and more explicitly paternal rhetoric, will follow that Avitus to the grave in 8.23 (Bernstein 2008: 220 n.51). **amaui...tam ardenter quam nunc impatienter requiro** 'I loved as passionately as I now miss unbearably' (*OLD ardenter* 2, *requiro* 5), chiastic. On P.'s friendly love, see 2.2.1n. *amor*; *ardenter* is a natural accompaniment to *amare* at 3.2.4, 3.9.7 and to *diligere* at 1.14.10, 6.4.3, 7.20.7, *Pan.* 85.8 (as e.g. Cic. *Fam.* 9.14.4 *in amore... ardentius*). The rarer *impatienter* is contemporary (*OLD*), and associated by P. with loss: 6.1.1 *impatientius careas*, 9.22.2 *dolet... impatientissime*; also [Quint.] *Decl. mai.* 1.17, 16.4. **consummatissimum** 'most perfect', only here and in Sid. *Epp.* (4×), the most splendid superlative (§2n. *ferocissimam*) saved for last. **erit...**

pergratum mihi 'it will give me great delight' (cf. 3.5.1 *pergratum est mihi*, 9.40.1 *pergratas*), a common phrase in Cicero, who widely used and coined adjectives in *per-* as (effectively) superlatives; P. by contrast has just two such possible coinages, 3.9.28 *perdecorus* and 9.31.1 *percopiosus* (cf. Sid. *Ep.* 4.7.3 *percopiose*): full survey in André 1951. *mihi* pursues the claim of *priuatim*: P. depicts himself (alone) as the ideal viewer of Cottius' portrait.   **hanc ... commeare** blends anaphoric tricolon (*hanc ... hac ... hanc*) with two antithetical pairs (*subinde ... subinde* and *sub hac ... praeter hanc*).   **effigiem:** from here the letter, like P., keeps its gaze fixed on Cottius' statue, ignoring that of Vestricius (beside it?). He will acquire a truly *immortalem effigiem* in 3.10.6 (§4n. *hac*).   **subinde intueri, subinde respicere, sub hac consistere, praeter hanc commeare** 'now to gaze at [this statue of his], now to look round at it, to stand below it, to come and go past it', two actions (stand contemplating it, glance round at it while passing) distributed across equal cola (13~13 syllables) of opposite construction: first *subinde* is repeated while the verbal prefixes vary (*intueri ... respicere*), then the verbal prefix is repeated (*consistere ... commeare*) while *sub hac* and *praeter hanc* vary. Double *subinde ... subinde* (= *modo ... modo*) is first here (K–S II 70). For *intueri* of contemplating statues, cf. Sall. *Jug.* 4.5, Tac. *An.* 2.37.2. *respicere* means 'look round at', not just backwards (e.g. Pl. *Mil.* 361 *respicedum ad laeuam*). One stood literally 'below' a statue, which was mounted on a base typically 1.2–1.8m high (Fejfer 2008: 18, 25).

7 etenim introduces a closing truism (2.5.11n.).   **defunctorum imagines domi positae:** ancestral masks were displayed in the *atria* of noble houses (*OCD* '*imagines*', Flower 1996).   **dolorem nostrum leuant:** the consolatory function of statue and letter (cf. §5 *tam gloriosa solacia*) climaxes with a stock phrase of consolation (e.g. Cic. *Fam.* 5.16.1, Sen. *Marc.* 16.8; cf. 8.19.1 *doloris leuamentum*) for this miniature *laudatio funebris* (intro.). *nostrum* implies people in general (true pl.), but abets P.'s private project too (§6n. *priuatim*).   **quanto magis ... !** 'how much more ... !', exclamatory question (*OLD quanto* 1b).   **hae** sc. *imagines dolorem nostrum leuant*. *imago*, covering all artistic likenesses (*OLD* 1), refers to death-masks and statues alike.   **quibus** 'by which', abl. of instrument.   **in celeberrimo loco:** where the most people will see them (*OLD celeber* 1a), a stock desiderandum for a statue: Cic. *II Verr.* 2.159, *Tab. Siar.* IIb.27 *quam celeberrimo loco*, *SC de Pisone patre* line 171 *in ... celeberrimo loco*, and examples in Stewart 2003: 138–9; also 3.6.4 *celebri loco*. Senatorial statues at this period might be in any imperial forum, on the Capitol, in temples and elsewhere (Alföldy 2001, Fejfer 2008: 51–63); P.'s words perhaps imply the Forum Romanum (cf. 1.17.4 *in foro populi Romani* and §1n. *triumphalis*), specifically the area near the rostra (Pl. *NH* 34.24 '*quam oculatissimo loco*', *eaque est in rostris*), as is likely if Cottius was next to his father (see Alföldy 2001: 19–20 for triumphal statues *in rostris*).   **non modo species et uultus illorum | sed honor etiam et gloria refertur** 'not only their appearance and features, but also their honour and glory is brought to mind' (*OLD species* 3a–b, *uultus* 4, *rĕfero* 19) or perhaps 'not only are their appearance and features brought to mind, but also due honour and glory is paid' (*OLD rĕfero* 13c, Ov.

Met. 2.285–6 *hunc fertilitatis honorem* | *officiique refers,* Stat. *Theb.* 12.819 *meriti post me referentur honores* – neither a perfect parallel), a sylleptic (2.1.4n. *pari*) use of *refertur* if so, both between the clauses, and because *gloriam referre* is unparalleled; for its agreement in number either way see G–L §285.2. Like domestic *imagines,* these statues recall a man's appearance; unlike them, their display in a prestigious location recalls in addition his great deeds. Isocolon (12~12 syllables) opposes two redundant noun-pairs (the first surprisingly unique, the second common), chiastic in length (3+2 ~ 2+3 syllables); *illorum* and *refertur* are distributed in double *apo koinou.* Cottius' distinctions were literally proclaimed (*OLD rĕfero* 18) by the inscription on the base: cf. 3.6.5 *nomen meum honoresque* with Henderson 2002a: 162–4; Pl. *NH* 34.17 *propagarique memoriā hominum et honores legendi aeuo basibus inscribi* [*coeperunt*]; Woolf 1996, esp. 25–7; Fejfer 2008: 25–33. But that goes without saying, and would make a flat close. On the consolation of fame, cf. 2.1.11 and Tac. *Ag.* 46.3–4; unlike the latter (and Sall. *Jug.* 4.6: §5n. *tanta*), P. talks down the value of physical likenesses but does not dismiss them altogether (*non modo,* not *non*). **sed ... etiam:** for the split (quite rare), cf. e.g. Cic. *Phil.* 3.34, Livy 1.40.3, Quint. 1.1.19. *non modo ... sed etiam* is only here in P. (Trajan in 10.32.1), varying §5 *uerum etiam.*

8

How are you spending your leisure time in Comum? I long to be there: the slavery of obligations at Rome is unending.

After the public grandeur of 2.7 comes a brief, intimate letter reversing the scenario of 2.2: P. is now busy, his addressee presumed to be enjoying *otium.* Longing for the country and release from urban cares is an old motif (Hor. *Sat.* 2.6.60 *o rus, quando ego te aspiciam?*) developed by P. already in 1.9 ('how time is wasted in the city! how much more fruitful my leisure at Laurentum!'). That letter gets an immediate response in 1.10, where P. is consoled by Euphrates' advice that public duty (1.10.10 *agere negotium publicum ...*) is the finest form of philosophy. 2.8 is less explicitly answered, but public duty is on spectacular display in the Priscus trial (2.11), while 2.17 will outweigh these complaints with abundant *otium.* Another 'partner' letter in *Epistles* 1–2 is 1.3, where the same Caninius' leisure is threatened by business (1.3.2); P. meets that threat with upbeat exhortation to immortality through literature. The contrasting movement of 2.8 from cheer to gloom, ending with a bleak image of P. enslaved, casts the first of several shadows over the book, so presaging, perhaps, a narrative of retreat (Intro. 16–17, 19–20).

P.'s claim of unending occupations is characteristically belied by his minute craftsmanship. It moves in three stages (30~25~30 words = 65~49~73 syllables). In §1 P. situates Caninius in his blessed retreat at Comum, precisely polarised against his own life of urban slavery, §2 (*numquamne* to the end); between these two worlds (§2 *sed ... fontes*) comes the central equivocation between P.'s refusal to show envy and his anguish that he cannot share Caninius' *otium.*

Lefèvre 1987: 254–8 = id. 2009: 239–42 explores the pairing of villa and *studia*, and diagnoses 'decadence' in P. (see Whitton 2011b). See also Hoffer 1999: 29–44 and Marchesi 2008: 30–6 on 1.3, Henderson 2002a: 102–24 on 3.7 (esp. 105–8 on Caninius), and G–M 172–9 on 1.9–10. See too 2.2.2n. *otio*.

CANINIO: Caninius Rufus (*PIR*² C 394), an equestrian in P.'s native Comum, receives seven letters: 1.3, 2.8, 3.7, 6.21, 7.18, 8.4, 9.33. Another (7.25) to 'Rufus' is a potential candidate (S-W, Syme 1985a: 341, Birley 2000a: 47), spoiling the pattern of distribution, and breaking the rule that P. uses the same single name for any one person throughout (Barwick 1936: 428–35: see Intro. 40; so does 9.38, below). The *inscriptiones* usually reduce an addressee to his *cognomen* (2.1n. C. PLINIVS) but *Rufi* abound, hence perhaps the less ambiguous *gentilicium* here and in 2.10 (Octavius Rufus) and 2.20 (Calvisius Rufus) – though other correspondents with common *cognomina* are not so helpfully distinguished (2.13n. PRISCO, 2.14n. MAXIMO). Caninius has an important role in the collection as 'an *alter ego* who will make the perfect reader for *all* the *Letters*' (Henderson 2002a: 105). Epistle 1.3 sites him in Comum (1.3.1 *quid agit Comum, tuae meaeque deliciae?*), urging him to enjoy the *otium* that P. (implicitly) misses; 3.7 (on the death of Silius Italicus) ends with an image of Caninius and P. as literary partners (3.7.15). His next letter (6.21) also concerns a poet (Julius Romanus); 8.4 (on his *Dacian War*) and 9.33 (the dolphin) reveal that poetry is Caninius' own *métier*. Epistle 9.38 praises the *librum omnibus numeris absolutum* of *Rufus noster*, surely Caninius, who thus rings the collection (1.3 ∼ 9.38, third from the end) as a key figure of and for Plinian *otium litteratum* (Gibson forthcoming).

1 Studes 'are you at your books?' (Walsh). *studere* (*OLD* 4), like *studia* (2.2.2n.), signifies literary practice and composition in P.; it instantly frames the letter as a continuation of 1.3 (1.3.3 *studîs... hoc sit negotium tuum, hoc otium...*). The absence of -*ne* (G–L §453) seems conversational (cf. 2.15.1 *placent*, 2.20.9 *sufficiunt*). **an** 'or' (*OLD* 4a). **piscaris:** fishing is mentioned again at 9.7.4 (Como) and 9.33.3. The pairing with hunting is common. **uenaris:** P. routinely intertwines hunting with *studia* as a villa pursuit. Normally a pedestrian activity, it involved both physical exercise (5.6.46 *nam studîs animum, uenatu corpus exerceo*) and patient sitting by nets (e.g. Mart. 12.1), both of which stimulate composition, as P. famously tells Tacitus in 1.6 (Edwards 2008). Hence they can be combined: 5.18.2 *in Tuscis et uenor et studeo, quae interdum alternis, interdum simul facio.* Hunting was a popular aristocratic sport, not least with Trajan (*Pan.* 81.1–3, Dio Chrys. *Or.* 3.135 (probably Trajan), Dio Cass. 68.7.3, Aymard 1951: 492–8): see Anderson 1985, Green 1996, Woolf 2003: 213–15. **simul omnia:** P.'s fantasies reach hyperbole (simultaneous fishing and hunting sounds optimistic). **possunt... nostrum:** justifies *simul omnia* (chiastically repeated in *omnia simul*) in isocolon (16∼16 syllables). **ad Larium nostrum** 'beside our (Lake) Como' (*OLD ad* 13a–b); *Larius noster* again at 6.24.2, 7.11.5. The ellipse (for *Larius lacus*, as at 4.30.2, 9.7.1) is Plinian; together with *noster*, it affectively marks a common delight (cf. 1.3.1 *Comum, tuae meaeque deliciae*) and sets the scene for the over-reader. **lacus piscem, feras siluae quibus lacus cingitur, studia altissimus iste secessus affatim suggerunt:** rising AB~BA~BA tricolon (4~11~17 syll.), varied sg. sg. ~ pl. pl. ~ pl. sg. (*piscem* is collective sg.). The three elements reprise *studes an piscaris an uenaris* in the order BCA, making *studes... studia* ring §1. **altissimus iste secessus** 'that most profound retreat'; *OLD altus* 10b (as 2.1.4), *iste* 3, implying 'that you/we know so well': cf. 1.3.3 *alto isto pinguique secessu*, 9.3.1 *pingue illud altumque otium* (both to Caninius). *secessus* is both absence from Rome (*OLD* 1b) and the site of that absence (*OLD* 2b). It defines *otium*, the leisure from metropolitan *negotia* that gives time for *studia* (2.2.2n. *otio*): 2.11.1n. *quietis*, 2.17.2n. *decem*. Alliteration of *s* marks the whole of *studia... suggerunt*. **affatim suggerunt** 'supply in abundance' (*OLD suggero* 3a): cf. 2.17.26 *suggerunt affatim ligna... siluae*, Ammianus 27.7.6 *alimenta affatim... suggerentibus locis* (with 2.6.5n. *quibus*). For the ending -*im*, see 2.6.2n. *gradatim*. The verb is natural with *piscem, feras*, but sylleptic (2.1.4n. *pari*) with *studia* (what Caninius' retreat provides is the right backdrop for writing: 1.6.2 *siluae et solitudo... magna cogitationis incitamenta sunt*).

2 omnia simul completes a trio (AB~BA~BA) with §1 *simul omnia... omnia simul*, while *facis* inverts *fieri*. **aliquid:** any one of them. **non possum dicere 'inuideo':** envy is not P.'s style: cf. 1.10.12 *neque enim ego, ut multi, inuideo aliis bono quo ipse careo*, amidst comparable equivocation (1.10.9–12). **angor tamen non et mihi licere** 'yet it pains me that I cannot (do so) too' (*OLD angor* 4 + acc. + inf.): *angor*, at the centre of the letter, is the key word. The verb is strong (mostly used of death or illness: 4.21.2, 5.5.2, 7.19.1; also 5.1.12); the whole phrase resonates with 1.10.9 'why do I talk of Euphrates when I have no time to hear him?' *ut magis angar quod non licet?*, referring to P.'s duties as prefect of the treasury of Saturn, Jan. 98 – Aug. 100 (S-W 75–8; on this post see Millar 1964, Corbier 1974); the echo perhaps implies that they are in mind here too. It is court work, by contrast, which fills his time in 2.14, a letter whose gloomy end develops the sour note here. See also 4.23.4 (eighth from the end of book 4) *quando mihi licebit [sc. otio frui]?* Ever-busy P. assures himself that old age will compensate (3.1.11–12, 4.23.2) – without conviction. **concupisco:** 2.3.7n. **ut aegri uinum balinea fontes** *sc. concupiscunt.* Abstinence from wine and bathing was common 'treatment' for illness (recurrent in Celsus' medical tract): cf. 7.1.4–6 (P. refuses drink and a bath), 7.21.3 *balineum... uinum*, Sen. *Ep.* 68.7, 78.11 *carere assuetis uoluptatibus* with Summers. The addition of *fontes* makes a typical asyndetic tricolon (2.3.1n. *facultas*) and a less prosaic expression; cf. 7.26.2 *balinea imaginatur et fontes [sc. infirmus]*. His desire is presumably for the cool draughts of a (rustic) spring (cf. 4.30.3, on the *fons* near Comum: *iuxta recumbis... ex ipso fonte (nam est frigidissimus) potas*), rather than a swim (8.8.6). On medical similes see 2.7.3n. *cuius*. **numquamne hos artissimos laqueos, si soluere negatur, abrumpam?** 'will I never break these bonds so tight, if I am refused permission to cast them off?' (*OLD artus* 1a, *laqueus* 2b, *soluo* 1a, *nego* 5b, *abrumpo* 1); cf. 6.6.9 *abrumpe si qua te retinent* (conversely summoning his addressee to Rome). The bonds are his duties, 'casting them off' (lit. 'untying them') is to complete them, 'breaking' them is to abandon them incomplete and escape the city headlong (Gierig); the latter is of course unthinkable. Seneca seems to be in mind: *Tranq.* 10.1 *fortuna . . . laqueum impegit quem nec soluere possis nec rumpere*, *Ep.* 22.3 *quod male implicuisti soluas potius quam abrumpas, dummodo, si alia soluendi ratio non erit, uel abrumpas*. Both texts prescribe responses to life's burdens (*negotia, occupationes*), the former endurance, the latter withdrawal into *otium*. *Tranq.* 10.1–3 develops at length a slavery metaphor (*tota uita seruitus est*), imagery adopted by P. here (*OLD laqueus* 1d, 2b) and in §3; cf. 9.28.4 for similar imagery, now jocular (Morello 2007: 184–5 and G–M 185 see rather a metaphor of hunting). Where Seneca gives firm guidance, P. indulges in a moment of human self-pity. For the 'fetters' of city life, cf. also Cic. *De or.* 2.22 *cum rus ex urbe tamquam e uinclis euolauissent*, Hor. *Ep.* 1.7.67 (an auctioneer's *mercennaria uincla*). **artissimos:** a bitter reply to §1 *altissimus*. Paired with *laqueus* at Cic. *II Verr.* 1.13 *artioribus . . . laqueis*, Sen. *Phoen.* 148 *artis . . . laqueis*. **si . . . negatur:** tantamount, with the present tense, to '*since* I cannot'. Alternatively, pres. for fut. pf., as 2.9.2 *obtinet* (Ritchie 1902: 7). **numquam, puto** 'no, never, I suppose' (*OLD puto* 8): *numquam* repeats the question (2.6.4n. *etiamne*).

3 ueteribus negotiis noua accrescunt resembles Sen. *Breu.* 17.5 *nouae occupationes ueteribus substituuntur* on the ceaseless round of ambition (cf. *occupationes* below), but P.'s *negotia* are piled up, not substituted. For *accrescunt* 'are added to' (rare) see *Pan.* 62.8 (*TLL* 1 337.83–338.9); it governs *negotiis* (dat.). For the duties of senatorial life see Talbert 1984: 66–76; on P.'s particular burden, §2n. *angor*. **nec tamen priora peraguntur** alliteratively explains what is already implicit in *accrescunt*. **tot nexibus, tot quasi catenis maius in dies occupationum agmen extenditur** 'so many are the knots, so many (as it were) the chains with which the procession of duties stretches daily longer': *OLD nexus* 2a, *quasi* 9a, *dies* 3b, *occupatio* 2b (= *negotium*), *agmen* 3 (personifying), *extendo* 5b. The slavery metaphor (§2n. *numquamne*) is developed, but the referent shifted (2.4.4n. *ita*): the slaves are now his occupations, personified as an ever-growing chain gang (Walsh 302; cf. Sen. *Tranq.* 1.8 *agmen seruorum*, Asc. on Cic. *Mil.* §28 Clark). Similar imagery in Mart. 1.15.7–8 *curaeque* <u>catenatiue</u> *labores;* | *gaudia . . .* <u>fugitiua</u> *uolant*. For *occupationes* personified, cf. Cic. *Fam.* 7.33.2 *maximarum quasi concursum* ['crowding together'] *occupationum*. A gloomy end (intro.), and one resonant with 2.9.1. **occupationum:** an echo perhaps of 2.2.2 *occupatior* (Merwald 1964: 57), underlining a contrasting pair of short 'leisure' notes 2.2~2.8 (Intro. 14–15).

9

I am worried about Clarus' candidature. My reputation is at stake, not least with the emperor. In any case he is a fine man of good family. So I am canvassing like mad, and ask that you consider helping. Just show your support and others will follow.

P. seeks support for a protégé who is standing as tribune of the plebs, in a model letter of patronage and an instance of the *negotia* lamented in 2.8 (§1n. *anxium*). Having benefited from the *suffragium* of a senior generation (2.1.8n. *candidatum*), he now takes on the role of *suffragator* himself. Being patronised is a young senator of equestrian stock, whose father received 1.16 and whose uncle Septicius Clarus is dedicatee of the *Epistles* (§4): like Voconius Romanus (2.13), Clarus typifies the interweaving of P.'s political and literary lives.

This is the first of three substantial electioneering letters: P. lobbies for Asinius Bassus as quaestor in 4.15 and for Julius Naso, perhaps for the same position, in 6.6 (with an appendix in 6.9). All three give a rare impression of 'the liveliness of elections' in the early imperial senate (S-W 157) and the concomitant importance of such interventions as this. Within the book it finds a close partner in 2.13, a more relaxed letter of recommendation for Romanus (2.13.intro.), while it also looks back at 2.7 (praise of a young man, there dead) and 2.1 (where P. was beneficiary of the patronage he now exercises): see Intro. 14–15.

Patronage is central to P.'s world, as to Roman society (Saller 1982, Wallace-Hadrill 1989, Garnsey 2010). Besides these electoral letters, he looks to advance *amici* in e.g. 1.19, 3.2, 3.8, 4.4, 7.22, 10.4, 10.12, 10.26, 10.87, 10.94. Many of these are, or contain elements of, letters of recommendation, a genre which abounded: Cugusi 1983: 40–1, 110–14. Cicero's are mostly collected in *Fam.* 13 (with Déniaux 1993); see also Hor. *Ep.* 1.9, Fronto *passim* (Champlin 1980: 29–44), and for non-literary letters Cotton 1981b. Those of P. are discussed by Pavis-d'Escurac 1992, Bérenger-Badell 2000, Rees 2007; see also 2.13. There is literary precedent and perhaps a model for P.'s electoral canvassing in Cic. *Fam.* 11.16–17 (§1 notes); certainly Ciceronian language pervades the letter.

APOLLINARI: L. Domitius Apollinaris, *cos. suff.* 97 (*PIR*² D 133, Birley 2000a: 56–7) from Vercellae (mod. Vercelli) in P.'s native Transpadana, is also blessed with P.'s longest letter, the *Tusci* villa (5.6), and at least five of Martial's epigrams (4.86, 7.26, 7.89, 10.30, 11.15, perhaps 10.12). Epistle 9.13.13 reveals that he spoke on the wrong side in the Certus debate of 97, casting a late shadow over any 'warm friend[ship]' (S-W 157) implied here and by 5.6.

1 Anxium me et inquietum habet 'is keeping me anxious and worried'; for the use of *habere*, see e.g. [Caes.] *B.Afr.* 71.2 *anxium . . . atque sollicitum*, Tac. *An.* 2.65.1 *anxium*, Juv. 10.296 *miseros trepidosque* (*TLL* VI.3 2429.58–69); for P.'s doublet, Tac. *D.* 13.1 *inquieta et anxia oratorum uita*. P. approaches his request indirectly and with no mention of the addressee (contrast 6.6.1 *si quando, nunc praecipue cuperem esse te Romae, et sis rogo*). The insistence on cares (*anxium . . . inquietum . . . cura . . . sollicitudinem . . . patior . . . discrimen*) resonates with the previous letter: here is yet another of P.'s *occupationum agmen* (2.8.3); cf. also Cic. *Fam.* 11.17.1 *pertimescam*. For the idiomatic position of *me*, leaning on (so 'focusing') *anxium* and generating hyperbaton, see Adams 1994b: 112–22. The run of five trochees (*anxium . . . habet pet-*) is striking but does not seem pointed; for a run of seven (at sentence-end) see Cic. *Or.* 224. Like clausulae, openings were the site of attention to rhythm (Quint. 9.4.62), but less so, and the phenomenon is less well understood (Wilkinson 1963: 150); see also 2.10.1n. *hominem*, 2.17.1n. *miraris*. Bornecque 1900 studies sentence-openings in *Pan*. **petitio** 'candidature' (*OLD* 5); P. does not yet specify the office (sometimes he never does: 3.2, 6.6). Electioneering is frequent in Cicero's letters (right from *Att.* 1.1.1 *petitionis nostrae*), though canvassing letters are few (*Fam.* 11.16–17); it is more rarely mentioned by P. (2.1.8, 1.14.7, 3.20, 4.25, 6.6, 6.9, 6.19). Magistrates were elected in the senate (under heavy influence from the emperor: see below and 10.12.1), and ratified in the popular assembly (Talbert 1984: 341–5). **Sexti Eruci:** Sextus Erucius Clarus (*PIR*² E 96, Birley 2000a: 58), *cos. suff.* 117, died in office as *cos.* II in 146; Gell. *NA* 13.18.2–3 calls him *uir morum et litterarum ueterum studiosissimus* (see also *NA* 7.6.12). P. usually reserves this naming style (*praenomen* and *gentilicium*) for formal introductions (S–W on 1.12.9, Jones 1991: 158; Birley 2000a: 22–3); here it distinguishes Sextus from his father, also called Erucius Clarus. One of the two, or Sextus' uncle, may have been defended in a speech by Voconius Romanus (9.28.5, where †*proclamo*†, conventionally emended to *Pro Clario*, could be *Pro Claro*: S–W, Syme 1968: 138, 147, Birley 2000a: 49). **mei:** a standard assertion of the intimacy that usually features in letters of recommendation. **quam pro me sollicitudinem non adii** 'the anxiety that I did not undergo on my own account' (*OLD adeo*¹ 11 = *patior*); *sollicitudinem*, object of *patior*, is attracted into the relative clause (G–L §616.1). Epistle 7.16.2 reveals that P. was *quaestor Caesaris*, one of the emperor's personal quaestors, who were usually guaranteed election as *candidati Caesaris* (Millar 1977: 304); this passage confirms that he was such a *candidatus*, and for his other early magistracies too (S–W 73–5, 419), so revealing, if hardly emphasising, advancement by Domitian (Intro. 6). For the idea, cf. Cic. *Fam.* 11.20.1 *quod pro me non facio, id pro te facere amor meus in te tuaque officia cogunt ut timeam.* **pro me altero** 'for another me'. A cliché of friendship (Arist. *NE* 9.4.5 = 1166a ἔστι γὰρ ὁ φίλος ἄλλος αὐτός 'for a friend is another self', Cic. *Lael.* 23 with Powell, Otto 1890: 26, Tosi 1991: 602–3) recurrent in Cicero's letters (*Att.* 3.15.4 with Shackleton Bailey). **et alioqui** 'and besides' (*OLD alioqui* 2b), a synonym for *praeterea* popular with P. (e.g. 2.15.2, 3.9.19) and his uncle. **meus pudor, mea existimatio, mea dignitas:** tricolon (4~7~5 syllables) with asseverative anaphora ('it is *my* . . . that is . . . ') and three synonyms for 'honour, reputation' (2.4.2n. *famam*; *OLD existimatio* 3), extending and justifying *pro me altero*. **in discrimen adducitur** 'is being put to the test' (*OLD discrimen* 4, *adduco* 9). A common Ciceronian phrase (often with *res*); for the subject 'reputation', cf. *Pan.* 10.1 (*auctoritas*), Cic. *Planc.* 8 (*dignitas*). P. develops this conceit of virtual candidature in 6.6.2 *rursus mihi uideor . . . candidatus*, 6.6.9 *ego ambio, ego periclitor . . . si negatur, mea repulsa est*; cf. Cic. *Fam.* 11.16.3 *persuade tibi . . . me petere praeturam*. It is a cliché of recommendation that the patron's reputation is most at stake: 10.26.3 *gaudere me exornata quaestoris mei dignitate, id est per illum mea* and e.g. Cic. *Fam.* 2.14 *eius negotia sic uelim suscipias ut si esset res mea* (Cotton 1981b: 19–20); see §5n. *quantumque*.

2 ego Sexto latum clauum a Caesare nostro, ego quaesturam impe-traui 'I obtained for Sextus the broad stripe and the quaestorship from our Caesar', bicolon with anaphora of *ego* (picking up §1 *meus*..., and itself extended to tricolon by *meo*), and with *a Caesare nostro* and *impetraui* distributed in double *apo koinou*. For the construction of *impetrare* (*OLD* 1a), cf. Cic. *Fam.* 13.36.1 *ei Dola-bella rogatu meo ciuitatem a Caesare impetrauit*. P. similarly obtains imperial favours at 2.13.8 (*ius trium liberorum*), 6.25.3 (equestrian rank), 10.6.1 (citizenship); the lan-guage makes no bones about the emperor's executive power or the need for *suffragium* (2.1.8n. *candidatum*). **latum clauum:** the laticlave (a broad stripe of crimson on the toga), metonym for senatorial rank (*OLD clauus* 4); only members of that rank could stand for senatorial magistracies and so (with the quaestorship) enter the senate. Sons of senators had it by birth; the promotion of equestrians like Clarus was in the emperor's gift. See Chastagnol 1975 (distinguishing the laticlave from *allectio*); also S-W, Talbert 1984: 11–15, Millar 1977: 290–3, 299–313. P. apparently acquired it for Junius Avitus (8.23.2, 6), and tries to do so for Romanus in 10.4 (2.13.intro.). **a Caesare nostro:** a contemporary formula: 6.31.1, Mart. *Spect.* 30.3, 9.36.9, Balbus *Ad Celsum* 92.12 L. (*c.* AD 90s/100s); the grander *deus Caesar noster* at Scrib. *Comp. ep.* 13 (AD 40s), Sen. *Tranq.* 14.9. P. uses *Caesar* of emperors dead or alive, including Nerva (alive) at 2.1.3 and 9.13.22, but *noster* implies a reigning *princeps* (cf. 1.17.1 *ab imperatore nostro* with S-W), almost certainly Trajan (Syme 1958: 660–1, Mynors 352, *contra* S-W 158–9, though see S-W 65 'may be either Nerva or Trajan'; Birley 2000a makes him Nerva on p.29, Trajan on p.93), since Clarus could hardly have made this progression within Nerva's sixteen-month principate. This incidentally shows that 10.1–14, which includes no letter about Clarus, is not a complete dossier (cf. 2.13.8n. *et*). Clarus could have become *laticlauius* in late Jan. 98 (after Nerva's death) and been elected quaestor that month, have served in 99, and be planning to stand in Jan. 100 for the tribunate of 101 (for the late January election and these intervals see S-W 158, 292, Talbert 1984: 18): our letter would thus date to 99, shortly before 2.11 (Jan. 100). These dates could easily be shifted back a year; any further, and the 'book-date' for *Epistles* 2 would go past 100 (Intro. 16). On P.'s practice in naming emperors see 2.1.3n. *reliquit*. **quaesturam:** the quaestorship (*OCD* 'quaestor'), evidently held by Clarus as *candidatus Caesaris* (§1n. *quam*) soon after he obtained the laticlave (previous n.). He must have been already 28 or so: he has skipped the vigintivirate and military tribunate which would normally precede the quaestorship (S-W, Talbert 1984: 12–13). **meo** turns *ego...ego* to tricolon, and adds the topical item. **suffragio** 'support' (2.1.8n. *candidatum*). **ius tri-bunatūs petendi** 'the right to stand for tribune' (*OLD ius* 11 + gerundive). A rising senator served as tribune of the plebs (*OCD* '*tribuni plebis*') or aedile no less than a year after the quaestorship. Evidently imperial permission was required to stand (Millar 1977: 303, citing *Pan.* 69.1), even if one was not the emperor's personal candidate. Some MSS (α) have *tribunatum*, but P. routinely prefers the gerundive: 10.9.1 *petendi commeatus* and e.g. 2.11.3 *mouendarum lacrimarum*, 2.18.5 *in eligendo praeceptore*, 1.8.9, 7.6.8, 9.37.2, *Pan.* 55.4 (exceptions at 2.10.7n. *ulteriora*,

2.13.1n. *occasiones*). **quem:** the *tribunatus*. **nisi obtinet:** present tense (fut. pf.
would be expected) 'by anticipation' (G–L §595 n.2), with a sense of immediacy:
cf. 2.10.3, 2.11.25, 9.13.17, 9.19.5 (the last two in direct speech). It is common in,
but not restricted to, colloquial Latin (*pace NLS* §194): for a range see Cic. *II Verr.*
1.6 *si condemnatur*, Hor. *Sat.* 2.8.34, *C.* 3.9.17, Livy 6.15.6, Sen. *Clem.* 1.6.1, Tac.
An. 4.35.3 (with Martin–Woodman), Juv. 3.239. **in senatu:** §1n. *petitio.* Clarus
is not *candidatus Caesaris* for his next post, meaning he faces some, perhaps slight,
competition (S-W on 1.14.7, Talbert 1984: 18–19). **uereor ne decepisse Caesarem uidear** 'I fear that I will seem to have misled Caesar' by recommending
Clarus to him in the past: a stronger reason to be *anxium . . . et inquietum* than
P.'s general repute. *uereor* + clause of fearing does duty for a future tense in the
apodosis. One of the rare glimpses in the *Epistles* of P.'s personal interaction with
an emperor (Intro. 7; cf. 2.11.15, 2.13.8); with the piety cf. Quint. 4.*pr.*3 on his
own appointment by Domitian, ['I must prove my worth'] *ne fefellisse in iis uidear
principem.*

3 proinde 'therefore' (*OLD* 3). **ut talem eum iudicent omnes qualem
esse princeps mihi credidit** 'that everyone judge him to be such as the
emperor believed him to be on my word', chiastic (*iudicent omnes ~ prin-
ceps . . . credidit*), with *eum* and *esse* distributed *apo koinou*. With *qualem . . . credidit*
compare Quint. 4.*pr.*5 [*Caesar*] *me qualem esse credidit faciat* (a few lines after the
quotation in §2n. *uereor*); where Quintilian invokes Domitian as a god, P. keeps his
reverence secular (contrast 2.4.3n. *decurrit*). **quae causa si studium meum
non incitaret** 'even if I did not have this powerful incentive' (after Radice), *OLD
causa* 7a, *studium* 1a (and 5a), *incito* 5; for *si . . . non* 'even if . . . not' (before *tamen*),
see K–S II 420–1 §3a. *studium incitare* is otherwise only at Cic. *Tusc.* 5.68, *Diu.*
2.5. **adiutum . . . cuperem** 'I would be keen [to see] . . . helped': for *cupere* +
predicative adj./participle (perhaps *sc. esse*), cf. 2.13.2 *impetratum*, 7.17.9 *commutata*,
OLD 1a, *TLL* IV 1433.57–1434.3. **probissimum grauissimum eruditissi-
mum omni denique laude dignissimum:** extended tetracolon (4~4~6~11
syllables), with capping *denique* (2.3.8n.), in a sonorous string of accusatives (assonance already begun in *adiutum . . . iuuenem*). *probus* (*OLD* 4a) is 'upright, honest'.
Similar commendations in 10.94.1 (Suetonius) *probissimum honestissimum eruditissimum uirum*; also 7.22.2 (Minicianus) *idem rectissimus iudex, fortissimus aduocatus, amicus
fidelissimus*; cf. also 5.3.3 and, flattering the addressee, 9.25.2 (tricolon) and 4.26.2
(tetracolon). For *grauissimum*, see 2.7.4n. *sanctitas*; for *eruditissimum* 'extremely well
read' see 2.19.9n.; *laude dignissimus* is again at 7.15.2, 9.19.3. Typically, professional
qualifications as we know them are all but absent, though P. (like Fronto) often
emphasises literary/oratorical ability (*eruditissimum* here; §4 *disertus . . . exercitatus*,
2.13.6–7; Bérenger-Badell 2000: 177–8), and this phrase (central in the letter) is
the only direct comment on Erucius himself. See Rees 2007 on praise inflation;
P. cheerfully admits to it in 7.28.2 (to Septicius Clarus) *quid enim honestius culpa
benignitatis?* **et quidem cum tota domo** 'and along with his entire family

too', *OLD domus* 6a (preferred by P. over *familia*: Saller 1994: 84, 87). The 'extending' *quidem* reinforces and adds to what precedes (*OLD quidem* 5a, Solodow 1978: 110–20; 2.11.23n. *foedissimo*), commonly as here with *et* (e.g. 2.13.11n. *rogat*, 1.6.1 *apros tres et quidem pulcherrimos*, 1.12.1 *decessit. . . et quidem sponte*).

4 nam: explains *cum tota domo* (P. specifies just two of them). **pater ei** *sc. est* (possessive dat.). **Erucius Clarus:** *PIR*[2] E 94, an equestrian, as §2 *latum clauum* shows. He receives 1.16, in praise of the young advocate Pompeius Saturninus. **uir sanctus antiquus disertus atque in agendis causis exercitatus:** extended tetracolon of adjectives (2 ~ 3 ~ 3 ~ 11 syllables), now nominative, to replicate in father the qualities of son (§3); the first three roughly corresponding (*sanctus ~ probus, antiquus ~ grauis, disertus ~ eruditus*). For the honorific use of *uir*, see 2.11.5n.; for *sanctus* (*OLD* 4a), 2.7.4n. *sanctitas*; for *disertus*, 2.3.7n. *disertissimum*. Such qualities tend to cluster in redundant groups: §3, 2.7.4 *sanctitas grauitas auctoritas*, and e.g. 1.22.1 *nihil est enim illo grauius sanctius doctius*, 4.4.1, 4.15.7 (six), 4.17.4, 5.14.3 *quid melius, quid sanctius, quid. . . ad exemplar antiquitatis expressius?*, 7.19.4 (four). **antiquus** 'of pristine character', 'as people used to be' (*OLD* 9a): cf. Cic. *Rosc. Am.* 26 *homines antiqui*, Vell. 2.49.3 *uir antiquus et grauis*. Implying both ancient and superior (Bettini 1991: 117–19), it is high praise in P.'s lexicon of values (Intro. 8–9): *Pan.* 83.5 (Plotina) *quid enim illa sanctius, quid antiquius?*, 1.22.2 (Aristo) *quantum antiquitatis tenet!*, 3.1.6 (chez Spurinna) *quantum ibi auctoritatis!*, 4.3.1 *consul fuisti similis antiquis*, 5.1.11 *factum meum antiquum*, 5.14.3 (previous n.). **summa fide, pari constantia nec uerecundia minore:** rising AB~AB~BA tricolon (4~6~9 syllables), with three ways of saying 'utmost'. For asyndetic *par*, see 2.1.1n., for 'X, Y *nec* Z', 2.1.2n. *triginta. fides* (2.5.3n.) and *constantia* 'steadfastness' (*OLD* 2) are canonical lawyerly virtues, often combined in P. (1.7.2, 3.9.23, etc.). *uerecundia* 'modesty, restraint', another Plinian favourite, tempers its antonym *constantia* (for the opposition, cf. Cic. *Fin.* 2.114, *SHA Marc. Ant.* 12.6): Clarus knows how not to take steadfastness too far. **defendit** 'he pleads', *OLD* 7a. **habet auunculum:** in varied antithesis to *pater ei*. **C. Septicium:** Gaius Septicius Clarus (*PIR*[2] S 411), recipient of 1.1 and thus dedicatee of that book and of the whole collection (addressee too of 1.15, 7.28, 8.1); he was also dedicatee of Suetonius' *Lives of the Caesars*. Originating perhaps, like P. and Apollinaris, in Transpadana (Syme 1985a: 344), he was praetorian prefect under Hadrian, but was dismissed, perhaps in 122 (Wallace-Hadrill 1983: 1 n.1), at the same time as Suetonius (another of P.'s correspondents: 1.18 and 1.24 with S-W, Hoffer 1999: 211–25). For the *praenomen* see §1n. *Sexti*. **nihil. . . fidelius:** a third tetracolon, this time a straight sequence (5~6~6~6 syllables) of virtual synonyms, enshrines his direct honesty. For *nihil* (a grander gesture than *neminem*, and not rare) see e.g. 1.22.1 (above on *uir*), 4.2.8, 5.16.1. **noui** 'I know' (*OLD nosco* 10, 12).

5 omnes me certatim et tamen aequaliter amant, | omnibus nunc ego in uno referre gratiam possum: isocolon antithesis (14~16 syllables) verbalises the reciprocity (*omnes me* ~ *omnibus nunc ego*). **certatim et tamen**

aequaliter: leaving no chink in the armour of praise.   **in uno** 'through one [of them]', *OLD in* 42. The opposition 'one ~ all' is an unsurprising rhetorical favourite (e.g. Cic. *Rosc. Am.* 22 with Dyck; Livy 6.17.5 with Oakley; ps.-Sen. *Oct.* 551 with Boyle); it recurs only twice in *Epp.* (1.22 *omnes . . . uno*, 3.20.12 *cuncta . . . unius*) but often in *Pan.* (13.5, 23.5, 26.3 etc., all with *omnes*).   **prenso amicos, | supplico ambio, | domos stationesque circumeo** 'I accost friends, I petition and canvass, I do the rounds of houses and meeting places', extended tricolon (4~5~11 syllables), with a breathless accumulation of first-person verbs for P.'s whirlwind canvassing. All are common electoral terms; for *prenso* see *OLD* 2, *TLL* x.2 1186.5–20. Cf. Mart. 12.29 (the ambitious senator treads sixty thresholds in a morning), Epictetus *Discourses* 4.10.20–1 'If you want to be consul, you must stay up at night, run around, kiss hands, waste away at other men's doors . . .' (a topos minted under the Republic; in fact the consulate was by now in the personal gift of the emperor: Millar 1977: 307–9).   **supplico ambio:** probably used absolutely, given the position of *amicos* and given that *supplico* usually takes dat. (though cf. Suet. *Aug.* 56.1 *tribus . . . circumibat supplicabatque*): *OLD supplico* 1b, *ambio* 2a and 6.6.9 *ego ambio, ego periclitor*, 1.14.7 and e.g. Cic. *Att.* 4.3.2. Some prefer to take *ambio domos* together, without parallel, and leaving *supplico* looking lonely.   **stationesque** 'meeting places' (lit. 'resting places', *OLD* 2a) such as porticoes and baths: 1.13.2 with Merrill and S-W, Juv. 11.4 with Courtney.   **circumeo:** *OLD* 6a, *Pan.* 69.2 *senatum circumirent*.   **quantumque . . . experior** 'and I test the strength of my authority and influence through my entreaties': *OLD experior* 1b + abl. + ind. question, as 1.17.2 *quantumque gratia ualeas aliorum honoribus experiri* (cf. Cic. *Phil.* 6.3 *quantum senatus auctoritas . . . ualiturus esset per legatos experiremur*). The clause glosses *itaque . . . circumeo* (with 'epexegetic -que', *OLD* 6a) in isocolon (23~23 syllables). 'From the point of view of the individual patron, the ability to persuade others of his power to secure access to benefits was the basis of social credibility' (Wallace-Hadrill 1989: 85).   **precibus** 'entreaties', common in P. of canvassing (2.13.11, 3.20.5, 4.15.11 etc.).   **teque obsecro** 'and I beg you', turning at last, with a simple *-que* (*OLD* 4) and fronted *te*, to Apollinaris and P.'s request. *obsecro te* is common in comedy and Cicero's letters; for the emphatic turn, cf. Cic. *Planc.* 104 (perorating) *teque, C. Flaue, oro et obtestor*.   **ut . . . tanti putes** 'to consider it worthwhile to shoulder part of my burden', indirect command after *teque obsecro* (see *OLD obsecro* 1a for the double construction), in studiously polite circumlocution. For *tanti putes*, see 2.3.8n.   **oneris mei:** a theme of the letter; of course P. does not profess to enjoy wielding influence.   **suscipere** '(willingly) take on (a burden)' (*OLD* 8a), P.'s favourite use of the verb: e.g. 2.10.5 *tantum curae*, 1.8.11 *taedium laboremque*, 3.6.5 *hanc curam*, *Pan.* 5.6 *imperium*.

6 reddam uicem si reposces, reddam et si non reposces: isocolon (8~7 syllables) with the same words beginning and ending each colon (*complexio*: Lausberg §633); *uicem* is *apo koinou*. For *reddam uicem* 'I shall return the favour' (*OLD uicis* 5), see Ov. *Am.* 1.6.23 *redde uicem meritis* with McKeown, adding Tac. *An.* 15.66.1.   **reposces:** future for fut. pf. (the verb has no attested pf. forms).

Elsewhere P. has fut. in protasis only for simultaneous actions (as is normal): 4.14.4, 6.20.20, 9.25.3, *Pan.* 28.7, 40.1, all verbs of wanting; 2.14.8n. *si*, 10.61.3 *coget* (1.22.12 is probably *quereris*). **et si** 'even if' (*OLD etsi*). *si non* (instead of *nisi*) negates *reposces* because the same word has just been used positively (G–L §591.a.1, Mayor on 3.1.4). **diligeris coleris frequentaris** 'you are loved, revered, sought out' (lit. '. . . much attended on', *OLD frequento* 6a), moving from inner to external show of respect. *colo* + *diligo* is a common Ciceronian doublet, usually in that order, as in P. 7.19.10 (but cf. *Lael.* 85 *diligendis et colendis*); *colo* + *frequento* is a rising pair in Sen. *Ep.* 79.17, Stat. *Silu.* 2.7.126. For the asyndetic tricolon see 2.1.12n. *cogito*, and cf. Sid. *Ep.* 5.5.3 (beginning a run of eight verbs) *amaris frequentaris expeteris*. P. has reserved flattery for his peroration.   **ostende modo uelle te** 'just show you are willing', *OLD ostendo* 7a; *modo* (*OLD* 1b) implies 'all you need do is'.   **nec deerunt:** as *Pan.* 27.2 'let there only be a good emperor' *nec deerunt qui filios concupiscant.*   **tu uelis:** chiastic polyptoton with *uelle te* for closing point.   **uelis cupiant:** both generic subjunctives. The closing assurance, with its juxtaposed synonyms, may evoke the famous adage *idem uelle atque idem nolle, ea demum firma amicitia est* (Sall. *Cat.* 20.4; Tosi 1991: 589–90): canons of friendship thus frame the letter (§1n. *pro*).

10

Why refuse us the pleasure of your poetry? Set it free to roam the world, before more of it escapes: this alone will guarantee you immortality. If you will not publish yet, at least hold a recital and enjoy the pleasure of performance.

Feigning exasperation, P. tries a series of arguments to persuade Octavius to publish his poetry at last; subject-matter and jovial tone contrast with the anxious 2.9 and grandiose 2.11. As suits his addressee (§2n. *sine*), he piles up poetic clichés, to the point perhaps of self-parody, including allusion to famous poetic epitaphs of Ennius (§2n. *sine*), Horace (§4n. *monimento*) and Ovid (§2n. *isdem*), and a reworking of the 'book as slave' motif (§3). These topoi all find a special place in the *sphragis*, the closing 'seal' of a poetic book; here, however, P. deploys them in the middle. 2.11 is an obvious centre to book 2 (Intro. 13–14) but 2.10 has an equal claim in terms of letter-number (not to mention Horatian precedent: cf. Hor. *C.* 2.10.5 *auream . . . mediocritatem*, in a twenty-letter book); and within the posterity-obsessed *Epistles* the theme of literary immortality gives this piece a weight belied by the banter. Indeed, it can be seen as the keystone in a three-book arch spanning *Epistles* 1–3 (Merwald 1964: 79–80; cf. again Horace, *Odes* 1–3): 1.1 (P.'s publication) ∼ 2.10 → 3.21 (Martial's death, P. as a new Cicero, and eternity), or better 1.1 ∼ 2.10–11 ∼ 3.21, since 2.10–11, for all their apparent contrasts, make a complementary centre-spread. The evocation of Octavius' future performance both resembles and glosses the picture of P. advocating at Priscus' trial (§2n. *frustrari*, §7n. *imaginor*), as P. urges his friend to self-memorialisation while memorialising himself as statesman, orator and epistolographer. Poetry and oratory thus emerge as paired, not competing, paths to glory, in direct contradiction of Aper's arguments in Tacitus' *Dialogus* (§7n. *imaginor*).

Our epistle also invites comparison with another tenth letter, 5.10, urging on a reluctant poet (§3n. *ut*); within *Epistles* 1–2 it finds a partner in 1.7 through the addressee (below). On P. as literary 'tastemaker' here, see Johnson 2010: 54–5.

OCTAVIO: Octavius Rufus, who receives 1.7 and perhaps also 7.25 (cf. 2.8n. CANINIO). The earlier letter established him as a close friend with whom P. could banter, and a poet whose verses he longs to receive (1.7.5). S-W's identification of this intimate with C. Marius Marcellus Octavius P. Cluvius Rufus, *cos. suff.* 80 and so by now a senior consular, has rightly been doubted (Jones 1968: 125, Syme 1985a: 347, *PIR*² O 53, Birley 2000a: 76–7). His origin is unknown; Champlin 2001: 126 makes him Etruscan, Krieckhaus 2001: 183–5 African.

1 Hominem te patientem uel potius durum ac paene crudelem 'what a long-suffering man you are, or rather stubborn and almost cruel!', acc. of exclamation: e.g. Plaut. *Poen.* 1032 *at hercle te hominem et sycophantam et subdolum*, Cic. *Fam.* 5.2.8 *hominem nequam*, Sen. *Ep.* 46.3 *o te hominem felicem* (*TLL* VI.3 2888.28–48); for the lack of *o*, cf. 2.20.2, 4.21.1, *Pan.* 19.4, Plaut. (above) and Flickinger 1913: 290. For *hominem* (mock-indignant), cf. 2.6.1n., 2.20.2n. *impudentiam*; for the position of *te*, 2.9.1n. *anxium*. The opening rhythm sounds stylised: two ionics and a choriamb (◡◡‒‒|◡◡‒‒|‒◡◡‒) make a recognisable if rare lyric sequence (for the combination, albeit on a larger scale, see e.g. Eur. *Bacchae* 370–85, 556–75). Another letter to a poet strongly resembles the cadence of an Alcaic stanza in its close (3.15.5 *pronuntio, de partibus experiar legendo*). **patientem . . . durum . . . crudelem:** graded tricolon, moving from Octavius' self-denial (*OLD patiens* 3, though *patientia* is an ambiguous virtue: Kaster 2002) to his cruelty; *durum* faces both ways (*OLD* 3 'hardy . . . ', 4 'unimpressionable . . . stubborn', 5 'harsh, pitiless'). The cruelty is both to his readers (§2) and to his poems (next n., and §8 *desine studia tua . . . fraudare*). **uel potius:** a favourite Ciceronian idiom (otherwise quite scarce) of self-correction (*reprehensio*: 2.1.10n. *si*), also at 6.13.5, 7.12.4, 8.6.12. **qui . . . teneas:** explanatory relative clause, for which P. usually has indicative (2.1.7n. *qui*) except with *ut qui* (5.16.8, 6.26.2 etc.), but cf. 2.20.2 *qui uenerit*, 2.20.7 *qui speraret*, 1.5.13 *uide hominis crudelitatem, qui se non dissimulet . . . uoluisse. teneas* 'hold on to' (*OLD* 18a 'prevent from leaving'), highlighted by the alliteration (*tam . . . tam diu teneas*), initiates or at least prepares the following personification of his poems. **libros:** books (of poetry): 2.1.5n.

2 quousque 'how long' (*OLD* 1b), marking impatience, as 2.20.8. So close to *patientem* and *nobis*, it might recall Cic. *Cat.* 1.1 *quousque tandem abutere, Catilina, patientia nostra?*, a famous line often quoted (Dyck ad loc.), with the *patientia* now that of addressee, not speaker. **nobis:** easily taken as a true plural, making P. spokesman for many. **inuidebis** 'deprive' (lit. 'begrudge') + dat. of person + abl. of thing (*OLD* 2c, K–S 1 310), P.'s routine construction (2.20.8, 1.10.12, etc.). The fear of envy (*inuidia*) from rivals was a poetic topos (Nisbet–Hubbard on Hor. *C.* 2.20.4 *inuidiāque maior*, adding V. *Georg.* 3.37–9), inverted here: it is Octavius, not any rival, who is guilty of it (besides being one of its victims). **tibi maxima laude, nobis uoluptate:** parallel antithesis expanding *et tibi et nobis*, with *maxima* construed *apo koinou*. *uoluptas* is spread liberally across the *Epistles*; again of poetry at 4.27.1 and 5.10.3, of oratory at 3.18.4, 11, 6.8.6 *uoluptatem . . . et gloriam* (cf. *laude* here). **sine per ora hominum ferantur . . . peruagentur:** subjunctives in paratactic indirect command (2.5.2n. *rogo*); supply *libri* as their subject. Although *per ora hominum* is matched (in a different context) at Livy 2.38.4, P. recalls Ennius' famous self-epitaph (Enn. *uar.* 18 V.; Courtney 1993: 43) *uolito uiuos per ora uirum* (quoted e.g. at Cic. *Tusc.* 1.34, 1.117, *Cato* 73), and/or its reworking in V. *Georg.* 3.9 *uictorque uirum uolitare per ora* and *Aen.* 12.235 *uiuusque per ora feretur* (P. quotes the former in 5.8.3; on Virgil's place in *Epp.* see Krasser 1993b, Schenk 1999, Marchesi 2008: 27–39 and her index s.v.); cf. also Ov. *Met.* 15.878 (next n.). As in 1.7, where P. quoted Homer twice, style reflects addressee (cf. 8.4.6 *cur enim non ego quoque poetice cum poeta?*), though P. replaces grand *uirum* (archaic gen. pl.) with homely *hominum*. **isdemque quibus lingua Romana spatiis peruagentur** 'let them range as far and wide as the Roman tongue' (i.e. *isdem spatiis peruagentur quibus lingua Romana [sc. peruagatur]*), personifying (*OLD peruagor* 1a), as the books do duty for 'fame/glory' (*OLD* 2a). For (*per*)*uagari* + abl. (rare), cf. Cic. *ND* 2.103 (*luna*) *isdem spatiis uagatur quibus sol*, *II Verr.* 3.129 (*scelus*) *tota Sicilia peruagatum*; for a comparable sentiment differently expressed (*peruagari* transitive) see 6.10.3 (on Verginius Rufus) *cuius memoriā orbem terrarum gloriā peruagetur*. Desire for, or claim to, worldwide fame is an ancient poetic topos (Hor. *C.* 2.20 with Nisbet–Hubbard, esp. pp. 332–3 and 344–5, Hor. *AP* 345–6, Mart. 1.1.2 *toto notus in orbe* with Howell); for this Romanocentric version, cf. esp. Ov. *Met.* 15.877–8 *quaque patet domitis Romana potentia terris,* | *ore legar populi* (contrast Cic. *Arch.* 23, arguing that Latin holds only limited sway). Books did indeed travel far: Martial has been found quoted on inscriptions from Spain, Germany and Africa (Howell, above); P.'s surprise that Lyons has booksellers (9.11.2) may be disingenuous, and does not address private forms of circulation. See also Parker 2009: 214 n.20, 217. **lingua Romana:** by now a synonym for *lingua Latina*, associated especially with the spread of Latin across the empire (e.g. Vell. 2.110.5, Tac. *Ag.* 21.2: Adams 2003b: 194–7, esp. 196). **magna et iam longa exspectatio:** *exspectatio* is often *magna* but rarely *longa* (10.25.1, Cic. *Fam.* 10.1.1; *TLL* v.2 1884: 38–41). **frustrari adhuc et differre** 'continue to cheat and defer' (Radice), a redundant couplet, both verbs unparalleled with *exspectatio* before the 4c. AD, by analogy with *spem frustrari* (*OLD* 2b, common) and *spem* (etc.) *differre* (i.e. defer its realisation: *TLL* v.1 1075.14–48). With *exspectationem . . . differre*, cf. 2.11.10 *auctāque dilatione exspectatio et fama*. For *adhuc* of future time, first in the younger Seneca (*TLL* 1 661.39–55), cf. 3.10.4 *an adhuc aliqua differrem*, 4.13.1 *pauculis adhuc diebus . . . commorabor.*

3 enotuerunt 'have become known', i.e. entered circulation. A rare verb, first in the elder Seneca; again in *Pan.* 5.2 (*fauor*), Suet. *Otho* 3.2 (*mimus*). **quidam tui uersus:** for the fronting of *quidam*, followed by adj. and noun, cf. 1.14.8

est . . . quidam senatorius decor, 4.16.2 *ad hoc quidam ornatus adulescens*, 7.17.10 *est quoddam magnum . . . consilium*, 8.16.5 *est enim quaedam . . . dolendi uoluptas* and e.g. Quint. 1.2.31 *est quaedam tacita dedignatio*, most of them (as here) after a main verb. Emendation to *quidem* (Griffith 1974) is unwelcome. **et** is epexegetic (*OLD* 11): the next phrase restates *enotuerunt* in different terms. **inuito te:** a common abl. abs. (*OLD inuitus* 2a). **claustra sua refregerunt** 'have burst their bonds' (lit. 'smashed open their bolts', *OLD claustrum* 1a, 2a, *refringo* 2a), common imagery, whether of animals, prisoners or slaves. The last is in play, as soon becomes clear; cf. Sen. *Ep.* 70.19 *seruitutis humanae claustra perrumperent*. Another Senecan slave metaphor at 2.8.2–3. **retrahis:** the *uox propria* for capturing fugitives (*OLD* 2b), with a hint perhaps of its frequentative *retractare* (*OLD* 6b), a stock verb of literary revision. The present tense is unexceptionable (2.9.2n. *obtinet*). **corpus:** both 'oeuvre, (literary) corpus' (*OLD* 16a) and, given verb and context, '(slave-)gang' (cf. *OLD* 15a–b; Ter. Clem. *Dig.* 40.9.24 *retrahi in seruitutem*). **quandoque** 'sooner or later' (*OLD* 2). **ut errones** 'like runaways' (*OLD ut* 7b), making the image explicit. *erro* was technically 'truant' vs *fugitiuus* 'runaway' (Ulp. *Dig.* 21.1.17.14), but they are as good as synonymous for Hor. *Sat.* 2.7.113 *fugitiuus et erro*. Books are often personified in Roman poetry (Citroni 1986), not least as runaway slaves: cf. famously Hor. *Ep.* 1.20 (v.5 *fuge* with Oliensis 1995: 212), ending his *Epistles* 1, and Mart. 1.3 (v.12 *i, fuge*), but already Cic. *Att.* 4.8a.3 *de poemate quid quaeris, quid si cupiat effugere? quid? sinam?* (*pace* Shackleton Bailey). In all three 'master' allows 'slave' to 'escape'; Mart. 1.52 legalises this to 'manumission' (Fitzgerald 2007b: 95–7, Seo 2009, next n.; Ovid's exile elegies, figured as both slaves and children (esp. *Tr.* 1.1, 3.1 with Nagle 1980: 82–91), travel on a mandate). P. varies the topos: Octavius has neither manumitted his poems nor connived in their escape. He hints at a manumission pun at 5.10.1 <u>*libera tandem hendecasyllaborum meorum fidem*</u>, a comparable tenth letter (urging Suetonius to publish poetry), which also personifies verses (Power 2010: 144 n.20). **aliquem cuius dicantur inuenient** 'will find someone [else] to be called their master (lit. ' . . . whose they may be said to be', *sc. esse*, relative purpose clause). A double reference to *plagium*, illegal possession of another person's slave (Crook 1967a: 60, 186; Robinson 1995: 32–5), and literary plagiarism. The two are first combined by Mart. 1.52, who complains that his 'manumitted' verses are being held against their will and passed off as the property of a *plagiarius*-poet; unlike Martial's captive freedmen, Octavius' naughty slaves are actively looking (cf. *inuenient*) for a new owner (Seo 2009: 569–73 finds P.'s imagery cliché). For the language of authorship see Mart. 1.52.7 *dicas esse meos*, 12.2.17–18 *clamabunt omnes te, liber, esse meum*, though P.'s *cuius dicantur* finds its closest match in Cat. 8.17 (to Lesbia) *cuius esse diceris?*

4 habe ante oculos mortalitatem 'keep mortality in view' (*OLD habeo* 15b, *oculus* 7b): cf. Sen. *Ep.* 12.6 *mortem ante oculos habere* (both 'see death around one' and 'have death in mind'), turned to paradox here. For *ante oculos habere* see also 8.24.4 (+ acc. + inf.), Ov. *Rem.* 564, Sen. *Ep.* 11.8, Quint. 10.7.15. Mortality has been repeatedly in view for P.'s reader (2.1, 2.4, 2.7). **a qua asserere te . . . potes** 'from which you can free yourself'. Cf. 3.5.4 (Pliny the Elder) *ut se ab iniuria obliuionis assereret*, Sen. *Polyb.* 2.6 *id egit ipse ut meliore sui parte duraret et compositis eloquentiae praeclaris operibus a mortalitate se uindicaret* '. . . free himself from mortality', also on literary composition and also recalling (see below) a famous poetic *sphragis* (Ov. *Met.* 15.875 *parte tamen meliore mei . . .*). Like *uindicare* there, *asserere* keeps live the imagery of manumission (*OLD assero* 2a–b), familiar esp. from Sen. *Ep.* 13.14 *Catoni gladium assertorem libertatis extorque* (the sword that 'frees' Cato from slavery to Caesar), 104.16 *animus ex miserrima seruitute in libertatem asseritur* (by philosophy), *Tranq.* 17.8; cf. also Mart. 1.52.5 *assertor*. The metaphor of §3 is thus extended, but now the slave is Octavius himself (for such shifts of referent see 2.4.4n. *ita*). **hoc uno** 'this and no other'. It is a leitmotif of the *Epistles* that literature alone will secure posthumous fame (e.g. 1.3.3–5, 5.5.4, 9.3, 9.14), at least for those to whom glory through *facta* is denied (3.7.14; cf. Sall. *Cat.* 3). So much for Cottius' statue (2.7.4n. *hac*). **monimento:** evoking Hor. *C.* 3.30.1 *exegi monumentum aere perennius* and with it a long tradition of imagining literary works as statues or monuments (Nisbet–Rudd ad loc., adding Cic. *Arch.* 30 *effigiem . . . summis ingeniis expressam et politam*). The spellings -*num*- and -*nim*- (representing the 'intermediary vowel': Allen 1978: 56–9) are interchangeable (*TLL* VIII 1461.9–26). **cetera fragilia et caduca** 'all else, (being) frail and fleeting' (*OLD fragilis* 3a, *caducus* 8): cf. 3.10.6 *non fragilem et caducam, sed immortalem . . . effigiem*, P.'s Life of Cottius (2.7.4n. *hac*). The adj. pair is a cliché of mortality (Cic. *Leg.* 1.24, *Lael.* 102, Sen. *Suas.* 7.7 etc.). **occidunt desinuntque:** an unparalleled redundant pair; *desinunt* enriches *occidunt*, cliché in context (*TLL* IX.2 350.53–63). For final -*que* (making a ditrochee, as often) see 2.1.4n. *durior*.

5 dices, ut soles: *occupatio* (2.3.9n. *dices*), with a reminder of their intimacy. **amici mei uiderint** 'my friends can see to that' (idiomatic fut. pf.: *OLD uideo* 18b, K–S I 149), *sc.* after my death. The need to publish rather than await a posthumous editor (as Cicero's letters had to) is a given throughout the *Epistles* (esp. 9.1; implicit from 1.1). **opto equidem . . . sed** 'I certainly hope . . . but'. *equidem* is a strengthened form of *quidem* used by P., as by Caesar, Cicero and Livy, only with first-person verbs (it was widely believed to derive from *ego quidem*: Solodow 1978: 19–29). It often softens an opinion (3.3.1, 6.16.3, etc.) with the modest implication, 'this is only my point of view' (*OLD* 1b); it can also do the work of concessive/contrasting *quidem* (2.1.7n. *et*; Solodow 1978: 53–5), as 2.11.11 *equidem . . . tamen*, 6.4.3 *equidem . . . nunc uero*, and (with the contrast implicit) 2.13.8. Here it does both, as at 7.29.3. **tibi** *sc.* *esse* or *fore* 'that you (will) have', possessive dat. **tam fideles, tam eruditos, tam laboriosos** 'so faithful, so learned, so industrious', rising and graded tricolon (4~4~6 syllables, with each adjective a higher demand). **tantum curae intentionisque suscipere** 'to undertake so great and laborious a task' (after Radice), literally 'take on so much care and devotion' (partitive genitives). *cura* is both 'care'

(*OLD* 3a) and a task entrusted (3.6.5 *suscipe hanc curam*); for *intentio* see 2.5.2n. For the combination, cf. Pl. *NH* 10.118 (on parrots) *curam atque cogitationem intentionem*. **dispice ne** 'consider whether... not' (*OLD dispicio* 2, *ne* 9). P. favours this courteous verb with ind. question (1.5.10 *dispicies ipse quid*, 1.18.5 *dispice an*, 7.33.5 *dispice num*; several times in book 10); for the delicate *ne*, cf. Sen. *Polyb.* 18.4 *dispice ne hoc iam... sit*. **sit parum prouidum sperare** 'it is short-sighted to hope' (*OLD prouidus* 2b, 2.1.5n. *parum*). That friends cannot be relied upon was a truism: 6.10.5 *tam rara in amicitiis fides... ut ipsi nobis debeamus... heredum officia praesumere*; Gell. *NA* 2.29.18–20 *in nobis tantum ipsis nitamur...*, quoting Ennius (= *Sat.* 58 V.) *ne quid exspectes amicos, quod tute agere possies*. So too Mart. 4.33.3–4 urges a poet to publish: *'edent heredes' inquis 'mea carmina'. quando?* | *tempus erat iam te, Sosibiane, legi*. **quod... praestes:** namely *cura intentioque* (cf. 2.5.2 *sollicitudinem praestare*, 2.11.15 *studium... curam... sollicitudinem praestitit*). *praestes* is generic subj. (and subordinate in acc.+inf.).

6 de editione quidem interim ut uoles 'as for publishing, in the meantime, do as you wish'. *editio* is 'the final placing of the much revised book in the hands of the *librarii* or *bibliopolae* to copy and sell' (S-W 91); *quidem* (2.1.7n. *et*) contrasts publication with the recitation in the next clause (for the lack of *sed/tamen* see 2.7.3n. *et*). For the elliptical use of *ut uoles*, cf. e.g. Cic. *Att.* 12.12.2 *de Epicuro ut uoles*, 12.18.4, *Phil.* 2.118. **recita:** recitation is a recurrent theme of the *Epistles*. It was by now the norm at least for poetry, a regular stage in the process of literary production (esp. 7.17.7), but P. is exceptional in emphasising it so heavily (Johnson 2010: 42–3). For poetic recitals see 1.13, 3.15, 4.27, 5.17, 6.21, 9.22, 9.34; also §7n. *cum dico*. For ancient testimonies see Mayor on Juv. 3.9 (ten pages) and Funaioli *RE* II.1 435–45; modern discussions of the recitation/publication process include Starr 1987, Small 1997: 26–40, Johnson 2000 and 2010 (33–79 on P.), Parker 2009. See also 2.19.1n. *recitem*. **quo magis:** *quo* routinely replaces *ut* before a comparative, as 2.13.10, 2.19.4 (*OLD quo²* 1b, *NLS* §150; exceptions in 2.20.4n. *quod*). **emittere** 'publish' (9.1.1, *OLD* 1c). **percipias... praesumo:** framing verbs, the antithesis pointed by *per-* ~ *prae-*. A new argument: Octavius will derive pleasure himself (contrast §1... *inuidebis... nobis uoluptate*); cf. Tac. *D.* 6.4 *quod illud gaudium* (§7n. *qui*). **quod ego olim pro te non temere praesumo** 'which I have enjoyed anticipating for you for a long time now [*OLD olim* 2a + pres.], with good reason [*OLD temere* 2b]'. *praesumere* implies not just anticipating (*OLD* 4) *gaudium* for Octavius (*OLD pro* 3b), but feeling it too: cf. 8.11.1 *praesumpta laetitia*, *Pan.* 79.4 *praesumo laetitiam*; *OLD praesumptio* 1 (= 4.15.11 *praesumptio ipsa iucunda est*, 9.3.1), *TLL* x.2 962.58–68. Cf. also 3.1.11 *hanc ego uitam uoto et cogitatione praesumo* (happy dreams of retirement, with Mayor) and, differently, 6.10.5 *heredum officia praesumere* (perform in life the duties of one's heirs).

7 imaginor enim qui concursus, quae admiratio te, | qui clamor, quod etiam silentium maneat: evoking the buzz of performance in *enargeia* (2.11.11n. *imaginare*), to explain *non temere* (hence *enim*); four indirect questions are arranged in isocolon (16~14 syllables), with *te* and *maneat* distributed *apo koinou*. Manner, content and construction invite comparison with two passages. First, Cic. *Diu. Caec.* 42 (feigning nerves at the forthcoming trial of Verres) *iam nunc mente et cogitatione prospicio* [cf. *imaginor*] *quae tum studia hominum, qui concursus futuri sint, quantam exspectationem magnitudo iudici sit allatura, quantam auditorum multitudinem infamia C. Verris concitatura, quantam denique audientiam* [a rare word; cf. *quod etiam silentium*] *orationi meae improbitas illius factura.* Second, Tac. *D.* 6.4 (Aper, on the delights of oratory): *iam uero qui togatorum comitatus et egressus* [cf. *concursus*], *quae in publico species, quae in iudiciis ueneratio* [cf. *admiratio* and perhaps *clamor*], *quod illud gaudium consurgendi assistendique inter tacentis* [cf. *silentium*] *et in unum conuersos . . . !* P. is closer to Cicero in some respects ('I imagine' + ind. questions; *qui concursus*), to Tacitus in the tetracolon (*qui . . . quae . . . quae . . . quod*); the climax with silence is common to all three. The persuasion resembles, and inverts, Aper's attempt to seduce Maternus away from poetry recitals to oratory. If this is appropriation, it is witty, but also cuts to the heart of P.'s manifesto for the compatibility of oratory and recital, as instantiated in his own practice (cf. below, *cum dico uel recito*). On the relative dating of *D.* and *Epp.* 2 see Intro. 33. **clamor:** the normal form of audience appreciation (2.14.5n. *Laudiceni*, 2.14.13n. *plausus*). **quod etiam silentium:** *etiam* caps the tetracolon (2.1.6n. *etiam*), pointing the apparent paradox that silence is welcome, and leading to the next sentence. If Tacitus is in mind (above), there may be a frisson of name-play: the cycle of letters to him is framed by 1.6.2 *silentium* ~ 9.14 *silentio*. Tacitus may play with his own name at *Ag.* 2.3 *tacere*, 3.2 *silentium*; Tert. *Apol.* 16.2 and Sid. *Ep.* 4.22.2 (also *Carm.* 2.192, 23.153–4) saw its potential (see also 2.1.6n. *laudator*, 2.1n. C. PLINIVS). **quo ego . . . delector** 'from which I (certainly) take pleasure': *OLD delecto* 4a with *quo* (antecedent *silentium*) abl. of instrument; *ego* adds authority ('I speak from experience'). Like Aper (Tac. *D.* 7.1 *equidem . . .*), P. allures Octavius with recollection of the pleasure that follows his own successes, a pleasure he is never loath to share (e.g. 7.4.10 *de aliorum iudicio loquor; qui siue iudicant siue errant, me delectat*, 4.12.6, 5.1.12, 9.11.2). **cum dico uel recito:** 'whenever I plead or recite' (*OLD cum*[2] 2a, *dico*[2] 1b), a significant combination (above on *imaginor*). The first sure indication of P.'s recital activities (implied perhaps at 1.13.6 *scribere aliquid quod non recitem*), which become a major theme of the collection (§6n. *recita*). He mentions reciting poetry at 5.3.7–8, 8.21, a (prose) Life of Cottius at 3.10.1, oratory frequently (2.19.1n. *recitem*). **sit modo:** 2.7.5n. *digni*. **acre et intentum et cupidum ulteriora audiendi** 'keen and attentive and eager to hear more' (*OLD acer* 7, *intentus* 1a–b, *cupidus* 1a–b), rising tricolon (1/2 [*acre* is elided] ~ 4 ~ 11) with intensifying personification, as the silence is invested with the audience's emotion. For *acre* cf. Quint. 8.2.23 *acrem iudicis intentionem*; for *intentum* cf. Val. Flacc. 4.257 *intenta silentia* (at a duel) and esp. Quint 4.2.37 *illud intentionis silentium*, scorning crowd-pleasers who do not realise that silence is superior to applause. *silentium cupidum* is unparalleled; for the personifying adj., see *OLD cupidus* 1b, *TLL* iv 1428.8–17. *cupidus audiendi* is at Cic. *De or.* 2.16, *Brut.* 305, Livy 3.71.5, Gell. *NA* 1.23.7, all describing people. For the expectant hush, see also Cic. *II Verr.* 2.74 *summum silentium, summa exspectatio, De or.* 3.33 *exspectatione et silentio,* V. *Aen.* 2.1, Phaedrus 5.5.15, Cic. *Diu. Caec.* 42 and Tac. *D.* 6.4 (quoted above). **ulteriora audiendi:** *ulteriora* is a neuter adjective used as a noun (*OLD ulterior* 5); P. has the gerund with such objects, a standard usage to keep the gender visible (K–S I 736): e.g. 2.11.10 *inusitata noscendi, Pan.* 6.5 *paria accipiendo* (so too with *aliquid* in 1.5.16, 6.27.4). Other things being equal, he prefers gerundives (2.9.2n. *ius*).

8 hoc fructu tanto tam parato 'given this enjoyment so great and so certain' (abl. abs.). *hoc fructu* summarises §7, but *hoc* also draws the letter to a close (2.1.6n. *huius*), helped by light ring-composition in *tanto tam parato* (~ §1 *tam insignes . . . tam diu*). *parato* implies 'that you can count on': cf. 6.10.5 *tam parata obliuio mortuorum,* 7.25.2, 8.11.3, 8.16.5; Cic. *Fam.* 10.8.7 (Plancus) *fructus meritorum . . . satis magnus est paratus, TLL* x.1 426.26–65. **desine studia tua . . . fraudare** 'stop cheating your work' (*OLD desino* 2a); for *studia,* see 2.2.2n. The inanimate object is not rare (*TLL* VI.1 1264.2–26) but personification is easily felt after §1 *teneas,* §2 *peruagentur* etc. No longer disobedient (§3), the (slave-)poems are being deprived by their cruel master. **infinita ista cunctatione:** abl. of means (*NLS* §43.1). P.'s own (modest) hesitation in publishing is thematised in 1.8 (see also 2.19.intro.) and recurs in 5.10.2, but he plays the friend's role in dissuading it again in 5.10.2 and 9.1.4. The hyperbolic *infinita* (cf. Sen. *Breu.* 9.3 *infinitam cunctationem*) and *ista* ('that . . . of yours') resume the impatience of §1–2. **quae cum modum excedit** 'when hesitation exceeds the (proper) limit', moving smoothly into a generalising *sententia* for the finish. For closing limits, see 2.4.4n. *etiamsi.* **uerendum est ne** 'there is a danger that' (Radice), impersonal gerundive of obligation. **inertiae et desidiae uel etiam timiditatis** 'of idleness and laziness, or even cowardice' (genitives of definition: *NLS* §72.5), graded tricolon to match §1 *patientem . . . durum . . . ac paene crudelem,* and/or isocolon (8~9 syllables). The first two nouns, a common couplet (e.g. Cic. *Brut.* 8 *non inertiae neque desidiae*), are undesirable traits, even if P. occasionally confesses to them (2.2.2n. *desidia*); the third is one to which he would never admit (1.5.1, 9.26.13) and (like §1 *crudelem*) the ultimate provocation. **nomen accipiat** 'be given the name'; the subject is *quae* (= *cunctatio*). Cf. 4.23.4 *quando secessus mei non desidiae nomen sed tranquillitatis accipient?, TLL* I 317.37–45; also Sall. *Jug.* 4.3 *nomen inertiae imponant.*

I I

The second-longest letter of book 2, narrating P.'s prosecution of Marius Priscus in AD 100. Straddling the centre of the book, it features a senate revived, Trajan as paradigmatic *ciuilis princeps,* and P. in the role of Ciceronian orator and defender of right, triumphing in a rare criminal case.

P. shapes his narrative rhetorically, not as historical source, and elides substantial time gaps in his smooth presentation (e.g. §8n. *uenerunt*); a brief summary of the events may be helpful (details follow in the notes). Marius Priscus was proconsul of Africa in 97–8; on his return he was accused of corruption in office. P. was appointed prosecutor in late 98 (10.3A–B), and a first hearing was held some time in 99 (§§2–7). Priscus pleaded guilty to extortion, hoping to receive summary justice (a fine and expulsion from the senate), so escaping full trial on more serious, capital charges. P. and his co-prosecutor Tacitus, however, successfully argued for full trial, alleging the wrongful execution of two Roman knights. Accomplices were summoned from Africa (§8) and in December 99 a trial was opened but adjourned (§9). The case was finally heard in a three-day senatorial session chaired by Trajan, 13–15 January 100 (§§10–22), at which Priscus was found guilty and sentenced to relegation (§8n. *exsilium*). During the trial evidence emerged incriminating one of Priscus' deputies, the ex-praetor Hostilius Firminus (§§23–4); his case was deferred to 3 February, when, despite manifest guilt, he received only slight censure (2.12).

Outside P.'s letters, Priscus is known only from Juvenal. In *Satires* 8.119–20 he features as corrupt governor *par excellence*, as the satirist offers advice to a prospective proconsul: *quanta autem inde feres tam dirae praemia culpae,* | *cum tenuis nuper Marius discinxerit Afros?* 'And what rewards will you bring back for such terrible guilt? | It's not long since Marius emptied the pockets of the starving Africans.' In another passage Juvenal condemns the meaningless trials from which senators emerged unscathed (*Sat.* 1.47–8 *damnatus inani* | *iudicio*); even the relegated Priscus has an easy life while Africa suffers (*Sat.* 1.49–50): *exsul ab octaua Marius bibit et fruitur dis* | *iratis, at tu uictrix, prouincia, ploras* 'Marius in his exile drinks from mid-afternoon and enjoys the gods' | anger; but you, province, weep in your victory.' Whether this letter is what reminded Juvenal of Priscus (Syme 1958: 500; cf. Intro. 34–5) is hard to say, given the lack of verbal allusion; in any case, his cynical exposé of senatorial justice is piquant for readers of P. and his proud claim to have set a shining example. Did he really see Priscus' relegation as a triumph? Perhaps so, and perhaps rightly: given the corporate sense of senatorial self-preservation that outrages the outsider Juvenal, relegation may have been the harshest verdict that could reasonably be expected. Whether P. himself saw this as an institutional failing is unclear. He emphasises how close Priscus came to an even lighter penalty (§21), whether to heighten the drama or (also) defensively; but 2.11–12 together channel any disappointment away from Priscus, as P. vents in the latter Juvenalian indignation at the soft treatment given to Firminus – a safely less significant defendant. 2.11 is too easily caricatured as naïve celebration: together with its appendix letter, at least, it presents a more nuanced view of the senate, if not of P. himself.

Certainly 2.11 is celebratory: P. promises a famous, salutary and eternal trial (§1) and holds up for display, in a long and prominent letter, a paradigmatic senatorial transaction – a promised source of delight (§1 *gaudio*) to his equestrian addressee Arrianus (and the over-reader beyond). This happy picture invites contrast with the 'fearful and tongue-tied' senate of Domitian's day (8.14.8), a contrast which P. draws explicitly in *Pan.* 75. Fighting the good fight with P. is Tacitus, whom the reader has already met in public (2.1.6) and in private (1.6, 1.20), and friend and soon-to-be fellow consul Cornutus Tertullus, whose proposed verdict on Priscus wins the day. Trajan earns a special place, presiding over the trial *qua* consul and giving personal support to P. in paradigmatically civilian guise (§10n. *princeps*). A central letter of book 1 featured at its mid-point the death of Domitian (1.12.8 *affuit tamen deus uoto*); 2.11 displays in its central panel Trajan overseeing exemplary justice, with P. as avenger. The implication is subtle but clear: the return of good governance, and the cardinal role of P. in its execution.

For all this, P.'s senate is by no means whitewashed. Priscus may be expelled, but Firminus remains. P. generally avoids criticism of living contemporaries (S-W 54–5), but this senator earns a savage attack (§§23–4) and wrathful indignation in 2.12. Senators who speak or vote in Priscus' and Firminus' favour receive a range of treatment. The consulars Catius Fronto and Salvius Liberalis earn honourable mention for their speeches. Although Pompeius Collega and Acutius Nerva are not directly criticised for proposing light penalties, the proposals themselves are damned, one in passing (§21 *uel solutiore uel molliore*), one at length (2.12.3–4). The last sting, however, is reserved for Aquillius Regulus, exposed as the alleged originator of the proposal that would effectively have acquitted Priscus (§22). This paradigmatic 'bad senator' will feature prominently in the final letter of the book, with its bitter coda (2.20.12–14); similarly here the senatorial narrative, for all its glory, ends not with celebration, but with Regulus skulking in the shadows. The diptych as a whole, too, ends on a note of frustration at the moral weakness of the senatorial majority (2.12.intro.).

Senatorial impropriety surfaces more than once in the *Epistles* (Lefèvre 2003 ≈ id. 2009: 93–101): 3.20 and 4.25 lament first the shambolic handling of elections and second an anonymous senator's outrageous spoiling of his ballot; in 6.5 a shameful quarrel is staged by two ex-praetors; and in 6.13 named individuals are criticised for their 'irreverent' and hypocritical behaviour in the Varenus case. It climaxes in 9.13, where P. attacks the shameful behaviour of Publicius Certus. That letter looks to the past (Certus' misdeed in 93, and P.'s attack in 97), but by virtue of its late place in the collection it presents the epistolary climax of the sequence of senatorial 'trials'. The narrative there ends with a scene of congratulation, as fellow senators applaud P. for single-handedly clearing the senate's name: 9.13.21 *quod denique senatum inuidia liberassem qua flagrabat apud ordines alios*. His self-proclaimed role as *defensor morum* is clear – a role which, under Trajan as under anyone, depends for its existence on the presence of other, less perfect senators.

As throughout the collection, then, the senatorial stage in 2.11 serves primarily as backdrop for P., star of the show. The structure of the letter makes this clear:

§1 proem		42 words
§§2–9 pre-trial sessions		262 words
§§10–16 trial: first day	>§14 *dixi horis paene quinque*	214 words
§§17–24 rest of trial; Firminus		328 words
§25 coda		31 words

The first day of the full trial, on which he delivered his set-piece speech, is the central panel, comprising a quarter of its length (§10–16). More precisely still, the lapidary notice of his speech, *dixi horis paene quinque* (§14), stands almost exactly at the mid-point of a minutely constructed structure (leaving no room to imagine, with S-W 19, that 2.11 is a patchwork of shorter notes). Epistle thus memorialises speech and stakes P.'s claim to *gloria dicendi* (cf. Mayer 2003). At the same time, it functions as a quasi-historiographical miniature (§1n. *personae*), although, like many features of historiography, the interested narrative – an apparently transparent account which in fact pushes the reader to a given judgment – is of course classic oratorical technique (e.g. Yunis 2001: 23 on Demosthenes' *On the crown*, and see Eco 1992 and Berry 2008 on the Vesuvius letters). Certainly 2.11, and even more 2.12, are themselves rhetorical showpieces, ranging from a plain narrative (§3n. *respondit*) through emotive *enargeia* (§§10–11), invective (§§23–4) and ultimately high indignation in the grand style (2.12.3–4): the reader is prevailed upon to share P.'s judgment of Priscus, of the senate and of himself, as the orator simultaneously records and re-performs his prosecution on the page.

To prosecute a corrupt governor in person and in writing is to evoke a clear Ciceronian paradigm: 'it recalled (the astute Pliny did not need to be specific) the ancient days and the classic indictment of Verres' (Syme 1979b: 258). The prosecution of Sicilian governor Verres in 70 BC was the acme of Cicero's pre-consular career; it was also performed above all through publication (five of the seven speeches were never delivered). Though there had been many famous extortion trials since then, the situational parallel with Priscus, and with this letter, is inescapable. In fact P. is more specific (Pflips 33–159, partly reworked in Philips [*sic*] 52–89): language and perhaps rhythm (§2n. *petit*) is modelled to an unusual extent after Cicero's. Although the clearest Verrine intertext falls in 3.9 (§15n. *uoci*), allusions to the *Verrines* and other speeches, and to an autobiographical comment in the *Brutus* (§15n. *gracilitas*), repeatedly invite the comparison, as does the choice of addressee (see below). Cicero presented the prosecution of Verres as an opportunity to rid the senate of *inuidia* (*I Verr.* 1), indeed to save the state itself from collapse (*Diu. Caec.* 70), and offered himself as Rome's moral safeguard. Only later does P. stake an explicit claim that he has redeemed the senate (9.13.21, quoted above), but in 2.11–12 the project of constructing an analogous Ciceronian ethos is well under way. Yet this is not just Cicero the orator: obtrusive recall of epistolary Cicero at the ends of both letters, and allusions to his *philosophica* in 2.12 (2.12.intro.), join to make 2.11–12 a climax, not just for book 2 but for the whole

Epistles, of P.'s self-presentation as latter-day orator, statesman and *littérateur* in the Ciceronian mould.

For an overview of P.'s later trial letters, see 2.12.intro. He makes Priscus the first big case in the *Epistles*, though he had already prosecuted Baebius Massa for extortion in 93 (1.7.2, 7.33.4–8). On the counterweighting of 2.11–12 and the villa letter, see Intro. 13–14, 2.17.intro. The extortion trials of the time are studied by S-W, Brunt 1961 (= id. 1990: 54–95) and 1990: 492–506, Bleicken 1962: 35–44 and 158–66, Talbert 1984: 460–87.

ARRIANO: Maturus Arrianus (*PIR²* M 378), an equestrian living in Altinum (§1n. *quietis*), is the fourth most frequently addressed individual in the *Epistles*: he receives seven letters and is the subject of an eighth (3.2) in which P. seeks a post for him, perhaps in Italy (Syme 1957b: 483–4) rather than Egypt (S-W). He may be Marius Maturus (*PIR²* M 306), procurator of Alpes Maritimae in 69 and thereafter Tarraconensis (Syme 1985a: 326 n.17); if so, he was a coeval and social equal of Pliny the Elder (for whose Spanish service see 2.13.4n. *scis*). He is the only recipient of major trial letters who is not probably resident in P.'s native Transpadana (Syme 1985a: 335 n.66), but his other letters make him an abundantly qualified reader of the Priscus diptych. Epistles 1.2 and 4.8 associate him with P.'s self-modelling after Cicero in both literature (1.2.4, 4.8.4) and life (4.8 compares their augurates and consulates), making him a fitting recipient of this most Ciceronian panel. Related themes are touched on in 6.2 (court oratory and *uitia ciuitatis*) and 8.21 (P.'s double life as forensic orator and literary composer); 4.12, reporting the scrupulous behaviour of a provincial quaestor in returning unspent moneys, is an apt counterpart to the exposé of corruption here. Arrianus is one of several individuals whom P. names by two *cognomina*, e.g. Cornutus Tertullus (§19), Libo Frugi (3.9.33), Catullus Messalinus (4.22.5), most of them senators (Vidman 1981: 588–9, and generally on naming Adams 1978, Salway 1994). The order of those names is uncertain: he is Maturus Arrianus twice in the index to book 4, Arrianus Maturus in 3.2.2 (perhaps inversion: §3n. *Fronto*). His presence in 2.11, along with any overt epistolary markers, is confined to the opening and the pointedly languid coda (§25; so too 2.12.6–7).

1 Proem

1 Solet: for the main verb to open, see 2.2.1n. *irascor*. The prefatory §1 comprises three sentences in rising tricolon (22~33~40 syllables).   **gaudio:** predicative dative (*NLS* §68, G–L §356). Like Cicero, P. often begins a letter with a statement of his own delight (4.13.1, 4.16.1, 6.26.1, 7.23.1); for the promise of delight to his reader, justifying (and framing) the letter to come, cf. 4.19.1 *non dubito maximo tibi gaudio fore cum cognoueris...*   **si quid acti est** 'if anything has been done', 'if there has been any transaction' (*OLD ago* 38). For *acti*, partitive gen. of *actum* (neuter participle used as a noun) cf. Sen. *BV* 17.4, Juv. 10.155 with Housman, and *TLL* 1 1406.74–81; with other verbs at e.g. Cic. *Att.* 8.3.4 *quid... est parati?* (Löfstedt 1956: 1 139), Livy 9.16.7, Sen. *Med.* 995. **ordine illo:** the senate. P. implies that it spent most of its time doing things unworthy of itself (intro.). **quietis amore secesseris:** Arrianus lives in wealthy Altinum (3.2.2 with Mayor, Mart. 4.25), modern Altino, at the mouth of the Po in Venetia; his distance from Roman *negotia* frames the letter (cf. §25). P. often uses *secedere* in this sense of 'withdraw from Rome' (*OLD* 3): 2.8.1n. *altissimus*, 2.17.2 *secessit*. With *quietis amore* he implies that Arrianus had opted out of a senatorial career (cf. 3.2.4, S-W 170; on such abstention see S-W 118–19, Talbert 1984: 76–80). **insidet tamen animo tuo maiestatis publicae cura** 'yet you are deeply concerned about the dignity of the state' (*OLD insideo* 5 'lie heavy on' + dat.). For *insidet... cura* cf. Livy 1.21.1; *in animo insidere* is Ciceronian (e.g. *Att.* 1.11.1) but the dative *animo* Livian (8.6.12, 28.26.7, 45.1.5); *maiestas publica* is first attested in Livy 2.40.3. *maiestas* refers to (senatorial) dignity again at 3.20.4, 8.6.4, to history (grandly) in 9.27.1, to the state at *Pan.* 12.1, 60.2; its common contemporary meanings 'treason' and '(imperial) majesty' are confined to *Pan.* 4.6, 11.1, 42.1 (etc.) and to a letter of Trajan, 10.82.1. On the term (a Ciceronian favourite) see Hellegouarc'h 1972: 314–20, Seitz 1973, Philips ad loc., who suggests that *maiestas publica* is shorthand for *maiestas rei publicae* (on *publicus* see 2.1.7n. *non*). Here it heralds a parable on the dignity of the senate (and so, by common extension, of Rome). Arrianus' noble concern for the state (Vretska on Sall. *Cat.* 6.6) is reaffirmed at 6.2.9 *nam tu quoque amore communium soles emendari cupere quae iam corrigere difficile est.* **accipe** 'let me tell you', with a relative clause as object (*TLL* 1 307.10–15; indirect question, by contrast, at 4.20.1). The imperative, widely common, introduces narrative and description again at 2.20.1, 5.6.3. **per hos dies:** probably 13–15 January 100 (S-W 166). The Ciceronian phrase (again at 4.9.1) gives the letter topicality, as if written immediately afterwards. **actum est** varies (*quid*) *acti est.* **personae claritate famosum, seueritate exempli salubre, rei magnitudine aeternum:** the 'proem' climaxes in a tricolon of three-word phrases, ABC~BAC~ABC (10~10~9 syllables). The first and third members respond closely in lexis, word-order, clausula (cretic–spondee) and rhyme; the second varies (ditrochee). The buoyant tricolon returns, varied, in 6.33.2 [*oratio*] *et dignitate personae et exempli raritate et iudici magnitudine insignis*; for a strong contrast, see 2.14.1 [*causa*] *uel personarum claritate uel negoti magnitudine insignis* (with note). This is the kind of great criminal trial that gave republican orators such scope for eloquence (Maternus in Tac. *D.* 37.4–5, on *splendor reorum* and *magnitudo causarum*), a rarity for P., who is mostly occupied in the civil courts (even if he later finds splendour there too: 2.14.intro.). Talking up one's material (*amplificatio*) is a prefatory device familiar from historical works since Thucydides 1.1: e.g. Sall. *Cat.* 4.4, Tac. *H.* 1.2.1 (Marincola 1997: 34–40). Like the *Epistles* as a whole, 2.11 is not overtly historiographical, but is open to reading as a historical contribution in miniature (see generally Traub 1955, Ash 2003, Tzounakas 2007). Yet – like most historiographical devices – *amplificatio* is a stock rhetorical trick (Lausberg §§400–9; Frazel 2009: 28–31), equally familiar from oratorical prefaces (e.g. Cic. *I Verr.* 1–3, portraying the case as a trial of the senate itself). **personae claritate** 'the distinction of the individual' (*OLD persona* 5a–b), i.e. defendant. *claritas* may be a nod to Priscus' senatorial rank (2.1.1n. *maximi*); cf. 6.29.3 *claras et illustres* [*causas*], referring to this case among others. **famosum** 'famous, celebrated' (*OLD* 1); cf. 6.23.1 *causam . . . pulchram . . . et famosam.* **seueritate exempli salubre** 'salutary in the severity of the example it set'. For *seueritas exempli*, cf. Cic. *II Verr.* 5.7, for *salubre exemplum* Livy 8.7.17 etc.; might a famous line of Livy's also be in mind (*pr.*10 *hoc illud est praecipue in cognitione rerum salubre ac frugiferum, omnis te exempli documenta in illustri posita monumento intueri*)? According to P., Thrasea Paetus said an orator should preferably undertake trials *ad exemplum pertinentes* (6.29.1; cf. Quint. 4.1.7); P. is similarly motivated in his attack on Publicius Certus (9.13.3 *exempli ratio incitabat*, 25 *interest . . . exempli*) and hopes for *seueritas* in the trial of Caecilius Classicus (3.9.19). He takes a different view when defending (4.9). The severity of Priscus' punishment is debatable (intro.), but with due allowance for exaggeration this proclamation may be taken to imply that milder penalties were the norm (Garnsey 1970: 55). **rei magnitudine** 'the immensity of the case' (*OLD res* 11, *magnitudo* 6): a vague, grand Ciceronian expression (*II Verr.* 4.105 etc.) for the climax. **aeternum:** thanks to this letter. The *aeternitas* conferred through historiography (5.8.1, 6.16) and other literature (2.10, 3.5, 3.21, 9.3.2, 9.14) is a favourite Plinian theme.

2–9 *Preliminary hearings*

2 Marius Priscus . . . petît: a miniature periodic sentence opens the narrative (subject, abl. abs., relative clause, abl. abs., predicate, in an arch: 5~7~9~8~5 syllables). P. first summarises the initial hearing some time in 99 (early enough for the African witnesses, §5n. *Mario*, to be summoned and arrive by December), omitting the sessions of 98 at which the charge was laid and advocates appointed (below on *adesse*). Perfect tenses (rather than pluperfect) bind it to the main trial, creating the sense of a single event. Like Trajan, Priscus was a senator from Baetica (southern Spain), a wicked counterpart to a good emperor, and with a doubly ill-omened name for this exemplary scrutiny of senatorial morals (no conquering general, nor a *priscus* Roman, though P. refrains from puns; cf. §23n. *superest*, 2.1n. C. PLINIVS). He occasioned a *bon mot* when Baetica itself suffered under the corrupt governor Classicus (3.9.3 *dedi malum et accepi*). Priscus was consul in the early to mid-80s, and held his proconsulate of Africa in 97–8 (Syme 1958: 658, S-W 56–7, *PIR*² M 315). He is known only from P. and Juvenal (intro.). **accusantibus Afris:** abl. abs. 3.9.4 specifies that Marius was prosecuted only by *una ciuitas* [Lepcis Magna: §23] *publice multique priuati*, not by the province corporately (as 3.9.4 and 7.6.1 with S-W), but the loose *Afris* is standard usage (see Fishwick 1972: 699–700, on Tacitus). The province of 'Africa Proconsularis', governed from Carthage (in modern Tunisia), by now stretched along the coast from Numidia (eastern Algeria) to Tripolitania (north-western Libya). Its agricultural wealth and importance made it a prestigious governorship, the only public (or 'senatorial') province except Asia given to a proconsul, rather than a propraetor (2.12.2n. *in*). Dondin-Payre 1989 surveys known prosecutions of African governors. **pro consule** 'as proconsul', predicative. Literally 'standing in for a consul' (*OLD consul* 1c), it is treated as an indeclinable noun, here nominative. **omissa defensione** 'offering no defence', effectively pleading guilty (as Tac. *An.* 13.33.2; cf. *H.* 3.9.5). The first and last mention of Priscus' participation: the spotlight is not so much on him as on the senate, and above all on P. **iudices petît** 'requested assessors'. At this period the *iudices* (or *recuperatores*) were a panel of five who assessed the damages after a senator had been found guilty of extortion (a development of arrangements instituted by the *SC Caluisianum* of 4 BC). *iudices accipere* seems to be an idiom for condemnation on a charge of extortion (Brunt 1961: 200, Bleicken 1962: 42 n.3), which entailed, besides financial penalty, expulsion from the senate (S-W 166–7). That this sanction was automatic is clear from P.'s comments on Julius Bassus (4.9.16, 19; 6.29.10), the exception who proves the rule; it also underlies the rhetoric of 2.12.3–4. If Priscus succeeded in his request, he would evade full senatorial trial on criminal charges and the prospect of capital punishment (exile). The precise remit of the *iudices* remains uncertain, thanks in part to the avoidance of technical terms in ancient accounts; the explanation here follows Brunt 1961: 199–200, Bleicken 1962: 41–2, 163, and Crook 1967b: 312–13, against S-W 161. Tac. *An.* 4.22.2 *datis iudicibus*, uniquely used of a trial not for extortion, remains a mystery (Martin–Woodman 1989: 155), and a reminder that idiom is flexible. **petît:** the MSS are divided between *petit* (Fγ) and *petiit* (α), which, together with evidence elsewhere, speaks in favour of the former. The short form is transmitted unanimously at 1.5.11 (surely perfect) and 5.20.2 *Varenus petit* (similarly opening a senatorial trial scene), and supported elsewhere when the MSS disagree (2.1.5n. *male*). Perhaps P. was flexible: here and in 8.23.5 *praereptus est pet(i)it* the longer form (usually printed) gives a more familiar clausula (cretic + resolved spondee); but *petit* makes a respectable cretic – iamb, moderately common in P. (Intro. 29 n.164); see 2.2.2n. *studîs* for a similar problem. Pflips 393–5 calculates that cretic + resolved spondee, the only one of P.'s favourite clausulae that is infrequent in Cicero (Intro. 30), is significantly rarer at sentence-end in 2.11 (5.4%) than it is in the *Epistles* as a whole (10.1%), a reflex perhaps of Ciceronian style (the other 'trial' letters show similar reductions; his figure for *Pan.* is 7.4%). With *petit* here it becomes rarer still; but one letter is a small statistical sample. **ego et Cornelius Tacitus:** the last record of Tacitus' public career before his proconsulship of Asia in (probably) 112–13. He is now a consular, senior to P. (2.1.6n. *laudatus*); here the name is left to speak for itself. It is often suggested that the outcome of this trial (as seen by Juvenal) turned Tacitus away from advocacy in disillusionment, but his supposed retirement from oratory is argued *ex silentio* and from a risky assumption that Maternus' rejection of advocacy in the *Dialogus* is autobiographical. **adesse**

prouincialibus: *adesse* + dat. 'assist, represent' as advocate (*OLD* 12, *TLL* 11 923.30–79), presenting them less as prosecutors and more as defenders of the weak. P. routinely uses *prouinciales* in the *Epistles*; *Pan.* has only the more elevated *socii* (Lavan 2013: 63–4). **iussi:** advocates were appointed by senatorial vote (the 'lot' in 10.3A.2 must be a formality or a fossilised idiom: cf. Talbert 1984: 348 'puzzling'; Bablitz 2009: 199–201 seems confused). In summer 98 the senate had appointed P. *in absentia*; he initially refused because of his duties as prefect of the treasury of Saturn, but was forced in a second session, with Trajan's permission, to relent (10.3A–B). So *iussi* is accurate, but it is also tasteful: one should never be keen to prosecute (Cic. *Off.* 2.50, Quint. 11.1.57, 4.1.7), especially a fellow senator, hence the defensive *fidei... conuenire* below; cf. 3.4.7 *quod in eius modi causis solet esse tristissimum, periculum senatoris*, 6.29.7 and P.'s restraint at 7.33.4–5; S–W 94–5. On the other hand, the duty should not be shirked when necessary (Quint. 12.7.1–4) and protecting provincials was the *ratio accusandi... honestissima* (Cic. *Diu. Caec.* 63; Frazel 2009: 160–4). **existimauimus:** a formal verb for a pompous sentence (next n.), placed early as often. **fidei nostrae conuenire | notum senatui facere | excessisse Priscum...** 'that it was in keeping with our integrity to make it known to the senate that Priscus had surpassed...' (for *fides* see 2.5.3n. *diligentia*): a ponderous chain of infinitival phrases, each dependent on the last, in extended tricolon (9~9~26 syllables). The AB~AB~BA order is typical but sets dramatic emphasis on *excessisse* after the bureaucratic language that precedes: *fidei conuenire* (only here and 1.7.2) sounds like a barrister's cliché, and *notum... facere* (8× in P., four of them in book 10) is officialese (Adams 2003c: 557–8). On *fides* see 2.5.3n. *diligentia*. **excessisse Priscum immanitate et saeuitiā crimina quibus dari iudices possent** 'that in his monstrous cruelty Priscus had sur-passed [*OLD excedo* 6b] the charges for which assessors could be appointed': his offences were too serious to avoid full senatorial trial. Cf. 6.29.9 *utebatur* [*Priscus*] *clementia legis, cuius seueritatem immanitate criminum excesserat*. P. alternates between 'Priscus' and 'Marius', perhaps for the sake of variety (Vidman 1981: 593); there is no such flexibility in 3.9 or 4.9. **immanitate et saeuitia:** an emotive pair, perhaps a hendiadys. *immanitas* 'brutality, monstrosity' is a Ciceronian favourite, not least in the *Verrines* (4×). P. uses it again of Priscus in 6.29.10 (previous n.), and of Domitian in 4.11.6 and *Pan.* 47.1. *saeuitia* is often treated by modern his-torians as a formal term for 'aggravated' extortion (cf. Tac. *H.* 4.45 *damnatur lege repetundarum et exilio ob saeuitiam*), but P.'s usage does not seem technical: cf. 3.9.2, where the same charge is expressed *proconsulatum... non minus uiolenter quam sordide gesserat*, with *sordide* referring to extortion, *uiolenter* to the criminal abuse here called *saeuitia*. The coupling with *immanitas* (which for Cicero often implies 'sub-human') evokes wild animal imagery. **crimina** covers both 'charges' (*OLD* 1, the usual Ciceronian meaning) and 'crimes' (*OLD* 4, as 6.29.9 above). **quibus:** indi-rect object of *dari*. Elsewhere 'judges are given' to the person, not the charge (§5 *Mario*, 4.9.16). **possent:** generic subjunctive (also subordinate within acc. + inf.). **cum ob innocentes condemnandos interficiendos etiam**

pecunias accepisset: for *accipio* of bribes see *OLD* 2b. *etiam* bolsters *interficiendos*, second and last in a list (2.1.6n., §15 *tantam etiam curam*, §20 *omnes etiam consulares*). *ob* + gerund(ive) 'in return for' is standard in Cicero for allegations of bribery (e.g. *I Verr.* 38 *acceptae pecuniae ob rem iudicandam*; K–S I 531, 751). *innocentes* is advocate's rhetoric: it presumably remained to be proved that the victims had in fact been innocent. If they had tried to appeal to the emperor and were prevented, Priscus was guilty of violating the *lex Iulia de ui*, but P. makes no such suggestion (Garnsey 1966: 175).

3 Fronto Catius: Tiberius Catius Caesius Fronto (*PIR²* C 194), *cos. suff.* 96, perhaps the rich patron of Mart. 1.55.2 and Juv. 1.12. P. inverts *gentilicium* (Catius) and *cognomen*, as at §18 and perhaps 6.13.3 (the MSS differ; at 4.9.15 he is plain *Fronto*). Such flexibility is familiar from Cicero and Livy (Axtell 1915: 392–7, Oakley on Livy 6.18.4); P. has it far more rarely than Tacitus. Fronto is remembered for his remark (as given in Dio 68.1.3) that 'it is bad to have an emperor under whom no one is allowed to do anything, but worse to have one under whom everyone is allowed to do everything', an oblique criticism of the frenzied attacks of late 96 on Domitianic 'collaborators'. He apparently specialised in defending governors on corruption charges (4.9.15, 6.13.3). **deprecatusque est** 'and made a plea' (*OLD* 3c). For the connection X Y*que* Z*que*, cf. §10n. *causae*, 2.19.9n. *omnesque*. **ne quid ultra repetundarum legem quaereretur** 'that there should be no trial beyond that for extortion', indirect command. *repetundae* [*sc. pecuniae*] 'money to be reclaimed' (*OLD repeto* 10b) is a stock term for an extortion trial (*causa de repetundis*), and by extension for extortion (*OCD* '*repetundae*'). The older form of the gerundive (*-und-*) is typical of legal jargon. While scholars often speak of 'aggravated extortion' or 'extortion with *saeuitia*' (§2n. *immanitate*), Catius speaks as if the proposed trial should be on separate charges. **omniaque actionis suae uela | uir mouendarum lacrimarum peritissimus | quodam uelut uento miserationis impleuit:** with (P. implies) little legal basis for defence, Fronto appeals to the senate's compassion (or class solidarity, §6n. *fauor*). Rising tricolon (11~14~15 syllables) with three noun-phrases each of four words; the first two are chiastic (ABCD~DCBA), the third varies. **actionis** 'oratory', covering both 'performance, delivery' (*OLD* 4, as 2.14.10) and 'speech' (*OLD* 5, as §16, etc.; see 2.5.1n.). **uela:** a nautical metaphor common in Cicero (*De or.* 2.187 *unde aliquis flatus ostenditur, uela do, Or.* 75 with Sandys; cf. *Tusc.* 4.9 *uela orationis*), developed with P.'s bold 'wind of pity' and a gust of onomatopoeia (*uēla ŭir mouĕndarum . . . uĕlut ŭento . . . implēuit*). In oratory as in poetry the *genus grande* 'grand style' was considered especially emotive (Lausberg §1079; Bramble 1974: 166–8): cf. Quint. 6.1.52 (on perorating) *e confragosis atque asperis euecti tota pandere possumus uela*. Similar imagery at 6.33.10, one of P.'s finest moments in the civil courts, and 9.26.4, a grand defence of the grand style; also 4.20.2 and 8.4.5. Fronto's oratory receives further praise at §18 (*insigniter*), 4.9.15 (*mirifice*), 6.13.3 (*grauiter et firme*). **uir mouendarum lacrimarum peritissimus:** in apposition with

Fronto Catius. A high compliment: only a consummate orator should attempt to move his audience to tears (Quint. 6.1.44). Picone 1978: 45 sees irony. On *uir*, see §5n.; on the gerundive, 2.9.2n. *ius.* The textbook claim that good Latin ('Ciceronian' or not) always avoids *-orum -orum* uel sim. with gerundives is not quite true (Macdonald 1961): cf. 9.37.1 *locandorum praediorum*, 10.54.1 (but some instances in 2.13.1n. *occasiones*). Here the sonority is apt, raising P.'s prose to match Fronto's grandeur.   **quodam uelut:** the hedging is doubled (2.5.13n. *dulcedo*, 2.4.3n. *ex*) for a bold usage, fitting bulk, and balance (above on *omniaque*).   **miserationis:** a synonym for *misericordia*, increasingly popular after Cicero (*TLL* VIII 1112.20–35).

4 magna contentio, magni utrimque clamores *sc. erant*, 'many strong words, much shouting on both sides'; *utrimque* is *apo koinou*. Isocolon (6~7 syllables) with parallel alliteration (*m- c- m- c-*) and gradation in nouns (lit. 'raising of the voice [*OLD contentio* 2b] ~ shouts') and number (sg. ~ pl.). Crisp scene-painting: cf. 2.14.11n. *clamor*, Hor. *Sat.* 1.9.77 *rapit in ius; clamor utrimque,* | *undique concursus.*   **aliis ... | aliis ... dicentibus** 'with some saying that the senate's judicial powers were circumscribed by law, others that it was free and unrestricted' (after Radice), abl. abs. with *cognitionem* and *dicentibus* distributed *apo koinou*. Rules are one thing, their interpretation another: cf. 4.9.17 *cum putaret licere senatui (sicut licet) et mitigare leges et intendere* with S-W 278.   **cognitionem senatūs:** lit. 'enquiry of the senate', *OLD cognitio* 3.   **conclusam** (*OLD* 5) *sc. esse.* This group was arguing that the senate was obliged to grant Priscus' request for assessors. The legalities are uncertain; such a provision would expedite justice for the provincials, but allow anyone to evade capital trial by pleading guilty to the lesser charges as Priscus does.   **liberam solutamque** *sc. esse*, 'free and unrestricted', a common Ciceronian pair (Gudeman on Tac. *D.* 39.2) also at 8.17.4, *Pan.* 80.4.   **quantumque admisisset reus tantum uindicandum** *sc. esse*, 'and that the penalty inflicted upon the defendant should correspond to the full extent of his crimes' (Merrill), a further indirect statement after *dicentibus*; for *admittere* 'commit [crime]' cf. 10.78.3, *OLD* 13a. The argument favouring the position of P. and Tacitus is reported second, at greater length and so worded as to seem self-evidently right.

5 nouissime 'eventually' (*OLD* 4).   **consul designatus:** consuls designate were invited to speak first in debates, followed by consulars in descending order of seniority.   **Iulius Ferox:** Tiberius Julius Ferox (*PIR*² I 306, Syme 1979a: 257), *cos. suff.* 99 (known from here), proconsul of Asia *c.* 116–17. He is mentioned again in 10.87.3 and may be the Ferox with whom P. is intimate in 7.13 (quoted in 2.2. intro.). The word-order, name following rank (cf. 5.13.4, Tac. *An.* 12.53.2), is far rarer than §19 *Cornutus Tertullus consul designatus* (4.9.16, 4.17.1, 5.20.6, 9.13.13, Tac. *H.* 4.4.3, *An.* 4.42.3 etc.), but without obvious nuance (unlike 2.1.6n. *laudatus*).   **uir rectus et sanctus** 'a just and scrupulous man' (*OLD rectus* 10c, *sanctus* 4a). Such appositional phrases with clustered epithets (2.9.4n. *uir*) are especially common in the trial letters (§§17, 19; 3.9.7 etc.). 'The defendants are *homines*, but the attorneys are *uiri*' (Santoro-L'Hoir 1992: 152). *rectus* (again in 7.22.2, 7.31.1; cf. 2.19.6) is rare in Cicero, *sanctus* common. **Mario quidem iudices interim censuit dandos, euocandos autem quibus diceretur innocentium poenas uendidisse** 'proposed that for the meantime Marius be condemned on the extortion charge [§2n. *iudices*], but that those to whom he was alleged to have sold the punishment of innocent men should be summoned'. Ferox's dual proposal is set in antithesis, articulated by *quidem*... *autem* (= μέν... δέ, 2.1.7n. *et*); *Mario* provides the prop for *quidem* despite not being the primary term of contrast (2.5.11n. *non*). Priscus will get the quick justice he requested, but those accused of bribing him will be summoned from Africa as witnesses (*OLD euoco* 3b); since such summonses were permitted only in full criminal trials, Ferox is implicitly proposing that Priscus face criminal charges in addition. For the latter procedure, cf. 6.29.8 *quaesitum est, an danda esset* [*Massae*] *inquisitio* ('whether to subject Massa to full trial'), 5.20.2 with S-W, Talbert 1984: 481. **censuit dandos:** *censeo* (*OLD* 4a) is the technical term for stating one's opinion or proposal (*sententia*) in the senate, construed here as often with a gerundive. Its placement between *iudices* and *dandos* ('verbal hyperbaton', in Cicero a sign of elaborate style) reflects a widespread mannerism in early imperial prose (Adams 1972c), used quite sparingly by P. (2.17.5n. *longinquos*). It generates a cretic–spondee and typical juxtaposition of verbs (*dandos, euocandos*) at the clause-break (2.1.2n. *triginta* and e.g. §14 *collegi, coepi*, §23 *commodasse, stipulatusque*).

6 quae sententia non praeualuit modo | sed omnino... fuit sola: rising bicolon (12~16 syllables), ABC~CBA (noun, verb, adverb), with framing alliteration *sententia ~ sola*. For *sententia* see previous n.; *praeualuit* 'prevailed' is first in Livy; with *sententia* (where Cicero would use *ualere*) several times in P. **sed omnino** 'but... at all', a Ciceronian favourite after *non* (*modo*), as here. **post tantas dissensiones** = §4 *magna contentio* etc.; the phrase adds weight and delay before the sharp finish. **fuit sola** 'was the only one', a pointed way to say 'received unanimous support'. Editors have always punctuated '*fuit sola frequens.*', problematic on several counts: (*i*) *frequens* cannot be 'unanimous' (*pace OLD* 4a), which would be flatly tautologous with *sola*, and 'strongly supported' (Talbert 1984: 281 n.18) is unparalleled. (*ii*) Making *annotatumque* first word in the following sentence puts great strain on -*que*. Words for 'and' can begin a brief parenthesis (H–S 473, von Albrecht 1964: 56–7), e.g. 3.14.3 *et iam tutum erat*, 3.18.10 *utinamque iam uenerit*, Cic. *Off.* 1.95 *idque intellegitur in omni uirtute*, but this excursus (down to §7 *teguntur*) is far from brief. (*iii*) As Michael Reeve observes, *fuit sola frequens* would make a very rare clausula, whereas *fuit sola* completes a routine cretic–spondee (cf. 3.9.27 and, also with penultimate *fui(t)*, 3.11.2, 8.2.8, 8.14.10, 10.21.1, *Pan.* 28.2, 30.5, 70.3). The scribe of M had it right, with a punctuation mark after *sola*. **frequens annotatumque experimentis** sc. *est*, 'it is common and observed from experience'; the narrative is suspended for a confirmatory general observation, introduced in asyndeton. For this use of *frequens* cf. Quint. 3.6.8 *frequens est ut ... omittamus*, Tac. *An.* 2.33.1 *erat ... frequens senatoribus ... promere*, Paul. *Dig.* 44.2.6 *parere ... frequens est*. With *annotatum experimentis* P. varies the historical/technical formula *cognitum experimento/-is* (Sall. *Jug.* 46.3, Celsus, Pl. *NH*, Tac.). **quod:** an early instance of *quod* + indic. (or subj.) replacing the acc. + inf. in formal prose, as at 3.9.6 (*NLS* §35, H–S 576–7, Kraut 1872: 31). At 3.16.1 P. construes *annotare* with acc. + inf., as Tacitus does *frequens* in *An.* 2.33.1 (previous n.). **fauor et misericordia:** respectively bias towards and sympathy for the defendant; the doublet is contemporary ([Quint.] *Decl. mai.* 17.8, Tac. *An.* 2.73). Priscus apparently benefited from both: some consider his indictment for extortion sufficient (§13) and he narrowly misses receiving a lighter sentence (§21). P.'s quasi-prosecution of the senator Publicius Certus faces similar opposition in *gratia* and *amicitiae* (9.13.11). Of course the rhetoric is tendentious, talking up the challenge faced by P., but senatorial bias seems likely enough (Brunt 1961; Garnsey 1970: 50–8). **acres et uehementes primos impetus habent, paulatim consilio et ratione quasi restincta considunt** 'have a fierce and violent initial onslaught, but gradually abate, quelled as it were by rational thought'. The first of a trio of *sententiae* rounding off this first episode (for such clustering see Intro. 28), a rising bicolon (14~19 syllables), ABC~ABC with the first two elements syntactically varied (*acres et uehementes* ~ *consilio et ratione* / *primos impetus* ~ *quasi restincta*) in 'false parallelism' (Kraus on Livy 6.33.1). The pairs *acer et uehemens* and *consilium et ratio* are Ciceronian, and for the contrast between the onset of emotion and its abating cf. Cic. *Cluent.* 5 *falsa inuidia ... uehementes habeat repentinos impetus* [~ P.'s *uehementes primos impetus habent*], *spatio interposito et causa cognita consenescat*. In place of Cicero's *consenescat* 'grows old' P. has a thoroughgoing disease metaphor (softened by *quasi*: 2.6.5n. *illa*): *OLD acer* 11c, *uehemens* 3d, *impetus* 3b, *restinguo* 2b, *consido* 7b (where *Pan.* 8.5 and Tac. *An.* 14.61.4 are also metaphorical: Woodman 2006: 318); for *primus impetus* of illness see Pl. *NH* 26.101 (gout) and, of emotions, Sen. *Ira* 2.29.1 (anger), *Ep.* 99.1 (grief). The image of emotion as disease, famous from love poetry (e.g. Cat. 76), is widespread (Braund–Gill 1997 *passim*).

7 unde 'and so' (lit. 'from which cause', *OLD* 11b). **euěnit ut** 'it comes about that' (*OLD euenio* 3a). **quod multi clamore permixto tuentur | nemo tacentibus ceteris dicere uelit** 'what many speak up for [*OLD tueor* 4b] in the mass of shouting, no one is willing to say when everyone else is silent', isocolon (12~14 syllables) again with varied ABC~ABC parallelism: *multi* (pl.) ~ *nemo* (sg.) / *clamore permixto* (abl. of circumstance) ~ *tacentibus ceteris* (abl. abs., and chiastic with *clamore permixto*) / *tuentur* (indic.) ~ *dicere uelit* (subj.). Cf. 9.13.4 *incondito turbidoque clamore*, in a similar context (§6n. *acres*), and Tac. *An.* 14.45.1 *sententiae Cassi ut nemo unus contra ire ausus est, ita dissonae uoces respondebant ...* The hecklers occupy the moral low ground, and know it. **patescit enim, cum separaris a turba, contemplatio rerum quae turbā teguntur** 'for consideration of things which are obscured by a crowd becomes clear once you detach [lit. 'when you have detached'] it from the crowd'. The preceding maxim is continued with the explanatory *enim* and a third, differently formed epigram. The key-word *contemplatio* is roughly central; the final words *turba* (abl. of instrument) *teguntur* (pl.) chiastically reprise *patescit* (sg.) . . . *a turba* (abl. of separation) and seal the sentence with typical Latin alliteration. *contemplatio rerum* is a recurrent pair, especially in Cicero. For *patescere* (*OLD* 3b) with abstract subject, cf. Lucr. 5.614 *ratio . . . recta patescit*. **separaris:** pf. subj. (= *separaueris*), the usual mood for generalising second person ('you/one') in temporal clauses (G–L §567, *NLS* §217c.ii): cf. 1.9.3 *haec . . . inania uidentur, multo magis cum secesseris*. An object *eam* must be supplied from the following *contemplatio*. P. usually prefers *-aueris* but syncopates also at 1.7.1 *collocaris, Pan.* 91.3 *ornaris*. The final *i* was originally long (poets had long been unsure or flexible: Owen on Ov. *Tr.* 2.323), and it may be felt so in *Pan.* 7.7 *genueris an elegeris*, 68.4 *iuraueris omnibus* and perhaps 2.17.25 *loco moueris humum*, making if so a dispondee rather than the ubiquitous cretic–spondee here. Nevertheless, pres. pass. *separaris* 'you are separated' (so most translators) is unlikely: the tense may be defensible (cf. e.g. 2.17.4 *includitur*, and Maec. *Dig.* 49.17.18.4 *cum hoc peculium a patris bonis separetur* 'is separate from') but the indicative, if not unheard of (H–S 419, Juv. 3.289 with Courtney), is unparalleled in P. **turba** embraces both 'confusion, disorder' (*OLD* 1) and a disordered 'mass' of people (*OLD* 2); its often contemptuous tone (*OLD* 6) makes for a less than complimentary reference to the senatorial majority (cf. 2.12.5).

8 Venerunt: from Africa. The single word bridges several months between the indictment and the next hearing in December 99, a characteristic ambiguity (e.g. 5.1.6 *post hoc* = 2 years; S-W 275–6) imposing unity on the series of debates (§2n. *Marius*). **adesse erant iussi** 'had been summoned' (*OLD adsum* 8), varying §5 *euocandos* and contrasting in meaning with §2 *adesse . . . iussi*. **Vitellius Honoratus et Flauius Marcianus:** two local aristocrats in Lepcis Magna (§23) with Roman citizenship (as the form of name indicates). Their *gentilicia*, well attested in African inscriptions, may imply patronage by recent imperial families (Thompson 1970: 64–6). **ex quibus** introduces a parallel antithesis *Honoratus . . . | Marcianus . . . arguebatur emisse* (31~33 syllables), with the main verb *apo koinou*. Word-order is varied between the cola, chiastic within the first: A (*Honoratus*) B (*trecentis milibus*) c (*exsilium*) D (*equitis Romani*) D (*septemque amicorum eius*) c (*ultimam poenam*) ~ A (*Marcianus*) D (*unius equitis Romani*) B (*septingentis milibus*) c (*plura supplicia*). In customary gradation, the higher price and more heinous charge come second. **trecentis milibus** sc. *sestertium*, abl. of price with *emisse*. A large but not astronomical sum (P. gives gifts of similar value: 2.4.2n. *in*). Classicus allegedly extorted four million from Baetica (3.9.13), Verres 40 million from Sicily (Cic. *I Verr.* 56). **exsilium:** used loosely for relegation (in this case from Africa), as commonly (Garnsey 1970: 111–22, esp. 114–15). Unlike *exsilium* proper (a capital punishment), *relegatio* did not entail loss of civic rights. **equitis Romani:** oratorical indignation; what matters is less the victims' identity than their rank. Inflicting such penalties on equestrians was certainly abnormal, possibly illegal (contested: S-W 164–5, Brunt 1961: 190–3; Garnsey 1966; Cloud 1988 and 1989). **septemque amicorum:** evidently of lower status, their seven executions subordinated to the exile of a single *eques.* **ultimam poenam** translates a Greek euphemism (ἐσχάτη δίκη) for death; cf. 8.14.24 *ultimum supplicium* (first in Caesar), and *ultima poena*, first in Livy. **unius** 'a single', contrasting with *plura supplicia.* **arguebatur emisse** 'was accused of having bought' by bribery. **enim** explains *plura.* **fustibus caesus, damnatus in metallum, strangulatus in carcere:** rising AB~BA~BA tricolon (5~7~8 syllables) with emotive gradation. **fustibus caesus** 'beaten' (lit. 'struck with cudgels'), a punishment usually reserved for lower social orders and non-citizens and commonly applied, as here, before hard labour or execution (Garnsey 1970: 136–41, Millar 1984: 127–30). **damnatus in metallum:** condemned to hard labour in a mine or quarry (*metallum*), a capital punishment second only to death and abnormal for anyone of high status, certainly an *eques* (Garnsey 1970: 131–6, Millar 1984: 137–43, Salerno 2003). The citizen (but probably not *eques*) Flavius Archippus had been sentenced *in metallum*, legally it seems, by a proconsul in the 80s (10.58.3 with S-W). **strangulatus in carcere:** an old form of execution regarded by now as brutal; it features extensively in Suet. *Tib.* Incarceration was a temporary measure (Garnsey 1970: 147–52, Millar 1984: 130–2): the victim was presumably awaiting transportation to the *metallum.* The word-order throws stress onto *carcere* (one might at least be strangled *en plein air*) and makes a double cretic.

9 sed Honoratum . . . Marcianus: parallel antithesis again (§8n. *ex*), now with differing syntax; for the varied cases cf. 2.17.13 *turbati maris . . . | hortum* and 2.17.14 *gestatio . . . | hortum.* **cognitioni senatūs mors opportuna subtraxit:** a timely death 'stole, rescued' (*OLD subtraho* 5) him from the trial (§4n. *cognitionem*, dative of disadvantage) between his arrival in Rome and the day of the hearing. *mors opportuna* is Livian (Kraus 1994: 91), as is the whole expression: cf. Livy 6.1.7 *cui iudicio eum mors, adeo opportuna ut uoluntariam magna pars crederet, subtraxit.* It often describes suicide (Oakley ad loc.) but need not (e.g. Sen. *Marc.* 36.2), and P. makes no such intimation here (contrast Classicus at 3.9.5: *accusationem uel fortuita uel uoluntaria morte praeuertit*). **inductus est** sc. *in senatum* (cf. 2.12.2), 'was brought in [as a defendant]' (*OLD induco* 1b), bringing us to the next hearing (December 99). **absente Prisco:** chiastic with *Marcianus inductus est* (and making a ditrochee). P. leaves the reason implicit, that Priscus had been found guilty by the *iudices* (§13 *damnatum*) and accordingly stripped of his senatorial status (§2n. *iudices*). That business could proceed in his absence reflects the nature of proceedings, not simply a 'trial' but (also) a senatorial debate (S-W 339–40; Talbert 1984: 463 'no rigid distinction was ever drawn by contemporaries between the judicial and non-judicial business of the House'). **itaque:** referring just to *absente Prisco*. **Tuccius Cerialis:** probably *cos. suff.* 90. The transmitted *Tuccius*, not *Tullius*, seems right despite inscriptional evidence (Syme 1968: 137; Birley 2000a: 94–5). Perhaps not the Cerialis who receives 2.19, even if that letter concerns P.'s speech against Priscus (2.19n. CERIALI). **consularis:** 2.1.9n. *senes*. **iure senatorio** 'by senatorial right'; a special request before the debate (S-W 166, 493–4; Talbert 1984: 231–4), which otherwise began only after the advocates' speeches and presentation of evidence.   **ut Priscus certior fieret** 'that Priscus be informed' (*OLD certus* 12b, Kraus on Livy 6.33.7) *sc.* and invited to attend.   **siue quia miserabiliorem siue quia inuidiosiorem:** isocolon (11~11 syllables) for the first two alternatives, with matching comparatives ('more pitiable', 'more odious').   **fore** *sc. eum* (= Priscus), a common Plinian ellipse in indirect statement, e.g. 2.12.2 [*eum*] *mouendum*, 2.20.13 [*se*] *habiturum*; Kraut 1872: 9–10.   **si praesens fuisset** 'if he were present', plpf. subj. representing fut. pf. in direct speech (*NLS* §272.3d).   (**quod maxime credo**): the antecedent of *quod* is all of *quia ... defendi* (2.7.2n. *quod*). The parenthesis underlines what one would in any case expect, that the third and longest option is preferred.   **quia aequissimum erat** 'because it was most just that ... ' + acc. + inf. (*OLD aequus* 6a). A proper, 'safely procedural' (Morello 2007: 184) explanation for Cerialis' intervention.   **crimen** means 'charge' with *defendi* 'be contested' and *dilui* 'be refuted' (*OLD* 4), both Ciceronian; with *puniri* (not in Cicero) the sense must include 'crime' (§2n.).   **ab utroque defendi ... in utroque puniri:** equal anaphoric phrases (7~7 syllables) for the *commune crimen*.   **potuisset:** tense as *fuisset* above (it is subordinate to the indirect statement after *aequissimum erat*).

10–16 Main trial: first day

10 The style rises. Painting the scene was a standard narrative technique in oratory, known as ἐνάργεια, *euidentia* or *repraesentatio* (Quint. 8.3.61), *sub oculos subiectio* (Quint. 9.2.40; cf. Cic. *De or.* 3.202) or *demonstratio* (*Rhet. Her.* 4.55): see Lausberg §810–19, Innocenti 1994, Squire 2011: 327–8 with n.51. It was similarly prized in historiography: e.g. Lucian *How to write history* 51; Walker 1993. Quintilian (8.3.64) praises Cicero as the master, and P.'s evocation is in his mould: cf. Cic. *Sest.* 72 *ueniunt Kalendae Ianuariae ... quae tum frequentia senatus, quae exspectatio populi, qui concursus legatorum ex Italia cuncta* etc.; *Diu. Caec.* 42 (quoted in 2.10.7n. *imaginor*). In other trial letters P. is explicit about his *enargeia*: 3.9.26 *non potui magis te in rem praesentem perducere* (cf. Quint. 4.2.123 *credibilis rerum imago quae uelut in rem praesentem perducere audientes uidetur*); 6.33.7 *ut ... non legere tibi sed interesse iudicio uidereris*; Mayer 2003: 230–1.   **Dilata res est:** we are left to infer that Cerialis' proposal was agreed.   **in proximum senatum** 'to the next sitting of the senate' (*OLD senatus* 2a), probably 13 Jan. 100 (S-W 166).   **cuius:** the relative clause transports us to that next meeting and the central panel of the letter (§§10–16), featuring P.'s star turn as advocate. In all his reported extortion trials he is the first to plead (S-W

276). **conspectus** 'appearance' (*OLD* 2), Ciceronian; for the picture cf. Tac. *An.* 3.60.3 *magnaque eius diei species fuit* (in the senate). **augustissimus:** the sole appearance of *augustus* 'majestic', 'dignified' in the *Epistles*; it occurs seven times in the grander *Pan.* (superlative at *Pan.* 60.2) and heightens the style here. There may be wordplay on *Augustus* (a title of Trajan, as of all emperors), as perhaps in Tac. *Ag.* 3.1 *augeatque cotidie felicitatem temporum Nerua Traianus.* Is it coincidence that the last word of book 10 is *augere* (10.121)? **princeps praesidebat ... | ad hoc Ianuarius mensis ... | praeterea causae amplitudo ...** : three justifications for *conspectus augustissimus* in rising tricolon (12~31~49 syllables), each leading with the subject. The unique alliterative pairing *princeps praesidebat* marks the occasion (on terms for 'emperor' see 2.1.3n. *reliquit*). P. has said nothing of Trajan's adoption, accession or triumphal entry to Rome: his first appearance in the *Epistles*, save a passing mention at 2.9.2, is in perfect senatorial guise (Intro. 7–8). **(erat enim consul):** the parenthetic explanation (2.4.2n. *erat*), scarcely necessary for Arrianus, delicately emphasises Trajan's constitutional exercise of office (*Pan.* 76.1 *nihil praeter consulem ageres*, labouring the contrast with Domitian); for such courtesy to readers, cf. 2.20.7n. *quia.* He was *cos.* III *ord.* in Jan.–Feb. 100 (having been *cos. ord.* 91, *cos.* II *ord.* 98); he held three further consulates (Kienast 2004: 123), a modest total compared with Flavian practice (Vespasian 9×, Titus 8×, Domitian 17×). The emperor could probably sit on the dais in any case (Dio 54.10.5, Talbert 1984: 122), but individual protocol varied (Talbert 1984: 174–84). Trajan is apparently absent from P.'s other grand performances (Talbert 1984: 181–3). **ad hoc** 'besides', 'in addition' (*OLD ad* 23b), a popular alternative to *praeterea* from Sallust (26×) on. **Ianuarius mensis ... celeberrimus** *sc. erat,* 'it was January, a very busy month' (*OLD celeber* 1c, usually of place). Rome was particularly crowded in January, a bad season for travel and the time of magisterial inaugurations, elections, and the annual oath of loyalty (Talbert 1984: 144, 200–6, and cf. Cic. *Sest.* 72, quoted above in §10n.). All the same, this is *amplificatio* (§1n. *personae claritate famosum*), not reportage. **cum ceterā tum praecipue senatorum frequentiā** 'when Rome is full of people, especially senators', literally 'both with the other crowding and especially with the crowding of senators', similar to the Greek idiom ἄλλος τε ... καί, as at *Pan.* 41.3 *cum ceteris omnibus tum uel maxime auaris adulationibus.* That parallel, and the sense, supports *ceterā* (*sc. frequentiā, apo koinou*) over *ceterā* neut. acc. pl. 'in other respects' (*OLD* 4). **praeterea** varies *ad hoc*, as at 6.33.4 (in similar *enargeia*), 8.1.3 and several times (esp.) in Sallust (e.g. *Cat.* 14.3, 17.4). Similar chains of reasoning at 2.19.5–6 *accedit his ... porro ... et sane,* 4.14.6 *sane ... praeterea.* **causae amplitudo | auctaque ... exspectatio et fama | insitumque ... studium ... noscendi:** the third member of the long tricolon (above on *princeps*) itself comprises three noun-phrases in rising tricolon (5~14~21 syllables). For X Yque Zque see §3n. *deprecatusque.* **auctāque dilatione exspectatio et fama:** *aucta* modifies *exspectatio et fama* (2.1.8n. *coniunctae* for the agreement); *dilatione* (cf. 2.10.2 *exspectatio ... differre*) picks up *dilata res est.* For the noun-pair, cf. Quint. 4.1.31 *fama iudiciorum, exspectatio uulgi*; for *aucta* *fama*, Livy 9.38.9 and Tac. *H.* 2.1.2 with Heubner. Cf. Cic. *De or.* 1.120 on *exspectatio hominum* as a cause of nerves, and passages quoted above, §10n. **insitumque mortalibus studium magna et inusitata noscendi** 'the desire, ingrained [*OLD insero* 3] in mankind, to discover what is great and unfamiliar'. On the gerund see 2.10.7n. *ulteriora*; the pair *magna et inusitata* recurs at *Pan.* 3.3. *insitus mortalibus* is first in Lucr. 5.1165 and common in the early books of Tac. *H.* (1.55.1, 2.20.1, 2.38.1: Ash 2007: 130). *mortales*, a 'choice and dignified variant for *homines*' (Oakley on Livy 6.16.4; cf. Marouzeau 1962: 198–202), is otherwise restricted to *Pan.* (5.9, 80.4, 85.1). **omnes undique exciuerat** 'had brought people from all around' (lit. 'everyone from everywhere'). For the abstract subjects (*amplitudo* etc.) cf. Livy *per.* 91.18 *fabros cura conquisitos undique exciuerat*; for the phenomenon cf. 9.33.5 and 10 (the dolphin), Cic. *Opt. gen.* 22, Apul. *Met.* 4.28.3.

11 imaginare: the *enargeia* (§10n.) intensifies with a direct appeal to the reader's imagination: see Quint. 9.2.41 and Lausberg §814.2a on 'alerting formulae', e.g. Cic. *Rosc. Am.* 98 *nonne uobis haec quae audistis cernere oculis uidemini?* This is a favourite of P.'s (also Sen. *Ep.* 102.28), again at 8.6.11–12 *imaginare... imaginare* (another senatorial scene), 5.6.7 *imaginare* (a vista). The present passage contrasts with the previous letter 2.10.7 (*imaginor...*): there P. summons up ego-boosting *concursus, admiratio, clamor* and *silentium*; here he focuses (for a moment) on *sollicitudo* and *metus*. **quae sollicitudo... qui metus:** the orator's nervousness was a topos, e.g. Cic. *De or.* 1.119–21 (Crassus), Sen. *Ira* 2.3.3, Tac. *D.* 6.5 (Aper); Quint. 11.3.158 recommends showing signs of it. P.'s picture heightens the success that follows, but could also be read as re-performing his speech with this stock element of *captatio beneuolentiae* (winning over the audience), e.g. Cic. *Rosc. Am.* 9 *huc accedit summus timor, Diu. Caec.* 41–2, *Deiot.* 1. He may specifically recall *Cluent.* 50–1, likewise describing a speech of his: *hic ego tum ad respondendum surrexi qua cura, di immortales!, qua sollicitudine animi, quo timore* [~ *quae sollicitudo... qui metus*]*! semper equidem magno cum metu incipio dicere* [~ *equidem in senatu non semel egi*]*... tum uero ita sum perturbatus ut omnia timerem* [~ *tunc me tamen... permouebant*]*... collegi me aliquando* [~ §14 *utcumque tamen animum cogitationemque collegi*] (some of this in Philips). *Pro Cluentio* was one of Cicero's longest speeches, which would commend it to P. (1.20.4 *M. Tullium... cuius oratio optima fertur esse quae maxima*). **nobis** *sc. fuerit*, possessive dative, probably authorial plural (2.3.8n. *nosque*): Tacitus has not been mentioned since §2, including him would be tactless, and the spotlight is fixed on P. (*contra* Lilja 1971: 94). For the variation with the following singular (*egi*), see 2.4.3n. *sunt*. Ellipse of subordinate verbs (2.2.1n. *quod*) is allowed already by Cicero in indirect questions, where it becomes increasingly common (H–S 421–2 §223d). **quibus:** dat. of agent with *dicendum erat*; pl. as for *nobis* above. **super tanta re | in illo coetu | praesente Caesare:** graded tricolon of varied ablative phrases (5~5~6 syllables), chiastically reprising the tricolon of §10 (§10n. *princeps*). *Caesare* varies §10 *princeps* (2.1.3n. *Caesares quibus*). P. uses *super* 'about' (instead of *de*) twice, both times in the formula *super tanta re* (the other is 2.18.4).

It tends to be confined to such formulae and to official contexts (Adams 1972a: 358), though Cic. *Att.* has it 3×. **equidem** 'of course': contrasting with *tamen* (2.10.5n. *opto*) as a concessive ('it is true that'). **non semel** 'more than once', litotes. **egi** 'I have pleaded' (*OLD* 44). **quin immo** '[and] what is more' (*OLD quin* 3e), popular with the elder Pliny and Quintilian. **nusquam audiri benignius soleo:** cf. Cic. *Cluent.* 63 *etsi a uobis sic audior ut numquam benignius neque attentius quemquam auditum putem.* Cicero's self-praise there, as often (e.g. *Dom.* 32, *Sest.* 31, *Phil.* 1.15), functions as a *captatio beneuolentiae*, as perhaps does P.'s here (above on *quae*). Strictly, P. says only that no other audience gives him a kinder hearing, not in itself a boast (unlike 9.23.2 *frequenter e senatu famam qualem maxime optaueram rettuli*). On Plinian immodesty, see 2.4.intro., 2.10.7n. *quo.* **tunc me tamen:** *tamen* is exceptionally relegated from second place by *me*, which 'focuses' the emphatic *tunc* (cf. Adams 1994b). **ut noua omnia nouo metu permouebant** 'everything filled me, as if it was new, with new fear' (*OLD ut* 8a). Content, parallelism and polyptoton recall Cic. *Mil.* 1 *haec noui iudici noua forma terret oculos*, while the intensified form of *mouere*, dear to Cicero, heightens the drama and generates a ditrochee (cf. also *Cluent.* 51, above on *quae*).

12 obuersabatur '(before my eyes/in my mind) there appeared' (*OLD* 2), intensifying the *enargeia* (§10n.): having been shown the scene, we now enter P.'s mind (cf. 8.23.6 *obuersantur oculis cassi labores*, 4.17.4). This absolute use is first in Livy (*TLL* IX.2 312.76–313.7); cf. Tac. *An.* 16.29.2 *ipsius Thraseae uenerabilis species obuersabatur.* **causae difficultas:** cf. Cic. *Cluent.* 2 *perspicio quantum in agendo difficultatis et quantum laboris sit habitura* [*sc. altera pars causae*]. **stabat** 'there stood', painting the scene, with the first indication that Priscus, stripped of senatorial and a fortiori consular rank (§9n. *absente*), is present. The tables have been turned since 1.18.3 *eram acturus adulescentulus adhuc . . . contra potentissimos ciuitatis.* **modo consularis** '[a man who had] just recently [been] a consular' = *qui modo consularis fuerat.* For this compendious usage, the adverb modifying a noun, see K–S I 218–20, von Nägelsbach 1963: 412–14, Oakley on Livy 6.15.7 (with addendum in IV 520) and (on P.) Kraut 1872: 46, Merrill on 1.2.5 *fortasse.* For the pathos (present plight set against former greatness) and detail, cf. Cic. *De or.* 2.195 *quem enim ego consulem fuisse . . . meminissem, hunc cum afflictum . . . uiderem* (Guillemin 1929: 117); Gierig compares V. *Aen.* 2.274 *quantum mutatus ab illo . . .* **modo septemuir epulonum:** the 'board of seven in charge of sacred feasts' was one of the four senior priestly colleges (2.1.8n. *illo*; Beard–North–Price 1998: I 100–1). Syntax as for *modo consularis.* **iam neutrum** 'now neither'; neuter because referring to his status (*OLD neuter* 1c).

13 erat ergo: still explaining *causae difficultas.* **perquam** 'extremely', popular with P. (12×). **onerosum:** rhetorically loaded but probably based on fact (senatorial solidarity: §2n. *iussi*, §6n. *fauor*). **accusare damnatum:** tendentious oxymoron: Priscus had been 'condemned' by the *iudices* (§9) but not on the more serious charges now in question. To describe the defendant as already proved guilty was good lawyerly technique (e.g. Cic. *II Verr.* 1.1–3). **ut . . . ita**

'while . . . at the same time' (*OLD ut* 5b). Chiastic rising bicolon (ABC~CBA, 11~21 syllables) with each element longer in the second clause.   **quem . . . premebat atrocitas criminis** 'the enormity of the charge was bearing hard on him'. The elements are Ciceronian (e.g. *Rosc. Am.* 28 *atrocitate criminis, II Verr.* 2.49 *criminibus prematur*), but for the abstract subject cf. Hor. *Ep.* 1.18.79 *culpa premet,* [Quint.] *Decl. mai.* 9.11 *premere atrocitas criminum non potest.* P. assumes the veracity of the charges throughout.   **quasi peractae damnationis miseratio** 'pity for what they saw as a condemnation fully complete' (*OLD peragere* 5). *quasi* + participle gives the justification without endorsing it (*OLD* 1c, G–L §602 n.4, K–S I 790–1). *peractae damnationis* is objective genitive; for *miseratio* see §3n.

14 utcumque 'somehow or other'. P. has it 7×, three in this adverbial use (*OLD* 2, Petr. 92.13 with Habermehl), as e.g. 6.20.19 *curatis utcumque corporibus,* three as a conjunction (*OLD* 1), e.g. 9.13.24 *postea actionem meam utcumque potui recollegi, addidi multa* (at 1.12.2 it means *utique* 'at all events'). The passage from 9.13 is closely comparable: did the adverbial use arise through ellipse of *posse?*   **animum cogitationemque collegi, coepi dicere** 'I pulled myself together and began to speak'; cf. Cic. *Cluent.* 51 *collegi me aliquando* (in §11n. *quae*). The pair *animus et cogitatio* is also Ciceronian, though *animum colligere* is first in Livy 35.35.18. For the main verbs juxtaposed in asyndeton, cf. 9.13.24 (previous n.), §5n. *censuit.*   **non minore audientium assensu quam sollicitudine mea:** chiastic. *audientes* for *auditores* is common since Cicero, especially in this context (Adams 1973a: 124; cf. 2.3.9n. *dicentis*). *assensu* and *sollicitudine* are ablatives of attendant circumstances (2.1.4n. *pari*; cf. 9.13.7 *dico . . . maximo assensu*). P. does not hold back from reporting the fair reception his performances receive, e.g. 8.21.4 *recitaui biduo: hoc assensus audientium exegit,* 4.5.2 *hoc studio, hoc assensu,* 4.19.3 *laudesque nostras,* 7.6.13, 9.13.18. Cicero gives ample precedent, e.g. *Att.* 1.16.10 *magnis clamoribus, Q. fr.* 2.3.6 *magno assensu omnium*; see also Fronto *Ad M. Caes.* 2.2.1 (pp. 17.18–18.3 vdH², mentioning unfavourable reaction too). As usual, P.'s immodesty is filtered through apparent objectivity by his reporting others' opinions: e.g. 7.4.10, 9.23.6 *neque enim uereor ne iactantior uidear, cum de me aliorum iudicium non meum profero* (Ludolph 1997: 115; Mayer 2003: 229–30).   **dixi horis paene quinque:** a lapidary statement of P.'s speech almost precisely at the mid-point (434 words precede, 439 follow): the focal point of the trial, as we see it. For similarly precise centering, cf. 1.12.8 (intro.; Whitton 2013: n.94). There is not a word about the content: the reader is presumed to have access to the speech (not that Arrianus did), or the letter substitutes for it. P. spoke 'for nearly five hours' (*horis* is his usual abl. of duration: Schuster 460–1), in modern terms a little under four hours. Defined as one-twelfth of daylight, an hour varied by season; Rome has around 9½ hours' daylight in mid-January, so that each of P.'s 'hours' is 45–50 modern minutes. The prosecution in an extortion trial had six hours in total (4.9.9), of which P. had half (*duodecim clepsydris*), but his allowance was doubly extended, as he next explains.   **duodecim clepsydris** 'twelve clocks', indirect object of *additae*. The water-clock (κλεψύδρα) was the standard device for timing court speeches; 'one clock' was the time it took to drain, believed on the basis of this passage to be a quarter of a Roman hour (Marquardt 1886: 794–5, *pace OLD clepsydra* 2). It is possible, but never attested, that a *clepysdra* was a fixed amount of time in Rome (as it had been in Greece: Marquardt 1886: 792–4), in which case a legal *hora*, unlike an ordinary *hora*, was a fixed length (so Talbert 1984: 500–1). Otherwise (as *spatiosissimas* here suggests) the clock was adjusted throughout the year to keep it in proportion with the changing hours. Plinian clocks are discussed by Ker 2009 and Riggsby 2009. **quas spatiosissimas acceperam:** *spatiosus* 'ample' refers here to both space and time, the clock being filled up about a quarter more than the volume normal for January. **sunt additae quattuor:** making sixteen *clepsydrae*. P. received these extensions 'perhaps to deal with the extra complications' (S-W 167), on whose authority it is unclear: if that of Trajan as president, P. allows a delicate compliment (Ker 2009: 293). Mart. 6.35.1–2 and 8.73–4 show that an advocate could 'ask for *n* clocks' of the judge. **adeo** 'so completely' (*OLD* 5): the length of P.'s performance was the product of his confidence. **dura et aduersa:** synonymous couplet (cf. Cic. *Fin.* 4.59 *dura difficilia aduersa*). **dicturo . . . dicenti** *sc. mihi*, 'before I spoke . . . when I was speaking'. For similar polyptoton cf. 4.9.18 *diceret . . . dicturus*, 4.19.3 *acturus . . . egi*, Wills 1996: 303; see also 2.1.12n. *et*, 2.17.2n. *peractis*. **secunda:** a glancing name-pun, perhaps (*Secund*[*o*] *dicenti*; cf. 6.16.12 *auunculus meus secundissimo* [*uento*] *inuectus*)?

15 Caesar quidem 'the emperor in particular', picking out the most important of the *dura et aduersa* (cf. 6.5.4 *Iuuentius quidem Celsus*, 8.1.2 *Encolpius quidem*) with 'extending *quidem*' (Solodow 1978: 110–18, esp. 114). **tantum mihi studium, tantam etiam curam (nimium est enim dicere sollicitudinem) praestitit** 'showed me so much goodwill [*OLD studium* 5], so much concern even (for it would be too much to say anxiety)'. Rising bicolon (7~23 syllables) with *mihi* and *praestitit* in double *apo koinou*; for *praestitit* see 2.5.2n. *sollicitudinem*, for *est* 'would be' 2.6.1n. *longum*. The parenthesis (affecting to explain the word-choice *curam*: 2.4.2n. *erat*) makes a graded trio of nouns *studium* ~ *cura* ~ *sollicitudo*, displacing onto Trajan precisely the sentiments that P. might have felt pleading before him (*studium* in his case being 'effort', *OLD* 1). For form and manner (suggesting *sollicitudo* while claiming not to), cf. Cic. *De or.* 2.364 *uel pudentius uel inuitius* (*nolo enim dicere de tam suaui homine fastidiosius*). **libertum meum post me stantem:** the only record of a non-imperial freedman in the senate. It can hardly have been allowed to all, given space constraints, but might have been normal for an advocate, as it was in court (cf. Cic. *Diu. Caec.* 52 and Quint. 6.4.9 *monitoribus* 'prompters', 11.3.131 *librarios* 'clerks', 11.3.132 *suos*). Talbert 1984: 156, taking P.'s rhetoric literally (see below on *gracilitas*), speculates that this was a concession to his health. **admoneret . . . consulerem** 'warned (him) [to tell me] to watch', paratactic indirect command (2.5.2n. *rogo*); for *consulo* + dat., see 2.6.5n. *quibus*. We have no idea how far apart P. and Trajan were; perhaps P. is standing just in front of the consuls' dais (on which see Talbert 1984: 121–2), so that his freedman is close enough for the emperor to speak to. Otherwise

Trajan perhaps beckoned him over, or used a freedman of his own as messenger. **uoci laterique** 'voice and lungs' (*OLD latus* 2b), a Ciceronian couplet (*II Verr.* 4.67 *quae uox, quae latera*; Quint. 10.7.2). To profess anxiety at the physical demands of a trial is good rhetoric ('how could I ever list *all* his crimes?'): Cic. *Diu. Caec.* 39, *II Verr.* 2.52 *me dies uox latera deficiant*... (reworked by P. in a particularly clear allusion at 3.9.9 *uerebamur ne nos dies, ne uox, ne latera deficerent*). P. shifts the fear from himself onto Trajan (cf. above on *tantum*), but with similar implication. **cum... putaret:** naturally taken as part of the indirect statement (*putaret* would be subjunctive either way). **uehementius** 'more forcefully'. *uehemens* is approximately synonymous with *acer* (2.3.9n. *acriora*), e.g. §6 *acres et uehementes*. P. pulls out the stops when necessary: cf. 2.19.5 *oratio... pugnax et quasi contentiosa*, 1.2.4 *acres enim esse... uolebamus*, Picone 1978: 43. **intendi** 'exerting myself' (*OLD* 4c), middle voice; cf. 5.12.1 *ut sollicitudine intendar* (passive), Quint. 1.10.27 *modos* ['pitches'] *quibus deberet intendi* (*TLL* VII.1 2115.28–33). At 2.19.2 P. gives a vigorous description of the *gestus incessus discursus etiam* of an advocate (himself?) in full swing. **gracilitas** 'slenderness'. The rare word suggests allusion to Cicero, who refers to similar physical weakness early in his career (Pflips 365): Cic. *Brut.* 313 *erat eo tempore in nobis summa gracilitas et infirmitas corporis... eoque magis hoc eos quibus eram carus commouebat, quod omnia... totius corporis contentione dicebam*, reworked in Plut. *Cic.* 3.7, and itself recalling Demosthenes: Plut. *Dem.* 4.5–8 etc. (Moles on Plut. *Cic.* 3.7). Trajan's concern for Pliny corresponds to that of Cicero's friends there. The implied self-comparison to a specifically young Cicero is perhaps modest, and/or fitting for this early point in the collection. Besides his slight figure (at 10.18.1 Trajan refers to *corpusculi tui*) we know little of P.'s physique, but he had suffered a *grauissima ualetudo* in 97 (10.5.1, 10.8.1; other ailments in 7.1.4, 7.21). His uncle, by contrast, was ample (6.16.13), as perhaps was his mother (6.20.11 *corpore grauem*). **perpeti:** a strengthened form of *pati* which makes an alliterative clausula with *posset* (cf. *Pan.* 82.1 *perpeti poterat*). **respondit mihi pro Marciano Claudius Marcellinus:** P.'s speech dealt with both Priscus and Marcianus (§9), but it takes two defence advocates to reply (§§16–17). Marcellinus' identity is uncertain (possible family connections in Corbier 1981); P. accords his speech only brief notice. Marcianus receives the customary single name at his second mention (2.1.1n. *Vergini*).

16 missus *sc. est*, 'was dissolved' (*OLD* 2b). **posterum** *sc. diem* (*OLD* 2a). **actio** 'a[nother] speech' (*OLD* 5; cf. §3n.). **nisi ut... scinderetur** 'without being broken up' (*nisi ut = nisi ita ut*). 4.9.11 expands on the disadvantages such a break could cause. **noctis interuentu** 'by the interruption of night' (Caes. *BG* 3.15.5, *OLD interuentus* 4b).

17–22 Main trial: second and third days

17 Postero die dixit: 14 January (§10n. *in*). P.'s performance over, the following speeches are covered in swift sequence: §17 *dixit, respondit*, §18 *dixit*, each heading its clause (cf. §16 *respondit*). **Saluius Liberalis:** C. Salvius Liberalis Nonius Bassus (*PIR²* S 138), *cos. suff.* in or before 86, prosecuted and perhaps exiled under Domitian (3.9.33 with S-W). **subtilis dispositus acer disertus** 'precise, methodical, powerful, eloquent': generous tribute. The asyndetic group contains three specifics followed by a general compliment (2.3.7n. *disertissimum*). *subtilis* implies acute thought (*OLD* 3–4; 4.14.7 *sapiens subtilisque lector*) and/or the precision of the *genus subtile* 'plain style' (*OLD* 5) recommended especially for narration and proof (Lausberg §1078.1). *dispositio* 'arrangement' is a canonical element of rhetoric (Lausberg §§443–52); *dispositus* of a speaker is first attested here (cf. Quint. 10.7.12 *disposite* and *TLL* v.1 1430.10–19). For *acer*, see 2.3.9n. *acriora*. Salvius' power is seen again at 3.9.36 *ut est uehemens* [= *acer*. §15n. *uehementius*] *et disertus*. Though he is defending the villain on both occasions, this consular (and potential reader?) is treated with respect.   **in illa uero causa:** *uero* adds a climax (2.1.7n. *mihi*): Salvius was always a superlative speaker, but in this trial he excelled himself.   **protulit** 'displayed' (*OLD* 2).   **Cornelius Tacitus:** the repetition of his double name, like that of Fronto (§18), adds formality (Jones 1991: 156) and dignity, and recognises his absence since §2. At §19 he is plain *Tacitus*.   **eloquentissime:** high praise, for a second time (2.1.6n. *laudator*). Ludolph 1997: 81 unaccountably detects disparagement.   **quod eximium orationi eius inest** '– the outstanding feature of his style –', lit. '[that] which is the remarkable [quality] present in his style', *OLD insum* 3 + dat. (K–S 1 328); *eximium* is used predicatively, as Sen. *Ep.* 85.22 *quod habet eximium* [*uita*]. The parenthetical clause, describing '[the fact that he speaks] σεμνῶς' (2.3.3n. *quod*), emphasises σεμνῶς through delay (2.7.2n. *quod*). For *oratio* '(oratorical) style' (= *elocutio*), see Cic. *Brut.* 8, Sen. *Ep.* 114.1, *TLL* ix.2 883.53–82.   **σεμνῶς** 'gravely, solemnly', *grauiter* (*TLL* vi.2 2302.32–79). Hermogenes (late 2c. AD) lists σεμνότης 'solemnity' as one of the constituents of μέγεθος 'grandeur'; it requires directness, concision, dignified assurance and a preponderance of long syllables (*On types of style* 1.6 = 242–54 Rabe) as well as choice vocabulary (*On invention* 4.11 = 200–2 Rabe); cf. also Philostratus *Lives of the sophists* 504 (with examples from Demosthenes and Isocrates). Readers of Tacitus' historical works may see something familiar here (Norden 1898: 329–35, Leeman 1963: 321–3). The Greek critical term (cf. 1.2.1 *eodem* ζήλῳ *scripsisse*, 6.22.2 *egit . . .* κατὰ κεφάλαιον) typifies a wider phenomenon (not least in Cicero's letters) of turning to Greek for rhetorical description (Adams 2003a: 323–9). This one also appears in Lucilius *Sat.* 1.15 M. (on borrowing Greek words) and Cic. *Att.* 2.1.3 (of Demosthenes; Demosthenes himself applies it ironically to Aeschines in *On the crown* 35). Here the short, heavy, choice word instantiates what it describes, and offers high praise (cf. 6.31.11 *locutus est Caesar summa grauitate*); it occasioned the dissertation of Berger 1725.

18   Fronto Catius: §3n.   **insigniter** 'splendidly' (cf. 9.29.1, Quint. 8.5.15).   **utque iam locus ille poscebat** 'as he had to at that point' (lit. 'as that moment/situation demanded by this stage', *OLD iam* 6, *locus* 22; for *locus poscere* cf. 5.17.2, Quint. 10.1.17). The *locus* is Priscus' now dire position and the late stage of the defence, a moment when *deprecatio* was in order (Quint. 7.4.3). *ut iam* is Ciceronian, *utque iam* a Plinian variant (8.21.2, *Pan.* 72.7). **plus in precibus temporis:** the hyperbaton (*plus . . . temporis*, partitive gen., as e.g. 2.18.1 *quantum apud illos auctoritatis*, 5.6.37 *tantum stibadio reddit ornatūs*), makes the word-order match *quam in defensione consumpsi*. For the antithesis *in precibus . . . in defensione* cf. 5.13.3 *deprecari magis . . . quam defendi*. **actionem:** §16n. **uespera inclusit:** *OLD includo* 6 'bring to an end', with *uesper(a)* only here. **abrumperet:** first in Virgil for breaking off a speech (*TLL* I 141.9–18). **in tertium diem probationes exierunt** 'the presentation of evidence spilled over to a third day', perhaps a liquid metaphor (*OLD exeo* 2b). *probationes* (πίστεις, 'proofs') were either 'technical' (divisions of a speech) or 'non-technical', i.e. other evidence, such as documents, decrees and witness statements (Quint. 5.2–7); P. refers to the latter, as at 4.9.15 *quartum diem probationes occuparunt* (after three days of speeches), Tac. *D.* 39.3. Although the advocates were still involved, interpreting evidence and cross-examining (Quint. 5.7), this stage of the trial was demarcated from the *actiones* (set-piece orations) that preceded. Given that Fronto's second speech closed proceedings on the second day, the *probationes* began only on the third, so that *exierunt* cannot mean 'extend into' (*pace OLD exeo* 10b, similarly *TLL* v.2 1365.16–23). **iam hoc ipsum pulchrum et antiquum . . . !** 'here already a splendid and traditional thing in itself . . . !', accusative of exclamation (or sc. *erat/fuit* for a statement). *iam* implies 'my main point is yet to come [*viz.* the judgment], but here already is a remarkable fact', as *Pan.* 22.1 *iam hoc ipsum, quod ingressus es, quam mirum laetumque!* (before describing Trajan's reception in Rome, P. celebrates the fact that he entered on foot). *Contra TLL* VII.1 121.42–3, glossing our passage as 'deinde'. Cf. *Pan.* 76.1 (on the Priscus trial) *iam quam antiquum, quam consulare, quod triduum totum senatus sub exemplo patientiae tuae sedit . . . !* On *antiquus*, high praise, see 2.9.4n. and cf. *Pan.* 61.1 *illum antiquum senatum* (probably the same occasion: Paladini 1958: 725–7). P. is anything but implying that three-day trials were 'entirely normal' (*pace* Talbert 1984: 215). In later trial-letters (with Trajan no longer presiding) he makes ever less capital out of such continuation (3.9, 4.9.9–10, 14–15, 5.20.6). **senatum nocte dirimi, triduo uocari, triduo contineri** 'for a senate/senatorial meeting to be interrupted by nightfall, summoned for three days, kept convened for three days': graded, slightly rising AB~AB~AB tricolon (5~6~7 syllables). For *dirimi* 'be interrupted' (*OLD* 4a) cf. 4.9.9 *actionem meam, ut proelia solet, nox diremit* (it is indeed a cliché of battle narrative: *TLL* v.1 1260.1–12), Cic. *Q. fr.* 2.12(11).2 (of a senatorial debate) *actum est eo die nihil; nox diremit*. For the abl. *triduo* of duration, see §14n. *dixi* (contrast *Pan.* 76.1 *triduum totum*). For *senatum contineri* cf. Livy 26.10.2. Fellow senators, sitting on hard benches in an unheated chamber, may have been less appreciative (Talbert 1984: 194–5).

19 Cornutus Tertullus consul designatus: asyndeton carries us from the *probationes* to the ensuing debate. C. Julius Cornutus Tertullus (*PIR*² I 273, Halfmann 1979: 117), of Pamphylian origin, was P.'s colleague as prefect of the treasury of Saturn (2.8.2n. *angor*), soon to hold a suffect consulship, again together with P., in Sept.–Oct. 100 (5.14.5). P. repeatedly mentions his close friendship (5.14.4 *artissima familiaritate*) with the man he calls *collega carissime* (7.21.1; cf. 7.31), an allied opponent of Domitian (*Pan.* 90–2, esp. 90.5) and intimate of grandee Corellius Rufus (4.17.9; cf. 1.12 and 2.1.intro.); see G–M 154–7. For his naming (two *cognomina*) see above on ARRIANO. The suffect consuls had been elected just a few days before, perhaps on 9 or 12 January (S-W 23–6, Talbert 1984: 206–7 respectively); P. refrains from mentioning that he was one of them, so avoiding any hint (to the first-time reader) of his imminent high office before its revelation in book 3 (explicitly in 3.13 and 3.18 on *Pan.*, implicitly in the honorific statue of 3.6: Henderson 2002a). **uir egregius:** for the appositional phrase see §5n.; for the praise, 5.14.3 *Cornuto autem quid melius, quid sanctius, quid in omni genere laudis ad exemplar antiquitatis expressius?* His proposal naturally has P.'s approval, as again in 2.12.2. **pro ueritate firmissimus** 'unwavering in his defence of truth' (*OLD firmus* 9); cf. Cic. *Mil.* 91 *in suscepta causa firmissimus.* For *firmus pro* see e.g. Sen. *Ira* 3.28.6 *pro libertate . . . pertinacissimum,* Mart. 11.5.7 *inuictus pro libertate.* **censuit:** §5n. *censuit,* §5n. *consul.* Cornutus was not the most senior of the several consuls designate; Trajan (as president) perhaps chose the first speaker (S-W 172). **septingenta milia . . . inferenda, | Mario . . . interdicendum, | Marciano . . . Africa** sc. *esse,* parallel antithesis with three proposals in falling tricolon (21~12~10 syllables), or one might say two proposals (the second bipartite) in isocolon (21~22 syllables), in either case with gradation (rising intensity). **quae acceperat Marius:** the bribe from Marcianus (§8). For the indicative see 2.3.8n. *uiderat.* **aerario inferenda:** be confiscated by the treasury of Saturn, i.e. the state. Profits from extortion were usually returned (the nearest a province got to compensation: Brunt 1961: 204), but Marcianus had given this money willingly, and criminally. The 300,000 from Honoratus (§8) goes unmentioned and there seems to be no other fine beyond any imposed by the *iudices* (§2). **Mario urbe Italiaque interdicendum** 'that Marius should be banned from Rome and Italy': impersonal gerundive of obligation (*NLS* §204) with *Mario* dat. object and *urbe Italiaque* abl. of separation. The pleonasm (expulsion from Italy obviously included Rome) sounds like legal archaism, but is found first here or in Livy *per.* 54; it creates a graded trio *urbe Italiaque . . . Africa* (each further from Rome). The suggested punishment is perpetual *relegatio,* gentler than *exsilium* (§8n.) and milder too than relegation to a specified destination. Priscus chose Marseille, no hardship in Juvenal's view (intro.). **hōc amplius** '(and) in addition', *OLD amplius* 4: Marcianus was to be banned likewise from Italy, but also from his native province, a routine stipulation. **in fine sententiae** 'at the end of his statement/speech'. *sententiae* (§5n. *censuit*) could be substantial: at 5.13.4 P. reduces one to its *summa* 'essentials'; Quint. 3.8.65, 67 uses the word of full-scale Ciceronian speeches. **quod . . . functi essemus** 'that, because we had discharged . . . ', subordinate in indirect statement. The subjunctive, with due modesty, avoids endorsing Cornutus' view (but cf. *acceperat* above). **iniuncta aduocatione** 'the duty of advocacy enjoined upon us', *OLD iniungo* 2a, *aduocatio* 2. Both words are common in P.; the verb ranges from friendly favours (2.18.111.) to formal assertions of public duty: 3.18.1 *officium consulatus iniunxit mihi*..., 7.33.4 *'iniunctam nobis accusationem'* (an advocate speaking in the senate), *Pan.* 95.1 *officiis quae studiis nostris circa tuendos socios iniunxeratis* (referring to trials like this one) and e.g. Frontin. *Aq.* 1.1 (many more are scattered in *TLL* VII.1 1666.34–1667.57). It also reminds us that P. and Tacitus were acting out of obligation (§2n. *iussi*). **diligenter et fortiter** 'with diligence and resolve', *OLD fortiter* 7a, alliterative with *functi*. Cf. Cic. *Att.* 8.6.3 *fortiter et diligenter.* **arbitrari senatum** 'the senate judged', an official formula (e.g. *SC de Pisone patre* lines 68, 71, 115, 163 and possibly 26). Cornutus is not speaking on its behalf (as often translated), but offering the statement for endorsement as part of his *sententia* (e.g. Cic. *Phil.* 9.16 *senatui placere*; Sall. *Cat.* 51.43 *'senatum existumare'*), in effect proposing a vote of thanks like the one passed in P.'s next trial (3.9.23 *eodem senatus consulto industria fides constantia nostra plenissimo testimonio comprobata est*); *Pan.* 95.1 (above on *iniuncta*) mentions corresponding honorifics. **ut dignum mandatis partibus fuerit** 'as was worthy of the role entrusted [to us]', *OLD pars* 10; cf. Tac. *An.* 1.12.1 *pars*... *mandaretur* (in the senate), Hor. *AP* 177 (dramatic roles). *fuerit* represents *fuit* in direct speech, breaking the normal 'sequence of tenses' (*fuisset* would be expected) in *repraesentatio*, familiar esp. from Livy (Andrewes 1951: 143–4). Further nuance is hard to determine (speculations in *NLS* §284 and G–L §654); here it makes a common clausula (§2n. *petit*).

20 omnes etiam consulares 'and all the consulars'; for *etiam* see §2n. *cum*; for the order of speeches, §5n. *consul.* **usque ad** 'up to'. **Pompeium Collegam:** *cos. ord.* 93 (Tac. *Ag.* 44.1, *PIR²* P 601). The unusually spondaic ending (ten heavy syllables) is owed in part to the name, but the gravity is perhaps not unwelcome. **et septingenta... inferenda | et Marcianum... relegandum, | Marium... relinquendum** *sc. esse.* Parallel antithesis in extended tricolon (14~13~23 syllables), with polysyndeton for the first two elements, largely identical to Cornutus' *sententia*, asyndeton and a longer colon for the third, different one. **in quinquennium relegandum:** the penalty proposed by Cornutus (§19 *Mario*), but limited to five years. This is still harsher than what Collega proposes for Priscus, more culpable but of high rank. **Marium** 'but that Marius'. **repetundarum:** §3n. *ne.* **poenae... relinquendum:** be left to (*OLD relinquo* 12b + dat.), i.e. suffer no more than, the penalties already inflicted by the *iudices* (a fine and loss of senatorial status), tantamount to acquittal on the criminal charges. *poenae/-is relinquere* (also at 6.31.6) is hitherto preserved only in poetry: Ov. *Met.* 7.41, 14.247, [Sen.] *Herc. Oet.* 811–12.

21 in utraque sententia multi, fortasse etiam plures in hac: chiasmus. Collega's proposal (*hac*) is faring slightly better. **uel solutiore uel molliore** 'whether more indulgent or more complaisant'. P. affects to leave the choice of word open (e.g. 3.9.35 *uel constantiam uel audaciam*), but neither condones a

proposal which could more neutrally be called the *mitior* 'milder' of the two
(cf. 2.12.1, 4.9.2). For the judgmental tone, cf. Cic. *Cat.* 1.30 *mollibus sententiis* and
OLD mitis 13b, Cic. *Cat.* 2.27 *lenitas . . . solutior* and *OLD solutus* 5–6. **nam** explains
fortasse etiam plures. **Cornuto:** dative object of *assensi*. **uidebantur assensi** *sc.*
esse 'seemed to have agreed with', in their own *sententiae*. **hunc:** Collega. **ipsos**
sc. se. **sequebantur** 'were supporting' (*OLD* 13); the idea of 'following' is live,
since one supported a *sententia* by going to sit near its proponent (Talbert 1984:
124–5, 282–3).

22 discessio 'division', when the presiding consul put his choice of *sententiae*
to the vote. They were taken one at a time, in the order they had been made,
until one gained an outright majority (cf. 8.14.19; Talbert 1984: 279–85). Only
Cornutus' *sententia* is voted on, since it wins a majority, leaving Collega's necessarily defeated. *Pan.* 76.2 commends Trajan's liberal chairing on this occasion:
uicitque sententia non prima sed melior ('not [because it was] first, but [because it was]
better'). **qui sellis consulum astiterant** 'those who had gone to stand/were
standing beside the consuls' chairs'. While other senators had gathered around
Cornutus or Collega (§21), this group had moved to the centre, reserving judgment. Talbert 1984: 150 sees rather a sign of overcrowding, suggesting that a
senator showed neutrality rather by remaining in his place, but that would be difficult if he had happened to be seated near Cornutus or Collega in this instance,
and it is hard to imagine these men standing for three nine-hour days. The plural
consulum is the closest P. comes to acknowledging the other consul present, Sextus
Julius Frontinus, *cos. suff.* 72/3, *cos.* II *suff.* 98, and now *cos.* III *ord.* with Trajan;
also author of *De strategematis* and *De aquaeductu*. P. elsewhere offers high praise
(5.1.5, *Pan.* 62.2) and advertises intimacy (4.8.3). *Pan.* 61.1 celebrates his place on
the consular dais, apparently at the Priscus trial (§18n. *iam*); here he is eclipsed
by the emperor (and by P.). **in Cornuti sententiam ire coeperunt** 'began
to go over to Cornutus' proposal', literally (§21n. *sequebantur*). **illi . . . Collega:**
parallel antithesis. **qui se Collegae annumerari patiebantur** 'who were
letting themselves be counted alongside [*OLD adnumero* 3a] Collega': *patiebantur* lets Collega's supporters save face by implying that they had never been
enthusiastic anyway. **in diuersum transierunt** 'went over to the other side',
perhaps a military metaphor (cf. Livy *per.* 80 *in diuersas partes transiebant*), continued in *deseruisset*. **Collega cum paucis relictus** *sc. est*, leaving 'Colleague'
ill named for the occasion. **impulsoribus** 'instigators', pejorative or at best
neutral (*TLL* VII.1 717.42–73). **Regulo:** the anti-hero of the *Epistles*, Marcus
Aquillius Regulus (*PIR*² A 1005; for the spelling *Aquillius* see Birley 2000a: 37–8):
see 2.20.intro. Quaestor before 70 (Tac. *H.* 4.42.4), he was probably born *c.* 42–5,
making him around 15–20 years P.'s senior. Here, casually introduced, he makes
his only Plinian appearance in the senate, ending the central panel of book 2 as
he ends the whole book. P. gives him a double name, *M. Regulus* (an unusual style:
Aquillius Regulus, as in Tac. *H.* 4.42.1, would be normal; cf. Birley 2000a: 24–5),
only in 1.5.1 and 6.2.1, the first and last letters to mention him, encouraging a

reading of these letters as a sequence (Jones 1991: 154–5). **qui se in sententia quam ipse dictauerat deseruisset** 'who, he said, had abandoned him in the proposal that he [Regulus] himself had given him to deliver' (*OLD dicto* 2c, 3a), virtual *oratio obliqua* (part of an indirect statement implied by *questus est*): cf. 2.13.8n. *daret*, 3.9.29 *iratus quod euocatus esset inuitus*, 6.5.3 *fuerunt quibus haec eius oratio . . . displiceret, quae . . . castigaret peractum, NLS* §§240, 242b. For the indicative *dictauerat* see 2.3.8n. *uiderat* and §19 *acceperat*; euphony may be a factor, avoiding *dicta(ui)sset deseruisset*. Regulus is very likely to have served as consul, and probably in the 80s (Syme 1953: 161, id. 1979a: 259, Jones 1970: 98 n.7; *contra* S-W); the allegation (not strictly endorsed as fact) that he preferred to make the more junior Collega (*cos.* 93) his spokesman is in keeping with his shady dealings throughout the *Epistles*. **deseruisset:** heroic clausula (2.3.3n. *narrat*). **alioqui** 'certainly' (*OLD* 2 ' . . . according w. or emphasizing a general tendency'), implying 'whether or not Collega's claim is true, it is likely enough'. The cadential remark combines epistolary casualness with historiographical content and typically tight sententious form. **Regulo:** dat. of possession. **mobile ingenium:** a characteristic of Rome's enemies in Sallust (*BJ* 46.3, 66.2) and Livy (2.37.5, 43.22.6) and of weak-minded emperors in Tacitus (*Ag.* 13.2, *H.* 1.7.2, 1.24.1, 2.57.2, 3.84.4). **ut plurimum audeat, plurimum timeat** 'that he is extremely daring, but extremely cowardly', anaphoric isocolon (6~6 syllables) making epigram from incongruity. P. borrows a second historiographical cliché, that of the primitive Gauls and Britons whose 'courage in demanding battle' is matched by their 'fear in avoiding it' (Tac. *Ag.* 11.3; cf. Caes. *BG* 3.19.6, Livy 10.28.4, Tac. *H.* 1.68.1). Both qualities are abundantly displayed in 1.5, P.'s first major epistolary assault on Regulus; 4.7.3 calls his *audacia* the product of ignorance.

23–4 Appendix: Firminus

23 Hic finis *sc. fuit* (cf. V. *Aen.* 10.116 *hic finis fandi*; Livy 45.9.2 *hic finis belli*). Having ended the narrative proper with the tableau of the disappointed Collega (and the villainous Regulus stalking backstage), P. begins a brief epilogue. He has not specified the outcome of the vote – the last we saw of it was when the senators 'began' (*coeperunt*) to support Cornutus' *sententia* – but it is clear enough, not least from §1 *seueritate exempli*, that the harsher *sententia* won. For a similarly allusive conclusion, cf. 8.14.25 with Whitton 2010: 118 n.3. **cognitionis amplissimae** varies the Ciceronian *causa amplissima* (6.33.10, Cic. *De or.* 1.181). P. likes the superlative *amplissimus* (26×); though it can be applied widely, its use as an epithet for the senate (*ordo amplissimus* in 8.6.13, etc., as often in Cicero's speeches: *TLL* I 2010.62–8) may be resonant in this most senatorial trial. **superest tamen λιτούργιον non leue, Hostilius Firminus** 'but there remains the little trifle, no trivial one, of Hostilius Firminus'. λιτούργιον is transmitted here and at 2.12.1 only in F (though ΛΙΤΟΥΡΓΙΟΝ is also a likely origin for ΔΙΗΟΥΡΓΙΟΝ in the index to B: Intro. 40); although unique, it looks right. Formed from λῑτός 'minor, petty' (LSJ s.v. iii) + ἔργον 'work, deed' (analogous to αὐτουργία, καιν-ουργία, μεγαλουργία, etc.), with the diminutive ending -ιον, it makes a punning, alliterative oxymoron with *non leue*, since λιτός = *leuis*, at *Firm*inus' expense (for *leuis~firmus* see e.g. Quint. 7.10.12; on bilingual wordplay, 2.2.1n. *haec*). Perhaps a coinage (as e.g. Cic. *Att.* 2.1.3 ἀποσπασμάτια), it may also play on λειτουργία 'public duty' (also spelled λιτουργία, LSJ s.v.; ι and ει were now aurally indistinguishable), whose diminutive λειτούργιον is transmitted in γ and added to the margin of F (Merrill 1903: 53). Reekmans 1969, missing the joke, emends to λιπούργιον 'little tumour'. **Hostilius Firminus:** in apposition to λιτούργιον, 'another case, (namely) Firminus' (cf. Cic. *Att.* 3.8.3 with Shackleton Bailey). Probably an ex-praetor (Thomasson 1960: 61–4), he is otherwise unknown (*PIR²* H 225). **legatus** 'deputy' (*OLD* 2; fully *legatus pro praetore*). Priscus probably had three. **Mari Prisci:** given two names for the first time since §2, adding weight to this new charge through formality (§17n. *Cornelius*). As in 2.1.1 *Vergini Rufi*, the cretic-spondee guarantees *Mari* (not *Marii*). The gen. sg. form of nouns in -*ium/*-*ius* varied in antiquity (N–W I 134–54, K–H 451–3) and MSS are no safe guide (cf. 2.1.5n. *male*, 2.2.2n. *studis*). Those of P. tend to follow the ancient rule of single -*i* for proper names, rightly (though F has *Marii* here and e.g. 2.3.8 *Liuii*, 2.7.6 *Coctii*, and Π already has 3.4.2 *Caecilii Classici*, at the cost of the clausula). For other nouns the MSS prefer -*ii*, largely followed by modern editors. Yet some clausulae push strongly for -*i*, e.g. 1.20.21 *ingeni uitium (e)st*, 3.4.4 *patrocini foedus*, 7.19.6 *exsili causam*, 8.6.14 *fastidiosissimi mancipi*, *Pan.* 16.2 *Dānŭbi ripa*, 54.4 *imperi finibus* (mostly printed -*i* or -*î* by Mynors). See also (less strongly) 1.1.2 *ut nec te consili* and *paeniteat obsequi*, 5.8.6 *reliquum (e)st stud(i) addidero*, 7.12.6 *ullius pret(i) esse*; others are indifferent (e.g. 3.4.2 *aerari commeatu*, 3.12.4 *apparatūs et impendi*, 8.1.3 *quantum oti pollicentur*), several involving a choice between dactyl–cretic (with -*ii*) and cretic–iamb (with -*i*), neither of which is particularly common, though the latter (Intro. 29 n.164) is less rare (e.g. 1.5.10 *consili ducem*, 3.14.8 *exiti fuit*, 7.17.10 *iudici parum*, *Pan.* 72.5 *Caesar, ingeni*). A clausula clearly demanding -*ii* is yet to be found. Accordingly, though P. may, like versifiers, have varied his use (2.2.2n. *studis*), -*i* seems the more likely norm (cf. Brakman 1925: 92–3, Stout 1954: 138–9; also Müller 1954: 736, 771 on Curtius Rufus; *contra* Housman 1917: 43 with Winterbottom 1998b: 243 n.1): hence *unguentari* below, 2.14.1 *negoti*, 2.17.7 *triclini*, 2.20.5 *fili*. **permixtus causae** 'deeply implicated in the case' (*OLD permisceo* 3 + dat.). **grauiter uehementerque uexatus est** 'was given very harsh treatment', i.e. was the object of harsh words (in his absence: §24), as he will be now; there is perhaps another dig at *Firm*inus (*grauis* + *firmus* is common, e.g. 6.13.3 *grauiter et firme*). The doublet *grauiter uehementerque* and the phrase *grauiter uexare* are Ciceronian. **et rationibus . . . et sermone . . . | operam . . . commodasse | stipulatusque . . . probabatur, | ipse praeterea accepisse . . . unguentari:** an unusually long sentence, but with a simple syntactical skeleton. The main verb is *probabatur* 'he was being proved (to have)', with a pair of instrumental ablatives in the first colon, and governing an infinitival phrase in each of the following three (*commodasse, stipulatus* [*esse*], *accepisse*, in rising tricolon, 20~26~33 syllables). *et . . . et* is a parallel rising bicolon (10~18 syllables, abl. gen. ~ abl. gen.). **rationibus Marciani** 'by Marcianus' account-books' (*OLD ratio* 2), which he was obliged to produce as evidence (S-W on 7.6.2). **sermone quem ille habuerat** 'by a speech which he [Marcianus] had given', known either by report or from council records sent to Rome. Perhaps a speech in which Marcianus accused the *eques Romanus* (§8) and claimed to have Firminus' support in the prosecution. P. uses *sermo* for 'speech' 3×, all in municipal councils (here, 1.8.2, 5.7.5); elsewhere it means 'language', 'conversation', or 'statement' (3.4.5, 9.13.7, in the senate). **in ordine Lepcitanorum:** as *ordo* can mean the senate in Rome (§1), so it can be used of a local council (*curia*) elsewhere. Lepcis Magna (in modern Libya) was an important coastal city, by now a *ciuitas libera* or possibly a *municipium*; it was to gain the status of *colonia* under Trajan in 109 or 110 (Thompson 1970: 56–7, 64 n.52). Its name was variously spelled *Leptis* (after the grecisation Λέπτις) and *Lepcis* (closer to the native Phoenician *L(e)pqi*) in texts and inscriptions (Bücheler 1904; Dessau *RE* XII.2 2074–5) and P.'s MSS are divided, *Lepc-* (α) *Lept-* (Fγ). It is easier to explain 'correction' of the unusual cluster -*pc*- to -*pt*- in Fγ (whether independently or by contamination) than the opposite in α (*pace* Stout 1954: 153). Schuster and Mynors both printed -*pc*- (cf. Schuster 1928: 413), but -*pt*- crept into Schuster's third edition at the hands of Hanslik. **operam suam Prisco ad turpissimum ministerium commodasse . . . probabatur** 'he [Firminus] was shown [*OLD probo* 7a] to have offered his assistance to Priscus for a most disgraceful service', as an intermediary in the crooked justice (below on *stipulatusque*). **turpissimum:** the moralising adjective (2.6.7n.) opens an exceptional assault on a fellow senator. Although P. freely criticises senatorial impropriety (intro.), the *ad hominem* criticism here and in 2.12 is surpassed only by his treatment of Regulus (§22n.). He probably published only after Regulus' death (Intro. 19–20); whether Firminus was still alive is a matter for speculation. **stipulatusque de Marciano quinquaginta milia denariorum** 'and to have contracted to receive 50,000 *denarii* [= 200,000 sesterces] from Marcianus', specifying the *turpissimum ministerium* with 'epexegetic' (explanatory) -*que* (*OLD* 6a). For the use of *de*, cf. *OLD* 6a, Just. *Inst.* 7.1.36.1 *stipulatus sum de Titio fundum*. Firminus had arranged a bribe from Marcianus on Priscus' behalf (not for himself, as the antithesis with *ipse . . . accepisse* shows), presumably part of the 700,000 specified in §8 (S-W). **ipse praeterea accepisse** 'and that in addition he himself had received' (*OLD accipio* 2b, 2.4.2n. *acceptum*), a separate bribe. Adversative asyndeton (for the structure see above on *et*), with *accepisse* still governed by *probabatur*. **sestertia decem milia:** 10,000 sesterces (*sestertia* is adjectival: *OLD* 3a), Firminus' commission for fixing the bribe. **foedissimo quidem titulo, nomine unguentari** 'and under an utterly disgusting heading, the entry "perfume-money"', *OLD titulus* 4a, 5, *nomen* 22a, 24 + gen.; on the spelling *unguentari* see above on *Mari*. Evidence from Marcianus' accounts (above on *rationibus*). For *unguentarium* (*sc. argentum*) and its use to conceal an illegal or informal payment in the books, cf. Cic. *II Verr.* 3.181 *cerario* 'wax-money', *Pis.* 86 *quasi uasari nomine* 'equipment-money', Suet. *Vesp.* 8.3 *calceari nomine* 'shoe-money', Tac. *H.* 3.50.3 *clauarium (donatiui nomen est)* 'bootnail-money'. The moralising continues with 'extending' *quidem* (2.9.3n. *et*), often paired with a superlative (e.g. 6.16.13 *et quieuit, uerissimo quidem somno*, 7.7.1 *gratias egi, libentissime quidem*). Perfume was widely used (Griffin 1985: 10–11) but a stock source of invective (Edwards 1993: 68–9, 187 n.44), e.g. Cic. *Pis.* 25, comparing Gabinius to a perfume-seller (*unguentarius*). **qui titulus a uita hominis compti semper et pumicati non abhorrebat** 'a heading which matched well enough [lit. 'was not incompatible with', *OLD abhorreo* 5b, in litotes] the lifestyle of a man who was always slick and smooth-skinned', another parting shot (cf. §22n. *alioqui*). Two charges of effeminacy; any pun on '*delicatus/mollis* Firminus' is left implicit. As in Cicero's letters, *homo* is often neutral in P. (2.6.1n.), but this 'lowest form of social designation' (Kraus on Livy 6.41.9) is well suited to pejorative remarks, especially – again as in Cicero – in a forensic context (cf. 3.9.2 *homo foedus*, 3.9.32; Santoro-L'Hoir 1992: 21–8, 151–2; also 2.20.2 *impudentiam hominis* and, in banter, 2.10.1 *hominem te patientem*). For *comptus* 'with hair made up' in invective, see again Cic. *Pis.* 25 (Gabinius' *compti capilli*), Sen. *Breu.* 12.3 (so-called men who prefer to be *compti* than *honesti*). *pumicare* 'to pumice' is a rare term for depilation, regarded in men, in the terms of invective, as a still surer sign of deviant sexuality (Mart. 14.205, Juv. 8.16, 9.95; cf. Hor. *Ep.* 1.2.29) – though Pl. *NH* 36.154 remarks that pumice is used 'these days' by men as well as women, and Sen. *Ep.* 114.14 takes male depilation of the armpits (but no more) as a respectable norm.

24 placuit 'it was resolved' (*OLD* 5b). **censente Cornuto** 'on Cornutus' proposal', probably in his *sententia* on Priscus (§19), though P. has detached this element to make a self-standing appendix. **referri de eo proximo senatu** 'that his case be considered at the next session' (*OLD refero* 7a, §10n. *in*), probably on 3 February (S–W 169). A teaser for Arrianus, and for the reader. **casu an conscientia** 'whether by chance or guilty conscience' (*OLD conscientia* 3d, *TLL* IV 367.26–368.23; cf. 1.5.8 *conscientia exterritus*), a compressed indirect question with *incertum* or similar omitted (and predictably interpolated in some MSS), as 5.4.2 *lapsine uerbo, an quia ita sentiebant*. The idiom appears in Cic. *Ac.* 2.63 *iocansan ita sentiens*, increasingly in Livy and often in Tacitus (H–S §273, *TLL* II 6.70–8). P.'s alliterative, unbalanced pair offers a 'weighted alternative' like many in Tacitus (Sullivan 1976), leaning on the second, less kind interpretation. **afuerat:** the pluperfect looks back on the trial/debate as already complete, aiding the impression that Firminus was a separate matter.

25 Coda

25 Habes res urbanas 'there you have the news from Rome'; *res urbanae* (common in Cicero's letters) again at 4.11.15. For *habes* drawing a longer letter to a close, cf. 1.8.18, 1.22.12 etc.; it also ends the collection (9.40.3). P. reintroduces his addressee and his rustic situation, framing the letter (§1 *quietis*, §1 *accipe*) and easing the tone for a *leggero* finish (cf. 6.2.10, also to Arrianus). If Cicero the orator has underlain much of 2.11, here we shift to the epistolographer for a coda which is 'exquisitely Ciceronian' (Cugusi 1983: 224) in tone, if not in specifics (unlike 2.12.7). As P. elsewhere tells Arrianus, one should always blend *seueritas* and *comitas*, and he himself likes to set off *grauiora opera* with *lusibus iocisque* (8.21.2). **inuicem rusticas scribe:** chiasmus points the contrast. The pair *urbanus~rusticus* is common; P. takes the opposite position at 9.15.3 *nobisque sic rusticis* [at his Etruscan villa] *urbana acta perscribe.* **quid arbusculae tuae, quid uineae, quid segetes agunt?** 'how are your little trees doing, your vineyards, your crops?', anaphoric tricolon with subjects of 6~3~3 syllables. *arbusculae* is an 'affective' diminutive, as in 1.24.4 (at 5.6.27 it is probably literal, 'shrubs'); cf. 2.17.29 *uillulae*. The rustic content may be enhanced by a glancing recall in *quid segetes* of V. *Georg.* 1.1 *quid faciat laetas segetes* (also in a series of questions). *agunt* offers framing contrast with §1 *acti... actum*, but also recalls, with the repeated question and pathetic personification, the villa letter 1.3.1 *quid agit Comum, tuae meaeque deliciae? quid suburbanum amoenissimum...? (quid* ×10). A hint, perhaps, at the end of the great *negotium* letter, of the *otium* to come in 2.17. **quid oues delicatissimae?** *sc. agunt*, 'how are your sheep so tender?', making a tetracolon. Sheep are literally *delicatae* 'delicate' (*OLD* 7; Hor. *Epod.* 2.16 *infirmas oues* with Watson), but the word also has apt overtones of lazy country life (4.14.1 *ex aliqua peregrina* ['out of town'] *delicataque merce*, 8.17.3 *Anio, delicatissimus amnium*, 9.10.2 *delicate... ut in secessu*; Phaedrus 4.5.26 *delicatos hortulos*, Mart. 7.17.1 *ruris... delicati*). The sheep of Altinum were outstanding, according to Col. *RR* 7.2.3. **in summa** 'in short' (*OLD summa* 7c), a repeated closing formula (e.g. 1.12.12, 3.4.8, 6.33.11). **nisi... reddis:** for the present tense see 2.9.2n. **aeque longam** 'equally long', with tongue in cheek, since this letter has been exceptional, second only to 1.20 in the collection so far (on epistolary length see 2.2.2n. *plurimas*, 2.5.13n. *longius*). For the jocular demand, cf. 2.12.7n. *litteris*, 1.20.25, 4.11.16, 9.28.5; for an attempt to justify P.'s sense of humour against cynics see Thompson 1942. Another long and grave senatorial narrative ends with a similarly self-reflexive joke (9.13.26: if my letter is too long, you have only yourself to blame: you asked for it!), and the even longer Classicus trial-letter is enlivened with games over false endings (3.9.27–8 and 37: Whitton 2013 at n.15). **non est quod postea nisi breuissimam exspectes** 'you needn't expect any letter to follow except a very short one'. For *non est quod* see 2.4.3n. *nec.* In the event Arrianus does not reply before 2.12 (cf. 2.12.6), so evoking a reality of letter transmission (2.12 follows too soon for P. to have heard back: Merwald 1964: 170 n.28, Pflips 33); seen another way, P. does (nearly) keep to his threat: 2.12 is indeed *breuis*, if not quite *breuissima*.

12

The promised postscript: Firminus' case was heard in the senate, and he escaped with light censure – though to remain a senator under censure is the worst disgrace of all. But such was the majority view. I trust you have received my last letter by now: now it is your turn to write!

A pendant to 2.11 concerning Hostilius Firminus, the 'little trifle' arising from Priscus' trial (2.11.23–4). It is addressed again to Arrianus, making a unique diptych: unlike Cicero's editors, P. is fastidious in avoiding runs of letters to one addressee. Other thematic pairs are juxtaposed but addressed to different people (7.7–8, 8.9–10), or address the same person but are placed separately (e.g. 6.4 and 6.7, 7.29 and 8.6, 1.6 and 9.10); another unique pair bridges the division from books 2 to 3 with different themes but the same addressee (2.20.intro.). Other trial letters are arranged in carefully varied configurations (cf. S-W 18–20). The prosecution of Caecilius Classicus was chronologically intertwined with the Priscus case (S-W 58–60) but is reserved for book 3; there it receives, like 2.11, a long epistle (3.9, to Minicianus) at the centre of the scroll, bolstered this time not by a sequel but by the preliminary 3.4 (to a different addressee, Macrinus). Book 4 features P.'s defence of Julius Bassus (AD 103) in a single large letter, 4.9 (to Ursus). The case of Varenus Rufus (AD 106/7) is spread through a series of shorter letters across three books (5.20, 6.5 and 6.13 to Ursus, 7.6, 7.10 to Macrinus – chiastically reprising the recipients of 3.4 and 4.9). The pattern of books 2–4, though not the chronology, resumes with the long 8.14 to Capito (the debate over Afranius Dexter's slaves in AD 105) and 9.13 to Quadratus (P.'s quasi-prosecution of Publicius Certus in AD 97). It may be no accident that 8.14, at the centre of the penultimate book, corresponds closely in length to the pair 2.11–12: two salutary interventions by P. (and Tacitus) in the re-empowered Trajanic senate (Whitton 2010: 120 n.13).

In itself the diptych is marked by multiple contrasts, most obviously of length, reflecting the difference between celebrity defendant Priscus and small fry Firminus. Success in 2.11 contrasts with failure in 2.12: whatever P. contributed to the latter debate (he mentions nothing), here in 'private' he professes strong disapproval of Firminus' effective acquittal. Narrative, which occupies the majority of 2.11, is quickly dispensed with (§2), making way for expansive comment; correspondingly, the mostly moderate style of 2.11 is capped in the sequel by a striking burst of *genus grande* (§§3–4). The 'grand style' was prescribed for indignation, especially in a peroration (Quint. 1.6.52; Lausberg §§1079, 1126–8): not just appendix, then, 2.12 is the climax of the para-oratorical performance in the diptych. Yet whereas the first letter repeatedly evoked Cicero as orator, P. now directs a string of intertexts towards Cicero's *Republic* (§5), making for a striking combination of high oratory and political theory. At the same time an elaborate series of horticultural metaphors (§§1, 3, 6) and the relatively long coda, evocative of epistolary Cicero, reprise and develop the close of the first letter (2.11.25).

Ambivalence towards the senate, already present in 2.11 (intro.), here sharpens. On the one hand, the paradoxes that P. develops out of a situation in which a condemned man remains a senator (§§3–4) depend for their force on an idealised view of the senate as honoured dispenser of justice. On the other, criticisms are not restricted to Firminus: the majority of senators are found wanting for endorsing a proposal that P. professes to find too mild. A democracy within the senate, where each vote counts equally, is no guarantee of justice when the senatorial 'mob' has so little sense. Though P. criticises individuals liberally enough (2.11.intro.), here his displeasure extends much further. Again 9.13 is enlightening: in that debate P. alone (we learn) had the courage to stand up for justice in a senate tainted with complaisance. In 2.12, similarly, the reader is invited to see in P. not just an honest senator, but a *princeps uir* within the miniature society of the senate. Yet here the tone is one of resignation at a system that cannot be changed (§5). So the body of the letter, and the triumphant diptych as a whole, ends on a sour note, just as book 2 itself, for all its breeziness, closes with bitter reflections about Regulus (2.20.12–14). An airy coda lightens the tone before the final *uale*.

ARRIANO: 2.11n. ARRIANO. He is the only recipient of more than one letter in book 2, and P.'s only addressee to receive two letters in a row (see above), a peculiarity wittily recast by Sidonius, as Roy Gibson observes: Sid. *Ep.* 2.11 is to Rusticus, 2.12 to Agricola (Sidonius, like P. elsewhere, never addresses successive letters to the same person). This letter in particular vindicates Arrianus' decision to opt out of a senatorial career (2.11.1n. *quietis*).

1 Λιτούργιον illud quod superesse Mari Prisci causae proxime scripseram 'that "little trifle" which, I wrote in my last letter, remained in the case of Marius Priscus'. λιτούργιον . . . *superesse* picks up 2.11.23 verbatim, with *illud* as signpost. The prominent repetition binds the letters together and metatextually defines their relationship: 2.12 is the minor appendage to 2.11. For the explicit resumption of theme in trial sequences, cf. 3.9.1 (from 3.4), 5.13.1 (from 5.4), 7.10.1 (from 5.20, 6.13 and 7.6); for the repetition, cf. egregiously 8.6.1, which quotes in full a senatorial decree already cited in 7.29.2. **proxime** 'recently'. It often specifies '*most* recently' (*OLD* 2a) but need not: e.g. 3.6.1 *emi proxime . . . signum*; at 10.67.2 *proxime scripseram* refers not to 10.65 but to 10.63 (see also 2.13.4n. *proxime*). Nevertheless, it reinforces the bond with the preceding letter (cf. 2.11.24 *proximo senatu*). The interval is two or three weeks: 2.11 immediately follows the main trial (13–15 January: 2.11.10n. *in*), 2.12 a debate probably held on 3 February (2.11.24n. *referri*). **scripseram:** the pluperfect is justified (the writing of 2.11 predates 3 Feb.) independently of any 'epistolary' tense (2.5.1n. *exhibui*). **nescio an satis** 'perhaps not adequately' (2.2.1n. *nescio*). If P. shared Juvenal's dissatisfaction at Priscus' punishment he has displaced it onto sidekick Firminus (2.11.intro.): here is a man not even *damnatus inani | iudicio* (Juv. 1.47–8). **circumcisum tamen et arrasum est** 'but still, has been clipped round and trimmed': the rotten senator has not been uprooted altogether, but has at least been pruned, images corresponding to the milder and harsher penalties floated below. The verbs vary a Ciceronian metaphor, *circumcidere et amputare* (*Tusc.* 4.57 *ista . . . euellenda et extrahenda penitus, non circumcidenda nec amputanda sunt*; cf. *De or.* 1.165, *Ac.* 2.138, *Fin.* 1.44, and the imitation in Tac. *D.* 32.4). P. keeps the redundance but substitutes *arradere*, another technical term from horticulture (*OLD adrado* 2), and a novelty in this figurative use. The imagery helps graft the letter onto 2.11, which ended with Arrianus' *res rusticae* (2.11.25).

2 Firminus: 2.11.23n. *Hostilius*. A double name is normal for a character's first mention (2.1.1n. *Vergini*); though P.'s practice is not rigid, here is another prompt to read 2.11–12 as a (semi-)continuous pair (2.11.22n. *Regulo*). **inductus:** 2.11.9n. *inductus*, here with *in senatum* stated, since the context has not yet been established. **respondit crimini noto** 'he replied to the well-known charge' or 'to the charge you know about', as Arrianus does from 2.11.23. As with Priscus (2.11.2n. *omissa*), the defendant's comments are of little interest: what matters is the senate's action. A likely line of defence may have been 'following orders' (cf. 3.9.14–15 and S-W 232–3). Firminus seems not to have been formally charged (Talbert 1984: 480), there being no distinction between a debate and a trial (2.11.9n. *absente*); if he was, P. elides it. **sententiae** 'proposals, statements' (2.11.5n. *censuit*). **Cornutus Tertullus:** P.'s friend and colleague, who also gave the first, harsher *sententia* on Priscus (2.11.19). **censuit:** 2.11.5n. **ordine mouendum** *sc. eum* (2.11.9n. *fore*), 'that he be removed from the senate', i.e. expelled (*OLD moueo* 7b), the loss of status already suffered by Priscus (2.11.9n. *absente*). **Acutius Nerua:** *cos. suff.* July–August 100 and so senior to Cornutus: either the presiding consul chose the first speaker (2.11.19n. *censuit*) or P. has arranged the *sententiae* to suit the run of the letter. **in sortitione prouinciae rationem eius non habendam** 'that his name not be included [*OLD ratio* 8c] in the ballot for a(ny) province', *sc.* but that he go otherwise unpunished. This would censure him lightly while protecting provincials from future outrages (cf. Tac. *An.* 3.69.1 *mitius in ipsos* [*reos*], *melius in socios, prouideri ne peccaretur*). The modest penalty is similar to the outcome of 9.13, where Certus is not formally censured, but fails to proceed to the consulship he expected; there P. expresses himself satisfied (9.13.22 *obtinui ... quod intenderam*). Provincial governors were chosen by ballot, though tenure was effectively guaranteed for the most senior eligible candidates each year (Talbert 1984: 348–53; Dio 53.14.2 with Rich). 'Proconsuls' might be ex-consuls or, like Firminus (probably: 2.11.23n. *Hostilius*), ex-praetors, depending on the status of the province (Millar 1981: 55). The expression *sortitio prouinciae* is only here in this sense; more commonly it refers to the award of a province (Cic. *Att.* 1.17.1; cf. *Phil.* 3.24, Tac. *Ag.* 6.2). **tamquam mitior** 'as being the milder': *tamquam* indicates that it seemed *mitior* to the senators voting on it, without formally giving P.'s view (2.1.3n.). On *mitis*, see 2.11.21n. *uel solutiore*, and cf. Tac. *An.* 3.69.1 (previous n.). Their complaisance may reflect senatorial bias (2.11.6n. *fauor*) and/or Firminus' comparatively small role in the affair. **cum ... alioqui** 'though actually', 'when in fact'. For this use of *cum alioqui*, marking the preceding statement as incongruous, cf. 2.19.6, 9.35.1, 9.39.1; P. has adopted it from his uncle (e.g. Pl. *NH* 8.28 [*elephanti*] *gaudent amnibus maxime ... cum alioqui nare* *non possint* 'though they cannot actually swim', 9.86, 10.198); for *alioqui* 'in fact' (without *cum*) cf. 2.14.12. *OLD alioqui* 4 is only partly helpful; *TLL* I 1594: 27–44 is better but mixes this with other uses. Elsewhere (8.24.9, 10.8.5, 10.81.8) *cum alioqui* means 'since in any case'. **durior tristiorque**: one of a run of redundant pairs, redolent of Cicero (this one at *Tusc.* 2.29 *triste, durum*): §3 *exsectum et exemptum, labore et molestia, conspiciendum se monstrandumque*, §4 *congruens aut decorum*. There may be a whiff of a fruit metaphor (*OLD mitis* 1a 'sweet and juicy', *durus* 1a 'hard', *tristis* 8b 'sour'). For final *-que* see 2.1.4n. *durior*.

3 quid enim miserius quam . . . ? *sc. est* (modal indicative: 2.6.1n. *longum est*), 'what could be more pitiful than?', introducing acc. + inf. *quid enim* + comparative adverb (several times in P.) is a common rhetorical turn in Cicero; cf. esp. *Att.* 4.8a.2 *quid enim hoc miserius, quam eum qui tot annos quot habet designatus consul fuerit fieri consulem non posse. . . .?* Here it launches an elaborately worked passage of high outrage (§§3–4); for comparable *indignatio* at greater length see 8.6. **exsectum et exemptum honoribus senatoriis** 'excised and extracted from senatorial offices'; *honoribus* (*OLD* 5a) is dat. of disadvantage (cf. *OLD eximo* 5a–b). The rhyming participles contain elaborate imagery. *exsecare* 'excise' may nod to the surgical metaphor of cutting a cancerous person out of the body of the state (e.g. Cic. *Sest.* 135, *Att.* 2.1.7), but is also congruous with the horticultural metaphor of §1 (e.g. Plaut. *Rud.* 122 *exsicasque harundinem*), except that Firminus is no longer a plant being cut back, but an unwanted growth being removed (for such shifts see 2.4.4n. *ita*). *eximere* could have its common meaning 'exempt from' (*OLD* 5b), making a pair of metaphor plus non-metaphor, but this verb too has a horticultural use (*OLD* 1b; Cat. *Ag.* 42 has *eximere* and *exsecare* as synonyms). **labore et molestia:** abl. with *carere*, juxtaposed with *honoribus senatoriis* at the centre of a verb–noun chiasmus. This doublet is used several times by Cicero; for the contrast *honores~molestia*, cf. Cic. *Rab. Post.* 17 [*uita otiosa*] *quoniam honore caret, careat etiam molestia* (inverted here). P. complains often enough of the burdens of senatorial rank (2.8.2–3); Firminus will not have the prospect of advancement to compensate. **grauius** 'more unbearable' (*OLD* 10b). **ignominia** can refer, like *infamia*, to the loss of senatorial rights, though (as *tanta* indicates) not as a technical term (Crook 1967a: 83–5; Garnsey 1970: 185–7). The word is studied by Kaser 1956, Forssman 1967. **non in solitudine latēre** 'not to lie hidden in solitude', the infinitive rhyming with *carere* and *praebere*. The antithesis in the sentence is between obscurity and visibility, and a phrase like *in tenebris latere* or *in occulto latere* would have been predictable. Instead, P. takes a word easily associated with darkness (e.g. *Pan.* 48.5 *tenebras semper secretumque. . . solitudine*; Cic. *Cael.* 47 *solitudinem ac tenebras*) to make a novel combination. **in hac altissima specula** 'on this loftiest of pinnacles'. A *specula* is a look-out post (or any distant vantage point: V. *Aen.* 4.586 etc.; *alta specula* is also Virgilian), the origin therefore of a beacon (Cic. *II Verr.* 5.93, turned to metaphor by P. in 3.18.3) and so – in a novel extension that inverts its original meaning – the object of viewing. As a striking substitute for *fastigium* 'summit' (*OLD* 7, a common metaphor for social eminence), it points the paradox that Firminus will be exposed from on high not, as desirably, to admiration, but to a shaming gaze. For the thought, cf. Cic. *Off.* 2.44, Juv. 8.140–1 (on provincial extortion). This rare use of *specula* recurs in *Pan.* 86.4 *stetit Caesar in amicitiae specula* and Symm. *Ep.* 1.26 *uiro in specula honorum locato* (referring, as here, to high office, and so one of the strongest candidates for Plinian epistolary influence in Symmachus: Intro. 35). **conspiciendum se monstrandumque praebere** 'to expose oneself to be stared and pointed at', *OLD conspicio* 3b, *monstro* 1b, *praebeo* 3b, with predicative gerundives (*NLS* §207.3).

4 praeterea quid publice minus aut congruens aut decorum 'besides, what could be less fitting or seemly for the state', beginning the massive third member of a rising tricolon (14~19~40 words) of rhetorical questions, comprising a tricolon of its own, varied with negative comparatives. The adverb *publice* 'in/for public life' (2.1.7n. *non*) takes the place of a dative with *congruens* and *decorum* (cf. 1.8.12 *publice consulentem*). That adjective-pair occurs only here; for *congruens* in a matching context see 4.9.19. Cic. *II Verr.* 2.58 expands similarly on an agent of Verres who dared to show his face in Rome after being publicly shamed (*quid est turpius ingenuo, quid minus libero dignum...?*). **notatum...summotum...damnatumque:** each member of the tricolon begins with a perfect participle, and each time a key term early in the colon is reprised as its penultimate word (*notatum... notatus | summotum a proconsulatu...proconsulibus | damnatumque...damnare*) in a crafted indictment of the perversity of the scenario. **notatum a senatu in senatu sedere** '[than] that a man censured by the senate should sit in the senate' (*OLD sedeo* 3), chiastic. The lack of *quam* is paralleled in Cic. *ND* 1.107 *quid est quod minus probari possit, omnium in me incidere imagines...?* 'what is less probable [than] that all [these people's] images should appear to me...?', *Fin.* 5.31, *Pis.* 47 (*pace* Nisbet ad loc.), and in verse (where editors are not at liberty to add it) at [Virgil] *Aetna* 255–6 (with Goodyear). It can be explained by the feeling that a rhetorical question (*quid minus decorum?*) is equivalent – as indeed it is – to a statement (*minime decorum est*) that would naturally be followed by acc. + inf., as in 2.11.18 *iam hoc ipsum pulchrum et antiquum, senatum nocte dirimi* (Löfstedt 1956: II 166–70). Merrill 1909 had already drawn a parallel with Tac. *An.* 2.77.1 *quem iustius arma oppositurum qui* ['than the man who'] *legati auctoritatem... acceperit?*, where editors routinely (and needlessly) insert *quam*, as once did editors of our passage. 'Conversational' parataxis (H–S 471 §252b) seems unlikely. Mynors prints acc. + inf. of exclamation as a new sentence (*quid... decorum? notatum... absoluere!*). The punctuation adopted here (as by Schuster) makes a more likely rising tricolon (above on *praeterea*). **a senatu in senatu:** the repetition underlines the incongruity and, together with *sedere*, generates indignant *s* alliteration; cf. the still more studied 9.13.2 *in senatu senator senatori.* **ipsisque illis:** indirect object of *aequari.* **sit notatus:** subordinate within acc. + inf. **summotum a proconsulatu** 'removed from [the prospect of] a governorship', a compendious use of *OLD submoueo* 4 'dismiss (from an office)'. *proconsulatus* (first in Pl. *NH*), like *proconsul*, is used regardless of rank (praetorian or consular: §2n. *in sortitione*). **quia se ... gesserat:** the indicative perhaps affirms Firminus' guilt, though see 2.3.8n. *uiderat.* **legatione** 'in his office as legate' (*OLD* 5a). **turpiter:** cf. 2.11.23 *turpissimum ministerium.* **de proconsulibus iudicare:** in a similar future trial Firminus would be juror *qua* senator. **sordium** '(filthy) greed' (*OLD* 4b), an emotive term for bribery (cf. 3.9.2); genitive of charge. **uel damnare alios uel absoluere:** the former would be hypocritical (cf. Cic. *Phil.* 1.20 *ut enim quisque sordidissimus uidebitur, ita libentissime seueritate iudicandi sordis suas eluet*), the latter potentially conniving with fellow crooks. Cic. *Cluent.* 119 expresses similar outrage that a senator who had been struck off later rejoined the senate and indeed became censor.

5 pluribus uisum est 'was the majority verdict' (*OLD uideo* 23–4). **numerantur enim sententiae, non ponderantur:** antithesis in falling bicolon (10~5 syllables) pointed by rhyme in the framing verbs, the first in a cluster of three sharp *sententiae*. While accepting the one-man-one-vote system as inevitable (*nec aliud . . . potest fieri*), P. argues, with repeated reference to Cicero, that it is unjust. This first epigram perhaps recalls Cic. *Rep.* 6.4 Powell (= Nonius 519.17) *expendendos ciues, non numerandos puto*, another political application of a common quality/quantity antithesis (*De or.* 2.309 *non tam ea* [= *argumenta*] *numerare soleo quam expendere*, Cic. *Off.* 2.79 *non enim numero haec* [grievances] *iudicantur sed pondere* (lexically close to P. here), Sen. *Ep.* 29.12 *aestimes iudicia, non numeres*, Quint. 10.5.21 *numerantium potius declamationes quam aestimantium*). **publico consilio** 'government' (lit. 'public council' or 'public decision-making'), used as often by Cicero and others in grandiose (not technical) reference to the senate and/or senatorial debate (8.14.5, Tac. *An.* 6.15.3, *OLD consilium* 4b, Mommsen 1887–8: III 1028–9). **in quo** could refer to *publicum consilium*, or (as punctuated here) to the preceding main clause, the fact that votes are counted indiscriminately. **nihil est tam inaequale quam aequalitas ipsa** 'nothing is as unequal [i.e. unfair] as equality itself', paradoxical isocolon (7~6 syllables, or 6~6 reading *nil*). The wordplay recalls Cic. *Rep.* 1.43 *ipsa aequabilitas* ['even distribution of honours'] *est iniqua* and 1.53 *eaque quae appellatur aequabilitas iniquissima est: . . . ipsa aequitas* ['equality'] *iniquissima est*, but P. substitutes another Ciceronian noun, *aequalitas* 'equality of status', and the adjective *inaequale* (a later alternative to *iniquum*, rare in this ethical sense of 'unfair': *TLL* VII.1 810.48–57) for more precise paronomasia. Cf. 9.5.3 *nihil est ipsa aequalitate inaequalius*, referring (as does Cicero) to society at large; here P. brings the terms to bear on the miniature society of the senate itself. Similar wordplay in different contexts at 8.2.2, 8.2.6, Sen. *Ep.* 104.28, [Quint.] *Decl. mai.* 5.3. **nam cum sit impar prudentia, par omnium ius est** 'for although men have differing powers of judgment, they all have the same right (to vote)', ABC~BCA falling bicolon (9~6 syllables); *omnium* is *apo koinou*. Cicero again supplies a model: *Rep.* 1.49 *si ingenia omnium paria esse non possunt, iura certe* *paria debent esse eorum inter se.* Whereas the position advocated (but not endorsed) by Scipio there makes equality an ethical obligation (*debent esse*), P. regrets it. On his low view of the senatorial 'masses', see intro., 3.20.8 *multi famam, conscientiam pauci uerentur*, 6.5.5 *quo magis quosdam e numero nostro improbaui* (describing senators rushing around with no dignity as their loyalties shifted), and cf. Livy 21.4.1 on the 'senate' at Carthage: *ut plerumque fit, maior pars meliorem uicit.*

6 Impleui promissum 'I have fulfilled my promise' (*OLD impleo* 10, adding Cic. *Cluent.* 51). P. did not explicitly commit himself to a sequel, though it was implicit (2.11.24n. *referri*, 2.11.25n. *non*). 5.13.1 *ego promisi* similarly retrojects a promise to 5.4, where none is stated.   **fidem exsolui** 'kept my word' (*OLD fides* 2b, *exsoluo* 4), chiastically reprising *impleui promissum*.   **quam ex spatio temporis iam recepisse te colligo** 'which I assume [*OLD colligo* 11] from the time that has passed you have now received'. The period is two to three weeks (§1n. *proxime*). In Cicero's time letters from Rome to the Bay of Naples (less than half the distance to Altinum) were taking three to seven days (Cic. *Att.* 14.13.1, 14.18.1; White 2010: 11).   **tabellario** 'courier', a private messenger, the normal postal mechanism. Cicero's letters are heavily populated with them (White 2010: 11–15), *Epistles* 1–9 far less so (3.17.2, 7.12.6, 8.3.2): this rare 'reality reference' marks the turn, as in 2.11.25, to a specifically epistolary Ciceronian mode for the close.   **nisi quid impedimenti in uia passus est** 'unless he has been held up along the way' (lit. ' . . . has suffered any hindrance'; *impedimenti* is partitive gen.). The clause is tacked on as an afterthought (cf. 1.2.6 *nisi tamen . . .*), dependent on *recepisse te colligo* but informally construed as if the main verb had been *recepisti.*

7 tuae nunc partes, ut . . . remunereris 'now it is your turn to repay . . .', Ciceronian: cf. *Att.* 14.13b.4 *tuas partes esse arbitror ut . . . imbuas* (*OLD pars* 10c) and, for *remunerari* of letter exchange, *Att.* 8.1.4, *Fam.* 9.8.1.   **primum illam, deinde hanc** = 2.11, then 2.12 (2.14.2n. *hic*). The assumption that Arrianus has not yet replied to 2.11 cements the already strong sense of a diptych.   **litteris quales istinc redire uberrimae possunt** 'with the richest letter that can return from your parts'. *istinc* recalls again (2.11.25n. *habes*) Arrianus' distance from Rome, so completing a ring with 2.11.1 *secesseris*. *uberrimae* combines a final nod to Cicero (of long letters at *Att.* 4.16.7 etc.) with a reprise of the farming imagery of §1 (*OLD uber²* 1 '(of natural produce, growth, etc.)') and a sly dig: Altinum had good sheep (2.11.25n. *quid*) and a thriving sea-trade (*RE* 1.2 1697–8) but was too marshy to produce much of a land-crop (no impediment, though, to Arrianus' epistolary crop). Likewise *redire* (poetic, not Ciceronian, for letters: Ov. *Am.* 1.12.1 *tristes rediere tabellae*, *Her.* 20.172, Hor. *Ep.* 2.2.22) hints at *reditus* 'yield' (*reditus* + *uber/ubertas* is in Cic., Col., Vell., Fronto). The syntax *qualis* + superlative + *posse* ('the -est that can . . .') is a rare variant on *quantum maximum posse* (2.13.10n. *licet*): cf. Livy 8.39.1 *equitum acies qualis esse instructissima potest* (with Oakley); Sen. *Ep.* 85.40 *fecisset quale . . . fieri optimum posset*; Quint. 7.3.20 *duos ponere debemus fines* ['definitions'] *quales utrimque esse optimi poterunt.*

13

You are the perfect man to help a friend of mine. Voconius Romanus is an excellent man of fine extraction. I have been his patron, and recently won for him the three-child privilege. Please do all you can for him, but above all honour him with your friendship.

The second patronage letter of the book, making a pendant to 2.9, symmetrically placed around the long 2.11. Each addressed to a consul of 97, one assists a senatorial career (Clarus), the other an equestrian (Romanus); 2.9 is marked by anxiety, 2.13 persistent but blithe. Romanus is familiar as the addressee of 2.1, and Clarus' uncle received 1.1 (2.9.intro.): this, together with P.'s central praise for Romanus' letter-writing above all (§7), blurs the boundary between P.'s literary and social lives. The numerically matching 3.13 is addressed to Romanus.

P. presents a model letter of recommendation, a common genre in a world where careers depended above all on personal patronage (2.9.intro.). An introduction establishes the bond between P. and his addressee, and Priscus' qualification for receiving the request; the body of the letter (just over half its length) sketches a portrait of Romanus; finally, P. poses the request before a sententious sign-off. He names no post, but a likely one would be a military tribunate; as with election letters (2.9.1n. *petitio*), he varies his practice between specifying the position sought (3.8.1, 4.4, 7.22) and not (3.2.5 *dignitati eius aliquid astruere*). Recommendations frequently work through the '*amicitia* triangle' (Rees 2007): 'X is my friend, you are mine, so you should be his'. As in 2.9, P. does not dwell explicitly on his relationship to Priscus; but repetitions establish a parallel in their patronal positions: *auidissime* (§§1, 8), §2 *beneficiorum* ∼ §9 *beneficia*, §8 *quantum potui* ∼ §10 *quantum . . . potes*.

Together with 10.4, this letter has caused extensive debate among historians. In 10.4 (datable to 98), P. introduces Romanus to Trajan and requests his promotion to senatorial status. If that precedes 2.13, as now seems certain from the identity of Priscus (below), Trajan must have declined P.'s request; certainly there is no sign in the *Epistles* that Romanus is present in the senate or resident in Italy (as senators had to be): cf. 9.28.2 *in diuersissima parte terrarum*. For this view (against S-W and, differently, Vidman 1986), see Syme 1960: 365–7, Seelentag 2004: 158–79; also Jones 1968: 131.

PRISCO: L. Neratius Priscus, jurist, *cos. suff.* 97, governor of Germania Inferior (98/9 to mid-101) and of Pannonia (102/3 to *c.* 106): for his career see Camodeca 2007, superseding long debate (including Syme 1957a, *PIR²* N 60 and Bauman 1989: 194–213). The German command is attested by an inscription (*CIL* IX 2455 = *ILS* 1034, as revised by Camodeca 1976 and *AE* 1976: 195) and by a military diploma of March 101 (Pferdehirt 2004: 22–9). Neratius may also be the legate Priscus of the trio 7.7, 7.8, 7.15 and/or the Priscus of 6.8 and/or 7.19 (Schuster and Mynors, indexes; Birley 2000a: 83; other possibilities in Syme 1985a: 337–40). P. makes a similar recommendation to his brother Neratius Priscus Marcellus, governor of Britain, in 3.8.1. One of the brothers had as his first wife Corellia Hispulla, recipient of 3.3 and daughter of P.'s mentor Corellius Rufus (Syme 1985a: 339–40, id. 1991: 595–6, 641, Camodeca 2007: 308, 311); given that Corellius was a Transpadane like P. (Syme 1968: 147), the family tie may suggest the same origin for our Neratius.

A former contender for 2.13 was Javolenus Priscus (*PIR*² I 14), *cos. suff.* 86, governor of Syria some time in the 90s, a member of Trajan's *consilium* after *c.* 103, and object of unkind remarks in 6.15 (so S-W 173–5 and Berriman–Todd 2001: 320, dating the letter to 97; Syme 1957a: 488, dating it to *c.* 100). But Javolenus now seems to have been in Syria 92/3–95/6, too early for this letter (Dąbrowa 1998: 73–4, Seelentag 2004: 178–9). L. Neratius Priscus, *cos. suff.* 86, father of the Neratius above (Syme 1985a: 339 n.83), is unlikely, since he is not known to have governed any *exercitus amplissimus* (§2) in our period.

These difficulties would have been eased, though not obviated, by the two-name index that probably once accompanied book 2 (Intro. 39–41) – assuming P. was concerned to facilitate identification. 'Priscus' is a common *cognomen*, but makes a light link with the preceding 2.11–12, the Marius Priscus trial and its aftermath, and a suitable partner with 'Romanus' for this exemplary transaction.

1 Et tu . . . amplecteris, et ego . . . debeo: syntax implies reciprocity, though the unbalanced bicolon (18~13) weights Priscus' side. There is no sign that he needs any favours from P.; he can perhaps expect, however, to receive favours from others in turn, in 'indirect reciprocity' (Griffin 2003b: 116; cf. Lendon 1997: 63–9). **occasiones obligandi me** 'opportunities to oblige me', *OLD occasio* 2a, *obligo* 5a (a common verb in P.'s vocabulary of *beneficia*, e.g. 3.4.6, 4.4.2, 4.15.4). Genitive gerund, rather than P.'s usual gerundive (2.9.2n. *ius*), again at 7.12.1 *emendandi eum*, 9.19.7 *illum reprehendi . . . hunc tuendi*, all with pronoun objects (a common usage, K–S I 745–6); cf. also *Pan.* 85.8 *amicos tuos obligandi* (avoiding -*orum* -*orum*, K–S I 736, despite 2.11.3n. *uir*) and 9.13.2 *insectandi nocentes, miseros uindicandi, se proferendi* (where both factors pertain). See also 2.10.7n. *ulteriora.* **auidissime amplectĕris** 'welcome with all alacrity' (lit. 'very hungrily'): *OLD auide* 2, *amplector* 6a. Cf. Frontin. *Aq.* 73.3 *acquisitionem non auide me amplecti*; *Tab. Vind.* 225.4–5 Bowman–Thomas (*c.* AD 95–105) [*li*]*benter amplexus s*[*um do*]*mine salutandi te occassionem* (with Bowman–Thomas 1983: 129). **nemini** *sc. quam tibi.* **libentius** varies *auidissime*; cf. Cic. *Fam.* 13.28.1 *etsi libenter petere a te soleo.* The bright enthusiasm contrasts with the anxious start to 2.9. **debeo** 'am indebted to' + dat., *OLD* 3a.

2 duabus ergo de causis: the 'two' reasons just given, not the facts that follow. Like Cicero, P. has both *ex causa/-is* (2.1.10, 2.5.12, 2.7.6) and *de causa/ -is* (2.17.29), with a preference for the former (21:9). **quod** = *id quod* (2.1.10n. *qua*). **impetratum . . . cupio:** 2.9.3n. *adiutum* and Fronto *Ad M. Ant.* 1.2.1 (p.87.8 vdH²) *impetratum cupiam.* **regis** 'you command', *OLD* 11. **exercitum amplissimum:** a Plinian term for a consular province with several legions: cf. 9.13.11 (almost certainly Syria, with three legions), *Pan.* 9.2 (Germania, probably Superior: Pferdehirt 2004: 26–7). P. never names the province when writing to an army commander (Syme 1958: 96): what matters is the personal network, and the exemplary transaction. **hinc:** *OLD* 8a. **tibi** *sc. est*, possessive dat. **beneficiorum** 'favours', a genteel word for the giving of political or military advancement (*OLD* 2), as §9, 1.19.4, 3.4.6 etc.; cf. *Pan.* 39.3 *tot beneficiorum occasiones*. Governors had some autonomy in appointing at least junior staff members, both at the beginning of and during their command: S-W 175–6; 3.8 with S-W; Stat. *Silu.* 5.1.95–8 with Gibson. **longum praeterea tempus** *sc. fuit* 'besides, you have had a long time'. Priscus is evidently well settled, but the end of his term is not in sight. Given his tenure of Lower Germany (Prisco n.), P.'s request perhaps falls in late 99 or 100. **quo** 'in which' (*NLS* §54b). **exornare** 'advance' (*OLD* 3b), a 'semi-technical' term for promotion, as at 10.12.1, 13, 26.3 (S-W 579, echoing *TLL* v.2 1582.44–80, which gives several inscriptions). **conuertĕre** 'turn (your attention) to' (*OLD* 6c, Cic. *Fam.* 3.12.1 *ad me conuertat*), imperative. **nostros** *sc. amicos*, contrasting with *tuos*. **nec hos multos** 'and not many at that'. Like his uncle, P. favours appositional additions with *hic*: 5.6.34 *nec huic uni*, *Pan.* 54.4 *nec hos singulos*, and e.g. 1.14.9 *et his pluribus*; cf. e.g. Petr. 45.3 *nec haec sola*, Pl. *NH* 19.26 *nec haec tota* (*OLD nec* 4b, *TLL* vi.3 2724.80–2725.47).

3 malles tu quidem multos 'you would prefer [them to be] many'. For *quidem* (contrasting *tu* with *meae*) see 2.1.7n. *et.* **uerecundiae:** dat. with *sufficit*. See 2.9.4n. *summa.* **unus aut alter** 'one or two at most' (*OLD unus* 1d), as 3.11.6, 4.3.1, 4.4.3. **ac potius** 'or rather' (*OLD potius* 2b). **unus** completes a graded tricolon *multos* ~ *unus aut alter* ~ *unus*, homing in on the subject.

4 Is erit: the idiomatic future implies perhaps 'this (you will see) is', as Plaut. *Asin.* 734 *hic inerunt uiginti minae* (K–S 1 143 n.2). **Voconius Romanus:** 2.1n. C. Plinivs; for the two names at first mention see 2.1.1n. *Vergini* and 10.4.1 *Voconius Romanus* (vs 10.4.4 *Romani mei*). **pater . . . clarus, clarior uitricus . . . , mater e primis** *sc. est* ×3. AB~BA~AB tricolon; the family parade varies 2.9.4 (longer, but only father and uncle and with different syntax). The father is probably C. Voconius Placidus (*CIL* ii 3865). **in equestri gradu clarus** 'distinguished in the equestrian rank'. A *clarus* father is a recommendation at Hor. *Sat.* 1.6.58 *claro natum patre* and e.g. Cic. *Rosc. Am.* 147, Ov. *Met.* 13.513, Vell. 2.2.1. The qualification *in equestri gradu* (a rare alternative to *equester ordo*, also at 4.2.3, first in Livy 2.1.10) may be pointed, given the senatorial overtone at least of the superlative *clarissimus* (2.1.1n. *maximi*), but it seems oversubtle to conclude that Romanus by contrast was a senator (Vidman 1986: 71). In 10.4 P. asks Trajan to give him that rank, apparently unsuccessfully (intro.). **clarior uitricus:** for *clarus, clarior* see 2.3.1n. *magna*. The stepfather and adoptive father (below) may be C. Licinius Marinus (*PIR*² L 210; S-W 176 misprints 'Macrinus'). He can decently outshine the father, because the latter is dead. **immo** 'or rather' (2.3.1n.). **pater alius** 'a second father', with *alius* for *alter* (post-Augustan): cf. Ulp. *Dig.* 37.8.1.11 *alius filius*, *TLL* 1 1648.70–1649.38. **(nam . . .):** the parenthesis justifies *pater alius* (2.4.2n. *erat*). **huic quoque nomini pietate successit** 'he has taken over this title [*sc.* of *pater*] as well through his devotion' (*OLD nomen* 4c, *pietas* 3b, *succedo*

5b; cf. 8.18.6 *successit in locum patris*, Cic. *Ad Brut.* 1.13.1, Gai. *Inst.* 2.156), by adopting Romanus (10.4.4). He did so shortly after a gift to Romanus from his mother
(*pace* S-W on 10.4.4, who quibbles unduly with *statim*), thus (from the rest of 10.4)
late in Nerva's or early in Trajan's principate.   **e primis** 'from a leading family'.
Discreetly vague for a rich woman (her gift to Romanus was 4 million sesterces,
10.4.2), and perhaps trumping *pater* and *uitricus* with senatorial lineage.   **citerioris Hispaniae** 'Nearer Spain', renamed by Augustus as Tarraconensis, but the
old term is in regular use by the elder Pliny, Tacitus and (just here) P.   **(scis quod
iudicium prouinciae illius, quanta sit grauitas):** *scis* introduces two indirect questions with *prouinciae illius* and *sit* distributed *apo koinou*. The parenthesis
magnifies the statement it interrupts (2.7.2n. *quod*) – Romanus' flaminate is not
only prestigious but owed to a discrimating electorate – and appeals to Priscus by
asserting shared values: cf. 4.15.1 *Cornelium Tacitum (scis quem uirum) arta familiaritate
complexus est*. Tarraco produced among others Quintilian, Martial and Trajan's
wife Plotina (Trajan was from neighbouring Baetica). The elder Pliny served
there as procurator, probably in the early 70s (3.5.17; Syme 1969): hence perhaps
P.'s acquaintance with Romanus' family (Syme 1969: 230–1). *scis* may imply that
Priscus too has a connection there (cf. 1.14.4–6 *illa nostra Italia . . . nosti loci mores*).
A different judgment in Tac. *An.* 4.45.3 *barbari*.   **flamen:** priest of the imperial
cult (*OLD c*) and president of the provincial council, thus the highest-ranking
local official, elected annually (S-W 177, Étienne 1958, Alföldy 1973).   **proxime**
'recently' (2.12.1n.). P may (but does not necessarily) imply that Romanus was the
most recent *flamen* at Tarraco; Alföldy 1973: 76–7 deduces AD 97, Vidman 1986:
69 prefers 99.

5 cum simul studeremus: as boys or young men (*OLD studeo* 4): cf. 10.4.1
Romanus, ab ineunte aetate condiscipulus et contubernalis, 1.19.1 (Romatius Firmus)
condiscipulus et ab ineunte aetate contubernalis.   **artē familiariterque** 'closely and
intimately' (*OLD artē* 4b), a redundant doublet; cf. *art(issim)a familiaritate* at 3.11.5,
4.15.1, 5.14.4.   **dilexi:** P. uses *diligere* and *amare* (cf. §7 *amatur*) interchangeably
for friendship, often together: e.g. 1.14.10 *diligo . . . amantis*, 7.31.1 *amari a te cupit
dignus . . . quod ipse te diligit*, Pan. 85.4–5 *amari nisi ipse amet non potest; diligis ergo
cum diligaris*; Méthy 2007: 256–62. Intimacy is not a bar to good judgment, but
confirmation of it (3.3.5 *caritas . . . ex iudicio nata est*; cf. 1.14.10).   **ille meus in
urbe, ille in secessu contubernalis** 'he was my constant companion in and
out of Rome'. Asseverative anaphora with *meus* and *contubernalis* distributed in
double *apo koinou*. For *secessu* see 2.8.1n. *altissimus*; for *contubernalis*, above on *cum
simul*.   **cum hoc seria, cum hoc iocos miscui** 'with him I shared matters
both serious and light' (*OLD misceo* 10 'give and take'): anaphora again, now with
single *apo koinou*. Cf. Sid. *Ep.* 4.4.1 *saepe cum hoc seria, saepe etiam ioca miscui*; also
Auson. *Parent.* 7.11 *ioca seria mixti*, though *seria* and *ioci* are a proverbial pair for
intimacy (Cic. *Fin.* 2.85 *ioca seria, ut dicitur*; Otto 1890: 176–7): e.g. 4.17.5 *nihil a me
ille secretum, non ioculare non serium* [*sc. habebat*]. Ennius *Annales* 268–85 Sk. (a famous,

perhaps autobiographical, description of a friend) may be in mind: cf. *Ann.* 273–4 *quoi res audacter magnas paruasque iocumque | eloqueretur* and next n. **quid enim illo aut fidelius amico aut sodale iucundius?** 'for what [could be] more faithful than him as a friend, more pleasant as a companion?', chiastic, with *fidelius* and *iucundius* picking up *seria* and *iocos* in parallel; *enim* implies 'and this was only natural'. For the aggrandising neuter see 2.9.4n. *nihil.* Cf. Enn. *Ann.* 279–80 Sk. *doctus, fidelis, | suauis homo, iucundus, suo contentus, beatus* (~ *fidelius . . . iucundius . . .* §6 *suauitas,* and the asyndetic list of adjectives in §7); for *iucundius* cf. also Cic. *Fin.* 1.65 *nihil esse maius amicitia, nihil uberius, nihil iucundius,* Hor. *Sat.* 1.3.93–4, 1.5.44 with Gowers.

6 mira . . . , mira . . . suauitas: a third anaphora with *apo koinou* (§5n. *ille*). *suauitas* 'charm' is usually for P. a literary quality (1.16.4, 3.1.7, 3.15.3, 4.3.2, 5.8.10, 5.17.3, 6.7.3), but also depicts character (5.16.2, 6.8.7, *Pan.* 49.7; at 6.31.14 it describes dining chez Trajan); here it is both. P. likes *mirus* 'marvellous, wonderful' and cognates, not least in anaphora: 3.1.7 *mira illis dulcedo, mira suauitas, mira hilaritas,* 6.25.5 *pietate mira, mira etiam sagacitate,* 8.18.6 *mira illius asperitas, mira felicitas horum;* see also 2.17.1n. *miraris.* **ore ipso uultuque** 'his very face and expression', a common doublet: 5.16.9 and e.g. Cic. *De or.* 1.184, V. *Aen.* 10.821, Tac. *An.* 14.16.2. A distinction between *os* (natural features) and *uultus* (countenance) is suggested by Tac. *Ag.* 44.2 *nihil impetus in uultu: gratia oris supererat,* Serv. ad *Aen.* 9.249.

7 ad hoc: 2.11.10n.   **ingenium** *sc. est ei.*   **excelsum subtile dulce facile eruditum in causis agendis** 'lofty, sharp, charming, deft, learned in legal practice': *OLD excelsum* 2a (and 2.3.3n. *excelse,* Quint. 12.10.23 *Aeschines . . . excelsior*); 2.11.17n. *subtilis;* 2.3.1n. *tersae* (for *dulce*); *OLD facilis* 11 and Quint. 10.1.128; *OLD eruditus* b. P.'s usual practice, and 2.9.4 *atque in agendis causis exercitatus* (ending a list), suggest that *in causis agendis* modifies *eruditum,* so making an extended pentacolon. For the list form, and emphasis on *studia,* see 2.9.3n. *probissimum.* The adjectives are near-symmetrical in morphology (*ex–um, -īle, -ce, -īle, e–um*) and length. **epistulas quidem scribit** 'and as for his letters, he writes them [such]', *sc. tales* (Kraut 1872: 12) or *ita.* The 'adversative-extending *quidem*' (Solodow 1978: 85–7) marks a contrast with *in causis agendis* but also develops the preceding clause with yet stronger praise. Letter-writing might be relevant to a posting as procurator, but this climactic and central encomium (*epistulas* is 153rd word of 298) has a self-reflexive edge, valorising P.'s own literary form: cf. 1.16.6 *legit mihi nuper epistulas; uxoris esse dicebat. Plautum uel Terentium metro solutum legi credidi,* 7.13 (quoted in 2.2.intro.); also 7.9.8 and Stat. *Silu.* 1.3.104 with G–M 80–1. P.'s last letter to him dwells at length on three letters of his, *omnes elegantissimas amantissimas* (9.28.1), and ends with an echo (9.28.5 *litteras curiosius scriptas*) of his own letters (1.1.1 *si quas paulo curatius scripsissem*). Like 2.9, then, this letter patronises a man tightly sewn into the epistolarity of the collection. **ut Musas ipsas Latine loqui credas** '[such] that you would think the Muses themselves spoke Latin', *OLD Latine* 1a (standard idiom); *credas* is potential generalising subjunctive (2.3.3n. *dubites*). P.

varies a cliché of literary praise: cf. Cic. *Or.* 62 *Xenophontis uoce Musas quasi locutas ferunt* (reused in Quint. 10.1.33, 10.1.82); also Aelius Stilo (2c. BC) *apud* Quint. 10.1.99 (on Plautus) *Musas . . . Plautino . . . sermone locuturas fuisse si Latine loqui uellent*; Cic. *Brut.* 121 (on Plato) *Iouem sic aiunt philosophi, si Graece loquatur, loqui* (cf. Dion. Hal. *Dem.* 23); Hor. *Ep.* 2.1.27 (the lover of hoary Latin) *dictitet Albano Musas in monte locutas.*

8 amatur: §5n. *dilexi.* **nec tamen uincitur** 'and yet he is not surpassed' *sc.* by me: i.e. his love for me matches mine for him (cf. 4.1.5 *uinci in amore turpissimum est*). The framing *amatur . . . uincitur* encapsulates the reciprocity. **equidem** 'for my part' (2.10.5n. *opto*), leaving aside Romanus' proofs of friendship to focus on P.'s. **iuuenis statim iuueni** 'from the very beginning of our adulthood', later perhaps than §5 *cum simul studeremus*, as P. is now exercising social/political influence (below). For the polyptoton cf. 1.14.3 *qui me ut iuuenis iuuenem . . . diligit*; for *statim* 'right from', cf. *OLD* 3 and 2.17.23 *orientem statim*, 9.37.1 *Kalendis statim*, and the common *primo statim die* (etc.), e.g. *Pan.* 21.2, 23.3. Longevity is a topos of friendship in Cicero: e.g. *Fam.* 10.3.2, Hutchinson 1998: 17 n.28. **quantum potui per aetatem auidissime contuli** 'I conferred (on him) with all alacrity everything my age allowed'. The object of *contuli* (*OLD* 5) is *quantum potui per aetatem*: cf. 3.21.6 *dedit enim mihi quantum maximum potuit*, 6.12.2 *quantum plurimum potuero praestabo*. Both the rare superlative *auidissime* (3.1.11, Cic. ×1, Pl. *NH* ×2), repeated from §2, and *quantum potui . . . contuli*, reworked in §10 *tribuas ei quantum amplissimum potes*, establish a parallel between P. and Priscus as patrons (intro.). P.'s influence was limited by his youth, though naturally he strove to overcome such limitation (2.1.9n. *huius*). **et nuper** brings us to a recent and relevant *beneficium.* There is no hint of it in 10.4 or anywhere in book 10. Perhaps P. acquired it from Trajan in person on the latter's return to Rome in 99 (Seelentag 2004: 169, 175), or perhaps this is a sign that 10.1–14 is not comprehensive (2.9.2n. *a*). **optimo principe:** probably Trajan: if it had been Nerva, P. might have mentioned it in 10.4. In any case, P. routinely uses this phrase of Trajan (3.13.1, 3.18.3, 4.22.1, 5.13.7, *Pan.* 1.2 and often), who seems to have held *optimus* as an informal title (*Pan.* 2.7) and later, in 114, added 'Optimus' to his titulature (Fell 1992: 52–61). Though he also calls Nerva *optimus* (2.1.3n. *reliquit*), he never refers to him simply as '(the) *optimus princeps*', and that term seems not to be used elsewhere of a dead emperor. **trium liberorum ius** 'the three-child privilege'. Elite men and women with few or no children were legally disadvantaged, and the men achieved promotion more slowly (at 7.16.2 P. is pipped to the tribunate *liberorum iure*), unless they were awarded this exemption by the emperor. Trajan gave it to P. (10.2) and, on his request, to Suetonius (10.94–5). See S-W 558, Zabłocka 1988, Treggiari 1991: 66–80. **impetraui:** cf. §2 *impetratum.* **quod:** object of both *daret* and *indulsit*; the antecedent is *trium liberorum ius.* **quamquam parce et cum delectu daret** 'although (he said) he gave it sparingly and with discrimination' (*OLD dilectus² [sic]* 3); for the expansion of a single word (*parce*) with a phrase (*cum delectu*) see H–S 723. After *quamquam* P. chooses freely between indicative (e.g. 4.9.21 *probabatur*, 4.15.7 *soles*, 7.27.6) and subjunctive, e.g. 3.3.1 *contigerit*, 6.19.2 *occultaretur*, 7.1.1, 8.16.3 (Kraut 1872: 35, K–S II 442, H–S 602–3). The mood of *daret* is therefore unremarkable (*pace* S–W); less so the tense, which either refers to the dead Nerva or, if the emperor in question is Trajan (above on *optimo*), shows virtual *oratio obliqua* (2.11.22n. *qui se in*), where sequence demands the imperfect (again *pace* S-W). For the comment, cf. Trajan's words in 10.9 *quamquam eius modi honorum parcissimus* and 10.95 [*scis*] *quam parce haec beneficia tribuam* (on *trium liberorum ius*). **mihi tamen tamquam eligeret indulsit** 'nevertheless he granted it to me as though the choice were his own' (after Cowan), i.e. as if Trajan himself were nominating Romanus. Rhyme (*tamquam ~ quamquam*) and paired near-synonyms (*cum delectu* [< *deligere*] ~ *tamquam eligeret* and *daret* ~ *indulsit*) mark the antithesis. *indulsit* (*OLD* 5) has an official ring (10.6.1 *ius Quiritium*, 10.108.2, *Pan.* 39.2, Gai. *Dig.* 40.9.10, etc.; *TLL* VII.1 1253.61–72); *mihi* appropriates the favour as Pliny's (the dative is usually the recipient of the *ius*). For the subjunctive *eligeret* see 2.2.1n. *tamquam*.

9 haec beneficia: generalises from the significant one, the *ius trium liberorum*, whose value would be limited if no *cursus* followed. *beneficia mea* matches §2 *tibi beneficiorum*. **tueri** 'maintain, uphold' (*OLD* 7a), with *beneficium* also at Cic. *Cael.* 7, *Att.* 15.14.3, Sen. *Ben.* 4.15.4. In 1.19.4 *beneficium* . . . *tuendum*, conversely, it is the recipient of P.'s kindness who 'preserves its memory' (*OLD* 7c, also Ciceronian: e.g. *II Verr.* 3.9, *Phil.* 2.60). **quam ut augeam** 'than by compounding them', *OLD* augeo 2b; *NLS* §298 for *quam ut*. A 'tenet of Roman philanthropy' (S-W on 3.4.6 *antiquiora beneficia subuertas, nisi illa posterioribus cumules*): cf. 1.8.10 with S-W, 5.11 (esp. 5.11.3 *nescit enim semel incitata liberalitas stare*), Sen. *Ben.* 2.11 (esp. 2.11.5 *nisi illa* [= *beneficia*] *adiuueris, perdes; parum est dedisse: fouenda sunt*), 5.1.5 *nec recusabis conferre alia* [*beneficia*]; Guillemin 1929: 10–11, Griffin 2007: 474. **tam grate interpretetur** 'shows such appreciation of' (lit. 'regards so gratefully', *OLD* interpretor 4: cf. Sen. *Ep.* 63.7 *desine beneficium fortunae male interpretari, Ben.* 1.1.9, 2.28.4, 6.13.5). A claim for the past and promise for the future; cf. Sall. *Jug.* 63.5 *semperque in potestatibus eo modo agitabat, ut ampliore quam gerebat dignus haberetur* (Döring). **mereatur:** a key word to end the main body of the letter, and a stock technique of recommendation (Rees 2007: 157).

10 Habes 'you see' (*OLD* 11a), concluding the sketch (2.11.25n.). **qualis quam probatus carusque sit:** a rising pair of indirect questions (*qualis* [*sit*] and *quam probatus carusque sit*). Cf. 7.22.1 *cum scieris quis ille qualisque.* **nobis . . . rogo:** for the variation of plural and singular, cf. 2.4.3n. sunt. **pro ingenio, pro fortuna tua** 'as befits your nature and your position' (*OLD pro* 12a, *ingenium* 1a, *fortuna* 11b; supply *tuo* with *ingenio*), reprising in parallel §1 *tu . . . amplecteris* and §2 *regis exercitum amplissimum.* **exornes:** §2n. *exornare.* Subjunctive for paratactic indirect command (2.5.2n. *rogo*). **in primis:** *OLD imprimis* 1a. **ama** 'be kind to', 'look after', 'be (his) friend', as 4.27.5, 7.31.7; cf. Cic. *Att.* 3.23.5, *Q. fr.* 2.13.3

(both *ames*). The imperative perhaps signals intimacy. **hominem** = *eum*, as
e.g. 2.20.2, 7, 11, 3.3.5 (*OLD* 3b, *TLL* VI.3 2882.13–64). It is common in, but
not restricted to, comedy and casual prose (the preferred 'higher' alternative
is *uir*, *OLD* 6), not always derogatory (2.6.1n.). **licet tribuas ei quantum
amplissimum potes** 'though you may grant him the highest honour you can',
concessive (2.3.9n. *licet*); *OLD tribuo* 2a, *amplus* 7–8 (cf. *honor amplissimus*, common
in Cicero and e.g. *Pan.* 55.4). *quantum amplissimum potes* is a unique variant on
the idiom *quantum maximum/plurimum posse* (e.g. 3.21.6, 6.2.7; *OLD quantum*[2] 3a;
K–S II 479–80), echoing §2 *amplissimum* and §8 *quantum potui*. This is as specific
as P. gets: he probably refers to a military tribunate (*pace* Cotton 1981a: 237,
who assumes that tribunes were appointed only at a governor's arrival). On the
commissioning of officers see Birley 2003. **nihil ... amplius potes** *sc. tribuere*
'you can grant him no greater honour'. **amicitiā tuā:** abl. of comparison,
picking up *ama* in verb-noun modification (Wills 1996: 327–8) and with play on
amplius, in a flattering climax. *amicitia* encapsulates a whole discourse of Roman
patronage (Saller 1982, Konstan 1996: 122–48): P. smoothes away any edges to
present this transaction throughout as one of sentimental affection: cf. 7.7–8,
Cic. *Fam.* 7.5.3 *huic ego neque tribunatum neque praefecturam ... peto, beneuolentiam tuam
et liberalitatem peto* (producing the offer of a tribunate: *Fam* 7.8.1). On Plinian
amicitia see Guillemin 1929: 2–12, Castagna 2003 (p. 164 on 2.13). **cuius esse
eum usque ad intimam familiaritatem capacem quo magis scires**
'to make you more certain that he is capable of earning [*OLD capax* 3a] it and
indeed of the closest intimacy': a purpose clause (*quo magis*; cf. 2.10.6n. *quo*) in
which *scires* governs an indirect statement *cuius ... capacem*; for *capax* + gen., cf.
1.12.7, 10.50 (+ abl. at 2.17.3). **usque ad intimam familiaritatem:** cf. §4 *arte
familiariterque dilexi*, 7.8.2 *uirum ... quam familiarissime dilige*. If Romanus was intimate
with P., the implicit logic runs, he can be intimate with Priscus. **breuiter:** as
the genre dictates (2.2.2n. *plurimas*). **studia mores omnem denique uitam:**
extended tricolon (3~2~7 syllables), rising to the pointed claim (after *breuiter*) that
this miniature encapsulates a whole life (*OLD uita* 6a). *liberalia studia* commend
Romanus at 10.4.4 (just after *moribus*); *studia* and *mores* are paired again at 7.20.7
studia mores fama, 7.22.2, 10.94.1.

11 extenderem ... fecissem 'I would be continuing my entreaties, if you did
not dislike being asked at length, and I had not done this [i.e. made entreaties]
throughout my whole letter'; cf. 5.14.7 *in infinitum epistulam extendam, si ...* **et
tu ... et ego** reprises §1. **rogari diu nolles:** for the compliment, cf. Cic.
Lig. 38 (perorating) *longiorem orationem causa forsitan postulet, tua certe natura breuiorem*,
Fam. 3.2.2. P. affects such reluctance himself at 4.17.1 *quod rogas, queror ... rogari
non debeo*. **totā hoc epistulā:** idiomatic word-order (Adams 1994b: esp. 124–6,
138–9), referring tendentiously to §§4–9. **rogat ... rogandi** 'for to give one's
reasons for asking is [in itself] to ask, and indeed the most effective way' (lit.
'he who gives reasons for asking ...'); for *et quidem* see 2.9.3n. Framing verbal

polyptoton picks up *rogari* and marks the conceit. For *efficacissime*, cf. 6.6.8 *me efficacius... rogaturum*, 6.18.2 *quid enim precibus... efficacius?*, and (in a panegyric version of the *sententia* here) *Pan.* 70.9 *efficacissimum pro candidato genus est rogandi gratias agere*. The superlative adverb is 34× in Pl. *NH*, otherwise very rare; Sidonius borrows it and reworks the *sententia* to end a letter of recommendation, *Ep.* 8.13.4 *is efficacissime quemque commendat qui meras causas iustae commendationis aperuerit.*

14

I am busy with the centumviral court, and taking little pleasure in it. It is full of arrogant upstarts, and the audiences are no better. Claqueurs earn fees for cheering speeches of which they hear not a word. My teacher Quintilian told how Domitius Afer saw in this practice the death of oratory, but that was only the beginning: now it really has died, with speakers and audiences equally disgraceful. I feel obliged to continue my work there – but I have started to withdraw.

The third-longest letter of the book, set midway between the long 2.11 and 2.17, is the most pessimistic, a satirical attack on the fallen standards of advocates and audience alike in the most prestigious civil court (§1n. *centumuiralibus*). Lament at cultural decline is ubiquitous in antiquity, and the decline of oratory in particular is a live subject in the first century AD (Kennedy 1972: 446–64, Williams 1978: 6–51, Heldmann 1982), treated at around the same time in Tacitus' *Dialogus de oratoribus*. The frustrations of 2.14, however, also demand consideration in the context of the collection.

The opening flags up a contrast with 2.11 (§1n. *raro*): glorious senatorial advocacy is answered here with petty civil work, so making a second negative tail, after 2.12, to the long Priscus letter. Yet this condemnation of the centumviral court is at odds with the implication elsewhere that it was P.'s own primary area of renown. He does not mention that he had presided over this court at the age of around 20, as a *decemuir stlitibus iudicandis* (S-W 72–3); but book 1 recalls two appearances of former years, once as an *adulescentulus* (1.18.3) and once, more recently, against Regulus (1.5.4–7, the first trial mentioned in the *Epistles*), while book 3 ends with the epigram of Martial that flatters P. as a centumviral advocate to rival Cicero (*Epig.* 10.20(19).14–18). In books 4–6 these past glories are crowned by fresh successes. The 'death' of oratory in 2.14 (§12) is answered by resurrection in 4.16 (*gaude... adhuc honor studis durat*), where P. reports the rapt attention to his seven-hour speech in a centumviral case. We see him there again in 4.24 and 5.9, and by 6.12.2 he calls it *harena mea* 'my arena'; book 6 climaxes with the centumviral case of Attia Viriola, billed as one of his greatest speeches (6.33). In books 7–9 the topic falls quiet again, but 9.23.1 names the centumviral court alongside the senate as P.'s primary sphere of renown.

The disenchantment of 2.14 thus turns out to be temporary, 'redeemed' in books 4–6. In fact P.'s withdrawal, as 10.3A.1 reveals, was complete and pragmatic: he laid aside all advocacy, except for the senatorial trials of Priscus and Classicus (3.4, 3.9), during his time as prefect of the treasury of Saturn and the immediately ensuing consulate. This gives 2.14 a dramatic date before Jan. 98 (S-W), unless we allow book 2 to extend beyond Oct. 100 (Intro. 16). In any case, its position after the Priscus trial generates a decline in optimism and sense of withdrawal as book 2 proceeds. P. was already grumbling about city life in 2.8; the gloom reaches an acme in 2.20, where Regulus' continued influence draws letter and book to a remarkably resigned end (2.20.12–14): see Intro. 16–17.

As Gibson and Morello have shown, there seems to be a connection in the *Epistles* between the centumviral court and Regulus, another – perhaps the other – *doyen* of that arena (1.20.14 *cum simul adessemus*, 6.2.3 *una dicentibus*, Mart. 2.74, 4.16 and esp. 6.38): his retirement (implied in 4.24.3) and death (reported in 6.2) coincide with P.'s rise to lone supereminence (G–M 68–73). Though the noble Regulus is clearly not among the *obscuri adulescentuli* lambasted in 2.14, he is an emblem of the modern style and of 'bad' oratory for P. (2.20.intro.) as, it seems, for Quintilian (Winterbottom 1964: 93–5), who plays a significant role in this letter. The sorry state of affairs in book 2, then, may hint at an expression of the social ill caused by Regulus' activities – though given P.'s continued gripes in 6.2 (after Regulus' death) about court practice, the association is not crudely direct. Certainly the negative picture in 2.14, as in 6.2, provides a typical foil for the success that will attend our hero, P., in due course (Kennedy 1972: 548), just as the negative treatment of the senate (2.12) and society at large (2.20.12) creates a space for the exemplary performance of P. and his paraded friends.

The letter proceeds in two unequal stages. §§1–8 (254 words) work up the subject, including a topical anecdote (§6) and climaxing in the sententious claim that the worst oratory gets most applause. The shorter §§9–13 (132 words) is a variation on the theme, using an older anecdote to proclaim the death of oratory with (miniature) thundering denunciation. A coda (§14, 33 words) announces P.'s intended withdrawal.

MAXIMO: P. addresses thirteen letters to 'Maximus'; this is one of the eight for whom no *gentilicium* is preserved (see Intro. 39). S-W (180–1 and *passim*) identifies an 'Elder Maximus' who receives 2.14, 6.11, 8.19, 9.1 and 9.23, and who may also be the Novius Maximus of 4.20 and 5.5; Syme 1985a: 324–37 adds 7.26 to make eight letters and one of P.'s favourite correspondents. This is a coeval and fellow Transpadane (§2n. *ut*) with whom he exchanges compositions, 'probably a previous practitioner in the courts' (Syme 1985a: 335). The themes of 2.14 recur in his later letters, with contrast: 6.11 celebrates the oratorical performance of two noble tiros under P.'s wing, Fuscus Salinator and Ummidius Quadratus, the opposite of the *obscuri adulescentuli* here (§2); 9.23 makes a final, grandiose reference to the centumviral court (intro.).

1 Verum opinaris: P. refers to a letter from Maximus, typically admitting the secondary reader to a dialogue already under way: cf. 2.16 *admones*, 2.17 *miraris*, 2.19 *hortaris*; S-W 6–7. The tense (contrast 2.5.1n. *exhibui*) evokes the fiction of live

conversation (2.5.13n. *tecum*).   **distringor** 'I am heavily occupied', a metaphorical use of *distringo* 'strain apart' common since Cicero (*TLL* v.1 1551.12–64) and
11× in P.: e.g. 1.10.9 (treasury duties), 3.5.19, 7.15.1, 9.2.1, 9.25.3 (Bütler 1970:
41–3); within this book the complaint recalls 2.8. He tells a different tale to
Trajan in 10.3A.1 *aduocationibus, quibus alioqui numquam eram promiscue functus*.   **centumuiralibus causis:** the centumviral court heard (at least) all cases relating
to testamentary law, the majority of civil legislation: *OCD* '*centumviri*', Kelly 1976:
1–39, Bablitz 2007: 61–70; also Querzoli 2000 (89–91 on 2.14), Gagliardi 2002: 99–
502, 523–37. It now comprised 180 jurors, usually operating in four simultaneous
panels but occasionally combining for major cases (1.18.3, 4.24.1, 6.33.3).   **quae
me exercent magis quam delectant** 'which give me more trouble [*OLD
exerceo* 2b] than pleasure'.   **paruae et exiles** 'small and trivial' (*OLD exilis* 6);
cf. Sen. *VB* 13.1 *paruum et exile*. A notably damning verdict on a court in which P.
elsewhere takes great pride (intro.).   **raro incidit** *sc. causa*.   **uel personarum
claritate uel negoti magnitudine insignis:** cf. 2.11.1 *personae claritate famosum, seueritate exempli salubre, rei magnitudine aeternum* (and Tac. cited there), whose
terms and grandeur are here reversed (tricolon drops to bicolon): centumviral
pettiness counters senatorial pomp. This will be inverted in turn in 6.33.2 [*oratio*] *et
dignitate personae et exempli raritate et iudici magnitudine insignis*, heralding P.'s climactic
centumviral triumph (intro.). On the spelling *negoti* see 2.11.23n. *Mari*.

2 ad hoc: 2.11.10n.   **pauci:** including, perhaps, Clarus *pater* (2.9.4) and
Romanus (2.13.6). By 4.24.2 not one of P.'s former centumviral *socii laboris* is still
practising.   **cum quibus iuuet dicere** 'whom I like to plead alongside' (*OLD
dico*[2] 1b), generic/consecutive subjunctive (*NLS* §§155–7).   **audaces** '(over)bold',
pejorative as often, though not always (e.g. 7.9.4). Cf. 8.23.3 *statim sapiunt, statim
sciunt omnia, neminem uerentur, neminem imitantur, atque ipsi sibi exempla sunt*. In Cic. *De
or.* 1.173–84 Crassus condemns the *impudentia* of inexperienced advocates who pre-
sume to plead in the centumviral court; later he attacks the declamation schools
that teach only boldness (*ut auderent, De or.* 3.94), in a passage recalled by Messalla
in Tac. *D.* 35.1: he and P. are acting out a tried and tested script. See too Lucian
Rhet. praec. 15, ironically listing a beginner's virtues as 'ignorance, boldness, audacity, shamelessness'.   **adulescentuli obscuri:** the adj. confirms the damning
spin of the diminutive (2.6.2n. *paruulis*); cf. Cic. *Cato* 20 (quoting Naevius) *oratores
noui, stulti adulescentuli*. P. first performed *in foro* aged 18 (5.8.8) and pleaded in a
quadruple session of the centumviral court *adulescentulus adhuc* (1.18.3). To some
he was perhaps *obscurus* himself, but (like Tacitus) he does not let his origins as a
nouus homo stand in the way of social exclusivity now he is a senator. It is characteristic of him to set his own exemplary efforts to nurture and educate Roman
youth (2.6, 2.9, 2.18) against a backdrop of social failure.   **ad declamandum**
'to practise their school-exercises' (Merrill). Not an attack on declamation per
se (lauded in 2.3), but on bringing to court what belongs in school: cf. Cic. *Brut.*
311 *non ut in foro disceremus, quod plerique fecerunt, sed ut . . . docti in forum ueniremus;*

Quint. 10.5.17, 12.6. **huc transierunt:** from their schools. **irreuerenter et temere:** redundant synonyms. *irreuerenter* is first in P. (also 6.13.2, 8.21.3). **ut mihi Atilius noster expresse dixisse uideatur, sic in foro pueros a centumuiralibus causis auspicari ut ab Homero in scholis** 'that I think our dear Atilius captured it perfectly when he said that boys are starting with [*OLD ab* 12a, *auspicor* 3a] centumviral cases in the courts [*OLD forum* 5], just as they start with Homer in the schools'. Atilius Crescens, a fellow Transpadane (6.8.2; Syme 1985a: 332), is unknown outside the *Epistles*. P. praises and reuses another *sententia* of his in 1.9.8 (Intro. 27). **expresse dixisse uideatur:** lit. 'seems to have said precisely, appositely', i.e. hit the nail on the head (as one should with a good *sententia*). For *expresse* (rare) see *OLD* 1, *TLL* v.2 1796.1–27; it commends a quotation in Col. *RR* 11.1.29. The clausula, with semi-redundant *uideri*, evokes Cicero's notorious *esse uideatur* (Berry on Cic. *Sull.* 3.9), not much affected by P. (cf. §14 *fugisse uideamur* and 2.18.3 *audisse uidearis*, where *uideri* has more force, and cf. Intro. 30 n.175). **pueros** makes damning syllepsis (2.1.4n. *pari*): it is accurate for *in scholis*, patronising for the *adulescentes* in court. **ab Homero in scholis:** chiastic with *in foro . . . a centumuiralibus causis*. Homer was the canonical starting-point in studies with the *grammaticus* (the second stage of schooling): Quint. 10.1.46 *nos rite coepturi ab Homero uidemur*, Hor. *Ep.* 2.2.42 with Brink, Petr. 5.11–12. P. names and quotes him frequently (Deane 1918: 50–1; Mynors, index s.v. *Homerus*). **hic . . . illic:** *hic* pinpoints the 'more immediate object of Pliny's thought' (Merrill on 1.20.21; Cova 1969: 182–4, Ussani 1971: 84, K–S 1 623), as e.g. 2.12.7, 9.19.7, *Pan.* 55.7, rather than, as often, 'the latter'. **primum coepit esse quod maximum est** 'the most important thing now comes first'. That the centumviral court, like Homer, is *maximum* is implicit throughout P., as also at Cic. *De or.* 1.171–84 (above on *audaces*) and 1.238 *maximas centumuirales causas*, Tac. *D.* 7.1, 38.2 (Kelly 1976: 35–9, §1n. *centumuiralibus*). There were several other courts where beginners could cut their teeth (Crook 1995: 70–83, Bablitz 2007: 14–50).

3 at hercule: contrastive (past vs present) and affirmatory, as 1.13.3 (introducing an anecdote *memoria parentum*) and 7.24.7. For *hercule* see 2.6.5n. *et.* **ante memoriam meam** 'before my time' (*OLD memoria* 6a, *TLL* viii 680.57–681.60), too vague to pin to the 'age of Claudius' (S-W 182). **(ita . . . dicere):** forestalls the question, how he knew. On parenthesis see 2.3.2n. *sed.* **maiores natu** 'older people' (*OLD maior* 3a). **ne nobilissimis quidem adulescentibus:** contrasting with §2 *adulescentuli obscuri.* **nisi aliquo consulari producente** 'unless someone of consular rank [2.1.9n. *senes*] was presenting (them)' (*OLD produco* 2c), by inviting the debutant to plead alongside him. Consular P. single-handedly upholds the tradition in 6.23, as he proposes that young Cremutius Ruso share a brief with him (using the terms *ostendere foro, producere* and *prouehere*). Such apprenticeship is commended by Quint. 12.6.6–7. For *nisi* + abl. abs., cf. e.g. 2.17.22 *nisi fenestris apertis*, 1.23.3 *quasi eiurato magistratu*, 6.16.12 *quamquam nondum* *periculo appropinquante* (Steele 1904: 323). **tanta ueneratione . . . colebatur** 'so deep was the respect with which . . . was revered' (*OLD ueneratio* 1a, *colo* 6a), perhaps with religious overtones (§4n. *refractis*). **pulcherrimum opus** 'the finest profession' (*OLD opus* 3b). A cliché for oratory: Sen. *Contr.* 1.*pr.*7 *pulcherrima res*, Petr. 4, Quint. 1.10.7, 12.1.32 *rem pulcherrimam*, Tac. *An.* 11.6.1 *pulcherrimam . . . et bonarum artium principem*.

4 refractis pudoris et reuerentiae claustris: the religious hint is developed into a metaphor in which a shrine (such as the Shrines of Pudicitia Patricia and Plebeia, *LTUR* IV 168–9) is smashed open (e.g. Tac. *H.* 1.35.1 *refractis Palati foribus*), leaving *pudor* and *reuerentia* exposed (*patent*) to all (2.10.3 *claustra . . . refregerunt*, conversely, concerns captives escaping). *pudor* 'propriety' is a hint of the sexual moralising to come (§12n. *pudet*); the combination with *reuerentia* also at 7.17.8, Stat. *Ach.* 1.312, Tac. *H.* 3.41.2, Juv. 2.110; and cf. again (§2n. *audaces*) Messalla on the schools (Tac. *D.* 35.1–3 *ut ait Cicero, 'ludum impudentiae' . . . in loco nihil reuerentiae est*). **omnia patent omnibus:** polyptoton captures the elitist outrage. **nec inducuntur sed irrumpunt:** a rhyming pair, antithetical in meaning and voice. *inducuntur* varies §3 *producente*; *irrumpunt* continues the image of *refractis . . . claustris*. The unstated subject is the *adulescentuli* of §2. **auditores . . . redempti:** claqueurs. Analogous behaviour in the theatre stirs disgust at 7.24.7. The planting of supporters in court is first attested in Cic. *Sest.* 115 *emptos plausus* and *Ad Q.* 2.3.2 (Wiseman 1985: 36–7). See Cameron 1976: 234–49, Aldrete 1999: 135–7, Korenjak 2000: 124–7, Bablitz 2007: 126–33. **actoribus:** dat. with *similes*. P. routinely uses *actor* as 'advocate' (*OLD* 4); given, however, the theatrical associations of claques (§6n. *mesochorus*, §13 *theatris*, Cameron 1976: 235), the sense 'actor' (as 7.17.3) may also be live, as always in oratory (Fantham 2002). **conducti et redempti** 'hired and bought', with gradation. P. disdains the mercenary attitude of claqueurs and lawyers alike. Fees for advocacy were frowned upon in theory, taken in practice: cf. Quint. 12.7.8–12 (equivocal) and Crook 1967a: 90–1, id. 1995: 129–31, Bablitz 2007: 141–8. P. advertises his own – evidently atypical – rejection of all fees at 5.13.8, 6.23.1; likewise that of Atilius (§2n. *ut*) at 6.8.5–6. **manceps conuenitur** 'they go to meet the agent'; for transitive *conuenire* see 1.5.11, 7.33.4, *OLD* 2a. **conuenitur . . . dantur . . . transitur:** a trio of passive, clause-final verbs for the tricolon (6~21~17 syllables). **in media basilica:** not even subtly. The court sat in the Basilica Julia, a large and busy building on the Via Sacra in the Forum (*LTUR* I 177–9, Richardson 1992: 52–3). **sportulae** 'hand-outs'. *sportula*, literally 'little basket', was by now the standard term for a 'dole' of food or cash (here the latter) from patron to client. It seems conventionally to have accompanied dinner (next n.). Claqueurs earn it in court at Quint. 11.3.131 (advocates who, when applauded, *ad librarios* ['secretaries'] *suos ita respiciunt ut sportulam dictare uideantur*) and Juv. 13.31–3 *clamore . . . | quanto Faesidium laudat uocalis agentem | sportula* 'as loudly as the vocal dole praises Faesidius mid-speech', but only P. describes it actually being paid out there. **quam in triclinio:** Martial several times refers to evening distribution of cash 'dole' (1.80.1 with Shackleton Bailey), sometimes implying that it occurred at dinner (e.g. 3.30.1, 12.29(26).13–14 with Gérard 1976: 180). Slater 2000 attempts an explanation involving public feasts, hard to swallow. **ex iudicio in iudicium:** between the four sessions (§1n. *centumuiralibus*). Retained by specific advocates, claqueurs did not need to stay for an entire case. It is not known how the basilica was physically divided (possible scenarios in Bablitz 2007: 63–8), but it was evidently easy to come and go. **transitur** 'they pass', impersonal passive.

5 inde 'so' (*OLD* 10a). **non inurbane** 'rather wittily', litotes. The same phrase introduces droll remarks at Cic. *ND* 3.50 and Sen. *Contr.* 10.*pr.*10. On *urbanitas*, the wit of a man about town, see Quint. 6.3.17, 21, 102–12, Ramage 1963, id. 1973 (pp. 132–43 on P.), Winniczuk 1966. **Σοφοκλῆς** 'Sophocles', punning on the tragedian's name and an etymology explained below. For some other proper-name puns see Starkie on Ar. *Ach.* 75 ὦ Κραναὰ πόλις. **uocantur; isdem:** between these two words all MSS present the phrase ἀπὸ τοῦ σοφῶς καὶ καλεῖσθαι 'from [calling] "bravo!" and getting invitations [to dinner]' (LSJ σοφός III, καλέω I.2, passive). For the notion of earning dinners by cheering, cf. Mart. 2.27, 6.48 *quod tam grande sophos clamat tibi turba togata,* | *non tu, Pomponi, cena diserta tua est*; Lucian *Rhet. praec.* 21 'let your friends keep jumping to their feet and pay back the price of their dinner'; and (in poetry recitals) Petr. 10.2 *ut foris cenares poetam laudasti, Anth. Pal.* 11.394 'in truth the best poet of all is the man who dines his audience'. The cry σοφῶς (lit. 'cleverly') appears in Petr. 40.1 and 6× in Martial (with disdain, e.g. 1.76.10 *perinane sophos*). The Greek explanation is therefore apposite, but it has long been suspected as an intrusion (Deufert 2008: 70–1); it is defended by Barwick 1936: 441–3 and retained by Mynors. In favour of Plinian authorship is (*i*) the obscurity of the pun (first explained by Barwick): the obvious etymology of Sophocles is 'famed for wisdom' (σοφ + κλεϜ), and many (still) mistake P. as punning on καλεῖν, active ('bravo-callers'); (*ii*) the clausula (cretic–ditrochee), especially given the near match with *inurbane* Σοφοκλεῖς *uocantur*, with σοφ- and *uocantur*/καλεῖσθαι (lit. 'to be called') in corresponding positions. On the other hand, (*i*) the etymology is explained by *Laudiceni*; (*ii*) P. nowhere else glosses in Greek (he uses single words and quotes phrases); (*iii*) 'ἀπὸ suggests an editor's hand' (S-W); (*iv*) excision leaves a tidy isocolon (*inde... uocantur;* | *isdem... Laudiceni*) of 14~15 syllables. The problem is finely balanced, but tips in favour of deletion. The presence of the words in all MS families shows only that interpolation was in the archetype (Intro. 38–9). **Laudiceni** 'applause-diners', i.e. those who applaud to earn their dinner: a nonce-formation from *laus* + *cena* playing on 'Laudiceni', inhabitants of Laudicea (Laodicea) in Syria, and so a match for the proper-name pun Σοφοκλεῖς. The parallel is helped by its being nominative, against P.'s usual rule (3.9.31 *legati nomen*, 4.23.4 *desidiae nomen*; Stout 1954: 89). *laudare* is a standard verb for the shouts of praise (cf. §6 *clamores*) that were the usual form of audience appreciation: e.g. §6 *laudandum*,

§8 *laudant, laudabitur,* §13 *laudatio,* Mart. 2.27.1, Quint. 10.1.18 (in §9n. *corrogaret*), 11.1.131 *laudationum.* Derivation from *laus* + *dicere* (Dunlap 1919) is unlikely, as is Zehnacker's from *canere* (that verb forms compounds in *-cen, -cinis*). **et tamen** 'and yet', as if the monikers Σοφοκλεῖς and *Laudiceni* should be a deterrent. Schuster, Mynors and others begin §6 here, illogically and against older editions (e.g. Cortius, Gierig). **foeditas:** first in Cicero; only here in P. **utraque lingua:** Greek and Latin were 'the' two languages in the Roman elite: e.g. 3.1.7 *scribit… utraque lingua lyrica,* Hor. *C.* 3.8.5 with Nisbet–Rudd, Quint. 1.1.12–14, Suet. *Claud.* 42.1. **notata** 'censured' (*OLD* 3c).

6 here '[only] yesterday' (2.7.1n.). An anecdote exemplifies, and lends topicality. **duo nomenclatores mei** 'two of my namers'. A *nomenclator* was a slave who reminded his master of the names of those he met (testimony in *OLD* 2a; *Pan.* 23.1 extols Trajan's ability to remember some names without one). P. was evidently well supplied. **(habent sane aetatem…)** '– and they are only as old as… –', with affirmatory *sane* (*OLD* 3a, Risselada 1998: 232–4); cf. 5.13.3 *erat sane.* The parenthesis (2.3.2n. *sed*) is perhaps in part to avoid two successive relative clauses (*qui habent aetatem eorum qui…*). P. stresses perhaps the absurdity of such young boys feigning to understand oratory (Merrill), perhaps the shamelessness of the *manceps* in preying on vulnerable youths. **eorum qui nuper togas sumpserint:** generic subj. Were they citizens, they would be among those who have 'recently taken togas', i.e. received the *toga uirilis,* making them about 14–16 years old (Marquart 1886: 127–33). The ceremony took place not on the boy's birthday but on the Liberalia (17 March) or various other days in the year (1.9.2 with S–W; Marquardt 1886: 124): hence *nuper.* **ternis denariis** 'three *denarii* each', a generous price for a lad and for a single speech (§4n. *ex*): Martial repeatedly (1.59.1, 3.7.1, 4.68.1 etc.) specifies a daily *sportula* of 100 *quadrantes,* about half that amount (1 *denarius* = 16 *asses* = 64 *quadrantes*); in 9.100 he scorns an offer of three *denarii* for a long day's trailing around Rome. **trahebantur** 'were being lured' (*OLD* 9c): the imperfect paints the scene (P., we may imagine, intervened to stop it). With gerund also at Livy 21.41.6. **tanti constat ut sis disertissimus** 'that is what it costs to be eloquent' (*OLD* tantum 3, gen. of price, *consto* 11a), epigrammatic paradox. For *disertissimus,* see 2.3.7n. **hōc pretio… implentur, hōc… colligitur, hōc… commouentur:** tricolon (17~10~12 syllables) with anaphora and gradation (*numerosa ~ ingens ~ infiniti*). *hoc pretio* (understood three times) is a standard abl. of price, varying *tanti.* **quamlibet** = *quamuis* (K–S II 446), 10× in P. It modifies only *numerosa.* **subsellia** were movable wooden benches, used by judges, advocates, litigants and audience (Bablitz 2007: 53). The number varied with requirements (*numerosa subsellia* again for the great case in 6.33.3). **ingens corona colligitur** 'a great circle gathers' (*OLD* corona 4, *colligo* 14) of bystanders; court sessions were open to all (6.33.3, Bablitz 2007: 57–8). Bablitz 2007: 70 estimates a total capacity of around 500 for each of the four courts, not including the upper storey (6.33.4).

infiniti clamores: §5n. *Laudiceni*. The court was not a quiet place: Mart. 4.8.2 *raucos . . . causidicos*, Sen. *Contr.* 9.*pr*.5 *inter fremitum consonantis turbae*, Quint. 12.5.6 *omnia clamoribus fremerent*, Juv. 13.31–3 (in §4n. *sportulae*). To receive *clamor* was an index of success (Cic. *Brut.* 326 *Hortensius . . . clamores faciebat*, Mart. 6.38.5–6, on Regulus), to which P. did not object in his own case: 9.23.1 (to Maximus) *frequenter agenti mihi euenit ut centumuiri . . . omnes repente . . . consurgerent laudarentque*. **commouentur** 'are elicited' (*OLD* 13a). **mesochorus** 'chorus leader'. μεσόχορος 'mid-chorus' is found in a single inscription, where it is used of the *coryphaeus*, leader of a dramatic chorus (LSJ s.v.; see also LSJ *Suppl.* μουσόχορος). P. uses it metaphorically of the leader of the claque, an urbane sideswipe at their theatricality: cf. Lucian *Rhet. praec.* 21 'make sure you have your own well tuned chorus [χορόν]', Tac. *An.* 1.16.3 *dux olim theatralium operarum* 'once leader of a theatre claque' with Goodyear, §4n. *actoribus*. The word reappears, now for a dinner entertainer, in Sid. *Ep.* 1.2.9 (just before a Plinian close, *ego non historiam sed epistulam efficere curaui*: cf. P. 1.1.1, 6.16.22).

7 enim explains *signum*. **apud** 'among' (*OLD* 13a). **intellegentes . . . audientes:** substantival (2.3.9n. *dicentis*). **nam:** many editions begin §8 here, against older numbering (cf. §5n. *et*). **plerique non audiunt, nec ulli magis laudant:** pointed isocolon (7~7 syllables). Contrast the 'resurrection' letter (intro.) 4.16.3 *sunt qui audiant* 'there are people who listen [after all]'.

8 si quando transibis . . . et uoles 'if ever (*quando*) you are passing through . . . and want', fut. (rather than fut. pf.) because simultaneous with the main clause (2.9.6n. *reposces*). **per basilicam:** whether through the central area where the courts met, or down the double aisles either side (cf. *LTUR* I 178). The basilica was a likely place to be passing through (§4n. *in*). **quomodo:** how well. **dicat** 'is pleading' (§2n. *cum*). **nihil est quod tribunal ascendas** 'there is no need [2.4.3n. *nec*] to go up onto the platform'. Elite attenders could watch proceedings from there (like Tiberius in Tac. *An.* 1.75.1, Suet. *Tib.* 33), filling it for big cases or a popular speaker: 6.33.4 *stipatum tribunal* (*pace* Bablitz 2007: 67–9); Cic. *Brut.* 290 *locus in subselliis occupetur, compleatur tribunal*. **praebeas aurem:** a choice equivalent for *audire* (*OLD praebeo* 1c, *TLL* II 1510.47–58). **facilis diuinatio** sc. *est*. **scito** 'you can be sure', the regular imperative form. **eum pessime dicere qui laudabitur maxime:** chiastic isocolon (8~8 syllables) for a second paradoxical *sententia*, ending the 'paragraph' (for such clustering of aphorisms, see Intro. 28). The last word fits the addressee (cf. 8.24.10 . . . *maximum debet*, ending a letter to a(nother) Maximus).

9 An apparent digression, setting up the proclamation that oratory is dead (§12). **morem induxit:** *OLD induco* 5a. **Larcius Licinus:** a Julio-Claudian orator (*PIR²* L 95) who co-authored with Asinius Gallus a *Ciceromastix* 'Scourge of Cicero'; he was known personally to the elder Pliny (3.5.17). If Cicero was the instantiation of proper oratory, this anti-Cicero is a good place to pin the blame for modern decline. **hactenus tamen ut** 'but only so far as to'. *hactenus . . . ut* (4× in P.) is common in Cicero; first here with *tamen*. **corrogaret** 'invite along', not pay. The verb usually has a critical tone (Manuwald on Cic. *Phil.* 3.20; Quint. 10.1.18 *a corrogatis laudantur etiam quae non placent*), as in 6.2.3 [*Regulus*] *audituros corrogabat*, even if P. (as Regulus' fellow pleader) was happy to benefit from it. **ita certe** 'at least that is how'. **Quintiliano praeceptore meo:** M. Fabius Quintilianus (*PIR²* F 59), Vespasian's public professor of rhetoric, celebrated neo-Ciceronian and author of *Institutio oratoria* 'Training of the Orator' (introductions in Kennedy 1972: 487–514, López 2007); his dates are conventionally given as AD 35–96, though neither is secure (Kaster 1995: 333–6). He also wrote a lost *De causis corruptae eloquentiae* (§12n. *pudet*). On P. and Quintilian (named again in 6.6.3: §10n. *assectabar*), see 2.3, 2.5, 7.9, Cova 2003; also S–W 86–9, Gamberini 1983: 12–55, Weische 1989: 376–7, Roca Barea 1992, ead. 1998, Riggsby 1998, Mastrorosa 2010. **audisse me memini:** P. always has pf. infin. with *memini*, like Quintilian (Cicero varies: Austin on Quint. 12.5.6; G–L §281 n.2; K–S I 703). The phrase implies that Quintilian is dead, and not recently (no fresh grief). P. similarly reaches one generation back for anecdotes at 1.13.3 *at hercule memoria parentum*, 3.20.5 *supersunt senes ex quibus audire soleo*.

10 narrabat ille introduces an unusually long quotation, further sign of Quintilian's privileged place. Only Tacitus gets to tell a tale similarly (9.23.2 *narrabat*). For the tense see 2.3.10n. *fatebatur*. **assectabar:** cf. Quint. 5.7.7 *Domitio Afro . . . quem adulescentulus senem colui*, referring to the period of 'apprenticeship' sometimes called *tirocinium fori* (*RE* II VI.2 1450): Quint. 10.5.19 *deligat quem sequatur, quem imitetur*, Tac. *D.* 2.1 *assectabar*, 20.4 *iuuenes . . . qui profectus sui causa oratores sectantur*, Powell on Cic. *Cato* 10. P. refers similarly to his studies with Quintilian at 6.6.3 *frequentabam*. **Domitium Afrum:** Afer (*PIR²* D 126, Rutledge 2001: 220–3) was a renowned orator of the mid-first century (Tac. *D.* 13.3); he appears again at 8.18.5. Quintilian (10.1.118, 12.11.3) accords his old mentor unqualified praise (contrast Tac. *An.* 4.52.4 *prosperiore eloquentiae quam morum fama fuit*, 4.66.1, 14.19). He died in AD 59 (Tac. *An.* 14.19); given Quint. 5.7.7 (previous n.) and 6.1.4 (Quint. was *adulescens* in AD 57), this anecdote probably dates from the late 50s. **grauiter et lente:** weighing his words, a style P. admires (*lente* only here as a stylistic comment; *grauiter* at 1.10.5 and often; see also 2.11.17n. σεμνῶς). **(hoc enim . . .):** a characteristic parenthesis (2.4.2n. *erat*). **actionis** 'delivery' (2.11.3n.). **audît:** pf., like *reticuit, factum est, quaesit* and therefore presumably *repetît, coepit, inquit* (for the short form see 2.1.5n. *male*, 2.20.3n. *ubi*). Historic present would be acceptable sequence after *diceret* (G–L §509 2.1.a), but alternation between present and pf. is hard to parallel (contrast the normal interplay of historic present and imperfect at 7.27.8–9 *respicit . . . stabat . . . exspectaret . . . significat etc.*). **ex proximo:** from another of the four *consilia* in session in the basilica. **immodicum insolitumque:** rhyming doublet. **clamorem:** §5n. *Laudiceni*, §6n. *infiniti*. **admiratus reticuit** 'he broke off in surprise'. The rhythm (four heavy syllables, then four light) is perhaps expressive. **ubi** 'when', especially common in vivid narratives (e.g. 6.16.20, 7.27.7). **repetit quod abruperat** 'picked up where he had left off' (lit. 'what he had broken off', 2.11.18n. *abrumperet*); for the tense see above on *audit* (even if present + plpf. is unexceptionable in P.: Kraut 1872: 37–8).

11 iterum ... coepit: the sequence of events repeats itself, now with terse concision (but affective anaphora of *iterum*). **clamor** *sc.* e.g. *fit, exoritur*, compressing §10 *audit ... clamorem*. For the ellipse, cf. 5.9.2 *silentium longum*, 7.33.8 *horror omnium* etc. (Kraut 1872: 47, Niemirska-Pliszczyńska 1955: 115–19) and e.g. Cic. *Att.* 4.3.3 *clamor lapides fustes gladii*; more expansively 2.11.4 *magna contentio, magni utrimque clamores*. **post silentium** varies §10 *ubi silentium factum est*. Such concision with *post* (3.5.11 *post solem*, 7.18.1 *post te*, 9.25.2 *post iudicium tuum*) is widespread but not new in imperial Latin: see Nisbet–Hubbard on Hor. *C.* 1.18.5 *post uina* (citing Hom. *Il.* 18.96 μεθ᾽ Ἕκτορα 'after [the death of] Hector'), Summers 1910: lxix–lxx, Goodyear on Tac. *An.* 1.68.5, K–S I 534–5. **coepit** = *repetit quod abruperat*, also pf. (§10n. *audit*). **idem tertio:** maximum brevity for the third telling. The iterations §10 *audit ... abruperat*, §11 *iterum ... coepit* and *idem tertio* run 40~20~5 syllables. **nouissime:** 2.11.5n. **quaesît:** the MSS show *quaesiuit* (α), *quaesiit* (β), *quaesit* (γ), which speaks for the last (2.1.5n. *male*) amidst this series of verbs in *-it* (§10n. *audit*); either that or *quaesiit* makes a common clausula. **responsum est** 'the answer came'. **intermissa causa** 'leaving off his plea'; *intermittere* implies only temporarily, but the anecdote suggests rather finality. **'centumuiri':** vocative. **'hoc artificium'** 'this profession', advocacy. **'perît'** 'is dead' (pf.); cf. Sen. *Marc.* 22.4 *exclamauit Cordus tunc uere theatrum perire*. A pregnant one-liner concludes the anecdote (2.1.9n. *etiam*). On the short form see 2.1.5n. *male*; here MSS and rhythm (resolved cretic + cretic) are unanimous.

12 quod alioqui perire incipiebat cum perisse Afro uideretur; nunc uero prope funditus exstinctum et euersum est 'in fact it was [only] beginning to die when Afer thought it was dead; *now* it is almost utterly devastated and destroyed'. Asyndetic antithesis (21~19 syllables), with the double contrast 'then/now' and 'beginning/near-complete decline'; *quod* is connecting relative (antecedent *hoc artificium*). For *alioqui* 'on the contrary', 'in fact' introducing a clause (first in Livy), see *TLL* I 1593.50–1594.26 and 2.12.2n. (*TLL* I 1594.72–3 seems wrong on this passage). **perire ... perisse:** for the polyptoton see 2.1.12n. *et*. One need not press *perire incipiebat* to find praise of Claudian/Neronian Rome; it does, however, implicitly reject a view that the advent of the principate caused the decline of oratory. P.'s pessimism (Lefèvre 2009: 102–5) is temporary: resurrection follows in 4.16 (intro.). **funditus exstinctum et euersum est:** *funditus euertere* is a favourite, *funditus exstinctum* a preserve, of Cicero, though the two participles are paired only here and in [Quint.] *Decl. mai.* 6.22 *exstinctus euersus*. The expansive redundance draws us out of the Afer anecdote, pins the invective on the present, and sets the grand tone for the following invective. Cf. Tac. *An.* 14.20.4 *patrios mores funditus euerti* (his only use of *funditus*). **pudet referre** 'I am ashamed to mention'. *pudor*, the (sexualised) shame (Gunderson 2000: 205–8) that modern orators do *not* feel, opens a gendered attack on debased, 'effeminate' practice. The need for virility is a given in Roman oratorical theory (Gleason 1995: 103–30, Gunderson 1998, id. 2000, Connolly 2007), but anxiety about effeminacy comes to the fore in the first century AD: cf. Sen. *Contr.* 1.*pr*.8 *cantandi saltandique obscena studia effeminatos tenent*, Sen. *Ep.* 114 (an attack on mincing Maecenas) and above all Quint. (Winterbottom 1964, id. 1998a, Gleason 1995: 113–21; passages quoted below), who presumably developed the theme in his lost *De causis corruptae eloquentiae* (Brink 1989): this letter may include even stronger Quintilianic overtones than we hear.   **quae . . . dicantur, quibus . . . excipiantur** 'what is said, and with what mincing delivery, what the shouts, and how effeminate, that greet it': two double indirect questions distribute P.'s satirical indignation between orators and audience in rhyming isocolon (14~15 syllables). The sentence has a mannered economy which presumably contrasts with the histrionics he is attacking.   **fracta** 'mincing, effeminate': *OLD* 4, Bramble 1974: 44 n.1, 76 n.2, Summers on Sen. *Ep.* 90.19 *infractos*, Courtney on Juv. 2.111 *fracta uoce*; (κατα)κεκλασμένος 'broken' is analogous (LSJ κατακλάω B.II.2). Such effeminacy is the preserve of the theatre (*Pan.* 54.1 *cum laudes imperatorum . . . effeminatis uocibus modis gestibus frangerentur*, Quint. 1.10.31 *musice . . . effeminata et impudicis modis fracta*), undesirable in an orator: cf. Quint. 1.11.1 (the pupil must not *femineae uocis exilitate frangi*), Tac. *D.* 18.5 *fractum atque elumbem* (Brutus' judgment of Cicero).   **pronuntiatione** 'delivery' (2.3.9n.).   **teneris:** similarly gendered (cf. 10.96.2, *OLD* 7), as Quint. 9.4.31 *teneram delicatamque modulandi uoluptatem*, 11.3.23 *molli teneraque uoce*, Tac. *D.* 26.3 *tenere dicere*. P., however, is attacking the audience: cf. Quint. 11.3.60 *et sunt quidam qui . . . etiam hac ubique audiendi quod aures mulceat uoluptate ducantur*, and, with violent sexualisation, Persius 1.19–21 (Bramble 1974: 78–9).   **excipiantur:** Merrill envisages the frenzied responsion of priests and worshippers of Cybele (cf. §13). Heroic clausula (2.3.3n. *narrat*).

13 plausus 'clapping', with double sense. Although vocal appreciation was the default in court (§5n. *Laudicem*), applause is also sometimes attested: Cic. *Or.* 236 *eloquens . . . admirationes clamores plausus . . . mouere debet*, Tac. *D.* 39.4 *oratori autem clamore plausuque opus est*; cf. 6.17.2 (an unappreciative audience) *non labra diduxerunt, non mouerunt manum*. Yet *plausus* are also the rhythmical claps of a dancer (Merrill) such as a bacchant (Ov. *Met.* 11.17 *tympanaque et plausus et Bacchei ululatus* with Bömer; Livy below on *ululatus*), making invective of a piece with the following *cymbala* and *tympana*, and in line with Quint. 12.10.73 *corruptum dicendi genus . . . bacchatur* ('bacchises'; cf. Cic. *Or.* 99 *bacchari*, 'Longinus' *On the sublime* 3.5 παρένθυρσον 'bogus bacchanalian').   **ac potius:** 2.13.9n.   **sola** repeats and varies *tantum*.   **cymbala et tympana:** instruments associated with the *galli*, self-castrated priests of the Phrygian goddess Cybele (Cat. 63.21, 29; Lucr. 2.618 with Bailey; *tympana* alone at Juv. 6.515, 8.176), and accordingly staples of invective against 'effeminates', e.g. Plaut. *Truc.* 611 *tympanotribam*, Cic. *Pis.* 22, V.

Aen. 9.619, Sen. *VB* 13.3, Juv. 9.62. Quintilian sets a precedent in oratorical critique, with irony as savage as P.'s here: 5.12.21 *nos qui oratorem studemus effingere non arma sed tympana eloquentiae demus?*, 9.4.142 (*syntona*, another percussion instrument), 11.3.59 (*cymbala*). See also Phil. *VS* 520 'play the *tympanum* like a bacchant'. **illis canticis** 'those songs' (dat. with *desunt*), a damning reference to the 'sing-song' style (*uitium ... cantandi, modulatio scaenica*) condemned at length by Quint. 11.3.57–60 as well as by Isaeus (2.3.1n. *Isaeum*); cf. *OLD canticum* 3 and Tac. *D.* 26.3 *cantari*. **ululatūs** 'shrieks', specifically feminine wailing, frequent of bacchants (Ov. *F.* 4.186 with Bömer); Mart. 5.41.3 has it of a *gallus*, Cic. *Leg.* 2.39 of actors; cf. Cic. *Or.* 27 ('Asianic' orators) *inclinata ululantique uoce ... canere*. The effeminacy of actors is commonplace; P. extends it to the courtroom and to the audience. For the combination with *cymbala* and *tympana*, cf. Livy 39.8.8 and 39.10.7, on the Bacchanalia. **quidem** 'certainly', contrasting *ululatus* with *plausus*, but also extending the claim indirectly made by the previous phrase, that the courtroom is only one step away from being a show and/or rave (cf. 2.13.7n. *epistulas*). *Contra* Ludewig 1891: 68, Solodow 1978: 81 (overlooking *tantum*). (**neque enim ...**) justifies *ululatus* (2.4.2n. *erat*). **theatris quoque indecora** '[which would be] unseemly even in theatres', a compendious final sting, capping Quint. 2.2.10 *indecora et theatralis* (students' rowdy praise of a declaiming colleague). On the noise of theatrical crowds see Hor. *Ep.* 2.1.200–1 *nam quae peruincere uoces | eualuere sonum referunt quem nostra theatra?*, and for claqueurs there see 7.24.7 (in §4n. *auditores*) and Cameron 1976: 234–49. Theatres furnish another disdainful comparison in 4.25.5 (a senatorial debate) *ista ludibria scaena et pulpito digna*. **large supersunt** 'are in plentiful supply' (*OLD supersum* 7), in antithesis with *desunt*; the phrase again at 3.2.2.

14 Nos tamen: a closing turn to P. himself (in authorial plural: 2.3.8n. *nosque*) to excuse his continued involvement in such proceedings. **adhuc** hints at future change. **utilitas amicorum** 'the needs of my friends' (*OLD utilitas* 1b); cf. Cic. *Lael.* 75 *utilitates amicorum*. **ratio aetatis** = *aetas* (as 3.1.11, Cic. *Leg. Man.* 1 *uitae meae rationes*: see 2.5.8n. *in* for the periphrasis), i.e. P.'s relative youth. He dreams of retirement at 3.1.11–12 and in 4.23.4 *quando mihi licebit ... ?* (beside 4.24, a nostalgic letter on the centumviral court) – 'but his zeal in this direction is somewhat academic in character' (Merrill). **moratur ac retinet:** the couplet implies reluctance (cf. §1 *distringor*). **ne forte ... uideamur** 'that I would perhaps seem ...', sc. if I were to give up. **indignitates:** like Cicero, P. likes plurals of abstract nouns, e.g. 2.18.5 *offensas ... simultates*, 1.4.4 *nouitatibus*, 8.16.1 *infirmitates* (Kraut 1872: 3, Lagergren 1872: 89). **laborem fugisse uideamur:** cf. 3.1.12 *inertiae crimen effugero*. For the clausula, see §2n. *expresse*. **sumus tamen solito rariores** 'nevertheless, I am there less than usual' (*OLD solitus* 4a, *rarus* 4), with ellipse of e.g. *ibi* (cf. Tac. *An.* 2.57.3 *rarus in tribunali*, 14.56.3 *rarus per urbem*) or e.g. *in aduocationibus* (cf. Sen. *Ben.* 2.23.3 *rariores in ... officis sunt*). Assuming this is AD 97, P. gives no hint of his imminent and pragmatic break from all court work in Jan. 98, or that his heralded 'retirement' lasts only until book 4 (intro.): the effect is bleak. Beutel 2000: 253–8 strangely reads the letter as a call to P.'s fellow senators *not* to give up on the centumviral court. **quod initium est gradatim desinendi** 'and that is the beginning of gradual cessation' (*OLD gradatim* 2a), probably generalising for the close. A flat ending, except for a light epigrammatic twist (and reprise of §12 *perire incipiebat*) in the conceit *initium . . . desinendi*. That verb is a fitting final word (Herrnstein Smith 1968: 172–82), also in 7.27.16, but perhaps too obvious a closural device for frequent or ostentatious use.

15

How do you like your new land? My mother's is doing less than well, but I mustn't complain.

This brief grumble about country estates, the shortest letter of the book, makes a complementary pair with 2.8 (complaints about the city) and a strong contrast with 2.17, the long, sunny celebration of P.'s Laurentine villa (slightly varying the juxtaposition of longest and shortest letters in 1.20–21). It also makes an apt tail-piece to 2.14, a rustic breath after the tarnish of the courts (cf. 2.11.23, a coda – there within the same letter – to the Priscus trial), also exhibiting dissatisfaction, but pulling P. up after the indulgent pessimism of 2.14.14.

Language suggests intimacy, with a Ciceronian tone (§1n. *quomodo*, §2n. *occallui*), but the note is minutely structured. Its two parts, flagged by §1 *te* and §2 *me*, match closely in word-count (26~23), more closely still in syllables (50~53), and are sealed by two matching *sententiae* (17~16 syllables): the product is one of P.'s 'veritable epigrams in prose' (Guillemin 1929: 150).

VALERIANO: probably Julius Valerianus (*PIR*² I 612, Birley 2000a: 66), a senator (5.4.4 with S–W) who receives a pair of letters in book 5 on the trial of Tuscilius Nominatus. 5.4 (also next-but-one before a great villa letter) promises *res parua* [a reminder of 2.15?] *sed initium non paruae* (5.4.1), a promise on which 5.13 delivers. His name lends an audible frame to this short letter (. . . **VALE**).

1 Quomodo . . . ? quomodo . . . ? placent . . . ? tricolon of questions (11~7~11 syllables), or rising bicolon (since the third question only extends the second). **Quomodo te ueteres Marsi tui?** *sc. tractant* (from §2), 'how is your old Marsian place treating you?' The verb, conversationally elided here, personifies (cf. 1.3.1 *quid agit Comum, tuae meaeque deliciae? . . . possident te . . . ?*, Cic. *Fam.* 12.20 *uilla pusilla iniquo animo feret*, 2.17.2n. *decem*) and inverts its common meaning 'manage (property)' (*OLD tracto* 6). Like e.g. *Baiae* or *Sabini*, the plural *Marsi* is used for a people, for their region, and by further extension for a property there: so P. refers to his 'Etruscan' villa at Tusculum Tiberinum as *Tusci mei* (5.6.1, 45) and *Tusci* (3.4.2, 4.1.3 etc.); see Mayor on 3.4.2, Shackleton Bailey 1989: 140 on Mart. 7.31.11 (*pace* Nisbet–Hubbard 1978: 300). The region in question is around the Fucine Lake in what is now the Abruzzo (Letta 1972). *ueteres* (*OLD* 2) refers

to long ownership (vs *noua emptio*).   **emptio noua** 'your new purchase', chiastic
with *ueteres Marsi tui*; supply *tractat. emptio* (*OLD* 2a) is abstract for concrete: cf.
1.24.2 *mala emptio semper ingrata* (NB *gratum* below), Cic. *Fam.* 7.23.2.   **placent
agri, postquam tui facti sunt?** 'do you like the land, now it is yours?', *OLD
ager* 3 (plural at e.g. Cic. *Fam.* 7.20.2, Tac. *An.* 4.6.5); for omission of *-ne* see 2.8.1n.
studes; for *postquam* see 2.1.11n. The virtual repetition of the preceding question
sets up the following *sententia*.   **rarum id quidem** *sc. est*: cf. 2.7.3 *rarum id in
iuuene*. P.'s sole use of *id quidem* (*OLD quidem* 1c), a common marker of asseveration
whether conversational (e.g. V. *Ecl.* 9.37) or high-oratorical (e.g. Livy 25.33.6).
The cynicism casts a shadow over what looked set to be a jolly letter.   **nihil
enim aeque gratum est adeptis quam concupiscentibus** 'for nothing
is as attractive once you have acquired it as when you desire it' (lit. '. . . to those
who have acquired as to those desiring'), *OLD aeque* 3a, *gratus* 3a (+ dat.), 2.3.7n.
concupisco; for the substantival participles see 2.3.9n. *dicentis*. The *sententia*, a variant
on 'the grass is always greener' (e.g. Ov. *Ars* 1.348 *capiant animos plus aliena suis*, Petr.
93.1–2 . . . *quicquid quaeritur, optimum uidetur* with Habermehl; Otto 1890: 13, Tosi
1991: 581), resembles Sen. *Ep.* 15.11 (on worldly honours) *sperantibus meliora quam
assecutis*; where Seneca moralises (similarly *Tranq.* 12.1, Cic. *Tusc.* 5.54), P. accepts
human weakness as fact. The opposite in 3.2.6 *quamuis enim ista non appetat, tam
grate tamen excipit quam si concupiscat*. This letter presents a particularly clear case
of the tendency for *sententiae* to gravitate to the midpoint of letters, as to their end
(Gallent-Kočevar 1933).

2 me 'as for me . . . ': first position marks the contrast, splitting the letter in half
(intro.).   **praedia materna:** estates inherited from his mother, from where
(we imagine) P. has news just in. They were around P.'s native Comum, where
he had several (cf. 7.11.5 *ex praediis meis . . . exceptis maternis paternisque*). Plinia, sister of the elder Pliny, is seen alive in the Vesuvian drama of AD 79 (6.16.21,
6.20) and mentioned at 4.19.7. She has been dead some time (*longa patientia*).   **materna . . . tractant, delectant . . . materna:** chiasmus with *redditio* (2.2.1n. *irascor*) and rhyming verbs, typically juxtaposed (cf. 9.21.4 *iterum rogabo,
impetrabo iterum*).   **parum commode tractant** 'are treating me less than kindly'
(2.1.5n. *parum*); *commode* can be just 'well' (e.g. 1.9.5 *parum commode scribo*), but lends
itself to the personification in *tractant* (*OLD commode* 4). The (brief) 'unkindness' –
presumably poor returns (2.4.3n. *nescio*) – makes a sharp contrast with the ever-
obliging *Laurentinum* (2.17.2n. *decem*).   **delectant tamen ut materna** 'but they
give me pleasure by virtue of being my mother's' (*OLD ut* 21a). Similar *pietas* in
7.11.5 (above on *praedia*).   **et alioqui** 'and besides' (2.9.1n.).   **longa patientia
occallui** 'I have acquired a thick skin through long endurance'; cf. 6.2.10 *leuiora
incommoda [sunt] quod assueui*. Figurative *occallesco* (*OLD* 2) is used personally only
here and Cic. *Att.* 2.18.4 *angor equidem, sed iam prorsus occallui*.   **habent hunc
finem assiduae querellae, quod queri pudet** 'the end result of unremit-
ting complaints is that one is ashamed to complain' (*OLD finis* 13, *quod* 2b),

asyndetically explaining *occallui*. Chiasmus and paronomasia (*habent . . . querellae* ~ *queri pudet*) in falling bicolon (11~5 syllables): the brusque *quod queri pudet* proves its point, sharply curtailing letter and complaint. The cretic–iamb to close is relatively rare but not suspect (ten other letters, e.g. 1.18, 4.13, 6.9–10; none in books 7–9; cf. Intro. 29 n.164). The whole *sententia* (16 syllables) closely matches that of §1 (17 syllables). Self-conscious imposition of an end is a topos of longer letters (2.11.23 *hic finis*, 3.9.27 *hic erit epistulae finis, re uera finis*; 2.5.13n. *finem*), making for incongruity here: so too the oxymoron *finem assiduae*, since P.'s complaints comprised just three, understated words (*parum commode tractant*) – unlike Ovid's endless epistolary laments (cf. Ov. *Ex P.* 3.7.2 *iamque pudet uanas fine carere preces* and 3.4.45–6, next n.). Seen, however, as a tailpiece to the lengthy exasperation of 2.14 (NB 2.14.12 *pudet referre . . .*), P.'s apology can well be taken at face value; cf. Martial's placing of a short epigram of apology or defence after a long one (*Epig.* 1.109–110, 3.82–3, 6.64–5, 8.28–9, with Canobbio 2008: 170–3). **assiduae querellae:** cf. Aratus apud Cic. *Diu.* 1.14 *assiduas . . . querellas*, Ov. *Ex P.* 3.4.45–6 *assidue domini meditata querelas | . . . lyra*, Sen. *Ben.* 3.4.1 *assidue queritur*.

16

You remind me that Acilianus' codicil is not legally valid. I know, but I consider a dead man's wishes as good as the law, and my way of honouring them is quite legal.

Besides writing a will, Acilianus had made one or more legacies in a codicil, without having properly ratified it. P., who is one of the heirs, finds a way to respect both the law (which deems the codicil void) and the wishes of the deceased, by accepting his inheritance and then gifting money to the intended beneficiaries. Thus self-interest gives way to exemplary generosity, and P.'s moral, that the wishes of the dead matter more than the letter of the law, is upheld. The sequence 'testamentary fairness – villa' (2.16–17) is inverted in 5.6–7 (§2n. *ut*).

If the deceased is the Acilianus whom P. recommended to Mauricus in 1.14 as a husband for his niece (§1n.), the reader of books 1–2 learns of his death, sees P. duly rewarded for his earlier patronage and finds the villa letter framed by two letters concerned with Mauricus and the family of his brother, the 'Stoic martyr' Arulenus Rusticus (2.18.intro.).

The letter develops in a smooth sequence, building in the first half (57 words, up to §2 *tuerer*) to P.'s golden rule about *defunctorum uoluntates*, in the second (62 words) to a *sententia* on the compatibility of that rule with the law.

On inheritance see 2.4.intro., adding (on 2.16) Spruit 1973: 18–21, Tellegen 1982: 30–47.

ANNIANO: the MSS are divided between ANNIO (β, with *Annium* in the index of B), accepted by Mynors and in Anglophone scholarship since, and an otherwise unknown ANNIANO (αγ, preferred by Schuster and Zehnacker). In favour of the former is the thematic bond with 3.6 and 5.1, both to Annius Severus (*PIR²* A 689).

But the headings to those letters give his name as Severo, making Annio here anomalous (2.1n. C. Plinivs); for other Severi the *cognomen* is routine (3.18, 4.28, 6.27, 9.22), except for Catilio in 1.22 and 3.12. Corruption of Anniano to Annio also seems the more likely in light of the MSS' tendency to abbreviate addressees (e.g. 1.15 Septio in B¹, 3.8 Sveto in F); β is similarly guilty in the preceding 2.15 (Valerio/*Ad Valerium*), as is γ in 2.11 (Arrio), and in general β is less accurate in its names (e.g. 2.7 *Ad Magnum*, 2.18 Martio/Mvrcio/*Ad Marcium*, though α sins at e.g. 2.8 Cannino). Annio is thus hard to defend in textual terms (best, perhaps, by supposing that it was corrupted under the influence of 2.15 Valeriano or §1 *Aciliani*). Annianus (or Annius), in any case, is unlikely to be Pliny's co-heir here (*pace* Tellegen 1982: 31: contrast §1 *qui me ex parte instituit heredem* with 5.7.1 *qui nos reliquit heredes*).

1 Tu quidem prepares the contrast with §2 *sed ego* (2.1.7n. *et*); cf. 7.14.1, 10.61.1. **pro cetera tua diligentia** 'in keeping with your usual assiduity' (lit. 'assiduity in other matters'), *OLD pro* 16b. Cf. 3.8.1 *facis pro cetera reuerentia . . .*, 8.21.6, *Pan.* 39.4, Fronto *M. Ant.* 3.4.1 (p. 102.9 vdH²) *pro cetera erga me beniuolentia tua*. A double-edged compliment, since Annianus is telling P. the obvious (below), with a possible implication of penny-pinching (2.4.2n. *non*). **admones:** a standard opening: 2.19.1 *hortaris*, 4.17.1 *et admones et rogas*, 5.8.1 *suades*; 2.5.1n. *efflagitatam*. **codicillos** 'codicil', pl. for sg. (*OLD* 4), a supplementary document commonly used to avoid the trouble involved in writing a new will (2.20.8n. *signatum*). It could add *fideicommissa* 'trusts' (*OCD* s.v.) and *legata* 'legacies' (2.20.5n. *legatum*) but not *hereditates* (the title of heir and a proportion of the estate): cf. 2.20.5, 6.31.7, Tac. *An.* 16.17.5, *RE* iv.1 174–9, Johnston 1988: 134–45, *BNP* 'codicilli'. **Aciliani:** probably the Minicius Acilianus of 1.14 (intro.): the name is rare, and P. uses only the *cognomen* at this second mention (despite the change of addressee; 2.11.22n. *Regulo*). **me ex parte instituit heredem** 'appointed me heir in part'. *ex parte* (*OLD pars* 3c) may mean 'half' (Cowan), but it is hard to be sure (Goodyear on Tac. *An.* 2.48.1). It was normal to nominate multiple heirs, not just family. Acilianus was perhaps childless (cf. Champlin 1991: 142–4); certainly he lacked a mature child if 1.14 concerned his first marriage. P. notes receipt of inheritances in 3.6.1, 4.10.1, 5.1.1, 5.7.1, 7.11.1, 10.75.2, 10.104, of legacies at 5.1.1 and 11, and (in general) 7.20.6. The specified sums alone total 1,450,000 sesterces (Duncan-Jones 1982: 21). **pro non scriptis habendos** 'should be treated as not having been written' (*OLD pro* 9a). **non sunt confirmati testamento** 'is not ratified in the will' (*OLD confirmo* 9). Codicils had to be ratified in the will, as anyone knew (§2 *quod ius . . .*); Johnston 1988: 135–6. A formula like *si quid codicillis . . . reliquero, ita ualere uolo* (Celsus *Dig.* 29.7.18) left room for doubt whether codicils written *before* the will were included, perhaps the problem in Acilianus' case (Tellegen 1982: 35–43). The heavy rhythm, to which *testamentum* lends itself (cf. Hor. *Sat.* 2.5.85), suits the topic (2.20.6n. *pueri*). The MSS are split between *sunt* (αγ) and *sint* (β); both are good Latin (2.3.8n. *uiderat*), and one could argue either way for precise or varied repetition in §3 *non sint confirmati testamento*.

2 ne mihi quidem ignotum est, cum sit iis etiam notum qui nihil aliud sciunt: P. positions himself (not perhaps without acerbity) as an amateur in jurisprudence: cf. 4.10.2 *contuli cum peritis iuris*, 5.7.2 *uereor quam in partem iuris consulti quod sum dicturus accipiant*, 8.14.1. Similar self-depreciation in 3.6.1 (on artistic taste) *fortasse in omni re, in hac certe perquam exiguum sapio*.   **propriam quandam legem mihi dixi** 'I have laid down for myself a kind of private law': *OLD proprius* 3, *quidam*[1] 3a, *dico* 10a; *lex* can mean 'rule' (*OLD* 5c), but it is framed against *ius* and prepares the *sententia* in §4. For the clausula see 2.6.4n. *magno*.   **ut defunctorum uoluntates, etiam si iure deficerentur, quasi perfectas tuerer** 'to uphold the wishes of the deceased as if valid, even if they lack (full) legality': *OLD ut* 39b, *ius* 1d, *deficio* 2a, *quasi* 1a, *tueor* 7b; for *perfectus* 'legally valid', see *TLL* x.1 1373.10–29, 1379.51–64; for the tenses, 2.5.2n. *deberem*. The crux of the letter, ending its first half (57 words of 120), with *defunctorum . . . deficerentur* ~ *perfectas* underlining the point. P. makes the same point at 4.10.3 *defunctorum uoluntatem, quam bonis heredibus intellexisse pro iure est* ('. . . is as good as law') and 5.7.2 *mihi autem defuncti uoluntas . . . antiquior iure est* (each following the longest letter of its book, making chiasmus, intended or not, with 2.16–17). He thus lays claim to *humanitas* – a claim which depends on the concession that Acilianus' codicil was not defensible in law (*pace* Tellegen 1982: 43–7) – and to a Ciceronian respect for natural over human law (Cic. *Leg.* 1, esp. 1.42). In fact (as P. well knew) the conflict of *scriptum* and *uoluntas* ('letter' and 'spirit') was a stock debating point (cf. Quint. 7.6; Bonner 1949: 47–8), not least in the centumviral court (e.g. the *querela inofficiosi testamenti* of 6.33, and Quint. 7.6.9–11). For the heroic clausula *deficerentur* see 2.3.3n. *narrat*.   **autem** 'furthermore' (*OLD* 3a).   **manu scriptos:** this was no legal requirement, though the will of Longinus Castor (late 1c. AD) ratifies only codicils τῇ χειρί μου γεγραμμένα 'written in my own hand' (Tellegen 1982: 36, 41).

3 licet: concessive (2.3.9n.).   **non sint confirmati testamento:** P. 'quotes' Annianus (§1), to trump him with an equally spondaic *ut confirmati obseruabuntur*.   **ut** 'as if' (*OLD* 8a).   **praesertim cum:** introduces a further point, bridging to *nam* (2.3.6n. *senibus*).   **delatori locus non sit** 'there is no scope [*OLD locus* 14a] for a legal challenge' (lit. 'denouncer'). A will could be contested by *delatio* 'denunciation', initiating a trial (as e.g. Quint. 9.2.73–4); if it was found invalid, the estate was confiscated by the treasury of Saturn (2.8.2n. *angor*; it was properly called *aerarium populi Romani*), i.e. the public purse, with a portion going as reward to the *delator*. In Acilianus' case there is no risk of that, as P. will explain (§4); it is not his style to be taken to court (cf. 5.1.6, where he is specifically excluded from an action). The fact that Trajan curbed excesses of *delatio* (*Pan.* 34–5, focusing on inheritance: Giovannini 1987: 221–6) is at most tangentially relevant to the point of law here.

4 si uerendum esset ne quod ego dedissem populus eriperet 'if there were a risk that the state would confiscate what I gave'; *dedissem*, subjunctive by attraction (G–L §663.1), stands for *dedero* in primary sequence (2.11.9n. *si praesens*).

For *populus eriperet*, see §3n. *delatori*, 2.11.19 *aerario inferenda*, 4.12.3 *praefecti aerari populo uindicabant* '... claimed for the state'. S-W 185 detects a hint that P. has finished his stint as prefect of the treasury (2.14.intro.): perhaps so, but the (official) phrasing hardly excludes his being one of the confiscating *praefecti* (would he let us see him bending rules for private reasons?). **cunctantior fortasse et cautior:** varied at 9.13.6 *erat enim cunctantior cautiorque*; cf. Livy 22.12.12 *pro cunctatore . . . pro cauto*, Amm. 14.10.14 and 31.12.6 *cunctator et cautus*, not compelling evidence that Ammianus knew Pliny (Adkin 1998: 594, against Cameron 1967: 422; see 2.6.5n. *quibus*); for *cunctantior* cf. (only) Lucr. 3.192. **esse deberem** 'I would have to be'. **cum uero liceat heredi donare quod in hereditate subsedit** 'but since an heir is free to give away the residue of his inheritance' (*OLD subsido* 3b 'come to rest'). Heirs paid legacies and other charges (2.4.2n. *famam*) out of their share: hence 'residue'. P. will not invite legal challenge by disbursing the legacy or legacies specified in the codicil, but will give the same amount(s) as a free gift – technically different, but identical in result (on gifts see 2.4.3n. *ne*). P.'s own right to inherit, which came with his *ius trium liberorum* (2.13.8n. *trium*) in AD 98 (10.2), seems to be immaterial (*pace* Tellegen 1982: 36), given the generalising *heredi* (not *mihi*). **nihil est quod obstet illi meae legi, cui publicae leges non repugnant** 'there is nothing to impede that law of mine, with which the laws of the state do not conflict', *OLD repugno* 7. A final bicolon (12~10 syllables; 11~10 if P. heard or wrote *nil*) with chiasmus (ABCD~CDAB: *nihil obstet . . . meae legi ~ publicae leges . . . non repugnant*; the varied lexis sets the polyptoton *legi . . . leges* in relief) reworks the conceit of §2 *propriam quandam legem* for a triumphant final proof. P.'s selflessness is left implicit: not so 4.10.4 . . . *heredes* [*sc. nos*] *bene elegit*, 5.1.12–13, 7.11.8.

17

This letter describes, or rather recreates in words, P.'s suburban villa on the coast at Laurentum, his primary winter residence outside Rome. At 1,083 words it is the longest letter of book 2 and the fourth longest in the *Epistles*. Together with 5.6 (the Etruscan villa and P.'s longest letter, at 1,520 words), the *Laurentinum* dominates the collection and rivals even the letters on Vesuvius (6.16, 6.20) and Christians (10.96–7) for scholarly interest. Much effort has been spent on reconstructing the villa in models and plans, as well as imitating it in architecture (du Prey 1994), on matching P.'s account with archaeological evidence of villas (Förtsch), and on identifying its location (below). Though we have no reason to doubt that P.'s villa really existed, to read 2.17 purely for documentary value misses much of its meaning: this is, above all, a textual villa.

It is a challenge, however, to modern readers. Apart from the considerable difficulties of language, the question arises, why lavish so many words on describing a house? Why make 2.17 and 5.6 equal to or even weightier than the great 'trial' letters? Villas played a large part in elite Roman life, both for agriculture and for pleasure (see *OCD* 'villa', adding Purcell 1995, Bodel 1997, Frazer 1998). The suburban villa in particular, within a day's travel from Rome (Champlin 1982), was central to politicking, leisure and literature, as Cicero's letters and philosophical works amply demonstrate (Agache 2008), the 'not-quite-absolute retreat' from the urban bustle that allowed a man to be himself (Hor. *Ep.* 1.14.1 *mihi me reddentis agelli* with Mayer 1994: 46–7). The importance of the villa is attested by the extensive moralising discourse around it (Edwards 1993: 137–72), in which property became not just a source of *dignitas* (Cic. *Att.* 1.13.6; Marzano 2007: 15–33) but representative, metonymic even, of its owner: *la villa, c'est l'homme même* (e.g. Plautus *Mostellaria* 84–156 with Leach 1969). This is clear to see in Seneca's villa letters (Henderson 2004a): in *Ep.* 12 house and Seneca have aged in tandem, in *Ep.* 86 Scipio's villa instantiates the *mores* of a statesman of old, and Vatia's villa in *Ep.* 55 turns to parable on its owner's misspent retirement. Statius' lavish descriptions of villas in *Siluae* 1.3 and 2.2 (Newlands 2002: 119–98; Van Dam and Newlands on *Silu.* 2.2) double as encomia of their owners, emblematised in the words *dominique imitantia mores* (*Silu.* 2.2.29). Martial too praises owners through villas, in his case with a more Horatian ethic of simplicity, in 3.58 and 4.64 (Deremetz 2008).

P. in turn makes the villa, and with it 'villa as owner', central to his autobiographical project. The resulting picture conforms with the tension running throughout the *Epistles*: a parade of proud moderation by a writer unashamed to let us glimpse him putting *ego* front and centre. It is significant that 5.6 ends with celebration not just of the *gaudium* the Etruscan villa affords but also its *gloria* (5.6.46): P.'s self-display is directed as ever towards posterity as he builds his *monumentum aere perennius* (Hor. *C.* 3.30.1). In contrast to Seneca's villas, breathing antiquity and senility, and the half-built edifices of Cicero *Ad Quintum fratrem* 3.1.1–6, these are captured in bloom, preserved like their owner at their apogee. Yet moderation, as ever, is key: unlike the lavish villas of the *Siluae*, the *Laurentinum* (in its epistolary form) is devoid of rich adornment; instead, P. presents a long series of rooms and spaces defined mostly by their orientation and views (§6n. *altera*). Alongside the luxury of *otium* (Leach 2003; 2.2.2nn.), the most ostentatious consumption is verbal: what marks this villa out, besides sheer size, is the extreme (yet economical) elegance of P.'s language, an urbane textualising of suburban bliss.

Like the villa, the letter avoids exuberance – no rhetorical declamation here (Gamberini 1983: 295) – and presents a façade of studied elegance, combining choice diction with small-scale but mannered phrasing, *simplex munditiis* (Hor. *C.* 1.5.5). As Guillemin 1928 and 1929: 117–27 first demonstrated, allusivity plays an unusually prominent role, targeted especially towards Seneca (notes on §§4 *egregium*, 5 *hilare*, 6 *altera*, 9 *suspensus*, 12 *calidissimo*, 27 *quod non*) and Statius (on §§1 *miraris*, 5 *mare*, *leuiter*, *quasi*, *longinquos*, 6 *quod*, 11 *spatiosa*, *natantes*, 12 *possidet*, 13 *quod*, 16 *prope*, 20 *re uera*, 24 *studiis*). This letter would become in turn a prime allusive target for P.'s epistolary epigone, Sidonius Apollinaris, who treats 2.17

and 5.6 to a witty reworking in his *Ep.* 2.2 (notes on §§8 *non legendos*, 9 *dormitorium*, 10 *plurimo*, 11 *balnei, baptisteria*, 12 *calidissimo*, 14 *quamquam*, 16 *cryptoporticus, prope*, 22 *andron*). P. emulates neither the censoriousness of Seneca nor Statius' extravagant play with myth, luxury and the conquest of nature, but constructs his own *Romanitas* of moderation between luxury and asceticism. The villa of Pollius Felix (Stat. *Silu.* 2.2) is the most insistent intertext: of similar length to our letter, Statius' poem too leads the reader through environs, house (empty of inhabitants) and inner sanctum to a climactic presentation of the owner(s) themselves. Despite their ethical differences, P. shares Statius' aesthetic of nature mediated and harnessed by human ingenuity (§5n. *Africo*, §5n. *quasi*), and the literary aesthetic too: it is no accident that this can fairly be called the most poetic letter of the book. (On P.'s closeness to Statius, often forgotten, see Vollmer 1898: 26–7, Guillemin 1929: 125–7, Schuster 1951: 450, Syme 1958: 97.)

'Poetic' can be a misleading term given the ongoing domestication of poetic vocabulary in prose (e.g. Hine 2005), but it is a label P. would surely not eschew for this letter: *descriptiones locorum . . . non historice tantum sed prope poetice prosequi fas est* (2.5.5), and much of his diction finds parallels only in poetry. Such descriptions fell within ancient concepts of 'ecphrasis', the description of a real or imaginary place, work of art or other object (widely discussed: e.g. Bartsch–Elsner 2007, Webb 2009, Squire 2013). Ecphrasis was at home in oratory as well as in poetry, but P. clearly sets his villa letters in the latter context when he ends the second (5.6.43) with explicit comparison to two canonical epic ecphrases, the shields of Achilles (*Iliad* 18) and Aeneas (*Aeneid* 8). Wonder is a hallmark of such descriptions (§1n. *miraris*), though P.'s version has sufficient imperfection (§15n. *malignior*, §25n. *deficitur*) to protect it from a fall into fantasy. Fundamental to ecphrasis is the blurring of boundaries between the described object and the describing text, and 2.17 is no exception (McEwen 1995): letter and villa have merged into an indivisible work of art, with P. as master textual architect.

A further reason why villas are the site of such intense literary art in 2.17 and 5.6 lies in the deep conceptual bond of 'villa' and composition that underpins the *Epistles*. P. establishes it early, in 1.3 (Hoffer 1999: 29–44), and our first encounter with the *Laurentinum* is a paean to the inspiring *otium* it affords (1.9.5–6): *nulla spe, nullo timore sollicitor, nullis rumoribus inquietor: mecum tantum et cum libellis loquor. o rectam sinceramque uitam! o dulce otium honestumque ac paene omni negotio pulchrius! o mare, o litus, uerum secretumque* μουσεῖον ['shrine of the Muses'], *quam multa inuenitis, quam multa dictatis!* Similarly, 1.22.11 finds P. looking forward to an escape from Rome: *qua* [*sollicitudine*] *liberatus Laurentinum meum, hoc est libellos et pugillares studiosumque otium, repetam*; that the *Epistles* says so little about his urban *domus* on the Esquiline (3.21.5) may be telling in this regard. At 2.2.2 he is enjoying *studia* and *desidia* in a villa which we have no reason not to identify as this one (2.2.2n. *ad*). By the time we reach 2.17, then, the Laurentine villa is not just strongly associated with, but actually defined as, the pleasure of literary endeavour (cf. also 4.6.2 *ibi enim plurimum scribo*). Although the Etruscan villa is hinted at in 1.4.1 (S-W ad loc.), the reader is not introduced to it until book 3, and then gradually (3.4.2 *in Tuscos*, 3.19; 4.1 names the town; the villa gets its full showing in 5.6), while we wait until 9.7 to hear about the Comum properties implied or mentioned in passing in 1.3, 2.8 and 2.15. For the reader of the collection, then, suburban Laurentum, primarily a winter residence (§3n. *tepore*), turns out to be a junior partner to the great *Tusci* (§29n. *uillulae*) with its deeper, remoter tranquillity. Yet in books 1–2 it stands proud as the very instantiation of *otium*. The importance of both major villas is underlined at the end of the collection: P. concludes book 9 with a pair of letters describing his daily routine in summer at *Tusci* (9.36) and in winter at Laurentum (9.40), emphasising literary composition and so ending the *Epistles*, like the tour here, in the *penetralia* of Plinian *studia* (§24n. *in*). Although 2.17 has made way for the yet grander 5.6, this closing, chiastic reprise leaves us with our last sight of P. back on the Laurentine shore, dictating away into oblivion.

Within book 2, the villa-letter and its carefully filtered aura of *otium* (§24n. *studîs*) makes for a sharp (and numerically precise) contrast with the parade of *negotium* in 2.11–12 (Intro. 13–14), as well as with the urban and social business that frames it in 2.16 and 2.18. At the same time, Cicero's presence, so dominant in 2.11–12, fades into the background: 2.17 could be taken as a reply to *Ad Atticum* 12.9, where Cicero is at Astura enjoying *uilla litore prospectu maris* but adds *neque haec digna longioribus litteris* (Guillemin 1929: 116), but substantive engagement with his most obvious villa letter (*Q. fr.* 3.1.1–6, *me refeci…*) is less evident, and P. seems not to exploit any circumstantial overlap between Cicero's *otium litteratum* at Tusculum and his own at Laurentum. Within the pair of villa letters 2.17∼5.6, abundant common ground (partly reflecting, no doubt, standard villa vocabulary) is typically complemented with variety in both structure and content. The parallel relationships 2.15+17 ∼ 5.4+6 (2.15.intro.) and 2.16–17 ∼ 5.6–7 (2.16.intro.) seem unlikely to be coincidence.

The letter itself is constructed – of course – with great care. What first strikes the reader is the linearity of the 'tour' (§4n. *in*): after a proemial sentence (§1), P. transports us from Rome and shows us the surroundings (§§2–3); we visit in turn the central part of the house (§§4–5), the south-east wing (§§6–9) and the north-west wing, including the baths and a 'tower' (§§10–12; for the orientation of the villa see §6n. *huius*). We then move to a second 'tower' (§§13–15) from which we view the *gestatio* (driving circuit) and gardens, and catch a second sight of the front entrance (§§14–15). From here we proceed to the two *pièces de résistance*, first the cryptoportico (§§16–19) and then, at its end, P.'s pavilion, a private suite detached from the main house (§§20–4). There, in his inner sanctum, the tour ends, leaving time for some snapshots of locality, landscape and seascape (§§25–8), before a closing invitation to Gallus to see it for himself (§29).

Linearity, however, is not the only organising device. An elaborate structure matches epistle to edifice:

§1 proem (Gallus)	23 words
§§2–3 arrival; landward topography	92 words
§§4–15 main house	463 words
(ends with *turris* 2, framing a view of *gestatio* and garden)	
§§16–24 cryptoportico and pavilion	326 words
§§25–8 locality, landscape, seascape	147 words
§29 peroration (Gallus)	32 words

While avoiding precise symmetry, P. mounts his villa in a double frame: within the outer pair of addresses to Gallus (§§1, 29), descriptions of the surroundings on land and sea (§§2–3, 25–8) encircle the buildings. The villa itself divides into main house (§§4–15) and outbuildings (§§16–24) in a ratio of roughly 3:2. The main house, defined by ring-composition (§15n. *uestibulum*), is itself further subdivided into four roughly equal parts:

§§4–5 central wing	100 words
§§6–9 south-east wing	124 words
§§10–12 north-west wing, incl. *turris* 1	116 words
§§13–15 *turris* 2, including gardens	123 words

At its end, and at the centre of the letter, is the garden (§15n. *hortum*), encircled by the *gestatio* that lies between main house and pavilion. Epistolary and domestic architecture are finely in tune.

The bibliography on 2.17 is substantial (Anguissola 2007). Bergmann 1995 and G–M 200–33 make helpful introductions; see also Henderson 2002a: 15–20 and 2003: 120–5, Leach 2003, Riggsby 2003, Myers 2005, Spencer 2010 (esp. 62–134) and (in German) Lefèvre 1977 and 1987 (≈ 2009: 223–45). For archaeological commentary see Förtsch (superseding Lehmann-Hartleben). Unlike the 'Etruscan' villa near Tifernum Tiberinum, which seems to have been identified (G–M 225–30), efforts to match the *Laurentinum* with properties excavated on this stretch of coast have proved inconclusive (e.g. Salza Prina Ricotti 1984, ead. 1985, ead. 1988, persuading few, and Ramieri 1995; De Franceschini 2005: 260–7 gives a digest; rebuilding after P.'s time complicates the quest). Nevertheless, studies of the area have built up a valuable architectural and social context (§12n. *latissimum*, §26n. *uicus*) and give us a sense of scale (e.g. §1n. *gratiam*, §13n. *gestationem*). To avoid adding to the plethora of reconstructions, the plan of Winnefeld 1891: 212 is reproduced in this volume (p. xii) despite some points of disagreement (§12n. *sub*, §13n. *est*, §19n. *tum*, §20n. *alia*, §23n. *hypocauston*). To attempt such a bird's-eye view at all is to miss the point of P.'s fluid, experiential textualisation (§4n. *in*); nevertheless, for modern readers it may be a useful guide in their own tour of P.'s architexture.

GALLO: almost certainly the same Gallus who receives another descriptive letter, 8.20 (Lake Vadimon), a natural wonder to complement the man-made marvels here. Placed near the end of second and penultimate books, 2.17 is the 41st letter in the collection, 8.20 the 45th from the end. The opening aphorism of 8.20 (we are prone to overlook *miracula* close to Rome) resonates with 2.17; less so perhaps its close, *nam te quoque ut me nihil aeque ac naturae opera delectant*, only half borne out to modern taste by 2.17, where nature is fetishised, but through man's mediation. Closer identification of the addressee is difficult. P. mentions a Gallus in 1.7.4, and addresses 4.17 to Clusinius Gallus, perhaps the same man (Birley 2000a: 50–1); but any overlaps are unclear, and Gallus is a common name (Syme 1968: 148 hazards five suggestions, including consuls of 101 and 108). If we knew more about the 1C. BC poet Gallus, we might be better able to judge whether his name is relevant. Whoever he is, this man, like the recipient of 5.6 (2.9n. APOLLINARI), is one of P.'s less frequent correspondents. As in the long Priscus trial (2.11n. ARRIANO), overt epistolarity is confined to the outer frame (§§1, 29), but here more frequent second-person verbs, albeit generalising, reach out to the reader-visitor (§2n. *possis*) along the way.

1–3 Proem and arrival

1 Miraris cur me Laurentinum uel: ten heavy syllables make an exceptionally ponderous opening for the longest letter yet; P. rarely allows even three heavy syllables to open (2.6, 2.13), and only the four of 2.2 come close in this book (runs of seven in 8.18, 9.12 and probably 7.29). The letter justifies itself as reply to an implied precursor (2.5.1n. *efflagitatam*, 2.16.1n. *admones*). In context *miraris* is prosaic, 'you wonder why' (*OLD* 2c; cf. 7.11.1 *miraris quod*, 7.22.1 *minus miraberis*), and *mirus* words are common in P. (2.13.6n. *mira*), but 'you wonder' (*OLD* 3) is an apt start for this marvellous villa (cf. §11 *mirifica*, §25 *mira natura*). Wonder is recurrent in his descriptive letters (e.g. 4.30, 6.16, 6.20, 8.20), and is apt as a hallmark of utopias (Mankin on Hor. *Epod.* 16.53). It is also a key word of ecphrasis (intro.), introducing and/or framing the shields of Achilles (*Iliad* 18.467 θαυμάσσεται 'will wonder': see Becker 1995), Heracles (Hesiod *Shield* 140, 224, 318 θαῦμα ἰδεῖν/ ἰδέσθαι 'a wonder to behold') and Aeneas (V. *Aen.* 8.619 and 8.730 *miratur*), as well as Europa's basket (Moschus 2.38 θηητόν, μέγα θαῦμα 'wondrous, a great marvel'), the Ariadne tapestry (Cat. 64.51 *mira . . . arte*) and the temple at Carthage (V. *Aen.* 1.456 *miratur*, 1.494 *miranda*). Given P.'s explicit comparison of his villa letters to the Homeric and Virgilian shields (as well as to Aratus' *Phaenomena*) near the end of 5.6 (intro.), this first word is surely loaded, joining 5.6.43 to make an epic ecphrastic frame. Yet the hint is delicate, as P. goes on to promise that Gallus will *cease* to wonder (*desines mirari*; contrast 3.5.7 *miraris . . .; magis miraberis si scieris . . .*): as throughout the letter, poetic magic is set off against prosaic realism. **Laurentinum** 'Laurentine (place)', n. sg. substantival adjective (perhaps *sc. praedium*) < *Laurentum*, the regular formation from the name of a town (as Cicero's *Tusculanum* < *Tusculum*; contrast *Tusci* from the

name of a region, Etruria: 2.15.1n. *quomodo te*).   **uel, si ita mauis, Laurens:**
the near-repetition (2.2.1n. *irascor*) adds suitable weight to this 'headline'; Gallus
apparently wrote *Laurens*, showing poetic and/or antiquarian taste: dating back
to Ennius and Cato, it was by now exclusively poetic, leaving *Laurentinum* (first in
1c. AD), as P. implies, the everyday term. For the banter, cf. Cic. *Att.* 15.13.3 *quod
ad te antea atque adeo prius scripsi (sic enim mauis)*; for double-naming, Cat. 44.1 *o funde
noster seu Sabine seu Tiburs*, addressing a suburban villa (Guillemin 1929: 145). The
ager Laurens, on the coast southwest of Rome (Talbert 1985: 122 gives a map), was
an area of rich mythohistorical connotations, the landing-place of Aeneas, and
the site of archaic Latin settlements including Lavinium (Ogilvie on Livy 1.1.10,
Purcell 1998). It was now also a prestigious site for villas, including the imperial residence at Tor Paterno (Marzano 2007: 316–23): §12n. *latissimum*.   **tanto
opere:** a pun for this great work? *opus* serves both architectural (*OLD* 10) and
literary (*OLD* 9) achievement. The adverb (alternatively spelled *tantopere*) recurs
only at 1.7.3 and *Pan.* 10.2.   **delectet:** the phrase began with wonder and ends
with delight, like V. *Aen.* 8.730 <u>*miratur rerumque ignarus imagine gaudet*</u> (Aeneas viewing the shield). Delight, a keynote of both villa letters, also furnishes the last
word of 8.20, to Gallus (8.20.10 *delectant*). The cadence is Ciceronian: *I Verr.* 1.35
tanto opere delectat and e.g. *Pis.* 59, *Att.*15.13.3.   **cognoueris:** fut. pf.   **gratiam
uillae, opportunitatem loci, litoris spatium** 'the charm [*OLD* gratia 6a]
of the villa, the convenience of the location, the extent of the shore', AB~AB~BA
tricolon, a headline varied in 5.6.3 *temperiem caeli, regionis situm, uillae amoenitatem*
(AB~BA~BA). *opportunitas loci* is a common phrase (again at 10.70.2), especially in
historians; cf. also 1.24.3 *uicinitas urbis, opportunitas uiae . . .* (a villa for Suetonius).
litoris spatium unqualified by a measurement (*tantum, ingens*, etc.) is unique; for
the pair, cf. Prop. 1.20.9 *spatiabere litoris ora* (addressing Gallus). Villas surveyed
in the area each claimed around 400m of coastline; P. had the benefit both of
his own stretch and of the view beyond (§12n. *latissimum*). The three elements
will receive unequal coverage: convenient location (§§2–3, 26) frames a long
description of the villa itself (§§3–25), with the shore featuring briefly at the end
(§§25–8).

2 Decem septem milibus passuum ab urbe secessit 'it is seventeen miles
withdrawn from Rome' (17 Roman miles = *c.* 25km). *decem septem = septemdecim*
(for such forms see K–H 640, though many are now edited away). *secessit* (whose
subject is *Laurens meum*) establishes the governing aura of *otium* (2.8.1n. *altissimus*,
2.11.1n. *quietis*) and launches a serial personification of the villa and its rooms,
which alternately stand in for their owner/visitor (e.g. 'enjoying' vistas: §5n. *quasi*)
and work like good slaves to make his stay pleasant ('intensifying' the sunlight,
'blending' views: Niemirska-Pliszczyńska 1955: 80, Maselli 1995: 97–9); cf. §29n.
dotibus. Personification continues in the Etruscan villa (e.g. 5.6.2 *hi procul a mari
recesserunt*); see also 2.15.1n. *quomodo te* and 8.17.3 *Anio . . . adiacentibus uillis uelut
inuitatus retentusque*. At this modest distance, the villa combines seclusion with

convenience; cf. Mart. *Ep.* 6.43.9 *urbis uicina iuuant facilesque recessus.* **peractis quae agenda fuerint** 'after concluding your business', literally 'with the business that had to be done having been completed' (*OLD ago* 38): abl. abs. (*sc. eis*: *NLS* §93.1); *fuerint* is generic subjunctive (G–L §625) and/or by attraction within the result clause (G–L §567). For the jingle *-act-* ~ *ag-*, cf. 4.19.3 *acturus... egi*, 6.29.4–6 *agerent agendo... agendo... agerem, Pan.* 53.6 *actiones agant*; see 2.1.12n. *et*, 2.11.14n. *dicturo.* Barring senatorial meetings, the elite working day usually ended around noon (Balsdon 1969: 24), so that one could complete all affairs (*peractis*) and still have time to get to the villa. The first and last mention of *negotium* in the letter. **saluo iam et composito die** 'when the day is now safely set to rest' (abl. abs.), a poetic way of saying, more or less, 'with the setting sun' (Boyle). The villa is half a day's journey from Rome, and one arrives at nightfall. For *composito*, cf. V. *Aen.* 1.374 *diem... componet* 'will set the day to sleep' with Austin, *TLL* III 2116.16–22. Editors, translators and *OLD saluus* 7a have preferred 'without cutting short your working day', ignoring *iam* and making tautology with *peractis quae agenda fuerint.* The sense of *saluo* is hard to parallel, but *saluo iam* implies completion (once finished, the day can suffer no harm; cf. the late antique bath-motto *saluum lotum* 'well washed'). **possis** refers to Gallus and/or, in the generalising second person (2.6.5n. *si gulae*), to any reader-visitor. P. enters the stage as owner-occupier just once (§24), leaving it largely as an empty space for viewing and inhabitation by the reader (albeit with evaluative prompts). This is achieved by varied means: the generalising second person (§11 *cogites*, §25 *moueris*, §27 *utare*; cf. §26 *si forte... dissuadeat*), an unspecified *frugi homini* (§26), a generalising plural (§11 *natantes*), the attribution of enjoyment to rooms instead of their occupants (§5n. *quasi*), and implicit focalisation (below on *iunctis*, §3n. *modo*, §12n. *longissimum*, §19n. *tum maxime*). P. thus invites Gallus and the eavesdropping reader to share the experience, a less obtrusive form of Virgil's ecphrastic technique in the shield of Aeneas (*Aen.* 8.650 *aspiceres*, 676 *uideres*, 691 *credas*); such encouragement becomes most prominent in §§25–7, as the end nears. While sharing all these traits, 5.6 also addresses the reader directly (5.6.7 *imaginare*, 13 *capies uoluptatem... uideberis*). **manere:** spend the night (*OLD* 2a). **aditur non unā uiā:** a common litotes (*OLD non* 12c, *unus* 2a). Our tour begins with the journey from Rome; we literally have two roads to choose between, but *uia* 'way' (*OLD* 7–10) is a common metaphor (e.g. 3.18.2 *qua potissimum uia*, Sen. *Ep.* 91.5 [*fortuna*] *non unā uiā semper... incurrit*, Quint. 7.2.22 *non unā uiā ducitur*), offering a hint, perhaps, at the varied riches of this letter. Road imagery makes a famous poetic manifesto in Callimachus (*Aetia* fr. 1.25–8 'walk on the tracks that are not trodden by wagons, and do not drive your chariot in the common paths of others or along the broad highway...'; cf. Prop. 3.1.14 *non datur ad Musas currere lata uia*). P. does not specify which to take. **et Laurentina et Ostiensis** *sc. uiae.* The Via Ostiensis headed sixteen Roman miles west-southwest from Rome to Ostia (§26n. *suggerunt*); the Laurentina, though its exact route is uncertain, left Rome to the southwest (Radke 1971: 69–71; a reconstruction in Salza Prina Ricotti 1984: fig. 3 at p.347). P.'s villa lies on the coast between the two, so combining the desideranda of *opportunitas uiae* (1.24.3; cf. Columella *RR* 1.3.3) and adequate distance from the disturbance of a highway (Col. *RR* 1.5.6–7). **ferunt** 'lead', *OLD* 6b. **a quarto decimo lapide** 'at [*OLD ab* 12a] the fourteenth milestone' (from Rome). **utrimque excipit iter** 'from both of these begins a road' (*OLD excipio* 16 'take up from'), *TLL* v.2 1254.49, 52–5 (esp. Caes. *BC* 1.66.4 *inde excipere loca aspera*, Livy 38.40.6 *a Cypselis* [a town] *uia... excipiebat*). **iunctis paulo grauius et longius, equo breue et molle** 'somewhat taxing and long by carriage, short and easy [*OLD mollis* 6a] on horseback', parallel (noun–adj. pair) ∼ noun–adj. pair) with chiasmus (*grauius et longius* ∼ *breue et molle*) and variety in *iunctis* (pl.) ∼ *equo* (sg.) and *grauius et longius* (comparative) ∼ *breue et molle* (positive). The comparative force of *grauius et longius* is weak (2.1.4n. *durior*); *paulo* is abl. of degree of comparison (*NLS* §82). The elliptical *iunctis* 'harnessed [mules, etc.]' is unique to P. (4.2.3 has ponies *et iunctos et solutos* 'for harnessing and for riding'). If it is abl., by analogy with *equo* 'on horseback' (*OLD equus* 3e), it is metonymic for 'by carriage'. Alternatively *iunctis*, and perhaps *equo*, are dat. ('for yoked animals... for a horse') and both metonymic, since we are interested in the experience of passenger or rider, not of the animals. Concrete and abstract are blurred, with focalisation: the *iter* 'road' is sandy, but the *iter* 'journey' *feels* long or short depending on the mode of transport (cf. Hor. *Sat.* 1.5.6 *minus est grauis Appia tardis*); *molle* covers both. P. gives a rare insight into his modes of travel (Cova 1999; on horseback again at 9.15.3), in which solitary simplicity is the effect: contrast the lavish arrangements satirised in Hor. *Sat.* 1.6.103–9 and Sen. *Ep.* 87.1–11. An accompanying retinue is doubtless elided (cf. 8.1.1; for Sen. *Ep.* 87.2 the height of restraint is to travel *cum paucissimis seruis, quos unum capere uehiculum potuit*). On types of vehicles, see Chevallier 1989: 178–81.

3 uaria hinc atque inde facies 'the view is varied all around' (*hinc atque inde* 'on every side': *Pan.* 22.4, 68.2) or '... on both sides', as in Statius, who first has the phrase (*Theb.* 4.220 etc.). The villa and letter in a nutshell: variety and views are P.'s two predominant concerns. **modo occurrentibus siluis uia coartatur, modo latissimis pratis diffunditur et patescit** 'now the road is narrowed by woods blocking its way, now it spreads out and extends over broad expanses of meadow'. Parallel antithesis, with extension in the second member: *patescit* (*OLD* 4) is a choice synonym for *diffunditur*. For the topographical use of *occurrere*, see *OLD* 4–5 and *TLL* ix.2 398.9–24. More focalisation: what narrows and broadens is not the road but the view (*modo... modo* is temporal) enjoyed by the traveller. *coartatur* (a real passive) and *diffunditur* ('middle' voice) make a 'false parallel' (2.11.6n. *acres*), as do *occurrentibus siluis* (instrumental abl.) and *latissimis pratis* (abl. of extent with *diffunditur et patescit*: *TLL* v.1 1107.35, x.1 703.51–4). **multi greges ouium, multa ibi equorum boum armenta:** ABC∼ACCB with polyptoton; *equorum boum* are in asyndeton; *ibi* is construed *apo koinou*. **montibus hieme depulsā | herbis et tepore uerno nitescunt**

'driven down from the mountains in/by winter, grow sleek [*OLD nitesco* 2] with the grass and the spring warmth'. A chain of ablatives in three different uses – *montibus* abl. of separation (*NLS* §41.8); *hieme* adverbial, 'in winter' (*TLL* VI.3 2779.12–31), or instrumental, 'by winter' (personifying season as herdsman); *herbis et tepore uerno* abl. of cause (*NLS* §45), the last combining concrete and abstract. A reference to 'vertical' transhumance, common in coastal areas, whereby livestock are pastured on low plains in the early months of the year, then moved upland, where grass grows later into the year (Gabba–Pasquinucci 1979, esp. 142–6, 152–5; Garnsey 2000: 689–91). This moment of rusticity 'seems almost a recovery of an ancestral past, in the midst of the modern world' (Mansuelli 1978: 61, translated; cf. 5.6.6 *putes alio te saeculo natum*), crafted into the most urbane language. **tepore uerno:** the (mild) warmth of spring, vs the *calor* of summer. Late winter/early spring is the default, but not unvarying, season for the letter: §5n. *Africo*, §6n. *altera*, §17n. *quantumque*, §24n. *Saturnalibus* (summer at §15n. *uinea*, §18n. *haec*; also §28n. *aquam* and 7.4.4). In the Etruscan villa (5.6), conversely, summer predominates but with glimpses of winter (e.g. 5.6.24 *cubiculum hieme tepidissimum*); these seasonal norms are restated in 9.36 (*Tusci* in summer) and 9.40 (*Laurentinum* in winter).

4–15 Villa: main building

We reach the main building, visiting in turn the central wing (§§4–5), the south-east wing (§§6–9), the north-west wing, including baths and a *turris* (§§10–12), and a second *turris*, from which we see the gardens (§§13–15). Mynors begins §4 at *cuius* (presumably a typesetting slip).

4 Villa usibus capax, non sumptuosa tutela *sc. est*, 'the villa is adequate for its purpose, but not costly in upkeep' (*OLD usus* 12, *capax* 2a + dat. (rare: *TLL* III 304.16–17), *tutela* 5), chiastic antithesis. Rhythm demands *sumptuosă*, with either *tutelă* (as Apul. *Met.* 4.13) or better *tutelā*, keeping *uilla* as the subject and antecedent to *cuius* (for *sumptuosus* + abl., cf. Varro *RR* 3.2.5 *deliciis sumptuosior*). Asyndeton, a simple six-word clause, and the headword *uilla* (as in 5.6.14) announce our arrival, with a programmatic statement of modesty: this property will embody in its own way the sort of *mediocritas uillae* endorsed in 1.24.3. P. freely uses *uilla* to refer to the buildings (e.g. 5.6.19) and/or the estate as a whole (e.g. §28). On the moral discourse around villas see intro.; P. may have in mind Cato's strictures *ut uillarum tutela non sit oneri* (Pl. *NH* 18.31). **in prima parte:** from the visitor's point of view. The tour begins at the entrance, works along the central axis of the main wing, then gradually progresses to the most intimate reaches. P. plays on this fusion of letter and guided tour in 5.6.41 (where he has undertaken 'to tour all the corners by letter in your company', *omnes angulos tecum epistula circumire*). In *Siluae* 1.3 and 2.2, by contrast, Statius himself is the tourist. The linearity of the tour is striking in both writers: the house is experienced not as a two-dimensional plan but as a dynamic, sequential flow of spaces. This may be inconvenient for modern reconstructions, but reflects a 'hodological' form of visualisation current now as in antiquity (Clay 2011: 96–100; see also Elsner 1995: 79–80, Purves 2010). With *in*, P. avoids any promise of exhaustive treatment: he omits the *uestibulum* (§15) and probably an entrance passage (*fauces*). **atrium frugi nec tamen sordidum:** the golden mean prevails from the outset, with the atrium 'modest' (*frugi*, a term of praise; cf. 5.6.15 *atrium ex more ueterum*) but not 'lowly' (*sordidum*, pejorative). For the modest pride, cf. §10n. *politissimum*, §11n. *elegantes*, §21 *eleganter*. As throughout (§5n. *satis*), detail is shunned, with not a word about the construction, furniture, decor or adjoining rooms. We need not doubt that arrangements were lavish (a passing hint in 3.19.3 *sumptus supellectilis*, probably in reference to the Etruscan villa). On contemporary *atria* see Förtsch 30–41, Leach 2004: 21–34. **deinde:** the first of a series of varied and often vague connecting words (Riggsby 2003: 169): P. is no more concerned to facilitate modern reconstructions than Virgil is in the shield ecphrasis (*Aen.* 8.635 *nec procul hinc* etc.). **porticus in D litterae similitudinem circumactae** 'colonnades curved into the shape of a letter D'; P. counts two *porticūs* (§5n. *a tergo*), presumably one curved and one straight (despite *circumactae*), making a D-shaped peristyle, a shape partly matched by the horseshoe-shaped Porticus Absidata in the Forum Transitorium (*LTUR* IV 116, fig. 42). See Förtsch 58–60 and, on peristyles generally, Leach 2004: 34–40. The reading *in D* is owed to one manuscript (F) and its copies (αγ have *inde*, an easy corruption). Early editors corrected it to the less likely 'O': hence the circular peristyle in many reconstructions. The phrase has been taken as a witty reminder of this villa's textuality (Drummer 1993: 138–40, with Bergmann 1995: 409–10; Henderson 2002a: 18). If so, it points up the ecphrastic stakes: for all its descriptive power, this visualised villa remains *litterae* on the page. For the expression, cf. 8.20.4 *lacus est in similitudinem iacentis rotae circumscriptus.* **paruula sed festiua area** 'a petite but jolly courtyard'. An *area* was an open precinct or yard, often planted as a garden (at least in Campania: Jashemski 1979: 25–54 and 1981). The affective and/or modest diminutive *paruula* (§29n. *uillulae*) is no safe indication of size: an *areola* in the Etruscan villa has room for four plane trees (5.6.20). For the shy pride, cf. §4 *capax, non sumptuosa* and *frugi nec tamen sordidum* and 3.6.1 *modicum quidem sed festiuum et expressum* (P.'s statue, and an acme of epistolary self-portraiture: 2.7.intro.). **includitur** 'is enclosed', *OLD* 4b. **egregium hae aduersus tempestates receptaculum** sc. *sunt*, 'these [sc. porticoes] make an excellent shelter from [*OLD aduersus*[4] 7] storms'; the winter/spring scene continues (§5n. *Africo*). Peristyles were suited among other things to literary meditation and composition (Hor. *Sat.* 1.4.134). The hyperbaton of *egregium . . . receptaculum* (mimetically enclosing the phrase?) throws the adjective into relief, as does the displacement of *hae*, usually first (e.g. §§6–7 *huius . . . huius . . . hoc*). The diction resembles Sen. *Ep.* 90.41 *aduersus saeuitiam hiemis aut imbris uili receptaculo tuti sub fronde uiuebant*, on the simple habits of former days, but P.'s shelter is *egregium*, not *uile*, and the comforts modern, not simple leaves. **specularibus** 'windows' (*OLD specularis* 2b, n. pl.), made from *specularis* (*sc. lapis*), a translucent mineral, probably selenite (Foy–Fontaine 2008: 444–9; older references in Courtney on Juv. 4.20), or from glass, used for windows from around the mid-1c. AD (Foy–Fontaine 2008: 405–30, superseding e.g. Forbes 1966, Harden 1969). Like the intercolumnar glazing in the peristyle of the House of the Mosaic Atrium at Herculaneum (Maiuri 1958: 291–2), these windows filled the gaps between columns, but presumably not all of them: *multo magis* implies a limited effect, access was needed to the *area*, and neither selenite nor glass of the time was sufficiently transparent to allow the long view through this courtyard (§5). Sen. *Prou.* 4.9 counts them an enervating luxury. **imminentibus tectis:** the 'overhanging' roofs of the peristyle extend beyond the columns over the *area* (as pictured in Maiuri, previous n.). The phrase is otherwise only at Sen. *Ep.* 90.8.

5 contra medias *sc. porticus*, 'in line with the centre (of the porticoes)'; for this use of *contra* see e.g. §21, 5.6.20, Vitr. 3.2.3 and often, *OLD* 12b and examples in *TLL* IV 744.2–51. **cauaedium:** a contraction, only here, of *cauum aedium* (Varro *LL* 5.161, Vitr. 6.3.1–2; on P.'s formation see Leumann 399); 'simply another designation for *atrium*' (Förtsch 30, translated). **hilare** 'bright, cheerful' (*OLD* 3); cf. 5.6.25, Sen. *Ep.* 55.8 *in uilla hilari et amoena*. For the pathetic fallacy, see *OLD rideo* 3, Thomas on Hor. *C.* 4.11.6 *ridet . . . domus*. **mox** 'then' (2.5.9n. *interim*). **triclinium:** the first of several dining-rooms, and a centre of gravity for this part of the house and tour. On *triclinia*, see Förtsch 100–16, Dunbabin 1991, Leach 2004: 41–7; by now it was common to set a large one, seating more than the traditional nine diners, on a central axis (Dunbabin 1996: 72–4). **satis pulchrum:** as much detail as P. will give on the decor of any room in this villa (again §10 *politissimum*); 5.6.22 is a sole mention of wall-paintings. **in litus** 'onto the shore', not necessarily to be taken literally. Building over the sea was fashionable (and deplored by moralisers: Hor. *C.* 2.18.21 with Nisbet–Hubbard). **excurrit** 'protrudes' (*OLD* 3; cf. 5.6.19), a common architectural term. For the design cf. 6.24.2 *cubiculum quod in lacum prominet* and Förtsch 100–1. **Africo** *sc. uento* (as often in both prose and verse), a stormy south-westerly wind: cf. V. *Aen.* 1.85–6 with Austin; Col. *RR* 11.2.4 *uentus Africus: tempestatem significat*. This is the first of several mentions of a stormy sea, already signalled by §4 *tempestates* (§13 *turbati maris*, §27 *frequens et contrarius fluctus*; the *Africus* appears again in §17), conjuring up a bracing wintry scene – at a comfortable distance (cf. Lucr. 2.1–2): as in Statius (Newlands 2002: 167–8), even hostile nature can be a source of pleasure to the villa-owner within. In 5.2.1 too storms are raging here in Laurentum (the Etruscan villa is a haven of calm, with a single, benign breeze, 5.6.29). **mare:** this villa is defined above all by the ever-present sea, 18× in the letter, and first among its charms in 1.9.6 (*o mare, o litus . . .*). Unlike Statius, who works hard to vary his sea words in *Siluae* 2.2 (Van Dam 1984: 226), P. prefers discreetly prosaic repetition of *mare*. **fractis iam et nouissimis fluctibus** 'by the very tips of the now broken waves', *OLD frango* 1d (as 6.31.16, 9.7.4), *nouissimus* 2c and 3 'the last of, dying' (cf. Ov. *Met.* 11.256 *admisitque suos in uerba nouissima fluctus*). It is the base of the exterior wall which is wetted, and probably a raised foundation (*basis uillae*) at that (for such structures see Marzano 2007: 33–4 and e.g. p. 315 on the 'Villa Magna' sometimes alleged to be that of P.); Radice's 'spray of the spent breakers' (after Cowan) perhaps encourages the fantasy, often repeated in the scholarship, that P.'s guests are spattered with brine over dinner. **leuiter alluitur** 'is lightly lapped', expressively alliterative. Even in a storm the villa feels only the gentle touch of the sea. Statius' Campanian home is similarly blessed, *quas imbelle fretum torpentibus alluit undis* '. . . laps with its lazy waters' (*Silu.* 3.5.84), as is Pollius' villa, where *ponunt . . . lassa furorem | aequora* (*Silu.* 2.2.26–7). **undique ualuas aut fenestras non minores ualuis habet** 'it has doors or windows no smaller than doors on every side', two sets of *ualuae*, folding doors (one from the house, one leading to a balcony?), and two windows – in our terms, empty openings protected by pairs of shutters (Blümner 1911: 102–3, citing Ov. *Am.* 1.5.3, Hor. *C.* 1.25.1 etc.; *RE* VI 2183–4) – left and right. The arrangement resembles a dining room in the Etruscan villa (5.6.19) and the *oecus Cyzicenus* of Vitr. 6.3.10 (Förtsch 100–1). **a lateribus, a fronte . . . maria prospectat, a tergo . . . respicit montes** 'at the sides and in front it looks out over . . . seas, while behind it looks back at . . . mountains'. Parallel antithesis, chiastically reprising the doors and windows already mentioned (*ualuas . . . fenestras* ~ *lateribus . . . fronte* + *tergo*), and with alliterative chiasmus in the final word-pairs *maria prospectat . . . respicit montes*. For *a* ('*at* the sides, *in* front, behind'), standard idiom, see K–S 1 492. P. defines the 'front' of a room by its principal view, here the sea (cf. §10 and 13 *post*; §15, 21 and 5.6.14 *a tergo*). It both has the obvious outlook and is aptly orientated for the evening sun in a primarily winter villa (as Vitr. 6.4 advises). **quasi tria maria prospectat** 'looks out as if over three seas'. Along with orientation (§6n. *altera*), it is above all the views that define the different spaces of P.'s villas, reflecting a wider Roman preoccupation in architecture (Elsner 1995: 49–87) as well as the ecphrastic drive powering these letters. These views are enjoyed by the rooms, personified, on their occupants' behalf, beginning here with a common expression (Heubner on Tac. *H.* 5.6.1, adding Hor. *Ep.* 1.10.23 *domus longos quae prospicit agros*; P. has [*triclinium*] *prospectat* again at 5.6.19); for the idea, cf. Stat. *Silu.* 2.2.3 *speculatrix uilla*. The conceit of 'three [different] seas', softened by *quasi* (2.6.5n. *illa*), resembles that of Stat. *Silu.* 2.2.74 *omni proprium thalamo mare* 'each room has its own sea'. Like the triple vista of §21, it has been taken to reveal a Roman desire to partition natural scenes into a series of framed pictures (Drerup 1959: 151; Lefèvre 1977: 521–2 = 2009: 225); cf. 5.6.13 *formam . . . pictam uideberis cernere*. This aesthetic of nature mediated was not universally shared: see Sen. *Ep.* 90.43 (with Summers) and Juv. 3.17–20 on 'spoiling' nature through artifice, and Carey 2003: 102–37 on the 'artifice of nature' in Pl. *NH*. **a tergo cauaedium porticum aream porticum rursus, mox atrium siluas et longinquos respicit montes:** the room 'looks back' at all the rooms so far visited (§§3–5) and now reprised in reverse order, then out into the woods and Alban hills beyond. Two contrasting groups are articulated by the juxtaposed adverbs (*rursus, mox*): first an asyndetic list of four spaces (*cauaedium*, portico, courtyard, 'portico again', i.e. the second of the two *porticūs*), then an extended tricolon of *atrium*, | *siluas* | *et . . . montes* (3~2~9 syllables). The accumulation of nouns mimics in text the long axial perspective, characteristic of Roman architecture (Bek 1980: 164–203, Jung 1984, Wallace-Hadrill 1994: 44–5). We could have seen it on our arrival, but P. prefers to savour the view from the comfort of the *triclinium*, with a 'lingering gaze . . . not in a momentary stiffening of surprise' (Bek 1980: 202). **siluas . . . montes:** a common pair evoking untamed countryside, remote from civilisation (cf. Quint. 9.4.4 *urbibus montes ac siluas mutari oportuit* (of primitive man) and e.g. V. *Ecl.* 2.5); see also 5.6.8 *siluae cum ipso monte.* **et: 2.1.2n.** *triginta.* **longinquos respicit montes:** the word-order creates hyperbaton (2.11.5n. *censuit*), chiasmus with *maria prospectat* (above), and a cretic–spondee. Cf. V. *Aen.* 8.697 *geminos a tergo respicit anguis* (Cleopatra on the shield), the only other attestation of *a tergo* + *respicit*. Unlike *prospectat*, *respicit* is rare in the context, making for more obtrusive personification; Statius seems to be in mind, apostrophising part of Vopiscus' villa: *ad siluas quae respicis, aula, tacentis* 'you courtyard looking back at the silent woods' (*Silu.* 1.3.40); cf. also Tiberius' villa in Phaedrus 2.5.10 *prospectat Siculum et respicit Tuscum mare* (as emended by Gronovius) with Henderson 2001b: 23.

6 Huius a laeua: on the left, as you look out to sea (§5n. *a lateribus*). We now enter the south-east wing. The villa front is aligned with the coast, which runs roughly NW to SE (*pace* S-W 189, who overlooks the compass rose in the figure he cites, Van Buren 1948: 35). **retractius paulo** 'set back slightly' from the sea (2.1.4n. *durior*), as Livy 34.9.2 *retractior a mari*. A *triclinium* was commonly flanked by a pair of recessed or projecting rooms (Förtsch 108–11). **cubiculum:** 'room' or perhaps 'private room' (not 'bedroom'), a relatively intimate place for sleep (cf. *cubare*), study or leisure (Riggsby 1997, Anguissola 2010). P. mentions eleven in this letter, distinguishing them from *diaetae* 'apartments' (§12n., though *diaetae* can contain *cubicula*, as in §20), dining-rooms (but see §10n. *uel cubiculum*), service-rooms, baths and other named spaces (*atrium* etc.: Förtsch 54–6). **est:** more often P. omits it. The usage and position (late, and separating *cubiculum amplum*) are matched in §10 *ex alio latere cubiculum est politissimum* (announcing the other wing). **amplum:** large, that is, for a *cubiculum*, and contrasting with *minus*. References to size are vague: P. is concerned with impressions, not Vitruvian calculations. **aliud minus** 'another, smaller one'. **alterā fenestrā admittit orientem, occidentem alterā retinet** 'admits the rising sun through one window and holds back the setting sun through the other' (ABC~CAB). The 'willing servant' motif (§2n. *decem*), continues, with the sun also personified, and poetically so: *oriens sc. sol* 'rising sun' (as opposed to 'east') is hitherto exclusive to poetry (e.g. V. *Georg.* 1.250, *Aen.* 5.42: *OLD oriens*[2] 1), *occidens* 'setting sun' unparalleled. Cf. Sen. *Ep.* 55.6 *altera [spelunca] solem non recipit, altera usque in occidentem tenet*, Stat. *Silu.* 2.2.45–7 *haec domus ortus | aspicit . . . illa cadentem | detinet*. The conceit of ushering in the dawn sun (cf. 5.6.15 *solem . . . quasi inuitat*) gets a satirical twist at Juv. 7.183 *algentem rapiat cenatio solem* 'a dining room grabs the shivering sun', perhaps inspired by P., though the exposé of a rich patron's villa at *Sat.* 7.178–85 does not otherwise point in his direction (*pace* Herrmann 1940). Orientation was vital (e.g. Cat. 26, Vitr. 6.4, Col. *RR* 1.6.1–2), and maximising sunlight at the *Laurentinum* is a primary concern, as dictated by winter occupancy, and perhaps by character: 'the obsession with catching sunlight . . . tells of Pliny's love of conventional approval, imperial benevolence, glory, and honour' (Henderson 2003: 123). **hac** 'through the latter (window)', *OLD hic* 11. **et subiacens mare** 'also . . . the sea lying below'. *subiacere* (*OLD* 1b, not rare) recurs at §15, 1.3.1 (*lacus*), 5.6.23 (*piscina*). **longius quidem sed securius intuetur** 'has a more distant but calmer view of '; *intuetur* 'looks out onto', continues the personification (cf. 5.6.28, also with *cubiculum* as subject), as might *securus* 'unconcerned, untroubled' (*OLD* 1–2). *longius* and *securius* are best taken as adverbs: *longe intueri* (uel sim.) is common (*TLL* VII.2 1644.50–64, 1645.51–72; NB Sen. *Phoen.* 67–8 *alta rupes . . . | spectatque longe spatia subiecti maris*), even if *secure intueri* is unmatched (and so typically adventurous: contrast Sen. *Ep.* 118.4 *qui . . . securus intuetur*). *quidem* is concessive (2.1.7n. *et*), but 'admittedly' (uel sim.) is a clumsy English equivalent for this unpretentious idiom (e.g. Petr. 46.6, a freedman speaking, *non quidem doctus sed curiosus*).

7 huius cubiculi et triclini illius obiectu includitur 'enclosed between this room and the dining room I mentioned earlier is' (§4n. *includitur*); *illius* points back to the *triclinium* of §5. For *obiectus* 'obstruction' and the idea (usually topographical), cf. V. *Aen.* 1.160, *OLD* 1b; on the spelling *triclini* see 2.11.23n. *Mari.* **angulus** 'nook', implying a secluded place of retreat (*OLD* 6a) and suggesting (more affectively than literally) a small space. **purissimum solem continet et accendit** 'holds on to and fires up the clearest sun', *OLD purus* 6a, *contineo* 2a, 6, *accendo* 3a; for *sol* 'sunlight' (*OLD* 4), cf. 5.6.24; also 5.6.33 *purissimum diem recipit*. Language and paradox vary §6n. *altera*; cf. §17 *teporem solis . . . auget, tenet solem*. This area faces due south. **hoc hibernaculum, hoc etiam gymnasium meorum** 'this is the winter retreat of my staff, and their exercise ground too.' In domestic terms a *hibernum* or *hibernaculum* was a 'winter apartment' (Col. *RR* 1.6.1–2, Vitr. 1.2.7, 6.3.2, 7.4.4), here an outdoor space. *etiam* suggests an area sometimes used for exercise, not a demarcated gymnasium (cf. Förtsch 69–72), and different from the *gymnasia* of Cicero's villas (Greek-style gardens for philosophising). In giving prime outdoor space over to his slaves, P. demonstrates his trademark *humanitas* (2.6.4n. *etiamne*), and avoids sunburn. **meorum:** slaves and freedmen, as §24, 1.4.1 *meis . . . tuis*, 8.14.12 *suorum* etc. and e.g. Cic. *Fam.* 13.20.1, Hor. *Sat.* 2.6.65 (*TLL* VIII 920.22–7). A villa required a large staff, some permanently resident (1.4.2), others in one's retinue (5.6.46). Hoffer 1999: 29 n.1 estimates P.'s slave force at a minimum of 500 (see also Gonzalès 2003: 144–62); like their owner, the Laurentine workers scarcely intrude on our tour. **silent** 'are still', *OLD* 1b, poetic except for Columella. **exceptis qui nubilum**

inducunt et serenum ante quam usum loci eripiunt: abl. abs. (common with *excepto*: *TLL* v.2 1248.73–1249.25) with *eis* understood (ibid. 1249.3–4, §2n. *peractis*). The winds bringing cloud (*OLD nubilus* 2a, neuter adj. as noun) above can deprive you of a clear sky (*OLD serenum*, another neuter adj. as noun), but the lack of breeze keeps the temperature pleasant. *silent* now becomes paradoxical, given its primary sense of 'be silent' (high winds being inaudible in any weather). For *inducere* (*OLD* 17a), cf. Germ. *Arat.* 4.84 *inducet nubila*, and the phrase *nubes inducere* (Livy 1.29.4 and 8× in Ovid).

8 annectitur angulo 'adjoining the nook is'.   **cubiculum in hapsida curuatum:** an apsidal room, i.e. with one of the walls curved in a bay (for this brevity, cf. §4n. *porticus*). The shape was common (Wallace-Hadrill 1994: 22–3), but here the curved wall contains several windows through which it 'follows the path of the sun' (a south wall, then), as room 14 in the Pompeian Villa of Diomedes (Förtsch 20). ἁψίς 'arc, arch' is latinised as *apsis* by the elder Pliny; here uniquely it is aspirated and declined *à la grecque* (acc. sg.). It begins a series of more or less obtrusive Greek terms (along with the naturalised *triclinium* and *balineum*): §8 *bybliothecae*, §10 *procoetone*, §11 *baptisteria, hypocauston, propnigeon*, §12 *sphaeristerium*, §13 *apotheca*, §17 *xystus*, §21 *zotheca*, §22 *andron*). Whether this was pointed or mundane in the elite of P.'s day is hard to judge: Varro *RR* 2.*pr*.2 is caustic about those who 'think they don't have a villa unless it rattles with Greek vocabulary', but that was over a century earlier; Cic. *Leg.* 2.2 is critical of *euripus*, Mart. 12.50.1 of *platanon* (both features of the villa in 1.3.1), but it is not clear whether they are censuring object or word (or both). At all events the Greek has proved exotic to more distant readers, including already Sidonius (§11n. *baptisteria*). For Hoffer 1999: 37 it reflects the artifice of villa design, for Riggsby 2003: 170 luxurious excess. See also 2.2.1n. μικραίτιος.   **parieti eius in bybliothecae speciem armarium insertum est** 'a cupboard is set into the wall [i.e. one of its walls; cf. §21] in the shape of a library' (8.20.5 *in speciem carinae*, *OLD species* 3d). Scrolls were stored horizontally in such cupboards, preferably (for Vitr. 6.4.1) in a sunny spot. This one, one of the very few pieces of furniture we see (§21n. *lectum*), seems a significant choice for this textual treasure-house (next n.). Formal libraries in villas were rare, hence the apparent diffidence ('in the shape of'); P. mentions only one private library in the letters (4.28.1, not his). The orthography *bybl-*/*bibl-* is debatable; the more exotic *y* seems likely (cf. above on *cubiculum*).   **non legendos libros sed lectitandos** 'books not for reading but for reading and re-reading'; for *libros* see 2.1.5n.; for the enclosing word-order (*coniunctio*), 2.1.11n. *in*. The frequentative implies repeated consultation (*OLD lectito* 2), suggesting serious study and/or that this is just a selection of favourites, not to be compared with the great library collections of a Ciceronian villa (on which see Casson 2001: 69–79). P. follows Seneca's advice (*Ep.* 2), to pick a few good books and stick to them; they perhaps include Asinius Gallus' work on Cicero which P. has been reading here in 7.4.3. He is surely also offering advice to the reader: only repeated study unlocks the riches of this epistolary villa, as of the *Epistles*. The verbal polyptoton (2.1.12n. *et*) caught Sidonius' eye: *Ep.* 2.2.13 *ubi . . . dormitandi potius quam dormiendi locus est* (see §22n. *andron* on the same phrase). On Sidonius see intro. and Intro. 35–7. **capit** 'holds' (*OLD* 25a).

9 adhaeret: linking expressions remain varied (§7 *includitur*, §8 *annectitur*). **dormitorium membrum** 'bedroom': for *membrum* 'room' see 1.12.6, 5.6.15, *OLD* 3b; singular only here, replacing *cubiculum* perhaps for variety's sake (Förtsch 20 n.98). *dormitorius*, again at 5.6.21, is a rare term which P. seems to have picked up from his uncle (Pl. *NH* 30.52 *cubiculum dormitorium*; cf. Sid. *Ep.* 2.2.10 *dormitorium cubiculum*). **transitu interiacente** 'with a passage between' (*sc.* it and the previous room), abl. abs. **suspensus et tubulatus** 'with a hollow floor and piped walls' (Merrill), i.e. heated by a hypocaust. Not a rare feature (*pace* Mielsch 2003: 323): heated rooms have been found in several Laurentine villas, not always near the bath-houses (e.g. C28 at Vicus: §23n. *hypocauston*), as in North Africa (e.g. Lézine 1961: 93–8). Hot air (*uapor*) is captured (*conceptus*) and distributed under the 'suspended' floor (cf. *OLD suspendo* 4b) and through pipes in the walls (cf. Sen. *Prou.* 4.9 *subditus et parietibus circumfusus calor*, *Ep.* 90.25 *impressos parietibus tubos*, *NQ* 3.24.3) to generate a controlled temperature (on the technology see Forbes 1958: 36–57, Yegül 1992: 356–95 and 2010: 80–100). *tubulatus* is another borrowing from P.'s uncle (*NH* 9.130). **salubri temperamento** 'healthy mix [of hot and cold]', i.e. 'healthy moderation'; cf. Sen. *Ep.* 86.10 *salubrem temperaturam* (on temperance in olden bathing); it returns in a political context at 3.20.12 (also with *ministrare*). **huc illuc:** to the rooms on each side. **digerit et ministrat** 'distributes and supplies': *ministrare* (*OLD* 2–3) perhaps continues the 'willing slave' motif (§2n. *decem*). **lateris** 'wing'. An unspecified number of mundane service rooms (accommodation for slaves, kitchens, storerooms), probably making up the bulk of this wing (Winnefeld 1891: 214), pass in a single sentence: our concern is with the elite experience. **seruorum libertorumque:** §7n. *meorum*. **detinetur** 'is reserved for' + dat. (*OLD* 4b). **plerisque tam mundis ut accipere hospites possint** 'though most [of the rooms] are smart enough to accommodate guests', abl. abs. (*sc.* e.g. *cubiculis*); *mundis* is surely 'elegant' (*OLD mundus*[1] 2a), rather than literally 'clean' (1a). A rare glimpse of social life in the villa: see §11n. *natantes*, §12n. *latissimum*. With *possint* ('can' or 'could') P. does not say whether they were in fact so used; if so, this demonstrates the flexibility of the rooms, if not, it shows the villa-owner's pride and slave-owner's humanity (§7n. *hoc*). Trimalchio boasts of the capacity of his guest-quarters in Petr. 77.4 (the numeral is corrupt).

10 Ex alio latere 'on the other side' (*OLD latus* 8a). Having toured the rooms to the left (SE) of the *triclinium* in §§6–9 (124 words), we now cross to the north-west wing for §§10–12 (116 words). **est:** §6n. **politissimum** 'very elegant', one of the stronger claims to fine decor, though details go unspecified (§4n. *atrium*). **uel cubiculum grande uel modica cenatio:** chiastic. *cenatio* is a 1c. AD synonym for *triclinium*; for the form (*-tio* normally forms an action noun) cf. §13n. *gestationem*, 5.6.26 *descensiones*, *OLD aratio* 2. Although a dining room was often marked out by its floor mosaics, the furniture was usually movable (Dunbabin 1991), and designation could be accordingly fluid. Evidently P. expected *triclinia* to be larger than *cubicula*. He mentions four dining rooms at Laurentum and three in *Tusci*; this small one is perhaps suited to more casual moments, like the *cotidiana amicorumque cenatio* of 5.6.21. Such abundance was not rare; they could offer different levels of intimacy (1.3.1 *triclinia illa popularia, illa paucorum*) or simply variety (Wallace-Hadrill 1994: 57), not least of view (§15n. *hac*). **plurimo sole, plurimo mari lucet** 'is bright with abundant sun and abundant sea' (*OLD luceo* 2 'to shine with reflected light'). The simple balance belies the bold syllepsis (2.1.4n. *pari*): *lucet* goes naturally with *sole*, not with *mari*, giving mannered expression to the wide sea view (or, more mundanely, describing the light reflected from the water's surface). Sid. *Ep.* 2.2.11 follows P. closely here, with room-names, watery view, mannered bicolon and (a different) syllepsis: *ex hoc triclinio fit in diaetam siue cenatiunculam transitus, cui fere totus lacus quaeque tota lacui patet* (*cenatiuncula* is attested only in P. 4.30.2, whose mysterious lake subtends Sid. *Ep.* 2.2.17). **post hanc** 'behind this', to the landward side (§5n. *a lateribus*). **procoetone** 'antechamber' (προκοιτών), with a Latin ending, as usual in the abl. sg. (contrast §8 *hapsida*). Censured by Varro *RR* 2.*pr.*2 as an affected Grecism, the word is otherwise preserved in Latin only here (§10 twice, §23) and scarcely in Greek. Förtsch 55 suggests a small ante-room for the use of slaves (what Sid. *Ep.* 2.2.13 calls a *consistorium*), alternatively this may be a pair of rooms, with the *cubiculum* felt to be more private than its *procoeton* (a common type: Wallace-Hadrill 1994: 57). **altitudine aestiuum** 'summery [i.e. suited to summer: *OLD aestiuus* 1c] in its height' (because a high room stays cooler), perhaps describing *cubiculum* and *procoeton* together, though height might vary between them (Förtsch 55), as it commonly did throughout (e.g. building C at Vicus: Claridge 1998: 119–23). **munimentis hibernum** 'but wintry [i.e. suited to winter: *OLD hibernus* 1c] in its protection'. For the antithesis and adjectives, cf. 5.6.31 *porticus ante medium diem hiberna, inclinato die aestiua* (i.e. warm a.m., cool p.m.), and (cynically) the declaimer in Sen. *Exc. contr.* 5.5 *scilicet ut domus . . . brumales aestus habeant, aestiua frigora*. Seven heavy syllables match the weight of the walls. **subductum omnibus uentis** 'brought in safe from every wind', with a touch of nautical metaphor: *subducere* (+ dat.) is a technical term for furling sails in the face of storms (*OLD* 1d; Petr. 114.1 *uelaque tempestati subducunt* with Vannini) and for beaching ships (*OLD* 1b; Servius on V. *Aen.* 1.551). Cf. Sen. *Ben.* 7.1.7 *subductus ille tempestatibus in solido . . . stetit*, [Quint.] *Decl. mai.* 12.23 (both metaphorical). **aliud** sc. *cubiculum*. **et procoeton** varies *cum procoetone*. **communi pariete iunguntur** 'are joined by a shared wall', a mundane detail turned to oxymoron (walls divide).

11 inde 'next', 'beyond this', yet another connecting expression (§4n. *deinde*). **balinei** 'of the baths' (gen. sg.), heading its section. They are a standard feature (Yegül 1992: 50–5); other literary treatments include Sen. *Ep.* 86.6–13 (moralising at Scipio's villa), Mart. 6.42 and Stat. *Silu.* 1.5 (ecstatic ecphrasis), Lucian *Hippias*, Sid. *Ep.* 2.2.4–8 (a reply to P.). **cella frigidaria:** P.'s term (again at 5.6.25–6) for the *frigidarium* 'cold-room'. If the bathing experience starts here, P. has omitted the changing-room (5.6.25). **spatiosa et effusa:** two post-Augustan synonyms for 'large'; *effusus* is used of a room only here and Stat. *Silu.* 4.2.23 (*aula*). For the doublet, cf. 7.27.5 *spatiosa et capax domus*, 8.6.2 *copiosum et effusum*, 9.21.4 *plenius et effusius*. **baptisteria** 'bath-tubs, pools', another Grecism (a place to βαπτίζειν 'dip, plunge'), again at 5.6.25 (big enough to swim in). Sidonius uses it – noting the linguistic pretension – for an outdoor swimming pool: *Ep.* 2.2.8 *piscina forinsecus seu, si graecari mauis, baptisterium.* **uelut eiecta sinuantur** 'thrust out, as it were, in a curve' (lit. 'curve as if thrown out', *OLD sinuo* 1c, middle voice): a paraphrase, softened by *uelut*, to avoid the Vitruvian technical term *proiectura* 'projection'. These projecting pools invert the common scheme of setting a curved basin within an apse (e.g. the imperial villa at Tor Paterno, Marzano 2007: 320–1; Yegül 1992: 376–7). **abunde capacia si mare in proximo cogites** 'quite large enough, given the proximity of the sea' (lit. 'if you consider the sea nearby'), *OLD abunde* 3a, *cogito* 8b; see 2.6.5n. *si gulae* for the generalising second person. The appended *si*-clause qualifies *abunde capacia* as a relative judgment: cf. 4.2.2 *incredibile, sed Regulum cogita*, 6.31.13 *modica [cena], si principem cogitares* ('a modest dinner, considering the emperor [*sc.* was hosting it]'), 9.13.26, *Pan.* 64.1 and e.g. Sen. *Ep.* 94.56. **adiacet unctorium hypocauston, adiacet propnigeon balinei** 'then come the oiling-room, the furnace and the ante-furnace of the bath-house', one asyndetic pair, one noun + genitive, split by the anaphora of *adiacet*. **unctorium:** a room for oiling and massage (the word only here; Sid. *Ep.* 2.2.4 has an *unguentaria*); for once P. chooses Latin over Greek (*aleipterion* or Vitr. 5.11.2 *elaeothesium*), making chiasmus of Latin–Greek–Greek–Latin nouns. **hypocauston** 'hypocaust' (ὑπόκαυστον), referring either to the furnace itself, heating water and air, a chamber for transmitting the latter (§23, 5.6.25, Stat. *Silu.* 1.5.59), or (unparalleled) a 'sauna' (S-W 192). **propnigeon balinei:** προπνιγεῖον (only here and at Vitruv. 5.11.2) appears to be a type of warm-room, though its precise meaning is elusive (Saliou 2009: 353–4). The addition of *balinei* may suggest unfamiliarity. **duae cellae:** perhaps the warm *tepidarium* and hot *caldarium* (Merrill); Förtsch 21 would rather see a steam-room. P. covers ground quickly: baths were familiar terrain, and thorough exposition is not his aim. **magis elegantes quam sumptuosae:** the refrain of tempered pride (§4n. *atrium*); for *sumptuosae* see §3n. *uilla*. For the contrast, cf. Nep. *Att.* 13.5 *elegans, non magnificus, splendidus, non sumptuosus.* **calida piscina mirifica:** a warm-water pool adjacent to the hot-rooms; *mirifica* (§1n. *miraris*) implies unusual size and/or highlights the view. Evidently indoors (*calida*, not *tepida*; and next n.); perhaps it had shutters or movable panes of glass (Broise 1991: 61). **natantes mare aspiciunt:** for substantival *natantes* cf. 2.3.9n. *dicentis*, here in a generalising plural, as at 5.6.32 *intrantium oculis*, 36 *cubantium*, 40 *ambulatione fessos*, unusually revealing some occupants besides P. The view is now seen through human eyes (cf. §5n. *quasi*). Stat. *Silu.* 1.5.51–6 and 2.2.9–20 proclaim the superiority of a man-made *piscina* over sea or natural pond. P. caps that with the best of both worlds, a sea-view without the discomfort (Lefèvre 2009: 226–7); *natantes mare* captures the point. Sea-bathing (also an option, to judge from *si mare . . . cogites* above) was for the hardy (Sen. *Ep.* 53.3; on its heroic associations see also Hall 1994: 44–7). Seneca is caustic (*Ep.* 86.8): people nowadays are not content *nisi et lauantur simul et colorantur* ['get a tan'], *nisi ex solio* ['tub'] *agros ac maria prospiciunt*. P.'s luxury finds a parallel on the shore at Herculaneum, a large indoor heated pool with windows out to sea on three sides (De Simone et al. 1998: 39–43, Guidobaldi et al. 2009: 91–124 (esp. p.93 figs 48–9), Wallace-Hadrill 2011: 163, 165).

12 nec procul *sc. est.* **sphaeristerium:** a court nominally for exercise with the *pila* (= σφαῖρα) 'ball' (e.g. 3.1.8 with Mayor), but P.'s Etruscan one *plura genera exercitationis . . . capit* (5.6.27). The word is well attested in Greek, and in Latin authors of P.'s time. **calidissimo soli . . . occurrit** 'faces the hottest sun'; *occurrere* is not uncommon of topography (*OLD* 4b) but is rare of buildings (5.6.23 *cubiculum triclinio occurrit*, Sen. *Ep.* 55.7 *occurrit* [*uilla*] *. . . Fauonio*). The court is open to the SW, perhaps between the buildings and the sea-front, so that it picks up the late afternoon sun (a favoured time for exercise: 3.1.8, 9.36.3, S-W 193). The superlative suggests that we are temporarily in summer. Sidonius (*Ep.* 2.2.11) pokes fun at P.'s seasonal inconsistency, describing a winter room before interrupting himself: *sed quid haec tibi, quem nunc ad focum minime inuito? quin potius ad te tempusque pertinentia loquar* (his season was clearly set as high summer). **inclinato iam die:** abl. abs. (lit. 'the day having now turned / started to sink': *OLD inclino* 4b), not evening but mid- to late afternoon, the hottest time (cf. 5.6.31, quoted in §10n. *munimentis*). Cicero refers to the time after siesta as *inclinato iam in postmeridianum tempus die* (*De or.* 3.17; cf. *Tusc.* 3.17); for simple *inclinato die*, see 5.6.31, 7.27.2 and e.g. Sen. *NQ* 1.8.6. **turris** 'tower', or more precisely 'upper storey(s)' (Döring; below on *sub qua*). It has two sets of rooms 'below' it (i.e. on the ground floor), and two sets of rooms 'in' it (on the upper floor), as well as a dining room with excellent views. P.'s *turres* are often imagined to resemble the slender quasi-defensive tower depicted (or imagined) on contemporary wall-paintings (Förtsch 48, 116–27, plates 33–9, with Bergmann 1995: 412). Deterring piracy had once been important (cf. Sen. *Ep.* 55.11, 86.4) and decorative mock-turrets are archaeologically attested (Marzano 2007: 22–3), such as the word *turris* might seem to fit, or seek to evoke. Yet the number and size of rooms described, in particular for the second tower (§13, esp. *lata*), warn against taking P.'s term too literally. **erigitur** 'rises' (middle voice), first in V. *Aen.* 8.417, with *turris* in Lucan 3.455. Sidonius has *comminus erigitur . . . turris* in his architectural-ecphrastic *Carm.* 22.211 (on reflexes of Statius and P. in which, see §23n. *quem*, Pavlovskis 1973: 45–8). **sub qua** *sc. sunt* 'beneath which are', in our terms 'on its ground floor'. Vitr. 5.12.6 *turris insuper* *aedificari* (also ibid. 10.13.6) shows the same conception of a tower as beginning not at ground level, but one storey up. The interpretation 'beside the base of which' (Winnefeld 1891: 215, Förtsch 48) is linguistically unproblematic (*OLD sub* 6a) but implausible given the parallel use of *sub hoc* [*sc. horreo*] in §13. **diaetae** 'apartments', a standard term (LSJ δίαιτα II); see Mau *RE* v.i: 307–8, Förtsch 48–52. It is often ambiguous whether *diaeta* refers to a single room or a suite (*pace OLD* 2). P. certainly means the latter in 2.17.20, 5.16.21, 31 (two *diaetae*, containing seven *cubicula* between them); here and 5.6.27–8 it is not clear, though arguments about the likely width of a 'tower' are immaterial (above). Stat. *Silu.* 2.2.83 is similarly ambiguous (see Van Dam ad loc.). **in ipsa:** on the upper floor. **cenatio:** an upstairs dining-room may be a boast for gauche Trimalchio (Petr. 77.4 *susum cenationem*, with Schefferus' emendation), bringing his total to five, against P.'s three or four (§10n. *uel cubiculum*). **latissimum mare, longissimum litus, uillas amoenissimas:** AB∼AB∼BA (as §1 *gratiam . . . spatium*), a broad panorama (and expansive phrase) to pause on as we complete our tour of this wing. With *longissimum litus*, cf. §1 *litoris spatium*; on *amoenitas* see §25n. *haec*. The vista may, but need not, suggest that this room is on a third storey. These other villas had inhabitants, of course, and 5.6.45 indirectly hints at a lively social life on the coast (*nemo accersitor ex proximo* [*sc. in Tuscis*], with Champlin 1982: 104–5); see §9n. *plerisque* and G–M 231 on this 'millionaires' row'; for the archaeological evidence see §26n. *uicus*. In 2.17, however, the emphasis is on remote tranquillity, and on the views. **possidet** 'owns', i.e. commands a view of. The conceit that a property owns the land around, and conversely that the surroundings are 'slaves' to the property, recurs at 1.3.1 *subiectus et seruiens lacus*, 5.6.23 [*piscina*] *seruit ac subiacet*, and is found already in Hor. *Ep.* 1.11.26 *locus effusi late maris arbiter*, Mart. 4.64.8 *luce nitet peculiari*, Stat. *Silu.* 2.2.74–5 *omni proprium thalamo mare . . . diuersis seruit sua terra fenestris*. It may recall the legal term *seruitutes* 'easements', which included the right of a house not to have its views blocked (Berger 1953: 702–3, Buckland 1963: 259–61). The juxtaposition with (other people's) *uillas amoenissimas* is piquant (too piquant for one copyist (β), whose correction *prospicit* was widely preferred until the twentieth century: Stout 1954: 122–3, reversing id. 1924: 67–8). For another play on *possidere* see 1.3.1 (there of the villa 'owning' its owner: cf. 2.15.1n. *quomodo te*).

13 Est et alia turris: a unique shift from physical sequence to conceptual link, breaking the mostly continuous tour as we come to the fourth and final segment of the main house. Since the *triclinium* of this 'tower' is the *cenatio* of §15n. *hac*, a position on the NE corner of the villa, near the entrance, can (with hindsight) be reconstructed. Winnefeld implausibly detaches it altogether from the main house, and puts it beside the rooms it contains (p. xii, no. 22; cf. §12n. *sub*). **in hac:** on the upper floor (as §12 *in ipsa*). **in quo sol nascitur conditurque** 'in which the sun is born and is laid to rest'. *nasci* 'rise' (*OLD* 3a) is poetic; so too *condere* in this context (V. *Ecl.* 9.52 *condere soles*; cf. *diem condere* at

9.36.4, *Pan.* 80.5, *OLD condo* 8). In a bold figure, capping §6n. *altera*, the room becomes not witness but site of this solar activity. It has windows facing E/SE and W/SW. For final *-que* see 2.1.4n. *durior*. **lata:** a clear sign that P.'s 'towers' are not slender. **post** 'behind' (adverb: *OLD post*[1] 1), to the NW (cf. §10n. *post*); also upstairs. **apotheca et horreum:** ἀποθήκη (latinised in Cicero) is a store-room usually for wine; *horreum* was originally a grain-store (Col. *RR* 1.6.9–10 advises that the latter be on an upper floor, facing NE, as this perhaps does) but could also by now be a general store room (8.18.11 has *horrea* full of unused furniture). S-W 194 suggests that upper floors were less suited to personal use given their heat, forgetting the dining-rooms, *diaetae* and *cubiculum* mentioned, and the frequent winter use of this villa. These are the only service rooms to be specified (contrast §9n. *lateris*): the *turris* earns fuller exposition. **sub hōc triclinium** sc. *est*, on the ground floor under the grain-store, facing NE into the grounds described next. **turbati maris non nisi fragorem et sonum patitur** 'is exposed [*OLD patior* 1b] only to the roaring noise of the stormy sea', opening a parallel antithesis *turbati maris . . . patitur* ∼ *hortum et gestationem uidet*, with varied cases in the opening nouns (cf. 2.11.9n. *sed*). Along with light, heat and wind, sounds add to the sensory experience: cf. §22–4 (noisy villa but silent pavilion), §7 *silent uenti*. For *non nisi* 'only', frequent in Pl. *NH*, see *OLD nisi* 9; for *fragorem et sonum*, cf. Fronto *Ad Ver.* 2.1.8 (p. 122.8 vdH²) *fragoribus nubium et sonoribus procellarum* and the commoner doublet *fragor* + *sonitus*. This dining-room provides maximum contrast with the sea-lapped *triclinium* of §5; on the stormy weather, see §5n. *Africo*. For a slightly different 'best of both worlds', cf. Stat. *Silu.* 2.2.50–1 *haec pelagi clamore fremunt, haec tecta sonoros | ignorant fluctus terraeque silentia malunt.* The roar of the sea is heard at 6.31.17 *uastus illic fragor* (Trajan's villa up the coast at Centumcellae); in this letter it is comfortably distant (§5n. *Africo*). **eumque** 'and that', qualifying *fragorem et sonum* (*OLD is* 7, Oakley on Livy 9.18.9). **languidum et desinentem** 'dying faintly away' (for *desinentem* 'dying' cf. 2.10.4); cf. Germ. *Arat.* 344 *languenti desinit astro.* **hortum:** the only land in this villa worth mentioning, according to 4.6.2 *nihil quidem ibi possideo praeter tectum et hortum statimque harenas.* On gardens, integral to the villa experience, see *OCD* 'gardens', Purcell 1996a, von Stackelberg 2009; on their place in literature, Beard 1998, Henderson 2004b, Myers 2005, Pagán 2006. **gestationem** 'ride, drive', for the taking of exercise by being conveyed in a *uehiculum* (3.1.5, 9.36.3), a small carriage drawn by horses or ponies (cf. Mart. 1.12.8 *gestatus biiugis . . . equis*, Juv. 7.179–80 *gestetur . . . iumenta*), or a *lectula*, a litter carried by slaves (Celsus 2.15.3, Courtney on Juv. 4.5–6). The practice (itself called *gestatio*) was considered healthy recreation (Blümner 1911: 86), and makes a daily constitutional at *Tusci* (9.36.3), sometimes varied with horse riding (9.36.5; cf. 9.15.3; that villa boasts a *hippodromus* 'riding course', 5.6.32, as well as an *ambulatio* 'walk' and *gestatio*, 5.6.17). Laurentine excursions perhaps extend to the coast too (§27n. *quod*). Like Seneca (*Ep.* 15.6), P. finds *gestatio* conducive to literary composition (9.36.3), meditating and dictating to a slave. He is the first to make the noun describe the circuit itself (1.3.1, 5.6.17; for the *-tio* form see §10n. *uel*),

which could take varying forms (9.7.4) but was not small: Spurinna manages seven
Roman miles a day (3.1.6–7), and the *gestatio* here encloses a substantial garden
(§15n. *morus*). The nearby 'Villa del confine' at La Chiesola (Lauro–Claridge 1998:
41, 43 fig. 7) has a garden and surrounding *gestatio* occupying about 200×100m
(information owed to Amanda Claridge). **uidet:** yet another expression for
'looks out onto'.

14 gestatio and §15 *hortum* chiastically take up §13 *hortum et gestationem* for a new
parallel antithesis *gestatio... ambitur ~ hortum... uestit* (obscured by the conventional section numbering); the cases of the opening nouns are again varied (§13n.
turbati). **buxo aut rore marino** 'box or rosemary', evergreens common for
borders. Although box was not to everyone's taste (*grauem praefert odorem*, Pl. *NH*
16.70), it was in common use (ibid.; Mart. 3.58.3), and features heavily in P.'s
Etruscan villa, especially for topiary (5.6.16–17, 32–6). McEwen 1995: 17 sees
(tenuous?) literary hints: box was used for writing-tablets; rosemary sharpens the
sight (Pl. *NH* 24.99) and thus (so McEwen) the memory. **nam... inarescit:**
explaining *ubi deficit buxus*. **qua parte defenditur tectis:** by the cryptoportico sheltering this part of the grounds from the sea (§15), by the pavilion at its
end (§§20–4), and perhaps by part of the main house. **aperto caelo apertoque uento** 'in the open sky and wind', i.e. where it is exposed to the elements,
with mannered anaphora: *aperto caelo* is an established pair, mostly poetic; *aperto
uento* is unprecedented (*OLD apertus* 3c performs contortions accordingly). The
abl. expresses place, with poetic omission of *in* (*NLS* §51), in antithesis to *qua parte
defenditur tectis* (10~9 syllables). The MSS (followed by all editions) transmit *et* after
uento. This seems to be an intrusion, easy but unwelcome between *aperto... uento*,
abl. of place, and *aspergine*, abl. of cause; it also obscures the parallel antithesis
of place + adverb/adverbial phrase + verb (*qua parte defenditur tectis* + *abunde* +
uiret ~ aperto caelo apertoque uento + *quamquam longinqua aspergine maris* + *inarescit*). The
interpolation must have been in the archetype, since all MSS transmit it (Intro.
38–9). **quamquam longinqua aspergine maris** 'because of the spray of
the sea, though distant', abl. of cause (*NLS* §45), as e.g. Pl. *NH* 16.89 [*folia*] *candore
[solis] inarescant*. *quamquam* modifies only *longinqua*, a verbless concession common
in this period (Kraut 1872: 35–6, K–S II 444–5, Madvig on Cic. *Fin.* 5.68). At the
end of the *gestatio* furthest from both house and sea, salinity in the air dries out the
box. The dry observation is set in paradox (*aspergine... inarescit*) and characteristically limpid language: *aspergo* for sea-spray is hitherto exclusively poetic (first
in V. *Aen.* 3.534); P. has it of fresh water in 5.6.20. Sidonius' oxymoron *asperginis
fragor impluat* (*Ep.* 2.2.15) may be a reflex of P. here (cf. §13 *fragorem*). **inarescit:**
common of plants or trees drying out (*TLL* VII.1 834.3–17).

15 adiacet interiore circumitu 'beside it on its inner circuit is'. *gestationi*,
transmitted in all MSS after *adiacet*, looks like an intrusion. P. does not normally
add a dative to words like *adiacet*; this one might seem justified by the parenthesis
on *buxus* (§23 *applicitum est cubiculo* looks similar but cancels a potential ambiguity,

not a risk here) and the desire for a signpost, but it disrupts the parallel antithesis *gestatio . . . hortum* (§14n. *gestatio*) and spoils the further antithesis *ambitur ~ adiacet interiore circumitu* (outside ~ inside, as at 5.6.33). It is an early interpolation if so (§14n. *aperto*). **uinea tenera et umbrosa nudisque etiam pedibus mollis et cedens** 'vines, delicate and shady, soft and yielding even to bare feet'. *uinea* (f. sg.), used in 5.6.29–30 for 'vineyard', here uniquely describes a pergola walk (Förtsch 66 n.761), comprising both the vines with frame above (cf. *OLD umbrosus* 2 'affording plentiful shade') and the ground below: there is an analogy in *porticus*, referring both to a portico and to the ground it shades (e.g. Ov. *Ars* 1.491 2 *spatiosa teretur | porticus,* Juv. 4.5–6). For *mollis* ground see §2 *molle* and e.g. Ov. *Ars* 3.688 *mollis humus,* Col. *RR* 4.4.3 *mollis ac tenera humus*; for *pedibus . . . cedens* cf. Ov. *Ars* 1.560 *imposito cessit harena pede* (Gierig); *tenera* can describe both plant (*OLD* 3c) and ground (*OLD* 5a), the latter tautological with *cedens*. Förtsch (plate 42.5) reconstructs a free-standing pergola describing a circuit between (uncovered) *gestatio* and (uncovered) *hortus,* odd but perhaps possible, though *adiacet* does not imply any particular length; for the letter, in any case, its intermediate place is elegant (centering the focus progressively through *gestatio – uinea – hortus*). Smaller vine-pergolas were common in Pompeian gardens (Jashemski 1979, index s.v.) and their pleasant shade a poetic commonplace (V. *Ecl.* 7.58, [Virgil] *Copa* 31 etc.). We have moved for a moment out of the default season (§3n. *tepore*), to see the garden on a summer's day. There is no call to emend *uinea* (in all MSS) to *uinca* 'periwinkle' (Sulze 1931; *uinca* in Aldus is a misprint, corrected in his 1518 edition) or *uia* (Schefferus 1675, S-W): *umbrosa* would be nonsense with the first, mysterious with the second. **tenera et umbrosa . . . mollis et cedens:** the two phrase-final adjective pairs are varied in application (previous n.), length and clausula. **hortum:** garden and description are plain by contrast with the elaborations of the Etruscan villa and letter (5.6.32–40), but this sentence takes central place in the letter (*hortum* is the 537th word of 1082), framed by *gestatio,* main house, cryptoportico and pavilion in the prose as in the architecture. On centres in (Virgilian) ecphrasis, see Thomas 1983. **morus et ficus frequens** 'numerous mulberry and fig trees'; *frequens* + collective sg. is used esp. by writers on nature: *TLL* VI.1 1299.47–72. The enclosure is evidently not small (§13n. *gestationem*). **uestit:** common of plants and trees (5.6.32, *OLD* 2b). **uel maxime** 'especially' (*uel* 'I dare say', *OLD* 5c). **malignior ceteris** 'unkinder to other [trees]', in chiastic antithesis, with varied cases, to *quarum arborum . . . ferax.* For *malignior,* cf. V. *Georg.* 2.179 *collesque maligni*; again in this context at *Pan.* 31.6. For S-W these words exclude the reading *uinea* (above); but the vine was not straightforwardly considered a tree (Columella *De arboribus* 1.2) and the ground is fertile enough (*pinguis* below). The acknowledgement of imperfection keeps us firmly in the real world: no fantasy ecphrasis here (contrast Alcinous' garden, Hom. *Od.* 7.112–32, or the Cyclopes' island, *Od.* 9.116–41). **hac non deteriore quam maris facie cenatio remota a mari fruitur** 'this is the view, no worse than that of the sea, which the dining room away from the sea enjoys', summing up

§§14–15, all of which we saw through the window of this *cenatio* (= the *triclinium* of §13). Polyptoton and alliteration combine in *maris facie . . . mari fruitur*. This inland view equals the sea-vista of the *triclinium* in the first *turris* (§12), giving the 'towers' matching but varied charm. **cingitur diaetis duabus a tergo:** chiastic antithesis with *facie . . . fruitur*. Two apartments 'enclose' the south and west sides of the dining-room ('behind', i.e. away from the view: §5n. *a lateribus*), completing the ground floor of this wing. **subiacet:** §6n. *et*. It need not imply an upper storey (cf. Col. *RR* 1.2.3 *campus . . . aedificio subiaceat*). **uestibulum uillae:** an entrance-court, or at least a structured approach to the main entrance (Förtsch 31, 127–35; Leach 1993). We have thus closed a spatial and textual ring from our entry at §4. **hortus alius pinguis et rusticus** 'a fertile country garden', apparently a kitchen garden (Grimal 1984: 422). Its location is left vague, but must be somewhere near the main entrance. The pair *hortus pinguis* finds a sole match in V. *Georg.* 4.118 *pinguis hortos* (glossed by Erren ad loc. as 'vegetable gardens'). There it heads a list of subjects which Virgil will *not* treat as his poem moves to its final stage; here it ends our tour of the main house on a characteristic paradox of rich simplicity (*pinguis* + *rusticus*).

16–19 Cryptoportico

16 Hinc 'from here', referring to the second *turris* as a whole, the focal (and viewing) point of §§13–15, and thus approximately the NE corner of the main building. Alternatively (the word is vague), 'from the vestibulum' (S-W 195); less persuasively, 'from the villa as a whole', as taken by Zehnacker 1 158 and apparently by Salza Prina Ricotti 1984: 340 (= Förtsch, plates 42.3–4). In any event, the tour of the main villa is now complete, and we proceed NW (see below on *extenditur*) along the cryptoportico – not without stopping to admire it – to the pavilion at its end. **cryptoporticus:** a walled and roofed arcade, usually called a *crypta* (< κρυπτή 'hidden, covered'). P. may have coined this bilingual compound (κρυπτο- + *porticus*): it appears only in his letters, and in a wry appropriation by Sidonius at the centre of his villa letter (*Ep.* 2.2.10 *longitudo tecta intrinsecus patet . . . quae . . . etsi non hippodromus* [∼ 5.6.32–6], *saltim cryptoporticus meo mihi iure uocitabitur*). The structure was now common in villa architecture (Förtsch 41–8, plates 4–8; Zarmakoupi 2011); P. has two in *Tusci*, one overground like this, one semi-subterranean (5.6.28–30). Like the Elizabethan 'long gallery', it was used for exercise and meditation, in P.'s case also for composition (by dictation: 9.36.3). It is a point of pride, described at length with unusual immodesty and with six statements of the bulky word itself (two each of nom., acc. and gen.). **prope publici operis** 'virtually [the size of] a civic building', gen. of description (*NLS* §85.1.a, as 3.1.5 and 8.5.1 *uxorem singularis exempli*). Suddenly changing the tone after the humble *hortus . . . rusticus*, the cryptoportico earns the boldest claim in the letter to (urban) grandeur. *publicum opus* is a common phrase, but in this context cf. Cic. *Q. fr.* 3.1.4 *uiam perspexi; quae mihi ita placuit ut opus publicum uideretur esse* and (*pace* S-W 196) the *porticus . . . urbis opus* of Stat. *Silu.* 2.2.30–1. As ever, P. is more modest than Statius: he compares his portico to a civic building, not an entire city, and adds a tempering *prope*. Even so, he remains vulnerable to moralising criticism, e.g. Hor. *C.* 2.15.14–16, Sen. *Exc. contr.* 5.5, Sen. *Ben.* 7.10.5, *Ep.* 90.43 (for the other side see Vitr. 6.5.2, advising ambitious senators *basilicas non dissimili modo quam publicorum operum magnificentia habeant comparatas*; see also Platts 2011: 251–65). Sidonius notes the risks: *Ep.* 2.2.5 *frigidaria . . . quae piscinas publicis operibus exstructas non impudenter aemularetur*. The length could be 100m or more, far greater than implied on most reconstructions. Porticoes are long enough for *gestatio* at Mart. 1.12.8, 1.82.5, Juv. 7.178–9, and the garden whose side this one flanks was substantial (§15n. *morus*). At the 'Villa del confine' (§13n. *gestationem*) a seafront *porticus* over 100m long, with windows on both sides, joins the main building to a set of baths.   **extenditur:** middle voice. It runs NW, perpendicular to the main axis of the villa and parallel to the shore. S-W 195–8 improbably makes it head south, running into difficulties in §18 (the shade over the *gestatio*) and §19, where he must deny the clear meaning of *in capite xysti*. Through a misunderstanding (§19n. *tum*) Winnefeld has it run due north.   **utrimque fenestrae** *sc. sunt*; cf. the 'Villa del confine' (above on *prope*).   **a mari . . . ab horto** 'facing the sea . . . facing the garden' (§5n. *a lateribus*).   †**singulae sed alternis pauciores**† 'one but to every two fewer', an unsolved crux. The MSS agree, except that αγ have *sed*, β *et*, and the gist is clear – there are fewer windows on the garden side, exposed to the north wind (§17 *Aquilonem*), than on the side facing the sea and its pleasant breezes (§19n. *patentibus*) – but the Latin seems corrupt. Solutions include: (*i*) *singulae et alternis pauciores* 'single-shuttered and fewer by half' (Cataneus): an unparalleled but plausible use of *singulus*, given that double shutters were the norm (§5n. *undique*), but *alternis* should mean 'alternately' (5.6.35, 5.18.2, *OLD* 1); (*ii*) *singulae et pauciores*, solving that problem (could *alternis* be the corruption of an interpolated *alteris*?); (*iii*) the transposition *pauciores sed alternis singulae* (Keil, Merrill 1922), which does little to help; (*iv*) excision of *singulae sed alternis* (Stout 1954: 155–6), leaving a balanced but pat antithesis *a mari plures, ab horto pauciores* (cf. e.g. §10 *altitudine aestiuum, munimentis hibernum*, 5.6.32 *ut summae suis, ita imae alienis*; Deufert 2008: 71 n.40 suggests that *sed* and *et* are different attempts to fix an interpolated *singulae alternis*); (*v*) excision of *pauciores*, an easy intrusion if P. had avoided balance for once, and of *et/sed* to leave *singulae alternis* 'one for every other [window on the other side]', taking *alternis* (*OLD alternus* 4a) as dative. Rhythm is less decisive than is sometimes claimed: *pauciores* is a safe ditrochee, but *singulae sed alternis* and *singulae alternis* are equally good cretic–spondees (the elision is unremarkable: e.g. 2.11.19 *sententiae adiecit*, 2.13.4 *prouinciae illius*, 2.14.1 *paruae et exiles*). 'Locus nondum videtur esse sanatus' (Schuster).   **hae, cum serenus dies et immotus, omnes, cum hinc uel inde uentis inquietus, qua uenti quiescunt sine iniuria patent** 'these [windows] stay open harmlessly, all of them when the sky is clear and still; when it is restless with winds on one side

or the other, those on the side where the winds are at rest'. Parallel antithesis with
paired *cum*-clauses; *hae* and *sine iniuria patent* are distributed in double *apo koinou*
(though *sine iniuria* pertains more to the second scenario). **cum serenus dies
et immotus** *sc. est*; for such omission in a *cum*-clause (twice in this sentence), cf.
8.14.7, 8.20.1; with other conjunctions, e.g. 1.12.5 *quoad uiridis aetas*, 5.6.25 *si dies
nubilus*, 6.20.12 (*donec*), 9.36.3 (*ubi*). Although the verbal ellipse is unremarkable
(2.2.1n. *quod*), the phrasing here seems poetic: cf. V. *Ecl.* 8.15 *cum ros . . . gratissimus*,
Hor. *Sat.* 1.10.33, Ov. *Ars* 2.315, 3.173. *dies* 'sky', i.e. weather (9.36.3; *OLD* 2c),
divides the adjectives in *coniunctio* (2.1.11n. *in*). *serenus dies* (replacing *serenum caelum*)
is common in the 1c. AD, especially in Pl. *NH*; *immotus* of weather, and this pair,
is matched only by Tac. *H.* 1.86.1 *sereno et immoto die*. It is varied at 5.6.14 *sereno
et placido die*. **hinc uel inde** 'on one side or the other'. **uentis inquietus**
sc. dies est. For *inquietus* of weather, cf. Livy 5.42.6 (*lux*) and Sen. *NQ* 2.11.1 (*aer*),
6.12.2 (*tempus*), etc.; for the two different winds, above on *singulae*. **quiescunt**
inverts *inquietus* and varies §7 *silent*. **sine iniuria:** without harm or detriment
(to the ambience within). For *iniuria* of weather, see *TLL* VII.1 1675.56–1676.5.
sine iniuria is common, but for the combination with *fenestrae*, cf. Sen. *Ep.* 86.8 on
the narrow chinks of olden days that *sine iniuria munimenti lumen admitterent* (i.e. did
not compromise the defensive function of the wall): a typical contrast between
Senecan moralising and Plinian comfort.

17 ante cryptoporticum xystus: cf. 5.6.16 *ante porticum xystus* (also *sc. est*). The
ξυστός 'garden terrace', usually adjacent to a portico, was a space for strolling
(or sitting: Mayor on 3.1.5) and meditation (cf. 9.36.3; Grimal 1984: 251–2, 266–7;
Förtsch 73–4). **uiolis odoratus:** after sight (*passim*) and sound (§13 *fragorem et
sonum*), the first and only mention of smell, though we have observed rosemary
(and box) at §14. Violets are 'a standard element in natural and artificial paradises'
(Nisbet–Hubbard on Hor. *C.* 2.15.5). **teporem solis infusi repercussu
cryptoporticūs auget** 'it magnifies the warmth of the sun streaming in with the
reflection of the cryptoportico': like the *angulus* of §7, the *xystus* actively enhances
the sun for its user's pleasure. *tepor solis* is first in Livy 41.2.4; for *sol infusus*, cf. V.
Aen. 9.461, Sen. *NQ* 5.1.2. The verbal noun *repercussus* (the fact of being reflected,
echoed, etc.) is a favourite of the elder Pliny, not least for the sun (also Sen.
Ben. 4.30.4, *NQ* 1.7.1); but P. makes it active, 'the cryptoportico's reflecting it', a
usage rare even with his uncle (e.g. *NH* 37.76 *angulorum*); similarly 10.61.4 *maris*.
Word order and rhythm (cretic–spondee) make *cryptoporticus* almost certainly
genitive. **quae:** the antecedent is *cryptoporticūs* (feminine, like *porticus*). **ut tenet
solem sic Aquilonem inhibet summouetque:** *ut . . . sic* 'just as . . . so too'
(*OLD ut* 5). Chiasmus with lengthening (two verbs) in the second member; *tenet
solem* varies §6 *retinet*, §7 *continet*. The *Aquilo* is the chill north (strictly NNE) wind.
inhibet summouetque 'curbs and drives back': the second verb obtrusively
personifies the cryptoportico as obliging servant (§2n. *decem*, §6n. *altera*). For final
-que see 2.1.4n. *durior*. **quantumque caloris ante tantum retro frigoris**

'and [keeps] as much heat in front as cold behind', supplying e.g. *retinet*. ABC~ACB, with the partitive genitives *caloris* and *frigoris* (the latter unwelcome chill, not pleasant cool, as §18 *hieme* shows) picking up *solem* and *Aquilonem* in parallel. Despite the balance, the experience is focalised only from the terrace side, where we feel the sun while shielded from the cold. **Africum:** §5n. **diuersissimos** 'wholly opposite', fairly common in prose. The two winds made a stormy pair: Hor. *C.* 1.3.12–13 *praecipitem Africum | decertantem Aquilonibus*, Pl. *NH* 2.125, 18.335 *contrarius Aquilo Africo*, Sen. *NQ* 5.18.2. **alium alio latere** 'with its two sides' (lit. 'one with the one side, the other with the other', *OLD alius*[2] 2b). **frangit et finit** 'breaks and bounds', i.e. weakens and delimits, with alliteration.

18 haec iucunditas eius hieme, maior aestate *sc. est.* Another shimmer of summer (§15n. *uinea*): this timeless account is not bounded by chronological literalism. Mynors' §18 begins at *nam*, presumably a slip (cf. §4n.). **nam ante meridiem . . . temperat:** parallel antithesis, with *umbra sua temperat* (*OLD* 5b 'moderate, regulate') understood twice, like §16 *sine iniuria patent*. In the morning the cryptoportico casts its cooling shade SW over the *xystus*, in the afternoon NE over part of the *gestatio* and garden. **quae** = *umbra sua.* **ut dies creuit decreuitue** 'as the day rises and falls' (lit. 'according as the day has increased or decreased', *OLD ut* 17), i.e. as the sun's height changes through the day (*TLL* v.1 219.82–3), with aural play (*dies creuit ~ decreuit*). The usage is unparalleled: at Pl. *NH* 2.151 *die decrescente . . . crescente* refers to change through the year (similarly *crescere* at Lucr. 5.680, Livy 37.41.2, Pl. *NH* 18.264). **modo breuior, modo longior hac uel illa cadit** 'falls now shorter, now longer, on one side or the other', picking up chiastically the two concepts of morning/afternoon and movement of the sun: A (*ante meridiem . . . post meridiem*) ~ B (*creuit decreuitue*) ~ B (*modo breuior, modo longior*) ~ A (*hac uel illa*). At the same time there is non-chiastic alternation (ABAB) of asyndeton and coordination (*ue/uel*) across the four phrases.

19 ipsa uero cryptoporticus: a climax marked by *ipsa* and *uero* (2.1.7n. *mihi*), as the cryptoportico returns in the nominative to show off its star feature. **tum maxime caret sole cum ardentissimus culmini eius insistit** 'it lacks the sun most of all when it is bearing down hottest on its roof'. A conceit contrived from ellipse and focalisation: the cryptoportico feels cool to someone inside, namely the reader, who is now invited to admire its star feature from within (Maselli 1995: 99–100). Winnefeld 1891: 215 (followed by Förtsch 21, 41) mistook P. to mean that it casts no shade at midday, and so made it run due north-south. **ad hoc:** 2.11.10n. **patentibus fenestris Fauonios accipit transmittitque:** with the shutters on both sides open, it allows the pleasant breeze through. The *Fauonius* was a westerly wind (equivalent to Greek Zephyr) associated with spring (Lucr. 1.11; Hor. *C.* 1.4.1 with Nisbet–Hubbard); unlike the *Africus* it was considered kind and nourishing (it was supposed to derive from *fouere*, Maltby 1991: 226), and a pleasant feature of the west coast (Sen. *Ep.* 55.7 on Vatia's villa); hence the greater number of windows on the west side (§16). The plural, first in Hor. *C.* 3.7.2, was by now regular in prose. For final *-que* see 2.1.4n. *durior*. **aëre pigro et manente** 'with inert and settled air'; for *aer piger* caused by the absence of wind, see Sen. *NQ* 7.21.1 *aeris pigri* (cf. *NQ* 1.2.6 *stabili aere et pigro uento*, 5.18.1 *aera... pigrescere*), Lucan 6.107. **ingrauescit** 'become heavy', 'be oppressive', transferring to the cryptoportico the quality of its air; for the latter, cf. Lucr. 6.570 (*uenti*), Sen. *NQ* 1.13.3 (*nubes*), 6.28.2 (*spiritus*, a noxious gas), *pace OLD ingrauesco* 1c.

20–4 *Pavilion*

20 In capite xysti, deinceps cryptoporticūs horti 'at the head of the terrace, then of the cryptoportico and of the garden'; the last two genitives in asyndeton. *caput* is common in architectural language (*OLD* 9–11) but aptly bolsters the personifying force of *amores mei*, not so much the villa's heart, as it were, as its head (detached from its main body by the cryptoportico); see also §21n. *a pedibus*. This final group of rooms is constructed along the far, NW end of the cryptoportico; P. will describe them, as *deinceps* implies, from west (the *xystus* side) to east (the *hortus* side). *hortus* here and in §22 refers to the garden surrounded by *gestatio* of §15 (*pace* S-W 195). **diaeta** 'apartment' (§12n.), in this case a pavilion detached from the main villa. **amores mei** 'my darling', 'my jewel'. A common phrase esp. in poetry for one's beloved, used here uniquely and extravagantly not of a person but of a building (cf. 1.3.1 *Comum, tuae meaeque deliciae*), a climax of the running personification (§2n. *decem*). Stat. *Silu.* 3.5.105, concluding praise of his villa and homeland, is a (loose) comparandum, *mille tibi nostrae referam telluris amores?* ('delights'). Like Statius there, P. may be alluding to the supposed etymology *amoenus* < *amor* (attributed to Varro by Isid. *Orig.* 14.8.33; cf. *TLL* I 1962.30–42, and perhaps underlying the opening of 5.6.1 *amaui*): amid the thematised *amoenitas* (§25n. *haec*), this pavilion is the ultimate *locus amoenus*. There is no trace in 2.17 of P.'s human darling, his second (or third) wife Calpurnia; she makes a late appearance in *Tusci* in 9.36.4, and by implication in the *Laurentinum*, at the last, in 9.40.2. If he was remarried by the dramatic date of book 2 (as most believe: Hoffer 1999: 232–3; G–M 33), the editing looks planned: Calpurnia is wholly absent from books 1–3, then book 4 opens with the first of several letters to her grandfather. Even in book 5, though, the Etruscan villa is a wife-free zone. **re uera amores:** repetition with *re uera* is a mannerism peculiar to P. (1.16.5, 3.9.37). The villa of Stat. *Silu.* 2.2 also culminates in a prized *diaeta* (vv.83–94) introduced with pathetic repetition: <u>una</u> *tamen cunctis procul eminet* <u>una</u> *diaetis* (v.83). **ipse posui** 'I built it myself'. Villas were often modified by successive owners; P. is planning extensions to two Como properties in 9.7. He may have inherited his Etruscan villa from his uncle (G–M 222–5); there he claims especial affection based on his (greater) personal involvement in the building: *indulsi amori meo; amo enim quae maxima ex parte ipse incohaui aut incohata percolui* (5.6.41). A timely reminder, as we penetrate this most intimate spot, of P.'s status as master-architect of villa, of letter and of self-image (cf. Hor. *C.* 3.30.1

exegi monumentum . . .). **heliocaminus quidem . . . cubiculum autem:** parallel antithesis (*quidem . . . autem* = μέν . . . δέ, 2.1.7n. *et*), 20~20 syllables. On the 'conservatory' (ἡλιοκάμινος, lit. 'sun-oven'), well suited to winter, see Förtsch 56–7; the name is given to a circular bathing room in Hadrian's Tivoli villa (MacDonald–Pinto 1995: 71–3, De Franceschini 2001: 180–1). It lies at the SW corner of the *diaeta*, filling in a corner between cryptoportico and the *cubiculum* next mentioned (Förtsch 56 n.647), or with the *cubiculum* wrapping around it in an L shape to the NW. **aliā xystum, aliā mare, utrāque solem** *sc. prospicit* (from sentence-end, *apo koinou*), 'looks out one way at the terrace, the other at the sea, both ways at the sun' (*OLD alius*[1] 8), i.e. SE and SW (*contra* Winnefeld). Supply perhaps *parte* with *aliā . . . aliā . . . utrāque* (*OLD aliā* b, *TLL* 1 1652.77–84), varying §6 *alterā fenestrā . . . alterā.* **ualuis cryptoporticum, fenestrā prospicit mare:** parallel antithesis with verbal hyperbaton (2.11.5n. *censuit*); for *prospicit*, see §5n. *quasi.* The room has folding doors (*ualuae*) onto the cryptoportico, and a single window facing SW.

21 contra parietem medium 'in the middle of the wall' (§5n. *contra*); this unspecified wall (as §8 *parieti*) is on the NW side of the room. **zotheca** 'niche' (ζωθήκη, contracted from ζωοθήκη: Leumann 120); 5.6.38 has a diminutive *zothecula.* It was originally a wall-niche for the placing (θήκη) of small statues (LSJ ζῷον ΙΙ, ζῴδιον), as in *ILS* 5449 *signis . . . dispositis in zothecis* (see also *ILS* 3452 (in a temple), 5549 (in a portico), LSJ ζωθήκη ΙΙ); *zothecula* returns in Sid. *Ep.* 8.16.3, 9.11.6 as a book-alcove. Blümner 1911: 44 cites comparable niches in Pompeian rooms. Like *angulus* (§7), it is an affective description, here for an especially intimate space. **perquam eleganter recedit** 'recedes extremely elegantly' (2.11.13n. *perquam*). Exceptional pride, surpassing §11 *elegantes.* The verb finds poetic precedent at Cat. 64.43–4 *recessit | regia,* V. *Aen.* 2.300, Stat. *Theb.* 5.242–3; P.'s present tense points the personification, as the niche 'withdraws' like its occupant from the *cubiculum* (cf. 5.6.38 *zothecula refugit*). **specularibus et uelis obductis reductisue:** abl. abs. Glazed panels (§4n. *specularibus,* Forbes 1966: 186) and curtains serve as a movable partition. Sen. *NQ* 4b.13.7 mentions *uelis ac specularibus* as dining-room fittings. **modo adicitur cubiculo, modo aufertur:** it can be shut off as required. **lectum et duas cathedras:** *lectus* is a couch for various uses (*OLD* 1a–c); *cathedrae* are 'easy-chairs, with long, sloping backs, but apparently without arms' (Merrill), not just a ladies' chair as commonly thought, at least by now (e.g. Mart. 12.18.18; see Marquardt 1886: 726, Blümner 1911: 123). The only free-standing furniture mentioned in the letter. **capit:** the subject is still *zotheca* (clearly substantial). **a pedibus mare, a tergo uillae, a capite siluae** *sc. sunt.* The niche has windows in three outer walls, facing the sea (SW), the villas up the coast (NW, glimpsed at §12) and the woods inland (NE: §§3, 5, 26). In an acme of personification, the zotheca is treated as if it were a person reclining on the couch (facing the cryptoportico): 'this luxurious niche fits Pliny like a second skin' (Spencer 2010: 117). Although *a tergo* and *a capite* are paralleled (§5n. *a lateribus,* §20n. *in capite*), *a pedibus* is unique in this use. The conceit surpasses the twin views of Faustinus' couch in Mart. 10.51.9–10 *et non unius spectator lectulus undae,* | *qui uidet hinc puppes fluminis, inde maris* (a villa set between river and sea). **tot facies locorum:** §3n. *uaria.* The triple view earns especial praise (*tot . . . totidem*), as does that of the sea-front *triclinium* (§6). **et distinguit et miscet** 'separates and blends at once', an oxymoron for the perfect (Plinian) variety of combination. The *zotheca* no longer enjoys them itself, but serves them up to its owner like a good slave (§2n. *decem*, §9n. *digerit*).

22 iunctum est cubiculum noctis et somni 'next to it [the *cubiculum* of §20] is a room of night and sleep'. *noctis et somni* could be taken as hendiadys for 'night sleep' as opposed to siesta, but is a common redundant pair, esp. in poetry (e.g. V. *Aen.* 6.390 *somni noctisque soporae*). Either way the phrase, more emotive than §9 *dormitorium membrum*, emphasises tranquillity: It is the penultimate room P. describes, and as a place of sleep carries appropriate closural force. The miniature tour of a Comum villa in 1.3.1 ended with *cubicula diurna nocturna* (Hoffer 1999: 32): as there, our tour gestures at linearity through a day, without rigidity (just as seasonal time has been only loosely constant: §18n. *haec*). **non illud uoces seruulorum, non maris murmur, non tempestatum motus, non fulgurum lumen, ac ne diem quidem sentit:** the room is marked out both by the anaphora of *non* and by *illud* (contrast e.g. §6 *huius*, §10 *huic*, §20 *in hac*). The objects of *sentit* comprise first a graded tricolon of sounds (slaves – sea – storm, 6~4~6 syllables), then move through the natural pair storm/lightning to light in a minute crescendo–diminuendo. The order of acc./gen. nouns is characteristic (AB~BA~BA~BA). **seruulorum:** an affective diminutive (2.11.25n. *quid arbusculae*) for one's own slaves, again at 3.16.8, 6.16.19 (pejorative at *Pan.* 7.6). **maris murmur:** an alliterative phrase current at least since Pacuvius (*trag.* fr. 417). **ac ne diem quidem** 'and not even the daylight' (cf. 5.6.33, *OLD dies* 2a), capping the *non*-tetracolon. Besides suiting sleep, extreme darkness is prized by P. as an incitement to contemplation: he describes in 9.36.1–2 how he spends the first hours of the day lying in bed, the shutters closed, mentally composing before calling in a slave to take dictation (there in *Tusci*, but his Laurentine routine is much the same, 9.40.1). As P. doubtless knew, this solitary meditation resembles (except for the lie-in) the practice of Demosthenes as reported and recommended by Quint. 10.3.25: *Demosthenes melius, qui se in locum ex quo nulla exaudiri uox et ex quo nihil prospici posset recondebat, ne aliud agere mentem cogerent oculi.* **nisi fenestris apertis** 'except when the shutters are open' (§5n. *undique*), probably of a single window in the NW wall. The phrase best qualifies only *ne diem quidem*; evidently rooms normally felt some daylight even with the shutters closed. For *nisi* + abl. abs., see 2.14.3n. **tam alti abditique secreti illa ratio, quod** 'the reason for such deep and hidden seclusion is that' (*OLD secretum* 2b, *ratio* 5a). Here is the *uerum secretumque* Μουσεῖον of 1.9.6 (quoted in intro.). The importance of *secretum* to composition is also stressed by Quint. 10.3.22–30, though he might have disapproved of P.'s allowing slave-scribes to interrupt him (cf. Quint.

10.3.18–21). In 9.40 P. paints his Laurentine existence as an acme of solitude (against the frequent socialising in *Tusci*, 9.36); see §12n. *latissimum*. **andron** 'passageway' (Vitr. 6.7.5), a radical change from its Greek meaning 'men's quarters' (ἀνδρών). Sidonius, tongue firmly in cheek, describes the somniferous qualities of a corresponding corridor in his villa: *interiecto consistorio perangusto, ubi somnulentiae cubiculariorum* ['chamber slaves'] *dormitandi potius quam dormiendi locus est* (Sid. *Ep.* 2.2.13: for *dormitandi . . . dormiendi* see §8n. *non legendos*). **parietem cubiculi hortique distinguit** 'separates the wall[s] of the bedroom and the garden': the passage runs between the bedroom wall and an exterior wall. The last mention of the *hortus* (here as in §20 the *gestatio* is taken for granted), which we know borders on all three cardinal structures: main villa, cryptoportico and pavilion. For *parietem* [sg.] . . . *distinguit*, cf. Cic. *Mur.* 76 *distinguit rationem officiorum ac temporum*. The verb looks pointed: walls generally separate, rather than being separated (§10n. *communi*). **media inanitate consumit** 'swallows up . . . with its intervening emptiness'; *inanitas* with this sense is a hallmark of the elder Pliny.

23 applicitum est: synonymous with *adiacet* (§11) and *cohaeret* (5.6.25). The participle in *-itus* (< *applicare*) was now common. **hypocauston perexiguum:** a small chamber heated with hot air supplied from the furnace (*suppositum calorem*; see §9n. *suspensus*, §11n. *hypocauston*) and admitted through a vent (*angustā fenestrā*). It resembles that of 5.6.25, different from the sauna of §11. It seems to be behind the NE wall of the *cubiculum* (as on Winnefeld's plan, p. xii, though Winnefeld has the vent on the wrong side of it); an analogous installation of the mid-2c. AD has been found in nearby Vicus Augustanus (C39, heating room C28: Claridge 1988: 62–3, ead. 1998: 118–19 and fig. 6, 128 fig. 25). **ut ratio exigit** 'as occasion requires' (2.5.4n. *quantum*). **procoeton inde et cubiculum:** §10n. *procoetone*, §11n. *inde*. Despite the closural overtones of the dark bedroom (§22n. *iunctum*), there is a final pair of rooms beyond. **porrigitur in solem** 'extends [middle voice] towards the sun', certainly east and perhaps SE around the corner of the cryptoportico. **quem orientem statim exceptum ultra meridiem obliquum quidem sed tamen seruat** 'which it catches right from its rising and holds on to beyond midday, albeit at an angle' (*OLD seruo* 7c; for *statim* see 2.13.8n. *iuuenis*). For the personification, see §6n. *altera* and Hor. *C.* 2.15.16 *excipiebat Arcton* with Nisbet–Hubbard; for the concise *quidem sed tamen* see §6n. *longius*. A possible echo of *solem . . . seruat* in Sid. *Carm.* 22.157 *et totum solem lunata per atria seruat* (with Delhey and §12n. *erigitur*). A window facing NE gets the dawn sun; another facing S/SE catches it in the afternoon.

24 in hanc ego diaetam: summing up the pavilion toured since §20. For the idiomatic position of *ego*, splitting *hanc diaetam*, see Adams 1994b: 134, 137–8, 143–4, Oakley 1997–2005: IV 565 (cf. 2.9.1 *anxium me et inquietum*). It is usually called 'unstressed', but hardly lacks emphasis here: P. inserted himself qua builder-owner in §20 (*amores mei . . . ipse posui*); now, uniquely and climactically, he walks onto his constructed stage. Our letter is thus synecdochic of *Epistles* 1–9, which closes with P.'s daily routine in *Tusci* (9.36) and, finally, Laurentum (9.40). **cum me recepi** 'when(ever) I withdraw' (*OLD recipio* 12a), generalising (*OLD cum²* 2a), with standard precision of tense (*recepi* must precede *uideor*: G–L §567). **etiam a uilla mea** 'even from my own villa', as well as from Rome. **magnamque eius uoluptatem praecipue . . . capio** 'and I take great pleasure from it especially . . . ' (*OLD capio* 13b). *magnam / non mediocrem* (etc.) *uoluptatem capere / percipere* is recurrent in P. (3.18.4, 4.23.1, 7.8.2, etc.), as in Seneca and above all Cicero (esp. epistles). It is usually construed with *ex* or a clause; for *eius*, cf. *Pan.* 23.4 *praecipuam uoluptatem operis sui percepisse*, Cic. *Fam.* 5.2.3. **Saturnalibus:** the Saturnalia, time of licence and social inversion (*OCD* 'Saturnus, Saturnalia'). Originally a single day (17 December), it was now an extended festival whose winter timing fits the seasonal frame (§3n. *tepore*). Like Seneca (*Ep.* 18), P. prefers to avoid the party; on his po-faced attitude to common entertainments, see 2.7.1n. *nisi.* **tecti** 'building'. **licentia dierum festisque clamoribus:** chiasmus; *festis* ('festive, merry', *OLD* 4) of course modifies *clamoribus*, but can also be felt with *dierum* (*dies festus* = 'holiday', *OLD festus* 1a). **personat** 'rings with' (*OLD* 1b); on the sense of sound, see §13n. *quod.* Joyous festival ends ecphrasis at Hom. *Il.* 18.604–6, V. *Aen.* 8.717–18. **nec ipse meorum lusibus nec illi studîs meis obstrepunt:** ABC~ACB isocolon (9~10 syllables); *obstrepunt* is sylleptic, since P. does not disturb the slaves with his silence. For *meorum* 'my staff', see §7n.; for the content, cf. 1.9.5 *nullis rumoribus inquietor: mecum tantum et cum libellis loquor . . .* (in intro.). Hor. *Ep.* 1.11.9 *oblitusque meorum obliuiscendus et illis*, a comparable balanced conceit, mocks the man who seeks solitude far away; P. finds it at home. **studîs** (2.2.2n.) climactically stakes literary endeavour as highest function of the villa, so replaying on a larger canvas the shift from villa to literature in the brief 1.3 (Hoffer 1999: 38–40). Both Statius' villa poems make the same closing move, lauding the poetry of Vopiscus and Pollius that their environs inspire (*Silu.* 1.3.99–104, 2.2.112–20). P., however, omits detail (and praise) of his productions: this sole reference to *studia* (apart from a hint in the 'library' room, §8) is brief and vague. Later in the collection (7.4) we glimpse P. writing poetry here one summer afternoon, but at the very end (9.40) he reveals that court business is what often keeps him working into the night, the *negotium* carefully filtered out of the *otium*-filled 2.17 (G–M 219–20); in the winter of 99–100 that had involved, especially, the Priscus and Classicus trials (2.11–12, 3.4 and 3.9). Yet we are (also) surely invited to imagine him, in *mise-en-abîme*, writing letters like this one.

25–8 Amenities; coast

25 Haec utilitas, haec amoenitas: cf. 5.6.28 *haec facies, hic usus*, 5.6.32 *hanc dispositionem amoenitatemque*. Abstracts for concrete, summing up. The marriage of practical and charming is in line with Quintilian's precepts for geographical encomia, *in quibus similiter speciem et utilitatem intuemur* (3.7.27; he goes on to associate *species* with *amoenitas*). The nouns loosely reprise §4 *usibus capax* and §2 *gratiam uillae* respectively. *amoenitas* is a quality routinely attached to villa paradise (e.g. 5.18.1 *uilla amoenissima*, Cic. *Q. fr.* 3.1.1 *amoenitate fluminis me refeci*, prefacing news of Quintus' villas, Van Dam on Stat. *Silu.* 2.2.32–3). **deficitur** 'lacks' + abl. (*OLD* 2a), as 10.90.1 *Sinopenses . . . aqua deficiuntur*. **aqua salienti** 'water jets', literally 'gushing water' (*OLD salio* 3): (*aquae*) *salientes* were water-features such as fountains and jets (Rodgers on Frontin. *Aq.* 9.9), an integral part of the *locus amoenus* (V. *Ecl.* 5.47 *aquae saliente . . . riuo*) and desirable in any garden (Purcell 1996b, Bannon 2009), e.g. Cic. *Q. fr.* 3.1.3 *mirifica suauitate te uillam habiturum piscina et salientibus additis*, Mart. 12.50.6 (sardonic) *pereuntis aquae fluctus*. The ingenuous concession (§15n. *malignior*) brings us back to earth and prepares a contrast with the lavish water features in summery *Tusci* (5.6.36–8, 40). Heroic clausula (2.3.3n. *narrat*). **ac potius fontes** 'or rather springs' (2.13.3n. *ac*), because the water is near ground level (*OLD summus* 3b): the land was marshy (and in modern times malarial). The hyperbole gives this villa something to match the Etruscan *fonticuli* (5.6.23, 40) after all. **et omnino litoris illius mira natura** 'in fact, that whole stretch of shore has a wonderful property' (*et omnino* lit. 'and altogether'). A reprise of ecphrastic wonder (§1n. *miraris*) for a marvel, this time, of nature (cf. 8.20 and GALLO n.). **moueris:** perfect subjunctive. Although *quicumque* normally takes an indicative (G–L §254 n.4), subjunctives appear by P.'s time (K–S II 198–9, Kraut 1872: 39), and are standard in any case for the generalising second person in indefinite clauses (*NLS* §195). This is the first use of a second-person verb since §11 *cogites*, beginning a cluster of terms which (also) reach out to Gallus/the reader (§26 *homini, dissuadeat, utare*), bringing to the fore the epistolary motive of temptation and invitation that will become explicit in §29. **obuius et paratus umor occurrit:** cf. Sen. *NQ* 3.30.3 *eruentibus terram umor occurrit*. **sincerus ac ne leuiter quidem . . . corruptus:** there is no trace of salinity. For *sincerus* (here 'pure', despite *OLD* 2), cf. Sen. *NQ* 3.5 *mare . . . in sinceram aquam transit*; for *corruptus* [Caes.] *B. Alex.* 6.3, Pl. *NH* 6.166. **tanta maris uicinitate** 'by the sea's being so close'.

26 suggerunt affatim ligna proximae siluae, ceteras copias Ostiensis colonia ministrat: ABC~BCA. The *proximae siluae*, supplying wood (cf. 2.8.1 *affatim suggerunt*) for the furnaces, are presumably those glimpsed in §5. Ostia (*OCD* s.v.) lies at the mouth of the Tiber, north of P.'s villa; for the periphrasis *Ostiensis colonia*, see e.g. Tac. *H.* 1.80.1, *CIL* XIV 34. **frugi quidem homini** 'but for a person of moderation', with adversative *quidem* (Solodow 1978: 75–81). 'Hic ilico se corrigit, frugalitatis suae memor' (Gierig); alternatively, taking *homo* to imply the potential visitor, a conditional (or challenge): 'if your needs are moderate . . .'. **uicus quem una uilla discernit** 'the village that [only] one villa divides [from mine]'. Almost certainly 'Vicus Augustanus' (previously, and perhaps still in P.'s day, the humbler 'Vicus Laurentium'), a coastal town around five miles south of Ostia identified in 1874 and extensively excavated 1875 to *c.* 1913. Since the 1980s Vicus and the surrounding coast has been a renewed focus of study: www.rhul.ac.uk/classics/laurentineshore. See Claridge 1985, ead. 1988, ead. 1998; also Patterson 1985 (historical context), Claridge 1997–8 (a summary) and Marzano 2007: 306–29 (a gazetteer of Laurentine villas). **balinea meritoria** 'baths for hire' (*OLD meritorius* a), i.e. public baths (Merrill) or perhaps baths which one could hire for sole use. Several baths have been excavated at Vicus, mostly of later date. **magna commoditas:** in apposition to *balinea*. **si forte . . . dissuadeat** 'if . . . should ever advise against' (*OLD forte* 3a), third-person generalising subjunctive (*NLS* §196). In 1.4.1 P. is surprised that the *balineum* at a friend's villa is ready for him when he is just passing through; cf. Cic. *Att.* 2.3.4, *Fam.* 9.16.9. **domi:** locative. **subitus aduentus:** arriving without giving the staff notice. **breuior mora** 'a shorter stay' *sc.* than would make it worth heating it, or simply 'a short stay' (2.1.4n. *durior*).

27 uarietate gratissima: shore, like road (§3 *uaria . . . facies*) and villa (*passim*), attracts with the variety of views. So does the letter: on the need for pleasant variety in composition see Quint. 10.1.58 *uarietas . . . grata*, 10.2.11 *compositio . . . uarietate gratissimā*, 8.3.52 *uarietatis gratia*, etc. The pleasure of variety is also a historiographical commonplace: see Oakley on Livy 9.17.1, esp. Val. Max. 1.6.*ext.*1 *gratae uarietatis.* **nunc continua, nunc intermissa** 'now right next to each other, now spread apart'. Like §3 *modo . . . modo*, the temporal *nunc . . . nunc* (introduced to prose by Livy: K–S ii 70) implies a moving viewer rather than a static scene. The pair *continua . . . intermissa* (and this adjectival use of *intermissa*) is Senecan, e.g. *NQ* 1.3.8 (*TLL* vii.1 2229.14–22). **tecta uillarum** 'villa buildings' (*uilla* referring to house and grounds together: §3n. *uilla*): cf. Cic. *Tull.* 21 *tectum uillamque*, Livy 7.39.14 *tectum uillae.* **praestant multarum urbium faciem:** they look like a series of cities. Villa as city is a cliché of Roman thought and art (Purcell 1987, esp. 196–8; Förtsch 28 n.224), and this effect was often sought by coastal villas, presenting their best face to the sea (Marzano 2007: 22–4). **siue mari siue ipso litore utare:** whether you look from a boat or the shore. For the generalising second person see 2.6.5n. *si gulae.* On the choice between *-re* and *-ris* see G–L §130.1b; *utare* (12× in Cicero, who never has *utaris*) is absent from prose between his death and P., who has it here and 1.19.4, but *utaris* in 2.6.5 (before a vowel). In general he overwhelmingly prefers *-ris* (e.g. 2.4.3 *uerearis*, 2.8.1 *piscaris*); *-re* forms, apparently restricted to subjunctives, are perhaps elevated (3.1.6 *imbuare*, 9.3.2 *meditere*, 9.25.1 *perfruare, Pan.* 10.3 *precarere*, 21.3 *uocarere*; also 7× impf. indic. *-bare*). **quod non numquam longa tranquillitas mollit, saepius frequens et contrarius fluctus indurat** 'which is sometimes softened by a period of calm [i.e. softens when the sea is calm], more often hardened by strong incoming waves' (for *frequens* see *TLL* vi.1 1297.39–69 'de rebus, quarum propter densitatem uis augetur'; for *contrarius*, next n.). The antithesis (abcd~abbcd of adverb, adjective(s), noun, verb) emphasises the more desirable thing, firm sand suitable for walking and perhaps *gestatio* (§13n., and below). For the balanced praise, cf. 1.3.1 *illa mollis et tamen solida gestatio* (firm and soft at once), and the oxymoron of Mart. 10.51.7–8 *solidumque madentis harenae | litus* 'solid shore of moist sand' (celebrating a villa at Anxur); for the antithesis *mollit . . . indurat*, cf. §2 *grauius . . . molle*. A close intertext is Seneca's description of the coast near Baiae in *Ep.* 55.2 *fluctus enim illud [sc. litus]*, *ut scis, frequens et concitatus exaequat, longior tranquillitas soluit*, an antithesis inverted and elaborated by P. The content is mundane (the scene, a bumpy *gestatio* across the sands, memorable), but it is piquant that, almost at the close, P. evokes the opening of a Senecan villa letter recalled already in 1.9 (Henderson 2004a: 84–6) and repeatedly here (intro.). Acerbic Seneca warns against stultifying *secessus*; no risk of that for affable P., whose *otium* here is amply matched by *negotium* elsewhere (Intro. 13–14). **contrarius fluctus:** a wave coming (hard) against you (Val. Max. 1.8.*ext*.11, 9.8.2), here against the shore. It is the product of a *contrarius uentus* (*Ep.* 6.16.12, 10.17a.2; cf. Ov. *Met.* 13.183–4), namely the stormy Africus, §5n. *Africo* (the Mediterranean is virtually non-tidal).

28 non sane pretiosis piscibus: the sea joins P. in eschewing luxury. *sane* is concessive (*OLD* 8a). **abundat:** common for 'abounds in' (*OLD* 2) but 'overflows with' (*OLD* 1) responds to the pun (*mare . . . abundat*; cf. Lucr. 5.262). **soleas . . . squillas:** sole and shrimps. *squillae* (any small shellfish) range from humble, as here, to a luxury item, as at Juv. 5.81 (Dalby 2003: 300–1). An anecdote in Cic. *De or.* 2.22 (and Val. Max. 8.8.1) has Laelius and Scipio collecting shellfish on the Laurentine coast in idyllic, infantile recreation; P. shows no sign of getting his own hands dirty. Purcell 1998: 13 n.66 gives other references to fishing here. **egerit** 'yields' (*OLD* 4, *TLL* v.2 243.57–62), but again with wit in its literal meaning, 'pours out' (liquids usually *egeruntur*, not *egerunt*: 4.30.8, 5.6.37, 8.20.9; *OLD* 3a). **uilla uero nostra:** *uero* is adversative (the villa produce contrasts with that of the sea), and climactic (2.1.7n. *mihi*), opening the third member of a tricolon (*litus . . . mare . . . uilla*) and the last sentence before the coda, and underlining this last statement of *uilla*. **etiam mediterraneas copias** 'even . . . inland produce', paradoxical language for a coastal estate. **illuc e pascuis pecora conueniunt** 'the herds come there from their pasture', the livestock and *latissima prata* seen in §3 return in ring-composition, now with the possible implication that the herds belong to P. **aquam umbramue:** on arrival we saw the animals 'driven down by winter', early in their lowland pasturage season (§3n. *montibus*); this parting glimpse is in the warmer weather nearer its end (§3n. *tepore*). Shade makes a suitably bucolic, and Virgilian, closing motif (*Ecl.* 1.83, 10.75–6, *Aen.* 12.952; cf. *Georg.* 4.566). Despite the wry disclaimer in 4.6.2 *nihil quidem ibi possideo praeter tectum et hortum statimque harenas*, P. seems to have enough land beyond his garden to supply water and the shade of trees.

29 Peroratio

29 Iustisne de causis: a rhetorical question expecting the answer 'yes' marks a conclusion, as 3.16.13 *uidenturne*, 3.21.6 *meritone*; *Pan.* 88.4 *iustisne de causis*. In all of these -*ne* does the work of *nonne* (common in comedy and not rare in

Cicero: K–S II 505). This long letter unusually makes no apology for its size (contrast 2.11.25); the Etruscan villa makes amends with P.'s most elaborate excursus on length (5.6.41–4 with Chinn 2007, Squire 2011: 353–5). For *de* (not *ex*), see 2.13.2n. *duabus*. **iam:** now that you have heard all this (*OLD* 6), as perhaps Hor. *Ep.* 1.16.15 *et, iam si credis* (concluding a brief sketch of his *rus amoenum*; some print *etiam si credis*). **tibi:** the return to the addressee and his implied question (§1) creates closure. **incolere inhabitare diligere:** reprising, inverting and expanding §1 *delectat*. The asyndetic trio rises first by word-length (*incolere inhabitare*), then by gradation (the emotion of 'love' trumps plain 'live'), though *diligere* perhaps also activates a latent sense in *incolere* of 'adorn, cherish, worship' (*OLD colo* 4–6). **secessum** '[my] retreat', sealing a ring (§2 *secessit*); cf. 6.10.1 *colere secessum*. **quem tu nimis urbanus es nisi concupiscis** 'you are too urban(e) if you do not long for it'. Though a common verb in P. (2.3.7n.), *concupiscis* inverts 2.8.2 *concupisco*, where it was P. who longed for villa life. It is associated again with the Laurentine coast at 4.6.3. *urbanus* puns: if Gallus is not stirred by this letter, then he is too urban-minded (to appreciate the country) and/or too urbane (to feel emotion). Yet P. has shown himself, in literary terms, to be as *urbanus* as they come. Other play on *urbanus* at 5.6.35 and Cic. *Q.fr.* 3.1.6 . . . *de rebus rusticis. urbanam expolitionem urget* . . . (ending discussion of Quintus' villas). The question *rusticane uita an urbana potior* was a debating cliché (Quint. 2.4.24). **atque utinam concupiscas** 'and I hope you will!' (lit. 'and would that you might desire it!'). *atque utinam* is esp. common in Cicero's and Ovid's letters; cf. also Cic. *Verr.* 2.1.61 *negare non potes. atque utinam neges!*, Sen. *Suas.* 6.25 *concupiscatis; concupiscite*. P. much likes reprise of a verb across sentences, e.g. 1.1.1 *colligerem publicaremque. collegi*, 1.2.6 *blandiuntur. sed sane blandiantur*. The attempt to lure Gallus, implicit throughout the letter, peaks in this urbane (still indirect) invitation to come and join P. in his wonderland. **dotibus** 'endowments, attractions' (*OLD* 4b); cf. 1.24.4 *praediolum istud, quod commendatur his dotibus*. There is perhaps a touch of personification (cf. 9.7.3, the ladylike Comum villas *Tragoedia* and *Comoedia*), although P. is not the first to attribute *dotes* to objects: e.g. Sen. *Ep.* 51.1 (*naturales dotes* of Baiae) with Summers, *TLL* v.1 2047.42–58. **uillulae:** affective diminutive (2.11.25n. *quid arbusculae*), first in Cat. 26.1, 4× in Cic. *Att.*, only here in P., a choice word for this closing moment (D'Agostino 1931: 126–7; also Hanssen 1953: 126–7). The false modesty (2.4.3n. *agellorum*) strains against the climactic satisfaction of *tot tantisque dotibus*, nearby *maxima*, and the *tour de force* of the letter as a whole. The reader who later visits the Etruscan villa will discover that the *uillula* of 2.17 was but a prelude to that *uilla* . . . *magna* (5.6.44). S-W, reading literally, concludes that this is no top-league mansion. **maxima commendatio ex tuo contubernio accedat:** all these delights would be as nothing to Gallus' company (for *contubernalis* cf. 2.13.5), with rhyme (*commendatio* ~ *contubernio*) making point. For the courteous self-disparagement, cf. Hor. *Ep.* 1.10.50 *excepto quod non simul esses, cetera laetus* (ending another epistolary paean of *rus amoenum*) and contrast Sen. *Ep.* 55.8 *animus est qui sibi commendet omnia* (the owner's character determines how he enjoys his villa), Mart. 4.64.25–6 *hoc rus . . . | commendat dominus*. The propriety of this proprietor, and its reflection in the villa, is taken as read.

18

What a pleasant task, to find a teacher for your nephews. I went back to the schoolroom, and discovered in what respect I was held – a sign that standards are still maintained. I shall make a tour and give you full results: I owe it to you and your dead brother. Nor shall I be put off by the risk of causing offence in the process.

After the solitary seaside sojourn of 2.17, we find P. back into the nexus of social relations at Rome, as he undertakes to find a teacher for the sons of Mauricus' deceased brother, Arulenus Rusticus.

Careful selection of teachers was important, and P. shows here his (Quintilianic) credentials, as he commits himself to a thorough search on Mauricus' behalf – or rather, on behalf of the dead Arulenus. Roman education was canonically the father's responsibility (cf. 4.13.4–9, 8.13, 8.14.6), with the elder Cato as exemplary beacon (Bonner 1977: 10–14; also e.g. Hor. *Sat.* 1.6.81–4, [Plut.] *De liberis educandis* 4C–F, and esp. Quint. 2.2 with Reinhardt–Winterbottom). P. had no children of his own, as the reader learns first in 4.13.5 *ego, qui nondum liberos habeo* (cf. 10.2) and later in the tragedy of Calpurnia's miscarriage, 8.10–11. Instead, and perhaps as a result, he offers himself as a substitute parent to others throughout his collection (Bernstein 2008 and 2009; §5n. *quam*), whether by offering a guiding hand to young men (as in 2.6), by usurping as here a dead parent's role, or even by inviting himself to share paternal obligations with a still living father (§5n. *quam*, 2.4.2n. *in*): thanks to Mauricus' request of a favour P. is flirting, by the closing analogy, with acquiring virtual children of his own.

As for the real father, P. uses the phrase *fratris tui* four times in this short letter. The reader of the collection can easily supply the name, given the strong recall of P.'s last letter to Mauricus, 1.14 (§1n. *quid*, §1n. *fratris*). There too he fulfilled paternal obligations and recommended a husband for Mauricus' niece (sister of the boys here), so 'producing the next deserving generation of the ruling class' (Hoffer 1999: 177–93), and in the process, all-importantly, propagating the family line of Q. Junius Arulenus Rusticus (*PIR*² I 730), one of the senators executed in the notorious treason trials of AD 93 (3.11.3, Tac. *Ag.* 45.1, Suet. *Dom.* 10.3); Mauricus himself was relegated (below). Like Tacitus (*Ag.* 2.1), P. mentions his trial and death early, in 1.5.2 *Rustici Aruleni periculum*. There, in his first substantial letter, P. builds common ground with Arulenus and Mauricus through a shared enmity with Regulus, 'wicked' creature of the Domitianic regime (2.20.intro.). He develops the association in 1.14.4, numbering the brothers, ten or twenty years his senior, among his *formatores*, and in 3.11.3 he claims that this acquaintance exposed him to danger under Domitian (cf. also 5.1.7–8). Our letter, then, is part of a serial effort by P. to graft himself onto the family of a prominent Domitianic victim (Hoffer 1999: 177; Carlon 2009: 38–43).

Besides making a pair with 1.14, the letter looks forward both to 4.13 (P. tasks Tacitus with finding a *praeceptor*) and more immediately to 3.3, where P. reveals (to a different addressee) the success of his search (§3n. *efficiamque*), so adding a symmetrical bond to the two books (2.18 is third from the end of its book; on the connection 2.20~3.1 see 2.20n. CALVISIO). More closely still, the political edge of 2.18 establishes a link with 2.20, so extending the attack on Regulus back into the book. If 2.19 is addressed to Velius Cerialis (whom 4.21, concerning the daughters of Helvidius the Younger, connects to another talismanic victim of the treason trials), that makes a triptych (2.19n. CERIALI).

MAVRICO: Junius Mauricus (*PIR*² I 771, Birley 2000a: 67) is an important figure in the collection. A fellow Transpadane (1.14.4 *illa nostra Italia*), older than P. (he was a senator by 68, Plut. *Galba* 8.5), he also receives 1.14 (above) and 6.14 (P. accepts an invitation to Formiae). He was relegated (2.11.8n. *exsilium*) in the trials of AD 93, and 1.5 makes much of his imminent return to Rome (1.5.5, 15, 16). Through that letter and his cameo in 4.22 (following hard on 4.21, about Helvidius' daughters: above) he is marked out as a fellow opponent of the so-called *delatores* (2.20.intro.), as he is in Tac. *H.* 4.40.3 (cf. Plut. *Galba* 8.5 'one of the best men').

1 Quid a te mihi iucundius potuit iniungi | quam ut praeceptorem fratris tui liberis quaererem? 'what more pleasant task could you have given me than to look for a teacher for your brother's children?', isocolon (15~15 syllables) and a clear parallel with 1.14.1 *petis ut fratris tui filiae prospiciam maritum, quod merito mihi potissimum iniungis*. Strong similarities (*mihi . . . potuit iniungi* ~ *mihi potissimum iniungis* and *fratris tui liberis* ~ *fratris tui filiae*) are offset by variation (*praeceptorem . . . quaererem* ~ *prospiciam maritum*, clause-order reversed); cf. also 1.14.2 *nihil est quod a te mandari mihi aut maius aut gratius . . . possit*. **iucundius:** a favourite Plinian word, esp. in later books. It perhaps makes a euphonious hint, fitting for *Jun*ius Mauricus, at a (false) etymology *iucundius . . . iniungi* (cf. 9.28.1 *iniungis mihi iucundissimum ministerium*) and eases us out of the world of the villa (2.17.18 *haec iucunditas*). It describes another pleasant duty, a summons to Trajan's council, in 6.31.2. **potuit:** indicative, as usual with modal verbs (*NLS* §125). **iniungi:** a verb of varied application in P. (2.11.19n. *iniuncta*), here in the world of personal favours and obligations (e.g. 4.28.2, 6.16.3, 9.28.1). Nevertheless, the repetition from 1.14.1 *iniungis* (above on *quid*) is striking; P. turns the tables in 3.6.5 *omnia quae a me tibi iniunguntur* and again in 4.13.10 *iniungo . . . ut . . . circumspicias praeceptores*, likewise seeking a teacher. **praeceptorem** 'teacher'. As *iuuenes* below shows, P. is referring to the *rhetor Latinus* (3.3.3; cf. Quint. 2.1.1 *praeceptoribus eloquentiae . . . rhetores*), who provided the third tier of childhood education (*OCD* 'education, Roman'). He is the subject of Quint. 2: see esp. *Inst.* 2.2 with Reinhardt–Winterbottom on choosing a *praeceptor* (§5n. *in eligendo*). P. is presumably in Rome, as he was in 1.14; his commission may imply that Mauricus is away, perhaps at his villa in Formiae (6.14). In 4.13 P., writing from Tusculum, asks

Tacitus (in Rome) to find a *praeceptor* to send to Comum. **fratris tui:** the first of four identical references to Arulenus Rusticus (§§2, 4, 5). P.'s last letter to Mauricus began similarly (1.14.1), but continued to a climactic statement of his name (1.14.2 *ex quo nasci nepotes Aruleno Rustico deceat*). Here that name is a loud absence. **liberis:** these boys (§2 *filios*) may include Q. Junius Rusticus, *cos.* 133, *cos. ord.* 162 (S-W; *PIR*² I 814 makes him Arulenus' grandson). On the assumption that this is to be their first *rhetor*, the eldest at least is perhaps around 13 years old (below on *iuuenes*), and they are still under the guardianship of Mauricus (2.1.8n. *tutor*). Allowing a letter-date of 97–100, Rusticus (praetor in 69, so born AD 39 or earlier) therefore fathered them in his forties: a late, or second, marriage (Hoffer 1999: 180, modified). **nam . . . in scholam redeo | et . . . aetatem quasi resumo:** the first half of a divided tetracolon (*redeo . . . resumo, sedeo . . . experior*), itself an isocolon (13~14 syllables) with paired colon-final verbs (*redeo ~ resumo*) and fem. acc. sg. nouns. P. reenacts the elder Seneca's *Controuersiae* 1.pr.1 *est, fateor, iucundum mihi redire in antiqua studia melioresque ad annos respicere* (~ *redeo . . . resumo*), 1.pr.4 *mittatur senex in scholas* (see Fordyce 1952), 10.pr.1 (opening the last book) *sinite me . . . ad senectutem meam reuerti*. P.'s return to the classroom looks at first to be similarly metaphorical, but is revealed, like that of Sen. *Ep.* 76.1–4 (*in scholam eo . . .*), to be literal. **beneficio tuo** 'by your kindness'. A paradox (P. is providing the *beneficium*), though at another level it is indeed P. who benefits from this paraded association with martyr blood (cf. Hoffer 1999: 183 on 1.14). On this favourite word of P.'s see 2.13.2n. *beneficiorum*; he turns it to paradox again in 7.12.3 *beneficio fastidi tui* 'the kindness of your fussiness'. **illam dulcissimam aetatem quasi resumo** 'I am reliving, as it were, that loveliest time of life' (*OLD resumo* 2 'regain the use . . . of, recover'). Cf. again Sen. *Contr.* 1.pr.1 (in previous n.) *iucundum . . . melioresque ad annos respicere*, but with bolder expression (*quasi* mitigates: 2.6.5n. *illa*), for which cf. Stat. *Silu.* 3.1.161 *si dulce decus uiridesque resumeret annos*. For the superlative, cf. 2.3.6 *quod dulcissimum est in iuuenta* (declamation in the *schola*), and contrast the oxymoron of Sen. *Ep.* 12.5 *iucundissima est aetas deuexa iam* '. . . an age in decline'. **sedeo . . . ut solebam | atque etiam experior quantum . . . habeam:** a rising bicolon (11~23 syllables) completes the tetracolon (above on *in*), now with the verbs colon-initial, and formally (not syntactically) paired subordinate verbs (*solebam ~ habeam*) at colon-end. On *atque etiam* see 2.1.1n. *insigne*. **iuuenes:** here boys in their teens. At Quint. 2.2.3 the *rhetor*'s pupils range from *adulti fere pueri* (around 13) to *iuuenes . . . facti* (around 18?). **illos** 'them' (only slightly more emphatic than *eos*, if at all), showing the pronoun's postclassical weakening (2.1.7n. *illis*). **auctoritatis:** partitive genitive, idiomatically divided from *quantum* by *apud illos* (2.11.18n. *plus*). **studîs** 'from my literary pursuits', *OLD ex* 18a, presumably here oratory; cf. 9.23.2 (Tacitus to a stranger) '*nosti me, et quidem ex studiis*'. On *studia* and the form *studîs*, see 2.2.2n.

2 nam . . . iocabantur: *sc. iuuenes*, an unannounced but easy change of subject. **proxime** 'recently' (2.12.1n.). **frequenti** 'crowded, packed', *OLD*

3a. **auditorio** 'performance hall', created ad hoc rather than a permanent fixture (cf. Tac. *D.* 9.3 *auditorium exstrui*). 'The rhetors like the *grammatici* kept school either in simple booths or under the colonnades and in the *exedrae* of the Roman Fora' (S-W). **coram multis ordinis nostri:** with many senators present (*OLD coram* 3a + abl., 2.11.1n. *ordine*). Adults came to hear the virtuosity on display (Quint. 2.11.3 *cuius rei gratia plenum sit auditorium, sententiis grandibus*). **clare** 'loudly' (*OLD clarus* 1). **intraui, conticuerunt:** asyndeton, parataxis and rhythm reenact P.'s grave entrance: the lapidary *intraui* (– – –), its brevity set off by the chain of five adverbial phrases in the preceding clause, cues instant silence. Heroic clausula (2.3.3n. *narrat*). **quod non referrem:** like Tac. *An.* 11.11.1 *quod non iactantia refero*, the protest is hard to swallow. We are invited to notice that the boys fell silent only for P., not for the other senators present. **sperare** implies an assumption that the boys would not be able to *probe discere*. For P.'s low view of modern morals, see 2.12 and 2.14 *passim*, 2.20.12n. *in ea*, 1.14.9 *cum publicos mores atque etiam leges ciuitatis intueor*, 3.3.5 *ut in hac licentia temporum*, 4.15.8 *uellem tam ferax saeculum bonis artibus haberemus*, 5.8.13 *in tantis uitís hominum*, 6.2.9 *ut de pluribus uitís ciuitatis*, 9.30.4; Lefèvre 2009: 80–109, 277–85. **probe** 'without impropriety'. For P. (as for Quintilian) morality and oratorical training go hand in hand (2.14.12n. *pudet*). In the case of hormonal teenagers and potentially corrupt teachers care was especially necessary: cf. 3.3.3–4 (handsome Corellius needs a teacher *cuius scholae seueritas pudor in primis castitas constet*), 3.3.7 *eloquentiam... quae male sine moribus discitur* (with S-W), 4.13.4 *pudicius*; Hor. *Sat.* 1.6.81–4; Juv. *Sat.* 7.238–42; [Plut.] *De liberis educandis* 4B–C, 12A–C; and esp. Quint. 2.2 (esp. §§2–4, 14–15) with Reinhardt–Winterbottom.

3 quod superest 'for the rest', *OLD supersum* 6d. **cum ... scribam | efficiamque ... uidearis:** rising bicolon (20~30 syllables), ABC~CAB: main verbs are juxtaposed mid-sentence (as often), and each colon contains two subordinate clauses, with different conjunctions but parallel verb forms (*cum*... fut. pf. | *quid*... pres. subj. ~ *quantum*... fut. pf. | *ut*... pres. subj.). Each element is longer in the second colon than in the first. At the same time, chiasmus operates: *omnes... audiero* | (P.'s writing) ~ (P.'s writing) | *omnes audisse*. **qui profitentur** 'lecturers' (*OLD profiteor* 5b), varying *praeceptores*. The absolute use is modern: 4.11.1, 14, Quint. 1.5.7, Suet. *Gramm.* 9.2. **quid de quōque sentiam scribam** 'I shall write what I think of each one'; cf. Cic. *Brut.* 231 *quid de quoque iudicarem*, Hor. *Ep.* 1.18.68 *quid de quoque uiro et cui dicas, saepe uideto*. **efficiamque, quantum tamen epistula consequi potero, ut ipse omnes audisse uidearis** 'I shall make it seem – so far, that is, as I can achieve in a letter – that you heard them all yourself': *OLD efficio* 3, *quantum*[2] 3a (and *quantum*[1] 7). *quantum tamen* (with 'limiting' *tamen*: 2.1.10n. *si*) makes an unmatched alternative to *quantum modo* (e.g. Sen. *Const. sap.* 2.2 *rem publicam, quantum modo una retrahi manu poterat, tenuit*; also Ov. *Met.* 2.434, Sen. *Polyb.* 17.1, *Helu.* 9.4); the variation is analogous to *si tamen = si modo* 'if, that is'. Additionally, *tamen* may signal a concession in *epistula* 'although this is only a letter' (for this elliptical and anticipatory use see Housman on Lucan 1.333, Fordyce on Cat. 68.118, Horsfall on V. *Aen.* 3.341), though the concession is implicit in any case. For the letter as substitute for immediate experience, see e.g. 3.9.26, 5.6.41 (quoted in 2.17.2n. *aditur*). To ask why no such letter ensues is to miss the point, and P.'s efficiency in compilation: this exemplary transaction is complete without a second missive; and 3.3 (to another addressee) advertises the success of his search, as he recommends the rhetor Julius Genitor.

4 debeo enim tibi, | debeo . . . tui: rising bicolon (6~11 syllables), with pathetic anaphora of *debeo* (cf. 2.13.5 *ille meus in urbe, ille in secessu contubernalis*) and paired *tibi~tui* at colon-end.   **memoriae fratris tui:** the kernel of the letter: keeping the death of Arulenus alive is central to P.'s purpose (intro.).   **hanc fidem, hoc studium:** anaphora with polyptoton (cf. 1.3.3 *hoc sit negotium . . . , hic labor, haec quies*, 5.6.46 *hoc . . . gaudium, hanc gloriam*). For the noun-pair, cf. Ov. *Am.* 1.10.57 *studiumque fidemque*; Suet. *Iul.* 71.1; Cicero often has them in longer lists.   **praesertim super tanta re** for this tail, setting up the following *nam*, see 2.3.6n. *senibus*; for *super* see 2.11.11n.   **interest uestrā** (*sc. re*) 'matters to you (both)' (*OLD intersum* 9b), the plural anticipating *illo patre, te patruo*.   **dicerem tui:** the parenthesis interrupts, as if P. were about to say *liberi tui*, but checks himself.   **nisi nunc illos magis amares** 'if you did not now love them more' *sc.* than if they were your own (taking *nunc* to mean 'since their father's death'): P. would have said 'your children', but that would be to understate Mauricus' affection for them. For the soft *illos* (= *eos*) see §1n.; for the conceit, 2.1.9n. *etiam*. Like Verginius there, Mauricus presumably had no children of his own. There is no need to emend *nunc* to *nec* 'not even' (Shackleton Bailey 1981: 50).   **digni illo patre, te patruo** 'worthy of a father like him, an uncle like you' (lit. 'of him as father, of you as uncle'): the paronomasia, with chiastic reprise of *te . . . fratris tui* above, binds Mauricus to Arulenus. Proving worthy of one's family and especially father was a natural topos: Oakley on Livy 7.10.3 (with addendum in IV 550–1).   **reperiantur** 'be found to be' (*OLD* 5).   **curam . . . mandasses:** common from Livy on (also in 1.3.3, 6.10.3); cf. 1.14.2 *mandari*.   **uindicassem** 'I would have laid claim to'; similarly insistent obligingness at 6.16.3 *deposco etiam quod iniungis*.

5 nec ignoro 'and I am well aware'. The first sentence had its two finite verbs at or near clause-end (§1 *potuit, quaererem*); this last has them at clause-beginning (*ignoro . . . oportet*).   **suscipiendas offensas** *sc. esse* 'that one has to accept [the risk of] resentment' (*OLD suscipio* 10, *offensa* 5b), varying the common phrase (esp. in Cicero) *inimicitias suscipere*, cliché in such claims of selflessness: cf. Tac. *An.* 3.54.6 (Tiberius) *'offensionum . . . quas . . . suscipiam'*, and below on *subire*. The offence in question is not with *rhetores* but with their patrons, P.'s social equals (S-W): such patronage is apparent in 3.3 (P. recommends Genitor) and 4.13 (Tacitus is asked to recommend a *rhetor*). P. likes plurals of abstract nouns (2.14.14n. *indignitates*).   **in eligendo praeceptore:** the clausula (six heavy syllables) underlines the gravity of the task and perhaps an echo: cf. Quint. 2.2.15 *in eligendo fili praeceptore* (concluding the subject); also Quint. 1.2.5 *praeceptorem eligere*, 1.3.17 *in eligendis . . . praeceptorum moribus. praeceptor* is repeated from §1 to ring the letter.   **non modo . . . uerum etiam:** 2.7.5n. *non.*   **simultates** 'animosity' (*OLD* 1); see above on *suscipiendas* for the plural.   **fratris tui filiis:** the fourth statement of *fratris tui*, the second of *fratris tui filii*, and a variation on §1 *fratris tui liberis.*   **tam aequo animo** 'as cheerfully' (Radice): *OLD aequus* 8a, *Pan.* 9.5 [*muneris*] *aequo animo paratoque subeundi.* Another eighteenth letter in a book of twenty ends *aequum mi animum ipse parabo* (Hor. *Ep.* 1.18.112).   **subire** 'endure' (*OLD* 4), synonym of *suscipere.* Cf. 3.9.26 *offensas subierimus* and also 4.17.11 *nec subire offensas recusabo*, 9.13.21 *susceptis propriis simultatibus*, two comparable finales: in the former P. is helping Corellia, daughter of his patron and fellow Domitian-hater Corellius (1.12), in the latter he is 'avenging' Helvidius. Here too the assertion may be politically pointed, as he sides with Arulenus against unspecified forces.   **quam parentes pro suis** *sc. simultates subire oportet.* The letter closes with an implied *sententia* (that parents should risk any offence on behalf of their children) and an analogy which sets P., not Mauricus, as father to the young Junii. For similar appropriation, cf. 6.26.3, looking forward to the time when he can *nepotes tuos ut meos . . . ex uestro sinu sumere et quasi pari iure tenere*, 6.32.2 to Quintilianus, on a dowry for his daughter: *tamquam parens alter puellae nostrae confero . . .* 'as if I were a second father, I am giving our girl [50,000 sesterces]'; in 9.12 he offers avuncular advice to a father. Even a woman can fill a dead father's shoes in 4.19.1 *nec tantum amitae ei affectum uerum etiam patris amissi repraesentes.*

19

You urge me to recite a speech. It is hard to interest a recital audience, especially with a speech like this. Yet its very dryness should appeal to the cognoscenti I mean to invite. So tell me: should I recite it or not?

The first time that P. suggests reciting a speech, an activity implied to be innovative, and one which will recur – without the diffidence expressed here – throughout the collection (§1n. *recitem*). The speech in question probably derives from the trial of Marius Priscus (§8n. *nobis*), but, as often, P. avoids identifying it, so keeping the question general, the treatment exemplary. Within book 2 it makes a triptych with 2.5 (writing up a speech) and 2.10 (urging Octavius to recite his poetry); within books 1–2 it is a pendant to 1.8, which scrutinises at contorted length P.'s anxieties about self-promotion through publication. Among his arguments here the omission of Quintilian's views is striking. The recitation of speeches violates the master's fundamental tenet, that oratory should exist for the purpose of pleading a case, not for its own sake (e.g. Quint. 8.*pr.*32 *sciamus tamen nihil uerborum causa esse faciendum, cum uerba ipsa rerum gratia sint reperta*): in other words, forensic should always be privileged over epideictic. In rewriting his court speeches for recitation and publication, P. turns forensic *into* epideictic (Leeman

1963: 324, Cova 2003: 87–8; 2.5.5n. *descriptiones*). Of course the publication of court speeches was nothing new (and Quintilian would hardly prefer Cicero's not to survive); the novelty lies in adding a preliminary phase of recitation, and the stated aim of producing something more than a *monumentum actionis* 'the record of a speech delivered' (Quint. 12.10.51).

The letter proceeds in three movements: general disadvantages of recitation (§§2–4); difficulties peculiar to this speech (§§5–6); why it may nevertheless please at least the right sort of audience (§§7–9a). It is topped and tailed by appeals to Cerialis as adviser (§§1, 9b). P. works through his reasoning in clear but complex prose, testing his epistolary audience as much as those he will invite to scrutinise the speech (§9 *eruditissimum quemque*).

CERIALI: a common *cognomen* in inscriptions but not in P.; this is perhaps Velius Cerialis, who receives 4.21 about the daughters of Helvidius the Younger, and about whom we know nothing more. Between 2.18, on the sons of Arulenus Rusticus, a victim like Helvidius of the treason trials of AD 93, and 2.20, on Regulus, a villain of those trials, the presence of Velius may be pointed (2.18.intro.). The only other Cerialis in *Epp.* is Tuccius, the consular seen speaking in one of the preliminary meetings to the Priscus trial (2.11.9). The latter is preferred by S-W because this letter apparently concerns 'the *In Priscum*' (§8n. *nobis*) and because 'his rank requires *obsequium*'; the first reason is uncompelling, the second unlikely (§8n. *nobis*). Birley 2000a is agnostic.

1 Hortaris: for the opening displacement of responsibility, see 2.5.1n. *efflagitatam*. The theme is swiftly set. **orationem:** 2.3.10n. **pluribus** 'several' (*OLD plures* 4). **recitem:** the first of several references to P. reciting speeches: 3.18 (*Pan.*), 4.5, 5.12 (*oratiunculam*), 9.34.1 (where Mynors' *rationes* should be *orationes*) and esp. 7.17, a bullish defence; publication (by contrast) has been a given since 1.2. Though the recitation of speeches (as opposed to poetry, history et al.) had distinguished precedent, not least Aeschines on Rhodes (2.3.10; cf. 7.17.4 *orationes quoque et nostri quidam et Graeci lectitauerunt*), it appears to have been relatively unusual (Suet. *Aug.* 89.3 *nec tantum carmina et historias sed et orationes et dialogos* [*recitantes audiit*]); certainly P. presents it here as cause for hesitation, and defends it at length. See also 2.10.6n. *recita*. **faciam** 'I shall' (*OLD* 26a). Despite the assertion, the weight falls on the *quamuis* clause: the letter is predicated on P.'s (feigned) *lack* of certainty. **addubitem:** subj. with *quamuis*. The compound makes a favourite clausula (cretic–resolved spondee). On P.'s 'modesty' about publication see 2.10.7n. *infinita*.

2 neque enim me praeterit 'for it does not escape me that' (*OLD praetereo* 8a), with acc. (*actiones*) + inf. (*perdere*). **actiones:** the term emphasises speech as performance (2.5.1n.). Cf. Isoc. *Phil.* 26–7 'for when a discourse is robbed of the prestige of the speaker, the tones of his voice, the variations which are

made in the delivery . . . it is natural, I think, that it should make an indifferent impression upon its hearers' (tr. Norlin), Cic. *Att.* 1.16.8, *Or.* 130 *carent libri*
[written-up speeches] *spiritu illo propter quem maiora eadem illa cum aguntur quam cum*
leguntur uideri solent. P. advances comparable claims about speech vs letter in 5.7.6,
the opposite at 5.20.3. At 7.17.6 he presents the difficulty as a challenge to the
reciter.   **recitentur:** generic subjunctive (also subordinate within acc. + inf.,
where P. is flexible: 2.3.8n. *uiderat*). The division of MSS (*-antur* αF, *-entur* Bγ)
gives no reason to prefer the indicative printed by all recent editors: F is heavily
interpolated, and the often underrated γ is quite capable of containing a better
reading than α (e.g. *ut quas soleant* and §6 *aliud auditores aliud iudices*, both mangled
in αβ). Aldus printed *-entur*.   **impetum omnem caloremque . . . perdere**
'lose all their driving force and heat'. On *impetus* in oratory see Winterbottom
1995. Metaphorical *calor* (again at 4.9.11) is especially common in Quintilian (cou-
pled with *impetus* at Quint. 9.4.113, 10.3.17); here it is transferred from speaker to
speech. For image and theme, cf. Cic. *Brut.* 93 *ardor animi . . . cum consedit* ['calmed
down'], *omnis illa uis et quasi flamma oratoris exstinguitur*, describing why an able but
untrained orator fails to impress in writing; Sen. *Contr.* 10.*pr*.3 on the lack of *calor*
in Scaurus' published speeches.   **nomen suum:** the name of *actio*. They do not
quite lose it (hence *prope*), as e.g. 2.5.1 shows (reading an *actio*).   **ut quas soleant**
commendare simul et accendere 'for what generally makes speeches attractive and also exciting is', literally 'as being things which . . . make attractive and
at the same time fire up' (*OLD commendo* 6a, *accendo* 3c). Causal relative clause
(*ut qui* + generic subj.: *OLD ut* 21b; *NLS* §157b); the subject of *soleant* is the
long list *iudicum . . . corporis* (next n.). For (*actiones*) *commendare* cf. 4.22.2 (*actionem*),
5.20.8 (*oratiunculam*); also Cic. *Brut.* 240 (*orationem*) and Quint. 11.3.5 (*orationem*),
both, as here, describing performance. *accendere*, which normally has a person or
emotion as object, continues the gentle personification of the speech (above on
impetum).   **iudicum consessus, celebritas aduocatorum, exspectatio**
euentus, | fama non unius actoris diductumque in partes audien-
tium studium, | ad hoc dicentis gestus incessus discursus etiam,
omnibusque motibus animi consentaneus uigor corporis: nine factors which encourage a performing orator, elaborately arranged. An extended
tricolon (21~23~35 syllables) comprises (*i*) an AB~BA~BA tricolon of word-pairs,
(*ii*) rising bicolon (9~14 syllables) with chiasmus (nominatives frame genitives);
(*iii*) a longer rising bicolon (16~20 syllables) with the opposite chiasmus (genitives
frame nominatives), whose first member itself contains an asyndetic tricolon (*gestus*
incessus discursus etiam).   **consessus:** an assembly, usually of senators or jurors.
iudices and *aduocati* (below) evoke the centumviral court, P.'s principal lawyerly
arena (2.14.1n. *centumuiralibus*), rather than the senate, though the latter seems
to have been the stage for the speech now in hand (§8n. *nobis*).   **celebritas**
aduocatorum 'the great numbers of supporters', the older meaning of *aduocatus*
(Mayer on Tac. *D.* 1.1); usually (as in Quintilian and Tacitus) it means 'counsel,
advocate'.   **exspectatio euentus:** cf. Sall. *Jug.* 44.3, though *euentum exspectare*

(usually military) is common. **non unius actoris** 'of more than one advocate' (2.17.2n. *non*, 2.14.4n. *actoribus*). **diductumque in partes audientium studium** 'the sympathies of the audience drawn apart into factions', with substantival *audientium* (2.11.14n. *non*). The quickening rhythm (seven heavy syllables to start, a light cadence to end) perhaps evokes the excitement; the following phrase responds closely (except *gestūs*). **ad hoc** (2.11.10n.) reinforces the third member of the overarching tricolon (above on *iudicum*). **dicentis:** substantival (2.3.9n.). **gestus incessus discursus etiam:** all three singular, as is clear from the rhythm and e.g. *gestus* in 2.3.9 (see 2.3.9n. *pronuntiatio* for the whole sentiment here); *etiam* caps the tricolon (2.1.6n.). *incessus* 'pacing about' is recommended in moderation by Cic. *Or.* 59 and Quint. 11.3.125–6, but Quintilian (ibid.) condemns *discursare* 'running about' as *ineptissimum*. On the dangers of overacting see also Quint. 6.3.54 *discursantem salientem*, 11.3.56 and 118 (excessive arm gestures), Lucian *Rhet. praec.* 20. P. disregards these precepts, whether because of his sympathies for sophistic flamboyance (2.3), or because he is here evoking with maximum flair the excitement of the courtroom. **omnibusque motibus animi consentaneus uigor corporis:** ABC~ABC (adj., noun, gen.). *consentaneus* 'appropriate to, matching' governs *motibus* (dat.). The term *animi motus* is esp. common in Cicero; for the idea that the orator's physical movements visibly express his thoughts, cf. Cic. *De or.* 3.216 *omnis enim motus animi suum quendam a natura habet uultum et sonum et gestum . . .* , 3.223, Quint. 1.2.31 *illum . . . animi et corporis motum*. P. praises Trajan's total-body oratory at *Pan.* 67.1 *quae asseueratio in uoce, quae affirmatio in uultu, quanta in oculis habitu gestu toto denique corpore fides!*

3 unde accidit ut 'and so it comes about that' + subj. (*OLD unde* 11b, *accido* 7a). **ii qui sedentes agunt:** some advocates performed sitting down, especially in minor cases (Quint. 11.3.134–5 *iis qui sedentes agent . . .* , 11.1.44); perhaps physical disability (never mentioned in this context) played a part. P. is not yet talking about reciters (*pace* S-W et al.): *agere* (*OLD* 43–4) is proper to court action, and §4 *recitantium uero* draws the contrast. **quamuis illis maxima ex parte supersint eadem illa quae stantibus** 'although they may for the most part have the same abilities as people who [advocate] standing up' (*OLD quamuis* 3b, *supersum* 7). For the soft *illis/illa* (= *iis/ea*) see 2.1.7n. The substantival *stantibus* (2.3.9n. *dicentis*), dat. governed by an implied *supersint* or -*sunt*, varies *ii qui sedentes agunt*. **tamen:** clause-initial only here and in 10.2.1 (also Trajan in 10.9). **hōc quod sedent** 'by the fact that they are seated' (*OLD hic* 12b). **quasi debilitentur et deprimantur** 'are, so to say, weakened and undermined', subjunctive after *ut*; for *quasi* see 2.6.5n. *illa*; for *deprimere* 'undermine', cf. Cic. *Inu.* 1.22 *aduersariorum causam . . . deprimemus*. Cf. Quint. 11.3.134 (on seated pleaders) *et idem impetus actionis esse non possunt, et quaedam uitia fiunt necessaria*.

4 recitantium uero: *uero* brings us to the heart of the matter (2.1.7n. *mihi*); *recitantium* is again substantival (§3n. *quamuis*). Reciters not only performed sitting down (6.6.6 *dicenti mihi . . . assistit, assidet recitanti*, 9.34.2 *sedeam*, Pers. 1.17 *sede* *leges celsa*), so disadvantaged like the seated pleaders of §3 (a point left implicit), but had the further impediment next noted. **praecipua pronuntiationis adiumenta, oculi manus:** *oculi manus* is in apposition to *adiumenta*. On the importance of the eyes see Cic. *De or.* 3.221 *imago animi uultus, indices oculi,* Quint. 11.3.75 *oculi, per quos maxime animus emanat;* on the hands, Quint. 11.3.85 *ceterae partes loquentem adiuuant, hae* [= *manus*] *prope est ut dicam ipsae loquuntur.* For *pronuntiatio* see 2.3.9n. **praepediuntur** 'are impeded' (lit. 'fettered'), by holding and reading a scroll. P. takes for granted that advocates, by contrast, would perform from memory, the Quintilianic ideal if not ubiquitous practice (e.g. Quint. 11.3.142). Heroic clausula (2.3.3n. *narrat*). **quo minus mirum est si** 'and so it is hardly [lit. less] surprising if' (2.10.6n. *quo, OLD mirus* 3d). **auditorum intentio relanguescit** 'the attention of the audience flags' (*OLD relanguesco* c). Cf. Quint. 11.3.2 *affectus omnes* languescant *necesse est, nisi uoce uultu totius prope habitu corporis inardescunt:* Quintilian talks about the speaker's concentration, P. that of the audience. For *intentio* see 2.5.2n., 4.9.11 (*audientis*). **nullis extrinsecus aut blandimentis capta aut aculeis excitata** 'with no external allurements to charm it or barbs to prick it' (lit. 'charmed by . . . ', *OLD capio* 17a, *excito* 5b). *extrinsecus* is an adverb (*OLD* 2a 'from an extraneous source'), referring to performance as opposed to content; together with *nullis* it modifies both nouns. The rhythm seems expressive, seven heavy syllables of smooth blandishment followed by the spiky *aculeis excitata* (◡◡◡−−◡−◡). For this last combination, cf. 4.5.3 *aculeis excitabantur,* again on the recitation of speeches. **aculeis** 'stings, barbs', *OLD* 3a, a metaphor common since Cicero (*TLL* I 457.79–458.19) evoking arrows or insects (Leeman–Pinkster–Rabbie on Cic. *De or.* 2.222). Berry on Cic. *Sull.* 47.3 insists on the former, but in 1.20.17–18 (as in Cic. *De or.* 3.138, *Brut.* 38, Val. Max. 8.9.*ext*.2) *aculeus* translates κέντρον in a quotation of Eupolis, which Plato at least took as apian (*Phaedo* 91c ὥσπερ μέλιττα τὸ κέντρον ἐγκαταλιπών 'leaving his sting behind like a bee').

5 Accedit his quod 'then there is the fact that' (*OLD accedo* 17b + dat.), opening a rising tricolon of further points (*accedit . . . porro . . . et sane,* 23~32~34 syllables; for the varied formulae see 2.11.10n. *praeterea*). *his* refers to §§2–4. **pugnax** 'polemical' (*OLD* 2), first of literary style in Cic. *De or.* 2.317. In 6.33.8 P.'s speech for Attia Viriola contains *multa pugnacia;* 7.9.7 advises against excessive use of *pugnacem hunc et quasi bellatorium stilum.* **et quasi contentiosa** 'and I might say quarrelsome'. *contentio* 'quarrel' is named as a type of speech in *Rhet. Her.* 3.23; the adj. *contentiosus* first appears here and in the *Major declamations* attributed to Quintilian (also [Varro] *Sententiae* 140 Riese). For this adjective-pair, with *quasi* softening (2.6.5n. *illa*) the second, bolder term, cf. 3.1.2 *confusa . . . et quasi turbata,* 3.18.10 *hilarius et quasi exsultantius,* 8.2.4, 9.18.2, 9.37.1 (Stout 1954: 157–8, who unduly faults *quasi* here). P. leaves implicit the (questionable?) claim that this quality will make the speech unattractive. **ita natura comparatum est** 'it is in the nature of things'; similarly introducing an aphorism at 5.19.5, 8.20.1, and abbreviated in 3.4.6; *natura (com)paratum* is otherwise rare (Cic. *Diu.* 2.122, Livy

3.68.19, Col. 12.*pr.*1, Apul. *Flor.* 9.96). **ea quae scripsimus cum labore |
cum labore etiam audiri putemus** 'we think that what took hard work to
write is also hard work to listen to', chiastic *sententia*. The MSS omit the second
cum labore (αγ) or have it after *etiam* (β), but the text adopted here (as by most, *contra*
Goold 1964: 323) puts *etiam* in its usual second place (2.1.6n.) and before the word
it stresses, and explains the haplography in αγ (Postgate 1926: 378, anticipated
by Cortius).

6 et sane 'and indeed' (*OLD sane* 3a), introducing the third member of the
tricolon (§5n. *accedit*). *sane* is often concessive, but P. always uses *et sane* in this
affirmatory sense (1.14.9, 4.14.6 etc.), common also in Quintilian and [Quint.]
Decl. min. **quotus quisque tam rectus auditor quem non potius dulcia
haec et sonantia quam austera et pressa delectent?** 'how many listeners
really exist [*sc. est*] who are so sound that they do not take pleasure in all this
sonorous charm rather than in severe restraint?' The idiom *quotus quisque*, lit. 'one
of how many is each?', makes a rhetorical question (or exclamation) implying
'there is scarcely anyone': *OLD quotus* 2, Wackernagel 2009: 540–1 (also at 8.14.3,
8.23.3, *Pan.* 43.5, 63.3). **rectus** 'upright', 'sound' (2.11.5n. *uir*), morally loaded
(on morality in oratory see 2.14.12n. *pudet*, 2.18.2n. *probe*); a hint too, perhaps, of
the unembellished *rectus sermo* desired by purists (Quint. 2.5.11 with Reinhardt–
Winterbottom). **quem . . . delectent:** relative result clause. **dulcia haec et
sonantia:** *haec* gestures at the trend of the day (*OLD hic* 2a). *dulcis* 'attractive',
'charming' (*OLD* 7c; cf. γλυκύς, ἡδύς) is common in literary criticism and often a
compliment (e.g. 2.3.1 *praefationes . . . dulces*), as *sonans* can be (1.16.2 *sonantia uerba et
antiqua*). Here, however, P. is dismissing the easy charms of bombast: cf. Cic. *Or.* 42
(on sophists) <u>*dulce*</u> . . . *orationis genus . . . sententiis argutum, uerbis* <u>*sonans*</u>. He expresses
similarly pious hopes in 3.18.10 (on *Pan.*!), that public taste will soon revert from
dulcia haec blandaque to *austeris illis seuerisque*; at 4.14.3 *modo pressius, modo elatius*
and 7.12.4 he embraces a characteristic middle way. If Quintilian kept P. on the
straight and narrow, studies with the crowd-pleasing sophist Nicetes of Smyrna
(6.6.3) perhaps taught him the value of indulging modern taste (on Nicetes see
Tac. *D.* 15.3, Phil. *VS* 511–12, Anderson 1993: 19–20). **austera et pressa:** a
weighty reply to *dulcia haec et sonantia*. For *austerus* 'austere, plain', see *OLD* 4 and
3.18.10 (in previous n.); its literal meaning 'bitter' (*OLD* 1a), opposed to *dulcis*,
may also be in play: cf. Cic. *De or.* 3.103, where Crassus prefers oratorical charm
austeram et solidam 'bitter and firm', not *dulcem atque decoctam* 'sweet and over-ripe'.
pressus 'restrained, moderated' (*OLD* 6b; 9.26.12 *custoditius pressiusque*) is a term
commonly associated with 'Atticists' (e.g. Cic. *Brut.* 51, Tac. *D.* 18.4; Sandys on
Cic. *Or.* 20; Gamberini 1983: 171–2). P. uses it frequently in literary criticism
(Mayor on 3.18.10), usually in praise (though see 7.12.4, in previous n.); of a
speech of his own at 1.8.5. **est . . . est** 'is . . . does exist'. **quidem omnino:**
quidem is concessive; *omnino* emphasises the whole clause (2.4.3n. *sunt*). **turpis:**
2.6.7n. *turpissima*. **ista discordia:** *ista* (*OLD* 3) implies that the dispute is well

known; given what follows, it must be the variance of taste between judges in a courtroom and the audience in a recital (intro.). Elsewhere P. contests the view *aliud est actio bona, aliud oratio* in terms of content (1.20.9–10; cf. Quint. 12.10.49–57); here he focuses on poor taste in the audience. **euĕnit ut** (2.11.7n.) varies §3 *accidit ut.* **cum alioqui** 'when in fact' (2.12.2n. *cum*). **iis praecipue auditor affici debeat quibus idem, si foret iudex, maxime permoueretur** 'a listener ought to be affected especially by the things that would sway him most if he were a judge', instead of being interested (P. implies) in easy entertainment. P. does not hold back from judging his audience's judgment: cf. 3.18.8 *ego cum studium audientium tum iudicium mire probaui.* **foret:** only three times in P., who much prefers *esset* (47×), like e.g. Cicero and Seneca and unlike Tacitus (88~76), and uses no other forms of *forem.* Here it generates a cretic–spondee; the others are 4.13.10 *gratum mihi foret* (euphony?) and *Pan.* 76.6 *consul foret... consulem esset* (varying, and perhaps avoiding homophony). **permoueretur:** 2.11.11n. *ut.*

7 Potest... fieri ut 'it may be that' (also at 1.5.16). **quamquam in his difficultatibus** 'despite these difficulties' (2.17.14n. *quamquam*). **libro:** 2.5.3n. **lenocinetur** 'will assist' (+ dat.), subj. after *ut.* **nouitas apud nostros** corrects *nouitas* (*reprehensio:* 2.1.10n. *si tamen*), restricting it to novelty in Rome (*OLD noster* 7b). **apud Graecos... dissimile** 'for the Greeks have something which, although opposite, is not altogether dissimilar'; cf. Quint. 5.10.64 *ratio, quamuis sit ex diuerso, eadem est.*

8 ut illis... arguebant aliarum collatione conuincere, | ita nobis... postularemus... aliis colligendum fuit: a thoroughly worked antithesis (39~35 syllables) with corresponding arrangement and some rhyme (*aliarum collatione conuincere... aliis colligendum*) but varied lexis. Each half has *lex* twice (*leges... legibus* ~ *legi... lege*). The referents have shifted from *nostri* [i.e. *Romani*] ~ *Graeci* in the previous sentence to *Graeci* ~ *ego.* **illis erat moris** 'it was their custom'. *illis* is possessive dat.; *moris* predicative gen. of quality (G–L §366 R.2). **leges quas ut contrarias prioribus legibus arguebant** 'laws which they challenged as contradicting earlier laws' (*OLD arguo* 4b, *ut* 10). For *arguere ut*, cf. 8.21.3, Suet. *Iul.* 81.4 *ut falsum arguens*, *Nero* 7.1; also Quint. 9.3.67 *quasi falsum*, [Quint.] *Decl. min.* 264.3 *tamquam impium*, the latter two both legal. P. refers here to the γραφὴ παρανόμων 'indictment for illegality' used in Athens from *c.* 415 BC to challenge a law or decree on the ground that it conflicted with pre-existing laws (*OCD 'graphē paranomōn'*; MacDowell 2009: 152 n.1), as in the case involving Demosthenes' famous *On the crown* (2.3.10n. λαμπροφωνότατος; Yunis 2001: 7–12). The problem was not peculiar to Greece, of course: cf. Quint. 7.7 on *antinomia* (conflict of laws). **aliarum collatione** 'by comparing them with others', *OLD collatio* 4a–b, with *aliarum* objective gen. **conuincere** 'refute' (*OLD* 3b). **nobis inesse repetundarum legi quod postularemus cum hac ipsa lege tum aliis colligendum fuit** 'I had to infer that my accusation was covered by the extortion law not only from that law itself but also from other

[laws]', *OLD colligo* 11, *postulo* 3, *insum* 2, *cum* 14a. *inesse . . . postularemus* is indirect statement, with [*id*] *quod postularemus* (lit. 'what I was prosecuting', subjunctive because subordinate within it) the subject of *inesse*. P. has switched to authorial plural (2.5.3n. *nostra*). His speech clearly stemmed from an extortion trial (cf. *repetundarum*, with 2.11.3n. *ne*), naturally identified with P.'s prosecution of Priscus in 2.11 (S-W). **quod nequaquam blandum** 'which, being in no way appealing'; the non-existent present participle of *esse* must be assumed. *quod* (referring to the whole preceding idea) is the subject of *debet* and *habet*. *blandum* covers anything which wins over an audience (cf. §4 *blandimentis*), with a tone ranging from neutral ('charm') to damning ('flattery'). It is not necessarily to be rejected, then, but here as in 3.18.10 (§6n. *dulcia*) it is easily dismissed, in contrast to the grittier stuff that should appeal to the *docti*. **imperitorum** 'the untrained'. P.'s own *imperitia* is safely confined to art criticism (3.6.4). **tanto maiorem apud doctos . . . quanto minorem apud indoctos:** a snob's polarity: the less the ignorant like it, the more the learned should. For *tanto . . . quanto* see *OLD quanto* 2b. The antithesis *docti ~ indocti* is common; less so *imperiti ~ docti*, for which cf. Quint. 8.2.22 and esp. 12.10.50 (distinguishing the *imperiti* in a jury from the *docti* who read published speeches).

9 nos autem, si '– and if I', explaining the previous sentence and preparing for the closing turn (*si placuerit recitare* 'prompts' the question *adhuc an sit recitandum*). *nos* and *ego* freely alternate (2.4.3n. *sunt*). **si placuerit** *sc. mihi*, 'if I decide' (fut. pf.). **adhibituri sumus** 'I mean to invite', periphrastic future (2.2.2n. *non*); P. often uses *adhibere* in this sense (*OLD* 4); of *recitatio* also at 1.5.4, 6.15.4. **eruditissimum quemque** 'all the best read people' (*OLD quisque* 4a), rather than 'legal experts' (Radice): *eruditus* 'learned, well educated' (*TLL* v.2 831.18 '*i. q.* πεπαιδευμένος') is the opposite of *barbarus* (3.13.3), *imperitus* (Quint. 1.6.45) or *stultus* (Quint. 10.7.21). The point of *recitatio* is to elicit critique (5.3.8–11, 5.12.1, 7.17.1; Mayor 1886: 175–7), which demands a select audience: 7.17.12 *ego . . . non populum aduocare sed certos electosque soleo quos intuear, quibus credam*; cf. 3.18.9 *non multis recitasse*, 5.12.1 *aduocaui . . . paucos*, 7.4.7 *sodalibus legi*. The common-or-garden recital audience earns P.'s disdain (1.13.2), as does the wider reading public (2.5.4n. *ad*). The world of P.'s recitations – of which the *Epistles* grants only select glimpses – is thus characteristically exclusive.

Sed plane: a strengthened 'but' (10.42.1, *TLL* x.1 2345.43–55, esp. favoured by Cicero), pulling the discussion short and returning to the main question. **adhuc an sit recitandum examina tecum** 'weigh up yourself whether [I] should still hold a recital [at all]'. For *examinare* (*OLD* 4) + indirect question, cf. 3.15.1 *examinem an editione sint digni*, *TLL* v.2 1169.16–31; for *examina tecum*, Sen. *Ep.* 81.10 *sapiens omnia examinabit secum*. The imperative and *recitandum* bring us back to §1 *hortaris ut orationem . . . recitem*: after all P. has said, is Cerialis still as sure in his encouragement as P. is in his doubts (§1 *uehementer addubitem*)? The desired answer, of course, is 'yes'. Cowan and *TLL* I 661.47–8 take *adhuc* to have future reference (2.10.2n. *frustrari*), without clear justification. For the passing heroic clausula *sit recitandum*, see 2.3.3n. *narrat.* **omnesque quos ego moui in utraque parte calculos pone** 'and tally up all the points I have raised for and against', literally 'place all the pebbles that I have moved on each side [*OLD pars* 14a]'. A shift of metaphor after *examina*: *calculi* are pebbles used for arithmetic, *ponere* is to set them out on an abacus or 'reckoning board' (*OLD calculus* 3b, *pono* 18c; Menninger 1969: 315–18). Accounting metaphors are common: 1.14.9, 5.2.1, *Pan.* 20.5, *TLL* III 143.61–74, Vannini on Petr. 115.16 (*album calculum* at 1.2.5 is a voting image). With exemplary diffidence P. has given the arguments against (§§2–6) significantly more coverage than those for (§§7–9b); Cerialis is evidently intended to err the other way. For the fairly rare combination X Y*que* Z*que* see 2.11.3n. *deprecatusque.* **uicerit:** fut. pf., since the imperative *elige* refers to a future action. **ratio . . . ratio:** a smooth exit from the metaphor: the first *ratio* means 'calculation' (*OLD* 1–2), the second, opposed to *obsequium*, (also) means 'reason, justification' (*OLD* 5, 7). **a te enim ratio exigetur, nos excusabit obsequium:** ABC~ACB isocolon (9~9 syllables), with variety in voice of verbs (but matching *ex-* prefix), case of pronouns and clausula. **nos excusabit obsequium** 'I will have the excuse of compliance'. P. ends where he began, deflecting self-promotion onto Cerialis' request. For thought and form, cf. 1.1.2 *superest ut nec te consili nec me paeniteat obsequi* (justifying the *Epistles*), 1.8.18 *habes cunctationis meae causas; obsequar tamen consilio tuo, cuius mihi auctoritas pro ratione sufficiet* (on publishing a speech). *obsequium* is a word of which P. and Tacitus are unusually fond (Pani 1993, esp. 172–7 on P.). In both it has considerable semantic range, but while Tacitus tends to a critical view of *obsequium* as flattery (e.g. *H.* 1.15.4; Vielberg 1987: 131–4), that sense is rare in P. (e.g. 8.6.12). Rather, it is either (*i*) due obedience in vertical power relations, as of slave/freedman to master (8.14.2), soldier to general (8.14.7), province to Rome (*Pan.* 16.3), subject to emperor (*Pan.* 45.5) etc.; or (*ii*) the 'horizontal' compliance between friends familiar from late republican discourse (Pani 1993: 160–3, Beutel 2000: 95–8), a social lubricant in the elite world of courteous favours (8.23.5, 9.13.6), as of advocate to client (3.4.8, 10.3.3, 10.4). Here it is clearly the latter (*pace* S-W 201), as in 1.1.2, 1.8.18 (above).

20

Here are some pretty tales. Regulus tricked Verania into giving him a legacy, swearing falsely on the life of his own son. He was as shameless during Velleius Blaesus' terminal illness, without success. When Aurelia was making her will he even demanded that she leave him her clothes. What a society we live in, when a man like Regulus can rise from rags to riches on such perverse practices!

Book 2 began with a grave letter commemorating the death of Verginius Rufus, exemplary senior statesman and true friend to P. It ends with a (purportedly) light-hearted letter of similar length regretting the continued success of Aquillius Regulus, counter-exemplary senator and false friend to the dying.

Regulus (2.11.22n.) is an important figure in *Epistles* 1–6, a *bête noire* who embodies everything P. is not, and the inversion of the ideal senator (Hoffer 1999: 55–91, Méthy 2007: 141–51, Lefèvre 2009: 50–60, G–M 68–73). He is subject of four other letters: 1.5 establishes him as political enemy and oratorical polar-opposite; 4.2 and 4.7 mock Regulus' ostentatious mourning for the death of his son; 6.2 reports his death. He is mentioned, in addition, in 1.20.14 and 2.11.22. The trio of anecdotes in this letter thus caps his three previous appearances in books 1–2 (Bodel n.d.), while responding in style and content to 1.5 (the first substantial letter of the collection) and illuminating the dark hint of Regulus' *flagitia . . . tectiora* with which that letter began (§1n. *nec*).

Both letters smear Regulus with allegations of immoral behaviour, but where 1.5 opens with *Schadenfreude* at his reduced political influence after Domitian's death, 2.20 ends with impotent rage at his ongoing accumulation of wealth, and whereas 1.5 dwelled on *delatio* '(malicious) prosecution', a topic shared especially with Tacitus (Rutledge 2001, Whitton 2012: 353–9), 2.20 turns to *captatio*, a theme best known from satire. In a society with low survival rates and a custom of making substantial bequests outside one's family, allegations of 'legacy hunting', the cynical grooming of (especially) the rich and childless in the hope of a legacy or inheritance, were unsurprisingly common. Censured by P. (4.15.3, 5.1.3, 8.18, 9.30.1–2) and Seneca (*Ben.* 4.20.3, *Ep.* 19.4 *et passim*) as a feature of modernity, this subversion of the ideals of *amicitia* was a favourite butt of satire and epigram: see esp. Hor. *Sat.* 2.5 with Muecke (and Rudd 1966: 224–42), Petr. 116–17, 124–5, 140–1, Mart. 1.10 *et passim*, Juv. 1.37–9 *et passim* and (in Greek) Lucian *Dialogues of the dead* 15–18, 21; cf. Tracy 1980, Hopkins 1983: 238–42, Champlin 1991: 87–102 and 201–2. P.'s own calumny (for Calvisius) is duly satirical, both in its mocking of Regulus' failure (§8n. *Regulo*) and in its combination of (faux-)levity and indignation (§1n. *assem*).

From apparently light beginnings the letter climaxes in a miniature peroration worthy not just of Juvenal but of Demosthenes or Cicero (§12n. ἀλλά, §12n. *nequitia et*), ending the book on a note of angry impotence, more akin with the gloom of 2.14 than the optimism that tends to dominate: an arresting effect for the reader of *Epistles* 1–2. Yet the invocation of Demosthenic/Ciceronian *auctoritas* is also a muscular assertion of P.'s oratorical and literary power over his nemesis. 'Exposure' as a *captator* is particularly damaging to a man renowned as a leading light of the centumviral court, and thus of inheritance law (2.14.1n. *centumuiralibus*). That status is celebrated particularly by Martial, who addresses or mentions Regulus in fourteen poems (Howell on Mart. 1.12). One of those is *Epigrams* 2.93, which seals books 1–2 with a retrospective dedication (Maltby 2008: 256, 262–3). Do we see Martial's courtesy to Regulus overturned in this 'inverted dedication' (cf. Cat. 116 with Macleod 1973: 308), as P. seals book 2, and *Epistles* 1–2, with this damning critique?

P.'s gloom is also reframed by what follows. The very next letter unpicks the closure of book 2 through its shared addressee (CALVISIO n.); and book 3 as a whole, with P. as consul and Regulus wholly absent, invites a reading of book 2 as

a fall before the consular rise (Intro. 19–20). Subsequently the death of Regulus'
son in 4.2 inflicts divine (and poetic) justice on a perjurer (§6n. *qui*), and 4.7 twists
the knife with a devastating (though again 'light-hearted') critique of Regulus as
the definitive bad orator; but it is his death in 6.2, and with it the revival of the
centumviral court, which finally overturns the pessimism of 2.20 as well as of 2.14
(2.14.intro.). For *captatio* too, the tables will be turned in 8.18, a counterweight to
this letter, in which morality wins out (§1n. *fabulas*). In this way the 'meaning' of
2.20 proves radically different for the reader of the collection than for the reader
of the single letter, or of books 1–2.

   Dominated as it is by death, a favourite closural device (though also the
opening motif of this book: 2.1.intro.), 2.20 makes an apt book-end. Book 3 will
end with the death of Martial (3.21), together with another common motif of
closure, literary eternity (reprised in 7.33, to Tacitus), and book 5 closes with
another friend's death (5.21): the beginnings perhaps of a characteristic half-
buried pattern (Intro. 11–13). On the less emphatic closure of book 1, see Merwald
1964: 31, Hoffer 1999: 221–5.

   After a jaunty opening, P. presents three tales in a ratio of 2:1:1 (136 words for
Verania, 135 for Blaesus and Aurelia together), followed by a 77-word peroration.
The triptych, combining parallel and variation, is self-consciously flagged (§9)
and finely varied; the first act shows Regulus triumphant, the second foiled and
the third with result pending. In each he commits a different atrocity: perjury on
his son's life, advocating euthanasia, taking the shirt off Aurelia's back.

   The letter is discussed in treatments of Regulus (above) and receives acute
remarks in Scarcia 1984.

CALVISIO: the equestrian Calvisius Rufus (*PIR*² C 349) was a decurion (councillor)
in P.'s native Comum. Like Voconius, the equestrian recipient of 2.1, he receives
several letters (3.1, 3.19, 5.7, 8.2, 9.6) dealing with 'politics, gossip, and business,
but not literature' (S-W 202); all the Regulus letters seem to be addressed to
similarly close friends (G–M 140). As addressee of both 2.20 and 3.1, he forms a
unique bridge between books, undoing the closure of book 2 (§9n. *sufficiunt*); this
connection also invites us to draw a contrast between arch-villain Regulus and
model senator Vestricius Spurinna, the honorand of 3.1, and further between the
impotent frustration that closes this book (§§12–14) and the consular authority on
show in book 3 (above).

1 Assem para et accipe auream fabulam 'get a penny ready and hear
a golden tale', chiasmus, with the hint of a pun in *assem* ~ *auream* (cf. *OLD
aureus*², a high-value gold coin). 'Golden tale', elevating anecdote or gossip (*fabula*:
5.6.6, 6.15.1, 8.18.11) into (mock-)grandeur, is paralleled only by *Asinus aureus*,
Augustine's (light-hearted?) name for Apuleius' *Metamorphoses* (Aug. *Ciu.* 18.18;
also Fulg. *Serm. ant.* 17 and 40: *RE* II.1 250). P. plays the role of a beggar who will
sell his story for a coin (Pers. *Sat.* 1.88–9 *cantet si naufragus, assem | protulerim?* 'am

I supposed to produce a penny if a washed-up sailor starts to sing?'; cf. Suet. *Aug.* 91, begging for an *as*); alternatively, of a 'strolling mountebank' (Cowan), the *circulator* who declaimed to impromptu crowds (Peterson on Quint. 10.1.8). The intimate imperative (2.13.10n. *ama*) and jaunty mood belie the slander to follow and the dark conclusion: cf. Juv. 4, professedly *de factis leuioribus* (4.11) but ending in bitter rage (4.150–4). **fabulas immo** 'or rather stories' (*OLD immo* e), in self-correction (2.1.10n. *si*). For the polyptoton *fabulam . . . fabulas* see 2.2.1n. *irascor* (repetition as opening device) and cf. 8.18.11 *fabulas . . . fabulae*, concluding a pendant letter in the penultimate book, in which Domitius Tullus foils his *captatores*, so overturning the pessimism here: esp. 8.18.3 *quos* [*sc. captatores*] *sic decipi pro moribus temporum est.* **nam me priorum noua admonuit** 'for a/the new story has reminded me of earlier ones' (*OLD admoneo* 1b + acc. + gen.), justifying the letter with 'news value' in a natural move (Ov. *Met.* 6.316 *utque fit, a facto propiore priora renarrant*). **nec refert a qua potissimum incipiam** 'and it does not matter which one in particular I start with' (*OLD refert* 1a, *ab* 12a, *potissimum* 2). Like *Epistles* 2 (Intro. 15–16), the anecdotes are professedly disordered but may be chronological. Verania's death is undatable, that of Blaesus may be early 90s (§7n. *Velleius*); Aurelia, still alive, is presumably the *noua fabula*. One, two or perhaps all may then be among Regulus' *flagitia . . . tectiora* (1.5.1) under Domitian.

2 Verania Pisonis grauiter iacebat 'Verania, wife of Piso, lay seriously ill', *OLD iaceo* 2c, 5.21.2 (also terminal illness). For the gen. (standard) see 6.16.8, K–S 1 414. Each tale opens with asyndeton, the victim's name in the nom., and efficient scene-setting (§7 *Velleius . . . conflictabatur*, §10 *Aurelia . . . sumpserat*); cf. 3.16.3 *aegrotabat Caecina . . . 7 Scribonianus arma . . . mouerat* (two of a trio of tales). Verania Gemina (Raepsaet-Charlier 1987: §788) was daughter of Q. Veranius, *cos. ord.* 49. This first tale resembles a satirical epigram of Agathias (*Anth. Pal.* 11.382, 6c. AD), in which a 'doctor' visits an ill man (vv.1–5 κεῖτο μὲν Ἀλκιμένης . . . ἦλθε δὲ Καλλίγνωτος 'Alcimenes lay ill . . . along came Callignotos [the *captator*]' ~ *Verania . . . iacebat . . . Regulus uenit*), performs calculations about the 'critical days' of his illness (v.11 ~ §§3–4), assures him he will survive (v.17 ~ §4 *euades*), and requests an inheritance (vv.19–22 ~ §5 *legatum . . . scribit*): had Agathias read P., or was there a common source? The similarities are strong (Schuster 1927, Scarcia 1984: 297–8; *contra* Cameron 1965: 289 n.3, who doubts Agathias' competence in Latin). **huius dico Pisonis quem Galba adoptauit:** L. Calpurnius Piso Frugi Licinianus (*PIR*² C 300), on whose adoption by Galba in January 69, fatal to both, see Tac. *H.* 1.14–19, Plut. *Galba* 23, Suet. *Galba* 17, Dio 63(64).5. As *princeps manqué* he has something in common with Verginius Rufus (2.1.2nn.). Piso died poor (Tac. *H.* 1.48.4); Verania presumably had independent wealth to make her a worthwhile victim (cf. §7 *locuples*, §10 *ornata*). For the informal specification *huius dico* (*OLD dico* 8), cf. 1.16.1 *hunc dico nostrum*, 9.30.1 *amicis dico pauperibus*. It is necessary: Pisones were numerous. The bare *Galba* is typical of P.'s practice in naming non-deified emperors (Jones 1991: 161–3). **ad hanc Regulus uēnit** 'along came Regulus' (*ad hanc* lit. 'to (see) her', 'to her house': *OLD ad* 1b); pf. *uēnit* is likelier than *uĕnit*, given *uenerit* and the rhythm (though P. is content with 2.3.8 *audias uĕni*). Second in his short clause, Regulus walks into Verania's *cubiculum*, and the letter, unannounced. For his single name, see 2.11.22n. **primum:** adverbial (*OLD primum²* 1a). Outrage boils over, interrupting the narrative almost before it has begun. **impudentiam hominis:** acc. of exclamation, like Plaut. *Men.* 713 *hominis impudentem audaciam!* Cf. 1.5.13 (also of Regulus) *uide hominis crudelitatem.* The word *homo* can be neutral but is well suited to indignation (2.11.3n. *qui*). **qui uenerit:** explanatory relative with pf. subj. (2.10.1n.). **ad aegram:** justifying *impudentiam* and inviting sympathy for Verania. *captandi* ('victims') could be vilified no less than *captatores* (e.g. Tac. *An.* 15.19.2; see Tracy 1980: 401–2, Champlin 1991: 212), but P. directs our indignation squarely at the stalker. **cuius marito inimicissimus, ipsi inuisissimus fuerat** 'when he had been most hostile to her husband, most hateful to herself', bicolon with paired superlatives and heavy *i* assonance; supply *cui* with *ipsi* by syllepsis (2.1.2n. *legit*). Regulus provokes strong views: cf. 1.5.14 (quoting Modestus) *omnium bipedum nequissimus* 'most evil of all two-footed creatures'. He was blamed for the deaths of Piso's brother M. Licinius Crassus Frugi, *cos.* 64, and his father-in-law Q. Sulpicius Camerinus, *cos.* 9 (1.5.3, Montanus' speech in Tac. *H.* 4.42.1); he stands accused (also by Montanus) of rewarding Piso's murderers and even of biting the dead man's head (Tac. *H.* 4.42.2).

3 esto, si uenit tantum 'very well, if he merely came', picking up *uenit . . . uenerit.* For *esto* (3 sg. imperative: *OLD sum* 8b) with a condition, cf. 9.13.11 *esto . . . dum malis,* Hor. *Sat.* 2.1.83 *esto, si quis . . . ;* it is a form of *concessio* (Lausberg §856). The indicative is disingenuous (evidently he did not 'merely come'), the rhythm (all heavy syllables) portentous. **at ille etiam . . . sedit, | . . . interrogauit** 'but he went so far as to sit . . . and to ask . . . ', isocolon (12~13 syllables). For picture and motive, cf. Sen. *Ep.* 95.42–3 *amico aliquis aegro assidet: probamus* [~ *esto*]. *at hoc hereditatis causa facit: uultur est, cadauer exspectat* (so too *Ben.* 4.20.3). Visiting the sick was a friend's duty (Hor. *Sat.* 1.1.81–2 *habes qui | assideat . . . ;* Sen. *Ep.* 1.9.8; Yardley 1973) and so a route to bequests (Ov. *Ars* 2.332). **quo die, qua hora nata esset:** two indirect questions (= *quo die et qua hora*). **ubi audît** 'when he heard [her answer]': unpictorial and so brief, unlike the rest of the sentence. Most MSS have *audiit* (αβ) and *audiuit* (γ), but at 2.14.10 they are unanimous for *audit* (see n.), also read here by one γ MS, u (Urbinas Lat. 1153); it seems unlikely that P. varied his forms (2.1.5n. *male*). At 5.16.8 α has *quae audiit,* γ *quaerit* (corrupted from *quae audit?*). **componit uultum, intendit oculos, mouet labra, agitat digitos, computat** 'he looks serious, narrows his eyes, moves his lips, works his fingers, calculates'. *uultum componere* is 'to assume whatever expression is suitable to the context' (Westcott, echoing Döring), e.g. of calm (3.16.5) or resolve (7.1.6). It often involves deceit (*OLD compono* 11) but need not (Bömer on Ov. *Met.* 13.767, Martin–Woodman on Tac. *An.* 3.44.4): here it suggests feigned concentration. *agitat digitos* happens to be matched only by Lucr. 3.653 (a severed foot) *digitos agitat.* The accumulation evokes in miniature Verania's suspense, as Regulus' activity, crystallised in *computat* (breaking the pattern of two-word cola), gradually becomes clear. Historic present (2.3.2n. *poscit*) assists the *enargeia* (2.11.10n.). For the asyndetic string of pairs, see 2.3.3n. *prohoemiatur... excelse* (also non-chiastic), 4.25.4 *poposcit tabellas, stilum accepit, demisit caput, neminem ueretur, se contemnit* (another malevolent senator). Finger-calculations were sophisticated, used for complex sums: Mayor on Juv. 10.249, Thomas 1951: 31 5, Williams–Williams 1995. Mart. 11.29 turns finger-work in a similar situation to an unsavoury pun.   **nihil:** he says nothing, and P. scarcely more. For the ellipse, see 2.14.11n. *clamor.*   **ut diu miseram exspectatione suspendit** 'when he had kept the poor woman in suspense for a long time' (*OLD ut* 26a, *suspendo* 7).   **habes** 'you are in' (lit. 'living through', *OLD* 19c and Sid. *Ep.* 8.11.9, next n.). Each anecdote features a direct speech from Regulus, each shorter and blunter than the last.   **climactericum tempus** 'a climacteric time', astrological jargon. The 'climacteric' (κλιμακτήρ 'rung'; the adj. κλιμακτηρικός is latinised first here) was a critical moment in one's life, commonly the 63rd year (Pl. *NH* 7.161, Gell. *NA* 3.10.9, 15.7, Cens. *Nat.* 14), but Regulus' calculations (*quo die, qua hora nata esset*) concern something more specific than Verania's age; cf. Sid. *Ep.* 8.11.9 on predictions of a murder: [*mathematici*] *constellatione percontantis inspecta pariter annum mensem diemque dixerunt quos, ut uerbo matheseos utar, climactericos esset habiturus* (the parenthesis, 'to use the astrological term', may flag allusion: cf. 2.17.11n. *baptisteria*, 16n. *cryptoporticus*). On astrology, often outlawed and always popular, see *OCD* s.v.; Manilius 3.560–617 advises on zodiacal calculations of longevity.   **euades** 'you will survive' (*OLD* 5a).

4 quod ut tibi magis liqueat 'to rid you of doubt', literally 'so that this may be clearer of doubt for you' (*OLD liqueo* 3a): cf. Ov. *Tr.* 3.11.73 *quod magis ut liqueat.* P. usually prefers *quo*, not *ut*, with comparatives and result clauses (2.10.6n. *quo*), but *ut* is also at e.g. 1.10.9, 5.16.10, 6.33.7; *quod quo* would be ungainly here.   **haruspicem** 'a diviner', probably not one of the official college of Etruscan *haruspices* (*OCD* s.v.) or a local college (9.39.1 with S-W), but an unregulated (and unrespected) quack: cf. Cic. *Diu.* 1.132 *uicanos haruspices* (with Wardle), Haack 2002: 112 n.6.   **quem sum frequenter expertus** 'whom I have often used' (*OLD experior* 4a), i.e. one whom he (and so she) can trust. Regulus' consultations are seen in §13 and 6.2.2 (*nimia superstitio*, in P.'s view).

5 nec mora *sc. est* 'and [there is] no delay', jaunty brevity. This syntactically independent formula is common in poetry, esp. Ovid, and in casual prose narrative (Sen. *Apoc.* 11.6, Petr. 49.10, 64.7; Apul. *Met.* ×18). Tacitus varies it in *An.* 14.57.4 *nec ultra mora.*   **sacrificium facit:** *haruspices* prophesied by extispicy (inspecting animal entrails): Beard–North–Price 1998: II 175–8. Still in historic present, P. is compendious: two words cover Regulus' departure, consultation and return. Private diviners might be found in market-places (Jer. *Ep.* 127.9), as in the Velabrum (Plaut. *Curc.* 483). **facit, affirmat:** typical juxtaposition (2.1.2n. *triginta*). **affirmat exta cum siderum significatione congruere** 'declares that the entrails accord with the planetary signs' (Radice), *OLD significatio* 2b, *congruo* 2a–b. The diviner has confirmed Verania's horoscope (§3n. *climactericum*). **ut in periculo credula** 'credulous, as [to be expected] at a time of danger' (*OLD ut* 21a), excusing Verania's misplaced trust in the prognosis. S-W 1967 ad loc. compares the scoffing at 9.33.9 *religione praua*, 10.96.8 *superstitionem prauam et immodicam*, but P. is angling for sympathy. **poscit... scribit:** framing verbs, contrasting with *facit, affirmat.* **codicillos** 'a writing tablet' (*OLD* 2a) and/or 'a codicil' (2.16.1n.). **legatum:** a fixed bequest, as opposed to the whole or a fraction of the estate (*hereditas*), and potentially slight (Champlin 1991: 89, 142–50, 184–6, *BNP* 'legatum'). Verania's motive is presumably gratitude for the concern and for happy news (*euades*). **scribit:** not necessarily herself (2.16.2n. *manu*): dictation to slaves (whose presence is implicit in *poscit*) was doubtless common. Women's rights to make wills were circumscribed, apparently more in theory than in practice (on their legal rights, see 2.4.1n. *etiam*). **ingrauescit** 'gets worse', usually used of the disease, here of the patient (Cic. *Att.* 10.4.2, Tac. *H.* 3.54.1). **clamat moriens:** introducing a dramatic *ultima uox*, as Ov. *Am.* 2.6.48 (mock-tragic) *clamauit moriens.* **hominem... periurum:** cf. Plaut. *Mil.* 1066 *hominem periurum!*, Cic. *Phil.* 2.77 *o hominem nequam!* etc. (*TLL* VI.3 2888.28–48). Verania's words are acc. of exclamation in indirect statement (as *peierasset* shows): cf. Hor. *Sat.* 1.2.130 *miseram se conscia clamet*, Ov. *Ars* 1.531 *Thesea crudelem... clamabat.* **nequam perfidum ac plus etiam quam periurum** 'wicked, deceitful and even more than perjurous', extended tricolon (2~3~9 syllables; even without *ac plus etiam quam* the adjectives run ‒‒, ‒◡‒, ‒‒‒) with gradation. P. reserves *nequam* (indeclinable adj.) and cognates for Regulus (§12 *nequitia*, 1.5.14 *nequissimus*) and another delator, Messalinus (4.22.6 *nequitia*); he has *perfidus* and *periurus* only here. For the emotive hyperbole *plus etiam quam*, cf. Cic. *II Verr.* 3.6 *plus etiam quam inimicus*, Livy 21.4.9 *perfidia plus quam Punica*, Lucan 1.1 *bella... plus quam ciuilia.* For the combination X Y *ac* Z, see 2.1.2n. *triginta.* **qui sibi per salutem fili peierasset** 'who (she said) had perjured himself to her [i.e. sworn her a false oath] on the life of his son'. Explanatory relative clause (2.10.1n. *qui*), still in indirect statement, justifying *plus etiam quam periurum* (with paronomasia in *periurum ∼ peierasset*). The plpf. shows the historic present *clamat* being felt as a past tense (2.14.10n. *repetit*). *sibi* refers to Verania, subject of the sentence; *peiero* + dat. is probably first here (*TLL* X.1 987.46–50). Swearing on a son's life (because he is one's most precious possession) was unexceptional (MacDowell on Dem. *Fals. leg.* 292 (adding Dem. *Or.* 29.56, 54.40), Pease on V. *Aen.* 4.357, *Digest* 12.2.3–4 *per caput tuum iurasti uel filiorum tuorum*). Doing so falsely is particularly shocking, for the same reason. On the spelling *fili* see 2.11.23n. *Mari.*

6 facit hoc = *per salutem fili peierat* (2.5.6n. *laetius*), turning allegation (*peierasset*) into (alleged) fact, and specific into general (*frequenter... cotidie*). **scelerate:**

another strong term, only here in P. **quod** 'because', explaining *scelerate*. **iram deorum:** that divine anger follows perjury was an ancient motif (e.g. *Iliad* 3.276– 80; cf. *Pan.* 64.3). On Plinian gods see 2.2.2n. *nec.* **in caput infelicis pueri detestatur** 'calls down onto the head of the ill-starred child', *OLD detestor* 1b. This son's death is reported in 4.2 (beginning *Regulus filium amisit*) and 4.7, where P. throws in a rumour (4.2.2) that Regulus had even courted him for a legacy (the boy had already inherited his mother's estate): a strong contrast with Mart. 6.38, praising the same boy and praying for his survival. To the reader of book 4, the current passage proves retrospectively prophetic: Regulus' provocation of the gods has incurred disaster, as *infelix* (only here) perhaps hints (for the religious overtone, see 2.1.1n. *perinde*). See Intro. 19–20. **pueri detestatur:** one of a series of unusually heavy clausulae (−−−−−), suited perhaps to the subject (2.16.1n. *non*): cf. §7 *conflictabatur*, §7 *testamentum*, and the run of 15 heavy syllables in §8 *postquam signatum (e)st testamentum, mutat personam, uertit* (see also §3n. *esto*).

7 Velleius Blaesus: asyndeton for Act 2 (§2n. *Verania*). Perhaps the Blaesus recently deceased in Stat. *Silu.* 2.1.191 and 2.3.77 (*c.* AD 90–1), commemorated also in Mart. 8.28.10 (*c.* AD 94); possibly P. Sallustius Blaesus, *cos. suff.* 89 and still alive in May 91; surely not, however, Sallustius Lucullus, legate of Britain in 89 or 94, whose execution by Domitian (Suet. *Dom.* 10.2) fits ill with *ualetudine* here (*pace* Champlin 1976: 86). On this tricky nexus, see Syme 1958: 648, id. 1979c: 297, id. 1980: 42–7. A mid-Domitianic date for our man's death is thus likely but not certain. **ille** 'the well known' (*OLD* 4a–b). **locuples** 'wealthy', direct and pertinent. Regulus himself is *locuples* at 1.5.15. **consularis:** 2.1.9n. *senes.* **nouissima ualetudine conflictabatur** 'was in the throes of his final illness' (cf. 2.1.9 *nouissima ualetudine*, *OLD conflicto* 2–3) matching §2 *grauiter iacebat* and capping it with emotive foreknowledge. **conflictabatur, cupiebat:** §5n. *facit.* **Regulus:** asyndetic antithesis. *Blaesus... Regulus* begins the tale, §8 *Blaesus... Regulo* ends it. For the brash entry cf. §2n. *ad hanc* and §10 *Regulus*, each the second sentence of its tale. **qui speraret aliquid ex nouis tabulis:** explanatory relative (2.10.1n. *qui*); cf. Quint. 6.3.92 (in another *captatio* anecdote) *sperans aliquid ex mutatione tabularum*. In Verania's case there was no mention of hope, as Regulus ruthlessly took what he wanted; this time he will be foiled. **nouis tabulis** 'a/the new will' (*OLD tabula* 8b), perhaps punning on the common phrase *nouae tabulae* 'clearing of debts' (7b). **quia nuper captare eum coeperat** 'because he had recently begun to court him for a legacy': *captare* 'try to catch' (underlined by alliteration with *coeperat*) is the *uox propria* for 'legacy hunting' (*OLD capto* 9b, *captatio* 1b): 4.2.2 *captabat* (Regulus again), 8.18.2 *captandum*; the metaphor is from hunting or fishing (9.30.2 *uiscatis hamatisque muneribus*, Hor. *Sat.* 2.5.23–6, 44, Sen. *Ben.* 4.20.3 etc.). A rather clumsy phrase, both in form (*quia* following hard on *qui*) and in stating what is already (more elegantly) implicit; on the other hand, the alliteration, word order and rhythm of *captare eum coeperat* argue at least against pedestrian interpolation, as perhaps does the large-scale balance of the letter (intro.). If it is authentic, we see P. being considerate to his

wider audience, as in 2.11.10n. *erat* and (still more so) in 4.11.3 *carent enim togae iure,*
quibus aqua et igni interdictum est, a generous if not crass gloss; cf. 2.14.5n. *uocantur*,
6.33.3. **medicos:** patients in P.'s elite world do not settle for a single doctor
(1.22.8, 11, 5.16.4, 7.1.3 etc.). On Roman physicians see Jackson 1988, id. 2005,
BNP 'medicine IV'. **hortari rogare** 'set about asking and urging'. Regulus is
playing the *amicus*: Hor. *Sat.* 1.1.81–2 *habes qui | . . . medicum roget* (see §3n. *at*). For
the paired historic infinitives, cf. 6.20.12 (in next n.), [Caes.] *B.Afr.* 33.1 *orare et*
petere, Sall. *Cat.* 27.2 *iubere hortari*, *Jug.* 51.4 *orare et hortari*, Flor. 2.13.82 *orare hortari*
increpare. P. usually has them bunched in vivid narratives to depict simultaneous
or swiftly succeeding actions: six at 6.20.11–14 (Vesuvius), twelve at 7.27.8 (ghosts),
one at 9.13.7 (*ultio Heluidi*), nine at 9.33.4–5 (dolphin), four at *Pan.* 22.3 (Trajan's
aduentus). Ash on Tac. *H.* 2.5.1 lists comparable Tacitean clusters. Despite their
name, historic infinitives find a place in (e.g.) comedy, Cicero's letters, and oratory (Quint. 9.3.58 *breuitatis nouitatisque maxime gratiam petunt*; on Cicero's usage
see Hutchinson 1998: 133 n.30). See *NLS* §21, G–L §647, Rosén 1995 and (on
P.) Menna 1902: 134–41, Rosén 1980: 46–7 and 1995: 543, Calboli 1986. **quo-**
quo modo spiritum homini prorogarent 'to prolong his life in any way
possible' (*OLD quisque* 8b, *spiritus* 3b, *prorogo* 2a), in parataxis after *hortari rogare*
(2.5.2n. *rogo*): cf. 6.20.12 *orari hortari iubere quoquo modo fugerem.* **homini** = *ei* (§2n.
impudentiam).

8 signatum est: a will had to be sealed (*OLD signo* 8b) by five or seven witnesses:
1.9.2, *RE* II/v.1 998–9, Tellegen 1982: 9–17, Champlin 1991: 75–80. The ceremony passes briskly in four words. **testamentum, mutat** inverts §7 *mutare*
testamentum. **mutat personam** 'he changes role' (*OLD persona* 2); the tense
changes too, back to historic present. The theatrical metaphor (*OLD persona* 1a,
an actor's mask; cf. Sen. *Contr.* 9.3.13 *quasi persona mutata*, Sen. *Marc.* 6.1, *Ep.* 120.22)
is not pejorative per se (1.23.5 with Guillemin 1929: 52–3, 8.7.2), but suits Regulus'
deception here (cf. Bartsch 2006: 225–7 on deceptive *persona* in Seneca). **uer-**
tit allocutionem 'alters his tone', literally 'reverses his (manner of) address'
(*OLD uerto* 7a, *allocutio* 1), in parallel with *mutat personam*. **isdemque medicis**
sc. 'says'. *isdem* points the indignation. **quousque miserum cruciatis** 'how
long will you torment the poor man?', (faux-)indignant brevity for 'how long
will you allow the poor man's disease to torment him?' (*OLD crucio* 2a; *miser* 3a,
unsurprisingly cliché in the context of illness). *quousque* takes a present only here
in P. (future at 2.10.2, 7.3.2, *Pan.* 59.4), but it is contemporary (e.g. Sen. *Ep.* 33.7,
[Quint.] *Decl. mai.* 7.8, Calp. Flac. 52.19). **quid?** 'why?' **inuidetis . . . morte**
| . . . uitam . . . potestis: chiastic. For the syntax of *inuidetis [sc. ei] morte*, see
2.10.2n. *inuidebis*. **bona morte** 'a good death', i.e. an easy one (Cic. *Tusc.* 3.47,
Sen. *Contr.* 1.3.12; also Cic. *Att.* 16.7.3 and Suet. *Aug.* 99.2 εὐθανασία); cf. 6.20.12
bene morituram, 3.16.11 *male moriar*. **moritur:** as if Regulus' intercessions have
instant effect. **tamquam omnia audisset** is illogical: Blaesus rewrote his will
halfway through the tale (Gierig). **Regulo ne tantulum quidem** 'to Regulus

[he left] not even the slightest [amount]', reversing §5 *legatum Regulo scribit*. The phrase *ne tantulum quidem* is Ciceronian (*II Verr.* 2.125, *Att.* 15.27.3 etc.), the ellipse (*sc.* e.g. *legauit*) Plinian, adding epigrammatic kick: cf. Mart. 6.63 *hicine deflebit uero tua fata dolore? | si cupis ut ploret, des, Mariane, nihil*. For the '*captator* foiled' motif see also 8.18.3, Hor. *Sat.* 2.5.66–9, Petr. 141, Mart. 9.9, Lucian *Dialogues of the dead* 15–18, 21. We are invited to share the glee – and the indignation that will follow. It was normal for friends to receive legacies (7.20.6, 7.31.5, Champlin 1991: 146–50); omission could be construed as intentional insult (S-W 203, though note §7 *nuper*; Champlin 1991: 13–14). Blaesus exerts a degree of control denied to the ladies (Carlon 2009: 127).

9 Sufficiunt duae . . . tertiam poscis? chiasmus. For the lack of *-ne* see 2.8.1n. *studes*. The question invites meta-epistolary reading (Merwald 1964: 170 n.31): we are nearing the end of book 2 (*sufficiunt duae?*), and Calvisius will indeed receive 3.1 (*tertiam*). But the hint is typically light (2.1.1n. *post*). **fabulae:** a third statement of the word (§1 *fabulam, fabulas*) preceding the third tale. **scholastica lege** 'according to the schoolmen's rule' (*OLD lex* 6) that good things come in threes: a wry advertisement of this scrupulous triptych (for the disparaging tone see 2.3.5n. *scholasticus*). In a different context, Quint. 4.5.3 criticises those who insist *uelut lege* that the 'partition' of a speech be limited to three items (e.g. *Rhet. Her.* 1.17; cf. Quint. 4.2.49–50, Lausberg §347). Yet of course threes abound in rhetoric (Lausberg §443.2a, 1244 s.v. *tres*), and (so) in the *Epistles*, at every level. Other larger-scale trios are 6.31.1–12 (three days at Centumcellae), 7.27 (three ghost stories), 9.28 (three letters) and, more loosely structured, 3.16 (three noble deeds of Arria); this letter is itself perhaps the third of a triptych (2.18.intro.). **est unde fiat** 'I have the means', literally 'there is from where it may come' (*OLD sum* 6b, *unde* 3a; *fiat* is subjunctive of result/purpose), as Ter. *Ad.* 122 *est unde haec fiant*.

10 Aurelia: one of just eleven women named by P. in their own right (contrast §2 *Verania Pisonis*): Jones 1991: 166–7. It is a common noble name (S-W 204 suggests possible consular relatives); it fits the third *aurea fabula*, and resonates with the following *ornata*. Juv. 5.98 has a *captanda* called Aurelia, perhaps the same woman (*pace* Courtney and Braund ad loc.), given his apparent use of 8.18 (on *captatio*) in *Sat.* 10.232–9 (Syme 1979b: 253–5; Intro. 34–5). Unlike Juvenal, P. attacks only the *captator* (cf. §2n. *ad*). **ornata femina** 'distinguished lady' (*OLD ornatus* 4a), matching §7 *locuples consularis*. P. prefers *femina* to *mulier* 'woman' by 5:1, several times (as often in Latin) with an epithet (e.g. 6.33.2 *splendide nata*, 9.28.1 *sanctissimam*, 10.5.2 *ornatissimae*: Adams 1972b: 234–6). Here *ornata* honours a living woman and supplies like *locuples* (but more discreetly) a relevant fact (*OLD ornatus* 1b 'rich'). **signatura:** §8n. *signatum*. On the free use of the fut. participle see 2.1.5n. *acturus*. **sumpserat** 'had put on', a scene-setting tense like §2 *iacebat*, §7 *conflictabatur*. **pulcherrimas tunicas:** making her literally *ornata* 'adorned' (*OLD orno* 4a). Clearly she took the occasion seriously. For the wearing of two (or more) tunics, cf. 4.16.2 *scissis tunicis*, *OLD tunica* 1a, *BNP* 'tunica'; on female dress see Wilson 1938: 146–66, Scholz 1992. **Regulus:** §7n. This third tale proceeds through a trio of antitheses: *Aurelia ~ Regulus, Aurelia ~ ille* (×2). **ad signandum** 'for the sealing, to seal (it)', gerund of purpose. **'rogo ... has mihi lēgēs'** 'please leave me these' (< *legare* 'bequeath'), paratactic indirect command (2.5.2n. *rogo*). Regulus' third and shortest direct speech, and bluntest method (§3n. *habes*). That he wants her clothes (presumably for their value) is ungallant and perhaps redolent of effeminacy (cf. Ov. *Ars* 3.447–8 with Gibson). Women's clothes were a standard bequest – but from husband to wife (*Dig.* 34.2 *passim*). It was legal for a witness to receive a legacy (Ulp. *Dig.* 28.1.20). For the clausula see 2.6.4n. *magno*.

11 Aurelia ... putabat,   ille ... instabat: rhyming parallel antithesis. **hominem** = *eum* (§2n. *impudentiam*). **serio instabat** 'insisted in all seriousness' (*OLD serio* 1a, *insto* 11a). **ne multa** *sc. dicam* 'to cut a long story short' (*OLD ne* 13b), a lively device otherwise unique to Cicero (speeches, dialogue and letters). **coegit mulierem ... obseruauit ... inspexit:** tricolon of initial verbs. *coegit* 'compelled' (*OLD* 11a) ratchets up the outrage (*rogo ... instabat ... coegit*), as does the 'victim vocabulary' *mulierem* (Santoro-L'Hoir 1992: 151). **aperire ... legare:** framing verbs. The demand is impolite but legal (Tellegen 1982: 53–8). **quas erat induta** 'that she was wearing'; *induta* is 'middle' voice, with a 'retained' acc. object *quas*: *NLS* §19.iii, Courtney 2004: 425–6. The clause adds indignation, not information: Regulus wants the shirt off her back. **obseruauit scribentem, inspexit an scripsisset:** isocolon antithesis (7~7 syllables) with verbal polyptoton (2.1.12n. *et*). **inspexit an** 'he looked to see whether' (for *an* see 2.2.1n. *nec*). Evidently Aurelia was writing by hand (2.16.2n. *manu*). In Hor. *Sat.* 2.5.51–5 the *captator* is advised to decline to inspect any will he is witnessing, but to check that he can see his name all the same. **et Aurelia quidem ... ille tamen:** *quidem ... tamen* articulates a contrast between Aurelia and Regulus, and also between *uiuit* and *tamquam morituram* (2.5.11n. *non*). **istud ... morituram coegit:** chiastically reprises *coegit mulierem ... legare*. For *istud* '[to do] this', internal object of *coegit*, cf. 8.6.3 *nemo ... illa cogatur*, *TLL* III 1528.39–61, Horsfall on V. *Aen.* 3.56. **hic ... hic** 'this man [of all people]', in emotive anaphora. **hereditates ... legata:** §5n. *legatum*. The plurals, and *accipit* (generalising like §6 *facit*), gesture at continuing acquisitions. **quasi mereatur accipit** 'receives ... as if he deserved it' (*OLD quasi* 1a, *mereo* 5d), in violation of the moral code that legacies follow the deserving (Phaedrus 4.5, Apul. *Apol.* 23.7 *immeritis hereditatibus*; Pavis d'Escurac 1978: 287, Champlin 1991: 13 n.34), namely one's friends: the third tale ends by pinpointing the corruption of *amicitia* which Regulus' misdeeds embody.

12 Ἀλλὰ τί διατείνομαι ... ? 'but why do I get exercised ... ?', evoking Demosthenes *On the crown* 142 τί οὖν ταῦτ' ἐπήραμαι καὶ διετεινάμην οὑτωσὶ σφοδρῶς; 'now, why did I utter that prayer and get so greatly exercised?', following a unique outburst (Yunis 2001: 193) in that most famous speech (2.3.10n.

λαμπροφωνότατος), from which P. borrows again in 4.7.6 (another Regulus letter). Usually P. quotes Greek word for word, but cf. 4.25.5 ἀλλὰ ταῦτα τῷ ὑπὲρ ἡμᾶς μελήσει ~ Plato *Phaedo* 95b ἀλλὰ δὴ ταῦτα μὲν τῷ θεῷ μελήσει (a politic adjustment) and the equally loose allusion to Cic. *Verr.* below. Oratorical grandeur – albeit with epistolary brevity – bursts in on (what claimed to be) casual gossip, heralding the close of letter and of book, and aligning P. just for a moment with the greatest speaker of them all (2.3.10n. *orationem*). **in ea ciuitate in qua** 'in a town in which' (*ea* lit. 'the sort of', *OLD is* 10); again at 4.15.11 (mildly critical) and 8.6.3 (censorious). *ciuitas* is 'citizenry' (vs *urbs*, the physical city), in P.'s use the (elite) society of Rome, e.g. 4.2.6 *uexat... ciuitatem* '[Regulus] is annoying everyone in town', 8.18.3 (cf. *OLD* 1–2, Mankin on Hor. *Epod.* 16.18). For present-day Rome as a *ciuitas* of vice, see 2.18.2n. *sperare* (esp. 6.2.9, ending the last Regulus letter), and for the inevitability of *captatio* in it, Tac. *H.* 1.73 *pecunia et orbitate, quae bonis malisque temporibus iuxta ualent* (contrast 8.18.3, in §1n. *fabulas*). The complaint is hardly new: e.g. Sall. *Jug.* 4.9 *dum me ciuitatis morum piget taedetque*, Hor. *Epod.* 16.18 and 36 *exsecrata ciuitas*, Sen. *Clem.* 1.15.2 *in qua ciuitate numquam deest patronus peioribus*, and at monstrous length Juv. 3. The broadening of scope from *cubiculum* to *ciuitas* inverts the move of 2.1 from public to private stage (2.1.intro.). **non minora praemia, immo maiora:** object of *habent*. **nequitia et improbitas quam pudor et uirtus habent** 'wickedness and shamelessness have... than decency and honour', reworking the indignant redundance of Cic. *II Verr.* 3.7 (addressing Hortensius) *quod ad tuam ipsius amicitiam ceterorumque hominum magnorum atque nobilium faciliorem aditum istius* [i.e. *Verris*] *habet nequitia et audacia quam cuiusquam nostrum uirtus et integritas?*; the pair *nequitia et improbitas* is in *II Verr.* 3.155, 5.141 and as part of a list in *Cat.* 2.11. Like Cicero, P. positions himself as the lone, authoritative voice against both the single malefactor Verres/Regulus and society at large. Both the pose and the Verrine intertext bind this finale to 2.11, P.'s central parade of Ciceronian ethos (2.11.intro.). **nequitia:** §5n. *nequam* and previous n. Montanus attacks Regulus with the same word at Tac. *H.* 4.42.5, its sole appearance in Tacitus: a nod to P. (Martin 1967)? **improbitas** 'shamelessness'; cf. §14 *improbissimum*, 8.18.3 *improbas spes* (of *captatores*). **pudor et uirtus:** *OLD pudor* 2a, *uirtus* 2a (merit) and 3 (moral excellence). Another natural pair (e.g. V. *Aen.* 5.455), often combined in Ciceronian lists. Contrast 5.14.6 *quod tandem homines non ad pericula ut prius uerum ad honores uirtute peruveniunt.* **habent** 'have had' (present continuous with *iam pridem*).

13 aspice Regulum 'take Regulus' (*OLD aspicio* 9a), in lively imperative (cf. §1 *accipe*). This is his sixth and final naming. **ex paupere et tenui** 'from a poor and humble background' (*OLD ex* 13, *tenuis* 10; cf. Cic. *Vat.* 29 *ex pauperrimo diues factus*), with continued redundancy, as Gell. *NA* 16.10.10 *tenuissimi pauperrimique*, and chiastically alliterative with *ad ṯantas opes*. Regulus' father had been exiled and his estate confiscated (Tac. *H.* 4.42.3), leaving the boy to start from nothing (by elite standards, anyway), like the notorious delators Eprius Marcellus and

Vibius Crispus (Tac. *D.* 8.2), to whom he is compared (*H.* 4.42.5; cf. *An.* 1.74.2 (on delators) *ex pauperibus diuites, ex contemptis metuendi*). Such *nouveau* mobility is to be disdained, even by equestrian stock like P. (2.14.2n. *adulescentuli*, Scarcia 1984). **opes** 'wealth'. P. has more tasteful 'means' (2.4.3 *facultates*); see also §7n. *locuples*. **per flagitia processit** 'has progressed . . . through his outrageous deeds': cf. 1.5.1 *flagitia* (Regulus), 9.13.12 *flagitiosissimum*, 16 *flagiti manifestissimi*, both alleging complicity with *delatio* (cf. Montanus' accusations against Regulus in Tac. *H.* 4.42.3–4). P.'s advancement, by contrast, was genteel: 4.24.4 *studiis proces-simus*. Part-way through *processit* begins the fragmentary Π, the oldest surviving manuscript of the *Epistles* (Intro. 38). **ut ipse mihi dixerit** 'that he himself said to me', pf. subj. in primary sequence (after *processit*), introducing indirect statement in secondary sequence (hence *consuleret*). The result clause is elliptical: Regulus has done so well that he is already looking forward to acquiring his six-tieth million. For all the rhetoric of division, P. does not hide his social proximity to Regulus (cf. 1.5.11–14, 1.20.14, 6.2.1–3). **consuleret** *sc. haruspicem* (*OLD* 1d; cf. §4 *haruspicem consulam*): for this absolute use, cf. *consultare* in Tac. *An.* 2.30.1, 2.54.3, 6.21.1, 16.30.2. The first of those concerns a comparable enquiry: *An.* 2.30.1 (an absurd allegation) *ut consultauerit Libo an habiturus foret opes quis uiam Appiam Brun-disium usque pecunia operiret*. **sestertium sescentiens** 'sixty million sesterces'. *sestertium* (gen. pl., *sc. centena milia*) = 100,000 sesterces, a convenience in the mon-eyed world (cf. English 'a grand'), multiplied by a numeral adverb, here *sescentiens* '600×'. The target is several multiples of P.'s likely wealth (2.4.3n. *modicae*), but below that of super-rich delators Vibius Crispus and Eprius Marcellus at Tac. *D.* 8.1 (200 and 300 million respectively). Cf. the epitaph of gauche Trimalchio (Petr. 71.12) *ex paruo creuit* [∼ *ex paupere et tenui*]; *sestertium reliquit trecenties* (thirty million), and for the calumny, the allegation (Tac. *An.* 13.42.4) that Seneca's fortune was amassed through *captatio* (Scarcia 1984: 301–2, 316). **impleturus esset** 'would attain', fut. periphrastic subj. For *implere* (*OLD* 8a), cf. 1.19.2 *ad implendas equestres facultates*, Hor. *Ep.* 1.6.34 *mille talenta rotundentur*. **exta duplicia** 'double entrails', i.e. a cleft liver, considered an especially good portent (Val. Max. 1.6.9 *caput ioci-noris duplex*; Pl. *NH* 11.189 [*iocinoris caput*] *geminum*, 190 *iocinora replicata*; Dio 46.35.4 διττὰ τὰ ἥπατα). Cic. *Diu.* 2.33–4 is duly sceptical: 'you surely don't think that if there is a cleft of some sort in the liver, it is a sign of profit?' **quibus portendi** 'an omen, he said, that' (lit. 'by which (he said) that it was portended', impersonal passive), continuing the indirect statement with a connecting relative (G–L §635, *NLS* §230.6n., §289). **miliens et ducentiens** '120 million', double the money for a 'double' liver; cf. Pl. *NH* 11.190 (a double liver portends the doubling of Augustus' *imperium*). **habiturum** *sc. se* (2.11.9n. *fore*) and *esse*, indirect statement after *portendi*. Heroic clausula (2.3.3n. *narrat*).

14 et habebit 'and he will', affirming *habiturum* with a bleak prophecy of Regulus' ongoing rise; it will prove satisfactorily wrong with his death in 6.2. At the same time, the polyptoton of *habere* seems to point fleetingly back to

2.1.12 *et habemus et habebimus*, ring-composing book 2 and pointing the gulf that divides exemplary Verginius from counter-exemplary Regulus. **si modo** 'if only' (*OLD si* 8a) implies an easy task, though the long, jerky conditional clause (*si . . . ut . . .* object *. . . quod . . .* indirect object *. . . quorum . . .* verb) makes for an uncomfortable close. It is hard to see how Regulus would make millions from perhaps trivial legacies such as mentioned here (§5n. *legatum*). P. for his part collected at least 1.5 million sesterces in inheritances (2.16.1n. *me*). **aliena** 'other people's'. **quod est improbissimum genus falsi** '– the most shameless form of fraud –', a tendentious parenthesis commenting on the sentence it interrupts and emphasising what follows (2.7.2n. *quod*). Fraud (*OLD falsum* 3) was a capital crime (e.g. 10.58.3 with S-W, Tac. *H.* 2.86.1 with Ash) – one which Regulus shows no sign of having committed, since Aurelia acted legally and with free will (Tellegen 1982: 58–9); the allegation of having extorted a legacy, however, was always an easy calumny (Champlin 1991: 82–7). **ipsis quorum sunt illa dictauerit** 'dictates [fut. pf.] to the very people whose [wills] they are'. *illa*, subject of *sunt*, is only slightly (if at all) more emphatic than *ea* (2.1.7n.), but by redundantly restating *aliena testamenta* it points the perversity and makes a double cretic. Wills could legally be dictated on someone's behalf (e.g. Just. *Codex* 6.23.22 (Zeno) *dictantibus testamenta . . . legatum . . . testatorem posse relinquere minime dubitandum est* 'there is no doubt that a testator may leave a legacy to people dictating wills') but P. speaks of dictating to the testator, a tendentious way to describe requests or demands for legacies. Regulus was similarly writing other people's scripts in 2.11.22 *sententia quam ipse dictauerat*. That verb, also a term of literary composition (e.g. 1.9.6, quoted in 2.17.intro.; 9.40.2 *illa quae dictaui identidem retractantur*, ending the *Epistles*), thus makes a doubly if subtly apt last word.

WORKS CITED

More familiar journal titles are abbreviated, largely after *l'Année Philologique*. For editions of *Epistles* 1–9, see pp. ix–x.

Adamietz, J. 1972. *Untersuchungen zu Juvenal*, Wiesbaden

Adams, J. N. 1972a. 'The language of the later books of Tacitus' *Annals*', *CQ* 22: 350–73

1972b. 'Latin words for "woman" and "wife"', *Glotta* 50: 234–55

1972c. 'A type of hyperbaton in Latin prose', *PCPS* 17: 1–16

1973a. 'The substantival present participle in Latin', *Glotta* 51: 116–36

1973b. 'The vocabulary of the speeches in Tacitus' historical works', *BICS* 20: 124–44

1978. 'Conventions of naming in Cicero', *CQ* 28: 145–66

1994a. *Wackernagel's law and the placement of the copula* esse *in classical Latin*, Cambridge

1994b. 'Wackernagel's law and the position of unstressed personal pronouns in classical Latin', *TPS* 92: 103–78

2003a. *Bilingualism and the Latin language*, Cambridge

2003b. '*Romanitas* and the Latin language', *CQ* 53: 184–205

2003c. 'The new Vindolanda writing-tablets', *CQ* 53: 530–75

2005. 'The *Bellum Africum*', in Reinhardt–Lapidge–Adams 2005: 73–96

and M. Lapidge and T. Reinhardt. 2005. 'Introduction', in Reinhardt–Lapidge–Adams 2005: 1–36

Adkin, N. 1998. 'The Younger Pliny and Ammianus Marcellinus', *CQ* 48: 593–5

2011. 'A new echo of Pliny the Younger in Jerome?', *Philologus* 155: 193–5

Agache, S. 2008. 'La villa comme image de soi (Rome antique, des origines à la fin de la République)', in P. Galand-Hallyn and C. Lévy, eds. *La villa et l'univers familial dans l'Antiquité et à la Renaissance* (Paris) 15–44

Aili, H. 1979. *The prose rhythm of Sallust and Livy*, Stockholm

Albaladejo, T., E. del Rio and J. A. Caballero, eds., 1998. *Quintiliano: historia y actualidad de la retórica*, 3 vols, Calahorra

von Albrecht, M. 1964. *Die Parenthese in Ovids Metamorphosen und ihre dichterische Funktion*, Hildesheim

1989. *Masters of Roman prose from Cato to Apuleius. Interpretative studies* (tr. N. Adkin), Leeds

1997. *A history of Roman literature from Livius Andronicus to Boethius* (tr. G. Schmeling), 2 vols, Leiden

2003. *Cicero's style: a synopsis*, Leiden

Aldrete, G. S. 1999. *Gestures and acclamations in ancient Rome*, Baltimore

Alföldy, G. 1973. *Flamines provinciae Hispaniae Tarraconensis*, Madrid

1995. 'Bricht der Schweigsame sein Schweigen?' Eine Grabinschrift aus Rom', *MDAI(R)* 102: 251–68

2001. '*Pietas immobilis erga principem* und ihr Lohn: öffentliche Ehrenmonumente von Senatoren in Rom während der frühen und hohen Kaiserzeit', in id. and S. Panciera, eds. *Inschriftliche Denkmäler als Medien der Selbstdarstellung in der römischen Welt* (Stuttgart) 11–46

Allain, E. 1901–4. *Pline le Jeune et ses héritiers*, 4 vols, Paris

Allen, W., Jr. 1954. 'Cicero's conceit', *TAPA* 85: 121–44

Allen, W. S. 1978. *Vox Latina. A guide to the pronunciation of classical Latin*, 2nd edn, Cambridge

Altman, J. 1982. *Epistolarity: approaches to a form*, Columbus, OH

Ameling, W. 2010. 'Pliny: the piety of a persecutor', in J. Dijkstra, J. Kroesen and Y. Kuiper, eds. *Myths, martyrs and modernity. Studies in the history of religions in honour of Jan N. Bremmer* (Leiden) 271–300

Amherdt, D. 2001. *Sidoine Apollinaire. Le quatrième livre de la correspondance*, Bern

Anderson, G. 1993. *The Second Sophistic. A cultural phenomenon in the Roman empire*, London

Anderson, J. K. 1985. *Hunting in the ancient world*, Berkeley

Anderson, R. D. 2000. *Glossary of Greek rhetorical terms connected to methods of argumentation, figures and tropes from Anaximenes to Quintilian*, Leuven

André, J. 1951. 'Les adjectifs et adverbes à valeur intensive en *per-* et *prae-*', *REL* 29: 121–54

André, J.-M. 1966. *L'otium dans la vie morale et intellectuelle romaine des origines à l'époque augustéenne*, Paris

1975. 'Pensée et philosophie dans les lettres de Pline le Jeune', *REL* 53: 225–47

Andreau, J. 1999. *Banking and business in the Roman world* (tr. J. Lloyd), Cambridge

Andrewes, M. 1951. 'The function of tense variation in the subjunctive mood of oratio obliqua', *CR* n.s. 1: 142–6

Anguissola, A. 2007. 'L'epistolaria di Plinio il Giovane tra letteratura e archeologia: aggiornamento bibliografico (1936–2006)', in Lehmann-Hartleben (unpaginated)

2010. *Intimità a Pompei*, Berlin

Armisen-Marchetti, M. 1990. 'Pline le jeune et le sublime', *REL* 68: 88–98

Ash, R. 2003. '"Aliud est enim epistulam, aliud historiam ... scribere" (*Epistles* 6.16.22): Pliny the historian?', *Arethusa* 36: 211–62

2007. *Tacitus. Histories book II*, Cambridge

Aßfahl, G. 1932. *Vergleich und Metapher bei Quintilian*, Stuttgart

Aubrion, E. 1975. 'Pline le Jeune et la rhétorique de l'affirmation', *Latomus* 34: 90–130

1989. 'La "Correspondance" de Pline le Jeune: Problèmes et orientations actuelles de la recherche', *ANRW* II.33.1: 304–74

Austin, R. G. 1948. *Quintiliani Institutionis oratoriae liber XII*, Oxford

1971. *P. Vergili Maronis Aeneidos liber primus*, Oxford

1977. *P. Vergili Maronis Aeneidos liber sextus*, Oxford

Ax, W. 1930. Review of Guillemin 1929, *Philologische Wochenschrift* 50: 740–8

Axtell, H. L. 1915. 'Men's names in the writings of Cicero', *CP* 10: 386–404

Aymard, J. 1951. *Essai sur les chasses romaines, des origines à la fin du siècle des Antonins*, Paris

Bablitz, L. 2007. *Actors and audience in the Roman courtroom*, London

2009. 'The selection of advocates for repetundae trials. The cases of Pliny the Younger', *Athenaeum* 97: 197–208

Bailey, C. 1947. *Lucretius. De rerum natura*, 3 vols, Oxford

Baldwin, B. 1992. 'Greek in Cicero's letters', *Acta Classica* 35: 1–17

Balsdon, J. P. V. D. 1969. *Life and leisure in ancient Rome*, London

Bannon, C. J. 2009. *Gardens & neighbors: private water rights in Roman Italy*, Ann Arbor, MI

Barbuti, N. 1994. 'La nozione di fides in Tacito e Plinio il Giovane', in M. Pauri, ed. *Epigrafia e territorio. Politica e società. Temi di antichità romane. III* (Bari) 271–99

Barchiesi, A. 2005. 'The search for the perfect book: a PS to the New Posidippus', in Gutzwiller 2005a: 320–42

Barnes, T. D. 1976. 'The *Epitome de Caesaribus* and its sources', *CP* 258–68

Bartsch, S. 2006. *The mirror of the self: sexuality, self-knowledge, and the gaze in the early Roman empire*, Chicago

and J. Elsner. 2007. *Ekphrasis*, Chicago = *CP* 102.1

Barwick, K. 1936. 'Zwei antike Ausgaben der Pliniusbriefe?', *Philologus* 91: 423–48

Bauman, R. A. 1989. *Lawyers and politics in the early Roman empire: a study of relations between the Roman jurists and the emperors from Augustus to Hadrian*, Munich

Beard, M. 1998. 'Imaginary horti: or up the garden path', in M. Cima and E. La Rocca, eds. *Horti Romani* (Rome) 23–32

2002. 'Ciceronian correspondences: making a book out of letters', in T. P. Wiseman, ed. *Classics in progress* (Oxford) 103–44

2007. *The Roman triumph*, Cambridge, MA

and J. North and S. Price. 1998. *Religions of Rome*, 2 vols, Cambridge

Becker, A. S. 1995. *The shield of Achilles and the poetics of ekphrasis*, Lanham, MD

Bek, L. 1980. *Towards paradise on earth. Modern space conception in architecture: a creation of Renaissance humanism*, Odense

Bell, A. A. 1989. 'A note on revision and authenticity in Pliny's letters', *AJP* 110: 460–6

Bell, S. and I. L. Hansen, eds. 2008. *Role models in the Roman world: identity and assimilation*, Ann Arbor, MI

Bennett, J. 2001. *Trajan: optimus princeps*, 2nd edn, London

Bérenger-Badell, A. 2000. 'Les critères de compétence dans les lettres de recommandation de Fronton et de Pline le Jeune', *REL* 78: 164–79

Berger, A. 1953. *Encyclopedic dictionary of Roman law*, Philadelphia

Berger, J. G. 1725. *Τὸ σεμνόν in oratione Corn. Taciti ad Plin. Lib. II. Epist. XI. ex Hermogenis disciplina expensum*, Wittenberg

Bergmann, B. 1995. 'Visualizing Pliny's villas', *JRA* 8: 406–20

Bernstein, N. W. 2008. 'Each man's father served as his teacher: constructing relatedness in Pliny's letters', *CA* 27: 203–30

2009. '*Cui parens non erat maximus quisque et uetustissimus pro parente*: parental surrogates in imperial Roman literature', in S. R. Hübner and D. M. Ratzan, eds. *Growing up fatherless in antiquity* (Cambridge) 241–56

Berriman, A. and M. Todd. 2001. 'A very Roman coup: the hidden war of imperial succession, AD 96–8', *Historia* 50: 312–31

Berry, D. H. 1996. *Cicero: Pro P. Sulla oratio*, Cambridge

2008. 'Letters from an advocate: Pliny's "Vesuvius" narratives (*Epp.* 6.16, 6.20)', *PLLS* 13: 297–313

Bettini, M. 1991. *Anthropology and Roman culture: kinship, time, images of the soul* (tr. J. Van Sickle), Baltimore, MD

Beutel, F. 2000. *Vergangenheit als Politik. Neue Aspekte im Werk des jüngeren Plinius*, Frankfurt

Birley, A. R. 2000a. *Onomasticon to the Younger Pliny. Letters and Panegyric*, Munich

2000b. 'The life and death of Cornelius Tacitus', *Historia* 49: 230–47

2003. 'The commissioning of equestrian officers', in J. J. Wilkes, ed. *Documenting the Roman army: essays in honour of Margaret Roxan* (London) 1–18

Bleicken, J. 1962. *Senatsgericht und Kaisergericht. Eine Studie zur Entwicklung des Prozeßrechtes im frühen Prinzipat*, Göttingen

van der Blom, H. 2010. *Cicero's role models: the political strategy of a newcomer*, Oxford

Blümner, H. 1911. *Die römischen Privataltertümer*, Munich

Bodel, J. 1997. 'Monumental villas and villa monuments', *JRA* 10: 5–35

n.d. 'The publication of Pliny's letters' (revised version in Marchesi fthc.)

Bolkestein, A. M. 1998. 'Between brackets: (some properties of) parenthetical clauses in Latin. An investigation of the language of Cicero's letters', in R. Risselada, ed. *Latin in use: Amsterdam studies in the pragmatics of Latin* (Amsterdam) 1–15

Bömer, F. 1957–8. *P. Ovidius Naso. Die Fasten*, 2 vols, Heidelberg

1969–86. *P. Ovidius Naso. Metamorphosen. Kommentar*, 7 vols, Heidelberg

Bonner, S. F. 1949. *Roman declamation in the late republic and early empire*, Liverpool

1977. *Education in ancient Rome: from the elder Cato to the younger Pliny*, London

Bornecque, H. 1900. 'Les lois métriques de la prose oratoire latine d'après le Panégyrique de Trajan', *Revue de philologie* 24: 201–36

1907. *Les clausules métriques latines*, Lille

Bourgery, A. 1910. 'Sur la prose métrique de Sénèque le philosophe', *Revue de philologie* 34: 167–72

Bowersock, G. W. 1969. *Greek sophists in the Roman empire*, Oxford

2003. 'Seneca's Greek', in De Vivo–Lo Cascio 2003: 241–52

Bowie, E. L. 1982. 'The importance of sophists', *YCS* 27: 29–59

Bowman, A. K. and J. D. Thomas. 1983. *Vindolanda: the Latin writing-tablets*, London

1994. *The Vindolanda writing-tablets (tabulae Vindolandenses) II*, London

Boyle, A. J. 2008. *Octavia attributed to Seneca*, Oxford

Bradley, K. R. 2010. 'The exemplary Pliny', in C. Deroux, ed. *Studies in Latin literature and Roman history* 15 (Brussels) 384–422

Brakman, C. 1925. 'Pliniana', *Mnemosyne* 53: 88–100

Bramble, J. C. 1974. *Persius and the programmatic satire*, Cambridge

Braund, S. H. (= S. M. Braund). 1996a. *Juvenal. Satires book I*, Cambridge

    1996b. 'The solitary feast: a contradiction in terms?', *BICS* 41: 37–52

    1997. 'Roman assimilation of the other: *humanitas* at Rome', *Acta Classica* 40: 15–32

    2009. Seneca *De clementia*, Oxford

    and C. Gill, eds. 1997. *The passions in Roman thought and literature*, Cambridge

de Brauw, M. 2007. 'The parts of the speech', in I. Worthington, ed. *A companion to Greek rhetoric* (Malden, MA) 187–202

Brink, C. O. 1982. *Horace on Poetry III. Epistles book II: the letters to Augustus and Florus*, Cambridge

    1989. 'Quintilian's *De causis corruptae eloquentiae* and Tacitus' *Dialogus de oratoribus*', *CQ* 39: 472–503

    1994. 'Can Tacitus' *Dialogus* be dated?', *HSCP* 96: 251–80

Briscoe, J. 1981. *A commentary on Livy books XXXIV–XXXVII*, Oxford

Broise, H. 1991. 'Vitrages et volets des fenêtres thermales à l'époque impériale', in *Les thermes romains. Actes de la table ronde organisée par l'École française de Rome* (Rome) 61–78

Bruère, R. T. 1954. 'Tacitus and Pliny's Panegyricus', *CP* 49: 161–79

Brunt, P. A. 1961. 'Charges of provincial maladministration under the early principate', *Historia* 10: 189–227

    1990. *Roman imperial themes*, Oxford

Bücheler, F. 1904. 'Lepcis', *RM* 59: 638–40

Büchner, K. 1964. *Tacitus und Ausklang. Studien zur römischen Literatur IV*, Wiesbaden

Buckland, W. W. 1963. *A text-book of Roman law from Augustus to Justinian*, 3rd edn (rev. P. Stein), Cambridge

Burnyeat, M. F. 1994. 'Enthymeme: Aristotle on the logic of persuasion', in D. Furley and A. Nehemas, eds. *Aristotle's rhetoric: philosophical essays* (Princeton) 3–55

Bütler, H.-P. 1970. *Die geistige Welt des jüngeren Plinius. Studien zur Thematik seiner Briefe*, Heidelberg

Cain, A. 2008. '*Liber manet*: Pliny, *Ep.* 9.27.2 and Jerome, *Ep.* 130.19.5', *CQ* 58: 708–10

Calboli, G. 1969. *Rhetorica ad C. Herennium. Introduzione, testo critico, commento*, Bologna

    1986. 'A struggle with a ghost and the contrast between theme and rheme', in id., ed. *Papers on grammar II* (Bologna) 183–97

Cameron, A. D. E. 1965. 'The fate of Pliny's letters in the late empire', *CQ* 15: 289–98

    1967. 'Pliny's letters in the later empire: an addendum', *CQ* 17: 421–2

1976. *Circus factions: blues and greens at Rome and Byzantium*, Oxford

2010. *The last pagans of Rome*, New York

Camodeca, G. 1976. 'La carriera del giurista L. Neratius Priscus', *Atti dell'Accademia di scienze morali e politiche, Napoli* 87: 19–38

1999. *Tabulae Pompeianae Sulpiciorum. Edizione critica dell'archivio puteolano dei Sulpicii*, 2 vols, Rome

2007. 'Il giurista L. Neratius Priscus *cos. suff.* 97: nuovi dati su carriera e famiglia', *Studia et documenta historiae et iuris* 73: 291–311

Cancik, H. 1967. *Untersuchungen zu Senecas Epistulae Morales*, Hildesheim

Canobbio, A. 2008. '*Epigrammata longa* e *breves libelli*: dinamiche formali dell'epigramma marzialiano', in A. M. Morelli, ed. *Epigramma longum. Da Marziale alla tarda antichità / From Martial to late antiquity* (Cassino) 1 169–93

Carey, S. 2003. *Pliny's catalogue of culture: art and empire in the* Natural History, Oxford

Carlon, J. 2009. *Pliny's women: constructing virtue and creating identity in the Roman world*, Cambridge

Casanova, G. 1998. 'Incollare, arrotolare, maneggiare, restaurare papiri: note filologiche e bibliologiche', *Aegyptus* 78: 117–22

Casson, L. 2001. *Libraries in the ancient world*, New Haven

Castagna, L. 2003. 'Teoria e prassi dell'amicizia in Plinio il Giovane', in Castagna–Lefèvre 2003: 145–72

and E. Lefèvre, eds. 2003. *Plinius der Jüngere und seine Zeit*, Munich

Centlivres Challet, C.-E. 2008. 'Not so unlike him: women in Quintilian, Statius and Pliny', in F. Bertholet, A. Bielman Sánchez and R. Frei-Stolba, eds. *Egypte – Grèce – Rome. Les différents visages des femmes antiques* (Bern) 289–324

Chahoud, A. 2010. 'Idiom(s) and literariness in classical literary criticism', in E. Dickey and ead., eds. *Colloquial and literary Latin* (Cambridge) 42–64

Champlin, E. 1976. 'Hadrian's heir', *ZPE* 21: 79–89

1980. *Fronto and Antonine Rome*, Cambridge, MA

1982 [1985]. 'The suburbium of Rome', *AJAH* 7: 97–117

1989. '*Creditur vulgo testamenta hominum speculum esse morum*: why the Romans made wills', *CP* 34: 198–215

1991. *Final judgments: duty and emotion in Roman wills, 200 BC–AD 250*, Berkeley

2001. 'Pliny's other country', in M. Peachin, ed. *Aspects of friendship in the Graeco-Roman world* (Portsmouth, RI) 121–8

Chaplin, J. D. 2000. *Livy's exemplary history*, Oxford

Charney, B. L. 1943. 'Ellipsis of the verb in Seneca's *Epistulae morales*', *CP* 38: 46–8

Chastagnol, A. 1975. '*Latus clavus* et *adlectio*: l'accès des hommes nouveaux au Sénat romain sous le Haut-Empire', *Revue historique de droit français et étranger* 53: 375–94 = C. Nicolet, ed. *Des ordres à Rome* (Paris, 1984) 199–216

Chevallier, R. ²1989. *Roman roads* (tr. B. T. Batsford), London

Chinn, C. M. 2007. 'Before your very eyes: Pliny *Epistulae* 5.6 and the ancient theory of ekphrasis', *CP* 102: 265–80

Citroni, M. 1986. 'Le raccomandazioni del poeta: apostrofe al libro e contatto col destinario', *Maia* 38: 111–46

Claridge A. 1985. 'Il Vicus di epoca imperiale nella tenuta di Castelporziano: indagini archeologiche 1984', in *Castelporziano I. Campagna di scavo e restauro 1984* (Rome) 69–75

1988. 'Il Vicus di epoca imperiale: indagini archeologiche nel 1985 e 1986', in *Castelporziano II. Campagna di scavo e restauro 1985–1986* (Rome) 61–73

1997–8. 'The villas of the Laurentine shore', *Rendiconti della Pontificia Accademia Romana di Archeologia* 70: 307–17

1998. 'Il Vicus di epoca imperiale. Campagne di ricerche 1987–1991', in *Lauro 1998*: 115–36

Clay, J. S. 2011. *Homer's Trojan theater: space, vision, and memory in the* Iliad, Cambridge

Cloud, J. D. 1988. '*Lex Iulia de vi*: part 1', *Athenaeum* 66: 579–95

1989. '*Lex Iulia de vi*: part 2', *Athenaeum* 67: 427–65

Cole, T. 1992. 'Initium mihi operis Servius Galba iterum T. Vinius consules . . .', *YCS* 29: 231–45

Coleman, K. M. 2000. 'Latin literature after AD 96: change or continuity?', *AJAH* 15: 19–39

2012. 'Bureaucratic language in the correspondence between Pliny and Trajan', *TAPA* 142: 189–238

Connolly, J. 2007. 'Virile tongues: rhetoric and masculinity', in *Dominik–Hall 2007*: 83–97

Consoli, S. 1900. *Il neologismo negli scritti di Plinio il Giovane*, Palermo

Corbeill, A. 2004. *Nature embodied: gesture in ancient Rome*, Princeton

Corbier, M. 1974. *L'aerarium Saturni et l'aerarium militare: administration et prosopographie sénatoriale*, Rome

1981. 'Ti. Claudius Marcellinus et le procuratèle du Patrimoine', *ZPE* 42: 75–87

1985. 'Idéologie et pratique de l'héritage (Ier s. av. J-C – IIe s. ap. J-C)', *Index: Quaderni Camerti di Studi Romanistici* 13: 501–28

Corbinelli, S. 2008. *Amicorum colloquia absentium: la scrittura epistolare a Roma tra communicazione quotidiana e genere letterario*, Naples

Cotton, H. M. 1981a. 'Military tribunates and the exercise of patronage', *Chiron* 11: 229–38

1981b. *Documentary letters of recommendation in Latin from the Roman empire*, Königstein

Courtney, E. 1980. *A commentary on the Satires of Juvenal*, London

1993. *The fragmentary Latin poets*, Oxford

2004. 'The "Greek" accusative', *CJ* 99: 425–31

Cousin, J. 1979. *Quintilien. Institution oratoire*, VI (*Livres* X–XI), Paris

Cova, P. V. 1966. *La critica letteraria di Plinio il Giovane*, Brescia

1969. 'Problemi della lettera pliniana sulla storia', *Aevum* 43: 177–99

1972. 'Arte allusiva e stilizzazione retorica nelle lettere di Plinio. A proposito di vi, 31, 16–17; ii, 6; viii, 16; viii, 24; vii, 33, 10', *Aevum* 46: 16–36

1978. 'La misura umana di Plinio il Giovane', in id., *Lo stoico imperfetto. Un'immagine minore dell'uomo nella letteratura latina del principato* (Naples) 86–113

ed. 1992. *Letteratura latina dell'Italia settentrionale: cinque studi*, Milan

1997. 'La presenza di Seneca in Plinio il Giovane', *Paideia* 52: 95–107

1999. 'I viaggi di Plinio il Giovane', *Bollettino di Studi Latini* 29: 136–40

2001. 'Plinio il Giovane contro Plinio il Vecchio', *Bollettino di Studi Latini* 31: 55–67

2003. 'Plinio il Giovane contro Quintiliano', in Castagna–Lefèvre 2003: 83–94

Crook, J. A. 1967a. *Law and life of Rome*, London

1967b. 'Pliny plain' (review of S-W), *CR* 17: 311–14

1995. *Legal advocacy in the Roman world*, London

Cugusi, P. 1983. *Evoluzione e forme dell'epistolografia latina nella tarda repubblica e nei primi due secoli dell'impero*, Rome

1989. 'L'epistolografia. Modelli e tipologie', in G. Cavallo et al., eds. *Lo spazio letterario di Roma antica. II. La circolazione del testo* (Rome) 379–419

Dąbrowa, E. 1998. *The governors of Roman Syria from Augustus to Septimius Severus*, Bonn

D'Agostino, V. 1931. 'I diminutivi in Plinio il Giovane', *Atti della Reale Accademia delle Scienze di Torino (classe di scienze morali, storiche e filologiche)* 66: 93–130

Dalby, A. 2003. *Food in the ancient world from A to Z*, London

Damon, C. 2003. *Tacitus. Histories book I*, Cambridge

D'Arms, J. H. 1990. 'The Roman *convivium* and the idea of equality', in O. Murray, ed. *Sympotica* (Oxford) 308–20

Deane, S. N. 1918. 'Greek in Pliny's letters', *Classical Weekly* 12: 41–4, 50–4

De Franceschini, M. 2001. *Villa Adriana: mosaici – pavimenti – edifici*, Rome

2005. *Ville dell'agro romano*, Rome

De Groot, A. W. 1921. *Der antike Prosarhythmus*, Groningen

Delhey, N. 1993. *Apollinaris Sidonius, Carm. 22: Burgus Pontii Leontii*, Berlin

De Neeve, P. W. 1990. 'A Roman landowner and his estates: Pliny the Younger', *Athenaeum* 68: 363–402

1992. 'A Roman landowner and his estates: Pliny the Younger', *SIFC* 10: 335–44

Déniaux, É. 1993. *Clientèles et pouvoir à l'époque de Cicéron*, Rome

Deremetz, A. 2008. 'Descriptions des villas: Horace et Martial', in P. Galand-Hallyn and C. Lévy, eds. *La villa et l'univers familial dans l'Antiquité et à la Renaissance* (Paris) 45–60

De Simone, A., F. Ruffo, M. Tuccinardi, U. Cioffi. 1998. 'Ercolano 1992–1997. La villa dei papiri e lo scavo della città', *Cronache Ercolanesi* 28: 7–60

Deufert, M. 2008. 'Interpolationen in den Briefen des jüngeren Plinius', *Hermes* 136: 61–71

De Vivo, A. and E. Lo Cascio, eds. 2003. *Seneca uomo politico e l'età di Claudio e di Nerone*, Bari

Dixon, S. 2001. *Reading Roman women: sources, genres and real life*, London

Dominik, W.J. andJ. C. R. Hall, eds. 2007. *A companion to Roman rhetoric*, Malden, MA

Dondin-Payre, M. 1989. 'Le proconsul d'*Africa* malhonnête: mythe et réalité', in A. Mastino, ed. *L'Africa Romana. Atti del VI convegno* (Sassari) I 103–11

Döpp, S. 1989. '*Nec omnia apud priores meliora*: Autoren des frühen Prinzipats über ihre eigene Zeit', *RM* 132: 73–101

Douglas, A. E. 1966. *M. Tulli Ciceronis Brutus*, Oxford

Drerup, E. 1923. *Demosthenes im Urteile des Altertums*, Würzburg

Drerup, H. 1959. 'Bildraum und Realraum in der römischen Architektur', *MDAI(R)* 66: 147–74

Drummer, A. 1993. 'Villa: Untersuchungen zum Bedeutungswandel eines Motivs in römischer Bildkunst und Literatur', diss. Munich

Duckworth, G. E. 1962. *Structural patterns and proportions in Vergil's Aeneid: a study in mathematical composition*, Ann Arbor, MI

Ducos, M. 1998. 'Les testaments dans les lettres de Pline leJeune', in B. Bureau, ed. *Moussylanea: mélanges de linguistique et de littérature anciennes offerts à Claude Moussy* (Louvain) 341–6

Dunbabin, K. 1991. '*Triclinium* and *stibadium*', in W.J. Slater, ed. *Dining in a classical context* (Ann Arbor, MI) 121–48

1996. 'Convivial spaces: dining and entertainment in the Roman villa', *JRA* 9: 66–80

Duncan-Jones, R. 1982. *The economy of the Roman empire*, 2nd edn, Cambridge

Dunkel, G. E. 2000. 'Remarks on code-switching in Cicero's letters', *MH* 57: 122–9

Dunlap, J. E. 1919. 'Note on *laudiceni* (Plin. *Epist.* ii.14,5)', *CP* 14: 85–7

Durry, M. 1938. *Pline leJeune. Panégyrique de Trajan*, Paris

Dyck, A. 2004. *A commentary on Cicero, De legibus*, Ann Arbor, MI
2008. *Cicero. Catilinarians*, Cambridge
2012. *Cicero. Pro Sexto Roscio*, Cambridge

Ebbeler, J. 2010. 'Letters', in A. Barchiesi and W. Scheidel, eds. *The Oxford handbook of Roman studies* (Oxford) 464–76

Eck, W. 1984. 'Senatorial self-representation: developments in the Augustan period', in R. Millar and E. Segal, eds. *Caesar Augustus: seven aspects* (Oxford) 129–67

2001. 'Die große Pliniusinschrift aus Comum: Funktion und Monument', in G. A. Bertinelli and A. Donati, eds. *Varia epigraphica* (Faenza) 225–35 = id. *Monument und Inschrift: Gesammelte Aufsätze zur senatorischen Repräsentation in der Kaiserzeit* (Berlin, 2010) 299–310

Eco, U. 1992. 'A portrait of the Elder as a young Pliny', in id. *The limits of interpretation* (Bloomington, IN) 123–36

Edwards, C. 1993. *The politics of immorality in ancient Rome*, Cambridge

2005. 'Epistolography', in S. J. Harrison, ed. *A companion to Latin literature* (Malden, MA) 270–83

2007. *Death in ancient Rome*, New Haven

Edwards, R. 2008. 'Hunting for boars with Tacitus and Pliny', *CA* 27: 35–58

Elsner, J. 1995. *Art and the Roman viewer. The transformation of art from the pagan world to Christianity*, Cambridge

Erren, M. 2003. *P. Vergilius Maro, Georgica, Bd. 2: Kommentar*, Heidelberg

Étienne, R. 1958. *Le culte impérial dans la péninsule ibérique d'Auguste à Dioclétien*, Paris

Fagan, G. G. 2006. 'Leisure', in D. S. Potter, ed. *A companion to the Roman empire* (Malden, MA) 369–84

Fairweather, J. 1981. *Seneca the Elder*, Cambridge

Fantham, E. 2002. 'Orator and/et actor', in P. Easterling and E. Hall, eds. *Greek and Roman actors: aspects of an ancient profession* (Cambridge) 362–76

2008. 'With malice aforethought: the ethics of *malitia* on stage and at law', in I. Sluiter and R. M. Rosen, eds. *Kakos: badness and anti-value in classical antiquity* (Leiden) 319–34

Fedeli, P. 1989. 'Il "Panegirico" di Plinio nella critica moderna', *ANRW* II.33.1: 387–514

Fejfer, J. 2008. *Roman portraits in context*, Berlin

Fell, M. 1992. *Optimus princeps? Anspruch und Wirklichkeit der imperialen Programmatik Kaiser Traians*, Munich

Fishwick, D. 1972. 'The institution of the provincial cult in Roman Mauretania', *Historia* 21: 698–711

Fitzgerald, W. 2007a. 'The letter's the thing (in Pliny, book 7)', in Morello–Morrison 2007: 191–210

2007b. *Martial: the world of the epigram*, Chicago

Flickinger, R. C. 1913. 'The accusative of exclamation in epistolary Latin', *AJP* 34: 276–99

Flower, H. 1996. *Ancestor masks and aristocratic power in Roman culture*, Oxford

Forbes, R. J. 1958. *Studies in ancient technology VI*, Leiden

1966. *Studies in ancient technology V*, 2nd edn, Leiden

Fordyce, C. J. 1952. '*Mittatur senex in scholas*', *Proceedings of the Classical Association* 49: 28

1961. *Catullus*, Oxford

Forssman, B. 1967. 'Ignominia', *Zeitschrift für vergleichende Sprachforschung* 81: 72–103

Fowler, D. 1995. 'Martial and the book', *Ramus* 24: 31–58 = A. J. Boyle, ed. *Roman literature and ideology: Ramus essays for John Sullivan* (Bendigo) 199–226

Foy, D. and S. D. Fontaine, 2008. 'Diversité et évolution du vitrage de l'Antiquité et du haut Moyen Âge. Un état de la question', *Gallia* 65: 405–59

Frazel, T. D. 2009. *The rhetoric of Cicero's 'In Verrem'*, Göttingen

Frazer, A., ed. 1998. *The Roman villa: villa urbana. First Williams symposium on classical architecture*, Philadephia, PA

Frei-Stolba, F. 1969. 'Inoffizielle Kaisertitulaturen im 1. und 2. Jahrhundert n. Chr.', *MH* 26: 18–39

Freudenburg, K. 2001. *Satires of Rome: threatening poses from Lucilius to Juvenal*, Cambridge

Froesch, H. H. 1968. *Ovids Epistulae ex Ponto I–III als Gedichtsammlung*, Bonn

Gabba, E. and M. Pasquinucci. 1979. *Strutture agrarie e allevamento transumante nell'Italia romana (III–I sec. a.C.)*, Pisa

Gaertner, J. F. 2005. *Ovid, Epistulae ex Ponto, book 1*, Oxford

Gagliardi, L. 2002. *Decemviri e centumviri: origini e competenze*, Milan

Galimberti Biffino, G. 2007. 'Pline et la culture grecque', in Y. Perrin, ed. *Neronia VII. Rome, l'Italie et la Grèce* (Brussels) 285–301

Gallent-Kočevar, H. 1933. 'Über die Sentenzen des jüngeren Plinius', *Mitteilungen des Vereines klassischer Philologen in Wien* 10: 58–62

Gamberini, F. 1983. *Stylistic theory and practice in the Younger Pliny*, New York
    1984. 'Materiali per una ricerca sulla diffusione di Plinio il Giovane nei secoli XV e XVI', *Studi classici ed orientali* 34: 133–70

Gardner, J. F. 1986. *Women in Roman law and society*, London

Garland, R. 2010. *The eye of the beholder: deformity and disability in the Graeco-Roman world*, 2nd edn, London

Garnsey, P. 1966. 'The *lex Iulia* and appeal under the emperor', *JRS* 56: 167–89
    1970. *Social status and legal privilege in the Roman empire*, Oxford
    2000. 'The land', *Cambridge Ancient History* XI² 679–709
    2010. 'Roman patronage', in S. McGill, S. Sogno, E. Watts, eds, *From the Tetrarchs to the Theodosians: later Roman history and culture, 284–450 CE* (Cambridge) 33–54

Gauly, B. M. 2008. '*Magis homines iuvat gloria lata quam magna*. Das Selbstlob in Plinius' Briefen und seine Funktion', in id. and A. H. Arweiler, eds. *Machtfragen. Zur kulturellen Repräsentation und Konstruktion von Macht in Antike, Mittelalter und Neuzeit* (Stuttgart) 187–204

Gavoille, L. 2000. '*Epistula* et *litterae*: étude de synonomie', in L. Nadjo and E. Gavoille, eds. *Epistulae antiquae 1: actes du 1er colloque 'Le genre épistolaire antique et ses prolongements'* (Leuven) 13–36

Gazich, R. 1992. 'Retorica dell'ostensione nelle lettere di Plinio', in Cova 1992: 141–95
    2003. 'Retorica dell'esemplarità nelle lettere di Plinio', in Castagna–Lefèvre 2003: 123–41

Geisler, E. 1887. 'Loci similes auctorum Sidonio anteriorum', in C. Luetjohann, ed. *Apollinaris Sidonii Epistulae et Carmina = MGH auctorum antiquissimorum* VIII (Berlin) 351–416

Gérard, J. 1976. *Juvénal et la réalité contemporaine*, Paris

Gibson, B. J. 2006. *Statius, Silvae 5*, Oxford
    and R. D. Rees, eds. 2013. *Pliny the Younger in late antiquity*, Baltimore, MD (= *Arethusa* 46.2)

Gibson, R. K. 2002. 'Cf. e.g.: a typology of parallels and the role of commentaries on Latin poetry', in C. S. Kraus and id., eds. *The classical commentary: histories, practices, theory* (Leiden) 331–58

2003a. 'Pliny and the art of (in)offensive self-praise', *Arethusa* 36: 235–54

2003b. *Ovid: Ars Amatoria book 3*, Cambridge

2011a. 'Elder and better: the *Naturalis Historia* and the *Letters* of the Younger Pliny', in id. and R. Morello, eds. *Pliny the Elder: themes and contexts* (Leiden) 187–206

2011b. '<Clarus> confirmed? Pliny, *Epistles* 1.1 and Sidonius Apollinaris', *CQ* 61: 655–9

2012. 'On the nature of ancient letter collections', *JRS* 102: 56–78

2013a. 'Pliny and the letters of Sidonius: from Constantius and Clarus to Firminus and Fuscus', in (B.) Gibson–Rees 2013: 333–55

2013b. 'Starting with the index in Pliny', in L. Jansen, ed. *Paratextuality and the reader in Roman literature and culture* (Cambridge)

2013c. 'Reading Sidonius by the book', in J. van Waarden and G. Kelly, eds. *New approaches to Sidonius Apollinaris* (Leuven)

fthc. 'Not dark yet: reading to the end of the nine-book collection', in Marchesi fthc.

and R. Morello, eds. 2003. *Re-imagining Pliny the Younger*, Baltimore, MD (= *Arethusa* 36.2)

and R. Morello. 2012. *Reading the letters of Pliny the Younger: an introduction*, Cambridge (= G–M)

and A. D. Morrison. 2007. 'Introduction: what is a letter?', in Morello–Morrison 2007: 1–16

and C. Steel. 2010. 'The indistinct literary careers of Cicero and Pliny the Younger', in P. Hardie and H. Moore, eds. *Classical literary careers and their reception* (Cambridge) 118–37

Giovannini, A. 1987. 'Pline et les délateurs de Domitien', in *Oppositions et résistances à l'empire d'Auguste à Trajan* (Vandoeuvres) 219–48

Gleason, M. 1995. *Making men: sophists and self-presentation in ancient Rome*, Princeton

Gnilka, C. 1973. 'Trauer und Trost in Plinius' Briefen', *SO* 49: 105–25

Goetzl, J. 1952. 'Variatio in the Plinian epistle', *CJ* 47: 265–8 and 299

Gonzalès, A. 2003. *Pline le jeune: esclaves et affranchis à Rome*, Paris

Goodyear, F. R. D. 1965. *Aetna*, Cambridge

1972–81. *The Annals of Tacitus Books 1–6*, 2 vols [on *Annals* 1–2 only], Cambridge

Goold, G. P. 1964. Review of Mynors 1963, *Phoenix* 18: 320–8

Gordon, A. E. 1952. *Quintus Veranius consul A.D. 49. A study based upon his recently identified sepulchral inscription*, Berkeley

Gowers, E. 1993. *The loaded table. Representations of food in Roman literature*, Oxford

2012. *Horace. Satires book I*, Cambridge

Gowing, A. M. 2005. *Empire and memory: the representation of the Roman republic in imperial culture*, Cambridge

Grainger, J. D. 2003. *Nerva and the Roman succession crisis of AD 96–99*, London

Green, C. M. C. 1996. 'Did the Romans hunt?', *CA* 15: 222–60

Green, R. P. H. 1991. *The works of Ausonius*, Oxford

Griffin, J. 1985. *Latin poets and Roman life*, London

Griffin, M. T. 1999. 'Pliny and Tacitus', *Scripta Classica Israelica* 18: 139–58

2000. 'Nerva to Hadrian', *Cambridge Ancient History* XI² 84–132

2003a. '*De beneficiis* and Roman society', *JRS* 93: 92–113

2003b. 'Seneca as a sociologist: *De Beneficiis*', in De Vivo–Lo Cascio 2003: 89–122

2007. 'The Younger Pliny's debt to moral philosophy', *HSCP* 103: 451–81

Griffith, J. G. 1974. 'Pliny *Ep.* ii.10.1–3', *CR* 24: 184

Grimal, P. 1955. 'Deux figures de la Correspondance de Pline: le philosophe Euphratès et le rhéteur Isée', *Latomus* 14: 370–83

1984. *Les jardins romains*, 3rd edn, Paris

Gudeman, A. 1914. *Cornelii Taciti Dialogus de oratoribus*, Leipzig

Guerrini, C. 1997. 'I diminutivi nell'epistolario di Plinio il Giovane. Una nota stilistica', in *Discentibus obvius. Omaggio degli allievi a Domenico Magnino* (Como) 53–71.

Guidobaldi, M. P., D. Esposito, E. Formisano. 2009. 'L'Insula I, l'Insula nord-occidentale e la Villa dei Papiri di Ercolano: una sintesi delle conoscenze alla luce delle recenti indagini archeologiche', *Vesuviana* 1: 43–180

Guillemin, A-M. 1928. 'Les déscriptions de villas de Pline le Jeune', *Bulletin de l'Association Guillaume Budé* 19: 6–15

1929. *Pline et la vie littéraire de son temps*, Paris

Gunderson, E. 1997. 'Catullus, Pliny, and love-letters', *TAPA* 127: 201–31

1998. 'Discovering the body in Roman oratory', in M. Wyke, ed. *Parchments of gender. Deciphering the body in antiquity* (Oxford) 169–89

2000. *Staging masculinity: the rhetoric of performance in the Roman world*, Ann Arbor, MI

Gurd, S. A. 2012. *Work in progress: literary revision as social performance in ancient Rome*, Oxford

Gutzwiller, K. 1998. *Poetic garlands: Hellenistic epigrams in context*, Berkeley

ed. 2005a. *The New Posidippus: a Hellenistic poetry book*, Oxford

2005b. 'The literariness of the Milan Papyrus, or "What difference a book?"', in ead. 2005a: 287–319

Haack, M.-L. 2002. '*Haruspices* publics et privés: tentative d'une distinction', *REA* 104: 111–33

Habermehl, P. 2006. *Petronius, Satyrica 79–141: ein philologisch-literarischer Kommentar*, Berlin

Habinek, T. N. 1985. *The colometry of Latin prose*, Berkeley

Hainsworth, J. B. 1964. 'The starting-point of Tacitus' *Historiae*: fear or favour by omission?', *G&R* 11: 128–36

Halfmann, H. 1979. *Die Senatoren aus dem östlichen Teil des Imperium Romanum bis zum Ende des 2. Jh. n. Chr.*, Göttingen

Hall, E. 1994. 'Drowning by nomes: the Greeks, swimming, and Timotheus' *Persians*', in H. A. Khan, ed. *The birth of the European identity* (Nottingham) 44–80

Hall, J. 2007. 'Oratorical delivery and the emotions: theory and practice', in Dominik–Hall 2007: 218–34

    2009. *Politeness and politics in Cicero's letters*, Oxford

Halla-aho, H. 2011. 'Epistolary Latin', in J. Clackson, ed. *A companion to the Latin language* (Malden, MA) 426–44

Hanssen, J. S. T. 1953. *Latin diminutives: a semantic study*, Bergen

Harden, D. B. 1969. 'Ancient glass, II: Roman', *Archaeological Journal* 126: 44–77

Hardie, A. 1997–8. 'Juvenal, Domitian, and the accession of Hadrian (*Satire* 4)', *BICS* 42: 117–44

Häusler, S. 2000. 'Parenthesen im Lateinischen am Beispiel der Pliniusbriefe', *Glotta* 76: 202–31

Heldmann, K. 1982. *Antike Theorien über Entwicklung und Verfall der Redekunst*, Munich

Hellegouarc'h, J. 1972. *Le vocabulaire latin des relations et des partis politiques sous la république*, 2nd edn, Paris

Henderson, J. G. 2001a. 'On Pliny on Martial on Pliny on anon . . . (*Epistles* 3.21 / *Epigrams* 10.19)', *Ramus* 30: 57–88

    2001b. *Telling tales on Caesar: Roman stories from Phaedrus*, Cambridge

    2002a. *Pliny's statue. The Letters, self-portraiture and classical art*, Exeter

    2002b. 'Funding homegrown talent: Pliny *Letters* 1.19', *G&R* 49: 212–26

    2003. 'Portrait of the artist as a figure of style: P.L.I.N.Y's Letters', *Arethusa* 36: 115–25

    2004a. *Morals and villas in Seneca's* Letters*: places to dwell*, Cambridge

    2004b. *Hortus. The Roman book of gardening*, London

    2011. 'Down the Pan: historical exemplarity in the *Panegyricus*', in Roche 2011: 142–74

Hendrickson, G. L. 1905. 'The origin and meaning of the ancient characteristics of style', *AJP* 26: 249–90

Herrmann, L. 1940. 'Juvenaliana', *REA* 42: 448–52

Herrnstein Smith, B. 1968. *Poetic closure: a study of how poems end*, Chicago

Heubner, H. 1963–82. *P. Cornelius Tacitus. Die Historien. Kommentar*, 5 vols, Heidelberg

Highet, G. 1961. *Juvenal the satirist. A study*, New York

Hinds, S. 1998. *Allusion and intertext: dynamics of appropriation in Roman poetry*, Cambridge

Hine, H. M. 1981. *An edition with commentary of Seneca* Natural Questions, *book two*, Salem, NH

2005. 'Poetic influence on prose: the case of the younger Seneca', in Reinhardt–Lapidge–Adams 2005: 211–37

Hofacker, K. 1903. 'De clausulis C. Caecili Plini Secundi', diss. Bonn

Hoffer, S. 1999. *The anxieties of Pliny the Younger*, Atlanta, GA

    2006. 'Divine comedy? Accession propaganda in Pliny, *Epistles* 10.1–2 and the *Panegyric*', *JRS* 96: 73–87

Holford-Strevens, L. 2003. *Aulus Gellius: an Antonine scholar and his achievement*, Oxford

Hömke, N. 2002. *Gesetzt den Fall, ein Geist erscheint. Komposition und Motivik der ps.-quintilianischen Declamationes maiores X, XIV und XV*, Heidelberg

Hopkins, K. 1983. *Death and renewal*, Cambridge

Horsfall, N. 2006. *Virgil, Aeneid 3: a commentary*, Leiden

Housman, A. E. 1917. 'The *Thyestes* of Varius', *CQ* 11: 42–8 = *Collected Papers* III 941–9

    1940. *M. Annaei Lucani Belli civilis libri decem editorum in usum*, Oxford

    1945. *D. Iunii Iuuenalis Saturae editorum in usum*, London

Howell, P. 1980. *A commentary on Book One of the* Epigrams *of Martial*, London

Hutchinson, G. O. 1995. 'Rhythm, style and meaning in Cicero's prose', *CQ* 45: 485–99

    1998. *Cicero's correspondence. A literary study*, Cambridge

Innes, D., H. Hine and C. Pelling, eds., 1995. *Ethics and rhetoric. Classical essays for Donald Russell on his seventy-fifth birthday*, Oxford

Innocenti, B. 1994. 'Towards a theory of vivid description as practiced in Cicero's Verrine orations', *Rhetorica* 12: 355–81

Inwood, B. 2007a. *Seneca. Selected philosophical letters*, Oxford

    2007b. 'The importance of form in Seneca's philosophical letters', in Morello–Morrison 2007: 133–48

Jackson, R. 1988. *Doctors and diseases in the Roman world*, London

    2005. 'The role of doctors in the city', in A. MacMahon and J. Price, eds. *Roman working lives and urban living* (Oxford) 202–20

Janson, T. 1964. *Latin prose prefaces: studies in literary conventions*, Stockholm

Jashemski, W. F. 1979. *The gardens of Pompeii, Herculaneum and the villas destroyed by Vesuvius*, New Rochelle, NY

    1981. 'The Campanian peristyle garden', in E. MacDougall and W. F. Jashemski, eds. *Ancient Roman gardens*. Dumbarton Oaks colloquium on the history of landscape architecture 7 (Washington, DC) 31–48

Johnson, D. 1912. 'The manuscripts of Pliny's letters', *CP* 7: 66–75

Johnson, W. A. 2000. 'Toward a sociology of reading in classical antiquity', *AJP* 121: 593–627

    2004. *Bookrolls and scribes in Oxyrhynchus*, Toronto

    2010. *Readers and reading culture in the high Roman empire*, Oxford

Johnston, D. 1988. *The Roman law of trusts*, Oxford

Jones, C. P. 1968. 'A new commentary on the letters of Pliny' (review of S-W), *Phoenix* 22: 111–42

1970. 'Sura and Senecio', *JRS* 60: 98–104

Jones, F. 1991. 'Naming in Pliny's letters', *SO* 66: 147–70

Jung, F. 1984. 'Gebaute Bilder', *Antike Kunst* 27: 71–122

Kaser, M. 1956. 'Infamia und ignominia in den römischen Rechtsquellen', *Zeitschrift der Savigny-Stiftung für Rechtsgeschichte (Romanistische Abteilung)* 73: 220–78

Kaster, R. A. 1995. *C. Suetonius Tranquillus. De grammaticis et rhetoribus*, Oxford

2001. 'The dynamics of *fastidium* and the ideology of disgust', *TAPA* 131: 149–83

2002. 'The taxonomy of patience, or When is *patientia* not a virtue?', *CP* 97: 133–44

Kelly, G. 2013. 'Pliny and Symmachus', in (B.) Gibson–Rees 2013: 261–87

Kelly, J. M. 1976. *Studies in the civil judicature of the Roman republic*, Oxford

Kemper, S. 2000. '*Neglegit carpitque posteritas*: Plinius Minor van Oudheid tot Renaissance', in Z. von Martels, P. Steenbakkers, and A. Vanderjagt, eds. *Limae labor et mora: Opstellen voor Fokke Akkerman ter gelegenheid van zijn zeventigste verjaardag* (Leende) 8–19

Kennedy, D. F. 2002. 'Epistolarity: the *Heroides*', in P. R. Hardie, ed. *Cambridge companion to Ovid* (Cambridge) 217–32

Kennedy, G. 1972. *The art of rhetoric in the Roman world*, Princeton

1999. 'Encolpius and Agamemnon in Petronius', *AJP* 99: 171–80

Kenney, E. J. 1962. 'The first satire of Juvenal', *PCPS* 8: 29–40

1971. *Lucretius. De rerum natura book III*, Cambridge

1982. 'Books and readers in the Roman world', in E. J. Kenney and W. V. Clausen, eds. *The Cambridge history of classical literature. II Latin literature* (Cambridge) 3–32

1990. *Apuleius. Cupid & Psyche*, Cambridge

Ker, J. 2009. 'Drinking from the water-clock: time and speech in imperial Rome', *Arethusa* 42: 279–302

Kienast, D. 1968. 'Nerva und das Kaisertum Trajans', *Historia* 17: 51–71

2004. *Römische Kaisertabelle. Grundzüge einer römischen Kaiserchronologie*, 3rd edn, Darmstadt

Kierdorf, W. 1980. Laudatio funebris. *Interpretationen und Untersuchungen zur Entwicklung der römischen Leichenrede*, Meisenheim am Glan

Kindstrand, J. F. 1982. *The stylistic evaluation of Aeschines in antiquity*, Uppsala

Kirchner, R. 2000. *Sentenzen im Werk des Tacitus*, Stuttgart

Kloft, H. 1970. *Liberalitas principis*, Cologne

Konstan, D. 1996. *Friendship in the classical world*. Cambridge

Kooreman, M. 1996. 'The use of the active periphrastic future in some biblical translations', in H. Rosén, ed. *Aspects of Latin* (Innsbruck) 323–30

Korenjak, M. 2000. *Publikum und Redner. Ihre Interaktion in der sophistischen Rhetorik der Kaiserzeit*, Munich

Krasser, H. 1993a. '*claros colere viros* oder über engagierte Bewunderung. Zum Selbstverständnis des jüngeren Plinius', *Philologus* 137: 62–71

1993b. 'extremos pudeat rediisse – Plinius im Wettstreit mit der Vergangenheit. Zu Vergilzitaten beim jüngeren Plinius', *Antike und Abendland* 39: 144–54

Kraus, C. S. 1992. 'How (not?) to end a sentence: the problem of -*que*', *HSCP* 94: 321–9

1994. *Livy. Ab urbe condita book VI*, Cambridge

and A. J. Woodman. fthc. *Tacitus. Agricola*, Cambridge

Kraut, K. 1872. *Über Syntax und Stil des jüngeren Plinius*, Schönthal

Krevans, N. 2007. 'The arrangement of epigrams in collections', in P. Bing and J. S. Bruss, eds. *Brill's companion to Hellenistic epigram* (Leiden) 131–46

Krieckhaus, A. 2001. 'Vermutungen zu zwei Korrespondenten des jüngeren Plinius', *RM* 144: 175–85

Kroon, C. 1995. *Discourse particles in Latin. A study of* nam, enim, autem, uero, *and* at, Amsterdam

Kunst, C. 1917. 'De Aeschine Rhodi exulante', *WS* 39: 167–70

Lagergren, J. P. 1872. *De vita et elocutione C. Plinii Caecilii Secundi*, Uppsala

Lang, F. G. 1999. 'Schreiben nach Mass: Zur Stichometrie in der antiken Literatur', *Novum Testamentum* 41: 40–57

Laurand, L. 1911. 'Les fins d'hexamètre dans les discours de Cicéron', *Revue de philologie* 35: 75–88

Lauro, M. G., ed. 1998. *Castelporziano III. Campagne di scavo e restauro 1987–1991*, Rome

and A. Claridge. 1998. 'Litus Laurentinum: carta archeologica della zona litoranea a Castelporziano', in Lauro 1998: 39–62

Lausberg, M. 1991. 'Cicero – Seneca – Plinius. Zur Geschichte des römischen Prosabriefes', *Anregung* 37: 82–100

Lavan, M. 2013. *Slaves to Rome. Paradigms of empire in Roman culture*, Cambridge

Lavency, M. 2002. 'L'ablatif de modalité dans les *Lettres* de Pline le Jeune', in P. Defosse, ed. *Hommages à C. Deroux II* (Brussels) 240–52

Leach, E. W. 1969. '"De exemplo meo ipse aedificato": an organizing idea in *Mostellaria*', *Hermes* 97: 318–32

1990. 'The politics of self-presentation: Pliny's *Letters* and Roman portrait sculpture', *CA* 9: 14–39

1993. 'The entrance room in the House of Iulius Polybius and the nature of the Roman vestibulum', in E. M. Moorman, ed. *Functional and spatial analysis of wall painting* (Leiden) 23–8

2003. '*Otium* as *luxuria*: economy of status in the Younger Pliny's *Letters*', *Arethusa* 36: 147–66

2004. *The social life of painting in ancient Rome and on the Bay of Naples*, Cambridge

Leeman, A. D. 1963. *Orationis ratio. The stylistic theories and practice of the Roman orators, historians and philosophers*, 2 vols, Amsterdam

and H. Pinkster and M. L. W. Nelson. 1985. *M. Tullius Cicero: De Oratore libri III. Kommentar, 2. Band: Buch I, 166–265, Buch II, 1–98*, Heidelberg

and H. Pinkster and E. Rabbie. 1989. *M. Tullius Cicero: De Oratore libri III. Kommentar, 3. Band: Buch II, 99–290*, Heidelberg

Lefèvre, E. 1977. 'Plinius-Studien I: Römische Baugesinnung und Landschafts-auffassung in den Villenbriefen (2,17; 5,6)', *Gymnasium* 84: 519–41

1987. 'Plinius-Studien III: Die Villa als geistiger Lebensraum (1,3, 1,24, 2,8, 6,31, 9,36)', *Gymnasium* 94: 247–62

1988. 'Plinius-Studien IV: Die Naturauffassung in den Beschreibungen der Quelle am "Lacus Larius" (4,30), des "Clitumnus" (8,8) und des "Lacus Vadimo" (8,20)', *Gymnasium* 95: 236–69

1996. 'Plinius-Studien VII: Cicero das unerreichbare Vorbild (1,2; 3,15; 4,8; 7,4; 9,2)', *Gymnasium* 103: 333–53

2003. 'Plinius' Klage um die verlorengegangene Würde des Senats (3, 20; 4, 25)', in Castagna–Lefèvre 2003: 189–200

2009. *Vom Römertum zum Ästhetizismus: Studien zu den Briefen des jüngeren Plinius*, Berlin

Lendon, J. E. 1997. *Empire of honour. The art of government in the Roman world*, Oxford

Leo, F. 1878. *De Senecae tragoediis observationes criticae*, Berlin

Letta, C. 1972. *I Marsi e il Fucino nell'antichità*, Milan

Levick, B. M. 1967. *Roman colonies in southern Asia Minor*, Oxford

1985. 'Verginius Rufus and the four Emperors', *RM* 128: 318–46

Lézine, A. 1961. *Architecture romaine d'Afrique*, Tunis

Liberman, G. 2009a. Review of Zehnacker vol. 1, *BMCR* 2009.07.16

2009b. Response to Zehnacker 2009, *BMCR* 2009.09.44

Liebeschuetz, J. H. W. G. 1979. *Continuity and change in Roman religion*, Oxford

Lilja, S. 1969. 'On the nature of Pliny's letters', *Arctos* 6: 61–79

1971. 'The singular use of *nos* in Pliny's letters', *Eranos* 69: 89–103

Linde, P. 1923. 'Die Stellung des Verbs in der lateinischen Prosa', *Glotta* 12: 153–78

Lindholm, E. 1931. *Stilistische Studien zur Erweiterung der Satzglieder im Lateinischen*, Lund

Lo Cascio, E. 2003. 'L'economia dell'Italia nella testimonianza di Plinio', in Castagna–Lefèvre 2003: 281–302

Löfstedt, E. 1956. *Syntactica: Studien und Beiträge zur historischen Syntax des Lateins*, 2nd edn, 2 vols, Lund

López, J. F. 2007. 'Quintilian as rhetorician and teacher', in Dominik–Hall 2007: 307–22

Lowe, E. A. and E. K. Rand. 1922. *A sixth-century fragment of the letters of Pliny the Younger*, Washington, DC

Lübeck, A. 1872. 'Hieronymus quos noverit scriptores et ex quibus hauserit', diss. Leipzig

Ludewig, A. 1891. 'Quomodo Plinius maior, Seneca philosophus, Curtius Rufus, Quintilianus, Cornelius Tacitus, Plinius minor particula *quidem* usi sint', Prager philologische Studien 3, Prague

Ludolph, M. 1997. *Epistolographie und Selbstdarstellung. Untersuchungen zu den 'Paradebriefen' Plinius des Jüngeren*, Tübingen

MacArthur, E. J. 1990. *Extravagant narratives: closure and dynamics in the epistolary form*, Princeton

Macdonald, C. 1961. '"Heresies I" again', *G&R* 8: 188–9

MacDonald, W. L. and J. A. Pinto. 1995. *Hadrian's villa and its legacy*, New Haven

MacDowell, D. M. 2000. *Demosthenes: On the false embassy (oration 19)*, Oxford
    2009. *Demosthenes the orator*, Oxford

Macleod, C. 1973. 'Catullus 116', *CQ* 23: 304–9

Madvig, J. N. 1876. *Cicero: De finibus bonorum et malorum libri quinque*, 3rd edn,
    Copenhagen

Maiuri, A. 1958. *Ercolano. Nuovi scavi (1927–1958). Vol. I*, Rome

Maltby, R. 1991. *A lexicon of ancient Latin etymologies*, Leeds
    2008. 'Verbal and thematic links between poems and books in Martial', *PLLS*
    13: 255–68

Mankin, D. 1995. *Horace. Epodes*, Cambridge
    2011. *Cicero. De oratore book III*, Cambridge

Manning, C. E. 1985. '*Liberalitas*: the decline and rehabilitation of a virtue', *G&R*
    22: 73–83

Mansuelli, G. A. 1978. 'La villa nelle *Epistulae* di C. Plinio Cecilio Secondo', *Studi
    Romagnoli* 29: 59–76

Manuwald, G. 2007. *Cicero*, Philippics *3–9*, 2 vols, Berlin

Marchesi, I. 2008. *The art of Pliny's letters. A poetics of allusion in the private correspondence*,
    Cambridge
    ed. fthc. *Betting on posterity: Pliny as bookmaker*

Marincola, J. 1997. *Authority and tradition in ancient historiography*, Cambridge

Marouzeau, J. 1962. *Traité de stylistique latine*, 4th edn, Paris

Marquardt, J. 1886. *Das Privatleben der Römer*, 2 vols, Leipzig

Martin, R. H. 1967. 'The speech of Curtius Montanus: Tacitus, Histories IV, 42',
    JRS 57: 109–14
    and A. J. Woodman. 1989. *Tacitus. Annals book IV*, Cambridge

Marzano, A. 2007. *Roman villas in central Italy: a social and economic history*, Leiden

Maselli, G. 1995. 'Moduli descrittivi nelle ville pliniane: percezione, animazione,
    concezione dello spazio', *Bollettino di Studi Latini* 25: 90–104

Mastrorosa, I. G. 2010. 'La pratica dell'oratoria giudiziaria nell'alto impero:
    Quintiliano e Plinio il Giovane', in P. Galand et al., eds. *Quintilien ancien et
    moderne* (Turnhout) 125–52

Matthews, R. F. 1974. 'The letters of Symmachus', in J. W. Binns, ed. *Latin literature
    of the fourth century* (London) 58–99

Maxfield, V. A. 1981. *The military decorations of the Roman army*, Berkeley

Mayer, R. 1991. 'Roman historical *exempla* in Seneca', in P. Grimal, ed. *Sénèque et
    la prose latine* (Vandoeuvres) 141–69; revised in J. G. Fitch, ed. *Oxford readings
    in Seneca* (Oxford, 2008) 299–315
    1994. *Horace. Epistles book I*, Cambridge
    2003. 'Pliny and *gloria dicendi*', *Arethusa* 36: 227–34
    2005. 'The impracticability of Latin "Kunstprosa"', in Reinhardt–Lapidge–
    Adams 2005: 195–210

Mayer-Maly, T. 1984. Review of Tellegen 1982, *Gnomon* 56: 243–6

Mayor, J. E. B. 1886. *Thirteen Satires of Juvenal*, 4th edn, London

McDermott, W. C. 1970. 'Fabricius Veiento', *AJP* 91: 129–48

McEwen, I. K. 1995. 'Housing fame: in the Tuscan villa of Pliny the Younger', *Res: Anthropology and Aesthetics* 27: 11–24

McKeown, J. C. 1987–. *Ovid: Amores*, 4 vols, Leeds

Meister, R. 1924. 'Zur Frage des Kompositionsprinzips in den Briefen des Plinius', in Χάρισμα. *Festgabe zur 25jähr. Stiftungsfeier des Vereines klassischer Philologen in Wien* (Vienna) 27–33

Mellet, S. 1988. *L'imparfait de l'indicatif en latin classique: temps, aspect, modalité*, Paris

Melzani, G. 1992. 'Elementi della lingua d'uso nelle lettere di Plinio il Giovane', in Cova 1992: 197–244

Menna, P. 1902. 'De infinitivi apud Plinium minorem usu', diss. Rostock

Menninger, K. 1969. *Number words and number symbols. A cultural history of numbers* (tr. P. Broneer), Cambridge, MA

Merrill, E. T. 1903. 'Notes on Pliny's letters', *CR* 17: 52–5

1909. 'Plin. *Ep.* II.12.4', *CP* 4: 202

1917. 'On a Venetian codex of Pliny's letters', *CP* 12: 259–70

Merwald, G. 1964. 'Die Buchkomposition des jüngeren Plinius (*Epistulae* I–IX)', diss. Erlangen-Nuremberg

Méthy, N. 2003. '*Ad exemplar antiquitatis*: les grandes figures du passé dans la correspondance de Pline le Jeune', *REL* 81: 200–14

2006. 'Le portrait d'un empereur éphémère: Nerva dans le *Panégyrique de Trajan*', in J. Champeaux and M. Chassignet, eds. *Aere perennius: en hommage à Hubert Zehnacker* (Paris) 611–23

2007. *Les lettres de Pline le Jeune. Une représentation de l'homme*, Paris

2010. 'La religion d'un homme de lettres sous le règne de Trajan: le témoignage des lettres de Pline le Jeune', in D. Briquel, C. Février and C. Guittard, eds. *Varietates fortunae: religion et mythologie à Rome. Hommage à Jacqueline Champeaux* (Paris) 287–98

Mielsch, H. 2003. 'Traditionelle und neue Züge in den Villen des Plinius', in Castagna–Lefèvre 2003: 317–24

Millar, F. 1964. 'The aerarium and its officials under the empire', *JRS* 54: 33–44

1977. *The emperor in the Roman world*, London

1981. *The Roman empire and its neighbours*, 2nd edn, London

1984. 'Condemnation to hard labour in the Roman empire, Augustus to Constantine', *PBSR* 52: 124–47

Moles, J. L. 1988. *Plutarch. The life of Cicero*, Warminster

Mommsen, T. 1869. 'Zur Lebensgeschichte des jüngeren Plinius', *Hermes* 3: 31–136 = *Gesammelte Schriften* (Berlin, 1905–13) IV 366–468

1887–8. *Römisches Staatsrecht*, 3 vols in 5, Berlin

Montevecchi, O. 1953. *Papyri Bononienses (P. Bon.) I (1–50)*, Milan

Morello, R. 2003. 'Pliny and the art of saying nothing', *Arethusa* 36: 187–209

2007. 'Confidence, *inuidia*, and Pliny's epistolary curriculum', in Morello–Morrison 2007: 169–89

and A. D. Morrison, eds. 2007. *Ancient letters. Classical and late antique epistolography*, Oxford

Morford, M. 1973. 'Juvenal's thirteenth Satire', *AJP* 94: 26–36

Morgan, T. 2007. *Popular morality in the early Roman empire*, Oxford

Mouritsen, H. 2011. *The freedman in the Roman world*, Cambridge

Mratschek, S. 2008. 'Identitätsstiftung aus der Vergangenheit. Zum Diskurs über die trajanische Bildungskultur im Kreis des Sidonius Apollinaris', in T. Fuhrer, ed. *Die christlich-philosophischen Diskurse der Spätantike: Texte, Personen, Institutionen* (Freiburg) 363–80

Muecke, F. 1993. *Horace. Satires II*, Warminster

Müller, K. 1954. 'Textgestaltung – Klauseln', in id. and H. Schönfeld, *Geschichte Alexanders des Grossen: Lateinisch und Deutsch* (Munich) 734–82

Murgia, C. W. 1980. 'The date of Tacitus' *Dialogus*', *HSCP* 84: 89–125

1985. 'Pliny's letters and the *Dialogus*', *HSCP* 89: 171–206

Myers, K. S. 2005. '*Docta otia*: garden ownership and configurations of leisure in Statius and Pliny the Younger', *Arethusa* 38: 103–29

Mynors, R. A. B., ed. 1964. *XII Panegyrici latini*, Oxford

von Nägelsbach, K. F. 1963. *Lateinische Stilistik*, 9th edn, Darmstadt

Nagle, B. R. 1980. *The poetics of exile: program and polemic in the* Tristia *and* Epistulae ex Ponto *of Ovid*, Brussels

Nesselrath, H. G. 1990. 'Lucian's introductions', in D. A. Russell, ed. *Antonine literature* (Oxford) 111–40

Newlands, C. 2002. *Statius' Silvae and the poetics of empire*, Cambridge

2011. *Statius. Siluae book II*, Cambridge

Niemirska-Pliszczyńska, J. 1955. *De elocutione Pliniana in epistularum libris novem conspicua quaestiones selectae*, Lublin

Nisbet, R. G. 1923. '*Voluntas fati* in Latin syntax', *AJP* 44: 27–43

Nisbet, R. G. M. 1961. *M. Tulli Ciceronis in L. Calpurnium Pisonem oratio*, Oxford = id. (ed. S. J. Harrison) *Collected papers on Latin literature* (Oxford, 1995) 321–34

1990. 'Cola and clausulae in Cicero's speeches', in E. M. Craik, ed. *'Owls to Athens': essays on classical subjects presented to Sir Kenneth Dover* (Oxford) 349–59

and M. Hubbard. 1970. *A commentary on Horace* Odes, *book I*, Oxford

and M. Hubbard. 1978. *A commentary on Horace* Odes, *book II*, Oxford

and N. Rudd. 2004. *A commentary on Horace* Odes, *book III*, Oxford

Norden, E. 1898. *Die antike Kunstprosa vom VI. Jahrhundert v. Chr. bis in die Zeit der Renaissance*, 2 vols, Leipzig

Noreña, C. F. 2001. 'The communication of the emperor's virtues', *JRS* 91: 146–68

2007. 'The social economy of Pliny's correspondence with Trajan', *AJP* 128: 239–77

Oakley, S. P. 1997–2005. *A commentary on Livy books VI–X*, 4 vols, Oxford

2009. 'Style and language', in Woodman 2009b: 195–211

Ogilvie, R. M. 1965. *A commentary on Livy books 1–5*, Oxford

and I. Richmond. 1967. *Tacitus. De vita Agricolae*, Oxford

Oliensis, E. 1995. 'Life after publication: Horace *Epistles* 1.20', *Arethusa* 28: 209–24

Oliver, J. H. 1949. 'Two Athenian poets', in *Commemorative studies in honor of Theodore Leslie Shear* (Athens) 243–58

Orlandi, G. T. 2005. 'Metrical and rhythmical clausulae in medieval Latin prose: some aspects and problems', in Reinhardt–Lapidge–Adams 2005: 394–412

2008. *Scritti di filologia mediolatina* (ed. P. Chiesi), Florence

Otto, A. 1890. *Die Sprichwörter und sprichwörterlichen Redensarten der Römer*, Leipzig

Owen, S. G. 1924. *Ovid. Tristium liber secundus*, Oxford

Pagán, V. E. 2006. *Rome and the literature of gardens*, London

2010. 'The power of prefaces from Statius to Pliny', *CQ* 60: 194–201

Paladini, M.-L. 1958. 'Il processo di Mario Prisco nel *Panegirico* a Traiano di Plinio il Giovane', *Rendiconti dell'Istituto Lombardo (classe di lettere e scienze morali e storiche* 92): 713–36

Palmer, L. R. 1956. *The Latin language*, London

Panhuis, D. 1980. 'Gapping in Latin', *CJ* 75: 299–41

Pani, M. 1993. 'Sulla nozione di "obsequium" in Tacito e Plinio il Giovane', in id. *Potere e valori a Roma fra Augusto e Traiano*, 2nd edn (Bari) 159–80

1995. 'Sviluppi della tematica dell'*otium* in Plinio il Giovane', in A. S. Marino, ed. *L'incidenza dell'antico. Studi in memoria di Ettore Lepore. I* (Naples) 231–40

Parker, H. N. 2009. 'Books and reading Latin poetry', in W. R. Johnson and id., eds. *Ancient literacies: the culture of reading in Greece and Rome* (Oxford) 186–229

Patterson, J. R. 1985. 'Il vicus di epoca imperiale nella tenuta presidenziale di Castelporziano: contesto storico', in *Castelporziano I. Campagna di scavo e restauro 1984* (Rome) 67–9

Pausch, D. 2004. *Biographie und Bildungskultur. Personendarstellungen bei Plinius dem Jüngeren, Gellius und Sueton*, Berlin

Pavis d'Escurac, H. 1978. 'Pline le Jeune et la transmission des patrimoines', *Ktema* 3: 275–88

1992. 'Pline le Jeune et les lettres de recommandation', in E. Frézouls, ed. *La Mobilité sociale dans le monde romain* (Strasbourg) 55–69

Pavlovskis, Z. 1973. *Man in an artificial landscape: the marvels of civilization in imperial Roman literature*, Leiden

Pease, A. S. 1935. *Publi Vergili Maronis Aeneidos liber quartus*, Cambridge, MA

Pernot, L. 2006. *L'ombre du tigre: recherches sur la réception de Démosthène*, Naples

Perpillou, J.-L. 1995. 'Quelle sorte de θηρίον fut Démosthène?', *Revue de philologie* 69: 263–8

Peter, H. 1901. *Der Brief in der römischen Literatur*, Leipzig

Peterson, W. 1891. *M. Fabi Quintiliani Institutionis oratoriae liber decimus*, Oxford

Petrone, G. 2003. 'Plinio e il teatro', in Castagna–Lefèvre 2003: 15–22

Pferdehirt, B. 2004. *Römische Militärdiplome und Entlassungsurkunden in der Sammlung des Römisch-Germanischen Zentralmuseums*, Mainz

Philips, H. 1976. 'Zeitkritik bei Plinius dem Jüngeren. Interpretation zu epist. 2,6', *Anregung* 22.6: 363–70

Picone, G. 1978. *L'eloquenza di Plinio: teoria e prassi*, Palermo

Pinkster, H. 2005. 'The language of Pliny the Elder', in Reinhardt–Lapidge–Adams 2005: 239–56

Platner, S. G. 1888. 'Gerunds and gerundives in Pliny's Letters', *AJP* 9: 214–18

Platts, H. 2011. 'Keeping up with the Joneses: competitive display within the Roman villa landscape', in N. Fisher and H. van Wees, eds. *Competition in the ancient world* (Swansea) 239–77

Pollitt, J. J. 1974. *The ancient view of Greek art: criticism, history, and terminology*, New Haven

Posadas, J. L. 2008. 'Clientelas y amistades femeninas en Plinio el Joven', *Studia Historica: Historia Antigua* 26: 87–105

Postgate, J. P. 1926. 'Ad C. Caecilii Plini Secundi epistulas', *Mnemosyne* 54: 373–84

Powell, J. G. F. 1988. *Cicero. Cato maior de senectute*, Cambridge
  1990. *Cicero. On friendship and the dream of Scipio*, Warminster

Power, T. 2010. 'Pliny's *Letter* 5.10 and the literary career of Suetonius', *JRS* 100: 140–62

de Pretis, A. 2002. *'Epistolarity' in the first book of Horace's Epistles*, Piscataway, NJ

du Prey, P. de la Ruffinière. 1994. *The villas of Pliny from antiquity to posterity*, Chicago

Purcell, N. 1985. 'Wine and wealth in ancient Italy', *JRS* 75: 1–18
  1987. 'Town in country and country in town', in E. B. MacDougall and W. F. Jashemski, eds. *Ancient Roman villa gardens*. Dumbarton Oaks colloquium on the history of landscape architecture 10 (Washington, DC) 187–203
  1995. 'The Roman villa and the landscape of production', in T. J. Cornell and K. Lomas, eds. *Urban society in Roman Italy* (London) 151–79
  1996a. 'The Roman garden as domestic building', in I. Barton, ed. *Roman domestic buildings* (Exeter) 121–51
  1996b. 'Rome and the management of water: environment, culture and power', in G. Shipley and J. Salmon, eds. *Human landscapes in classical antiquity. Environment and culture* (London) 180–212
  1998. 'Discovering a Roman resort-coast: the *litus Laurentinum* and the archaeology of *otium*', at www.rhul.ac.uk/classics/laurentineshore/maritimefacade/mf_articles.html (author's translation of 'Alla scoperta di una costa residenziale romana: il *litus Laurentinum* e l'archeologia dell'*otium*', in Lauro 1998: 11–32)
  2005. 'The way we used to eat: diet, community and history at Rome', in B. K. Gold and J. Donahue, eds. *Roman dining* (Baltimore, MD) (= *AJP* 124) 329–58

Purves, A. C. 2010. *Space and time in ancient Greek narrative*, Cambridge

Querzoli, S. 2000. *I testamenta e gli* officia pietatis: *tribunale centumvirale, potere imperiale e giuristi tra Augusto e i Severi,* Naples

Quinn, K. 1970. *Catullus: the poems,* London (repr. Bristol 1996)

Radicke, J. 1997. 'Die Selbstdarstellung des Plinius in seinen Briefen', *Hermes* 125: 447–69

Radke, G. 1971. *Viae publicae Romanae,* Stuttgart

Raepsaet-Charlier, M.-T. 1987. *Prosopographie des femmes de l'ordre sénatorial (Ier–IIe siècles),* Leuven

Ramage, E. S. 1963. '*Urbanitas* in Cicero and Quintilian: a contrast in attitudes', *AJP* 84: 390–414

1973. *Urbanitas: ancient sophistication and refinement,* Norman, OK

1989. 'Juvenal and the establishment. Denigration of predecessor in the *Satires*', *ANRW* II.33.1: 640–707

Ramieri, A. M. 1995. 'La villa di Plinio a Castel Fusano', *Archeologia Laziale* 12: 407–16

Ramsey, J. T. 2003. *Cicero. Philippics I–II,* Cambridge

Rauzy, E. 2002. 'Les déplacements de point de vue dans la correspondance de Cicéron', in L. Nadjo and É. Gavoille, eds. *Epistulae antiquae II* (Leuven) 113–25

Raven, D. S. 1965. *Latin metre: an introduction,* Cambridge

Redford, B. 2012. 'The epistolary tradition', in D. Hopkins and C. Martindale, eds. *Oxford history of classical reception in English literature vol. 3 (1660–1790)* (Oxford) 427–45

Reekmans, T. 1969. 'Superest tamen λιτούργιον non leue', in *Hommages à M. Renard, I* (Brussels) 658–65

Rees, R. 2007. 'Letters of recommendation and the rhetoric of praise', in Morello–Morrison 2007: 149–68

2011. 'Afterwords of praise', in Roche 2011: 175–88

Reinhardt, T. 2003. *Marcus Tullius Cicero. Topica,* Oxford

and M. Lapidge and J. N. Adams, eds. 2005. *Aspects of the language of Latin prose,* Oxford

and M. Winterbottom 2006. *Quintilian book 2,* Oxford

Reynolds, L. D. 1965. *L. Annaei Senecae Ad Lucilium epistulae morales,* 2 vols, Oxford

1983. 'The younger Pliny', in id., ed. *Texts and transmission: a survey of the Latin classics* (Oxford) 316–22

and N. G. Wilson. 1991. *Scribes and scholars: a guide to the transmission of Greek and Latin literature,* 3rd edn, Oxford

Reynolds, S. fthc. '396', in ead., *Catalogue of the Holkham Hall manuscripts. I. Manuscripts produced in Italy to 1500,* Turnhout

Rich, J. W. 1990. *Cassius Dio. The Augustan settlement (Roman History 53–55.9),* Warminster

Richardson, L. 1992. *A new topographical dictionary of ancient Rome,* Baltimore

Richardson-Hay, C. 2006. *First lessons: book 1 of Seneca's* Epistulae Morales, Bern

Rieks, R. 1967. *Homo, humanus, humanitas. Zur Humanität in der lateinischen Literatur des ersten nachchristlichen Jahrhunderts*, Munich

Riggsby, A. M. 1991. 'Hiatus and elision in Latin prose', *CA* 10: 328–43

1995. 'Pliny on Cicero and oratory: self-fashioning in the public eye', *AJP* 116: 123–35

1997. '"Public" and "private" in Roman culture: the case of the cubiculum', *JRA* 10: 36–56

1998. 'Self and community in the Younger Pliny', *Arethusa* 31: 75–97

2003. 'Pliny in space (and time)', *Arethusa* 36: 167–86

2009. 'For whom the clock drips', *Arethusa* 42: 271–8

Risselada, R. 1998. 'The discourse functions of *sane*: Latin marker of agreement in description, interaction and concession', *Journal of Pragmatics* 30: 225–44

Ritchie, M. H. 1902. *A study of conditional and temporal clauses in Pliny the Younger*, Philadelphia

Rives, J. B. 1999. *Tacitus. Germania*, Oxford

Robbins, F. E. 1910. 'Tables of contents in the MSS of Pliny's letters', *CP* 5: 476–87

Robinson, O. F. 1995. *The criminal law of ancient Rome*, London

Roca Barea, E. 1992. 'La influencia de Quintiliano en los criterios retóricos de Plinio el Joven', *Helmantica* 43: 121–9

1998. 'La influencia de Cicerón y Quintiliano en las ideas sobre el estilo en las cartas de Plinio el Joven', in Albaladejo–del Rio–Caballero 1998: III 1053–8

Roche, P. 2006. 'Selling Trajan's saeculum. Destiny, abundance, assurance', *Athenaeum* 94: 199–229

2009. *Lucan. De bello ciuili book I*, Oxford

ed. 2011. *Pliny's praise: the* Panegyricus *in the Roman world*, Cambridge

Rodgers, R. H. 2004. *Frontinus. De aquaeductu urbis Romae*, Cambridge

Römer, F. 1989. *Kenntnis und Imitation des plinianischen Panegyricus bei italienischen Humanisten*, Graz

Rose, H. J. 1927. 'Mox', *CQ* 21: 57–66

Rosén, H. 1980. '*Exposition und Mitteilung* – the imperfect as a thematic tense-form in the letters of Pliny', in ead. and H. B. Rosén, *On moods and tenses of the Latin verb: two essays* (Munich) 27–48

1995. 'The Latin *infinitivus historicus* revisited', *Mnemosyne* 48: 536–64

Rosenmeyer, P. A. 2001. *Ancient epistolary fictions. The letter in Greek literature*, Cambridge

Roxan, M. M. 1994. *Roman military diplomas 1985–1993*, London

Rudd, N. 1966. *The Satires of Horace*, Cambridge

1976. 'Architecture. Theories about Virgil's *Eclogues*', in id., *Lines of enquiry: studies in Latin poetry* (Cambridge) 119–44 = P. Hardie, ed. *Virgil. Critical assessments of classical authors* (London, 1999) I 91–115

1992. 'Strategies of vanity: Cicero, *Ad familiares* 5.12 and Pliny's letters', in A. J. Woodman and J. Powell, eds. *Author and audience in Latin literature* (Cambridge) 18–32

Russell, D. A. 1983. *Greek declamation*, Cambridge

Rutherford, I. 1995. 'The poetics of the *paraphthegmata*: Aelius Aristides and the *decorum* of self-praise', in Innes–Hine–Pelling 1995: 193–204

Rutledge, S. H. 2001. *Imperial inquisitions: prosecutors and informants from Tiberius to Domitian*, London

Sailor, D. 2008. *Writing and empire in Tacitus*, Cambridge

Salerno, F. 2003. *Ad metalla: aspetti giuridici del lavoro in miniera*, Naples

Saliou, S. 2009. *Vitruve. De l'architecture livre V*, Paris

Saller, R. P. 1982. *Personal patronage under the early empire*, Cambridge

1994. *Patriarchy, property and death in the Roman family*, Cambridge

2000a. 'Status and patronage', *Cambridge Ancient History* XI² 817–54

2000b. 'Domitian and his successors. Methodological traps in assessing emperors', *AJAH* 15: 4–18

Sallmann, K. 2010. 'Pliny the Younger', in A. Grafton, G. W. Most, S. Settis, eds. *The classical tradition* (Cambridge, MA) 745–6

Salway, B. 1994. 'What's in a name? A survey of Roman onomastic practice from *c*. 700 B.C. to A.D. 700', *JRS* 84: 124–45

Salza Prina Ricotti, E. 1984. 'La c.d. Villa Magna: il Laurentinum di Plinio il Giovane', *Rendiconti Lincei* (*classe di scienze morali, storiche e filologiche*) 39: 339–58

1985. 'La Villa Magna a Grotte di Piastra', in *Castelporziano I. Campagna di scavo e restauro 1984* (Rome) 53–66

1988. 'Il Laurentino: scavi del 1985', in *Castelporziano II. Campagna di scavo e restauro 1985–1986* (Rome) 45–56

Salzman, M. R. and M. Roberts, 2012. *The Letters of Symmachus book 1. Introduction, text and commentary*, Leiden

Samuelsson, J. 1908. 'Der pleonastische Gebrauch von ille im Lateinischen', *Eranos* 8: 49–76

Sandys, J. E. 1885. *M. Tulli Ciceronis ad M. Brutum Orator*, Cambridge

Santirocco, M. 1986. *Unity and design in Horace's Odes*, Chapel Hill, NC

Santoro-L'Hoir, F. 1992. *The rhetoric of gender terms: 'man', 'woman', and the portrayal of character in Latin prose*, Leiden

Savon, H. 1995. 'Saint Ambroise a-t-il imité le recueil de lettres de Pline le Jeune?', *Revue des Études Augustiniennes* 41: 3–17

Scarcia, R. 1984. '"Ad tantas opes processit": note a Plinio il Giovane', *Labeo* 30: 291–316 = *Index: Quaderni Camerti di Studi Romanistici* 13 (1985) 289–312

Schefferus, J. 1675. *Lectiones academicae*, Hamburg

Scheid, J. 1978. 'Les prêtres officiels sous les empereurs julio-claudiens', *ANRW* II.16.1: 610–54

Schenk, P. 1999. 'Formen von Intertextualität im Briefkorpus des jüngeren Plinius', *Philologus* 143: 114–34

Scherf, J. 1998. 'Zur Komposition von Martials Gedichtbüchern 1–12', in F. Grewing, ed. *Toto notus in orbe: Perspektiven der Martial-Interpretation* (Stuttgart) 119–38

Schmidt, P. L. 1983. 'Die Rezeption des römischen Freundschaftsbriefes (Cicero–Plinius) im frühen Humanismus (Petrarca–Coluccio Salutati)', in F. J. Worstbrock, ed. *Der Brief im Zeitalter der Renaissance* (Weinheim) 25–59 = J. Fugmann, M. Hose, B. Zimmermann, eds. *Traditio Latinitatis. Studien zur Rezeption und Überlieferung der lateinischen Literatur* (Stuttgart, 2000) 142–65

Scholz, B. I. 1992. *Untersuchung zur Tracht der römischen matrona*, Cologne

Schuster, M. 1926. 'Kritische und erläuternde Beiträge zum jüngeren Plinius', *Mitteilungen des Vereines klassischer Philologen in Wien* 3: 50–61

1927. 'De Agathiae scholastici epigrammate quodam (*A.P.* XI 382)', *WS* 45: 120–2

1928. 'Kritisches zu den Pliniusbriefen I', *Philologische Wochenschrift* 48: 411–5

1951. 'Plinius der Jüngere', *RE* XXI.1: 439–56

Scivoletto, N. 1957. 'Plinio il Giovane e Giovenale', *GIF* 10: 133–46

Seelentag, G. 2004. *Taten und Tugenden Traians. Herrschaftsdarstellung im Principat*, Stuttgart

2011. 'Imperial representation and reciprocation: the case of Trajan', *CJ* 107: 73–97

Seitz, W. 1973. *Maiestas: Eine bedeutungsgeschichtliche Untersuchung des Wortes in der Republik und Kaiserzeit (bis ca. 200 n. Chr.)*, Innsbruck

Seo, J. M. 2009. 'Plagiarism and poetic identity in Martial', *AJP* 130: 567–93

Seyffert, M. L. 1855. *Scholae Latinae: Beiträge zu einer methodischen Praxis der lateinischen Stil- und Compositionsübungen. I. Die Formen der Tractatio*, Leipzig

Shackleton Bailey, D. R. 1965–70. *Cicero's Letters to Atticus*, 7 vols, Cambridge

1977. *Cicero: Epistulae ad familiares*, 2 vols, Cambridge

1981. 'Notes on the Younger Pliny', *PCPS* 27: 50–7

1989. 'More corrections and explanations of Martial', *AJP* 110: 131–50

1993. *Martial Epigrams*, 3 vols, Cambridge, MA

Shelton, J.-A. 1987. 'Pliny's letter 3.11: rhetoric and autobiography', *Classica et Mediaevalia* 38: 121–39

1990. 'Pliny the Younger, and the ideal wife', *Classica et Mediaevalia* 41: 163–86

Shotter, D. C. 1967. 'Tacitus and Verginius Rufus', *CQ* 56: 370–81

Sinclair, P. 1995. *Tacitus the sententious historian. A sociology of rhetoric in Annales 1–6*, University Park, PA

Slater, W. J. 2000. 'Handouts at dinner', *Phoenix* 54: 107–22

Small, J. P. 1997. *Wax tablets of the mind. Cognitive studies of memory and literacy in classical antiquity*, London

Smith, W. 1890. *A dictionary of Greek and Roman antiquities*, 3rd edn (rev. W. Wayte and G. E. Marindin), London

Smith, W. S. 1997. 'Juvenal and the sophist Isaeus', *CW* 91: 39–45

Sogno, C. 2006. *Q. Aurelius Symmachus: a political biography*, Ann Arbor, MI

Solodow, J. B. 1978. *The Latin particle quidem*, University Park, PA

Sörbom, G. 1935. *Variatio sermonis Tacitei aliaeque apud eum quaestiones selectae*, Uppsala

Soverini, P. 1989. 'Impero e imperatori nell'opera di Plinio il Giovane. Aspetti e problemi del rapporto con Domiziano e Traiano', *ANRW* II.33.1: 515–54

Spatharas, D. 2011. 'Self-praise and envy: from rhetoric to the Athenian courts', *Arethusa* 44: 199–219

Spatzek, F. 1912. 'De clausulis Plinianis' in Kukula: vii–xv

Spencer, D. 2010. *Roman landscape: culture and identity*, Cambridge

Spruit, J. E. 1973. *C. Plinius Caecilius en het erfrecht van zijn tijd. Een rechtshistorisch vertoog over Plinius' Epistulae V.7, II.16 en IV.10*, Deventer

Squire, M. J. 2011. *The Iliad in a nutshell: visualizing epic on the Tabulae Iliacae*, Oxford

   2013. 'Ekphrasis at the forge and the forging of ekphrasis: the "shield of Achilles" in Graeco-Roman word and image', *Word & Image* 29.2

von Stackelberg, K. T. 2009. *The Roman garden: space, sense, and society*, London

Stadter, P. E. 2006. 'Pliny and the ideology of empire: the correspondence with Trajan', *Prometheus* 32: 61–76

Starkie, W. J. M. 1909. *The Acharnians of Aristophanes*, London

Starr, R. J. 1987. 'The circulation of literary texts in the Roman world', *CQ* 37: 213–23

Steele, R. B. 1902. 'Chiasmus in the epistles of Cicero, Seneca, Pliny and Fronto', in *Studies in honor of Basil L. Gildersleeve* (Baltimore) 339–52

   1904. 'The ablative absolute in the epistles of Cicero, Seneca, Pliny and Fronto', *AJP* 25: 315–27

Stein-Hölkeskamp, E. 2002. 'Culinarische Codes: Das ideale Bankett bei Plinius d. Jüngeren und seinen Zeitgenossen', *Klio* 84: 465–90

   2005. *Das römische Gastmahl: eine Kulturgeschichte*, Munich

Stevens, P. T. 1976. *Colloquial expressions in Euripides*, Wiesbaden

Stewart, P. 2003. *Statues in Roman society: representation and response*, Oxford

Stout, S. E. 1924. 'The eight-book manuscripts of Pliny's letters', *TAPA* 55: 62–72

   1949. 'Did Pliny use epistolary tenses?', *Classical Weekly* 42: 139–40

   1954. *Scribe and critic at work in Pliny's letters. Notes on the history and the present status of the text*, Bloomington, IN

Strobel, K. 2003. 'Plinius und Domitian: Der willige Helfer eines Unrechtssystems? Zur Problematik historischer Aussagen in den Werken des jüngeren Plinius', in Castagna–Lefèvre 2003: 303–14

Strube, N. 1964. 'Plinius der Jüngere II 7. Eine sprachliche und stilistische Analyse', *WS* 77: 185–91

Strunk, T. E. 2012. 'Pliny the pessimist', *G&R* 59: 175–92

Sullivan, D. 1976. 'Innuendo and the "weighted alternative" in Tacitus', *CJ* 71: 312–26

Sullivan, J. P. 1968. *The Satyricon of Petronius: a literary study*, London

Sulze, H. 1931. 'Zu Plinius Epp. II.17.15', *Philologische Wochenschrift* 51: 733–5

Summers, W. C. 1910. *Select letters of Seneca*, London

Swain, S. 2002. 'Bilingualism in Cicero? The evidence of code-switching', in J. N. Adams, M. Janse and S. Swain, eds. *Bilingualism in ancient society. Language contact and the written text* (Oxford) 128–67

2004. 'Bilingualism and biculturalism in Antonine Rome: Apuleius, Fronto, and Gellius', in L. Holford-Strevens and A. Vardi, eds. *The worlds of Aulus Gellius* (Oxford) 3–40

Syme, R. 1953. Review of A. Degrassi, *I fasti consolari*, *JRS* 43: 148–61 = *Roman papers* I 231–55

1957a. 'The jurist Neratius Priscus', *Hermes* 85: 480–93 = *Roman papers* I 339–52

1957b. 'C. Vibius Maximus, Prefect of Egypt', *Historia* 6: 480–7 = *Roman papers* I 353–60

1958. *Tacitus*, 2 vols, Oxford

1960. 'Pliny's less successful friends', *Historia* 9: 362–79 = *Roman papers* II 477–95

1968. 'People in Pliny', *JRS* 58: 135–51 = *Roman papers* II 694–723

1969. 'Pliny the procurator', *HSCP* 73: 201–36 = *Roman papers* II 742–73

1979a. Appendix to Syme 1953, *Roman papers* I 255–9

1979b. 'Juvenal, Pliny, Tacitus', *AJP* 100: 250–78 = *Roman papers* III 1135–57

1979c. 'Ummidius Quadratus, capax imperii', *HSCP* 82: 287–310 = *Roman papers* III 1158–78

1980. *Some Arval brethren*, Oxford

1985a. 'Correspondents of Pliny', *Historia* 34: 324–59 = *Roman papers* V 440–77

1985b. 'The dating of Pliny's last letters', *CQ* 35: 176–85 = *Roman papers* V 478–89

1985c. 'Curtailed tenures of consular legates', *ZPE* 59: 265–79 = *Roman papers* V 499–513

1991. *Roman papers* VII (ed. A. R. Birley), Oxford

Talbert, R. J. A. 1984. *The senate of imperial Rome*, Princeton

1985. *Atlas of classical history*, London

Tellegen, J. W. 1982. *The Roman law of succession in the letters of Pliny the Younger, I*, Zutphen

Thomas, I. 1951. *Selections illustrating the history of Greek mathematics. I. From Thales to Euclid*, Cambridge, MA

Thomas, R. 1983. 'Virgil's ecphrastic centerpieces', *HSCP* 87: 175–84

2011. *Horace. Odes book IV and Carmen saeculare*, Cambridge

Thomas, Y. 1992. 'The division of the sexes in Roman law', in P. Schmitt Pantel, ed. *A history of women in the West, I* (Cambridge, MA) 83–137

Thomasson, B. E. 1960. *Die Statthalter der römischen Provinzen Nordafrikas von Augustus bis Diocletianus*, Lund

Thompson, G. H. 1942. 'Pliny's "want of humor"', *Classical Journal* 37: 201–9

Thompson, L. A. 1970. 'Pliny Epistulae II.11 and Lepcis Magna', *Nigeria and the Classics* 12: 55–67

Thraede, K. 1970. *Grundzüge griechisch-römischer Brieftopik*, Munich

Toner, J. P. 1995. *Leisure and ancient Rome*, Cambridge, MA

Tosi, R. 1991. *Dizionario delle sentenze latine e greche: 10,000 citazioni dall'antichità al Rinascimento nell'originale e in traduzione, con commento storico, letterario e filologico*, Milan

Townend, G. B. 1961. 'The reputation of Verginius Rufus', *Latomus* 20: 337–41

Toynbee, J. M. C. 1971. *Death and burial in the Roman world*, London

Tracy, V. 1980. 'Aut captantur aut captant', *Latomus* 39: 399–402

Trapp, M. 2003. *Greek and Latin letters. An anthology with translation*, Cambridge

Traub, H. W. 1955. 'Pliny's treatment of history in epistolary form', *TAPA* 86: 213–32

Treggiari, S. 1991. *Roman marriage: iusti coniuges from the time of Cicero to the time of Ulpian*, Oxford

Trisoglio, F. 1972. *La personalità di Plinio il Giovane nei suoi rapporti con la politica, la società e la letteratura*, Turin

   1973. 'San Girolamo e Plinio il Giovane', *Rivista di studi classici* 21: 343–84

Tzounakas, S. 2007. '*Neque enim historiam componebam*: Pliny's first epistle and his attitude towards historiography', *MH* 64: 42–54

Ussani, V. 1971. 'Leggendo Plinio il Giovane, II. Oratio–historia', *RCCM* 13: 70–135

   1981. 'Otium e pax in Plinio il Giovane', *Romanitas* 14–20: 37–58

Van Buren, A. W. 1948. 'Pliny's Laurentine villa', *JRS* 38: 35–6

Van Dam, H.-J. 1984. *P. Papinius Statius. Silvae book II. A commentary*, Leiden

Vannini, G. 2010. *Petronii Arbitri 'Satyricon' 100–115*, Berlin

Van Sickle, J. 1980. 'The book roll and some conventions of the poetic book', *Arethusa* 13: 5–42

Várhelyi, S. 2010. *The religion of senators in the Roman empire*, Cambridge

Venini, P. 1952. 'Le parole greche nell'epistolario di Plinio', *Rendiconti dell'Istituto Lombardo (classe di lettere e scienze morali e storiche)* 85: 259–69

Veyne, P. 1967. 'Autour d'un commentaire de Pline le Jeune' (review of S-W), *Latomus* 26: 723–51

Vidén, G. 1993. *Women in Roman literature*, Gothenburg

Vidman, L. 1981. 'Die Namengebung bei Plinius dem Jüngeren', *Klio* 63: 585–95

   1982. *Fasti Ostienses*, Prague

   1986. 'Zur Datierung von Plinius *Ep.* II 13', *Listy Filologické* 109: 65–71

Vielberg, M. 1987. *Pflichten, Werte, Ideale. Eine Untersuchung zu den Wertvorstellungen des Tacitus*, Stuttgart

   2003. 'Sentenzen im Werk des jüngeren Plinius', in Castagna–Lefèvre: 35–50

Vollmer, F. 1893. 'De funere publico Romanorum', *Jahrbücher für classische Philologie*, *Suppl.* 19: 231–64

   1898. *Publius Papinius Statius. Silvarum libri*, Leipzig (repr. Hildesheim 1971)

Voss, B.-R. 1963. *Der pointierte Stil des Tacitus*, Münster

Vretska, K. 1976. *C. Sallustius Crispus. De Catilinae coniuratione*, 2 vols, Heidelberg van Waarden, J. A. 2010. *Writing to survive: a commentary on Sidonius Apollinaris Letters book 7, vol. I*, Leuven

Wackernagel, J. 2009. *Lectures on syntax, with special reference to Greek, Latin, and Germanic* (tr. D. Langslow), Oxford

Walbank, F. W. 1957–79. *A historical commentary on Polybius*, 3 vols, Oxford

Walker, A. D. 1993. '*Enargeia* and the spectator in Greek historiography', *TAPA* 123: 353–77

Wallace-Hadrill, A. 1983. *Suetonius: a scholar and his Caesars*, London

 ed. 1989. *Patronage in ancient society*, London

 1994. *Houses and society in Pompeii and Herculaneum*, Princeton

 2011. *Herculaneum: past and future*, London

Wardle, D. 2006. *Cicero on divination:* De Divinatione *book 1*, Oxford

Waters, K. H. 1969. 'Traianus Domitiani continuator', *AJP* 90: 385–404

Watson, L. C. 2003. *A commentary on Horace's Epodes*, Oxford

Watt, W. S. 1990. 'Notes on Pliny's *Epistulae* and *Panegyricus*', *Phoenix* 44: 84–7

Webb, R. 2009. *Ekphrasis, imagination and persuasion in ancient rhetorical theory and practice*, Farnham

Weinreich, O. 1928. 'Trigemination als sakrale Stilform', *Studi e materiali di storia delle religioni* 4: 198–206

Weische, A. 1989. 'Plinius d. J. und Cicero. Untersuchungen zur römischen Epistolographie in Republik und Kaiserzeit', *ANRW* II.33.1: 375–86

West, M. L. 2007. *Indo-European poetry and myth*, Oxford

White, P. 2010. *Cicero in letters: epistolary relations of the late republic*, Oxford

Whitmarsh, T. J. M. 2005. *The Second Sophistic*, Cambridge

Whitton, C. L. 2010. 'Pliny, *Epistles* 8.14: poetics, politics and the *Agricola*', *JRS* 100: 118–39

 2011a. '*Dubitatio comparativa*: a misunderstood idiom in Pliny (*N.H.* 7.150), Tacitus (*H.* 4.6) and others', *CQ* 61: 267–77

 2011b. 'Pliny the aesthete' (review of Lefèvre 2009), *CR* 61: 147–9

 2012. '"Let us tread our path together": Tacitus and the younger Pliny', in V. E. Pagán, ed. *A companion to Tacitus* (Malden, MA) 345–68

 2013. 'Trapdoors: the falsity of closure in Pliny's *Epistles*', in F. Grewing, B. Acosta-Hughes and A. Kirichenko, eds. *The door ajar: false closure in Greek and Roman literature and art* (Heidelberg) 43–61

 fthc. 'Grand designs / unrolling *Epistles* 2', in Marchesi fthc.

Wilkinson, L. P. 1963. *Golden Latin artistry*, Cambridge

Williams, B. P. and R. S. Williams. 1995. 'Finger numbers in the Roman world and the early Middle Ages', *Isis* 86: 587–608

Williams, G. 1978. *Change and decline: Roman literature in the early empire*, Berkeley

Williams, G. D. 1991. 'Conversing after sunset: a Callimachean echo in Ovid's exile poetry', *CQ* 41: 169–77

 and A. D. Walker, eds. 1997. *Ovid and exile*, Bendigo = *Ramus* 26

Williams, W. 1990. *Pliny the Younger. Correspondence with Trajan from Bithynia (Epistles X)*, Warminster

Wills, J. 1996. *Repetition in Latin poetry: figures of allusion*, Oxford

Wilson, L. M. 1938. *The clothing of the ancient Romans*, Baltimore, MD

Wilson, M. 2001. 'Seneca's epistles reclassified', in S. J. Harrison, ed. *Texts, ideas and the Classics* (Oxford) 164–87

    2003. 'After the silence: Tacitus, Suetonius, Juvenal', in A. J. Boyle and W. J. Dominik, eds. *Flavian Rome: culture, image, text* (Leiden) 523–42

Winnefeld, K. 1891. 'Tusci und Laurentinum des jüngeren Plinius', *Jahrbuch des Kaiserlich Deutschen Archäologischen Instituts* 6: 201–17

Winniczuk, L. 1966. '"Urbanitas" nelle lettere di Plinio il Giovane', *Eos* 56: 198–205

    1975. 'The ending phrases in Pliny's letters (contribution to the epistolography)', *Eos* 63: 319–28

Winterbottom, M. 1964. 'Quintilian and the *vir bonus*', *JRS* 54: 90–7

    1970. *Problems in Quintilian*, London

    1975. 'Quintilian and rhetoric', in T. A. Dorey, ed. *Empire and aftermath. Silver Latin II* (London) 79–97

    1984. *The Minor Declamations ascribed to Quintilian*, Berlin

    1995. 'On impulse', in Innes–Hine–Pelling 1995: 313–22

    1998a. 'Quintilian the moralist', in Albaladejo–del Rio–Caballero 1998: I 317–34

    1998b. Review of H. M. Hine, *L. Annaei Senecae Naturalium quaestionum libri*, Stuttgart 1996, *Scripta classica Israelica* 17: 242–5

Wiseman, T. P. 1985. *Catullus and his world: a reappraisal*, Cambridge

Wolff, É. 2003. *Pline le Jeune ou le refus du pessimisme*, Rennes

Woodman, A. J. 1977. *Velleius Paterculus. The Tiberian narrative (2.94–131)*, Cambridge

    1983. *Velleius Paterculus. The Caesarian and Augustan narrative (2.41–93)*, Cambridge

    1995. 'A death in the first act: Tacitus, *Annals* 1.6', *PLLS* 8: 257–74 = id. 1998: 23–39

    1998. *Tacitus reviewed*, Oxford

    2006. 'Mutiny and madness: Tacitus *Annals* 1.16–49', *Arethusa* 39: 303–29

    2009a. 'Tacitus and the contemporary scene', in id. 2009b: 31–43

    ed. 2009b. *Cambridge companion to Tacitus*, Cambridge

    2012. *From poetry to history: selected papers*, Oxford

    and R. H. Martin. 1996. *The Annals of Tacitus book 3*, Cambridge

Woolf, G. D. 1996. 'Monumental writing and the expansion of Roman society in the early empire', *JRS* 86: 22–39

    2003. 'The city of letters', in C. Edwards and G. D. Woolf, eds. *Rome and the cosmopolis* (Cambridge) 203–21

    2006. 'Pliny's province', in T. Bekker-Nielsen, ed. *Rome and the Black Sea region: domination, Romanisation, resistance* (Aarhus) 93–108

Woytek, E. 2006. 'Der *Panegyricus* des Plinius. Sein Verhältnis zum *Dialogus* und den *Historiae* des Tacitus und seine absolute Datierung', *WS* 119: 115–56

Wright, N. 1997. 'Columbanus's Epistulae', in M. Lapidge, ed. *Columbanus: studies on the Latin writings* (Woodbridge) 29–92

Yardley, J. C. 1973. 'Sick-visiting in Roman elegy', *Phoenix* 27: 283–8

Yates, S. 1966. *The art of memory*, London

Yegül, F. 1992. *Baths and bathing in classical antiquity*, New York

2010. *Bathing in the Roman world*, Cambridge

Yuge, T. 1986. 'Die Einstellung Plinius des Jüngeren zur Sklaverei', in H. Kalcyk et al., eds. *Studien zur Alten Geschichte. Festschrift für Siegfried Lauffer, Bd. 3* (Rome) 1089–1102

Yunis, H. 2001. *Demosthenes. On the crown*, Cambridge

Zabłocka, M. 1988. 'Il "ius trium liberorum" nel diritto romano', *Bullettino dell'Istituto di Diritto Romano* 91 (series 3, vol. 30): 361–90

Zarmakoupi, M. 2011. '*Porticus* and *cryptoporticus* in luxury villa architecture', in K. Cole, E. Poehler, M. Flohr, eds. *Pompeii: art, industry and infrastructure* (Oxford) 50–61

Zehnacker, H. 2009. Response to Liberman 2009a, *BMCR* 2009.08.15

Zelzer, K. and M. Zelzer. 2002. '"Retractationes" zu Brief und Briefgenos bei Plinius, Ambrosius und Sidonius Apollinaris', in W. Blümer, ed. *Alvarium. Festschrift für Christian Gnilka* (Münster) 393–405

Zieliński, T. 1904. *Das Clauselgesetz in Ciceros Reden*, Leipzig

Zieske, L. 1972. *Felicitas. Eine Wortuntersuchung*, Hamburg

Zucker, F. 1928. 'Plinius epist. VIII 24 – ein Denkmal antiker Humanität', *Philologus* 84: 209–32

INDEXES

References are to page numbers in the Introduction and to letter or paragraph numbers in the Commentary; 'intro.' refers to the introductory note on a letter, 'add.' to the note on the addressee.

1. LATIN WORDS

Simple cross-references are generally omitted.

2. GREEK WORDS

Latinised words are listed in Index 1. See also Index 3 'Greek'.

3. GENERAL

Persons are listed by gentilicium where known, except in the case of authors and emperors.

meta-epistolarity (*cont.*)
   links between adjacent letters 15,
      2.5.intro., 8, 11, 13, 2.6.intro., 1,
      2.7.intro., 2.9.1, 2.12.intro., add., 1,
      2, 6, 7, 2.13.add., 2.15.2
   links across and between books 15,
      18–19, 2.1.1, 2.2.add., 2, 2.3.intro.,
      2.15.add., 2.20.intro., 9
metaphor and imagery 26
   accounting 2.4.4, 2.19.9
   animal 2.7.2, 2.11.2
   dining 2.5.8
   fruit 2.12.2, 2.19.6
   horticultural 2.5.3–4, 6, 2.12.intro., 1, 3,
      7
   hunting 2.20.7
   liquid 2.11.18
   medical 2.7.3, 2.8.2, 2.11.6, 2.12.3
   military 2.6.5, 2.11.22
   nautical 2.5.13, 2.11.3, 2.17.10
   pugna forensis 2.3.3
   religious 2.14.4
   road 2.17.2
   shift in referent 2.4.4, 2.8.3, 2.10.4,
      2.12.3
   slavery 2.5.3, 2.8.2–3, 2.10.3–4
   statue 2.5.11, 2.7.intro., 2.10.4
   theatre 2.14.6, 2.20.8
   water 2.4.3–4
   see also 'analogy', 'simile' *and* Index 1
      aculeus, calor, distringor, dulcedo, laetus,
      nota, ordo, perpolire, saxeus, specula
Metilius Sabinus Nepos 2.3.add.
middle *see* 'centre'
Minicius Acilianus 2.16.intro., 1
Minicius Macrinus 2.7.add.
modesty and immodesty 10, 2.4.intro., 3,
      2.9.4, 2.10.5, 7, 8, 2.11.11, 14, 15, 19,
      25, 2.17.4, 16, 22, 27, 29, 2.18.2,
      2.19.1
money 2.4, 2.20.13–14
morality *see* 'oratory'

Naevius 2.1.10
names and nomenclature 2.1.1, 2.3.8, 11,
      2.7.1, 3, 2.9.1, 2.11.add., 15, 17, 19,
      23, 2.13.4
   of emperors 7, 2.1.3, 2.9.2, 2.20.2
   omitted 1, 2.3.8, 2.6.1, 2.13.2
   see also 'addressees', 'wordplay'
'narrative of retreat' 16–17, 19–20,
      2.8.intro., 2.14.intro.
neologism 25–6, 2.3.3, 2.7.6, 2.11.23, 2.17.5,
      13, 16
Nepos *see* 'Metilius'

Neratius Priscus 2.13.add.
Nero 6, 2.1.intro., 2.14.12
Nerva 6–8, 2.1.intro., 1–4, 6, 9, 2.7.1, 2.9.2,
      2.13.8
   not named 7–8, 2.1.3
   optimus 2.1.3, 2.13.8
   see also 'Acutius'
Nicetes Sacerdos (of Smyrna) 2.2.1, 2.19.6
nostalgia 8–9, 2.7.1, 2.9.4, 2.14, 2.20.12
Novius (?) Maximus 2.14.add., 8

occupatio 2.3.9, 2.5.10, 2.10.5
Octavius Rufus 2.10.add.
officialese *see* 'technical and official
      language'
oratory 2.1.5, 7, 2.2.2, 2.3.intro., 5, 9, 2.5,
      2.10.intro., 7, 2.11, 2.12, 2.14, 2.18.1,
      2.19
   'death' of 20, 2.14.intro., 11–12
   and morals 2.3.5, 2.14, 2.18.2, 2.19.6,
      2.20.intro.
   styles of, critical terms for 2.3.1, 3, 9, 10,
      2.5.6, 7, 2.11.3, 17, 2.13.6–7, 2.14
Ostia 2.17.2, 26
Ovid 3–5, 12, 26, 33, 2.2.2, 2.10.2
oxymoron 26, 2.1.2, 2.6.1, 3, 7, 2.7.5,
      2.11.13, 23, 2.15.2, 2.17.10, 14, 21

parallelism 22, 2.2.2, 2.3.1, 3, 9, 2.4.2, 2.5.3,
      7, 10, 2.6.2, 3, 5, 2.10.2, 2.11.4, 7–9,
      11, 19, 20, 22, 23, 2.13.5, 10, 2.17.3,
      5, 13, 16–18, 20, 2.18.3, 2.20.3, 8, 11
   combined with chiasmus *see* 'chiasmus'
   'false' 2.11.6, 2.17.3
parataxis 21, 2.5.2, 2.10.2, 2.11.15, 2.12.4,
      2.13.10, 2.18.2, 2.20.7, 10
parenthesis 24, 2.3.2, 2.4.2, 2.5.6, 2.6.2,
      2.7.2, 2.11.6, 9, 10, 15, 17, 2.13.4,
      2.14.3, 6, 10, 13, 2.17.14, 15, 2.18.4,
      2.20.14
paronomasia *see* 'wordplay'
participle 21
   future 25, 2.1.5, 2.20.10
   substantival 25, 2.3.9, 2.4.2, 2.5.2,
      2.11.14, 2.14.7, 2.15.1, 2.17.11, 2.19.2,
      3, 4
paternity, real and virtual 9, 2.1.intro., 8, 9,
      2.4.add., 1, 2, 2.6.add., 6, 2.7.3, 5, 6,
      2.13.4, 2.18.intro., 4, 5
patronage 9, 16–17, 2.1.8, 2.4, 2.5.intro.,
      2.6.3, 2.9, 2.13, 2.14.4, 2.16.intro.,
      2.18.5
perfect tense
   effect of 2.1.1, 2.6.3, 2.11.2
   epistolary 2.1.12, 2.5.1

Lightning Source UK Ltd.
Milton Keynes UK
UKHW02f0351020918
328184UK00011B/107/P

9 780521 187275